ON
EXHIBIT

ART LOVER'S
TRAVEL GUIDE
TO
AMERICAN
MUSEUMS
1999

ON
EXHIBIT

ART LOVER'S
TRAVEL GUIDE
TO
AMERICAN
MUSEUMS
1999

BY JUDITH SWIRSKY

ABBEVILLE PRESS PUBLISHERS
NEW YORK LONDON PARIS

ISBN 0-7892-0454-1

First Edition

10 9 8 7 6 5 4 3 2 1

Library of Congress Cataloging-in-Publication Data available upon request.

To Leo, ever supportive in every way.

CONTENTS

ACKNOWLEDGMENTS

Even in the somewhat solitary process of writing a book, the help, counsel, and encouragement of others is essential. I owe a debt of thanks to Marjorie and Larry Zelner, who have solved numerous technical problems for us with their expertise. Paul Iskander's help in converting the masses of data into a database was invaluable.

The original idea for this book was Patti Sowalsky's. Her unique contribution will be missed in this and future issues.

In the years to come, On Exhibit promises to continue providing the art-loving traveler — and art professional — with the most factual, timely, and comprehensive guide available to the hundreds of treasure houses that preserve America's artistic heritage. I thank the thousands of art lovers and hundreds of participating museums who have enthusiastically supported our effort.

ACOUSTIGUIDE: THE FIRST 40 YEARS

1950's: Acoustiguide's First Tours: Mrs. Roosevelt at Hyde Park

Acoustiguide was founded in 1957 to produce audio tours for national museums and historic sites. From modest beginnings, we have grown to serve some seven hundred institutions around the world and have vastly extended our repertoire to include battleships, aquaria, zoos and commercial showrooms.

One of our first projects was at Hyde Park, Franklin Delano Roosevelt's New York residence. On the tour, Mrs. Roosevelt continues to guide visitors around her home, enlivening the experience with personal reminiscences including a memorable visit from King George VI and Queen Elizabeth. The tour is "like hearing a whispered confidence," one person commented.

1960's: Cassette Tours Become a Standard Component of the Museum Experience

In the 1960's, Acoustiguide tours became a strong presence in museums across the country. Using the brand new medium of audio cassettes, curators and directors began to reach out to their visitors. The Metropolitan Museum of Art, the National Gallery of Art, and the Fine Arts Museums of San Francisco, among others, offered tours of their permanent collections. Visitors soon came to expect this service and the authoritative voice of certain museum personalities. Even national publications recognized the trend, poking fun at headset-wearing art-lovers.

1970's: Blockbuster Exhibitions

The 1970's saw the first major "blockbuster" exhibition with an Acoustiguide, the immensely popular Treasures of Tutankhamun, which debuted at The Metropolitan Museum of Art and traveled throughout the country.

Blockbusters continue to this day - our most recent tour was Cézanne at the Philadelphia Museum of Art, where almost one million visitors attended the exhibition. Acoustiguide distributed a remarkable 3,000 tours a day!

1980's: Acoustiguide in Asia

With the introduction of a cassette tour at the Forbidden City in Beijing, Acoustiguide expanded into Asia. The tour is available in ten languages with one version of the English tour narrated by Peter Ustinov, another by Roger Moore. Each year, Acoustiguide leads more than 100,000 visitors through the majestic Gate of Heavenly Peace and into the private quarters of China's Imperial Family.

Acoustiguide continues to expand in Asia. In the last fifteen years, we have opened offices in Beijing, Taiwan, Singapore and Shanghai, with multi-lingual tours at the Shanghai Museum, the National Palace Museum in Taipei, and the National Museum of Natural Science in Taichung.

1990's: INFORM® Attracts New Clients

The 1990's marked a new age in interpretation with the introduction of INFORM. Acoustiguide's random access system has enjoyed success at over sixty sites throughout the world, from The Louvre to The Museum of Modern Art and the Roman Baths in England. INFORM is attracting nontraditional Acoustiguide users as well: zoos and aquaria, Kitt Peak National Observatory, Newcastle United Soccer Club, the Mercedes-Benz factory, Waste Management - a recycling plant, and Dallas Design, a furniture showroom.

The creative possibilities of INFORM are endless. Imagine walking through a zoo and hearing the rare sounds of a koala's mating call at the touch of a button; accessing baseball player's statistics at the ballpark; coordinating furniture and fabrics in a department store; learning which features are available on different models in a car dealership; or following the stars in a planetarium as an astronomer describes them. You can probably think of more...

Acoustiguide's commitment to research and development is leading the company to explore new technological directions. With the imminent introduction of two new random access tour systems and Acoustiguide's unparalleled service, we look forward to leading an ever-growing audience into the next millennium.

Acoustiguide Discount Coupon on Page 411

INTRODUCTION

Celebrating its seventh successful year of annual publication, On Exhibit's *Art Lover's Travel Guide to American Museums* is the comprehensive guide to art museums nationwide. Easy to use, up to date, and completely reliable, it is the ultimate museum reference.

Written for those who travel on business or for pleasure and love to explore interesting art museums, On Exhibit's annual travel guides allow you to "know before you go" with complete assurance. With this guide in hand, you will never again miss a "little gem" of a museum or an important exhibition for lack of information.

I encourage you to join the thousands of art lovers who are loyal fans of On Exhibit. Like them, you are certain to be completely delighted with this quick, yet comprehensive overview of the America's artistic riches.

IMPORTANT INFORMATION ON
HOW TO USE THIS GUIDE

- The On Exhibit *Art Lover's Travel Guide* has been designed to be reader-friendly.

- All museums are listed alphabetically by state, and then by city within each state.

- Most permanent collection and museum facility information is expressed in easily recognized standard abbreviations. These are explained in the front of the book – and, for your convenience, on the back of the enclosed bookmark.

- NOTE THE EXCLAMATION POINT ("!"). This is the symbol used to remind you to call or check for information or any other verification.

- All museums offering group tours require some advance notice. It is suggested that arrangements be made WELL in advance of your visit. When calling be sure to check on group size requirements and fee information. A group tour phone number is only included in cases where it is different from the regular museum number.

- As a reminder, it is recommended that students and seniors always present proper I.D.'s in order to qualify for museum fee discounts wherever they are offered (age requirements for both vary!).

- Admission and/or advance ticket requirements are included in the listings for certain special exhibitions.

- Please note that exhibitions at most college and university museums are only scheduled during the academic year. Due to the constraints of space student or faculty exhibits are rarely listed.
- Some museums that have no exhibition listings simply did not have the information available at press time, others did not respond to our request for information, and therefore have abbreviated listings.

- Every effort has been made to check the accuracy of all museum information, as well as exhibition schedules, at the time of publication. All hours, fees, days closed, and especially exhibitions, including those not already marked as tentative, are nonetheless subject to change at any time. We strongly suggest that you call to confirm any exhibition you wish to see.
- If you find any inaccuracies, please accept our apologies — but do let us know. Finally, if we have inadvertently omitted your favorite museum, a letter to us would be most appreciated, so we can include it in the 2000 edition.

EXPLANATION OF CODES

The coding system we have developed for this guide is made up primarily of standardized, easy to recognize abbreviations. All codes are listed under their appropriate categories.

MAIN CATEGORIES

AM	American	IND	Indian
AF	African	IMPR	Impressionist
AN/GRK	Ancient Greek	JAP	Japanese
AN/R	Ancient Roman	LAT/AM	Latin American
AS	Asian	MEX	Mexican
BRIT	British	MED	Medieval
BYZ	Byzantine	NAT/AM	Native American
CH	Chinese	OC	Oceanic
CONT	Contemporary	OM	Old Masters
DU	Dutch	OR	Oriental
EGT	Egyptian	P/COL	Pre-Columbian
EU	European	P/RAPH	Pre-Raphaelite
FL	Flemish	REG	Regional
FR	French	REN	Renaissance
GER	German	RUSS	Russian
IT	Italian	SP	Spanish

MEDIUM

CER	Ceramics	PHOT	Photography
DEC/ART	Decorative Arts	POST	Posters
DRGS	Drawings	PTGS	Paintings
GR	Graphics	SCULP	Sculpture
PER/RMS	Period Rooms	W/COL	Watercolors

17

SUBJECT MATTER

AB	Abstract	FIG	Figurative
ANT	Antiquities	FOLK	Folk Art
ARCH	Architectural	LDSCP	Landscape
CART	Cartoon	PRIM	Primitive
EXP	Expressionist	ST/LF	Still Life
ETH	Ethnic		

REGIONS

E	East	S	South
MID/E	Middle East	W	West
N	North		

PERM/COLL   Permanent Collection

The punctuation marks used for the permanent collection codes denote the following:

The colon (":") is used after a major category to indicate sub-listings with that category. For example, "AM: ptgs, sculp" indicates that the museum has a collection of American paintings and sculpture.

The semi-colon (";") indicates that one major category is ending and another major category listing is beginning. For example, "AM: ptgs; SP: sculp; DU; AF" indicates that the museum has collections that include American paintings, Spanish sculpture, and works of Dutch and African origin.

A number added to any of the above denotes century, i.e., "EU: ptgs 19, 20" means that the collection contains European painting of the nineteenth and twentieth centuries.

MUSEUM SERVICES

!	CALL TO CONFIRM OR FOR FURTHER INFORMATION
Y	Yes
☎	Telephone Number
℗	Parking Available
♿	Handicapped Accessibility: at least some of the facility is accessible
🍴	Restaurant Facilities Available
ADM	Admission
SUGG/CONT	Suggested Contribution — Pay What You Wish, But You Must Pay Something
VOL/CONT	Voluntary Contribution — Free Admission, Contribution Requested.
F	Free
F/DAY	Free Day
SR CIT	Senior Citizen, with I.D. (Age may vary)
GT	Group Tours
DT	Drop in Tours
MUS/SH	Museum Shop
H/B	Historic Building
S/G	Sculpture Garden
TBA	To Be Announced
TENT!	Tentatively Scheduled
ATR!	Advance Tickets Required - Call
CAT	Catalog
WT	Exhibition Will Travel - see index of traveling exhibitions
♩	Acoustiguide Tour Available

HOLIDAYS

ACAD!	Academic Holidays — Call For Information		
LEG/HOL!	Legal Holidays — Call For Information		
THGV	Thanksgiving		
MEM/DAY	Memorial Day		
LAB/DAY	Labor Day		
Mo	Monday	Fr	Friday
Tu	Tuesday	Sa	Saturday
We	Wednesday	Su	Sunday
Th	Thursday		

MUSEUMS AND EXHIBITIONS BY STATE

ALABAMA

BIRMINGHAM

Birmingham Museum of Art

2000 8th Ave. North, Birmingham, AL 35203

☎ 205-254-2566 or 2565   ◉ www.artsBMA.org

Open: 10-5 Tu-Sa, Noon-5 Su   **Closed:** Mo, 1/1, THGV, 12/25

& ℗ **Museum Shop** � Terrace Café

Group Tours: 205-254-2318   **Drop-In Tours:** 11:30 & 12:30 Tu-Fr; 2:00 Sa, Su   **Sculpture Garden**

Permanent Collection: AM: ptgs; EU: ptgs; OR; AF; P/COL; DEC/ART; PHOT; CONT; glass; REN: Kress Coll.

The Birmingham Museum of Art, with over 18,000 works in its permanent collection, is the largest municipal museum in the Southeast. In addition to the most extensive Asian art collection in the Southeast, the museum houses the finest collection of Wedgwood china outside of England. "Art & Soul", an 8 minute video presentation is available to familiarize visitors with the museum. **NOT TO BE MISSED:** Multi-level outdoor Sculpture Garden featuring a waterwall designed by sculptor Elyn Zimmerman and two mosaic lined pools designed by artist Valerie Jaudon; Hitt Collection of 18th C French paintings & decorative arts; Beeson collection of Wedgwood (largest of its kind outside of England); Contemporary Glass; Kress Collection of Renaissance Art.

ON EXHIBIT 1999

thru winter 1999   THE ARTIST IN THE STUDIO

Designed to allow the visitor to learn art processes and art history, both young and old will be able to enjoy a hands-on studio experience in an environment that features 3 learning stations. From time to time, various artists-in-residence will create art on site.

11/01/1998 to 01/03/1999   CHOKWE! ART AND INITIATION OF CHOKWE AND RELATED PEOPLES

In the first exhibition of its kind in the U.S., the 200 artifacts on view, gathered from important public and private collections here and in Europe, highlight the artistry of the Chokwe and related peoples of Angola, Zaire and Zambia. Interactive elements and innovative video techniques will be integrated into this gallery installation to provide a rich contextual setting for the items on view. *Will Travel*

01/31/1999 to 04/04/1999   ART AT THE END OF THE CENTURY: CONTEMPORARY ART FROM THE MILWAUKEE ART MUSEUM

About 30 European and American works mostly made in the last two decades by, among others, American Neo-Expressionist Susan Rothenberg, David Salle and Jenny Holzer, European figures such as George Baselitz and Francesco Clemente. In addition Neo-Conceptualists and younger artists from the 1990's with a variety of stylistic influences and no clear cut "ism". *Catalog Will Travel*

01/31/1999 to 04/04/1999   INFRA-SLIM SPACES: THE SPIRITUAL AND PHYSICAL IN THE ART OF TODAY

04/25/1999 to 07/04/1999   REMEMBERED PAST, DISCOVERED FUTURE: THE ALABAMA ARCHITECTURE OF WARREN, KNIGHT & DAVIS, 1901-1961

Architectural drawings, renderings and photographs illustrate the important role this firm played in the development and evolution of architecture in Alabama and the Southeast during the first half of the 20th century. *Catalog*

05/02/1999 to 07/04/1999   ROADS LESS TRAVELED: AMERICAN PAINTINGS 1833-1935

10/03/1999 to 01/16/2000   SEARCHING FOR ANCIENT EGYPT

From the display of the interior wall of a 4,300-year-old funerary chapel to an exquisite gold-covered mummy mask, this exhibition features more than 130 extraordinary objects from every major period of ancient Egypt. Many of those included have not been on public view for 30 years. *Catalog Will Travel*

American Sport Art Museum And Archives
Affiliate Institution: U.S. Sports Academy
One Academy Dr., Daphne, AL 36526
☎ 334-626-3303 ⊚ www.sport.ussa.edu
Open: 10-2 Mo-Fr **Closed:** Sa, Su, LEG/HOL, ACAD!
& ℗ **Museum Shop Group Tours Drop-In Tours**: Available upon request
Permanent Collection: AM: ptgs, sculp , gr all on the single theme of American sports heros

One of the largest collections of sports art in America may be found at this museum which also features works highlighting an annual sport artist of the year. Of special interest is the two-story high mural on an outside wall of the Academy entitled "A Tribute to the Human Spirit". Created by world-renowned Spanish artist Cristobal Gabarron, the work pays tribute to Jackie Robinson on the 50th anniversary of his breaking the color barrier in major league baseball. PLEASE NOTE: Works by Paul Goodnight, one of 15 official Olympic artists for the 1996 Atlanta Games, will be featured in the annual "Sport Artist of the Year" show (dates TBA!). **NOT TO BE MISSED:** "The Pathfinder", a large sculpture of a hammerthrower by John Robinson where the weight of the ball of the hammer is equal to the rest of entire weight of the body of the figure.

ON EXHIBIT 1999
Bi-monthly exhibitions are planned including participation in the local annual celebration of the arts organized by the City of Mobile.

Wiregrass Museum of Art
126 Museum Ave., Dothan, AL 36302-1624
☎: 334-794-3871
Open: 10-5 Tu-Sa, 1-5 Su **Closed:** Mo, LEG/HOL!
Sugg/Cont Adult: $1.00/visitor
& ℗ **Museum Shop Group Tours Drop-In Tours Historic Building** Located in former 1912 electric plant
Permanent Collection: REG

Featured on the main floor galleries of this regional visual arts museum are a variety of works that reflect the ever changing world of art with emphasis on solo exhibits showcasing important emerging artists of the south. The museum, located in the South East corner of Alabama, approximately 100 miles from Montgomery, recently renovated four galleries for the display of decorative arts, African art and works on paper. **NOT TO BE MISSED:** ARTventures, a "hands on" gallery for children, schools, & families

ON EXHIBIT 1999
ONGOING: AFRICAN ART

11/14/1998 to 01/17/1999 SHAHAR CAREN WEAVER: RECENT WORKS

12/19/1998 to 02/14/1999 BITS AND PIXELS: THE COMPUTER GRAPHICS OF JEFF BURDEN

01/23/1999 to 03/28/1999 THE TRANSPARENT PALETTE: WATERCOLORS FROM THE MINT MUSEUM OF ART COLLECTION

01/30/1999 to 04/18/1999 CH'ING DYNASTY JADE FROM THE COLLECTION OF THE COLUMBUS MUSEUM

04/03/1999 to 06/06/1999 THE CORPORATE COLLECTION OF BLOUNT, INC.

06/19/1999 to 08/29/1999 LOCAL COLOR: DOTHAN WIREGRASS ART LEAGUE

07/24/1999 to 10/17/1999 TIFFANY SILVER

09/04/1999 to 10/31/1999 WORKS BY WARHOL FROM THE COCHRAN COLLECTION

ALABAMA

Fayette Art Museum
530 Temple Ave. N., Fayette, AL 35555
📞: 205-932-8727
Open: 9-Noon & 1-4 Mo & Tu, Th & Fri; Su 1-4-folk art only **Closed:** We, Sa, Su, LEG/HOL!
Vol/Cont
♿ Ⓟ **Museum Shop**
Group Tours Drop-In Tours: daily during museum hours **Historic Building**
Permanent Collection: AM: ptgs 20; FOLK

Housed in a 1930's former school house, this collection consists mostly of 3,500 works of 20th century American art. Six new folk galleries, opened in 1996, are open Sundays 1-4. **NOT TO BE MISSED:** One of the largest collections of folk art in the Southeast.

Gadsden Museum of Fine Arts
2829 W. Meighan Blvd., Gadsden, AL 35904
📞: 205-546-7365
Open: 10-4 Mo-We & Fr, 10am-8pm T, 1-5 Su **Closed:** Sa, LEG/HOL!
Vol/Cont
♿ Ⓟ **Museum Shop**
Group Tours Drop-In Tours
Permanent Collection: EU: Impr/ptgs; CONT; DEC/ART

Historical collections and works by local and regional artists are housed in this museum.

Huntsville Museum of Art
700 Monroe St., S. W., Huntsville, AL 35801
📞: 256-535-4350 ◙ www.hsv.tis.net/hma
Open: 10-5 Tu-Fr, 9-5 Sa, 1-5 Su **Closed:** Mo, LEG/HOL!
Students: 0 **Seniors:** 0
♿ Ⓟ **Museum Shop**
Group Tours Drop-In Tours: selected Su afternoons
Permanent Collection: AM: ptgs, drgs, phot, sculp, folk, dec/art, reg 18-20; EU: works on paper; OR; AF

Focusing on American paintings and graphics from the 18th through the 20th century, as well as works by regional artists, the Huntsville Museum promotes the recognition and preservation of artistic heritage in its own and other Southeastern states, and serves as the leading visual arts center in North Alabama. PLEASE NOTE: A new museum building at 500 Church Street is being constructed and is tentatively scheduled to open in the spring of 1998. **NOT TO BE MISSED:** Large Tiffany style stained glass window.

ON EXHIBIT 1999
11/21/1998 to 02/07/1999 A TASTE FOR SPLENDOR: TREASURES FROM THE HILLWOOD MUSEUM
This is a rare opportunity to see the exquisite art collection of Marjorie Merriwether Post, heir to the Post cereal fortune, which never before has been seen outside her home at Hillwood. More than 160 decorative and fine arts objects created in Imperial Russia and Europe, dating from the 17th to the mid-20th c. range from 19th century French furniture to porcelains and gold boxes commissioned by Catherine the Great and treasures by Fabergé including two of the Imperial Easter Eggs.

MOBILE

Mobile Museum of Art

4850 Museum Dr., Langan Park, Mobile, AL 36608

☏: 334-343-2667

Open: 10-5 Tu-Su   **Closed:** Mo, LEG/HOL! CITY/HOL!

♿ Ⓟ   **Museum Shop   Group Tours   Drop-In Tours   Sculpture Garden**

Permanent Collection: AM: 19; AF; OR; EU; DEC/ART; CONT/CRAFTS

Beautifully situated on a lake in the middle of Langan Park, this museum offers the visitor an overview of 2,000 years of culture represented by more than 4,000 pieces in its permanent collection. PLEASE NOTE: Admission is charged for some traveling exhibitions. **NOT TO BE MISSED:** Boehm porcelain bird collection; 20th-century decorative arts collection

ON EXHIBIT 1999

11/07/1999 to 01/09/2000 TWENTIETH CENTURY AMERICAN DRAWINGS FROM THE ARKANSAS CENTER FOUNDATION COLLECTION

A great diversity of drawing styles and techniques spanning the greater part of the 20th c. of American art includes in their definition pencil, pen and ink, watercolor, silverpoint to acrylic and oil on paper. Among the artists represented in the 100 works are Avery, Brady, Burchfield, Cottingham, Curry, Davis, Dove, Frankenthaler, Francis, Guston, Hopper, Marsh, Pollock, Sheeler and Toby. *Catalog Will Travel*

Mobile Museum of Art Downtown

300 Dauphin St., Mobile, AL 36602

☏: 334-343-2667

Open: 8:30-4:30 Mo-Fr

Students: 0   **Seniors:** 0

♿ Ⓟ   **Museum Shop**

Group Tours   Drop-In Tours

A renovated early 1900's hardware store is home to this downtown art museum gallery.

MONTGOMERY

Montgomery Museum of Fine Arts

One Museum Dr., P.O. Box 230819, Montgomery, AL 36117

☏: 334-244-5700   ■ fineartsmuseum.com

Open: 10-5 Tu-Sa, till 9 Th, Noon-5 Su   **Closed:** Mo, LEG/HOL!

♿ Ⓟ   **Museum Shop**   ⛺ Tu-Sa 11-2 lunch, 2-4 coffee + desert

Group Tours: 334-244-5700   **Drop-In Tours**: 1:00 Sa, Su, 6:30 Th

Permanent Collection: AM: ptgs, gr, drgs 18-20; EU: ptgs, gr, sculp, dec/art 19; CONT/REG; BLOUNT COLLECTION OF AM ART

Set in a picturesque, English-style park, the Museum is noted for its holdings of 19th and 20th century American Paintings in the Blount Collection, its Southern regional art, and its Old Master prints. **NOT TO BE MISSED:** "A Peaceable Kingdom With Quakers Bearing Banners" by Edward Hicks; ARTWORKS, an interactive gallery for children

ALABAMA

Montgomery Museum of Fine Arts - continued
ON EXHIBIT 1999

11/07/1998 to 01/10/1999   IMAGES OF THE FLOATING WORLD: JAPANESE PRINTS FROM THE BIRMINGHAM MUSEUM OF ART
On view in this first time exhibition will be 100 contemporary and historic (Edo 1615-1868 & Meiji 1868-1912) Japanese prints, drawn from the Museum's extensive 500 piece collection acquired over the past 10 years. *Will Travel*

11/17/1998 to 01/17/1999   ALABAMA LANDSCAPES BY MONTGOMERY ARTISTS

01/30/1999 to 03/25/1999   EDWARD HOPPER: THE WATERCOLORS
Painted primarily during his trips away from NY during the 1920's and 30's, these early watercolors brought Hopper his original success. He continued to return to the New England landscape for inspiration. *Catalog Will Travel*

01/30/1999 to 03/28/1999   AKARI LIGHT SCULPTURES OF ISAMU NOGUCHI

01/30/1999 to 03/28/1999   THE LAMPS OF TIFFANY: HIGHLIGHTS OF THE EGON AND HILDEGARDE NEUSTADT COLLECTION
44 lamps and windows from this rarely seen collection.

03/27/1999 to 05/23/1999   ELAYNE GOODMAN

04/10/1999 to 05/23/1999   REMBRANDT PRINTS FROM THE WEIL COLLECTION

04/10/1999 to 05/23/1999   HOGARTH PRINTS FROM THE MCALLEN MUSEUM

06/05/1999 to 07/18/1999   REGIONS: JONI MABE

06/05/1999 to 07/18/1999   6TH INTERNATIONAL SHOEBOX SCULPTURE EXHIBITION

08/07/1999 to 11/07/1999   SPIRIT EYES, HUMAN HANDS: AFRICAN ART FROM THE SAMUEL HARN COLLECTION *Will Travel*

11/20/1999 to 01/02/2000   THE 33RD MONTGOMERY ART GUILD MUSEUM EXHIBITION

Anchorage Museum of History and Art

121 W. Seventh Ave., Anchorage, AK 99519-6650

☎: 907-343-4326

Open: 9-6 Mo-Su mid MAY-mid SEPT; 10-6 Tu-Sa, 1-5 Su rest of the year **Closed:** Mo winter, 1/1, THGV, 12/25

ADM Adult: $5.00 **Children:** F (under 18) **Seniors:** $4.50

& **Museum Shop** ⫙Café **Group Tours:** 907-343-6187 **Drop-In Tours:** 10, 11, 1 & 2 Alaska Gallery (summer)

Permanent Collection: ETH

The Anchorage Museum of History & Art is dedicated to the collection, preservation, and exhibition of Alaskan ethnology, history, and art.

ON EXHIBIT 1999

06/1998 to 05/1999   ONCE UPON A TIME: A CHILDREN'S EXHIBITION OF STORIES, MYTHS, AND LEGENDS IN ART

01/06/1999 to 01/24/1999   ALASKA POSITIVE

01/17/1999 to 02/28/1999   LYNN MARIE NADEN

02/1999 to 04/11/1999   BALTO EXHIBIT

02/02/1999 to 03/28/1999   EARTH, FIRE AND FIBRE

02/02/1999 to 03/28/1999   MATT JOHNSON

03/07/1999 to 04/04/1999   ANCHORAGE SCHOOL DISTRICT ART SHOW

03/07/1999 to 04/11/1999   ALASKA INAUGURAL BALL GOWN EXHIBIT

03/07/1999 to 04/11/1999   HAROLD WALLIN

03/07/1999 to 04/11/1999   COLORPRINT USA
One printmaker from each state was selected to submit a print to this prestigious exhibition. The works will be shown in all fifty states.

05/02/1999 to 09/19/1999   DRAWN FROM SHADOWS AND STONE: PHOTOGRAPHING NORTH PACIFIC PEOPLES (1897-1902)

05/06/1999 to 10/10/1999   STORIES FROM THE WATER: SMALL BOATS OF THE FAR NORTHWEST

06/1999 to 05/2000   ANIMALS AND ART

10/1999 to 11/1999   RAREFIED LIGHT

10/03/1999 to 11/14/1999   ALVIN AMAZON RETROSPECTIVE

11/07/1999 to 01/02/2000   TRASHFORMATIONS: RECYCLED MATERIALS IN CONTEMPORARY AMERICAN ART AND DESIGN
Works in various media featuring the varied and inventive use of recycled materials in American art and design. *Will Travel*

11/11/1999 to 12/05/1999   MARY VER HOEF

11/26/1999 to 01/02/2000   DOLLS AND TOYS
Antique dolls and toys from the Museum's collection will be on view in this annual holiday exhibition.

12/05/1999 to 02/27/2000   LIGHT ART: NEW ART FORMS USING LIGHT AS A MEDIUM

ALASKA

Totem Heritage Center

601 Deermount, Ketchikan, AK 99901

☎: 907-225-5900   ◉   www.ktn.net

Open: 8-5 Daily (5/15 - 9/30); 1-5 Tu-Fr (10/1 - 4/30 - no adm fee)   **Closed:** 1/1, EASTER, VETERAN'S DAY, THGV, 12/25

ADM   Adult: $3.00   **Children:** F (under 6)

& **Museum Shop**

Group Tours: (5/1-9/30 only)   **Drop-In Tours**

Permanent Collection: CONT: N/W Coast Indian art; Totem poles

Awe-inspiring Tlingit and Haida totem poles and pole fragments of the 19th century, brought to Ketchikan from Tongass and Village Islands and Old Kasaan during the totem pole revival project, are the highlight of this museum.

MESA

Mesa Southwest Museum
53 N. Macdonald, Mesa, AZ 85201
☎: 602-644-2230   ◙   www.ci.mesa.az.us/parkspec/msm/index.html
Open: 10-5 Tu-Sa, 1-5 Su   **Closed:** Mo, LEG/HOL!
Free Day: Varies   **ADM   Adult:** $4.00   **Children:** $2.00 (3-12)   **Students:** $3.50   **Seniors:** $3.50
&   ℗   **Museum Shop**
Group Tours: 602-644-3553 or 3071   **Drop-In Tours**: Reserved in Advance   **Historic Building**: Surrine House (1896)
Permanent Collection: ETH; P/COL; CER

Changing exhibitions of ancient to contemporary works based on Southwestern themes are featured in this multi-faceted museum. Undergoing a major expansion that will double its size, the new building of this 20 year old museum is scheduled to open in 2000. Please note that the museum will remain open during construction. **NOT TO BE MISSED:** "Finding The Way", by Howard Post; "Superstition Sunrise", full-color wall mural by Jim Gucwa; "Hohokam Life", by Ka Graves, a series of watercolor interpretations of Hohokam Indian life (300 B.C.-1450 A.D.) Some pieces not on exhibit during expansion

ON EXHIBIT 1999
03/28/1999 to 05/09/1999   REFLECTIONS OF A JOURNEY: ENGRAVINGS AFTER KARL BODMER
In 1833-34 Prince Maximilian a German Naturalist and explorer and Karl Bodmer, a Swiss Painter and illustrator, made an historic journey up the Missouri River. Works produced by both are considered a primary resource on the rich cultures of the North Plains Indians.

05/22/1999 to 07/18/1999   Home on the Range: Three Arizona Women Artists Interpret the Southwestern Landscapes, Social Life and Urban Myths

09/05/1999 to 10/24/1999   MEXICAN MASKS OF THE 20TH CENTURY: A LIVING TRADITION
Wearing a mask transforms the wearer. People have believed that masks work magic spells, inspire fears, etc. In this exhibition the versatility and diversity of masks in the 20th c is shown. Many here fall into two groups: Devic Masks, Tiger masks, Carnival Masks, and masks for the Dance of the Moors and Christians indicating the influence of Spanish Culture and religion on the Aztec civilization in early Mexico.

PHOENIX

Heard Museum
22 E. Monte Vista Rd., Phoenix, AZ 85004-1480
☎: 602-252-8840   ◙   www.heard.org
Open: 9:30-5 Mo-Sa, Noon-5 Su   **Closed:** LEG/HOL!
ADM   Adult: $6.00   **Children:** F (under 4) !   **Seniors:** $5.00
&   ℗   **Museum Shop   Group Tours   Drop-In Tours**: Many times daily!
Permanent Collection: NAT/AM; ETH; AF; OR; OC; SO/AM

The collection of the decorative and fine arts of the Heard Museum, which spans the history of Native American Art from the pre-historic to the contemporary, is considered the most comprehensive collection of its kind in the entire country. Named after the Heards who founded the museum based on their great interest in the culture of the native people of Arizona, the museum is housed in the original structure the Heards built in 1929 adjacent to their home called Casa Blanca. PLEASE NOTE: A new branch of the museum called Heard Museum North is now open at the Boulders Resort in Scottsdale (phone 602-488-9817 for information). **NOT TO BE MISSED:** Experience the cultures of 3 Native American tribes with hands-on family oriented "Old Ways, New Ways"

ARIZONA

Heard Museum - continued

ON EXHIBIT 1999

ON PERMANENT DISPLAY   NATIVE PEOPLES OF THE SOUTHWEST: THE PERMANENT COLLECTION OF THE HEARD MUSEUM
A magnificent display of superb Native American artifacts including pottery, baskets, jewelry, weaving and kachina dolls.

OLD WAYS, NEW WAYS
A state-of-the-art interactive exhibit that features enjoyable hands-on art activities for the entire family.

Through 03/1999   CRADLES, CORN AND LIZARDS
An exhibition that explores the cultures, landscape and wildlife of Arizona includes hands-on activities and an interactive multi-dimensional mural.

Through 09/1999   HORSE
Fully adorned horse replicas, artwork of horse imagery and hands-on activities are included in a presentation that examines the influences of the horse on the indigenous peoples of North America, from its introduction by the Spanish in the 1500's to the present day.

05/16/1998 to 10/1999   BLUE GEM, WHITE METAL: CARVINGS AND JEWELRY FROM THE C.G. WALLACE COLLECTION
A display of early 20th century Zuni and Navajo jewelry, silverwork and carvings from the largest collections of its kind features a wide variety of techniques including carving, mosaic overlay and inlay, casting, nugget work channel inlay and more.

05/30/1998 to 02/1999   RECENT ACQUISITIONS

10/10/1998 to 01/10/1999   MEMORY AND IMAGINATION: THE LEGACY OF MAIDU INDIAN ARTIST FRANK DAY
Frank Day (1902-1976) was a self-taught Konkow Maidu artist whose works were responsible for a revitalization of Native American ceremonialism in Northern California. In this exhibition 50 of his paintings will be featured with artifacts from his home and paintings by contemporary Maidu artists who were influenced by his work.

01/1999 to 10/1999   INVITATIONAL REUNION
A celebration of the creativity and innovation of contemporary Native American artists features the best works selected from those in the Museum's past 7 invitationals.

02/28/1999 to 05/1999   JEWELS OF THE SOUTHWEST
Documenting innovations in the transformation of contemporary Native American jewelry from craft to art will be pieces on loan from private and public collections as well as those from the Heard itself. The exhibition will be mounted in the Heard's new Lovena Ohl Gallery.

04/1999 to 08/2000   RISKY BUSINESS
Featured will be works by Native American artists who are risk takers and push the boundaries in their artistry.

05/1999 to 07/1999   TRANSITIONS: CONTEMPORARY CANADIAN INDIAN AND INUIT ART
Works by 13 Canadian artists will be seen in an exhibit designed to explore and challenge the perceptions of contemporary native art in Canada.

07/1999 to 10/2000   MICHAEL NARANJO: TOUCHABLE SCULPTURE
Bronze and stone sculptures are featured in a unique display that invites the visitor to touch and enjoy a hands-on experience.

10/1999   REMEMBERING OUR INDIAN SCHOOL DAYS: THE BOARDING SCHOOL EXPERIENCE
The controversial practice of removing Native American children from their homes and sending them to boarding school in order to facilitate education and assimilation is reflected in drawings reflecting their recollections and writings.

10/20/1999 to 12/20/1999   IMAGINING THE WORLD THROUGH NAIVE PAINTING
From public and private collections in Spain and throughout Latin America, this exhibition presents works by many of the most renowned Latin American naive artists.

11/13/1999 to 03/19/2000   POWERFUL IMAGES: PORTRAYALS OF NATIVE AMERICA
Pop and Native American cultures blend in the contemporary works on view.

Phoenix Art Museum
1625 N. Central Ave., Phoenix, AZ 85004-1685
☎: 602-257-1880
Open: 10-5 Tu-Su, till 9pm Th & Fr **Closed:** Mo, I/1, 7/4, THGV, 12/25
Free Day: Th **ADM Adult:** $6.00 **Children:** $2.00 6-18 **Students:** $4.00 full time **Seniors:** $4.00
⅊ ℗ **Museum Shop** ⑪ Eddie's Art Museum Café
Group Tours: 602-257-4356 **Drop-In Tours**: 2:00 daily & 6:00 on Th; Gallery Talks 12:00 daily
Permanent Collection: AM: Western, cont; AS; EU: 18-19;CONT Lat/Am; Fashion

The new 160,000 sq ft. Phoenix Art Museum is double its former size. The classically progressive design of the Museum integrates art and architecture with the southwestern landscape, accommodating large traveling exhibitions, a collection of over 13,000 works and a growing arts audience. Visitors enjoy an audiovisual orientation theater, an interactive gallery for children, a restaurant and Museum Store. Special admission prices apply to "Splendors of Ancient Egypt" and tickets will be available at Dillard's and the Museum. **NOT TO BE MISSED:** "Attack Gallery" for children and their families; Thorne miniature rooms of historic interiors.

ON EXHIBIT 1999
10/04/1998 to 03/27/1999 SPLENDORS OF ANCIENT EGYPT
From mummy cases and jewelry to wall carvings and ceramics, this major exhibition of 200 Egyptian masterpieces, one of the largest collections of its kind to ever visit the U.S., offers a panoramic view of 4500 years of Egyptian culture and history. Adm: Adults $10, Sen. $9, Children 6-18 $5, under 6 free. Tickets include Museum adm and audio tour. I/2 price tickets on Th after 5 on 1st come basis. Ticket available at the Museum or at Dilliards . *Catalog Admission Fee Will Travel*

10/24/1998 to 11/22/1999 34TH ANNUAL COWBOY ARTIST OF AMERICA SALE & EXHIBITION
Regarded as one of the most prestigious exhibitions and sales in the country, this exhibition unveils more than 100 new, important (and often quite costly) works that have never before been on public view.

12/19/1998 to 02/28/1999   COPPER AS CANVAS, TWO CENTURIES OF MASTERPIECE PAINTINGS ON COPPER, 1525-1775
This is the first ever exhibition of its kind in the world of spectacular works from public and private collections in the US and Europe. It will highlight the practice of painting on copper due to the copper's characteristics which lend to outstanding detail and luminescence. *Catalog Will Travel*

04/03/1999 to 06/27/1999 GREAT DESIGN: 100 MASTERPIECES FROM THE VITRA DESIGN MUSEUM
The first American venue for this world renowned collection of 19th and 20th century Furniture. It will present designs by Frank Lloyd Wright, Le Corbusier, Mackintosh, Saarinen, Eames, Noguchi and many others with early examples of mass production to most recent design innovations. *Catalog Will Travel*

07/22/1999 to 10/03/1999 CANTOS PARALELOS: VISUAL PARODY IN CONTEMPORARY ARGENTINE ART
Post World War II painting, sculpture and assemblage that parody Argentine middle class ideas of good taste. Large scale works by Berni, de la Vega, Grippo and Heredia are included. *Catalog Will Travel*

09/18/1999 to 01/02/2000 MONET: LATE PAINTINGS OF GIVERNY FROM THE MUSEE MARMITON
22 paintings on loan from the distinguished Musée Marmiton in Paris offer an overview of Monet's late works, considered by the artist to be the finest of his career. *Catalog Will Travel*

PRESCOTT

Phippen Museum
Affiliate Institution: Art of the American West
4701 Hwy 89 N, Prescott, AZ 86301
☎: 520-778-1385
Open: 10-4 M & We-Sa, 1-4 Su **Closed:** Tu, 1/1, THGV, 12/25
ADM Adult: $3.00 **Children:** F (12 & under) **Students:** $2.00 **Seniors:** $2.00
⅊ ℗ **Museum Shop Group Tours Drop-In Tours**
Permanent Collection: PTGS, SCULP

The Museum's collection of paintings and sculpture of Western America also includes contemporary works by Native American and Anglo artists. **NOT TO BE MISSED:** 3 foot high bronze of Father Keno by George Phippen; Spectacular view and historic wagons in front of the museum

ARIZONA

Fleisher Museum

17207 N. Perimeter Dr., Scottsdale, AZ 85255
☎: 602-585-3108   ▣ www.fleischer.org
Open: 10-4 Daily   **Closed:** LEG/HOL!
& ℗   **Museum Shop   Group Tours:** 602-585-3108   **Drop-In Tours:** Mo-Fr; 10-4 by Reservation Only
Historic Building All materials used in building indigenous to State of Arizona   **Sculpture Garden**
Permanent Collection: AM/IMPR; ptgs, sculp (California School)

Located in the 261 acre Perimeter Center, the Fleisher Museum was, until recently, the first and only museum to feature California Impressionist works. More than 80 highly recognized artists represented in this collection painted in "plein air" from the 1880's-1940's, imbuing their landscape subject matter with the special and abundant sunlight of the region. Russian & Soviet Impressionism from the Cold War era are represented in the permanent collection as well. **NOT TO BE MISSED:** "Mount Alice at Sunset" by Franz A. Bischoff, best known as the "King of the Rose Painters," "Alas Roses" by Franz A. Bischoff

ON EXHIBIT 1999

ONGOING: AMERICAN IMPRESSIONISM, CALIFORNIA SCHOOL FROM THE TURN OF THE CENTURY

WORKS OF RUSSIAN AND SOVIET IMPRESSIONISM FROM THE COLD WAR ERA

05/16/1998 to 06/1999   WORKS OF RUSSIAN AND SOVIET IMPRESSIONISM FROM THE POST WAR ERA.
A window to Russian life during the Soviet era.

05/16/1998 to 10/1999   AMERICAN IMPRESSIONISM: CALIFORNIA SCHOOL FROM THE TURN OF THE CENTURY
This art style was a blending of American artists who worked in California and painted internationally until they settled in the West. Characterized by plein air painting and an abundance of sunlight and brilliantly colored landscapes.

10/1999 to 05/2000   AMERICAN MASTERS: THEN AND NOW
Two centuries of sculpture from the National Sculpture Society.

10/1999 to 05/2000   NATIONAL SCULPTURE SOCIETY AT THE FLEISHER MUSEUM

Scottsdale Museum of Contemporary Arts

7380 E. Second St., Scottsdale, AZ 85251
☎: 602-994-2787   ▣ www.scottsdalearts.org
Open: WINTER: 10-5 Mo-Sa, till 8 Th, Noon-5 Su; SUMMER: 10-5 Mo-We, 10-8 Th-Sa, 12-5 Su   **Closed:** LEG/HOL!
Vol/Cont
& ℗   **Museum Shop** ¶ Arts Café (dinner only 2 hours prior to performances)
Group Tours: 602-874 4641   **Drop-In Tours:** 1:30 Su Oct-Apr, 3:00 Su (outdoor sculp) Nov-Apr
Permanent Collection: CONT; REG

Four exhibition spaces and a beautiful outdoor sculpture garden are but a part of this community oriented multi-disciplinary cultural center. The opening of a new museum called Gerard L. Cafesjian Pavilion will open a new and exciting concept with walls extending to the very limits of the city under the auspices of Scottsdale Museum of Contemporary art. It is scheduled for 2/14/99. **NOT TO BE MISSED:** "The Dance" a bronze sculpture (1936) by Jacques Lipchitz; "Ambient Landscape" by Janet Taylor; "Time/Light Fusion" sculpture (1990) by Dale Eldred

ON EXHIBIT 1999
09/11/1998 to 08/15/1999   THE WALL PROJECT
A large scale site specific work as a signature piece for the Museum will be commissioned annually.

Scottsdale Museum of Contemporary Arts - continued

12/05/1998 to 03/14/1999 BEVERLY MCIVER: ALL OF ME
Professionally trained as a clown, McIver explores issues of personal identity in these self-portraits depicting a black clown in white face.

12/18/1998 to 03/21/1999 MARK MCDOWELL
Bold and colorful still lifes of non traditional subjects in the tradition of pop art.

02/14/1999 STUDIO GLASS FROM THE GERARD L. CAFESJIAN COLLECTION
Only one facet of this collection is represented here. Fragile lampworked pieces as well as examples of bold forms of cast glass and metal show the versatility of the medium. Among the artists shown are Chihuly, Morris, Peiser and many others.

02/14/1999 MIXED MEDIA: SELECTIONS FROM THE SEGURA ARCHIVE COLLECTION
Over the years this publishing company has become well known for its limited editions and monotypes by leading artists. New prints by a diverse group of contemporary artists including Bernardi, Gaines, Serrano, Turrell, Carrie Mae Weems, William Wegman and others are presented in three segments: photographers and conceptual artists using photography, work by women and minority artists, and work that challenges romantic myths about the American West by addressing issues such as immigration and assimilation.

02/14/1999 to 05/09/1999 JIM WAID
Waid's large abstract canvases are lush explosions of light. They appear to be a compilation of fragments of phenomena from the environment rather than specific landscapes.

02/14/1999 to 05/09/1999 ART GUYS INSTALLATION
Described as a cross between Dada, David Letterman, John Cage and the Smother's Brothers, Jack Massing and Michael Galbreth are the court jesters of the modern age.

02/14/1999 to 05/09/1999 WILL BRUDER: POETRY, PRAGMATISM AND PLACE
A 25 year retrospective celebrating the virtuosity of Bruder's architectural studio. His is a significant international voice in contemporary architecture.

03/20/1999 to 06/06/1999 CRISTINA CARDENAS: WORKS ON PAPER
Her works are an assessment of personal identity and self-image. They combine images and icons from her cultural background with the human figure rendered against a background of violence and suffering.

04/03/1999 to 06/13/1999 COLLABORATIONS: WILLIAM ALLAN, ROBERT HUDSON, WILLIAM WILEY
Friends for more than 30 years, this exhibition features both collaborative and individual works by San Francisco Bay Area artists Allan, Hudson and Wiley. *Catalog Will Travel*

05/28/1999 to 08/29/1999 BLURRING THE BOUNDARIES: INSTALLATION ART 1970-1996
A study of installation art through the collections and exhibition record of the Museum of Contemporary Art, San Diego which has a unique heritage of such art dating back to the 60's

06/12/1999 to 09/18/1999 IAN VAN COLLER: NATURE OF DISPLACEMENT
His own perceptions of Africa and its people are scrutinized in these photogravures.

06/26/1999 to 09/03/1999 SELECTIONS FROM SCOTTSDALE'S COLLECTION OF FINE ART
A selection of work acquired since 1991.

11/28/1999 to 01/16/2000 AMERICA SEEN: PEOPLE AND PLACE
The images on view by Grant Wood, Norman Rockwell, John Stuart Curry, Thomas Hart Benton and other giants of American art working between the 1920's through the 1950's, document two world wars, the Great Depression, the New Deal, the growth of the American city and the nostalgia for simple rural life.

Sylvia Plotkin Judaica Museum

10460 N. 56th St., Scottsdale,, AZ 85253
☎: 602-951-0323   ◙   www.TempleBethIsrael.com
Open: 10-3 Tu-Th, Noon-3 (most) Su; OPEN AFTER FR EVENING SERVICES   **Closed:** Mo, Fr, Sa, LEG/HOL!; JEWISH HOL! JUL & AUG   **Sugg/Cont Adult:** $2.00
  ♿ ⓟ   **Museum Shop   Group Tours**: 602-443-4150   **Drop-In Tours**
Permanent Collection: JEWISH ART AND CEREMONIALS; TUNISIAN SYNAGOGUE PERIOD ROOM

ARIZONA

Sylvia Plotkin Judaica Museum - continued

Considered to be one of the most important centers of Jewish art and culture in the Southwest, the Sylvia Plotkin Judaica Museum has artifacts spanning 5000 years of Jewish history and heritage. The Museum hosts 3 special exhibitions a year, features guest speakers, Lecture Series, and interactive programs. It is advised to call ahead for summer hours. **NOT TO BE MISSED:** Reconstructed Tunisian Synagogue; To-scale Replica of a portion of the Western Wall in Jerusalem

ON EXHIBIT 1999

Fall 1998/ to Winter 1999   REDEDICATION OF PERMANENT EXHIBIT ON THEMES OF HOLIDAYS AND LIFE CYCLES

TEMPE

ASU Art Museum

Affiliate Institution: Arizona State University
Nelson Fine Arts Center & Mathews Center, Tempe, AZ 85287-2911
☎: 602-965-2787   ◙ http://asuam.fa.asu.edu
Open: SEPT THRU MAY: 10-9 Tu, 10-5 We-Sa, 1-5 Su; SUMMER: 10-5 Tu-Sa, 1-5 Su   **Closed:** Mo, LEG/HOL!
Vol/Cont
 & ℗ **Museum Shop**
Group Tours: 602-965-2787   **Drop-In Tours   Historic Building**; Award winning new building by Antoine Predock
Permanent Collection: AM: ptgs, gr; EU: gr 15-20; AM: crafts 19-20; LAT/AM: ptgs, sculp; CONT; AF; FOLK

For more than 40 years the ASU Art Museum, founded to broaden the awareness of American visual arts in Arizona, has been a vital resource within the valley's art community. The ASU Art Museum consists of the Nelson Center and the Matthews Center. **NOT TO BE MISSED:** Significant ceramics collection, new acquisitions on exhibition Jan - May; important and challenging collections and exhibitions of contemporary art.

ON EXHIBIT 1999

ONGOING   AMERICAN GALLERY:
An overview of the history of American art from early paintings by limners to works by Georgia O'Keeffe, Alexander Calder, Charles Demuth and other 20th century greats.

ONGOING   LATIN AMERICAN GALLERY: MEXICAN ART FROM THE LATIN AMERICAN COLLECTION
Superb paintings by such past masters as Rivera, Siqueiros and Tamayo, joined by those of contemporary artists are displayed with examples of vice-regal religious statuary and baroque-inspired Mexican retablos.

to 01/24/1999   HELME PRINZEN

01/29/1999 to 02/28/1999   DAVIS CERAMIC COLLECTION

01/29/1999 to 03/19/1999   LOS ANGELES EMERGING ARTISTS

01/29/1999 to 05/1999   DANCE AND TECHNOLOGY EXHIBITION

02/13/1999   CONTEMPORARY ART FROM THE PERMANENT COLLECTION
Works by regional contemporary artists

02/20/1999 to 05/30/1999   JULES HELLER

02/20/1999 to 05/30/1999   LEOPOLD MENDEZ

04/09/1999 to 05/29/1999   VEILED MEMORIES

08/28/1999 to 10/31/1999   RESONATING: DENISE GREEN

11/20/1999 to 02/13/2000   JEAN LIPMAN COLLECTION

12/1999 to 01/31/2000   SCHOOL OF ART FACULTY

Center for Creative Photography
Affiliate Institution: University of Arizona
Tucson, AZ 85721-0103
☎: 520-621-7968   ◉ www.ccp.arizona.edu/ccp.html
Open: 11-5 Mo-Fr, Noon-5 Su   **Closed:** Sa, LEG/HOL!
Vol/Cont
 ❤️ ℗ **Museum Shop Group Tours**: education dept **Drop-In Tours**
Permanent Collection: PHOT 19-20

With more than 60,000 fine prints in the permanent collection, the singular focus of this museum, located on the campus of the University of Arizona, on is on the photographic image, its history, and its documentation. **NOT TO BE MISSED:** Works by Ansel Adams, Richard Avedon, Imogen Cunningham, Laura Gilpin, Marion Palfi, & Edward Weston

ON EXHIBIT 1999

12/12/1998 to 01/24/1999 ANN MANDELBAUM: PROXIMITIES

01/30/1999 to 03/21/1999 BODIES OF WORK: SERIES AND OBSESSIONS FROM THE CENTER FOR CREATIVE PHOTOGRAPHY COLLECTIONS

03/27/1999 to 05/23/1999 PHILIPPE HALSMAN: A RETROSPECTIVE

Tucson Museum of Art
140 N. Main Ave. Tucson, AZ 85701
☎: 520-624-2333   ◉ www.tucsonarts.com
Open: 10-4 Mo-Sa, Noon-4 Su; Closed Mo MEM/DAY-LAB/DAY & all major holidays **Closed:** LEG/HOL!
Free Day: Th **ADM Adult:** $2.00 (Members F) **Children:** F (12 & under) **Students:** $1.00 **Seniors:** $1.00
 ❤️ ℗ **Museum Shop**
Group Tours: 520-696-7450 **Drop-In Tours**: daily during museum hours for current exhibitions
Historic Building; Located on the site of the original Presidio - 5 historic properties Sculpture Garden
Permanent Collection: P/COL; AM: Western; CONT/SW; SP: colonial; MEX

Past meets present in this museum and historic home complex set in the Plaza of the Pioneers. The contemporary museum building itself, home to more than 5,000 works in its permanent collection, is a wonderful contrast to five of Tucson's most prominent historic homes that are all situated in an inviting parklike setting. One, the historic 1860's Edward Nye Fish House on Maine Ave., has recently opened as the museum's John K. Goodman Pavilion of Western Art. PLEASE NOTE: 1. Tours of the Historic Block are given at 11am W e & Th from 10/1 through 5/1. 2. Free art talks are offered at 1:30 on Mo & Th in the Art Education Building. **NOT TO BE MISSED:** Modern & contemporary collection

ON EXHIBIT 1999

11/04/1998 to 01/03/1999 TUCSON COLLECTS: TRIBAL RUGS FROM ARIZONA COLLECTIONS

11/14/1998 to 01/03/1999 DIRECTIONS: DANIEL MARTIN DIAZ

11/21/1998 to 03/31/1999 EL NACIMIENTO
Over 200 hand-painted miniature Mexican figurines will be seen in the annual presentation of this traditional and intricate nativity scene recreated each year by Maria Luisa Tena.

01/16/1999 to 03/07/1999 MIRIAM SCHAPIRO WORKS ON PAPER
From traditional watercolors to cast paper pieces, Schapiro's wide-ranging works on view include such diverse elements as collaged fabrics, lace and glitter, stenciling, and Xerox reproductions or cutouts attached to the walls with Velcro.

03/06/1999 to 04/25/1999 TUCSON PHOTOGRAPHERS IN THE TMA COLLECTION

ARIZONA

Tucson Museum of Art - continued

03/13/1999 to 05/02/1999 CONTEMPORARY SOUTHWEST IMAGES XIII: THE STONEWALL FOUNDATION SERIES
Artist to be announced.

03/21/1999 to 03/21/1999 TMA 75TH ANNIVERSARY EVENT

03/21/1999 to 04/25/1999 TMA PERMANENT COLLECTIONS

05/15/1999 to 07/11/1999 ARIZONA BIENNIAL '99

09/11/1999 to 10/31/1999 DIRECTIONS: KATHERINE JOSTEN'S GLOBAL ART PROJECT

09/11/1999 to 10/31/1999 CONTEMPORARY SOUTHWEST IMAGES XIV: THE STONEWALL FOUNDATION SERIES

10/08/1999 to 11/07/1999 ARTIST OF THE YEAR

11/13/1999 to 01/09/2000 MEXICAN SILVER

11/19/1999 to 11/21/1999 HOLIDAY CRAFT MARKET

11/20/1999 to 01/09/2000 GOTTLIEB IN ARIZONA
Paintings and works on paper created by Adolph Gottlieb during his 8 month residency in Tucson will be featured in an exhibition that examines their effect on his later works.

11/20/1999 to 01/30/2000 MOUNTAIN OYSTER CLUB COLLECTION

University of Arizona Museum of Art

Olive And Speedway, Tucson, AZ 85721-0002
☞: 520-621-7567 ■ http://artmuseum.arizona.edu/art.html
Open: MID AUG-MID MAY: 9-5 Mo-Fr & Noon-4 Su; MID MAY-MID AUG: 10-3:30 Mo-Fr & Noon-4
Closed: Sa, LEG/HOL!; ACAD!
♿ Ⓟ **Museum Shop**
Group Tours   Drop-In Tours: upon request
Permanent Collection: IT: Kress Collection 14-19; CONT/AM: ptgs, sculp; CONT/EU: ptgs, sculp; OR: gr; CONT: gr; AM: ptgs, gr

With one of the most complete and diverse university collections, the Tucson based University of Arizona Museum of Art features Renaissance, later European and American works in addition to outstanding contemporary creations by Lipchitz, O'Keeffe and Zuñiga. **NOT TO BE MISSED:** 61 plaster models & sketches by Jacques Lipchitz; 26 panel retablo of Ciudad Rodrigo by Gallego (late 15th C); Georgia O'Keeffe's "Red Canna"; Audrey Flack's "Marilyn"

FORT SMITH

Fort Smith Art Center
423 North Sixth St., Fort Smith, AR 72901

☎: 501-784-2787

Open: 9:30-4:30 Tu-Sa **Closed:** Su, Mo, EASTER, 7/4, THGV, 12/21 - 1/1
ADM   Adult: $1.00

& ⓟ Museum Shop **Group Tours Drop-In Tours   Historic Building** Pilot House for Belle Grove Historic District
Permanent Collection: CONT/AM: ptgs, gr, sculp, dec/arts; PHOT; BOEHM PORCELAINS

Located mid-state on the western border of Oklahoma, the Fort Smith Art Center, housed in a Victorian Second Empire home, features regional and nationally recognized artists in changing monthly exhibits **NOT TO BE MISSED:** Large Boehm Porcelain Collection

ON EXHIBIT 1999

01/1999   PETER LIPPINCOTT: CERAMIC WORKS

02/1999   TEDDI STEYER: MIXED MEDIA PAINTINGS, PRINTS AND COLLAGES

04/1999   49TH ANNUAL ART COMPETITION
A national art competition.

05/1999   RIVER VISION: ARKANSAS RIVER AND RIVER HERITAGE

06/1999   FORT SMITH KENNEL CLUB DOG ART EXHIBITION

08/1999   SMALL WORKS ON PAPER
Works by Arkansas artists.

09/1999   5TH ANNUAL NATIVE AMERICAN INVITATIONAL EXHIBITION

10/03/1999 to 10/30/1999   PAUL JACKSON: WATERCOLORS

11/1999 to 11/1999   23RD ANNUAL PHOTOGRAPHY COMPETITION
Open to photographers nationwide

12/1999 to 12/1999   ANNUAL CHILDREN'S CHRISTMAS CARD COMPETITION

LITTLE ROCK

Arkansas Arts Center
9th & Commerce, MacArthur Park, Little Rock, AR 72203

☎: 501-372-4000

Open: 10-5 Mo-Sa, till 8:30 Fr, Noon-5 Su   **Closed:** 12/25
Vol/Cont

& ⓟ **Museum Shop** ⅋ The Vineyard in the Park Restaurant 11:15-1:30 M-F
Group Tours Drop-In Tours   Historic Building Housed in a 1840 Greek Revival building   **Sculpture Garden**
Permanent Collection: AM: drgs 19-20; EU: drgs; AM: all media; EU: all media; OR; CONT/CRAFTS

Housed in an 1840 Greek Revival building, this art center, the state's oldest and largest cultural institution, features a permanent collection of over 10,000 objects that includes a nationally recognized collection of American and European drawings, contemporary American crafts and objects of decorative art. **NOT TO BE MISSED:** "Earth", a bronze sculpture by Anita Huffington

ON EXHIBIT 1999
11/13/1998 to 01/03/1999   COLLECTOR'S SHOW AND GALA

ARKANSAS

Arkansas Arts Center - continued

11/13/1998 to 01/10/1999   EUROPEAN 20TH CENTURY ARTISTS' CERAMICS FROM THE COLLECTION OF THE KRUITHUIS MUSEUM
Works by Picasso, Miro, Braque, Chagall and Europe's CoBrA school will be among those featured in this unusual presentation of ceramics.

11/13/1998 to 01/10/1999   EUROPEAN 20TH CENTURY ARTISTS' WORKS FROM THE ARKANSAS ART GALLERY
Two-dimensional works from the Museum's collection will highlight works in the ceramics exhibition.

01/22/1999 to 03/21/1999   INNUENDO NON TROPPO: THE WORK OF GREGORY BARSAMIAN
Spinning constructions and strobe lights are employed in the creation of Barsamian's works of optical illusion some of which produce the appearance of vertical motion.

02/05/1999 to 04/25/1999   WILLIAM H. JOHNSON: TRUTH BE TOLD
Works by Johnson, an artist who lived in Harlem in the early part of this century and who attended the National Academy of Art in New York, will be seen in an exhibition that reflects many of his turbulent years as he traveled and worked in Europe.

03/26/1999 to 05/02/1999   YOUNG ARKANSAS ARTISTS

05/07/1999 to 06/23/1999   VICTOR KOULBAK: SILVERPOINT DRAWINGS, 1983-1997

PINE BLUFF

Arts & Science Center for Southeast Arkansas
701 Main St., Pine Bluff, AR 71601
📞: 870-536-3375
Open: 8-5 Mo-Fr, 1-4 Sa, Su   **Closed:** 1/1, EASTER, 7/4, THGV, 12/24, 12/25
  ♿ Ⓟ **Museum Shop**
Group Tours   Drop-In Tours
Permanent Collection: EU: ptgs 19; AM: ptgs, gr 20; OM: drgs; CONT/EU: drgs, DELTA ART; REG

The Museum, whose new building opened in Sept. '94, is home to a more than 1,000 piece collection of fine art that includes one of the country's most outstanding permanent collections of African American artworks. The museum also contains a noted collection of American drawings (1900 to the present) which are always on view. **NOT TO BE MISSED:** Talking Pictures: The Dawn of Sound, Forest Puzzles, Small Works on Paper, Changing Your Mind

ON EXHIBIT 1999

11/29/1998 to 01/17/1999   MEXICAN MASKS OF THE 20TH CENTURY: A LIVING TRADITION
Wearing a mask transforms the wearer. People have believed that masks work magic spells, inspire fears, etc. In this exhibition the versatility and diversity of masks in the 20th c is shown.   Many here fall into two groups: Devic Masks, Tiger masks, Carnival Masks, and masks for the Dance of the Moors and Christians indicating the influence of Spanish Culture and religion on the Aztec civilization in early Mexico.

03/1999   SMALL WORKS ON PAPER

09/01/1999 to 09/30/1999   ELIZABETH LAYTON: FACE TO FACE *Will Travel*

Bakersfield Museum of Art
1930 "R" St., Bakersfield, CA 93301
☎: 805-323-7219
Open: 10-4 Tu-Sa, Noon-4 Su **Closed:** Mo, LEG/HOL!
ADM Adult: $3.00 **Children:** F (under 12) **Students:** $1.00 **Seniors:** $1.00
& ℗ **Museum Shop Group Tours Drop-In Tours**
Permanent Collection: PTGS; SCULP; GR; REG

Works by California regional artists are the main focus of the collection at this museum, a facility which is looking forward to the results of an expansion project due to start in early 1998. Besides the sculptures and flowers of the museum's gardens where, with 3 days notice, box lunches can be arranged for tour groups, visitors can enjoy the 5-7 traveling exhibitions and 2 local juried exhibitions presented annually. **NOT TO BE MISSED:** The Artist Guild Show in the lobby where works by local professional artists are individually highlighted on a monthly basis.

ON EXHIBIT 1999

12/03/1998 to 02/28/1999 MARC CHAGALL12

04/08/1999 to 05/14/1999 DAVID MARTIN

05/20/1999 to 10/23/1999 WOMEN ARTISTS

07/08/1999 to 10/31/1999 LADDIE JOHN DILL

11/1999 JOYCE KOHL AND TED KERZLE

11/01/1999 to 02/28/2000 GEORGIA O'KEEFFE

Judah L. Magnes Memorial Museum
Russell St., Berkeley, CA 94705
☎: 510-549-6950 ▣ www.jfed.org/magnes/magnes.htm
Open: 10-4 Su-Th **Closed:** Fr, Sa, JEWISH & FEDERAL/HOL!
Sugg/Cont Adult: $5.00
& ℗ **Museum Shop Group Tours**: 510-549-6938 (by appt.) **Drop-In Tours**: 10-4 Su-Th
Historic Building 1908 Berkeley landmark building (Burke Mansion) Sculpture Garden
Permanent Collection: FINE ARTS; JEWISH CEREMONIAL ART, RARE BOOKS & MANUSCRIPTS; ARCHIVES OF WESTERN U.S. JEWS

Founded in 1962, the Judah L. Magnes Memorial Museum is the third largest Jewish museum in the Western Hemisphere and the first Jewish museum to be accredited by the American Association of Museums. Literally thousands of prints, drawings and paintings by nearly every Jewish artist of the past two centuries are represented in the permanent collection, which also includes ceremonial and folk pieces and textiles from antiquity to the present, from around the world. **NOT TO BE MISSED:** "The Jewish Wedding" by Trankowsky; Menorahs 14-20th C.; changing exhibitions

ON EXHIBIT 1999
Summer 1999 A SPECIAL MUSEUM-WIDE EXHIBITION

10/04/1998 to 02/15/1999 REMEMBERING BEN SHAHN: SELECTIONS FROM THE STEPHEN LEE TALLER COLLECTION
This commemorative exhibition spotlights the artist's impressive production of graphic art. 70 prints, posters and drawings have been chosen along with ephemera representing the range of his interests and stylistic development *Catalog Will Travel*

10/04/1998 to 02/15/1999 POSTER COMPETITION

03/07/1999 to 05/23/1999 TOBI KAHN

CALIFORNIA

University of California Berkeley Art Museum & Pacific Film Archive
Affiliate Institution: University of California
2626 Bancroft Way, Berkeley, CA 94720-2250
☎: 510-642-0808   ◙ www.bampfa.berkeley.edu
Open: 11-5 We-Su, 11-9 Th   **Closed:** Mo, Tu, LEG/HOL!
ADM Adult: $6.00   **Children:** F (under 12)   **Students:** $4.00   **Seniors:** $4.00
& ℗ **Museum Shop**   ‖Café 11-4 Tu-S   **Group Tours:** 510-642-5188   **Drop-In Tours   Sculpture Garden**
Permanent Collection: AM: all media 20; VISUAL ART; AS; CH: cer, ptgs; EU: Ren-20

The UC Berkeley Art Museum is the principal visual arts center for the University of California at Berkeley. Since its founding in the 1960's with a bequest of 45 Hans Hoffmans paintings, the BAM has become one of the largest university art museums in the US. International in scope, the Museum's 10,000 work collection emphasizes twentieth-century painting, sculpture, photography and conceptual art, with especially significant holdings in Asian art. **NOT TO BE MISSED:** Contemporary collection including masterpieces by Calder, Cornell, Frankenthaler, Still, Rothko, and others

ON EXHIBIT 1999
ONGOING   CHINESE CERAMICS: THE FIRST THREE THOUSAND YEARS
An ongoing exhibition of works from the Museum's collection.

09/26/1998 to 01/17/1999   TRANSFORMATION: THE ART OF JOAN BROWN
In the first major retrospective for Bay Area artist Brown (1938-1990), paintings representing all aspects of her career from her early works in the Bay Area Figurative style of the 60's, through her thickly painted abstract expressionist canvases, to her final mythical & spiritual works of the 70's and beyond will be on view. This exhibition will be shown in two parts; one part at the University of California Berkeley Museum and one part at The Oakland Museum of California. There will be as special ticket for admission to both Museums. Adults $9.00, Students and Seniors $7.00 *Catalog Will Travel*

10/21/1998 to 02/07/1999   RANCHO DESERTS: PHOTOGRAPHS BY TIM GOODMAN
A view of California's other desert, not the well watered one of Palm Springs and Rancho Mirage, but the harsh and inhospitable terrain that surrounds Twentynine Palms and Yucca Valley.

11/11/1998 to 02/28/1999   MATRIX/ PETER SHELTON: sixtyslippers
Shelton's work addresses notions of physical presence both of the art work and in relation to the spectator. This consists of 60 large iron cones suspended one-quarter inch from the gallery floor in random groupings. Each cone is unique and ranges from 50-four hundred pounds. Hung by pendulums, these become a perpetually moving mass.

01/1999 to 06/1999   MATRIX/RIGO 98
Rigo, his art alias, has created many public art projects throughout the bay area. This will create a vinyl wrap for the campus shuttle as well as other elements to be incorporated in the Museum's facade.

01/16/1999 to 04/25/1999   MATRIX: IRISH CONCEPTUAL WORKS ON PAPER
In conjunction with the major exhibition of Irish works, this will feature conceptual works on paper from the last decade.

02/10/1999 to 05/01/1999   WHEN TIME BEGAN TO RANT AND RAGE: TWENTIETH CENTURY FIGURATIVE PAINTING FROM IRELAND
Taking its title from a poem by William Butler Yeats, this is the most significant examination of modern Irish art ever to be held in the United States. It traces the development of a distinctly Irish identity in the visual arts from the 1890s to the present as well as the great independence movement from its beginning to the present day. The approximately 70 works include those by Sir John Lavery, Jack B. Yeats and contemporary artists. *Catalog Will Travel*

CLAREMONT

Montgomery Gallery
Affiliate Institution: Pomona College
Montgomery Gallery- 330 N. College Way, Claremont, CA 91711-6344
☎: 909-621-8283   ◙ www.pomona.edu/montgomery
Open: Noon-5 Tu-Fr; 1-5 Sa, Su   **Closed:** Mo, ACAD!, LEG/HOL!, SUMMER
& ℗ **Museum Shop   Group Tours   Drop-In Tours**
Permanent Collection: KRESS REN: ptgs; GR; DRGS, PHOT; NAT/AM: basketry, cer, beadwork

Montgomery Gallery - continued

ON EXHIBIT 1999

01/17/1999 to 02/14/1999 PROJECT SERIES 1: SOO JIN KIM

The first in a new series which will focus on an emerging Southern California artist.

01/17/1999 to 03/28/1999 DRAWING: AN EXPLORATION

This explores the medium of drawing based on works from the Museum's collection and important loans from neighboring institutions.

02/28/1999 to 03/28/1999 PROJECT SERIES II: LIZ YOUNG

The second in this series of emerging artists.

DAVIS

Richard L. Nelson Gallery & The Fine Arts Collection, UC Davis

Affiliate Institution: Univ. of California
Davis, CA 95616

: 916-752-8500

Open: Noon-5 Mo-Fr, 2-5 Su **Closed:** Sa, LEG/HOL! ACAD/HOL; SUMMER!

Vol/Cont

♿ Ⓟ **Museum Shop**

Group Tours Drop-In Tours

Permanent Collection: DRGS, GR, PTGS 19; CONT; OR; EU; AM; CER

The gallery, which has a 2,500 piece permanent collection acquired primarily through gifts donated to the institution since the 1960's, presents an ongoing series of changing exhibitions. **NOT TO BE MISSED:** "Bookhead" and other sculptures by Robert Arneson; Deborah Butterfield's "Untitled" (horse)

ON EXHIBIT 1999

01/11/1999 to 03/26/1999 JAPANESE WOODBLOCK PRINTS: SELECTIONS FROM THE COLLECTION

01/25/1999 to 02/13/1999 ARTIST'S VALENTINES

02/21/1999 to 03/26/1999 ART OF ASIA: SELECTED WORKS FROM THE FINE ARTS COLLECTION

04/12/1999 to 06/11/1999 WOMEN PRINTMAKERS: SELECTIONS FROM THE COLLECTION

DOWNEY

Downey Museum of Art

10419 Rives Ave., Downey, CA 90241

: 562-861-0419

Open: Noon-5 We-Su **Closed:** Mo, Tu, LEG/HOL!

Vol/Cont

♿ Ⓟ **Museum Shop**

Group Tours Drop-In Tours

Permanent Collection: REG: ptgs, sculp, gr, phot 20; CONT

With over 400 20th century and contemporary works by Southern California artists, the Downey Museum has been the primary source of art in this area for over 35 years.

CALIFORNIA

Fresno Art Museum
2233 N. First St., Fresno, CA 93703
☎: 209-441-4220
Open: 10-5 Tu-Fr; Noon-5 Sa, Su **Closed:** Mo, LEG/HOL!
ADM   Adult: $2.00 **Children:** F (15 & under) **Students:** $1.00 **Seniors:** $1.00
 ♿ ℗ **Museum Shop** ℍTh ONLY 12-2:00 **Group Tours:** 209-485-4810 **Drop-In Tours** **Sculpture Garden**
Permanent Collection: P/COL; MEX; CONT/REG; AM: gr, sculp

In addition to a wide variety of changing exhibitions, pre-Columbian Mexican ceramic sculpture, French Post-impressionist graphics, and American sculptures from the permanent collection are always on view. **NOT TO BE MISSED:** Hans Sumpfsumpf Gallery of Mexican Art containing pre-Columbian ceramics through Diego Rivera masterpieces.

ON EXHIBIT 1999
06/26/1999 to 08/22/1999   INTERACTION OF CULTURES: INDIAN AND WESTERN PAINTING (1710-1910) FROM THE EHRENFELD COLLECTION
This exhibition highlights the art created in India by Indian and Western artists between 1780 and 1910.The 95 works, primarily paintings on canvas have been drawn from this outstanding private collections. It will be the first exhibit in North America to consider the artistic interaction between these two cultures. *Catalog Will Travel*

Fresno Metropolitan Museum
1555 Van Ness Ave., Fresno, CA 93721
☎: 209-441-1444 ■ www.fresnomet.org
Open: 11-5 Tu-Su (open Mo during some exhibits!) **Closed:** Mo, LEG/HOL
Free Day: 5-8 Th **ADM Adult:** $5.00 **Children:** F (2 & under) **Students:** $4.00 **Seniors:** $4.00
 ♿ ℗ **Museum Shop**
Group Tours: 209-441-1444 **Drop-In Tours:** 9-4 daily during most exhibitions **Historic Building**
Permanent Collection: AM: st/lf 17-20; EU; st/lf 17-20; EU; ptgs 16-19; PHOT (Ansel Adams)

Located in the historic "Fresno Bee" building, the Fresno Metropolitan Museum is the largest cultural center in the central San Joaquin Valley. PLEASE NOTE: The museum offers $1.00 admission for all ages on the first Wednesday of the month. **NOT TO BE MISSED:** Oscar & Maria Salzar collection of American & European still-life paintings 17-early 20

ON EXHIBIT 1999
06/16/1999 to 08/29/1999   SHERLOCK HOLMES: THE CLOCKTOWER MYSTERY

Summer 1999   ZAP IT, MOVE IT, MAKE IT

09/15/1999 to 11/14/1999   REFLECTIONS IN A LOOKING GLASS: A LEWIS CARROLL CENTENARY EXHIBITION

09/15/1999 to 11/14/1999   THE WORLD OF PETER RABBIT: THE ART AND SCIENCE OF BEATRIX POTTER

12/03/1999 to 12/31/1999   CHRISTMAS AT THE MET 1999

Irvine Museum
18881 Von Karman Ave. 12th Floor, Irvine, CA 92612
☎: 949-476-2565 ■ www.ocartsnet.org/irvinemuseum
Open: 11-5 Tu-Sa **Closed:** S, M, LEG/HOL!
 ♿ ℗ **Museum Shop** **Group Tours:** 949-476-0294 **Drop-In Tours:** 11:15 Th
Permanent Collection: California Impressionist Art 1890-1930

Irvine Museum - continued
Opened in Jan. 1993, this museum places its emphasis on the past by promoting the preservation and display of historical California art with particular emphasis on the school of California Impressionism (1890-1930).

ON EXHIBIT 1999

09/24/1998 to 01/16/1999   CALIFORNIA IMPRESSIONIST CLOUD SCAPES AND SEASCAPES
These California cloud studies enticed artists to move to California for the magnificent sky, brilliant light and vibrant seas. Many artists chose to paint the cloud studies and seascapes. *Catalog Will Travel*

LA JOLLA

Museum of Contemporary Art, San Diego
700 Prospect St., La Jolla, CA 92037-4291
☎: 619-454-3541; DT 619-234-1001   ◉   www.mcasandiego.org
Open: 10-5 Tu-Sa, Noon-5 Su, till 8 We (La Jolla)   **Closed:** Mo, 1/1, THGV, 12/25
Free Day: 1st Tu & Su of month   **ADM   Adult:** $4.00   **Children:** F (under 12)   **Students:** $2.00   **Seniors:** $2.00
  ♿ ℗ **Museum Shop**   ⅋ Museum Café (at La Jolla location) 619-454-3945
Group Tours: ex 151   **Drop-In Tours:** LJ: 2pm Sa, Su & 6pm We
Historic Building Former Ellen Scripps Browning Home - Irving Gill Architecture   **Sculpture Garden**
Permanent Collection: CONT: ptgs, sculp, drgs, gr, phot

Perched on a bluff overlooking the Pacific Ocean, this 50 year old museum recently underwent extensive renovation and expansion, the results of which New York times architecture critic, Paul Goldberger, describes as an "exquisite project". Under the direction of noted architectural wizard, Robert Venturi, the original landmark Scripps house, built in 1916, was given added prominence by being cleverly integrated into the design of the new building. Additional exhibition space, landscaping that accommodates outdoor sculpture, a café and an expanded bookstore are but a few of the Museum's new features. Both this and the downtown branch at 1001 Kettner Blvd. at Broadway in downtown San Diego,(phone: 619-234-1001), operate as one museum with 2 locations where contemporary art (since the 1950's) by highly regarded national and international artists as well as works by emerging new talents may be seen. PLEASE NOTE: 1. Self-guided "Inform" audio tours of the Museum's permanent collection are available to visitors free of charge. 2. Downtown admission fees: $2.00 adults, $1.00 students & seniors, children free under 12 (a 3 day pass to both museums is available for $4.00.)

ON EXHIBIT 1999

09/20/1998 to 01/03/1999   KENNY SCHARF

09/20/1998 to 01/03/1999   DAVID REED PAINTINGS: MOTION PICTURES
The Museum of Contemporary Art in San Diego is presenting a first retrospective in the US of the work of this abstract artist. *Catalog Will Travel*

11/08/1998 to 01/31/1999   FABRIZIO PLEZZI

01/17/1999 to 03/28/1999   FRANCIS BACON: THE PAPAL PORTRAITS

01/17/1999 to 06/02/1999   LATERAL THINKING: A CONTEMPORARY COLLECTION

02/11/1999 to 04/25/1999   LANNAN GIFTS

04/07/1999 to 06/02/1999   ALEX GREY

06/12/1999 to 09/12/1999   A UNIQUE AMERICAN VISION: THE PAINTINGS OF GREGORY GILLESPIE

CALIFORNIA

Laguna Art Museum
305 Cliff Drive, Laguna Beach, CA 92651
☎: 949-494-6531   ◙ www.lagunaartmuseum.org
Open: 11-5 Tu-Su   **Closed:** Mo
Free Day: First Th 11-9   **Museum Shop**

ON EXHIBIT 1999
10/24/1998 to 01/03/1999   LIFE LESSONS: HOW ART CAN CHANGE YOUR LIFE

01/09/1999 to 04/11/1999   ART COLONIES AND AMERICAN IMPRESSIONISM *Catalog*

04/24/1999 to 07/11/1999   AFTER THE PHOTO-SECESSION: AMERICAN PICTORIAL PHOTOGRAPHY, 1910-1955
150 photographs documenting the social and artistic development of this pictorial medium between the World Wars, will be featured in the first major exhibition to focus on this subject.

Lancaster Museum/Art Gallery
44801 North Sierra Hwy., Lancaster, CA 93534
☎: 805-723-6250
Open: 11-4 Tu-Sa, 1-4 Su   **Closed:** Mo, LEG/HOL! & 1-2 WEEKS BEFORE OPENING OF EACH NEW EXHIBIT!
& ℗   **Museum Shop   Group Tours   Drop-In Tours**
Permanent Collection: REG; PHOT

About 75 miles north of Los Angeles, in the heart of America's Aerospace Valley, is the City of Lancaster Museum, a combined history and fine art facility that serves the needs of one of the fastest growing areas in southern California. The gallery offers 8 to 9 rotating exhibitions annually.

University Art Museum
Affiliate Institution: California State University, Long Beach
1250 Bellflower Blvd., Long Beach, CA 90840
☎: 562-985-5761   ◙ www.csulb.edu/~uam
Open: 9-4 Mo-Fr, 10-4 Sa   **Closed:** Su, ACAD/HOL! LEG/HOL!
Sugg/Cont   Adult: $3.00   **Students:** $1.00
& ℗   **Museum Shop   Group Tours   Drop-In Tours**: res req.   **Sculpture Garden**
Permanent Collection: CONT: drgs, gr; SCULP

Walking maps are available for finding and detailing the permanent site-specific Monumental Sculpture Collection located throughout the 322 acre campus of this outstanding university art facility. **NOT TO BE MISSED:** Extensive collection of contemporary works on paper

ON EXHIBIT 1999
01/25/1999 to 04/25/1999   GRAPHIC ABSTRACTION: A VIEW FROM THE FIRST CENTURY, THE WOMEN: FOUNDERS AND INNOVATORS
This is the first installation of a two-year collaborative exhibition designed to trace the development of abstraction in American printmaking from the early days of the 20th century to the present. Topics presented in 6 separate exhibitions celebrate the 200th anniversary of lithography, analyze abstraction in Pop images, highlight women in printmaking, investigate the reductive impulse, and look at sculptors and their works on paper.

University Art Museum - continued

01/26/1999 to 03/26/1999 CENTRIC 57: WALTON FORD
Watercolors from 1996-1997 follow the tradition of John J. Audubon. His depictions of birds are scientifically correct, exquisitely lush in color and superior in technique. *Catalog*

02/16/1999 to 04/25/1999 ARTISTS PROOF: PHOTOGRAPHS BY SIDNEY FELSEN
For more than 20 years photographer Felson has documented his friends and associates who Have been guest artists at Los Angeles renowned graphics workshop, Gemini G.E.I. For us his work has provided a unique window into the art world of the latter part of the 20th C.

06/29/1999 to 08/01/1999 GRAPHIC ABSTRACTION IN AMERICA: A VIEW FROM THE FIRST CENTURY, THE REDUCTIVE IMPULSE
Artists include Greene, Bolotovsky, Poons, Stella, Kelly, Mangold, Judd, LeWitt, Martin, Sylvia Mangold, Steir, etc. *Catalog*

06/29/1999 to 08/01/1999 CENTRIC 58: ROBERT BECHTLE
Bechtle's paintings of houses, cars, lawn chairs, palm trees and people freeze his subjects in brilliant California light. A founder of Photo-Realism in the late 60s he brings his own unique vision to his paintings. *Catalog*

08/17/1999 to 10/24/1999 CARLOTTA CORPRON: ILLUMINATIONS AND REFLECTIONS 1938-1978
Born in Minnesota and raised in India, Corpron used light as a paintbrush, a pencil and a mirror. Her provocative studies and sensitive portraits survey the range in this landmark exhibit. *Catalog*

08/17/1999 to 10/24/1999 SCULPTORS ON PAPER: GRAPHIC ABSTRACTION IN AMERICA, A VIEW FROM THE FIRST CENTURY
Artists include William Zorach, John Storrs, Alexander Calder, David Smith, Archipenko, Judd, Kelly and many others. *Catalog*

11/09/1999 to 12/19/1999 HISTORICALLY SPEAKING: LONG BEACH AT FIFTY
An exhibition looking at the 25 year history of the UAM and the important role it has played in Southern California. *Catalog*

LOS ANGELES

Autry Museum of Western Heritage
4700 Western Heritage Way, Los Angeles, CA 90027 1462
✆: 213-667-2000 ▣ www.autry-museum.org
Open: 10-5 Tu-Su and some Mo hols **Closed:** Mo, THGV, 12/25
ADM Adult: $7.50 **Children:** $3.00 (2-12) **Students:** $5.00 **Seniors:** $5.00
♿ ℗ **Museum Shop** ⍾ Golden Spur Café for breakfast & lunch (9am-4:30pm) **Group Tours Drop-In Tours**
Permanent Collection: FINE & FOLK ART

Fine art is but one aspect of this multi-dimensional museum that acts as a showcase for the preservation and understanding of both the real and mythical historical legacy of the American West. **NOT TO BE MISSED:** Los Angeles Times Children's Discovery Gallery; Spirit of Imagination

ON EXHIBIT 1999

09/19/1998 to 01/24/1999 GOLD FEVER! THE LURE AND LEGACY OF THE CALIFORNIA GOLD RUSH
In commemoration of the 150th anniversary of the discovery of gold in California, this presentation of 600 historical artifacts, artworks, photographs, and natural specimens traces the profound impact this occurrence had on the people, environment, economy and technological history of our country.

02/20/1999 to 05/16/1999 POWERFUL IMAGES: PORTRAYALS OF NATIVE AMERICA
Pop and Native American cultures blend in the contemporary works on view.

05/29/1999 to 09/1999 WESTERN COSTUMES

09/1999 to 12/1999 WESTERN AMENYKANSKI: POLISII POSTER ART

12/1999 to 03/2000 ON GOLD MOUNTAIN - CHINESE INFLUENCE ON THE DISCOVERY OF GOLD IN CALIFORNIA

CALIFORNIA

California African-American Museum
600 State Drive, Exposition Park, Los Angeles, CA 90037
☎: 213-744-7432 ◙ www.caam.ca.gov
Open: 10-5 Tu-Su **Closed:** Mo, 1/1, THGV, 12/25
♿ ℗ **Museum Shop Group Tours Drop-In Tours**
Permanent Collection: BENJAMIN BANNISTER: drgs; TURENNE des PRES: ptgs; GAFTON TAYLOR BROWN: gr; AF: masks; AF/AM: cont NOTE: The permanent collection is not on permanent display!

The primary goal of this museum is the collection and preservation of art and artifacts documenting the Afro-American experience in America. Exhibitions and programs focus on contributions made to the arts and various other facets of life including a vital forum for playwrights and filmmakers. The building itself features a 13,000 square foot sculpture court through which visitors pass into a spacious building topped by a ceiling of tinted bronze glass.

Fisher Gallery, University of Southern California
Affiliate Institution: University of Southern California
823 Exposition Blvd., Los Angeles, CA 90089-0292
☎: 213-740-4561 ◙ www.usc.edu/dept/Fisher_Gall
Open: Noon-5 Tu-Fr, 11-3 Sa (closed during summer) **Closed:** Mo, LEG/HOL! SUMMER
♿ ℗ **Museum Shop**
Group Tours: 213-740-4566 **Drop-In Tours**: 10-12 by appt.
Permanent Collection: EU: ptgs, gr, drgs; AM: ptgs, gr, drgs; PTGS 15-20,ARMAND HAMMER COLL; ELIZABETH HOLMES FISHER COLL.

Old master paintings from the Dutch and Flemish schools, as well as significant holdings of 19th century British and French, art are two of the strengths of the Fisher Gallery. Implemented in 1997 was a program on Saturdays entitled "Families at Fisher", which includes art tours and a variety of hands-on activities. PLEASE NOTE: The permanent collection is available to museums, scholars, students, and the public by appointment.

ON EXHIBIT 1999
01/06/1999 to 02/13/1999 SIXTY YEARS OF COLLECTING: SELECTIONS FROM THE PERMANENT COLLECTION
The Fisher Gallery's anniversary features the collection, donors, and the museum's history.

03/03/1999 to 04/17/1999 THE ARCHITECTURE OF SOCIAL CULTURE: MUSEUM ARCHITECTURAL PROJECTS
Architects plans, models and a full website focusing on theoretical and aesthetic underpinnings that led to various museum's creation and the success and social utility of those museums.

Gallery 825/Los Angeles Art Association
Affiliate Institution: Los Angeles Art Association
825 N. La Cienega Blvd., Los Angeles, CA 90069
☎: 310-652-8272
Open: Noon-5 Tu-Sa **Closed:** Su, Mo, LEG/HOL!
Vol/Cont
♿ ℗ **Museum Shop Group Tours Drop-In Tours**

For over 70 years Gallery 825/Los Angeles Art Association has been exhibiting and promoting some of the most important Southern California artists on the art scene today. Solo exhibitions are presented in the newly designed Helen Wurdemann Gallery.

Getty Center

1200 Getty Center Drive, Los Angeles, CA 90049-1681
☎: 310-440-3700 ◉ www.getty.edu
Open: 11-7 Tu, We, 11-7 Th, Fr, 10-6 Sa, Su **Closed:** Mo, LEG/HOL!
Ⓟ **Museum Shop** ⅋: Y
Group Tours Drop-In Tours: On the hour
Permanent Collection: AN/GRK; AN/R; EU: ptgs, drgs, sculp; DEC/ART; AM: phot 20; EU: phot 20; Illuminated Manuscripts

The Museum Complex, situated on one of the great public viewpoints in Los Angeles, consists of 6 buildings, designed by Richard Meier. These are joined by a series of gardens, terraces, fountains, and courtyards. An electric tram transports visitors from the parking area up the hill to the central plaza where a grand staircase welcome their arrival. The collections span the history of art and will be amplified by special exhibitions. The Museum at the Villa in Malibu will open in 2001. It will be devoted to the display, study and conservation of classical antiquities. Advance Parking reservations at the new facility are a MUST! There is a $5.00 per car charge. For information call 310-440-7300. **NOT TO BE MISSED:** "Irises" by Vincent Van Gogh, 1889; Pontormo's "Portrait of Cosimo I de Medici" c1537; "Bullfight Suerte de Varas" by Goya, 1824 (recently acquired)

ON EXHIBIT 1999

to 01/17/1999 BEYOND BEAUTY: ANTIQUITIES AS EVIDENCE
The variety of cultural, historical and scientific evidence within classical Greek and Roman works of art will be seen in an exhibition of objects from other cultures beyond the Mediterranean basin in which their influence is present. Many ancient Indian, Peruvian and Chinese artifacts will be on loan to the Getty for this show.

04/13/1999 to 07/04/1999 BRASSEI: THE EYE OF PARIS
A retrospective celebrating the centenary of the birth of Gyuyloa Halasz in Brasso, Transylvania know for photographs he made of Paris at night in the late 20s and 30s. Henry Miller described him as the 'eye of Paris'. His photographs reveal his remarkable sensitivity to light and atmosphere. *Catalog Will Travel*

Laband Art Gallery

Affiliate Institution: Loyola Marymount University
7900 Loyola Blvd., Los Angeles, CA 90045
☎: 310 338-2880 ◉ www.lmu.edu/colleges/cfa/art/laband
Open: 11-4 We-Fr, Noon-4 Sa **Closed:** Mo, Tu, JUN - AUG.; LEG/HOL, ACAD/HOL, RELIGIOUS/HOL
Vol/Cont
♿ **Museum Shop**
Group Tours Drop-In Tours
Permanent Collection: FL: om; IT: om; DRGS; GR

The Laband Art Gallery usually features exhibitions based on multicultural projects relating to Latin and Native American subjects, current social and political issues, and Jewish & Christian spiritual traditions.

ON EXHIBIT 1999

01/20/1999 to 02/27/1999 THE 15TH BIENNIAL OF THE LOS ANGELES PRINTMAKING SOCIETY
The Director of the Laband Art Gallery will be the Juror for the works for the biennial exhibition featuring the finest recent examples, both traditional media and digital expression-of printmaking throughout North America produced from 1995 to 1998. *Catalog*

03/11/1999 to 04/10/1999 INDEPENDENT SPIRIT: THE ART OF MABEL ALVAREZ (1891-1985
The career of this Los Angeles painter active from 1913-1973 is here shown in 40 works. Her drawing, prints and paintings reflect her interest-her early academic training and later embracing of the modernist style tinged with Theosophy and the occult. *Catalog Will Travel*

CALIFORNIA

Los Angeles County Museum of Art

5905 Wilshire Blvd., Los Angeles, CA 90036

📞: 323-857-6000   ◘ www.lacma.org

Open: 12-8 Mo, Tu, Th; 12-9 Fr; 11-8 Sa, Su   **Closed:** We, 1/1, THGV, 12/25

ADM   **Adult:** $6.00   **Children:** $1.00 6-17, F under5   **Students:** $4.00   **Seniors:** $4.00

 点 Ⓟ   **Museum Shop** ¶ Plaza Café

Group Tours: 213-857-6108   **Drop-In Tours**: Frequent & varied (call for information)

Permanent Collection: AN/EGT: sculp, ant; AN/GRK: sculp, ant; AN/R: sculp, ant; CH; ptgs, sculp, cer; JAP: ptgs, sculp, cer; AM/ART; EU/ART; DEC/ART

The diversity and excellence of the collections of the Los Angeles Museum offer the visitor to this institution centuries of art to enjoy from ancient Roman or pre-Columbian art to modern paintings, sculpture, and photography. Recently the Museum completed the first phase of the reorganization and reinstallation of major portions of its renowned American, Islamic, South & Southeast Asian and Far Eastern galleries, allowing for the display of many works previously relegated to storage. Always striving to become more user accessible, the Museum's hours of operation have been changed to create a better "business-and-family-friendly" schedule. **NOT TO BE MISSED:** George de La Tour's "Magdelene with the Smoking Flame", 1636-1638; "Under the Trees" by Cezanne.

ON EXHIBIT 1999

09/06/1998 to 01/04/1999   **PICASSO: MASTERWORKS FROM THE MUSEUM OF MODERN ART**   *Will Travel*

09/27/1998 to 01/03/1999   **AN EXPRESSIONIST IN PARIS: THE PAINTINGS OF CHAIM SOUTINE**
A major retrospective of focusing on the years between his arrival in Paris to his death. The works by this great French painter include 50 of his most important canvases, known for his highly expressive gestural and thickly painted work. *Will Travel*

12/20/1998 to 03/29/1999   **ANCIENT WEST MEXICO, ART OF THE UNKNOWN REGION**

01/17/1999 to 04/04/1999   **VAN GOGH'S VAN GOGHS: MASTERPIECES FROM THE VAN GOGH MUSEUM, AMSTERDAM**
70 paintings by Vincent van Gogh and two related works on paper is the largest survey of his career outside The Netherlands in more than a quarter of a century. This unique group of works, kept together by his brother Theo and his family are on loan from the van Gogh Museum, home to the largest collection of his work. *Catalog Will Travel*

Los Angeles Municipal Art Gallery

Affiliate Institution: Barnsdall Art Park

4800 Hollywood Blvd., Los Angeles, CA 90027

📞: 213-485-4581

Open: 12:30-5 We-Su, till 8:30 Fr   **Closed:** M, Tu, 1/1, 12/25

ADM   **Adult:** $1.50

 点 Ⓟ   **Museum Shop**

Group Tours   **Drop-In Tours**: house only $2.00 adult:1.00 Sr; We-Su Noon,1,2,3   **Historic Building** 1921 Frank Lloyd Wright Hollyhock House

Permanent Collection: CONT: S/Ca art

The Los Angeles Municipal Art Gallery in the Barnsdall Art Park is but one of several separate but related arts facilities. **NOT TO BE MISSED:** Frank Lloyd Wright Hollyhock House

ON EXHIBIT 1999

11/18/1998 to 01/17/1999   **ELEMENTS: WATER/FIRE/EARTH/AIR**

03/03/1999 to 04/18/1999   **THE MOURNING AFTER**

05/05/1999 to 06/20/1999   **COLA**

Museum of African American Art

4005 Crenshaw Blvd., 3rd Floor, Los Angeles, CA 90008

☎: 213-294-7071

Open: 11-6 Th-Sa, Noon-5 Su   **Closed:** Mo-We, 1/1, EASTER, THGV, 12/25

   ♿ Ⓟ **Museum Shop   Group Tours   Drop-In Tours**

Permanent Collection: AF: sculp, ptgs, gr, cer; CONT/AM; sculp, ptgs, gr; HARLEM REN ART

Located on the third floor of the Robinsons May Department Store, this museum's permanent collection is enriched by the "John Henry Series" and other works by Palmer Hayden. Due to the constraints of space these works and others are not always on view. The museum requests that you call ahead for exhibition information. **NOT TO BE MISSED:** "John Henry Series" and other works by Palmer Hayden (not always on view).

Museum of Contemporary Art, Los Angeles

250 S. Grand Ave., Los Angeles, CA 90012

☎: 213-626-6222   ◙ www.MOCA-LA.org

Open: 11-5 Tu, We, Fr-Su; 11-8 Th   **Closed:** Mo, 1/1, THGV, 12/25

ADM   Adult: $6.00   **Children:** F (under 12)   **Students:** $4.00   **Seniors:** $4.00

   ♿ Ⓟ **Museum Shop**   ¶ Café 8:30-4 Tu-F; 11-4:30 Sa, Su

Group Tours: 213-621-1751   **Drop-In Tours:** 12,1 & 2 daily; 6:00 Th

Historic Building First American building commission by Arata Isozaki

Permanent Collection: CONT: all media

The Museum of Contemporary Art (MOCA) is the only institution in Los Angeles devoted exclusively to art created from 1940 to the present by modern-day artists of international reputation. The museum is located in two unique spaces: MOCA at California Plaza, the first building designed by Arata Isozaki; and The Geffen Contemporary at MOCA, (152 North Central Ave., L.A., CA 90013), a former warehouse redesigned into museum space by architect Frank Gehry.

ON EXHIBIT 1999

ONGOING: MOCA at California Plaza: TIMEPIECES: SELECTED HIGHLIGHTS FROM THE PERMANENT COLLECTION

Designed to increase family involvement, this exhibition of permanent collection works by artists of international reputation, traces the development of contemporary art.

UCLA at the Armand Hammer Museum of Art and Cultural Center

10899 Wilshire Blvd., Los Angeles, CA 90024-4201

☎: 310-443-7000

Open: 11-7 Tu, We, Fr, Sa; 11-9 Th; 11-5 Su   **Closed:** Mo, 1/1, 7/4, THGV, 12/25

ADM   Adult: $4.50   **Children:** F (under 17)   **Students:** $3.00   **Seniors:** $3.00

   ♿ Ⓟ **Museum Shop**   ¶ Courtyard Café

Group Tours: 310-443-7041   **Drop-In Tours:** PERM/COLL 1:00 Su; CHANGING EXHS: 1pm Tu-Su   **Sculpture Garden**

Permanent Collection: EU: 15-19

With the largest collection of works by Daumier in the country (more than 10,000) plus important collections of Impressionist, Post-Impressionist, and Contemporary art, the Armand Hammer Museum is considered a major U.S. artistic cultural resource. Opened in 1990, the museum is now part of UCLA. It houses the collections of the Wight Art Gallery and the Grunwald Center for the Graphic Arts (one of the finest university collections of graphic arts in the country with 35,000 works dating from the Renaissance to the present). **NOT TO BE MISSED:** Five centuries of Masterworks: over 100 works by Rembrandt, van Gogh, Cassatt, Monet, and others; The UCLA Franklin D. Murphy Sculpture Garden, one of the most distinguished outdoor sculpture collections in the country featuring 70 works by Arp, Calder, Hepworth, Lachaise, Lipchitz, Matisse, Moore, Noguchi, Rodin and others.

CALIFORNIA

UCLA at the Armand Hammer Museum of Art and Cultural Center - continued

ON EXHIBIT 1999

ONGOING   THE ARMAND HAMMER COLLECTION

ONGOING   THE ARMAND HAMMER DAUMIER AND CONTEMPORARIES COLLECTION

ONGOING   THE UCLA GRUNWALD CENTER FOR THE GRAPHIC ARTS

ONGOING   THE UCLA FRANKLIN D. MURPHY SCULPTURE GARDEN
One of the most distinguished outdoor sculpture collections in the country.

10/07/1998 to 01/03/1999   SUNSHINE AND NOIR: ART IN L. A. 1960-1997
The exhibit examines art from a European perspective. Some of the groundbreaking works chosen because of their artistic sensibility and expression unique to Los Angeles, are by Baldessari, Dingle, Kelley, McCarthy, Nauman, Pastor and Turrell. Because of the size of this exhibition, the permanent collection will be deinstalled for Aug. 17, 1998-Jan, 25, 1999. *Only Venue Catalog*

02/24/1999 to 05/09/1999   THE QAJAR EPOCH: TWO HUNDRED YEARS OF ROYAL PERSIAN PAINTINGS
Catalog Will Travel

06/02/1999 to 08/22/1999   DEFINING EYE: WOMEN PHOTOGRAPHERS OF THE TWENTIETH CENTURY
Catalog Will Travel

06/02/1999 to 08/22/1999   STENBERG BROTHERS: CONSTRUCTING A REVOLUTION IN SOVIET DESIGN
The first retrospective of the works of Vladimir and Georgii Stenberg designers and colorful figures of the Russian avant-garde. Included are 100 works, many never before seen outside of Russia, including Posters, magazines, studies for posters, designs for theatrical sets, and several early Constructivist paintings, drawings and sculptures. *Catalog Will Travel*

Watts Towers Arts Center
1727 E. 107th St., Los Angeles, CA 90002
☎: 213-847-4646
Open: Art Center: 10-4 Tu-Sa, Noon-4 Su; (Watts Tower open Sa, Su! $1.00 adults)   **Closed:** Mo, LEG/HOL
& ℗ **Museum Shop**
Group Tours: 213-913-4157   **Drop-In Tours**
Permanent Collection: AF; CONT; WATTS TOWER

Fantastic lacy towers spiking into the air are the result of a 33 year effort by the late Italian immigrant visionary sculptor Simon Rodia. His imaginative use of the "found object" resulted in the creation of one of the most unusual artistic structures in the world. PLEASE NOTE: Due to earthquake damage, the towers, though viewable, are enclosed in scaffolding for repairs that are scheduled to be completed by the end of 1998.

MALIBU

Frederick R. Weisman Museum of Art
Affiliate Institution: Pepperdine Center for the Arts, Pepperdine University
24255 Pacific Coast Highway, Malibu, CA 90263
☎: 310-456-4851   ▣ www.pepperdine.edu
Open: 11-5 Tu-Su   **Closed:** Mo, LEG/HOL!
& ℗ **Museum Shop   Group Tours   Drop-In Tours**: call for specifics!
Permanent Collection: PTGS, SCULP, GR, DRGS, PHOT 20

Opened in 1992, this museum's permanent collection and exhibitions focus primarily on 19th & 20th-century art. **NOT TO BE MISSED:** Selections from the Frederick R. Weisman Art Foundation

Frederick R. Weisman Museum of Art - continued

ON EXHIBIT 1999

ONGOING: SELECTIONS FROM THE FREDERICK R. WEISMAN COLLECTIONS

05/1999 to/08/1999   CONTEMPORARY MALIBU
As a follow-up to the hit exhibition "Historic Landscapes of Malibu," members of the California Art Club will be exhibiting their new paintings of Malibu's picturesque landscape.

01/09/1999 to 03/28/1999   SANDRO CHIA: NEW WORK
Presented will be figurative works by contemporary Italian painter Chia, a Neo-Expressionist whose large scale figurative works reflect his love of bold color & brushwork and mythic content.

MONTEREY

Monterey Museum of Art
559 Pacific St., Location 2 -720 Via Miranda, Monterey, CA 93940
☎: 831-372-5477 Loc. 2 831-372-3689
Open: 11-5 We-Sa, 1-4 Su, until 8pm 3rd Th of the month   **Closed:** Mo, Tu, LEG/HOLS
Adult: $3.00   **Children:** F (under 12)
& Ⓟ **Museum Shop   Group Tours   Drop-In Tours**: 2:00 Su; 1:00 Sa & Su for La Mirada   **Historic Building**
Permanent Collection: REG/ART; AS; PACIFIC RIM; FOLK; ETH; GR; PHOT

With a focus on its ever growing collection of California regional art, the Monterey Museum is planning a modern addition to its original building, La Mirada, the adobe portion of which dates back to the late 1700's when California was still under Mexican rule. PLEASE NOTE: The suggested donation fee for La Mirada, located at 720 Via Miranda, is $3.00. **NOT TO BE MISSED:** Painting and etching collection of works by Armin Hansen

ON EXHIBIT 1999

ONGOING   BEHIND THE MASK: THE TEXTURES, SHAPES AND COLORS OF FOLK ART

ONGOING   SELECTIONS FROM THE RALPH K. DAVIES WESTERN COLLECTION

MORAGA

Hearst Art Gallery
Affiliate Institution: St. Mary's College
Box 5110, Moraga, CA 94575
☎: 510-631-4379
Open: 11-4:30 We-Su   **Closed:** Mo, Tu, LEG/HOL!
Vol/Cont   Adult: $1.00
& Ⓟ **Museum Shop   Group Tours   Drop-In Tours**
Permanent Collection: AM: Calif. Ldscp ptgs 19-20; IT: Med/sculp; EU: gr; AN/CER; CHRISTIAN RELIGIOUS ART 15-20

Contra Costa County, not far from the Bay Area of San Francisco, is home to the Hearst Art Gallery, built with the aid of the William Randolph Hearst Foundation. Located on the grounds of St. Mary's College, one of its most outstanding collections consists of Christian religious art representing many traditions, cultures and centuries. PLEASE NOTE: The museum is often closed between exhibitions. **NOT TO BE MISSED:** 150 paintings by William Keith (1838 - 1911), noted California landscape painter

49

CALIFORNIA

Orange County Museum of Art, Newport Beach
850 San Clemente Dr., Newport Beach, CA 92660
📞: 949-759-1122   ▣ www.ocartsnet.org/ocma
Open: 11-5 Tu-Su   **Closed:** Mo, 1/1, THGV, 12/25, 7/4, ESTR
Free Day: Th   **ADM   Adult:** $5.00   **Children:** F(under 16)   **Students:** $4.00   **Seniors:** $4.00
⚅ ℗   **Museum Shop**   ⑪ 11:00-3:00 Tu-Su
Group Tours   Drop-In Tours: 1:00 Th-Su, 2:00 Tu + Su   **Sculpture Garden**
Permanent Collection: REG: Post War Ca. art (PLEASE NOTE: The permanent collection is not usually on display).

With an emphasis on historical and contemporary art, the Orange County Museum of Art, with its late 19th and 20th century collection of California art, is dedicated to the enrichment of cultural life of the Southern California community through providing a comprehensive visual arts program that includes a nonstop array of changing exhibitions and stimulating education programs. Additional exhibitions are on view at the Museum's South Coast Plaza Gallery, 3333 Bristol Street in Costa Mesa (open free of charge, 10-9 Mo-Fr, 10-7 Sa & 11-6:30 Su)

ON EXHIBIT 1999

10/17/1998 to 01/10/1999   GOLD RUSH TO POP: 200 YEARS OF CALIFORNIA ART
100 works are featured in an exhibition that covers 200 years of artistic creativity in California, from historic paintings of the California wilderness, Gold Rush, and immigrant responses, to works reflective of the contemporary California scene.

01/16/1999 to 04/18/1999   RAUSCHENBERG IN TRANSPARENCY

01/16/1999 to 06/20/1999   HOUDIN'S HOUSE INSTALLATION BY TONY DE LAP

02/06/1999 to 05/06/1999   1999 BIENNIAL

05/09/1999 to 06/21/1999   MAJOR ART/MINOR ARTISTS

05/29/1999 to 09/12/1999   PETER ALEXANDER

07/03/1999 to 01/03/2000   MICHAEL BREWSTER

Oakland Museum of California
1000 Oak St, Oakland, CA 94607
📞: 510-238-2200   ▣ www.museumca.org
Open: 10-5 We-Sa, Noon-7 Su   **Closed:** Mo, Tu, 1/1, 7/4, THGV, 12/25
ADM   Adult: $5.00   **Children:** F (5 & under)   **Students:** $3.00   **Seniors:** $3.00
⚅ ℗   **Museum Shop**   ⑪: Y
Group Tours: 510-273-3514   **Drop-In Tours:** weekday afternoons on request; 12:30 weekends   **Sculpture Garden**
Permanent Collection: REG/ART; PTGS; SCULP; GR; DEC/ART

The art gallery of the multi-purpose Oakland Museum of California features works by important regional artists that document the visual history and heritage of the state. Of special note is the Kevin Roche - John Dinkaloo designed building itself, a prime example of progressive museum architecture complete with terraced gardens. **NOT TO BE MISSED:** California art; Newly installed "On-line Museum" database for access to extensive information on the Museum's art, history and science collections (open for public use 1:00-4:30 Th).

ON EXHIBIT 1999

05/02/1998 to 02/28/1999   URBAN FOOTPRINTS: THE PHOTOGRAPHS OF LEWIS WATTS
For more than 20 years Watts used his camera to explore the culture and history of urban environments in America. In this exhibition he explores the life and work, and the human and spiritual concerns of the largely African community of East Oakland.

Oakland Museum of California - continued

09/26/1998 to 01/17/1999   TRANSFORMATION: THE ART OF JOAN BROWN
In the first major retrospective for Bay Area artist Brown (1938-1990), paintings representing all aspects of her career from her early works in the Bay Area Figurative style of the 60's, through her thickly painted abstract expressionist canvases, to her final mythical & spiritual works of the 70's and beyond will be on view. This exhibition will be shown in two parts; one part at the University of California Berkeley Museum and one part at The Oakland Museum of California. There will be a special ticket for admission to both Museums. Adults $9.00, Students and Seniors $7.00 *Catalog Will Travel*

01/23/1999 to 01/09/2000   CALIFORNIA UNDERGROUND: OUR CAVES AND SUBTERRANEAN HABITATS
A family oriented exhibition exploring the types of caves located in California Cave Photography, a complex form involving collaborative effort will be explained and represented by some of the world's most famous cave photographers

02/20/1999 to 09/12/1999   AWAKENING FROM THE CALIFORNIA DREAM: AN ENVIRONMENTAL HISTORY
Photographer Robert Dawson and historian Gray Brechin present a sobering look at the changes over time in the California natural environment.

03/06/1999 to 07/25/1999   ART INTR'ACTIOON: WILLIAM T. WILEY AND MARY HULL WEBSTER AND FRIENDS *Catalog Will Travel*

03/20/1999 to 05/30/1999   ALL THINGS BRIGHT AND BEAUTIFUL: CALIFORNIA IMPRESSIONIST PAINTINGS FROM THE IRVINE MUSEUM
This is the first important exhibition of American Impressionists from California to be held on the east coast. It includes masterworks by leading artists, including Franz Bischoff, Alson Clark, Colin Campbell Cooper, Guy Rose and George Gardner Symons, all National Academicians. *Catalog Will Travel*

06/01/1999 to 08/15/1999   POSTERS: AMERICAN STYLE
The 100th anniversary celebration of an American popular art form brings together 120 compelling images by more than 90 graphic artists and designers on subjects from baseball games to rock concerts. The images demonstrate the ways in which graphic design is capable of eliciting specifically intended responses. *Will Travel*

08/21/1999 to 11/14/1999   REQUIEM: BY THE PHOTOGRAPHERS WHO DIED IN VIETNAM AND INDOCHINA *Catalog Will Travel*

10/16/1999 to 03/26/2000   MAIDU PAINTINGS BY DAL CASTRO: FROM THE AESSECHLIMAN COLLECTION OF THE OAKLAND MUSEUM OF CALIFORNIA
Castro's highly respected self taught Native American artist from Northern California depict Maidu creation myths, animal legends, ceremonies, historical events and portraits of tribal elders and ancestors. *Catalog Will Travel*

OXNARD

Carnegie Art Museum

424 S. C St., Oxnard, CA 93030
☎: 805-385-8157
Open: 10-5 T-Sa, 1-5 Su (Museum closed between exhibits)   **Closed:** Mo-We, MEM/DAY, LAB/DAY, THGV, 12/25
Sugg/Cont   Adult: $3.00   **Children:** F (under 6)   **Students:** $2.00   **Seniors:** $2.00
♿ ⓟ **Museum Shop**
Group Tours Drop-In Tours   Historic Building
Permanent Collection: CONT/REG; EASTWOOD COLL.

Originally built in 1906 in the neo-classic style, the Carnegie, located on the coast just south of Ventura, served as a library until 1980. Listed NRHP **NOT TO BE MISSED:** Collection of art focusing on California painters from the 1920's to the present.

ON EXHIBIT 1999

ONGOING: 8-10 works from the Museum's permanent collection of 20th century California art

CALIFORNIA

Palm Springs Desert Museum, Inc.
101 Museum Drive, Palm Springs, CA 92262

☏: 760-325-7186 ◙ www.psmuseum.org
Open: 10-5 Tu-Th & Sa, Noon-5 Su **Closed:** Mo, LEG/HOL!
ADM Adult: $7.50 **Children:** F (5 & under) **Students:** $3.50 **Seniors:** $6.50
♿ ℗ **Museum Shop** ❢ Toor Gallery Café open 11-3 Tu-S & 12-3 Su
Group Tours Drop-In Tours: 2 Tu-Su (Nov-May) **Historic Building** Architectural landmark **Sculpture Garden**
Permanent Collection: CONT/REG

Contemporary American art with special emphasis on the art of California and other Western states is the main focus of the 4,000 piece fine art and 2,00 object Native American collection of the Palm Springs Desert Museum. The museum, housed in a splendid modern structure made of materials that blend harmoniously with the surrounding landscape, recently added 20,000 square feet of gallery space with the opening of the Steve Chase Art Wing and Education Center **NOT TO BE MISSED:** Leo S. Singer Miniature Room Collection; Miniature of Thomas Jefferson Reception Room at the State Department

ON EXHIBIT 1999

07/25/1998 to 02/14/1999 RECYCLED RESEEN: FOLK ART FROM THE GLOBAL SCRAP HEAP
Ranging from adornment, utilitarian, religious, toys, and musical instruments, the 500 recycled objects on view, collected worldwide, demonstrate how the folk practice of recycling has become a global phenomenon.

10/21/1998 to 01/03/1999 PAUL KLEINSCHMIDT

10/21/1998 to 01/24/1999 MANUEL NERI: THE SCULPTOR'S DRAWINGS

02/17/1999 to 05/16/1999 EDWARD BOREIN

02/17/1999 to 05/16/1999 RODIN: SCULPTURE FROM THE IRIS AND B. GERALD CANTOR COLLECTION
On loan from the most important and extensive private collections of its kind will be 52 sculptures by celebrated 19th century French sculptor, Rodin.

02/23/1999 to 03/21/1999 ARTIST COUNCIL 30TH ANNUAL JURIED EXHIBITION

03/17/1999 to 01/23/2000 THE ROADRUNNER

03/26/1999 to 04/25/1999 9TH ANNUAL FINE ARTS CREATIVITY AWARDS EXHIBITION

03/30/1999 to 05/02/1999 ARTISTS COUNCIL MEMBERS JURIED EXHIBITION
Approximately 50 works created in a variety of media by Artist Council members will be featured in this juried exhibition.

04/30/1999 to 05/28/1999 MITOS, IMAGENES E IDIOMA: MYTHS, IMAGES AND LANGUAGE

06/1999 to 09/05/1999 JUNE WAYNE: A 50 YEAR RETROSPECTIVE
Paintings, drawings, tapestries and lithographs by this Los Angeles artist whose work is an investigation of time and space, of the genetic code and molecular energy, of stellar winds and magnetic fields as well as her concerns with texture, surface and color. *Will Travel*

Palo Alto Cultural Center
1313 Newell Rd., Palo Alto, CA 94303

☏: 650-329-2366 ◙ www.city.palo-alto.ca.us/palo/city/artsculture
Open: 10-5 Tu-Sa, 7-9 Th, 1-5 Su **Closed:** Mo, 1/1, 7/4, 12/25
♿ ℗ **Museum Shop Group Tours Drop-In Tours**: call for information
Permanent Collection: CONT/ART; HIST/ART

Located in a building that served a the town hall from the 1950's to 1971, this active community art center's mission is to present the best contemporary fine art, craft, design, special exhibitions, and new art forms.

Palo Alto Cultural Center - continued

ON EXHIBIT 1999

10/04/1998 to 01/10/1999   FIGURES AGAINST THE GRAIN
Contemporary figurative sculptures in wood.

10/04/1998 to 01/10/1999   FROM THE PHILIPPINES: FOLK OBJECTS
Objects of indigenous and European roots, celebrating the 100th anniversary of the independence of the Republic of the Philippines.

10/04/1998 to 01/10/1999   TEN THOUSAND THINGS THAT BREATHE: RENATO ORTEGA
Ballpoint pen meditations on paper by the Philippine born artist.

01/1999 to 04/1999   THE PRINT IS CAST
Cast lead, plastic and paper pulp pieces by Jasper Johns, Hockney, Noland, Arneson, Rauschenberg and others.

01/1999 to 04/1999   MAKING THE SELF
Modes of the self-portrait repeated in time by select artists such as Käthe Kollwitz to Duane Michaels.

05/1999 to 06/1999   RADIUS 1999
Juried exhibition of six area artists

08/1999 to 09/1999   LESLIE LERNER: THE IMAGINED CITY
Multi media installation with narratives on the travels from Delft to Venice of the 'Man With Wooden Arm'. *Will Travel*

PASADENA

Norton Simon Museum

411 W. Colorado Blvd., Pasadena, CA 91105
☎: 626-449-6840   ▣ www.nortonsimon.org
Open: Noon-6 Th-Su   **Closed:** Mo-We, 1/1, THGV, 12/25
ADM   Adult: $4.00   **Children:** F (under 12)   **Students:** $2.00   **Seniors:** $2.00
&   ℗   **Museum Shop   Group Tours**: ex 245   **Drop-In Tours   Sculpture Garden**
Permanent Collection: EU: ptgs 15-20; sculp 19-20; IND: sculp; OR: sculp; EU/ART 20; AM/ART 20

Thirty galleries with 1,000 works from the permanent collection that are always on display plus a beautiful sculpture garden make the internationally known Norton Simon Museum home to one of the most remarkable and renowned collections of art in the world. The seven centuries of European art on view from the collection contain remarkable examples of work by Old Master, Impressionist, and important modern 20th century artists. PLEASE NOTE: The Museum, undergoing interior renovation, is adding a wood and glass tea house, situated in a newly landscaped sculpture garden, where visitors will be able to enjoy light refreshment surrounded by sculptural masterworks. Due to the renovation project no exhibitions will be scheduled until Fall 1999. **NOT TO BE MISSED:** IMP & POST/IMP Collection including a unique set of 71 original master bronzes by Degas

Pacific Asia Museum

46 N. Los Robles Ave., Pasadena, CA 91101
☎: 626-449-2742   ▣ www.westmuse.org/Pacasiamuseum
Open: 10-5 We-Su   **Closed:** Mo, Tu, 1/1, MEM/DAY, 7/4, THGV, 12/25, 12/31
ADM   Adult: $5.00   **Children:** F (under 12)   **Students:** $3.00   **Seniors:** $3.00
&   ℗   **Museum Shop**
Group Tours: 626-449-2742   **Drop-In Tours:** 2pm Su
Historic Building California State Historical Landmark, National Register of Historic Places   **Sculpture Garden**
Permanent Collection: AS: cer, sculp; CH: cer, sculp; OR/FOLK; OR/ETH; OR/PHOT

CALIFORNIA

Pacific Asia Museum - continued

The Pacific Asia Museum, which celebrated its 25th anniversary in '96, is the only institution in Southern California devoted exclusively to the arts of Asia. The collection, housed in the gorgeous Chinese Imperial Palace style Nicholson Treasure House built in 1929, features one of only two authentic Chinese style courtyard gardens in the U.S. open to the public. **NOT TO BE MISSED:** Chinese courtyard garden, Carved Jade, Ceramics, Japanese paintings

ON EXHIBIT 1999

08/19/1998 to 01/03/1999 LILLIAN MILLER WOODBLOCK PRINTS
Paintings and prints by an American artist, born and raised in Japan. Her art offers insights into the Western fascination with Japanese culture. Tools and paints as well as woodblocks will also be shown.

02/1999 to 04/1999 ANCIENT CITIES OF THE INDUS VALLEY
American audiences will be introduced to the important and virtually unknown archeological remains of the Indus Valley civilization (2600-1900 BC). Many of the technologies used to create these objects are still practiced in India and Pakistan today.

05/1999 to 08/1999   JAPANESE FOLK PAINTINGS (0tsu-e) FROM THE PACIFIC ASIA MUSEUM COLLECTION

09/1999 to 01/2000 CHINESE CARPETS FROM SOUTHERN CALIFORNIA COLLECTIONS

PENN VALLEY

Museum of Ancient & Modern Art

11392 Pleasant Valley Rd., Penn Valley, CA 95946
☎: 916-432-3080
Open: 10-5 Mo-Sa   **Closed:** Mo, 1/1, EASTER, 7/4, LAB/DAY, THGV, 12/25
  ᕒ ℗ **Museum Shop   Group Tours   Drop-In Tours**: upon request if available
Permanent Collection: AN/GRK; AN/R; ETRUSCAN; GR; CONT; DU; FR; GER; CONT/AM; DEC/ART; PHOT

Although the permanent collection has been assembled in little more than a 20 year period, the scope and extent of its holdings is truly mind-boggling. In addition to the outstanding collection of ancient Western Asiatic artworks, the museum features a group of historical art books containing woodcuts, etchings and engravings printed as early as 1529, a wonderful assemblage of African masks and sculptures from over 20 different tribes, and a superb group of Rembrandt etchings and other European masterpieces. The museum is located approximately 50 miles north east of Sacramento. **NOT TO BE MISSED:** One of the largest collections of 18th Dynasty Egypt in the U.S.; Theodora Van Runkel Collection of Ancient Gold; Hall of Miniatures; the TIME MACHINE

RIVERSIDE

Riverside Art Museum

3425 Mission Inn Ave., Riverside, CA 92501
☎: 909-684-7111
Open: 10-4 Mo-Sa   **Closed:** Su, Last 2 Weeks Aug; LEG/HOL!
Sugg/Cont   Adult: $2.00
  ᕒ ℗ **Museum Shop**   ⑪ Open weekdays   **Group Tours   Drop-In Tours**: daily upon request
Historic Building 1929 building designed by Julia Morgan, architect of Hearst Castle
Permanent Collection: PTGS, SCULP, GR

Julia Morgan, the architect of the Hearst Castle, also designed this handsome and completely updated museum building. Listed on the NRHP, the museum is located in the Los Angeles and Palm Springs area. Aside from its professionally curated exhibitions, the museum displays the work of area students in May.

Riverside Art Museum - continued

ON EXHIBIT 1999

11/20/1998 to 01/02/1999   **DELOSS MCGRAW**

01/15/1999 to 03/15/1999   **JAMES WHISTLER**

01/15/1999 to 03/15/1999   **ARTISTIC DIALOGUE**

04/1999 to 06/1999   **WOMEN IN PRINT**

04/1999 to 08/1999   **LIGHT SHOW**

05/1999 to 08/1999   **MONOTHON EXHIBIT**

05/01/1999 to 05/05/1999   **MONOTHON 99**

09/1999 to 11/1999   **WATERCOLOR WEST**

11/1999 to 12/1999   **POTTERS OF MATA ORTIZ**

UCR/California Museum of Photography

Affiliate Institution: Univ. of California
3824 Main St., Riverside, CA 92521
☎: 909-784-FOTO   ▣   www.cmp.ucr.edu
Open: 11-5 We-Sa, Noon-5 Su   **Closed:** Mo, Tu, 1/1, EASTER, THGV, 12/25
ADM   Adult: $2.00   **Children:** F (under 12)   **Students:** $1.00   **Seniors:** $1.00
  Ġ   ℗   **Museum Shop   Group Tours   Drop-In Tours**
Permanent Collection: PHOT 19-20; CAMERA COLLECTION

Converted from a 1930's Kress dimestore into an award winning contemporary space, this is one of the finest photographic museums in the country. In addition to a vast number of photographic prints the museum features a 6,000 piece collection of photographic apparatus, and an Internet gallery. **NOT TO BE MISSED:** Junior League of Riverside Family Interactive Gallery; Internet Gallery

SACRAMENTO

Crocker Art Museum

216 O St., Sacramento, CA 95814
☎: 916-264-5423   ▣   www.sacto.org/crocker
Open: 10-5 Tu-S, till 9 Th   **Closed:** Mo, ¼, THGV 12/25
ADM   Adult: $4.50   **Children:** $2.00 (7-17)   **Students:** $4.50   **Seniors:** $4.50
  Ġ   ℗   **Museum Shop**
Group Tours: 916-264-5537   **Drop-In Tours:** 10-1 We-Fr, 5-8 Th, 12-4 Su, 12-3 Su, on the hour
Historic Building Over 100 years old
Permanent Collection: PTGS: REN-20; OM/DRGS 15-20; CONT; OR; SCULP

This inviting Victorian Italianate mansion, the oldest public art museum in the West, was built in the 1870's by Judge E. B. Crocker. It is filled with his collection of more than 700 European and American paintings displayed throughout the ballroom and other areas of the original building. Contemporary works by Northern California artists are on view in the light-filled, modern wing whose innovative facade is a re-creation of the Crocker home. Of special interest are two paintings, created by Charles Christian Nahl, that were commissioned for the spaces they still occupy. Both "Fandango" and "Sunday Morning in the Mines" are in their original frames (designed by I. Magnin of department store fame) and are so elaborate that one actually includes a high relief depiction of a pan of gold dust. **NOT TO BE MISSED:** Early California painting collection

CALIFORNIA

Crocker Art Museum - continued

ON EXHIBIT 1999

07/17/1998 to 04/01/1999   19TH-20TH CENTURY AMERICAN PAINTING FROM THE MUSEUM COLLECTION

10/1998 to 01/03/1999   HENRI DE TOULOUSE-LAUTREC: THE BALDWIN M. BALDWIN COLLECTION
The 108 works shown survey his work from his childhood sketches to the great posters of his final years. In addition to many masterpieces in the show, there is a complete set of 'Elles' depicting daily life in the Paris brothels, which is very rare today. *Will Travel*

11/13/1998 to 02/14/1999   DÜRER 1498
Organized around Dürer's famous drawing 'Woman with a Banner' this shows the evolution of his work from 1494-1505.

01/08/1999 to 04/1999   SEVENTEENTH CENTURY NETHERLANDISH DRAWINGS
Some of the Museum's finest drawings including those by Peter Paul Rubens and Rembrandt van Rijn

05/08/1999 to 07/25/1999   EL ALMA DEL PUEBLO: SPANISH FOLK ART AND ITS TRANSFORMATION IN THE AMERICAS
A major exhibition being presented jointly by the Americas Society and its neighbor, the Spanish Institute, will document the influence of Spanish folk art on the popular aesthetic of the Americas. Objects shown will be ceremonial in nature as well as decorative and domestic. They are borrowed from collections in Spain and the Americas. *Catalog Will Travel*

08/13/1999 to 10/10/1999   SILVER AND GOLD: CASED IMAGES OF THE CALIFORNIA GOLD RUSH
150 "cased" images (daguerreotypes and ambrotype), documenting the 19th century California gold rush, include vivid scenes of ship and overland travels, life in the mines, Gold Rush country landscapes, street scenes in San Francisco, and a cross-section of the ethnically diverse population.

10/1999   FIGURATIVE ART FROM ANCIENT ISRAEL
Found in archaeological discoveries in Israel, the human figures featured in this exhibition span more than 12 millennia, from the Natufian period (10th millennium B.C.E.) through the Christian Crusader period (12th century C.E.).

10/29/1999 to 12/24/1999   CREATIVE ARTS LEAGUE 40TH ANNIVERSARY CRAFTS EXHIBITION

SAN DIEGO

Mingei International Museum of Folk Art
Balboa Park - Plaza de Panama, San Diego, CA 92122
📞: 619-239-0003   ◉   www.mingei.org
Open: 10-4 Tu-Su   **Closed:** Mo, LEG/HOL!
Free Day: 3rd Tu of each month   **ADM   Adult:** $5.00   **Children:** $2.00 (6-17)   **Students:** $2.00   **Seniors:** $5.00
 ♿ Ⓟ   **Museum Shop   Group Tours   Drop-In Tours**: by appt
Permanent Collection: FOLK: Jap, India, Af, & over 80 other countries; international doll coll.

In Aug. 1996, this museum, dedicated to furthering the understanding of world folk art, moved its superb collection into a new 41,000 square foot facility on the Plaza de Balboa Park which is also close to the site of San Diego Museum of Art, the Timken Museum of Art, and numerous other art related institutions. It is interesting to note that Mingei, the name of this museum, (founded in 1974 to further the understanding of arts of people from all cultures), is a combination of the Japanese words for people (min) and art (gei).

ON EXHIBIT 1999

CONTINUING   A TRANSCULTURAL MOSAIC
Selections from the permanent collection.

01/29/1999 to 04/11/1999   SHAMANS, GODS AND MYTHIC BEASTS: COLUMBIAN GOLD AND CERAMICS IN ANTIQUITY
Presented for the first time to the American public new finds from the southwest and north coastal regions of Columbia focus on the important ceramic sculpture of ancient Columbia, the fabled land of gold "El Dorado" and the artistic qualities and themes found there. Also included are 44 exceptional gold masterpieces that share design motifs found in the ceramic figure. *Catalog Will Travel*

04/02/1999 to 05/16/1999   ART THAT HEALS: THE IMAGE AS MEDICINE IN ETHIOPIA

Museum of Photographic Arts

1649 El Prado, Balboa Park, San Diego, CA 92101
📞: 619-238-7559   ◙ www.mopa.org
Open: 10-5 Daily   **Closed:** Mo, LEG/HOL!
ADM   Adult: $3.50   **Children:** F (under 12)
&   ℗   **Museum Shop**
Group Tours   Drop-In Tours: 2:00 Su
Permanent Collection: PHOT

The Museum of Photographic Arts, dedicated exclusively to the care and collection of photographic works of art, is housed in Casa de Balbo, a structure built in 1915 for the Panama-California Exposition located in the heart of beautiful Balboa Park (designated as the number one urban park in America).

ON EXHIBIT 1999

Beginning Feb, 1, 1999 the Museum will be closed for renovation. The greatly expanded space is to open Spring 2000. During the renovation exhibitions will be presented at Museum of Contemporary Art Downtown, 1001 Kettner Blvd at Broadway.

11/15/1998 to 01/31/1999   ABELARDO MORELL AND THE CAMERA EYE
The first major exhibit to explore the most fundamental of photographic principles which while long understood have not been fully expressed as images. His subjects are familiar, yet his photographs reveal the extraordinary optical phenomena at work on the surface of commonplace subjects.. *Will Travel*

02/11/1999 to 04/25/1999   SEA CHANGE: THE SEASCAPE IN CONTEMPORARY PHOTOGRAPHY
The vast expanse of the sea is most often seen in paintings, poetry and literature. The 19 artists shown here share their preoccupation with the sea and the extraordinary possibilities of the seascape. *Will Travel*

05/02/1999 to 07/18/1999   SUSAN RANKAITIS
This Los Angeles based artist uses a unique hybrid of painting and photography and expands traditional notions of the photographic arts. She uses negatives, photograms, washes of photographic chemicals, and graphite, producing large, one of a kind images.

07/25/1999 to 10/17/1999   PHILLIPP SCHOLZ RITTERMANN
Tracing more than two decades of his work from Europe to the Western US and Baja Sur, this exhibition surveys the reoccurring themes and visual patterns that appear throughout his career.

San Diego Museum of Art

1450 El Prado, Balboa Park, San Diego, CA 92101
📞: 619-232-7931
Open: 10-4:30 Tu-Su   **Closed:** Mo, 1/1, THGV, 12/25
ADM   Adult: $8.00   **Children:** $3.00 (6-17)   **Seniors:** $6.00
&   ℗   **Museum Shop**   ❙❙ Sculpture Garden Café   10-3 Tu-F; 9-4:30 Sa, Su (619-696-1990)
Group Tours   Drop-In Tours: Many times daily
Historic Building; Built in 1926, the facade is similar to one at Univ. of Salamanca   **Sculpture Garden**
Permanent Collection: IT/REN; SP/OM; DU; AM: 20 EU; ptgs, sculp 19; AS; AN/EGT; P/COL

Whether strolling through the treasures in the sculpture garden or viewing the masterpieces inside the Spanish Colonial style museum building, a visit to this institution, located in San Diego's beautiful Balboa Park, is a richly rewarding and worthwhile experience. In addition to family oriented self-led discovery guides of the collection, available in both English and Spanish, the museum recently installed the Image Gallery, a Micro Gallery system developed to provide easy-to-use touchscreen interactive multimedia access to the permanent collection. PLEASE NOTE: There is a special admission fee of $4.00 for military with I.D. **NOT TO BE MISSED:** Frederick R. Weisman Gallery of Calif. art; Thomas Eakin's "Elizabeth With a Dog"; Works by Toulouse-Lautrec; World-renowned collection of Indian paintings

CALIFORNIA

Timken Museum of Art

1500 El Prado, Balboa Park, San Diego, CA 92101
📞: 619-239-5548 ▣ gort.uscd.edu/sj/timken
Open: 10-4:30 Tu-Sa, 1:30-4:30 Su **Closed:** Mo, LEG/HOL!; MONTH OF SEPT
Vol/Cont ♿ **Museum Shop Group Tours Drop-In Tours**: 10-12 Tu-Th
Permanent Collection: EU: om/ptgs 13-19; AM: ptgs 19; RUSS/IC 15-19; GOBELIN TAPESTRIES

Superb examples of European and American paintings and Russian Icons are but a few of the highlights of the Timkin Museum of Art located in beautiful Balboa Park, site of the former 1915-16 Panama California Exposition. Treasures displayed within the six galleries and the rotunda of this museum make it a "must see".
NOT TO BE MISSED: "Portrait of a Man" by Frans Hals; "The Magnolia Flower" by Martin Johnson Heade

ON EXHIBIT 1999

12/10/1998 to 04/11/1999 TURKISH FASHION IN 18TH CENTURY AMERICA

10/15/1999 to 02/15/2000 THE ART OF CONSERVATION
15-20 important works from public collections in the western US that have been treated by the Balboa Art Conservation Center, a regional, non-profit art center during the last two decades.

10/15/1999 to 02/15/2000 VENETIAN VIEWS: LUCA CARLEVARIJS

SAN FRANCISCO

Asian Art Museum of San Francisco

Affiliate Institution: The Avery Brundage Collection
Golden Gate Park, San Francisco, CA 94118
📞: 415-379-8801 ▣ www.asianart.org
Open: 9:30-5 We-Su, till 8:45pm 1st We each month **Closed:** Mo, Tu, 1/1, THGV, 12/25
ADM Adult: $7.00 **Children:** $4.00 (12-17) **Seniors:** $5.00
♿ Ⓟ **Museum Shop** ⑪ **Group Tours**: 415-379-8839 **Drop-In Tours**: frequent daily tours!
Permanent Collection: AS: arts; MID/E: arts; BRUNDAGE COLLECTION (80% OF THE MUSEUM'S HOLDINGS)

With a 12,000 piece collection that covers 40 countries and 6,000 years, the Asian Art Museum, opened in 1966 as a result of a gift to the city by industrialist Avery Brundage, is the largest of its kind outside of Asia. PLEASE NOTE: There are special hours during major exhibitions. Please call for specifics.

ON EXHIBIT 1999

11/21/1998 to 01/17/1999 HIROSHIGE: GREAT JAPANESE WOODBLOCK PRINTS FROM THE MOST RENOWNED MASTERS
In this second of two major exhibits, Hiroshige also specialized in landscapes placing mankind in the climactic conditions and scenic beauty that surround them. The collection of these prints from the James A Michener Collection at the Honolulu Academy of Arts is known the world over for its quality and breadth. Free audio tours are available.

Cartoon Art Museum

814 Mission St., San Francisco, CA 94103
📞: 415-CAR-TOON
Open: 11-5 We-Fr, 10-5 Sa, 1-5 Su **Closed:** Mo, Tu, 1/1, 7/4, THGV, 12/25
ADM Adult: $5.00 **Children:** $2.00 (6-12) **Students:** $3.00 **Seniors:** $3.00
♿ Ⓟ **Museum Shop Group Tours**: 415-227-8671 **Drop-In Tours**: Upon request if available
Permanent Collection: CARTOON ART; GRAPHIC ANIMATION

The Cartoon Art Museum, founded in 1984, is located in a new 6,000 square foot space that includes a children's and an interactive gallery. With a permanent collection of 11,000 works of original cartoon art, newspaper strips, political cartoons, and animation cells, this is one of only 3 museums of its kind in the country and the only West Coast venue of its kind. Over 7 exhibitions are mounted annually.

Coit Tower

1 Telegraph Hill, San Francisco, CA

📞: 415-274-0203

Open: WINTER: 9-4:30 daily; SUMMER: 10-5:30 daily

Ⓟ **Museum Shop Group Tours Drop-In Tours**

Permanent Collection: murals

Though not a museum, art lovers should not miss the newly restored Depression-era murals that completely cover the interior of this famous San Francisco landmark. 25 social realist artists working under the auspices of the WPA participated in creating these frescoes that depict rural and urban life in California during the 1930's. Additional murals on the second floor may be seen only at 11:15 on Saturday mornings. The murals, considered one of the city's most important artistic treasures, and the spectacular view of San Francisco from this facility are a "must see" when visiting this city.

Fine Arts Museums of San Francisco

Affiliate Institution: M. H. de Young Mem. Mus. & Calif. Palace of Legion of Hon.

Calif. Palace of the Legion of Honor, Lincoln Park, San Francisco, CA 94121

📞: 415-863-3330 ◙ www.thinker.org

Open: 9:30-5:00 Tu-Su **Closed:** Most holidays that fall on Mo, when the museum is regularly closed

Free Day: deYoung First We, Legion Second We

ADM Adult: $7.00 **Children:** $4.00 (12-17) **Students:** $10 Student Annual Pass **Seniors:** $5.00

♿ Ⓟ **Museum Shop** ❕⃓: 2 Cafes open 10am-4pm

Group Tours: 415-750-3638 **Drop-In Tours:** Tu-Su (deYoung) & Tu-Su (Palace)!

Historic Building Calif. Palace of Legion of Honor modeled on Hotel de Salm in Paris

Permanent Collection: DeYoung: PTGS, DRGS, GR, SCULP; AM: dec/art; BRIT:dec/art; AN/EGT; AN/R; AN/GRK; AF; OC.

Ca. Palace of Legion of Honor: EU: 13-20; REN; IMPR: drgs, gr

The de Young Museum: Situated in the heart of Golden Gate Park, the deYoung features the largest collection of American art on the West Coast ranging from Native American traditional arts to contemporary Bay Area art.

The California Palace of the Legion of Honor: One of the most dramatic museum buildings in the country, the recently renovated and reopened Palace of the Legion of Honor houses the Museum's European art, the renowned Achenbach graphic art collection, and one of the world's finest collections of sculpture by Rodin. **NOT TO BE MISSED:** Rodin's "Thinker" & The Spanish Ceiling (Legion of Honor); Textile collection (deYoung); Gallery One, a permanent art education center for children & families (deYoung)

ON EXHIBIT 1999

ONGOING AT THE de YOUNG:

GALLERY ONE: AN EXHIBITION FOR CHILDREN

ART OF OCEANIA GALLERY

09/19/1998 to 01/03/1999 IMPRESSIONS IN WINTER: EFFETS DE NEIGE

This exhibition of Impressionist winter landscape painting will provide the first thorough examination of the subject often called "effet de neige." It will focus primarily on works by Sisley, Monet and Pissarro.

10/31/1998 to 01/10/1999 ROBERT MOTHERWELL'S A la PINTURA: SELECTIONS FROM THE ANDERSON COLLECTION

10/02/1999 to 01/02/2000 WAYNE THIEBAUD: WORKS ON PAPER

CALIFORNIA

Friends of Photography, Ansel Adams Center

250 Fourth St., San Francisco, CA 94103

☎: 415-495-7000

Open: 11-5 Tu-Su, 11-8 1st Th of the month   **Closed:** Mo, LEG/HOL!

ADM   Adult: $5.00   **Children:** $2.00 (12-17)   **Students:** $3.00   **Seniors:** $2.00

  ᵫ ℗ **Museum Shop   Group Tours   Drop-In Tours**: 1:15 & 2 Sa

Permanent Collection: PHOT; COLLECTION OF 125 VINTAGE PRINTS BY ANSEL ADAMS available for study only

Founded in 1967 by a group of noted photographers including Ansel Adams, Brett Weston, and Beaumont Newhall, the non-profit Friends of Photography is dedicated to expanding public awareness of photography and to exploring the creative development of the media.

Mexican Museum

Affiliate Institution: Fort Mason Bldg.D.

Laguna & Marina Blvd., San Francisco, CA 94123

☎: 415-441-0405

Open: Noon-5 We-Fr, 11-5 Sa, Su   **Closed:** Mo-Tu, LEG/HOL!

ADM   Adult: $3.00   **Children:** F (under 10)   **Students:** $2.00   **Seniors:** $2.00

  ᵫ ℗ **Museum Shop   Group Tours**: 415-202-9704

Drop-In Tours   Historic Building Fort Mason itself is a former military site in Golden Gate Rec. Area

Permanent Collection: MEX; MEX/AM; FOLK; ETH; MORE THAN 300 OBJECTS FROM THE NELSON ROCKEFELLER COLLECTION OF MEX/FOLK ART

With more than 9,000 objects in its collection, the Mexican Museum, founded in 1975, is the first institution of its kind devoted exclusively to the art and culture of Mexico and its people. Plans are underway to open in a new museum building in the Yerba Buena Gardens district in 1998. This 50,000 square foot facility will house one of the most extensive collections of Mexican and Mexican-American art in the U.S. **NOT TO BE MISSED:** "Family Sunday", a hands-on workshop for children offered the second Sunday of each month (call 415-202-9704 to reserve).

ON EXHIBIT 1999

ZUÑIGA: HIGHLIGHTS FROM THE PERMANENT COLLECTION

Museo Italoamericano

Ft. Mason Center, Bldg. C, San Francisco, CA 94123

☎: 415-673-2200   ▣ www.well.com/~museo

Open: Noon-5 We-Su, till 7pm 1st We of the month   **Closed:** Mo, Tu, LEG/HOL!

Free Day: 1st We of month   **ADM   Adult:** $2.00   **Children:** F   **Students:** $1.00   **Seniors:** $1.00

  ᵫ ℗ **Museum Shop   Group Tours   Drop-In Tours**

Permanent Collection: IT & IT/AM: ptgs, sculp, phot 20

This unique museum, featuring the art of many contemporary Italian and Italian-American artists, was established in 1978 to promote public awareness and appreciation of Italian art and culture. Included in the collection are works by such modern masters as Francesco Clemente. Sandro Chia, and Luigi Lucioni. **NOT TO BE MISSED:** "Tavola della Memoria", a cast bronze sculpture from 1961 by Arnaldo Pomodoro

ON EXHIBIT 1999

02/17/1999 to 04/03/1999   GHIRARDELLI

04/08/1999 to 06/05/1999   JAN CAMP & JILL D'AGNENICA

06/10/1999 to 08/07/1999   ANDREA PONSI

08/12/1999 to 10/02/1999   MOSTRA 99: NEW ITALIAN AND ITALIAN-AMERICAN ARTISTS

10/07/1999 to 01/07/2000   GOTTARDO PIAZZONI

San Francisco Art Institute Galleries

800 Chestnut St,, San Francisco, CA 94133

: 415-771-7020

Open: 10-5 Tu-Sa, till 8 Th, Noon-5 Su **Closed:** Su, Mo, LEG/HOL!

♿ Ⓟ **Museum Shop** **Group Tours** **Drop-In Tours**

Founded in 1871, the Art Institute is the oldest cultural institution on the West Coast, and one of San Francisco's designated historical landmarks. The main building is a handsome Spanish colonial style structure designed in 1926 by architect Arthur Brown. Featured in the Walter/Bean Gallery are exhibitions by artists from the Bay Area and across the nation. **NOT TO BE MISSED:** Mural by Diego Rivera

San Francisco Craft & Folk Art Museum

Landmark Building A, Fort Mason, San Francisco, CA 94123-1382

: 415-775-0990

Open: 11-5 Tu-Fr, Su, 1-5 Sa, till 7pm 1st We of the month **Closed:** Mo, 1/1, MEM/DAY, 7/4, LAB/DAY, THGV, 12/25

Free Day: 10-12 every Sa, 1st We of month **ADM** **Adult:** $3.00 **Students:** $1.00 **Seniors:** $1.00

♿ Ⓟ **Museum Shop** 🍴 Right next door to famous Zen vegetarian restaurant, Greens

Group Tours: 415-775-0991 **Drop-In Tours**: 1:30 PM 2nd Fr of month **Historic Building** Building served as disembarkation center during WW II & Viet Nam

6 to 10 witty and elegant exhibitions of American and international contemporary craft and folk art are presented annually in this museum, part of a fascinating, cultural waterfront center in San Francisco. PLEASE NOTE: Group tours are free of charge to those who make advance reservations. The museum offers a special entry fee of $5.00 for families.

ON EXHIBIT 1999

01/09/1999 to 03/14/1999 THE LIGHT SHOW-ARTISTS WORKING WITH LIGHT/ BOXES BY TWO- JEFFREY KETCHUM AND LARRY JEFFERS

03/20/1999 to 05/30/1999 FURNITURE BY ART CARPENTER/ FOLK ART OF BRAZIL

08/14/1999 to 10/17/1999 AFRICAN TEXTILES/ PIERROT BARRA, HAITIAN ARTIST

10/23/1999 to 01/02/2000 BEYOND DESCRIPTION – CONTEMPORARY JEWELRY

San Francisco Museum of Modern Art

151 Third St., San Francisco, CA 94103-3159

: 415-357-4000 ◙ www.sfmoma.org

Open: 11-6 Fr-Tu, till 9 Th **Closed:** We, 1/1, 7/4, THGV, 12/25

ADM **Adult:** $8.00 **Children:** F (12 & under) **Students:** $4.00 **Seniors:** $5.00

♿ Ⓟ **Museum Shop** 🍴 Caffé Museo open 10-6 daily (except W), till 9pm T

Group Tours: 415-357-4191 **Drop-In Tours**: daily (call 415-357-4096) or inquire in lobby

Permanent Collection: AM: ab/exp ptgs; GER: exp; MEX; REG; PHOT; FAUVIST: ptgs; S.F. Bay Area Art; Video Arts

A trip to San Francisco, if only to visit the new home of this more than 60 year old museum, would be worthwhile for any art lover. Housed in a light filled architecturally brilliant and innovative building designed by Mario Botta, the museum features the most comprehensive collection of 20th century art on the West Coast. It is interesting to note that not only is this structure the largest new American art museum to be built in this decade, it is also the second largest single facility in the U.S. devoted to modern art. PLEASE NOTE: 1. Admission is half price from 6-9 on Thursday evenings; 2. Spotlight tours are conducted every Thursday and live jazz in the galleries is provided on the 3rd Thursday of each month; 3. Special group tours called "Modern Art Adventures" can be arranged (415-357-4191) for visits to Bay Area private collections, artists' studios, and a variety of museums and galleries in the area. **NOT TO BE MISSED:** "Woman in a Hat" by Matisse, one of 30 superb early 20th c. works from the recently donated Elise Hass Collection.

CALIFORNIA

San Francisco Museum of Modern Art - continued
ON EXHIBIT 1999

ONGOING: FROM MATISSE TO DIEBENKORN: WORKS FROM THE PERMANENT COLLECTION OF PAINTING AND SCULPTURE
Works from the museum's permanent collection, displayed in the vastly expanded gallery space of the new museum building, include prime examples of European & American Modernism, Surrealism, Abstract Expressionism, and California Art. In addition to highlighting individual artists such as Matisse, Klee, Still and Guston, the exhibition also features a room-sized light installation by James Turrell.

ONGOING: PICTURING MODERNITY: PHOTOGRAPHS FROM THE PERMANENT COLLECTION

ONGOING: CONTEMPORARY ART 1960-1996: SELECTIONS FROM THE PERMANENT COLLECTION

09/18/1998 to 01/03/1999 A PORTRAIT OF OUR TIMES: AN INTRODUCTION TO THE LOGAN COLLECTION
The first in a group of small focused exhibitions of works recently given to the Museum . This exhibit will encapsulate the overall vison of the collection/ *Catalog*

10/09/1998 to 01/19/1999   RICHARD DIEBENKORN *Catalog Will Travel*

10/23/1998 to 01/12/1999   NEW WORK: JULIA SCHER'S PREDICTIVE ENGINEERING
This is an updated version of the site-specific installation Scher did in 1993 for the architecture and environment of the new Museum building.

11/20/1998 to 02/23/1999   SITTING ON THE EDGE: MODERNIST DESIGN FROM THE COLLECTION OF MICHAEL AND GABRIELLE BOYD
This showcase of one of the most significant and comprehensive collections of modern furniture in private hands, it will explore issues in 20th c design. *Catalog*

01/08/1999 to 04/20/1999   MIRROR IMAGES: WOMEN, SURREALISM AND SELF-REPRESENTATION
Three generations of women artists associated with the surrealist movement of the 30's and 40's whose self-portraits are unique to 20th c. Modernism. *Catalog*

01/22/1999 to 04/06/1999   NEW WORK: KERRY JAMES MARSHALL
Works deeply influenced by the tradition of history painting and contemporary issues such as African-American identity.

02/04/1999 to 04/20/1999   GLENN MCKAY: ALTERED STATES – LIGHT PROJECTIONS 1966-1999
A concise survey of the work of the inventor of the liquid light show.

02/19/1999 to 04/27/1999   NEW WORK: DORIS SALCEDO'S UNLAND

02/26/1999 to 06/01/1999   INSIDE OUT: NEW CHINESE ART
Concepts of "modernity" and "identity" are undergoing rapid transformation in the Chinese world as Asian societies evolve in the post-1980s climate of radical social, economic and political change. This major exhibition is the first to bring together more than 100 works from various parts of the Chinese world including Taiwan, Hong Kong and outside of Asia. The political and economic change will be traced in the work of artists who worked in Asia before Tiananmen and outside after. Some of the works will be at the P.S. 1 Contemporary Art Center in New York *Catalog Will Travel*

03/19/1999 to 06/15/1999   ARCHIGRAM 1961-1974
Founded in the early 60's Archigram was active for over 12 years as a visionary English architectural collaborative, publishing a journal of the same name. This exhibition shows hundreds of drawings, models. Installations and multimedia environments that depict radical alternatives to houses, cities and other forms of architecture. *Catalog*

05/14/1999 to 08/03/1999   DAIDO MORIYAMA
The first retrospective of one of the major figures in 20th C. Japanese photography.

06/04/1999 to 09/07/1999   BILL VIOLA *Catalog Will Travel*

06/25/1999 to 09/14/1999   CARLETON WATKINS: THE ART OF PERCEPTION
The figure considered to be the greatest American photographer of the 19th century will be explored here. His landscape images informed an international audience of the natural beauty and abundant resources of California and the West. *Catalog*

Fall 1999   JULIA MARGARET CAMERON'S WOMEN
Cameron photographed many prominent figures of Victorian intellectual society in the 1860's and 70s. Her remarkable portraits of women constitute the bulk of her work. Her methods were unconventional for her time because they sought the "inner spirit" of the sitter. *Catalog Will Travel*

Yerba Buena Center for the Arts

701 Mission St., San Francisco, CA 94103-3138
☎: 415-978-ARTS (2787) ◉ www.YerbaBuenaArts.org
Open: 11-6 Tu-Su, till 8pm 1st Th of the month **Closed:** LEG/HOL!
Free Day: first Th of month **ADM Adult:** $5.00 **Children:** $3.00 **Students:** $3.00 **Seniors:** $3.00
    Ⓟ **Museum Shop** ‖ **Group Tours**: ex 114 **Drop-In Tours Sculpture Garden**

Opened in 1993 as part of a still evolving arts complex that includes the newly relocated San Francisco Museum of Modern Art, the Cartoon Art Museum, and the Ansel Adams Center for Photography, this fine arts and performance center features theme-oriented and solo exhibitions by a culturally diverse cross section of Bay Area artists. PLEASE NOTE: Admission for seniors is free from 11-3 on Thursdays. **NOT TO BE MISSED:** The building itself designed by prize-winning architect Fumihiko Maki to resemble a sleek ocean liner complete with porthole windows.

ON EXHIBIT 1999

11/14/1998 to 01/03/1999 ECOTOPIA

11/14/1998 to 01/03/1999 ALEXIS ROCKMAN AND KENJI YANOBE

11/14/1998 to 01/03/1999 ONE TREE BY NATALIE JEREMIJENKO

11/14/1998 to 01/03/1999 VICTOR BURGIN

01/16/1999 to 05/02/1999 FRED WILSON
A one-person show by Wilson, a celebrated New York artist.

01/16/1999 to 05/02/1999 THE MUSEUM OF JURASSIC TECHNOLOGY

01/16/1999 to 05/02/1999 CONTEMPORARY ART FROM CUBA

06/05/1999 to 08/22/1999 TRINH MINH-HA AND LYNN KIRBY
This presentation features a collaborative video installation by two local women artists.

09/03/1999 to 11/07/1999 SOUNDS LIKE ART

11/20/1999 to 02/2000 BAY AREA NOW

SAN JOSE

Egyptian Museum and Planetarium

Rosicrucian Park, 1342 Naglee Ave., San Jose, CA 95191
☎: 408-947-3636 ◉ www.rosicrucian.org
Open: 10-5 daily **Closed:** 1/1, THGV, 12/25
ADM Adult: $7.00 **Children:** $3.50 (7-15) **Students:** $5.00 **Seniors:** $5.00
Ⓟ **Museum Shop Group Tours**: 408-947-3633 **Drop-In Tours**: rock tomb only periodically during day
Permanent Collection: ANT: ptgs, sculp, gr

Without question the largest Egyptian collection in the West, the Rosicrucian is a treasure house full of thousands of objects and artifacts from ancient Egypt. Even the building itself is styled after Egyptian temples and, once inside, the visitor can experience the rare opportunity of actually walking through a reproduction of the rock tombs cut into the cliffs at Beni Hasan 4,000 years ago. **NOT TO BE MISSED:** A tour through the rock tomb, a reproduction of the ones cut into the cliffs at Beni Hasan 4,000 years ago; Egyptian gilded ibis statue in Gallery B

CALIFORNIA

San Jose Museum of Art
110 S. Market St., San Jose, CA 95113
📞: 408-294-2787   ▣ www.sjmusart.org
Open: 10-5 Tu-Su, till 8pm Th   **Closed:** Mo, LEG/HOL!
Free Day 1st Th; seniors 1st Tu; half price 5-8 pm Th   **Adult:** $7.00   **Children:** F (5 & under)   **Students:** $4.00
Seniors: $4.00   ♿ Ⓟ **Museum Shop**   ⅠⅠ Caffe La Pastaia al Museo   **Group Tours:** 408-291-6840, 408-291-5393
school tours   **Drop-In Tours:** 12:30 & 2:30 Tu-Su & 6:30 Th   **Historic Building** 1892 Richardsonian Romanesque.
Historic Wing; 1991 New Wing designed by Skidmore, Owings, & Merrill   **Sculpture Garden**
Permanent Collection: AM: 19-20; NAT/AM; CONT

Contemporary art is the main focus of this vital museum housed in a landmark building that once served as a post office/library. The museum added 45,000 square feet of exhibition space in 1991 to accommodate the needs of the cultural renaissance now underway in San Jose. Beginning in 1992, the Whitney Museum of American Art in New York agreed to send the San Jose Museum of Art four large exhibitions drawn from the Whitney's permanent collection. Each exhibition will be installed for a period of 12 months. PLEASE NOTE: Signed tours for the deaf are given at 12:30 on the 2nd Sat. of the month.

ON EXHIBIT 1999

10/04/1998 to 01/03/1999   CRIMES AND SPLENDORS: THE DESERT CANTOS OF RICHARD MISRACH
200 images of the American desert from Misrach's Desert Cantos series, begun in 1969, will be seen in the first photographic survey of this monumental series which acts as the artist's commentary on civilization and the environment.

11/15/1998 to 02/14/1999   GRONK X 3: MURALS, PRINTS, PROJECTS
This exhibition will showcase three facets of this prolific artist's work - murals, theatrical designs and prints. Central to the exhibition and located in the Museum's dramatic 26-foot-tall barrel-vaulted skylit gallery will be a large-scale, site-specific mural painted directly on the walls by Gronk.

01/17/1999 to 04/04/1999   JOHN REGISTER: A RETROSPECTIVE
More than 40 significant paintings by Register (1939-1996), an American realist artist will be presented in a major retrospective showcasing his trademark images of café interiors, empty chairs in hotel lobbies, phone booths and other scenes of the contemporary American urban landscape.

01/17/1999 to 04/04/1999   BYSTANDER: THE HISTORY OF STREET PHOTOGRAPHY

02/28/1999 to 05/04/1999   IMAGES OF THE SPIRIT: PHOTOGRAPHS BY GRACIELA ITURBIDE
A first retrospective of a range of Iturbide's work shown in the US, it is comprised of a range of her images of religious and cultural traditions of her native Mexico. *Will Travel*

02/28/1999 to 05/04/1999   MATERIAL ISSUES: RECENT GIFTS FROM THE COLLECTION OF KATHERINE AND JAMES GENTRY

04/16/1999 to 06/25/2000   INNUENDO NON TROPPO: THE WORK OF GREGORY BARSAMIAN
Spinning constructions and strobe lights are employed in the creation of Barsamian's works of optical illusion some of which produce the appearance of vertical motion.

04/18/1999 to 07/11/1999   STRIPES AND STARS: A VISUAL HISTORY OF AN AMERICAN ICON

05/04/1999 to 06/11/2000   A CENTURY OF LANDSCAPE: SELECTIONS FROM THE PERMANENT COLLECTION OF THE WHITNEY MUSEUM OF AMERICAN ART

05/20/1999 to 08/13/2000   BLURRING THE BOUNDARIES: INSTALLATION ART FROM THE SAN DIEGO MUSEUM OF CONTEMPORARY ART
Encompassing media as diverse as painting, sculpture, video and performance, installation art challenges viewers by asking them to participate in ways other than the purely visual. *Catalog Will Travel*

05/23/1999 to 09/12/1999   THE PERMANENT COLLECTION: INTO THE 21ST CENTURY

San Jose Museum of Art - continued

07/25/1999 to 10/10/1999 GIRLFRIEND! THE BARBIE SESSIONS BY DAVID LEVINTHAL

09/25/1999 to 01/10/2000 CATHERINE MCCARTHY

09/25/1999 to 01/10/2000 PIECING IT TOGETHER: PERSONAL NARRATIVE IN CONTEMPORARY ART

10/24/1999 to 01/09/2000 CARIOCA: A YEAR AMONG THE NATIVES OF RIO DE JANEIRO, NEW WORK BY SANDOW BIRK

SAN MARINO

Huntington Library, Art Collections and Botanical Gardens

1151 Oxford Rd., San Marino, CA 91108

☎: 626-405-2100   ▣   www.huntington.org
Open: 12-4:30 Tu-Fr, 10:30-4:30 Sa, Su; JUNE-AUG: 10:30-4:30 Tu-Su   **Closed:** Mo, LEG/HOL!
Adult: $8.50   **Children:** F (under 12)   **Students:** $2.00   **Seniors:** $7.00
&   ℗   **Museum Shop**   ∦ 1-4 Tu-F; 11:30-4:00 Sa, Su; ENGLISH. TEA 1-3:45 Tu-Fr; Noon-3:45 Sa, Su
Group Tours: 626-405-2126   **Drop-In Tours**: Introductory slide show given during day
Historic Building 1910 estate of railroad magnate, Henry E. Huntington   Sculpture Garden
Permanent Collection: BRIT: ptgs, drgs, sculp, cer 18-19; EU: ptgs, drgs, sculp, cer 18; FR: ptgs, dec/art, sculp 18; REN: ptgs; AM: ptgs, sculp, dec/art 18-20

The multi-faceted Huntington Library, Art Collection & Botanical Gardens makes a special stop at this complex a must! Known for containing the most comprehensive collections of British 18th & 19th century art outside of London, the museum also houses an outstanding American collection as well as one of the greatest research libraries in the world. A new installation of furniture and decorative arts, designed by California architects Charles & Henry Greene, opened recently in the Dorothy Collins Brown Wing which had been closed for refurbishing for the past 3 years. **NOT TO BE MISSED:** "Blue Boy" by Gainsborough; "Pinkie" by Lawrence; Gutenberg Bible; 12 acre desert garden; Japanese garden

ON EXHIBIT 1999

09/19/1998 to 01/11/1999   THE WISDOM OF THE TRAIL: JACK LONDON, AUTHOR AND ADVENTURER
Most often remembered for his dog stories, London lead a brilliant restless life which embraced many endeavors. As an author, prospector, foreign correspondent, sociologist, photo-journalist, socialist, rancher and adventurer this exhibit will seek to illuminate the two intertwined paths of his life.

10/06/1998 to 05/30/1999   THE GREAT EXPERIMENT: GEORGE WASHINGTON AND THE AMERICAN REPUBLIC
Using Washington's career and the 200th anniversary of his death as a vehicle, the exhibition will present the creation of the American republic as a genuinely revolutionary process, which produced the first successful republican nation in the modern world. *Catalog Will Travel*

11/21/1998 to 01/31/1999   ANTIQUITY REVISITED: ENGLISH AND FRENCH SILVER-GILT FROM THE COLLECTION OF AUDREY LOVE
More than 50 outstanding pieces from this world famous collection in the US will be shown here. Artists include Auguste, Boileau, Flaxman and Farrell.

mid 3/1999 to early 6/1999   TREASURES FROM MOUNT VERNON: GEORGE WASHINGTON REVEALED
Complementing the Washington exhibition will be a traveling exhibition of many priceless items including a full set of his dentures, the sword he wore during the French and Indian War, one of Martha Washington's favorite dresses, etc. *Will Travel*

07/27/1999 to 09/19/1999   CULTIVATING CELEBRITY: PORTRAITURE AS PUBLICITY IN THE CAREER OF SARAH SIDDONS, STAR OF THE GEORGIAN STAGE
The celebrity of Sarah Siddons will be shown at the same time as 'A Passion For Performance' at the Getty Center.

10/1999 to 09/2000   THE LAND OF GOLDEN DREAMS: CALIFORNIA AND THE GOLD RUSH DECADE, 1848-1858
A major exhibition of original material from the Museum's collection.

CALIFORNIA

Hearst Castle

750 Hearst Castle Rd., San Simeon, CA 93452-9741
📞: 800-444-4445 ◙ www.hearstcastle.org
Open: 8:20-3:20 (to reserve a tour call toll free 1-800-444-4445) **Closed:** 1/1, THGV, 12/25
ADM Adult: $14.00 **Children:** $8.00 (6-12)
⟨ ℗ **Museum Shop** ¶ **Group Tours:** 1-800-401-4775 **Drop-In Tours Historic Building**
Permanent Collection: IT/REN: sculp, ptgs; MED: sculp, ptgs; DU; FL; SP; AN/GRK: sculp; AN/R: sculp; AN/EGT: sculp

One of the prize house museums in the state of California is Hearst Castle, the enormous (165 rooms) and elaborate former estate of American millionaire William Randolph Hearst. The sculptures and paintings displayed throughout the estate, a mixture of religious, secular art and antiquities, stand as testament to the keen eye Mr. Hearst had for collecting. PLEASE NOTE: a 10% discount for groups of 12 or more (when ordered in advance for any daytime tour) has recently been implemented. Evening Tours are available for a fee of $25 adults and $13 for children ages 6-12 (hours vary according to the sunset). There are 4 different daytime tours offered. All last approximately 1 hour & 50 minutes, include a walk of ½ mile, and require the climbing of 150 to 400 stairs. All tickets are sold for specific tour times. Call 1-800-444-4445 to reserve BOTH, individual or group tours. For foreign language group tours also call 805-927-2020 for interpreters when available. Hours of operation may vary according to the season! **NOT TO BE MISSED:** Antique Spanish ceilings; a collection of 155 Greek vases; New IWERKS Theater presentation at the Visitor Center shows the 40 minute film "Hearst Castle: Building the Dream" on a 5-story high screen.

Bowers Museum of Cultural Art

2002 N. Main St., Santa Ana, CA 92706
📞: 714-567-3600 ◙ www.bowers.org
Open: 10-4 Tu-Su, till 9pm Th **Closed:** Mo, 1/1, THGV, 12/25
ADM Adult: $6.00 **Children:** $2.00 (5-12) **Students:** $4.00 **Seniors:** $4.00
⟨ ℗ **Museum Shop** ¶ Topaz Café **Group Tours:** 714-567-3680 **Drop-In Tours:** 1 & 2 most days
Permanent Collection: PACIFIC RIM 19-20; P/COL: cer; AM; dec/art 19-20; AF; N/AM: eth; S/AM: eth

Dedicated to the display & interpretation of the fine art of the indigenous peoples of the Americas, the Pacific Rim, & Africa, the Bowers, with its multi-faceted collection, is the largest museum in Orange County. Housed in a restored Spanish mission-style building (1932), the museum has a number of large galleries for the presentation of changing exhibits. PLEASE NOTE: Museum admission includes the KIDSEUM, an interactive, hands-on cultural art museum for children (open 2-5 We-Fr; 11-5 Sa & Su). **NOT TO BE MISSED:** "Seated Priest" from Oaxaca, Mexico (Classic Period); "Seated Shaman" from Colima, Mexico (200 BC-200 AD); Partners in Illusion: William and Alberta McCloskey

ON EXHIBIT 1999

ONGOING: PARTNERS IN ILLUSION: WILLIAM AND ALBERTA McCLOSKEY
A display of still lifes and portraits painted by the McCloskey's, a husband and wife artistic team.

ONGOING: EASELS IN THE ARROYOS: PLEIN AIR PAINTINGS
Created between 1900-1940, these important California plein-air and impressionist paintings from the Museum's collection are on permanent view with comparative works from before and after the period.

ONGOING: POWER AND CREATION: AFRICA BEYOND THE NILE
The power and sophistication of African art can be seen in the works on view from the Museum's extensive collection.

ONGOING: REALM OF THE ANCESTORS: ARTS OF OCEANA
Ritual objects, sculpture, costumes and artifacts in the Oceana Gallery tell of the culture of Southeast Asia and Pacific Oceana.

Bowers Museum of Cultural Art - continued

ONGOING: VISION OF THE SHAMAN, SONG OF THE PRIEST
A display of ancient pre Columbian Mexican and Central American ceramics and textiles.

ONGOING: ARTS OF NATIVE AMERICA
From beadwork to basketry, this exhibit showcases a rich display of Native American artifacts.

ONGOING: CALIFORNIA LEGACIES
The multi-cultural history of Orange County and the West is highlighted in a series of ongoing exhibitions.

ONGOING: CONTEMPORARY NETSUKE: MINIATURE SCULPTURE FROM JAPAN AND BEYOND
This exhibition of 500 miniature netsuke sculptures, created by 100 contemporary artists worldwide, is the largest display of its kind to ever be shown anywhere. Begun in Japan, the netsuke was originally designed as a clothing accessory.

10/04/1998 to 01/03/1999 TREASURES FROM THE ROYAL TOMBS OF UR
Mid-third millennium BC gold & silver jewels, cups, bowls and other ancient objects excavated from the royal burial tombs of Ur will be on exhibit. *Catalog Will Travel*

01/30/1999 to 03/21/1999 MUSICAL INSTRUMENTS FROM THE AGE OF BEETHOVEN
Revolutionary changes in the in music and the economic, political and social relationships of Europe at that time.

04/17/1999 to 06/06/1999 THE ART OF THE GOLD RUSH
Works of Gold Rush art by A.D.O. Browere, William Smith Jewett and Charles Christian Nahl are featured in an exhibition celebrating the Sesquicentennial of the discovery of gold in California *Catalog Will Travel*

07/01/1999 to 09/30/1999 A WINDING RIVER: JOURNEY OF CONTEMPORARY ART IN VIETNAM
Almost 80 paintings by 45 artists, this represents the first major cultural exchange since the diplomatic relations between the Us and Vietnam were resumed. *Will Travel*

10/29/1999 to 01/09/2000 SHAMANS, GODS AND MYTHIC BEASTS: COLUMBIAN GOLD AND CERAMICS IN ANTIQUITY
Presented for the first time to the American public new finds from the southwest and north coastal regions of Columbia focus on the important ceramic sculpture of ancient Columbia, the fabled land of gold "El Dorado" and the artistic qualities and themes found there. Also included are 44 exceptional gold masterpieces that share design motifs found in the ceramic figure. *Catalog Will Travel*

SANTA BARBARA

Santa Barbara Museum of Art

1130 State St., Santa Barbara, CA 93101-2746
: 805-963-4364 www.sbmuseart.org
Open: 11-5 Tu-W &, 11-9 Th, 11-5 Sa, Noon-5 Su **Closed:** Mo, 1/1, THGV, 12/25
Free Day: Th & 1st Su of month **ADM Adult:** $5.00 **Children:** F (under 6) **Students:** $2.00 **Seniors:** $3.00
♿ Ⓟ **Museum Shop Group Tours**: ex. 334 **Drop-In Tours**: 1:00 Tu-Su; (in-depth tours) Noon We, Th, Sa, Su
Permanent Collection: AN/GRK; AN/R; AN/EGP; AM; AS; EU: ptgs 19-20; CONT; PHOT; CA:reg

With 15,000 works of art, a considerable number for a community of its size, the Santa Barbara Museum, completing a major expansion project in 1/98, offers a variety of collections that range from antiquities of past centuries to contemporary creations of today. PLEASE NOTE: In addition to a rich variety of special programs such as free Family Days, the museum offers a monthly bilingual Spanish/English tour. **NOT TO BE MISSED:** Fine collection of representative works of American Art

ON EXHIBIT 1999

01/23/1999 to 03/21/1999 POSTERS: AMERICAN STYLE
The 100th anniversary celebration of an American popular art form brings together 120 compelling images by more than 90 graphic artists and designers on subjects from baseball games to rock concerts. The images demonstrate the ways in which graphic design is capable of eliciting specifically intended responses. *Will Travel*

CALIFORNIA

Santa Barbara Museum of Art - continued
02/14/1999 to 03/28/1999   CELEBRATING THE ANDERSON GRAPHIC ARTS COLLECTION *Will Travel*

04/17/1999 to 06/27/1999   SANTA BARBARA COLLECTS: ORIENTAL RUGS

07/31/1999 to 10/10/1999   THE CECIL FAMILY COLLECTS: FOUR CENTURIES OF DECORATIVE ARTS FROM BURGHLEY HOUSE
Burghley House is one of the oldest and grandest Elizabethan houses in England. The 120 crafted works from its collection will document the evolution of taste and collecting in Britain in the course of four centuries. *Catalog Will Travel*

University Art Museum, Santa Barbara
Affiliate Institution: University of California
Santa Barbara, CA 93106
☏: 805-893-2951
Open: 10-4 Tu-Sa, 1-5 Su & HOL   **Closed:** Mo, 1/1, EASTER, 7/4, THGV, 12/25
♿   **Museum Shop   Group Tours   Drop-In Tours**: acad year only: 2:00 Sa & 12:15 alternate Tu
Permanent Collection: IT: ptgs; GER: ptgs; FL: ptgs; DU: ptgs; P/COL; ARCH/DRGS; GR; OM: ptgs; AF

Outstanding among the many thousands of treasures in the permanent collection is one of the world's finest groups of early Renaissance medals and plaquettes. PLEASE NOTE: The museum will be closed for renovation during most of 1998. **NOT TO BE MISSED:** 15th through 17th century paintings from the Sedgwick Collection; Architectural drawing collection; Morgenroth Collection of Renaissance medals and plaquettes

---
SANTA CLARA
---

deSaisset Museum
Affiliate Institution: Santa Clara University
500 El Camino Real, Santa Clara, CA 95053-0550
☏: 408-554-4528   ◉   www.scu.edu/SCU/Departments/deSaisset
Open: 11-4 Tu-Su   **Closed:** Mo, LEG/HOL!
♿   ℗   **Museum Shop   Group Tours Drop-In Tours   Historic Building** Adjacent to Mission Santa Clara
Permanent Collection: AM: ptgs, sculp, gr; EU: ptgs, sculp, gr 16-20; AS: dec/art; AF; CONT: gr, phot, IT/REN: gr

Serving Santa Clara University and the surrounding community, the de Saisset, since its inception in 1955, has been an important Bay Area cultural resource. PLEASE NOTE: It is wise to call ahead as the museum may have limited hours between rotating exhibitions. **NOT TO BE MISSED:** California history collection

ON EXHIBIT 1999
ONGOING: CALIFORNIA HISTORY EXHIBIT

01/26/1999 to 03/28/1999   WE LIVE IN THE BIZARRO WORLD: ASSEMBLAGES BY DAVID GILHOOLY
Assemblages relating to myth, religion, and social commentary will be among the works on display by Gilhooly, an artist best known for his Dadaesque works, inspired, in part, by his association with ceramic artist, Robert Arneson, his late teacher and mentor.

01/26/1999 to 06/04/1999   PRINTS BY DAVID GILHOOLY FROM THE PERMANENT COLLECTION
To complement the assemblages exhibition on view at the same time.

05/1999 to 08/1999   OUR SAINTS AMONG US/NUESTROS SANTOS ENTRE NOSOTROS: 400 YEARS OF DEVOTIONAL ART IN NEW MEXICO
Included with some 10 historic pieces as well as children's work of today are contemporary New Mexican Santos-Hispanic religious wood carvings and the stories that go with each saint. Also included are santeros, Bullitos (carved statues), retablos (paintings on wood, and reredos (altar screens).

deSaisset Museum - continued
08/24/1999 to 12/03/1999   SMITH ANDERSEN EDITIONS EXHIBITION
This fine arts press is traced through the prints created there for the past three decades. Monotype,. etching, lithography and other media by Francis, Zirker, Shapiro, Gilliam and Gilhooly. *Catalog Will Travel*

09/25/1999 to 01/2000   ECO-TECH (working title)
This large scale interactive installation illustrates the "yarn ball theory of environmental complexity" which gives visitors the opportunity to experience the nature of systems theory first hand. These create a new way of thinking about technology etc.

Triton Museum of Art
1505 Warburton Ave., Santa Clara, CA 95050
✆: 408-247-3754   ◙ www.TritonMuseum.org
Open: 10-5 We-Su, till 9pm Tu   **Closed:** Mo, LEG/HOL
♿ ℗ **Museum Shop   Group Tours   Drop-In Tours   Sculpture Garden**
Permanent Collection: AM: 19-20; REG; NAT/AM; CONT/GR

Located in a seven acre park adjacent to the City of Santa Clara, the Triton has grown by leaps and bounds to keep up with the cultural needs of its rapidly expanding "Silicon Valley" community. The museum is housed in a visually stunning building that opened its doors to the public in 1987. **NOT TO BE MISSED:** The largest collection in the country of paintings by American Impressionist Theodore Wores; "Native Americans: Yesterday & Today" (on permanent display)

ON EXHIBIT 1999
11/15/1998 to 02/20/1999   DEWEY CRUMPLER: BAY AREA MASTER

03/01/1999 to 05/01/1999   IKU NAGAI

03/01/1999 to 05/01/1999   MARIE JOHNSON CALLOWAY: HOPE STREET REVISITED

05/14/1999 to 09/16/1999   FILIPINO-AMERICAN EXHIBITION

10/01/1999 to 10/21/1999   ARTS COUNCIL OF SANTA CLARA COUNTY FELLOWSHIP AWARD WINNERS

10/01/1999 to 01/06/2000   ELAINE BADGLEY ARNOUX: BACK TO THE GARDEN

10/31/1999 to 01/02/2000   TRITON MUSEUM OF ART BIENNIAL STATEWIDE COMPETITION AND EXHIBITION: PASTELS

SANTA CRUZ

Museum of Art and History at the McPherson Center
705 Front St., Santa Cruz, CA 95060
✆: 408-429-1964
Open: 12-5 Tu-Su, till 7 Fr   **Closed:** Mo, LEG/HOL
Free Day: 1st Fr of month   **ADM   Adult:** $3.00 ($2 for county residents)   **Children:** F   **Seniors:** $3.00
♿ ℗ **Museum Shop** ❙❙ Indoor courtyard/café   **Group Tours**: 408-429-1964 ext. 10
Drop-In Tours: Noon usually 1st Fr   **Historic Building** Museum store is housed in historic Octagon Building
Permanent Collection: CONT

Presenting visual and cultural experiences focused on regional history and modern art; art and history exhibitions from the permanent collection; changing exhibitions from the permanent collection; changing exhibitions of nationally and internationally renowned artists; group exhibitions that demonstrate various art techniques, mediums, crafts, and historic periods.

CALIFORNIA

Museum of Art and History at the McPherson Center - continued
ON EXHIBIT 1999

09/27/1998 to 08/1999   PICKS, PLOWS AND POTATOES: THE SANTA CRUZ REGION DURING THE GOLD RUSH

11/21/1998 to 02/1999   STITCHING STORIES: HISTORIC AND CONTEMPORARY QUILTS

11/21/1998 to 02/21/1999   PERSONAL CHOICE: THE MUSEUM, THE STAFF, AND THE PERMANENT COLLECTION

01/1999 to 03/1999   A GATHERING OF GLASS

02/1999 to 04/1999   CHINATOWN DREAMS: PHOTOGRAPHS BY SANTA CRUZ PHOTOGRAPHER GEORGE LEE

03/06/1999 to 06/1999   WHEN BORDERS MIGRATE

04/10/1999 to 06/27/1999   ALTERED: THE ANIMAL IN ART

05/1999 to 08/1999   A HISTORY OF WINE MAKING IN SANTA CRUZ COUNTY

06/27/1999 to 10/17/1999   WOOD/CUT/PAPER/INK, A RETROSPECTIVE: CAROL SUMMERS

SANTA MONICA

Santa Monica Museum of Art-Bergamot Arts Center
2525 Michigan Ave. Building G1, Santa Monica, CA 90404
✆: 310-586-6488   ◙   www.netvip.com/smmoa
Open: 11-6 We-Su, till 10 Fr   **Closed:** Mo, Tu, 1/1, 7/4, THGV, 12/25
Sugg/Cont   Adult: $3.00   **Students:** $2.00   **Seniors:** $2.00
&   Ⓟ   **Museum Shop   Group Tours   Drop-In Tours   Historic Building** Located in a renovated trolley station
Permanent Collection: NO PERMANENT COLLECTION

Recently relocated to a renovated trolley station in the historic Bergamont Station area, this museum, devoted to the display of art by living artists, is the only art museum in the area dedicated to making contemporary art more accessible to a culturally and economically diverse audience.

SANTA ROSA

Sonoma County Museum
425 Seventh St., Santa Rosa, CA 95401
✆: 707-579-1500
Open: 11-4 We-Su   **Closed:** Mo, Tu, LEG/HOL!
ADM   Adult: $2.00   **Children:** F (under 12)   **Students:** $1.00   **Seniors:** $1.00
&   Ⓟ   **Museum Shop**
Group Tours   Drop-In Tours   Historic Building 1910 Federal Post Office
Permanent Collection: AM: ptgs 19 ; REG

The museum is housed in a 1909 Post Office & Federal Building that was restored and moved to its present downtown location. It is one of the few examples of Classical Federal Architecture in Sonoma County. **NOT TO BE MISSED:** Collection of works by 19th century California landscape painters

Sonoma County Museum - continued

ON EXHIBIT 1999

01/18/1999 to 02/28/1999   OVERLAND EMIGRANT TRAIL

03/14/1999 to 05/16/1999   BEN E. CUMMINGS: A RETROSPECTIVE

05/28/1999 to 05/28/1999   ARTISTRY IN WOOD

07/23/1999 to 09/19/1999   REDWOODS OF SONOMA COUNTY; EARLY CALIFORNIA ART

07/23/1999 to 09/23/1999   ANSEL ADAMS

STANFORD

Iris and B. Gerald Cantor Center for the Visual Arts at Stanford University

Affiliate Institution: Stanford University
Stanford, CA 94305

✆: 650-723-4177
Open: OPENING 1/1999   **Closed:** Mo, 1/1, 7/4, THGV, 12/25
Vol/Cont
♿ Ⓟ **Museum Shop**
Group Tours   Drop-In Tours: Rodin Garden: 2pm We, Sa, Su; Outdoor sculp: 2pm 1st Su
Sculpture Garden
Permanent Collection: PHOT; PTGS; SCULP (RODIN COLLECTION); DEC/ART; GR; DRGS; OR; CONT/EU

In anticipation of the 1/1999 opening of the new Iris and B. Gerald Cantor Center for the Visual Arts at Stanford University, the former art gallery has become part of the university art department and is no longer open as a museum. Call for beginning of special tours, etc. **NOT TO BE MISSED:** Largest Rodin sculpture collection outside the Musée Rodin in Paris.

ON EXHIBIT 1999

winter 99   PICASSO: GRAPHIC MAGICIAN: PRINTS FROM THE NORTON SIMON MUSEUM *Catalog Will Travel*

Spring 1999   PACIFIC ARCADIA: IMAGES OF CALIFORNIA 1600-1915
The California dream is investigated here and the ways in which the State was promoted to outsiders and idealized by those who had a stake in California's development. *Catalog Will Travel*

WINTER 1999   BEFORE AND AFTER SCIENCE: THE PHOTOGRAPHS OF EADWEARD MUYBRIDGE

WINTER 1999 to 12/05/1999   A RENAISSANCE TREASURY: THE FLAGG COLLECTION OF EUROPEAN DECORATIVE ARTS AND SCULPTURE
This outstanding collection of later Medieval and Renaissance decorative arts was a gift to the Milwaukee Art Museum. Approximately 80 objects of diverse media, place of origin, and social function might provide insight into the Renaissance as well as the taste of an individual collector. Highlights of this collection are a number of rare secular objects like German and Swiss clocks, Limoges platters with classical scenes, marriage boxes, etc. as well as religious objects including the polychromed sculpture of 'St. George Slaying the Dragon'. *Catalog Will Travel*

CALIFORNIA

Haggin Museum

1201 N. Pershing Ave., Stockton, CA 95203

☎: 209-462-1566

Open: 1:30-5 Tu-Su; Open to groups by advance appt!   **Closed:** Mo, 1/1, THGV, 12/25
Sugg/Cont   Adult: $2.00   **Children:** $1.00   **Students:** $1.00   **Seniors:** $1.00
& Ⓟ **Museum Shop**
Group Tours   Drop-In Tours: 1:45 Sa, Su
Permanent Collection: AM: ptgs 19; FR: ptgs 19; AM: dec/art; EU: dec/art

Wonderful examples of 19th century French and American paintings from the Barbizon, French Salon, Rocky Mountain, and Hudson River Schools are displayed in a setting accented by a charming array of decorative art objects. **NOT TO BE MISSED:** "Lake in Yosemite Valley" by Bierstadt; "Gathering for the Hunt" by Rosa Bonheur

Ventura County Museum of History & Art

100 E. Main St., Ventura, CA 93001

☎: 805-653-0323

Open: 10-5 Tu-Su, till 8pm Th   **Closed:** Mo, 1/1, THGV, 12/25
ADM   Adult: $3.00   **Children:** F (under 16)   **Students:** $3.00   **Seniors:** $3.00
& Ⓟ **Museum Shop**
Group Tours   Drop-In Tours: 1:30 Su; "ask me" docents often on duty
Permanent Collection: PHOT; CONT/REG; REG

Art is but a single aspect of this museum that also features historical exhibitions relating to the history of the region. **NOT TO BE MISSED:** 3-D portraits of figures throughout history by George Stuart. Mr. Stuart has created nearly 200 figures which are rotated for viewing every 4 months. He occasionally lectures on his works (call for information)!

ON EXHIBIT 1999

ONGOING: VENTURA COUNTY IN THE NEW WEST
An exhibit that traces the county's history from before European contact to World War II.

Aspen Art Museum

590 N. Mill St., Aspen, CO 81611

☎: 970-925-8050 ▣ www.aspen.com/arm
Open: 10-6 Tu-Sa, Noon-6 Su, till 8pm Th **Closed:** Mo, 1/1, THGV, 12/25, & OTHER!
ADM Adult: $3.00 **Children:** F (under 12) **Students:** $2.00 **Seniors:** $2.00
& ℗ **Museum Shop Group Tours Drop-In Tours**
Historic Building The museum is housed in a former hydroelectric plant (c.1855) **Sculpture Garden**
Permanent Collection: SCULP

Located in an area noted for its natural beauty and access to numerous recreational activities, this museum, with its emphasis on contemporary art, offers the visitor a chance to explore the cultural side of life in the community. A free reception is offered every Thursday evening from 6-8pm for refreshments and gallery tours. PLEASE NOTE: The galleries may occasionally be closed between exhibits.

CU Art Galleries

Affiliate Institution: University of Colorado/Boulder
Campus Box 318, Boulder, CO 80309

☎: 303-492-8300
Open: 10-5 Mo-Fr, Tu 'til 8, 11-4 Sa **Closed:** Su, 1/1, 7/4, CHRISTMAS VACATION
Vol/Cont
& ℗ **Museum Shop Group Tours Drop-In Tours**
Permanent Collection: PTGS 19-20; GR 19-20; PHOT 20; DRGS 15-20; SCULP 15-20

ON EXHIBIT 1999

01/22/1999 to 03/20/1999 AFRO: POSTWAR ITALIAN ABSTRACTION

01/22/1999 to 03/20/1999 AMERICAN POP: SELECTIONS FROM THE COLORADO COLLECTION

Leanin' Tree Museum of Western Art

6055 Longbow Dr., Boulder, CO 80301

☎: 1-800-777-8716 ▣ www.leanintree.com
Open: 8-4:30 Mo-Fr, 10-4 Sa, Su **Closed:** LEG/HOL!
Vol/Cont
& ℗ **Museum Shop**
Group Tours: 303-530-1442 **Drop-In Tours**
Permanent Collection: WESTERN: sculp, ptgs, reg; CONT/REG; Largest collection of ptgs by actualist Bill Hughes (1932-1993) in the country.

This unusual museum, just 40 minutes from downtown Denver, is housed in the corporate offices of Leanin' Tree, producers of Western greeting cards. With 200 original oil paintings and 75 bronze sculptures by over 90 artist members of the Cowboy Artists of America, Leanin' Tree is home to the largest privately owned collection of contemporary cowboy and western art on public view in America. **NOT TO BE MISSED:** "Checkmate", by Herb Mignery, a monumental 10' high bronze sculpture depicting a mounted cowboy wrestling with a wild horse; "Invocation" by Buck McCain, a dramatic monumental 15' bronze sculpture of a horse and Native American rider.

COLORADO

Colorado Springs Fine Arts Center

Affiliate Institution: Taylor Museum For Southwestern Studies
30 W. Dale St., Colorado Springs, CO 80903

☎: 719-634-5581
Open: 9-5 Tu-Fr, 10-5 Sa, 1-5 Su **Closed:** Mo, LEG/HOL!
Free Day: Sa 10-5 **ADM Adult:** $3.00 **Children:** $1.00 (6-12) **Students:** $1.50 **Seniors:** $1.50
   Museum Shop ⑪ 11:30-3:00 Tu-F (summer only)
Group Tours: 719-475-2444 **Drop-In Tours**: by arrangement **Historic Building** **Sculpture Garden**
Permanent Collection: AM: ptgs, sculp, gr 19-20; REG; NAT/AM: sculp; CONT: sculp

Located in an innovative 1930's building that incorporates Art Deco styling with a Southwestern Indian motif, this multi-faceted museum is a major center for cultural activities in the Pikes Peak region. **NOT TO BE MISSED:** Collection of Charles Russell sculpture and memorabilia; hands-on tactile gallery called "Eyes of the Mind"; New sculpture acquisitions: "The Family", by William Zorach, "Hopi Basket Dancers", by Doug Hyde, "Resting at the Spring", by Allan Houser, "Prometheus" by Edgar Britton

ON EXHIBIT 1999

ONGOING: SACRED LAND: INDIAN AND HISPANIC CULTURES OF THE SOUTHWEST AND THE TALPA CHAPEL

ONGOING: CHARLES M. RUSSELL: ART OF THE AMERICAN WEST

ONGOING: EYES OF THE MIND, AN ADDED DIMENSION: SELECTIONS FROM THE TACTILE GALLERY COLLECTION

08/29/1998 to 11/29/1999 ON WITH THE SHOW: AMERICAN MUSICAL THEATRE

09/05/1998 to 11/22/1999 BANDITS AND BULLFIGHTERS: ART AND LIFE IN BROADSHEETS BY JOSÉ GUADALUPE POSADA

09/19/1998 to 01/10/1999 LAND AND WATER: ART ABOUT THE BASIC ELEMENTS

11/28/1998 to 03/14/1999 BY THE GRACE OF LIGHT: CONTEMPORARY IMAGES OF AN AGE-OLD FAITH, PHOTOGRAPHS BY CRAIG VARJABEDIAN

12/05/1998 to 01/03/1999 GALLERY OF TREES AND LIGHT

01/1999 SELECTIONS FROM THE PERMANENT COLLECTION

01/16/1999 to 03/07/1999 SOMETHING NEW: CONTEMPORARY REGIONAL ART

01/16/1999 to 04/11/1999 MASTER DRAWINGS FROM THE WORCESTER ART MUSEUM
More than 100 works including watercolors, pastels and illuminated manuscripts by European and American artists from 1275 to 1975 representing major trends of style and content. *Catalog Will Travel*

01/16/1999 to 04/18/1999 THE NATURE OF LOOKING

03/13/1999 to 05/31/1999 THE FLOWER SHOW: CONTEMPORARY BOTANICAL ILLUSTRATIONS

05/01/1999 HISPANIC WEAVING OF NEW MEXICO AND COLORADO

06/05/1999 to 08/1999 COWBOYS AROUND THE WORLD: PHOTOGRAPHS BY MARTIN SCHREIBER

06/05/1999 to 08/1999 ALLAN HOUSER: DRAWINGS & PRINTS

06/05/1999 to 08/1999 MARY CHENOWETH: A RETROSPECTIVE EXHIBITION

Gallery of Contemporary Art

Affiliate Institution: University of Colorado Springs
1420 Austin Bluffs Pkwy., Colorado Springs, CO 80933-7150
📞: 719-262-3567   ◉ harpy.uccs.edu/gallery/framesgallery.html
Open: 8:30-4 Mo-Fr, 1-4 Sa   **Closed:** Su, LEG/HOL!
ADM   Adult: $1.00   **Children:** F (under 12)   **Students:** $0.50   **Seniors:** $0.50
♿ ℗   **Museum Shop   Group Tours   Drop-In Tours**

This non-collecting university art museum concentrates on cutting edge group exhibitions of international, national and regional contemporary art with approximately 6 exhibitions each year. Attached to the second floor of the University science building, this is the only museum in the Colorado Springs (Pikes Peak) region dedicated exclusively to contemporary art.

DENVER

Denver Art Museum

100 West 14th Ave. Pkwy., Denver, CO 80204
📞: 303-640-4433   ◉ www.denverartmuseum.org
Open: 10-5 Tu-Sa, 10-9 W, Noon-5 Su   **Closed:** Mo, LEG/HOL!
Free Day: Sa (Colorado residents only)   **Adult:** $4.50   **Children:** F (under 5)   **Students:** $2.50   **Seniors:** $2.50
♿ ℗   **Museum Shop**   ⅠⅠTu-Sa 10-5; W 10-9, 12-5 S
Group Tours: 303-640-7591   **Drop-In Tours:** 1:30 Tu-Su, 11:00 Sa, 12-12:30 We & Fr
Historic Building Designed by Gio Ponti in 1971   **Sculpture Garden**
Permanent Collection: AM: ptgs, sculp, dec/art 19; IT/REN: ptgs; FR: ptgs 19-20; AS; P/COL; SP; AM: cont; NAT/AM; ARCH: gr

With over 40,000 works featuring 19th century American art, a fine Asian and Native American collection, and works from the early 20th century Taos group, in addition two newly renovated floors house the European, American and Western Paintings, sculpture, design and textiles. PLEASE NOTE: The Museum offers many free family related art activities on Saturday. Call 303-640-7577 for specifics! **NOT TO BE MISSED:** The outside structure of the building itself is entirely covered with one million grey Corning glass tiles.

ON EXHIBIT 1999

to 01/10/1999   ETERNAL COMPANIONS: ANIMAL FIGURES FROM CHINESE TOMBS IN THE SZE HONG COLLECTION
Objects collected from Chinese tombs from the Han through Tang dynasties.

to 01/09/2000   TREASURES FROM THE DR. S. Y. YIP COLLECTION: CLASSIC CHINESE FURNITURE, PAINTING & CALLIGRAPHY
On a rotating basis this exceptional collection is on long term loan to the Museum.

10/03/1998 to 08/08/1999   FORGING A NEW CENTURY: MODERN METALWORK, 1895-1935 • SELECTIONS FROM THE NORTHWEST COLLECTION
The second in a series of three modern design exhibitions showing metalwork by the world's leading designers.

10/03/1998 to 10/03/1999   WHITE ON WHITE: CHINESE JADES AND CERAMICS
On long-term loan to the Museum, the objects on view, from the Tang to the Qing dynasties (8th-19th centuries), reveal the many subtle variations of white.

10/10/1998 to 03/28/1999   600 YEARS OF BRITISH PAINTING: THE BERGER COLLECTION
This exceptional collection will be on view for the first time to Denver audiences. Included are a rare 14th c. painting of the "Crucifixion", a Book of Hours illuminated manuscript. as well as works by Turner, Gainsborough, Constable, Stubbs and more.

10/17/1998 to 01/10/1999   THE POINDEXTER COLLECTION OF MODERN AMERICAN MASTERS
This stunning collection of works by now legendary artists active in the 1950's and 1960's includes Pollock, de Kooning, Kline, Gorky and de Niro. They have been given to the Montana Historical Society and are known as "Montana's Best Kept Secret".

COLORADO

Denver Art Museum - continued
10/31/1998 to 01/24/1999   INVENTING THE SOUTHWEST: THE FRED HARVEY COMPANY AND NATIVE AMERICAN ART
Baskets, jewelry, paintings, and other art objects from this renowned collection will be displayed in an exhibit designed to tell the story of early American railroad travel and its effect on Native American people and their art.

10/31/1998 to 04/11/1999   CRAZY QUILTS
The highest levels of intricate handiwork and unparalleled creativity in a colorful presentation of the Museum's boldest and beautiful quilts.

11/14/1998 to spring 99   CONTEMPORARY BRITISH ARTISTS
Exciting creations by Britain's leading contemporary artists including Cragg, Gilbert and George, Hirst, Hockney, Parker. Quinn and others.

04/10/1999 to 07/04/1999   TOULOUSE-LAUTREC: FROM THE METROPOLITAN MUSEUM OF ART
More than 100 works will be on display including drawings, paintings, prints, posters, and illustrations by this observer of the Parisian demimonde. *Catalog Will Travel*

05/15/1999 to 08/15/1999   THE ROYAL ACADEMY IN THE AGE OF QUEEN VICTORIA (1837-1901): 19TH CENTURY PAINTINGS FROM THE PERMANENT COLLECTION
London's Royal Academy contributed major works throughout the 19th c. Included are Alma-Tadema, Blake, Millais, etc who are just now beginning to attract more attention from the art world.

09/02/1999 to 12/12/1999   COLLECTING IMPRESSIONISM: IMPRESSIONIST PAINTINGS FROM EUROPEAN MUSEUMS
This exhibition of impressionist works seeks to significantly deepen the understanding of how Europe finest museums assembled their collections of these paintings and turned them from objects of scandal to highly prized masterworks. Included are Manet, Cezanne, Degas, Morisot, Pissarro Sisley and Van Gogh. *Catalog Will Travel*

DENVER

Museo de las Americas
861 Santa Fe Drive, Denver, CO 80204
☎: 303-571-4401
Open: 10-5 Tu-Sa   **Closed:** Su, Mo, 1/1, 7/4, THGV, 12/25
ADM   Adult: $3.00   **Children:** F (under 10)   **Students:** $1.00   **Seniors:** $2.00
& ℗   **Museum Shop   Group Tours:** Call to arrange for certain exhibitions   **Drop-In Tours**
Historic Building; Housed in a former J. C. Penny store built in 1924
Permanent Collection: SPANISH COLONIAL ART; CONT LAT/AM

The Museo de las Americas, opened in 7/94, is the first Latino museum in the Rocky Mountain region dedicated to showcasing the art, history, and culture of the people of the Americas from ancient times to the present. PLEASE NOTE: Bilingual tours are available with admission price - call ahead to reserve.

ON EXHIBIT 1999
12/10/1998 to 03/1999   PERU: TRADITIONS OF YESTERDAY IN TRANSITION
Contemporary photographs of Peruvian photojournalist Mario Corvetto with traditional folk art retablos created by Nicario Jimenez.

05/1999 to 08/1999   CHICANO EXPRESSIONS
Local and national Chicano artists will be represented.

09/09/1999 to 12/27/1999   SPIRIT ASCENDANT, THE ART AND LIFE OF PATROCINO BARELA
40 wood carvings by this nationally recognized artist who was once known ads one o the most famous artists in the country.

12/09/1999 to 02/2000   HAITIAN VOODOO FLAGS
Sequined and beaded flags of satin, felt and other cloth are ritual objects in the practice of voodoo religion.

Museum of Outdoor Arts

7600 E. Orchard Rd. #160 N., Englewood, CO 80111
☎: 303-741-3609
Open: 8:30-5:30 Mo-Fr; some Sa from JAN-MAR & SEPT-DEC   **Closed:** LEG/HOL!
Vol/Cont   ADM   Adult: $3.00   **Children:** $1.00   **Students:** $1.00   **Seniors:** $1.00
& ℗   **Museum Shop**
Group Tours: 303-741-3609   **Drop-In Tours**: scheduled tours   **Sculpture Garden**
Permanent Collection: SCULP

Fifty five major pieces of sculpture ranging from contemporary works by Colorado artists to pieces by those with international reputations are placed throughout the 400 acre Greenwood Plaza business park, located just south of Denver, creating a "museum without walls". A color brochure with a map is provided to lead visitors through the collection.

Sangre deCristo Arts & Conference Center & Children's Center

210 N. Santa Fe Ave., Pueblo, CO 81003
☎: 719-543-0130
Open: 11-4 Mo-Sa   **Closed:** Su, LEG/HOL!
& ℗   **Museum Shop**
Group Tours   Drop-In Tours
Permanent Collection: AM: Regional Western 19-20; REG: ldscp, cont

The broad range of Western Art represented in the collection covers works from the 19th and early 20th century through contemporary Southwest and modern regionalist pieces. **NOT TO BE MISSED:** Francis King collection of Western Art; Art of the "Taos Ten"

A.R. Mitchell Memorial Museum of Western Art

150 E. Main St., P.O. Box 95, Trinidad, CO 81082
☎: 719-846-4224
Open: early APR-through SEPT: 10-4 Mo-Sa; OCT-MAR by appt.   **Closed:** Su, 7/4
Vol/Cont
& ℗   **Museum Shop**
Group Tours   Drop-In Tours: often available upon request   **Historic Building**
Permanent Collection: AM: ptgs; HISP: folk; AM: Western

Housed in a charming turn of the century building that features its original tin ceiling and wood floors, the Mitchell contains a unique collection of early Hispanic religious folk art and artifacts from the old west, all of which is displayed in a replica of an early Penitente Morada. The museum is located in southeast Colorado just above the New Mexico border. **NOT TO BE MISSED:** 250 works by Western artist/illustrator Arthur Roy Mitchell

CONNECTICUT

BRIDGEPORT

Discovery Museum

4450 Park Ave., Bridgeport, CT 06604

☎: 203-372-3521

Open: 10-5 Tu-Sa, Noon-5 Su, (Open 10-5 M during JUL & AUG)   **Closed:** Mo, LEG/HOL!

ADM   Adult: $6.00   **Children:** $4.00   **Students:** $4.00   **Seniors:** $4.00

♿ ℗ **Museum Shop** ‖ Cafeteria

Group Tours   Drop-In Tours

Permanent Collection: AM: ptgs, sculp, phot, furniture 18-20; IT/REN & BAROQUE: ptgs (Kress Coll)

18th to 20th century American works provide the art focus in this interactive art and science museum. **NOT TO BE MISSED:** 14 unique hands-on exhibits that deal with color, line, and perspective in a studio-like setting.

Housatonic Museum of Art

900 Lafayette Blvd., Bridgeport, CT 06608-4704

☎: 203-332-5000

Open: Mo-Fr 8:30 - 4:30 (By Appointment only)   **Closed:** Sa, Su, LEG/HOL! ACAD!

Free Day: Always   **Vol/Cont**

♿ ℗ **Museum Shop**

Group Tours   Drop-In Tours: by appointment

Sculpture Garden

Permanent Collection: AM 19-20; EU: 19-20; AF; CONT: Lat/Am; CONT: reg; ASIAN; CONT: Hispanic

With a strong emphasis on contemporary and ethnographic art, the Housatonic Museum displays works from the permanent collection and from changing exhibitions.

ON EXHIBIT 1999

11/19/1998 to 01/22/1999   SOL LEWITT: FORMS DERIVED FROM A CUBE

04/08/1999 to 05/14/1999   SHIRAZEH HOUSHIARY & SHIRLIN NESHAT: NUMBERS AND LETTERS

10/1999 to 12/1999   ROBERT PERLESS/SCULPTURE

BROOKLYN

New England Center for Contemporary Art, Inc.

Route 169, Brooklyn, CT 06234

☎: 860-774-8899

Open: (Open from 4/15-12/15 only) 10-5 Tu-Fr; Noon-5 Sa, Su   **Closed:** Mo, THGV

♿ ℗ **Museum Shop**

Group Tours   Drop-In Tours

Sculpture Garden

Permanent Collection: AM: cont/ptgs; CONT/SCULP; OR: cont/art

In addition to its sculpture garden, great emphasis is placed on the display of the contemporary arts of China in this art center which is located on the mid-east border of the state near Rhode Island. **NOT TO BE MISSED:** Collection of contemporary Chinese art; Collection of artifacts from Papua, New Guinea

FARMINGTON

Hill-Stead Museum
35 Mountain Rd., Farmington, CT 06032
📞: 860-677-9064
Open: MAY-OCT: 10-5 Tu-Su; NOV-APR: 11-4 **Closed:** Mo, 1/1, 12/25, Easter, 7/4
ADM Adult: $6.00 **Children:** $3.00 (6-12) **Students:** $5.00 **Seniors:** $5.00
🚹 ℗ **Museum Shop Group Tours:** 860-677-2940 **Drop-In Tours:** hour long tours on the hour & half hour
Historic Building National Historical Landmark
Permanent Collection: FR: Impr/ptgs; GR:19; OR: cer; DEC/ART

Designated a National Historic Landmark in 1991, Hill-Stead, located in a suburb just outside of Hartford, is a Colonial Revival home that was originally a "gentleman's farm." Built by Alfred Atmore Pope at the turn of the century, the museum still houses his magnificent collection of French and American Impressionist paintings, Chinese porcelains, Japanese woodblock prints, and original furnishings. PLEASE NOTE: Guided tours begin every half hour, the last one being 1 hour before closing. **NOT TO BE MISSED:** Period furnishings; French Impressionist paintings

GREENWICH

Bruce Museum
Museum Drive, Greenwich, CT 06830-7100
📞: 203-869-0376 ▣ www.brucemuseum.com
Open: 10-5 Tu-Sa, 1-4 Su **Closed:** Mo, LEG/HOL!
ADM Adult: $3.50 **Children:** F (under 5) **Students:** $2.50 **Seniors:** $2.50
🚹 ℗ **Museum Shop Group Tours:** 203-869-6786, x338 **Drop-In Tours:** various
Historic Building original 1909 Victorian manor is part of the museum
Permanent Collection: AM. ptgs, gr, sculp 19, AM. cer, banks; NAT/AM; P/COL; CH: robes

In addition to wonderful 19th century American works of art, the recently restored and renovated Bruce Museum also features a unique collection of mechanical and still banks, North American and pre-Columbian artifacts, and an outstanding department of natural history. Housed partially in its original 1909 Victorian manor, the museum is just a short stroll from the fine shops and restaurants in the charming center of historic Greenwich. **NOT TO BE MISSED:** Two new acquisitions: namely, "The Kiss", a 23 ½" bronze sculpture by Auguste Rodin, and an oil painting entitled "The Mill Pond, Cos Cob, CT., by Childe Hassam.

ON EXHIBIT 1999
09/19/1998 to 01/03/1999 SEEKING IMMORTALITY: EARLY CHINESE CERAMICS
Ancient Chinese Tomb sculpture from the Schloss Collection included ceramic funerary art depicting aspects from everyday life in all strata of Chinese society.

10/03/1998 to 01/03/1999 SPINNING SPHERES AND WHIRLING WHEELS: THE ART OF PLAY
An interdisciplinary family exhibition exploring the role of the sphere and the circle in the world of play.

Bush-Holly Historic Site
Affiliate Institution: The Historical Society of the Town of Greenwich
39 Strickland Rd., Greenwich, CT 06807
📞: 203-869-6899
Open: 12-4 We-Fr, 11-4 Sa, 1-4 Su (April - Dec) 11-4 SA, 1-4 Su (Jan-March) **Closed:** Mo, Tu (April - Dec), Mo-Fr (Jan - March), 1/1, THGV, 12/25
Free Day: Visitor center with exhibitions is always free **ADM Adult:** $6.00 **Children:** F (under 12)
Students: $4.00 **Seniors:** $4.00 🚹 ℗ **Museum Shop**
Group Tours: 203-869-6899 **Drop-In Tours Historic Building** 18th century house, home of Connecticut's first art colony
Permanent Collection: DEC/ART 18-19; AM: Impr/ptgs

CONNECTICUT

Bush-Holly Historic Site - continued

The National Historic Landmark Bush-Holley House was home of Connecticut's first art colony. The house features early American furniture reflecting the period of the 18th century Bush family and American Impressionist artwork of the area by artists who resided in the house at the turn of the 20th century **NOT TO BE MISSED:** "Clarissa", by Childe Hassam Changing exhibitions of local history may be seen in addition to the permanent collection of paintings and sculptures.

HARTFORD

Wadsworth Atheneum

600 Main St., Hartford, CT 06103-2990

📞: 860-278-2670

Open: 11-5 Tu-Su, till 8pm on selected 1st T of the month **Closed:** Mo, 1/1, 7/4, THGV, 12/25
ADM Adult: $7.00 **Children:** $3.00 6-17;F under 6 **Students:** $5.00 **Seniors:** $5.00
♿ ℗ **Museum Shop** ∥ Lunch Tu-Sa, Brunch S, Dinner till 8pm 1st T; (860-728-5989 to reserve)
Group Tours: ex 3046 **Drop-In Tours**: Noon Tu & Th; Noon & 2:00 Sa, Su **Historic Building Sculpture Garden**
Permanent Collection: AM: ptgs, sculp, drgs, dec/art; FR: Impr/ptgs; SP; IT; DU: 17; REN; CER; EU: OM 16-17, dec/art

Founded in 1842, the Wadsworth Atheneum is the oldest museum in continuous operation in the country. In addition to the many wonderful and diverse facets of the permanent collection, a gift in 1994 of two important oil paintings by Picasso; namely, "The Women of Algiers" and "The Artist", makes the collection of works by Picasso one of the fullest in New England museums. The museum is also renowned for its Hudson River School landscape paintings, the largest collection of its kind in the country. **NOT TO BE MISSED:** Caravaggio's "Ecstasy of St. Francis"; Wallace Nutting collection of pilgrim furniture; Colonial period rooms; African-American art (Fleet Gallery); Elizabeth B. Miles English Silver Collection

ON EXHIBIT 1999

09/11/1998 to 01/03/1999 NEW WORLDS FROM OLD: AUSTRALIAN AND AMERICAN LANDSCAPE PAINTING OF THE NINETEENTH CENTURY
This exhibition of 100 of the best landscape paintings from each of the two continents represented, provides the opportunity to discover the parallels and differences within the artistic traditions of each. Many of the works by the Australian painters will be on view for the first time in America.

12/18/1998 to 02/28/1999 PIETER DE HOOCH, 1629-1684

01/1999 to 04/1999 CARL POPE/MATRIX 138

03/18/1999 to 06/27/1999 NORMAN LEWIS: BLACK PAINTINGS, 1944-1977
This is the Studio Museum in Harlem's 30th Anniversary Exhibition. It will examine, via 75 paintings and works on paper, the aesthetic and social implications of black as a color and thematic symbol within the work of Lewis. Also examined will be his significant contributions to abstract art and American modernism.

MIDDLETOWN

Davison Art Center

Affiliate Institution: Wesleyan University

301 High St., Middletown, CT 06459-044nm

📞: 860-685-2500 ◉ www.wesleyan.edu/dac/home.html
Open: Noon-4 Tu-Fr; 2-5 Sa, Su (SEPT-early JUNE); closed June - August **Closed:** Mo, ACAD! LEG/HOL!
Vol/Cont ℗ **Museum Shop Group Tours:** 860-685-2500 **Drop-In Tours Historic Building**: 1830's Alsop House
Permanent Collection: GR 15-20; PHOT 19-20; DRGS

Historic Alsop House (1830), on the grounds of Wesleyan University, is home to a fine permanent collection of prints, photographs and drawings.

Davison Art Center - continued

ON EXHIBIT 1999
01/19/1999 to 03/05/1999 FANTASY AND REALITY: WORKS BY EIGHTEENTH-CENTURY VENETIAN PAINTERS

03/23/1999 to 05/30/1999 PRINTMAKING IN AMERICA, 1960-1990

07/19/1999 to 03/05/1999 L'ESTAMPE MODERNE: A CENTURY AFTER

NEW BRITAIN

New Britain Museum of American Art
56 Lexington St., New Britain, CT 06052
☎: 860-229-0257
Open: 1-5 Tu-Fr, 10-5 Sa, Noon-5 Su   **Closed:** Mo, 1/1, EASTER, 7/4, THGV, 12/25
ADM   Adult: $3.00   **Children:** F (under 12)   **Students:** $2.00   **Seniors:** $2.00
  Ⓟ   **Museum Shop**
Group Tours   Drop-In Tours
Permanent Collection: AM: ptgs, sculp, gr 18-20

The New Britain Museum, only minutes from downtown Hartford, and housed in a turn of the century mansion, is one of only five museums in the country devoted exclusively to American art. The collection covers 250 years of artistic accomplishment including the nation's first public collection of illustrative art. A recent bequest by Olga Knoepke added 26 works by Edward Hopper, George Tooker and other early 20th century Realist artworks to the collection. PLEASE NOTE: Tours for the visually impaired are available with advance notice. **NOT TO BE MISSED:** Thomas Hart Benton murals; paintings by Child Hassam and other important American Impressionist masters.

ON EXHIBIT 1999
01/30/1999 to 04/04/1999   !ESPANA!: AMERICAN ARTISTS AND THE SPANISH EXPERIENCE
Spain and Spanish art - especially the work of Velazquez, Goya, Fortuny, and Sorolla - played an important role in the development of American painting and this study will systematically explore these influences on the work of such artists as Mary Cassatt, William Merritt Chase, Childe Hassam, Robert Henri, Ernest Lawson, and John Singer Sargent. *Catalog*

NEW CANAAN

Silvermine Guild Art Center
1037 Silvermine Rd., New Canaan, CT 06840
☎: 203-966-5617
Open: 11-5 Tu-Sa, 1-5 Su   **Closed:** Mo, 1/1, 7/4, 12/25 & HOL. falling on Mondays
ADM   Adult: $2.00
  Ⓟ   **Museum Shop**
Group Tours Drop-In Tours
Historic Building: established in 1922 in a barn setting   **Sculpture Garden**
Permanent Collection: PRTS: 1959-present

Housed in an 1890 barn, and established as one of the first art colonies in the country, the vital Silvermine Guild exhibits works by well known and emerging artists. Nearly 30 exhibitions are presented yearly.

CONNECTICUT

Yale Center for British Art

Affiliate Institution: Yale University
1080 Chapel St, New Haven, CT 06520-8280
✆: 203-432-2800
Open: 10-5 Tu-Sa, Noon-5 Su   **Closed:** Mo, LEG/HOL!
 ♿   Ⓟ   **Museum Shop   Group Tours**: 203-432-2858   **Drop-In Tours**: Introductory & Architectural tours on Sa
Historic Building: Last building designed by noted American architect, Louis Kahn
Permanent Collection: BRIT: ptgs, drgs, gr 16-20

With the most comprehensive collection of English paintings, prints, drawings, rare books and sculpture outside of Great Britain, the Center's permanent works depict British life and culture from the 16th century to the present. The museum, celebrating its 20th anniversary in 1998, is housed in the last building designed by the late great American architect, Louis Kahn. PLEASE NOTE: The Museum will be closed until January 23, 1999 **NOT TO BE MISSED:** "Golden Age" British paintings by Turner, Constable, Hogarth, Gainsborough, Reynolds

ON EXHIBIT 1999

01/23/1999 to 03/21/1999   RE-INSTALLATION OF THE BRITISH ART COLLECTION
The re-installation with new vibrancy of the largest collection of British Art outside the United Kingdom including Hogarth, Stubbs, Turner, Constable, Bonnington, as well as Reynolds, Gainsborough and Zoffany.

01/23/1999 to 03/21/1999   FRANCIS BACON, LUCIEN FREUD, AND HENRY MOORE
The three artists being featured have changed the face of British art during the 20th C. Their reputation is world-wide, particularly for their representation of the human figure post-World War II . The paintings, etchings and sculpture are selected from collections throughout the world.

April 1999   RECENT ACQUISITIONS
The recent acquisitions by Joseph Wright, Gilliam Ayres, John Walker and Rachel Whiteread will be unveiled.

Yale University Art Gallery

Affiliate Institution: Yale University
1111 Chapel St., New Haven, CT 06520
✆: 203-432-0600   ✉   www.yale.edu/artgallery
Open: 10-5 Tu-Sa, 1-6 Su   **Closed:** Mo, 1/1, 7/4, 12/24, 12/25, 12/31
Vol/Cont: $5.00
 ♿   Ⓟ   **Museum Shop**
Group Tours: 203-432-8459 education dept.   **Drop-In Tours**: Sa 11, Su 3 or as requested
Historic Building: Louis I. Kahn's first museum building   **Sculpture Garden**
Permanent Collection: AM: ptgs, sculp, dec/art; EU: ptgs, sculp; FR: Impr, Post/Impr; OM: drgs, gr; CONT: drgs, gr; IT/REN: ptgs; P/COL; AF: sculp; CH; AN/GRK; AN/EGT

Founded in 1832 with an original bequest of 100 works from the John Trumbull Collection, the Yale University Gallery has the distinction of being the oldest museum in North America. Today over 100,000 works from virtually every major period of art history are represented in the outstanding collection of this highly regarded university museum. **NOT TO BE MISSED:** "Night Café" by van Gogh

ON EXHIBIT 1999

09/22/1998 to 02/15/1999   SPIRIT AND RITUAL IN ASIAN ART
Reinstallation of the Asian gallery exploring the Power and symbolism of Chinese paintings, ritual bronze vessels, jades, ceramics and pottery figures made for burial in tombs.

Yale University Art Gallery - continued
10/13/1998 to 01/03/1999   THE UNMAPPED BODY: THREE BLACK BRITISH ARTISTS
Since the post-World War II era, the migration of Africans, Afro-Caribbeans and Asians to the United Kingdom, has changed both perceptions and the reality of traditional "Britishness" beyond recognition. The London based artists in this challenging and provocative exhibition, Sonia Boyce, Sutapa Biswas, and Keith Piper bear witness to the far reaching cultural changes. *Catalog*

01/18/1999 to 04/11/1999   JAMES LATTIMEER ALLEN: PORTRAITURE AND THE HARLEM RENAISSANCE

02/02/1999 to 05/30/1999   WORLDS WITHIN WORLDS: THE RICHARD ROSENBLUM COLLECTION OF CHINESE SCHOLARS ROCKS

02/09/1999 to 06/13/1999   CLOSING: THE LIFE AND DEATH OF AN AMERICAN FACTORY

04/30/1999 to 08/15/1999   PLEASE BE SEATED: CONTEMPORARY CHAIRS AND BENCHES

NEW LONDON

Lyman Allyn Art Museum
625 Williams St., New London, CT 06320
☎: 860-443-2545
Open: 10-5 Tu-Sa, 1-5 Su   **Closed:** Mo, LEG/HOL!
ADM   Adult: $4.00   **Children:** F (6 & under)   **Students:** $3.00   **Seniors:** $3.00
& ℗ **Museum Shop**   ⅋ Bookstore Café
Group Tours: 860-443-2545 x112   **Drop-In Tours:** 2:00 weekly   **Sculpture Garden**
Permanent Collection: AM: ptgs, drgs, furn, Impr/ptgs; HUDSON RIVER SCHOOL: ptgs; 19th c. landscape, AM/CT DEC ART.

Founded in 1926 by Harriet U. Allyn as a memorial to her whaling merchant father, Lyman Allyn, the Lyman Allyn Art Museum was established for the community of southeastern Connecticut to use, enjoy, and learn about art and culture. The Museum is housed in a handsome Neo-Classical building designed by Charles A. Platt, architect of The Freer Gallery of Art in Washington DC, the Lyme Art Association Building, and several buildings on the campus of Connecticut College, with whom the Museum has recently affiliated. **NOT TO BE MISSED:** 19th century Deshon Allyn House open by appointment only

ON EXHIBIT 1999
OUTDOORS ON THE MUSEUM GROUNDS: SCULPTURE BY SOL LEWITT, CAROL KREEGER DAVIDSON, NIKI KETCHMAN, DAVID SMALLEY, GAVRIEL WARREN, JIM VISCONTI AND ROBERT TAPLIN

04/25/1999 to 06/13/1999   TREASURES OF DECEIT: ARCHAEOLOGY AND THE FORGER'S CRAFT
Objects representing ancient Near Eastern, Egyptian, Etruscan, Greek and Roman civilizations will be used as springboards in an exhibition designed to explain how art historians and classical archeologists determine the authenticity of antiquities. Visitors will be encouraged to examine many of the genuine, reworked and forged objects on view through a magnifying glass, enabling them to evaluate works utilizing some of the methodology of the experts. *Catalog Will Travel*

NORWICH

Slater Memorial Museum
Affiliate Institution: The Norwich Free Academy
108 Crescent St., Norwich, CT 06360
☎: 860-887-2506
Open: SEPT-JUNE: 9-4 Tu-Fr & 1-4 Sa, Su; JULY-AUG: 1-4 Tu-Su   **Closed:** Mo, LEG/HOL! STATE/HOL!
ADM   Adult: $2.00
℗ **Museum Shop   Group Tours:** ex 218   **Drop-In Tours**
Historic Building 1888 Romanesque building designed by architect Stephen Earle
Permanent Collection: AM: ptgs, sculp, gr; DEC/ART; OR; AF; POLY; AN/GRK; NAT/AM

CONNECTICUT

Slater Memorial Museum - continued
Dedicated in 1888, the original three story Romanesque structure has expanded from its original core collection of antique sculpture castings to include a broad range of 17th through 20th century American art. This museum has the distinction of being one of only two fine arts museums in the U.S. located on the campus of a secondary school. **NOT TO BE MISSED:** Classical casts of Greek, Roman and Renaissance sculpture

ON EXHIBIT 1999
01/24/1999 to 03/04/1999 LINCOLN AND THE CIVIL WAR EXHIBIT
The exhibition features the Norwich 'Lincoln Banner' and views of 19th c. Norwich.

03/14/1999 to 04/22/1999 56TH ANNUAL CONNECTICUT ARTISTS EXHIBITION

06/25/1999 to 08/19/1999 INVITATIONAL CONNECTICUT CRAFTS EXHIBIT

OLD LYME

Florence Griswold Museum
96 Lyme St., Old Lyme, CT 06371
☎: 860-434-5542   ◙ www.flogris.org
Open: JUNE thru DEC: 10-5 Tu-Sa, 1-5 Su; FEB through MAY: 1-5 We-Su   **Closed:** Mo, LEG/HOL!
ADM   Adult: $4.00   **Children:** F (under 12)   **Students:** $3.00   **Seniors:** $3.00
&. ℗   **Museum Shop   Group Tours   Drop-In Tours**: daily upon request   **Historic Building**
Permanent Collection: AM: Impr/ptgs; DEC/ART

The beauty of the Old Lyme, Connecticut countryside in the early part of the 20th century attracted dozens of artists to the area. Many of the now famous American Impressionists worked here during the summer and lived in the Florence Griswold boarding house, which is now a museum that stands as a tribute to the art and artists of that era. **NOT TO BE MISSED:** The Chadwick Studio: restored early 20th century artists' studio workplace of American Impressionist, William Chadwick. Free with admission, the Studio is open in the summer only.

ON EXHIBIT 1999
EACH DECEMBER   CELEBRATION OF HOLIDAY TREES
A month long display of trees throughout the house is presented annually. Every year a new theme is chosen and each tree is decorated accordingly.

01/16/1999 to 05/30/1999   THE LYME ART COLONY
The exhibit will focus on the Museum's collection of American Painting and sculpture and reveal the different approaches of members of the colony from Barbizon inspired canvases to Tonalism, full fledged Impressionism and Realism.

06/05/1999 to 09/05/1999   HENRY WARD RANGER: HIS ARTISTIC LEGACY
In the summer of 1999 Ranger's arrival at Miss Griswold's signaled the beginning of the Old Lyme Art Colony. During his lifetime Ranger was an important participant in the emerging art wold of the turn-of the century. This examination will reveal his significant contribution to American culture.

09/18/1999 to 11/28/1999   COLLECTING FOR THE FUTURE: GIFTS IN HONOR OF THE CENTENNIAL, 1899-1999

RIDGEFIELD

Aldrich Museum of Contemporary Art
258 Main St., Ridgefield, CT 06877
☎: 203-438-4519
Open: 1-5 Tu-Su   **Closed:** Mo-Tu, LEG/HOL!
ADM   Adult: $3.00   **Children:** F (under 12)   **Students:** $2.00   **Seniors:** $2.00
&. ℗   **Museum Shop   Group Tours   Drop-In Tours**: 2:00 Su   **Historic Building**   **Sculpture Garden**

Aldrich Museum of Contemporary Art - continued

The Aldrich Museum of Contemporary Art, one of the foremost contemporary art museums in the Northeast, offers the visitor a unique blend of modern art housed within the walls of a landmark building dating back to the American Revolution. One of the first museums in the country dedicated solely to contemporary art, the Aldrich exhibits the best of the new art being produced. Changing quarterly exhibitions of contemporary art featuring works from the permanent collection, collectors works, regional artists, and installations of technological artistic trends. **NOT TO BE MISSED:** Outdoor Sculpture Garden

STAMFORD

Whitney Museum of American Art at Champion

Atlantic St. & Tresser Blvd., Stamford, CT 06921
☎: 203-358-7630
Open: 11-5 Tu-Sa   **Closed:** Su, Mo, 1/1, THGV, 7/4, 12/25
& Ⓟ **Museum Shop**
Group Tours: 203-358-7641   **Drop-In Tours**: 12:30 Tu, Th, Sa

The Whitney Museum of American Art at Champion, the only branch of the renowned Whitney Museum outside of New York City, features changing exhibitions of American Art primarily of the 20th century. Many of the works are drawn from the Whitney's extensive permanent collection and exhibitions are supplemented by lectures, workshops, films and concerts.

ON EXHIBIT 1999

12/11/1998 to 02/24/1999 WALKER EVANS SIMPLE SECRETS: PHOTOGRAPHS FROM THE COLLECTION OF MARIAN AND BENJAMIN A. HILL

90 vintage photographic prints, some of which have never been published, will be featured in this career wide exhibition of works by Evans, one of the most important figures in the history of American photography.

03/05/1999 to 05/19/1999   INTIMATE INTERIORS: JANE FREILICHER AND FAIRFIELD PORTER

STORRS

William Benton Museum of Art, Connecticut State Art Museum

Affiliate Institution: University of Connecticut
245 Glenbrook Rd. U-140, Storrs, CT 06269-2140
☎: 860 486 4520 ◼ www.benton.uconn.edu
Open: 10-4:30 Tu-Fr; 1-4:30 Sa, Su   **Closed:** Mo, LEG/HOL
& Ⓟ **Museum Shop Group Tours**: 860-486-1711 or 486-4520   **Drop-In Tours**
Permanent Collection: EU: 16-20; AM: 17-20; KÄTHE KOLLWITZ: gr; REGINALD MARSH: gr

One of New England's finest small museums. Its Collegiate Gothic building, on the national register of Historic Places, is the setting for a wide variety of culturally diverse changing exhibitions. Call ahead for exhibition information and programs.

ON EXHIBIT 1999

01/19/1999 to 03/11/1999   AFTER THE PHOTO-SECESSION: AMERICAN PICTORIAL PHOTOGRAPHY, 1910-1955

150 photographs documenting the social and artistic development of this pictorial medium between the World Wars, will be featured in the first major exhibition to focus on this subject.

03/23/1999 to 04/25/1999   PETER GOOD/JANET CUMMINGS: GRAPHIC DESIGN AND ART WORKS

08/31/1999 to 10/10/1999   ART DEPARTMENT FACULTY SHOW

10/19/1999 to 12/19/1999   TOMIE dePAOLA'S CHILDREN'S BOOK ILLUSTRATIONS

DELAWARE

Sewell C. Biggs Museum of American Art

406 Federal Street P. O. Box 711, Dover, DE 19903
☎: 302-674-2111   **▣** www.biggsmuseum.org
Open: 10-4 We-Sa; 1:30-4:30 Su   **Closed:** Mo, Tu, LEG/HOL!
Vol/Cont
    ♿ **℗** **Museum Shop**   **Group Tours**: 302-674-2111   **Drop-In Tours**: ! Varies   **Historic Building**
Permanent Collection: AM; pntgs, sculp, Dec/Arts

A collection of about 500 objects assembled by one man. The focus is on the arts of Delaware and the Delaware Valley.

ON EXHIBIT 1999

ALL YEAR   A DELAWARE NATURE WALK: SELF GUIDED ART TOUR THROUGH PAINTINGS

01/13/1999 to 02/28/1999   PICTURE DELAWARE: PHOTOGRAPHS

03/28/1999   DELAWARE SAMPLERS: MADE BEFORE THE CIVIL WAR

04/07/1999 to 05/23/1999   DELAWARE LANDSCAPES

08/03/1999 to 09/05/1999   FRANK SCHOONOVER REMEMBERED

12/01/1999 to 01/02/2000   CHRISTMASES PAST

Delaware Art Museum

2301 Kentmere Pkwy., Wilmington, DE 19806
☎: 302-571-9590   **▣** www.udel.edu/delart
Open: 9-4 Tu & Th-Sa, 10-4 Su, 9-9 We   **Closed:** Mo, 1/1, THGV, 12/25
Free Day: 4-9 We; 9-12 Sa   **ADM**   **Adult:** $5.00   **Children:** F (6 & under)   **Students:** $2.50
  ♿ **℗** **Museum Shop**   **ⵢ** The Museum Café
Group Tours   **Drop-In Tours**: 11 am 3rd Tu & Sa of the month
Permanent Collection: AM: ptgs 19-20; BRIT: P/Raph; GR; SCULP; PHOT

Begun as a repository for the works of noted Brandywine Valley painter/illustrator Howard Pyle, the Delaware Art Museum has grown to include other collections of note especially in the areas of Pre-Raphaelite painting and contemporary art. **NOT TO BE MISSED:** "Summertime" by Edward Hopper; "Milking Time" by Winslow Homer

ON EXHIBIT 1999

07/25/1998 to 01/03/1999   HOLIDAY HAPPENINGS

12/10/1998 to 02/21/1999   WONDROUS STRANGE: PYLE, WYETH, WYETH AND WYETH
A major exhibition featuring more than 100 works focusing on an element of American Realism that goes through this families work. They give serious attention to the "wondrous" and "strange" that exist in the mind's eye and five life to that imagination. *Will Travel*

03/18/1999 to 05/09/1999   CHIHULY BASKETS
23 of Chihuly's glass basket sets accompanied by working drawings will be on view in an exhibition that juxtaposes them with examples of Native American baskets from which this contemporary glass master took his inspiration. *Will Travel*

06/04/1999 to 08/01/1999   SANDY SKOGLUND: REALITY UNDER SIEGE
Four life sized installation rooms, numerous prints, photographs, drawings and paintings by Skoglund, known for his large-scale, mixed media creations. His work has been described as dream-like, conceptual, and even surreal. *Catalog Will Travel*

Delaware Grand Exhibition Hall
along the Christina River, Wilmington, DE

☎: 888-395-0005 or 302-777-7769
ADM ♿ Ⓟ **Museum Shop** ⊤⊤ Coffee shop & restaurant
Group Tours   Drop-In Tours

In the process of being developed, the Delaware Grand Exhibition Hall (yet to be formally named), a major component of the revitalization along the Christina River in downtown Wilmington, is a facility being planned for the presentation of art and art related exhibitions. Special art trips are planned.

ON EXHIBIT 1999
FALL/1999   HISTORY AND TRADITION OF SCOTLAND

04/1999 to 09/1999   TREASURES OF THE IMPERIAL JAPANESE COURT

DISTRICT OF COLUMBIA

Art Museum of the Americas
201 18th St., N.W., Washington, DC 20006
☎: 202-458-6016
Open: 10-5 Tu-Su **Closed:** Su, Mo, LEG/HOL!
Vol/Cont
ⓟ **Museum Shop Group Tours:** 202-458-6301 **Drop-In Tours**
Permanent Collection: 20th C LATIN AMERICAN & CARIBBEAN ART

Established in 1976, and housed in a Spanish colonial style building completed in 1912, this museum contains the most comprehensive collection of 20th century Latin American art in the country. **NOT TO BE MISSED:** The loggia behind the museum opening onto the Aztec Gardens

Arthur M. Sackler Gallery
1050 Independence Ave., SW, Washington, DC 20560
☎: 202-357-2700 ⬛ www.si.edu/asia
Open: 10-5:30 Daily **Closed:** 12/25
♿ ⓟ **Museum Shop**
Group Tours: 202-357-4880 ex 245 **Drop-In Tours:** 11:30 daily
Permanent Collection: CH: jade sculp; JAP: cont/cer; PERSIAN: ptgs; NEAR/E: an/silver

Opened in 1987 under the auspices of the Smithsonian Institution, the Sackler Gallery, named for its benefactor, houses some of the most magnificent objects of Asian art in America.

ON EXHIBIT 1999
CONTINUING INDEFINITELY PUJA: EXPRESSIONS OF HINDU DEVOTION
Approximately 180 bronze, stone and wooden objects made in India as offerings in an essential element of Hindu worship known as "puja" will be seen in an exhibition focusing mainly on their functional use rather than their aesthetic beauty.

CONTINUING INDEFINITELY THE ARTS OF CHINA
Exquisite furniture, paintings, porcelain and jade from China's last two Imperial dynasties - the Ming (1368-1664) and Qing (1644-1911) will be on exhibit.

08/02/1998 to 01/03/1999 THE BUDDHA'S ART OF HEALING
Seen for the first time in the U.S., the 40 paintings featured in this exhibition from "The Blue Beryl", an early 20th century rendering of a 17th century medical treatise, were created as instructional aids for the training of Buryati doctors. Saved from destruction during the Cultural Revolution in Tibet, this medical atlas is considered to be one of the greatest surviving treasures of Tibetan civilization.

11/08/1998 to 02/07/1999 ROY LICHTENSTEIN: LANDSCAPES IN THE CHINESE STYLE
During the years from 1994-1997 Lichtenstein made a series of paintings, collages, drawings and even a scholar's rock, influenced by Chinese landscape paintings.

01/31/1999 to 08/01/1999 BEHIND THE HIMALAYAS: PAINTINGS OF MUSTANG BY ROBERT POWELL
Mustang is the thumb-like appendage of territory that thrusts northward from Nepal to Tibet. Here with tremendous altitudes and gale-force winds, Tibetan culture flourishes. Robert Powell, An Australian expatriate, lives in Katmandu, but has traveled extensively in that remote area. His watercolor paintings of that area are executed in blazing colors that the residents lavish on their buildings and monuments.

03/28/1999 to 09/06/1999 DEVI: THE GODDESS IN INDIAN ART

04/25/1999 to 07/18/1999 PAINTINGS BY NAINSUHK
This is the work of a single painter from India with a few selections from his family workshop. It gives an absorbing look at life in a particular Rajput court.

Arthur M. Sackler Gallery - continued

08/01/1999 to 10/17/1999   YOSHIDA HIROSHI: JAPANESE PRINTS OF INDIA AND SOUTHEAST ASIA

10/17/1999 to 01/17/2000   TREASURES FROM THE ROYAL TOMBS OF UR
Mid-third millennium BC gold & silver jewels, cups, bowls and other ancient objects excavated from the royal burial tombs of Ur will be on exhibit. *Catalog Will Travel*

11/07/1999 to Mid/2000   ANTOIN SEVRUGUIN AND THE PERSIAN IMAGE
Sevruguin operated a successful studio in Tehran from 1850's-1934. These come from the Freer Gallery Collection and the Arthur M. Sackler Gallery Archives Collection and offer an important pictorial record of the social history and visual culture in Iran. *Will Travel*

Corcoran Gallery of Art

17th St. & New York Ave., NW, Washington, DC 20006-4804
☎: 202-639-1700
Open: 10-5 Mo, We-Su, till 9pm Th   **Closed:** Tu, 1/1, 12/25
Adult: $3.00   **Children:** F (under 12)   **Students:** $1.00   **Seniors:** $1.00
   ᕷ   ℗   **Museum Shop**
⊪ Café 11-3 daily & till 8:30 Th; Gospel Brunch 11-2 S (202-639-1786)
Group Tours: 202 786 2374   **Drop-In Tours:** Noon daily; 7:30 Th; 10:30,12 & 2:30 Sa, Su
Permanent Collection: AM & EU: ptgs, sculp, works on paper 18-20

The beautiful Beaux Art building built to house the collection of its founder, William Corcoran, contains works that span the entire history of American art from the earliest limners to the cutting edge works of today's contemporary artists. In addition to being the oldest art museum in Washington, the Corcoran has the distinction of being one of the three oldest art museums in the country. Recently the Corcoran became the recipient of the Evans-Tibbs Collection of African-American art, one of the largest and most important groups of historic American art to come to the museum in nearly 50 years. PLEASE NOTE: There is a special suggested contribution fee of $5.00 for families. **NOT TO BE MISSED:** "Mt. Corcoran" by Bierstadt; "Niagra" by Church; Restored 18th century French room Salon Doré

ON EXHIBIT 1999

ONGOING   TREASURES OF THE CORCORAN: THE PERMANENT COLLECTION ON VIEW

10/10/1998 to 01/10/1999   IMPRESSIONS FROM NATURE, OIL SKETCHES BY AMERICAN LANDSCAPE PAINTERS 1830-1880

10/17/1998 to 01/04/1999   ROY DeCARAVA: A RETROSPECTIVE
Groundbreaking pictures of everyday life in Harlem, civil rights protests, lyrical studies of nature, and photographs of jazz legends will be among the 200 black & white photographs on view in the first comprehensive survey of DeCarava's works.

11/1998 to 03/1999   AT THE EDGE: A PORTUGESE FUTURIST - AMADEO DE SOUZA-CARDOSO

12/1998 to 01/1999   JYUNG MEE PARK

01/27/1999 to 04/20/1999   NEW WORLDS FROM OLD: AUSTRALIAN AND AMERICAN LANDSCAPE PAINTING OF THE NINETEENTH CENTURY
This exhibition of 100 of the best landscape paintings from each of the two continents represented, provides the opportunity to discover the parallels and differences within the artistic traditions of each. Many of the works by the Australian painters will be on view for the first time in America.

DISTRICT OF COLUMBIA

Dumbarton Oaks Research Library & Collection

1703 32nd St., NW, Washington, DC 20007-2961

☎: 202-339-6401　◉　www.doaks.org
Open: 2-6 Tu-Su, Apr-Oct; 2-5 Nov-Mar　**Closed:** Mo, LEG/HOLS
ADM　Adult: $4.00　**Children:** $3.00　**Seniors:** $3.00
♿　℗　**Museum Shop　Group Tours**: 202-339-6409　**Drop-In Tours**
Permanent Collection: BYZ; P/COL;　AM: ptgs, sculp, dec/art; EU: ptgs, sculp, dec/art

This 19th century mansion, site of the international conference of 1944 where discussions leading to the formation of the United Nations were held, is best known for its rare collection of Byzantine and Pre-Columbian art. Beautifully maintained and now owned by Harvard University, Dumbarton Oaks is also home to a magnificent French Music Room and to 16 manicured acres that contain formally planted perennial beds, fountains and a profusion of seasonal flower gardens. PLEASE NOTE: 1. Although there is no admission fee to the museum, a donation of $1.00 is appreciated. 2. With the exception of national holidays and inclement weather, the museum's gardens are open daily. Hours and admission from Apr to Oct. are 2-6pm, $3.00 adults, $2.00 children & seniors. From Nov. to Mar. the gardens are open from 2-5pm with free admission. **NOT TO BE MISSED:** Music Room; Gardens (open daily Apr - Oct, 2-6 PM, $4.00 adult, $3.00 children/seniors; 2-5 PM daily Nov-Mar, Free)

ON EXHIBIT 1999

ONGOING　PRE-COLUMBIAN COLLECTION
Prime works from Mesoamerica, lower Central America and the Andes collected by Robert Woods Bliss.

ONGOING　BYZANTINE COLLECTION
The recently re-installed and expanded collection of early Byzantine silver joins the on-going textile exhibit from the permanent collection.

Federal Reserve Board Art Gallery

2001 C St., Washington, DC 20551

☎: 202-452-3686
Open: 11-2 Mo-Fr or by reservation　**Closed:** LEG/HOL! WEEKENDS
♿　℗　**Museum Shop**
Group Tours　Drop-In Tours　Historic Building Designed in 1937 by Paul Cret
Permanent Collection: PTGS, GR, DRGS 19-20 (with emphasis on late 19th C works by Amer. Expatriates); ARCH: drgs of Paul Cret　PLEASE NOTE: The permanent collection may be seen by appointment only.

Founded in 1975, the collection, consisting of both gifts and loans of American and European works of art, acquaints visitors with American artistic and cultural values. **NOT TO BE MISSED:** The atrium of this beautiful building is considered one of the most magnificent public spaces in Washington, D.C.

Freer Gallery of Art

Jefferson Dr. at 12th St., SW, Washington, DC 20560

☎: 202-357-2700　◉　www.si.edu/asia
Open: 10-5:50 Daily　**Closed:** 12/25
♿　℗　**Museum Shop　Group Tours**: 202-357-4880 ext. 245　**Drop-In Tours**: 11:30 Daily　**Historic Building**
Permanent Collection: OR: sculp, ptgs, cer; AM/ART 20; (FEATURING WORKS OF JAMES McNEILL WHISTLER; PTGS

One of the many museums in the nation's capitol that represent the results of a single collector, the 75 year old Freer Gallery, renowned for its stellar collection of the arts of all of Asia, is also home to one of the world's most important collections of works by James McNeill Whistler. **NOT TO BE MISSED:** "Harmony in Blue and Gold", The Peacock Room by James McNeill Whistler

Freer Gallery of Art - continued

ON EXHIBIT 1999

ONGOING   ANCIENT EGYPTIAN GLASS
15 rare and brilliantly colored glass vessels created during the reigns of Amenhotep III (1391-1353 B.C.) and Akhenaten (1391-1353 B.C.) are highlighted in this small but notable exhibition.

ONGOING   KOREAN CERAMICS

ONGOING   ANCIENT CHINESE POTTERY AND BRONZE

ONGOING   SETO AND MINO CERAMICS

ONGOING   SHADES OF GREEN AND BLUE: CHINESE CELADON CERAMICS
Featured will be 44 celadon glazed Chinese ceramics presented with examples from Thailand, Korea, Japan and Vietnam.

ONGOING   ARMENIAN GOSPELS

ONGOING   ART FOR ART'S SAKE
Lacking a moral message, the 31 works on view by Whistler, Dewing, Thayer, and others working in the late 1880's, were created to be beautiful for beauty's sake alone.

06/06/1998 to 02/15/1999   JAPANESE ART IN THE AGE OF THE KOETSU
Reflecting the mastery of Hon'ami Koetsu (1558-1637), a Japanese artist greatly admired by Charles Freer and members of his artistic circle, the objects on view are considered some of the most beautiful and enduring works of Japanese art.

07/03/1998 to 06/30/1999   WHISTLER PRINTS I: THE LEYLAND CIRCLE, 1867-75
The first in a series of small exhibitions focused on James McNeill Whistler's printmaking career. These, mostly drypoints and etchings, were done in the period when Whistler worked under the patronage of Leyland, a Liverpool shipowner. *Will Travel*

10/11/1998 to 03/14/1999   BEYOND THE LEGACY: FREER GALLERY OF ART 75TH ANNIVERSARY
The results of a four year campaign to acquire extraordinary works of art in observance of the Freer's 75th anniversary. These represent a wide area of Asia and four millennia. *Catalog*

Spring 1999   WINGED FIGURES
Celebrating the sesquicentennial of artist Abbott B. Thayer's birth brings together three monumental winged figure paintings in the Freer Collection. All three represent his daughter and are examined here within his moral universe.

04/04/1999   JAPANESE ART: NEW SELECTIONS FROM THE PERMANENT COLLECTION

05/1999   MASTERPIECES OF CHINESE PAINTING
A selection is made of 10th-early 18th c painting and calligraphy from the Freer's collection. Included are books, hanging scrolls, murals, screen paintings, and albums.

Summer 1999   WHISTLER PRINTS II: THE HADEN CIRCLE, 1857-61
This Whistler exhibition shows his work as a printmaker also during a London stay with one oil painting produced during his early life in England.

Hillwood Museum

4155 Linnean Ave., NW, Washington, DC 20008
☎: 202-686-8500
Open: BY RESERVATION ONLY: 9, 10:45, 12:30, 1:45, 3:00 Tu-Sa   **Closed:** Su, Mo, FEB. & LEG/HOL!
ADM   Adult: $10.00   **Children:** $5.00   **Students:** $5.00   **Seniors:** $10.00
& ℗ **Museum Shop** ❙❙ Reservations accepted (202) 686-8893)
Group Tours: 202-686-5807   **Drop-In Tours   Sculpture Garden**
Permanent Collection: RUSS: ptgs, cer ,dec/art; FR: cer, dec/art, glass 18-19

The former home of Marjorie Merriweather Post, heir to the Post cereal fortune, is filled primarily with the art and decorative treasures of Imperial Russia which she collected in depth over a period of more than 40 years. PLEASE NOTE: Due to extensive renovation, the home will be closed to the public for the next several years. **NOT TO BE MISSED:** Carl Fabergé's Imperial Easter Eggs and other of his works; glorious gardens surrounding the mansion. NOTE: children under 12 are not permitted in the house.

DISTRICT OF COLUMBIA

Hirshhorn Museum and Sculpture Garden
Affiliate Institution: Smithsonian Institution
Independence Ave. at Seventh St., NW, Washington, DC 20560
☎: 202-357-2700   ▣ www.si.edu/hirshhorn
Open: Museum: 10-5:30 Daily; Plaza: 7:30am - 5:30 pm, S/G: 7:30am - dusk   **Closed:** 12/25
& Ⓟ **Museum Shop**   ❙❙ Plaza Café MEM/DAY to LAB/DAY only
Group Tours: 202-357-3235   **Drop-In Tours**: 10:30 + 12 Mo-Fr; 12 + 2 Sa, Su   **Sculpture Garden**
Permanent Collection: CONT: sculp, art; AM: early 20th; EU: early 20th; AM: realism since Eakins

Endowed by the entire collection of its founder, Joseph Hirshhorn, this museum focuses primarily on modern and contemporary art of all kinds and cultures in addition to newly acquired works. One of its most outstanding features is its extensive sculpture garden. PLEASE NOTE: No tours are given on holidays. **NOT TO BE MISSED:** Rodin's "Burghers of Calais"; works by Henry Moore and Willem deKooning, third floor

ON EXHIBIT 1999

10/15/1998 to 01/10/1999   CHUCK CLOSE
A major retrospective exhibition of works by Close, one of America's premier figurative artists.

01/28/1999 to 06/20/1999   DIRECTIONS - JULIAO SARMENTO

05/27/1999 to 09/06/1999   BRUCE MARDEN: WORKS OF THE 1990S *Catalog Will Travel*

07/15/1999 to 10/17/1999   DIRECTIONS - SAM TAYLOR WOOD

10/07/1999 to 01/17/2000   REGARDING BEAUTY: PERSPECTIVES ON ART SINCE 1950

Howard University Gallery of Art
2455 6th St., NW, Washington, DC 20059
☎: 202-806-7070
Open: 9:30-4:30 Mo-Fr; 1-4 Su (may be closed some Su in summer!)   **Closed:** Sa, LEG/HOL!
& Ⓟ **Museum Shop   Group Tours   Drop-In Tours**
Permanent Collection: AF/AM: ptgs, sculp, gr; EU: gr; IT: ptgs, sculp (Kress Collection); AF

In addition to an encyclopedic collection of African and African-American art and artists there are 20 cases of African artifacts on permanent display in the east corridor of the College of Fine Arts. PLEASE NOTE: It is advisable to call ahead in the summer as the gallery might be closed for inventory work. **NOT TO BE MISSED:** The Robert B. Mayer Collection of African Art

Kreeger Museum
2401 Foxhall Rd., NW, Washington, DC 20007
☎: 202-338-3552   ▣ www.kreegermuseum.com
Open: Tours only at 10:30 & 1:30 Tu-Sa   **Closed:** Su, Mo, LEG/HOL! & AUG; call for information on additional closures
Adult: $5.00
& Ⓟ **Museum Shop**
Group Tours: 202-338-3552   **Drop-In Tours**: 10:30 & 1:30 Tu-Sa   **Sculpture Garden**
Permanent Collection: EU: ptgs, sculp 19, 20; AM: ptgs, sculp 19, 20; AF; P/COL

Designed by noted American architect Philip Johnson as a stunning private residence for David Lloyd and Carmen Kreeger, this home has now become a museum that holds the remarkable art collection of its former owners. With a main floor filled with Impressionist and post-Impressionist paintings and sculpture, and fine collections of African, contemporary, and Washington Color School art on the bottom level, this museum is a "must see" for art lovers traveling to the D.C. area. PLEASE NOTE: Only 35 people for each designated time slot are allowed on each 90 minute tour of this museum at the hours specified and only by reservation. Children under 12 are not permitted. **NOT TO BE MISSED:** Collection of 9 Monet Paintings

National Gallery of Art
4th & Constitution Ave., N.W., Washington, DC 20565

☎: 202-737-4215   ◙ www.nga.gov

Open: 10-5 Mo-Sa, 11-6 Su   **Closed:** 1/1, 12/25

  ♿ Ⓟ **Museum Shop**   ⏹ 3 restaurants plus Espresso bar   **Group Tours:** 202-842-6247   **Drop-In Tours:** daily!

Permanent Collection: EU: ptgs, sculp, dec/art 12-20: OM; AM: ptgs, sculp, gr 18-20; REN: sculp; OR: cer

The two buildings that make up the National Gallery, one classical and the other ultra modern, are as extraordinary and diverse and the collection itself. Considered one of the premier museums in the world, more people pass through the portals of the National Gallery annually than almost any other museum in the country. Self-guided family tour brochures of the permanent collection as well as walking tour brochures for adults are available for use in the museum. In addition, advance reservations may be made for tours given in a wide variety of foreign languages. **NOT TO BE MISSED:** The only Leonardo Da Vinci oil painting in an American museum collection

ON EXHIBIT 1999

ONGOING   MICRO GALLERY

Available for public use, the recently opened Micro Gallery consists of 13 computer terminals that make it possible for visitors to access detailed images of, and in-depth information to, nearly every one of the 1700 works on display in the National Gallery's permanent collection.

10/04/1998 to 01/03/1999   VAN GOGH'S VAN GOGHS: MASTERPIECES FROM THE VAN GOGH MUSEUM, AMSTERDAM

70 paintings by Vincent van Gogh and two related works on paper is the largest survey of his career outside The Netherlands in more than a quarter of a century. This unique group of works, kept together by his brother Theo and his family are on loan from the van Gogh Museum, home to the largest collection of his work. *Catalog Will Travel* ◠

10/11/1998 to 01/03/1999   BERNINI'S ROME: ITALIAN TERRA COTTAS FROM THE STATE HERMITAGE MUSEUM, ST. PETERSBURG

This exhibition of rarely exhibited terra cotta 'bozzetti' is the first US exhibition of these rarely exhibited sculptures. The 14 artists represented present a rare opportunity to see these works including Bernini and Algardi, side by side. *Catalog Will Travel*

10/18/1998 to 01/03/1999   GIFTS TO THE NATION FROM MR. AND MRS. JOHN HAY WHITNEY.

Sixteen exceptional paintings from this once most important privately held collection of 19th and twentieth c paintings. Included are van Gogh's "Self Portrait" ,Toulouse Lautrec's' Marcelle Lender Dancing the Bolero in 'Chilperic' and Matisse's 'Open Window, Coilloure'.

11/08/1998 to 01/31/1999   LOVE AND WAR: A MANUAL FOR LIFE IN THE LATE MIDDLE AGES

The Housebrook Master was one of the most delightful artists of the waning middle ages. He was active in southern Germany from about 1465-1500 and is known primarily from two sources: one is the Houseboat and the other is 89 drypoints, the greater portion of which exist in a single collection at the Rijksmuseum.

11/15/1998 to 02/15/1999   EDO: ART JAPAN 1615-1868

The first comprehensive survey in the US of the Edo period will feature 300 works. More than forty of these have been declared National Treasures. The Edo period was one of great prosperity and peace in Japan and the works will be shown thematically in six section:' Edo Style',' Samurai', 'Work', 'Religion' 'Travel and Landscape' and 'Entertainment'.These will be public arts programs etc. Advance passes required for weekends, federal holidays *Only Venue Catalog*

01/24/1999 to 05/09/1999   AMERICAN IMPRESSIONISM AND REALISM: THE MARGARET AND RAYMOND HOROWITZ COLLECTION

One of the finest groups of American paintings of this period in private hands, this group, in forty years is at the top of the list of any group of works by their creators. This is the first exhibition since 1973. Included are Chase, Robinson, Hassam, Benson and Bellows. *Catalog*

01/31/1999 to 05/31/1999   FROM BOTANY TO BOUQUETS: FLOWERS IN NORTHERN ART

Flower still lifes ranging from Bosschaert, Breugel the Elder, de Heem, and Huysumk with related paintings and drawings by these and other seventeenth c Dutch and Flemish masters along with books and manuscripts from the collection of Mrs. Paul Mellon and the Folger Shakespeare Library. *Catalog*

DISTRICT OF COLUMBIA

National Gallery of Art - continued
02/21/1999 to 05/31/1999   JOHN SINGER SARGENT
This exhibition of more than 100 paintings and watercolors represents the artist's most significant and beautiful works. It will be the first time since the retrospective mounted after his death that so many works will be exhibited together. *Catalog Will Travel* ◠

SPRING 1999   NATIONAL GALLERY SCULPTURE GARDEN
Designed to offer year-round enjoyment of the preeminent space on the National Mall the Sculpture Garden will have flexible spaces to display a variety of works from the Gallery's growing collection of outdoor sculpture as well as works on loan for special exhibitions.

04/25/1999 to 07/05/1999   PHOTOGRAPHS FROM THE COLLECTION
An overview of the Gallery's collection of photographs. From the 19th and 20th c including Talbot, Sheeler, Kertsz as well as contemporary artist Robert Adams.

05/23/1999 to 08/22/1999   PORTRAITS BY INGRES: IMAGE OF AN EPOCH
Ingres captured the changing fashions of six decades during a career that spanned the closing years of the Revolutionary era, the First empire of Napoleon Bonaparte, the Bourbon Restoration, and the second empire in France. It is the first American showing and most comprehensive display since 1967. *Catalog Will Travel*

06/06/1999 to 09/06/1999   MARY CASSATT: MODERN WOMAN
Some 125 of Cassatt's most beautiful and compelling portraits, pastels, drawings and prints, are brought together here to place her at the heart of one of the most important Artistic movements in Western History and at the forefront of emerging modernism. *Catalog Will Travel* ◠

10/17/1999 to 01/16/2000   BRASSEI: THE EYE OF PARIS
A retrospective celebrating the centenary of the birth of Gyuyloa Halasz in Brasso, Transylvania know for photographs he made of Paris at night in the late 20s and 30s. Henry Miller described him as the 'eye of Paris'. His photographs reveal his remarkable sensitivity to light and atmosphere. *Catalog Will Travel*

National Museum of African Art
Affiliate Institution: Smithsonian Institution
950 Independence Ave., S.W., Washington, DC 20560
☎: 202-357-4600   ▣   www.si.edu/nmafa
Open: 10-5:30 Daily   **Closed:** 12/25
& Ⓟ   **Museum Shop   Group Tours   Drop-In Tours**
Permanent Collection: AF/ART

Opened in 1987, The National Museum of African Art is dedicated to the collection, exhibition, conservation and study of the arts of Africa.

ON EXHIBIT 1999
PERMANENT EXHIBITION   IMAGES OF POWER AND IDENTITY
More than 100 objects both from the permanent collection and on loan to the museum are grouped according to major geographical & cultural regions of sub-Saharan Africa.

PERMANENT EXHIBITION   THE ANCIENT WEST AFRICAN CITY OF BENIN, A.D.1300-1897
A presentation of cast-metal heads, figures and architectural plaques from the Museum's permanent collection of art from the royal court of the capital of the Kingdom of Benin as it existed before British colonial rule.

PERMANENT EXHIBITION   THE ART OF THE PERSONAL OBJECT
Aesthetically important and interesting utilitarian objects reflect the artistic culture of various African societies.

PERMANENT EXHIBITION   THE ANCIENT NUBIAN CITY OF KERMA, 2500-1500 B.C.
A semipermanent installation of 40 works from the Museum of Fine Arts in Boston celebrates Kerma, also known as Kush, the oldest city in Africa outside of Egypt that has been excavated.

PERMANENT EXHIBITION   CERAMIC ARTS AT THE NATIONAL MUSEUM OF AFRICAN ART

PERMANENT EXHIBITION   SOKARI DOUGLAS CAMP: THREE SCULPTURES

National Museum of African Art - continued
09/20/1998 to 02/28/1999   SOUTH AFRICA, 1936-1949; PHOTOGRAPHS BY CONSTANCE STUART LARRABEE

02/07/1999 to 05/09/1999   BAULE: AFRICAN ART/WESTERN EYES
125 of the greatest works of art from Baule culture, on loan from public and private collections in the U.S., Europe and Africa, will be featured in the first large museum exhibition of its kind. Known for their refinement, diversity and quality, the items on view will include examples of naturalistic wooden sculpture, objects of ivory, bronze and gold, and masks & figures derived from human and animal forms.

03/21/1999 to 06/20/1999   HEAVY METALS OR THE ALLOYED TRUTH: A TRIBUTE TO THE AFRICAN SMITH

05/23/1999 to 09/26/1999   MODERN ART FROM SOUTH AFRICA

07/18/1999 to 10/17/1999   HATS OFF: A SALUTE TO AFRICAN HEADGEAR

09/12/1999 to 01/02/2000   WRAPPED IN PRIDE: ASANTE KENTE AND AFRICAN-AMERICAN IDENTITY

12/19/1999 to 03/19/2000   THE ART OF AFRICAN MONEY

National Museum of American Art-Renwick Gallery
Affiliate Institution: Smithsonian Institution
8th & G Sts., N.W., Washington, DC 20560
☎: 202-357-2700   ◉ www.nmaa.si.edu
Open: 10-5:30 Daily   **Closed:** 12/25
  ♿ ⓟ   **Museum Shop**   ⅋ Patent Pending Café 11-3 Daily
Group Tours: 202-357-3111   **Drop-In Tours:** weekdays at Noon, 2 PM Sa & Su
Historic Building Housed in Old Patent Office (Greek Revival architecture) mid 1800s
Permanent Collection: AM: ptgs, sculp, gr, cont/phot, drgs, folk, Impr; AF/AM

The National Museum of American Art of the Smithsonian Institution, the first federal art collection, represents all regions, cultures and traditions in the United States. Today the collection contains over 37,500 works in all media, spanning more than 300 years of artistic achievement. The Old Patent Office Building, which houses the National Museum of American Art and the National Portrait Gallery, was built in the Greek Revival Style between 1836 and 1867 and is considered one of the finest neoclassical structures in the world. **NOT TO BE MISSED:** George Catlin's 19th C American-Indian paintings; Thomas Moran's Western landscape paintings; James Hampton's "The Throne of the Third Heaven of the Nation's Millennium General Assembly"

ON EXHIBIT 1999
09/25/1998 to 01/31/1999   EYEING AMERICA: ROBERT COTTINGHAM PRINTS
Gifted by the artist to the NMAA, this exhibition of Cottingham's full set of prints celebrates his printmaking career begun in 1972.

10/30/1998 to 03/07/1999   ART OF THE GOLD RUSH
On loan from public and private collections throughout the country, the 64 paintings, drawings and watercolors (1849 to the mid-1870's) on view reveal the origins of the development of California regional art with images of Gold Rush scenes, landscapes, genre scenes, mining activities, and scenes of San Francisco.

10/30/1998 to 03/07/1999   SILVER AND GOLD: CASED IMAGES OF THE CALIFORNIA GOLD RUSH
150 "cased" images (daguerreotypes and ambrotype), documenting the 19th century California gold rush, include vivid scenes of ship and overland travels, life in the mines, Gold Rush country landscapes, street scenes in San Francisco, and a cross-section of the ethnically diverse population.

04/02/1999 to 08/22/1999   IMAGE AND MEMORY: PICTURING OLD NEW ENGLAND
Approximately 180 magnificent paintings, sculptures, prints and photographs representing New England from 1865-1945 by artists such as Homer, Hassam, Prendergast, Bellows, Hartley, Hopper, Parish and Rockwell. *Catalog*

DISTRICT OF COLUMBIA

National Museum of American Art-Renwick Gallery - continued
04/23/1999 to 09/06/1999   ABBOT THAYER: THE NATURE OF ART
Thayer's "Angel" has become an icon of American art. The 60 paintings in this show will examine the work of this important artist in the context of the culture and artistic environment in which he worked.

10/22/1999 to 01/03/2000   EDWARD HOPPER: THE WATERCOLORS
Painted primarily during his trips away from NY during the 1920's and 30's, these early watercolors brought Hopper his original success. He continued to return to the New England landscape for inspiration. *Catalog Will Travel*

National Museum of Women in the Arts
1250 New York Ave., N.W., Washington, DC 20005
☎: 202-783-5000   ◙ www.nmwa.org
Open: 10-5 Mo-Sa, Noon-5 Su   **Closed:** Mo, 1/1, THGV, 12/25
Sugg/Cont Adult: $3.00   **Children:** F   **Students:** $2.00   **Seniors:** $2.00
& ℗   **Museum Shop**   ¶ Café 11:30-2:30 —Sa
Group Tours: 202-783-7370   **Drop-In Tours**
Historic Building 1907 Renaissance Revival building by Waddy Wood
Permanent Collection: PTGS, SCULP, GR, DRGS, 15-20; PHOT

Unique is the word for this museum established in 1987 and located in a splendidly restored 1907 Renaissance Revival building. The more than 2,000 works by more than 600 women artists in the permanent collection are the result of the personal vision and passion of its founder, Wilhelmina Holladay, to elevate and validate the works of women artists throughout the history of art. **NOT TO BE MISSED:** Rotating collection of portrait miniatures (late 19th - early 20th c.) by Eulabee Dix; Lavinia Fontana's "Portrait of a Noblewoman"; Frida Kahlo's "Self Portrait Dedicated to Leon Trotsky"

ON EXHIBIT 1999
ONGOING   ESTABLISHING THE LEGACY: FROM THE RENAISSANCE TO MODERNISM
A presentation of works from the permanent collection tracing the history of women artists from the Renaissance to the present.

06/15/1998 to 01/16/1999   BOOK AS ART X
57 imaginative, one of a kind, limited edition artists books focus on poetry illustrated with art, interactive books and morality fables.

10/15/1998 to 01/10/1999   TATYANA NAZARENKO: TRANSITION
One of the most talented realist painters working in Moscow today, and one of the most successful artists of the Moscow art wold in the past three decades.

10/22/1998 to 01/19/1999   BERENICE ABBOTT'S CHANGING NEW YORK 1935-1939
On view will be 125 of her New York City photographs which have come to define Depression-era New York in the popular imagination. These are from the benchmark CHANGING NEW YORK project of 1935-1939. *Will Travel*

12/14/1998 to 07/05/1999   PAINTING IN A LONELY AREA: JOYCE TREIMAN AND THE OLD MASTERS
In a period when modernist currents dominated the art world, Treiman fervently adhered to studying the European and American Old Masters and producing figurative painting.

DISTRICT OF COLUMBIA

National Portrait Gallery

Affiliate Institution: Smithsonian Institution
F St. at 8th, N.W., Washington, DC 20560-0213
☎: 202-357-2700   ▣ www.npg.si.edu
Open: 10-5:30 Daily   **Closed:** 12/25
 ⅄ ℗ **Museum Shop** ⅋ 11-3:30
Group Tours: 202-357-2920 ex 1   **Drop-In Tours**: inquire at information desk
Historic Building This 1836 Building served as a hospital during the Civil War
Sculpture Garden
Permanent Collection: AM: ptgs, sculp, drgs, photo

Housed in the Old Patent Office built in 1836, and used as a hospital during the Civil War, this museum allows the visitor to explore U.S. history as told through portraiture. **NOT TO BE MISSED:** Gilbert Stuart's portraits of George and Martha Washington; Self Portrait by John Singleton Copley

ON EXHIBIT 1999

01/29/1998 to 04/25/1999   PAUL ROBESON: ARTIST AND CITIZEN

08/07/1998 to 01/24/1999   RECENT ACQUISITIONS

10/27/1998 to 02/07/1999   THEODORE ROOSEVELT: ICON OF THE AMERICAN CENTURY

11/06/1998 to 02/07/1999   PHILIPPE HALSMAN: A RETROSPECTIVE

01/29/1999 to 10/03/1999   RECENT ACQUISITIONS

02/19/1999 to 08/08/1999   PORTRAITS OF GEORGE AND MARTHA WASHINGTON IN THE PRESIDENTIAL YEARS, 1789-1797

04/16/1999 to 09/06/1999   FRANKLIN AND HIS FRIENDS: PORTRAITURE AND THE MAN OF SCIENCE IN 18TH CENTURY AMERICA

04/30/1999 to 09/06/1999   HANS NAMUTH: PORTRAIT PHOTOGRAPHS

06/18/1999 to 10/03/1999   IN HIS TIME: A PORTRAIT OF ERNEST HEMINGWAY

07/02/1999 to 10/03/1999   AUGUSTUS WASHINGTON DAGUERREOTYPES

07/02/1999 to 10/03/1999   EDWARD SOREL

10/29/1999 to 01/02/2000   HENRI CARTIER-BRESSON

Phillips Collection

1600 21st St., N.W., Washington, DC 20009-1090
☎: 202-387-2151
Open: 10-5 Tu-Sa, Noon-7 Su, 5-8:30 Th for "Artful Evenings", (12-5 Su Summer)   **Closed:** Mo, 1/1, 7/4, THGV, 12/25
ADM   Adult: $6.50   **Children:** F (18 & under)   **Students:** $3.25   **Seniors:** $3.25
 ⅄ ℗ **Museum Shop** ⅋ Café 10:45-4:30 —Sa; Noon-6:15 S
Group Tours: ext 247   **Drop-In Tours**: 2:00 We & Sa
Historic Building   **Sculpture Garden**
Permanent Collection: AM: ptgs, sculp 19-20; EU: ptgs, sculp, 19-20

DISTRICT OF COLUMBIA

Phillips Collection - continued
Housed in the 1897 former residence of the Duncan Phillips family, the core collection represents the successful culmination of one man's magnificent obsession with collecting the art of his time. PLEASE NOTE: The museum fee applies to weekends only. Admission on weekdays is by contribution. **NOT TO BE MISSED:** Renoir's " Luncheon of the Boating Party"; Sunday afternoon concerts that are free with the price of museum admission and are held Sept. through May at 5pm.; "Artful Evenings" ($5.00 pp) for socializing, art appreciation, entertainment, drinks and refreshments.

ON EXHIBIT 1999
ONGOING   SMALL PAINTINGS AND WORKS ON PAPER

to April 1999   A CALDER CENTENNIAL AT THE PHILIPS COLLECTION
Calder's Centennial year is celebrated here with an outdoor and indoor installation of the artists work.

09/19/1998 to 01/03/1999   IMPRESSIONS IN WINTER: EFFETS DE NEIGE
This exhibition of Impressionist winter landscape painting will provide the first thorough examination of the subject often called "effet de neige." It will focus primarily on works by Sisley, Monet and Pissarro.

09/19/1998 to 01/06/1999   Whistler in Venice
20 prints done in 1879-80 will be shown from that productive trip.

01/23/1999 to 03/28/1999   AN AMERICAN CENTURY OF PHOTOGRAPHY: FROM DRY PLATE TO DIGITAL FROM THE HALLMARK PHOTOGRAPHIC COLLECTION
A deliberate mixture of famous and 140 little known images and artists. While the exhibition is focused on American themes and subjects it also suggests an international cross-pollination of ideas and influences.

04/17/1999 to 07/18/1999   GEORGIA O'KEEFFE; THE POETRY OF THINGS
O'Keeffe's aesthetics will be examined through her painting of object. Comprising about 60 works on paper and paintings done from 1908-1972. *Will Travel*

05/15/1999 to 05/15/1999   WORKS BY JUDITH ROTHCHILD
In the 31 rarely exhibited works created between 1945 and 1991 she shows the styles in which she pained duri9ng five decades. *Catalog Will Travel*

09/25/1999 to 01/23/2000   MODERN ART AT THE MILLENNIUM: THE EYE OF DUNCAN PHILLIPS (working title)
For the first time, for this exhibition it will be possible to enter the Phillips family house and presenting the galleries themselves as Phillips adapted them to his developing collection.

Renwick Gallery of the National Museum of American Art
Affiliate Institution: Smithsonian Institution
Pennsylvania Ave. at 17th St., N.W., Washington, DC 20560
☎: 202-357-2700 ▣ www.nmaa.si.edu
Open: 10-5:30 Daily   **Closed:** 12/25
♿ ⓟ **Museum Shop**
Group Tours: 10, 11 & 1 Tu-T 202-357-2531   **Drop-In Tours**: 12:00 weekdays
Historic Building French Second Empire style designed in 1859 by James Renwick, Jr.
Permanent Collection: CONT/AM: crafts; AM: ptgs

The Renwick Gallery of the National Museum of American Art, Smithsonian Institution, is dedicated to exhibiting American crafts of all historic periods and to collecting 20th century American crafts. The museum, which celebrated its 25th anniversary in 1997, rotates the display of objects from its permanent collection on a quarterly basis. It is housed in a charming French Second Empire style building across Pennsylvania Avenue from the White House that was designed in 1859 and named not for its founder, William Corcoran, but for its architect, James Renwick, Jr. **NOT TO BE MISSED:** Grand Salon furnished in styles of 1860'S & 1870'S

Renwick Gallery of the National Museum of American Art - continued

ON EXHIBIT 1999

09/11/1998 to 01/10/1999   DANIEL BRUSH: GOLD WITHOUT BOUNDARIES

The first exhibition to showcase the unparalleled jewels, precious objects and sculpture of Brush. Although he started as a minimalist painter, he mastered the art of goldsmithing and sculpting steel. *Catalog*

03/19/1999 to 07/25/1999   SHAKER: THE ART OF CRAFTSMANSHIP

Furniture and decorative arts from America's oldest and most influential Shaker community, established in 1785 at New Lebanon, New York.

03/19/1999 to 07/25/1999   DOMINIC DI MARE: A RETROSPECTIVE

A review of the evolution of forms from Di Mare's improvisational weavings will be seen in the first retrospective exhibition of his work.

09/24/1999 to 01/09/2000   THE ART OF JOHN CEDERQUIST: REALITY OF ILLUSION

30 major works featured in this mid-career survey consist of traditional furniture forms combined with pictorial images of perspective drawing, veneering, inlaying, and photo-realist painting to create a disorienting though surprising and amusing trompe-l'oeil effect of multi-layered reality.

Sewall-Belmont House

144 Constitution Ave.,N.W., Washington, DC 20002

☎: 202-546-3989

Open: 10-3 Tu-Fr; Noon-4 Sa, Su   **Closed:** Mo, 1/1, THGV, 12/25

Vol/Cont

Ⓟ   **Museum Shop**

Group Tours   Drop-In Tours: 10-3 Tu-Fr; Noon-4 Sa, Su   **Historic Building**

Permanent Collection: SCULP, PTGS

Paintings and sculpture depicting heroines of the women's rights movement line the halls of the historic Sewall-Belmont House. One of the oldest houses on Capitol Hill, this unusual museum is a dedicated to the theme of women's suffrage.

FLORIDA

Gulf Coast Museum of Art
222 Ponce DeLeon Blvd., Belleair, FL 34616

☎: 813-584-8634
Open: 10-4 Tu-Fr (Pilcher Gallery); 10-4 Tu-Sa, Noon-4 Su (Shillard Smith Gallery)   **Closed:** Mo, LEG/HOL!
 ⚀ Ⓝ   **Museum Shop**
Group Tours   Drop-In Tours: call for information   **Sculpture Garden**
Permanent Collection: AM: ptgs 1940-1950'S; CONT FLORIDA ART: 1960 - present; CONT/CRAFTS

In operation for over 50 years, this art center, just south of Clearwater, near Tampa, features a permanent collection of over 700 works of art (late 19th - 20th c) with a focus on American artists including I. Bishop, Breckenridge, Bricher, and Inness. PLEASE NOTE: The Pilcher Gallery houses works from the permanent collection while the Smith Gallery is host to traveling exhibitions.

ON EXHIBIT 1999

12/05/1998 to 01/31/1999   ARLINE ERDRICH: THE HEALING POWER OF ART; THE CHAOS SERIES

12/05/1998 to 01/31/1999   SEAN SEXTON: STILL LIFES

02/20/1999 to 04/18/1999   FROM THE COLLECTION: FLORIDA AND THE SOUTHEAST

02/20/1999 to 04/18/1999   FROM THE COLLECTION: FINE CRAFTS

05/08/1999 to 06/20/1999   FROM THE COLLECTION: LANDSCAPES

05/08/1999 to 06/20/1999   COAST TO COAST: THE CONTEMPORARY LANDSCAPE IN FLORIDA

07/05/1999 to 08/01/1999   STUDIOWORKS '99

07/05/1999 to 08/01/1999   FROM THE COLLECTION: E.K.K. WETHERILL

Boca Raton Museum of Art
801 W. Palmetto Park Rd., Boca Raton, FL 33486

☎: 561-392-2500
Open: 10-4 Tu, Th, Fr; 12-4 Sa, Su; till 9pm We   **Closed:** Mo, LEG/HOL!
ADM   Adult: $3.00   **Children:** F (under 12)   **Students:** $1.00   **Seniors:** $2.00
 ⚀ Ⓝ   **Museum Shop**
Group Tours: 561-392-2500   **Drop-In Tours**: daily!   **Historic Building** In Old Floresta Historic District
Sculpture Garden
Permanent Collection: PHOT; PTGS 20

An AAM accredited institution, the Museum boasts over 2000 works of art of the highest quality and distinction, including a superb assembly of modern masters Braque, Demuth, Glackens, Matisse and Picasso, to name but a few. Recent donations include superb photography from the 19th century to present, African and Pre-Columbian art and a broad range of contemporary sculpture portraying a variety of styles and media.

ON EXHIBIT 1999

01/21/1999 to 03/14/1999   "HOMMAGE A RENOIR"
A selection of paintings, drawings, and sculptures by Renoir from the his home in Cagnes-Sur Mer.

International Museum of Cartoon Art
201 Plaza Real, Boca Raton, FL 33432
☎: 561-391-2200 ◉ www.cartoon.org
Open: 10-6 Tu-Sa, Noon-6 Su (9/1-5/31); 11-5 Tu-Sa, Noon-5 Su (OTHER) **Closed:** Mo
ADM Adult: $6.00 **Children:** 6-12 $3; F under 5 **Students:** $4.00 **Seniors:** $5.00
  ♿ ℗ **Museum Shop** ❙❙: Y: Café **Group Tours Drop-In Tours**
Permanent Collection: CARTOON ART

Started by Mort Walker, creator of the "Beetle Bailey" cartoon comic, and relocated to Florida after 20 years of operation in metropolitan NY, this museum, with over 160,000 works on paper, 10,000 books, 1,000 hours of animated film, and numerous collectibles & memorabilia, is dedicated to the collection, preservation, exhibition and interpretation of an international collection of original works of cartoon art. PLEASE NOTE: On the many family weekends planned by the museum, event hours are 10-6 Sa, and 12-6 Su with admission at $4.00 per person. Call for information and schedule of programs.

ON EXHIBIT 1999
11/14/1998 to 01/17/1999 HOLIDAY CARTOON CELEBRATION
A cross-cultural winter holiday themed exhibition featuring the well known image of Santa Claus created by Thomas Nast, illustrative descriptions of Hanukkah, and original artwork by Ray Billingsley from the annual Kwanza series of his comic strip 'Curtis'.

01/23/1999 to 04/25/1999 IN LINE WITH AL HIRSCHFELD
Included in this exhibition are drawings, paintings, preliminary sketches, notebooks, movie posters, etc. chronicling the life of this famous New York Times caricaturist from the beginning of his career in the 1920's to the present.

CORAL GABLES

Lowe Art Museum
Affiliate Institution: University of Miami
1301 Stanford Dr., Coral Gables, FL 33146-6310
☎: 305-284-3535 ◉ www.lowemuseum.org
Open: 10-5 Tu, We, Fr, Sa; Noon-7 Th; Noon-5 Su **Closed:** Mo, ACAD!
Free Day: 1st Tu of the month **ADM Adult:** $5.00 **Children:** F (under 12) **Students:** $3.00 **Seniors:** $3.00
  ♿ ℗ **Museum Shop Group Tours:** 305-284-3535 **Drop-In Tours:** by appointment   **Sculpture Garden**
Permanent Collection: REN & BAROQUE: ptgs, sculp (Kress Collection); AN/R; SP/OM; P/COL; EU: art; AS. ptgs, sculp, gr, cer; AM: ptgs, gr; LAT/AM; NAT/AM; AF

Established in 1950, the Lowe recently underwent a multi-million dollar expansion and renovation. Its superb and diverse permanent collection is recognized as one of the major fine art resources in Florida. More than 9,000 works from a wide array of historical styles and periods including the Kress Collection of Italian Renaissance and Baroque Art, 17th - 20th century European and American art, Greco-Roman antiquities, Asian, African, pre-Columbian and Native American art. **NOT TO BE MISSED:** Kress Collection of Italian Renaissance and Baroque art

ON EXHIBIT 1999
12/17/1998 to 02/07/1999 WALTER O. EVANS COLLECTION OF AFRICAN AMERICAN ART
Portraits, landscapes and mythological imagery will be seen in this remarkable exhibition of historical and contemporary works of art by black artists.

02/18/1999 to 04/04/1999 TREASURES OF DECEIT: ARCHAEOLOGY AND THE FORGER'S CRAFT
Objects representing ancient Near Eastern, Egyptian, Etruscan, Greek and Roman civilizations will be used as springboards in an exhibition designed to explain how art historians and classical archeologists determine the authenticity of antiquities. Visitors will be encouraged to examine many of the genuine, reworked and forged objects on view through a magnifying glass, enabling them to evaluate works utilizing some of the methodology of the experts. *Catalog Will Travel*

FLORIDA

Lowe Art Museum - continued

02/18/1999 to 04/04/1999   ARTIST/AUTHOR: THE BOOK AS ART SINCE 1980
A survey of the entire spectrum of contemporary artists' book production including the fashion world, exhibition catalogs, 'fanzine' assemblies sketchbooks, etc.

04/15/1999 to 05/30/1999   MUSICAL CHAIRS: AN INSTALLATION BY EMILIE BENES BRZEZINSKI

06/10/1999 to 07/31/1999   THE VENERABLE BEAD: BEADED OBJECTS FROM THE PERMANENT COLLECTION

06/10/1999 to 07/31/1999   PURE VISION: AMERICAN BEAD ARTISTS
From intimate necklace forms to large wall constructions, this exhibition of works by 28 artists demonstrates the broad range of individual creativity and artistic expression possible through beadwork, a medium that is enjoying a renaissance among contemporary American artists.

08/05/1999 to 09/05/1999   4TH ANNUAL FLORIDA ARTISTS SERIES

08/05/1999 to 09/05/1999   UNIVERSITY OF MIAMI FACULTY EXHIBITION

09/16/1999 to 11/14/1999   DREAM WEAVERS: GUATEMALAN TEXTILES FROM THE PERMANENT COLLECTION

09/16/1999 to 11/14/1999   FIBERS AND FORMS: NATIVE AMERICAN BASKETRY OF THE WEST

11/02/1999 to 01/30/2000   CANADIAN SILVER FROM THE NATIONAL GALLERY OF CANADA

11/02/1999 to 01/30/2000   TREASURES OF CHINESE GLASS WORKSHOPS: PEKING GLASS FROM THE GADIENT COLLECTION
This exhibit contains exquisite examples of Chinese glass from the Qing Dynasty. The 60 works included reveal the brilliant range of glass-making abilities found in Peking and the surrounding region. *Will Travel*

DAYTONA BEACH

Museum of Arts and Sciences
1040 Museum Blvd., Daytona Beach, FL 32014
📞: 904-255-0285
Open: 9-4 Tu-Fr; Noon-5 Sa, Su   **Closed:** Mo, LEG/HOL!
ADM   Adult: $5.00   **Children:** $2.00   **Students:** $1.00
  ♿ ℗ **Museum Shop Group Tours**: 904-255-0285 ext.16   **Drop-In Tours**: daily 904-255-0285 ext. 22
Permanent Collection: REG: ptgs, gr, phot; AF; P/COL; EU: 19; AM: 18-20; FOLK; CUBAN: ptgs 18-20; OR; AM: dec/art, ptgs, sculp 17-20

The Museum of Arts and Sciences serves as an outstanding cultural resource in the state of Florida, recently added a wing designed to add thousands of square feet of new gallery space. The new Arts & Humanities Wing featuring the Anderson C. Bouchelle Center for the study of International Decorative Arts and the Helena & William Schulte Gallery of Chinese Art opened to the public in 11/96. A plus for visitors is the lovely nature drive through Tuscawill Park leading up to the museum, and interpreted nature trails. **NOT TO BE MISSED:** The Dow Gallery of American Art, a collection of more than 200 paintings, sculptures, furniture, and decorative arts (1640-1910).

ON EXHIBIT 1999

10/09/1998 to 01/09/1999   ON THE EDGE OF THE ABYSS: TAMPA BAY HOLOCAUST MEMORIAL MUSEUM

10/09/1998 to 01/09/1999   MARGOT BECKMAN WATERCOLORS

10/09/1998 to 01/09/1999   LATE MEDIEVAL AND RENAISSANCE ILLUMINATED MANUSCRIPTS PAGES FROM THE BLACKBURN COLLECTION *Catalog Will Travel*

10/09/1998 to 01/09/1999   27TH ANNUAL FLORIDA WATERCOLOR SOCIETY EXHIBITION

11/07/1998 to 04/11/1999   SETTING STANDARDS: PLACE SETTINGS FROM THE PERMANENT COLLECTION

Museum of Arts and Sciences - continued

01/24/1999 to 03/14/1999   THE STONEWARES OF CHARLES FERGUS BINNS: FATHER OF AMERICAN STUDIO CERAMICS
60 rarely seen works by a pioneer, potter, teacher and author who laid the foundation for the studio ceramics movement in this country. This ground breaking survey is the most comprehensive collection of his work ever assembled for a traveling exhibition. It includes the earliest documented stoneware vase signed and dated 1905. *Catalog Will Travel*

01/30/1999 to 03/21/1999   DAN GUNDERSON CERAMICS

04/10/1999 to 07/03/1999   HOCKNEY TO HODGKIN: BRITISH MASTER PRINTS *Catalog Will Travel*

05/22/1999 to 09/19/1999   HENRIETTA MARIE SLAVE SHIP

07/10/1999 to 09/19/1999   FROM THE AGE OF NAPOLEON

09/18/1999 to 01/09/2000   TREASURES FROM THE COLLECTION OF A LA VIEILLE RUSSIE

Southeast Museum of Photography

Affiliate Institution: Daytona Beach Community College
1200 West International Speedway Blvd., Daytona Beach, FL 32120-2811
☎: 904-254-5475   ▣   www.dbcc.cc.fl.us/dbcc/smp/welcome.htm
Open: 10-7 Tu; 10-4 We-Fr; 12-4 Sa, Su   **Closed:** Mo, LEG/HOL!
&   ℗   **Museum Shop   Group Tours**: 904-947-5469   **Drop-In Tours**: 20 minute "Art for Lunch" tours!
Permanent Collection: PHOT

Thousands of photographs from the earliest daguerreotypes to the latest experiments in computer assisted manipulation are housed in this modern 2 floor gallery space opened in 1992. Examples of nearly every photographic process in the medium's 150 year old history are represented in this collection. **NOT TO BE MISSED:** Kidsdays, a Sunday afternoon program for children and parents where many aspects of the photographic process can be experienced.

ON EXHIBIT 1999

10/14/1998 to 01/15/1999   INDOCHINE REQUIEM: PHOTOJOURNALIST WHO DIED IN VIETNAM

10/14/1998 to 01/15/1999   EVE ARNOLD

10/14/1998 to 01/15/1999   MEXICAN WOMEN: GRACIELA ITURBIDE, YOLANDE ANDRADE, LOURDES ALMEDA

10/14/1998 to 01/15/1999   MARY JEAN VIANO CROWE: SOMETIMES I FEEL LIKE A BEAUTIFUL PRINCESS

02/05/1999 to 05/07/1999   BLACK IN DAYTONA BEACH: PHOTOGRAPHS BY GORDON PARKS, 1940

02/05/1999 to 05/07/1999   FACING DEATH: PORTRAITS FROM CAMBODIA'S KILLING FIELDS
A partial record of the genocide perpetrated by Pol Pot's Khmer Rouge during the 1970's will be seen in this photographic documentation of women, babies, men and children sent to "S-21", a place of brutal internment, torture and execution.

02/05/1999 to 05/07/1999   DOCUMENTING BLACK DAYTONA

02/05/1999 to 05/07/1999   KENRO IZU: ANCIENT ANGKOR

Summer 1999   MARIANNE ALVAREZ: BARRIER ISLANDS

Summer 1999   LEE DUNKEL: CLAY WALL SERIES

Summer 1999   MARILYN BRIDGES: THIS LAND IS YOUR LAND

Summer 1999   LANDSHAPES: RECORD OF AN ACTION

Summer 1999   MARK MAIO WHEAT: A VISUAL SOCIOLOGY OF LABOR

Fall 1999   THE SEA AND SHIPS: SELECTIONS FROM THE JACK SAHLMAN COLLECTION OF MARITIME PHOTOGRAPHY

Fall 1999   KERTECZ: A RETROSPECTIVE

Fall 1999   LUCIAN PERKINS: RUNAWAY MADNESS

FLORIDA

DeLand Museum of Art
600 N. Woodland Blvd., DeLand, FL 32720-3447
☎: 904-734-4371
Open: 10-4 Tu-Sa, 1-4 Su, till 8pm Tu   **Closed:** Mo, LEG/HOL!
ADM   Adult: $2.00   **Children:** $1.00 (4-12)   **Students:** $1.00   **Seniors:** $2.00
  Ġ Ⓟ **Museum Shop   Group Tours   Drop-In Tours**: !
Permanent Collection: AM: 19-20; CONT: reg; DEC/ART; NAT/AM

The Deland, opened in the New Cultural Arts Center in 1991, is located between Daytona Beach and Orlando. It is a fast growing, vital institution that offers a wide range of art and art-related activities to the community and its visitors. PLEASE NOTE: The permanent collection is not usually on display.

Museum of Art, Fort Lauderdale
1 E. Las Olas Blvd., Ft. Lauderdale, FL 33301-1807
☎: 954-525-5500
Open: 10-5 Tu-Sa, till 8pm Fr, Noon-5 Su   **Closed:** Mo, LEG/HOL!
ADM   Adult: $6.00   **Children:** 5-18 $1.00,F under 4   **Students:** $3.00   **Seniors:** $5.00
  Ġ Ⓟ **Museum Shop   Group Tours**: ex 239/241   **Drop-In Tours**: 2:00 Tu, Th, Fr (Free with admission)
Historic Building Built by renowned architect Edward Larrabee Barnes   **Sculpture Garden**
Permanent Collection: AM: gr, ptgs, sculp 19-20; EU: gr, ptgs, sculp 19-20; P/COL; AF; OC; NAT/AM

Aside from an impressive permanent collection of 20th-century European and American art, this museum is home to the William Glackens collection, the most comprehensive collection of works by the artist and others of his contemporaries who, as a group, are best known as "The Eight" and/or the Ashcan School. It also is home to the largest collection of CoBrA art in the Western Hemisphere. **NOT TO BE MISSED:** The William Glackens Collection

ON EXHIBIT 1999
10/31/1998 to 01/17/1999   PICTURES OF THE TIMES: A CENTURY OF PHOTOGRAPHY FROM THE NEW YORK TIMES

10/31/1998 to 01/17/1999   JANET FISH: SELECTED WORKS 1970'S-1990'S
One of the leading realist painters of the late 20th century this exhibition surveys the past three decades of her career. Figures and New England landscapes are incorporated into her resplendent explorations of light and color.

12/15/1998 to 08/02/1999   AFRICAN COLLECTION
The selections from the masks and sculptures in the collection will illustrate the influence on modern painters with strong pattern, abstract form, and geometric designs.

12/18/1998 to 03/28/1999   GROPPER COLLECTION
Gropper studied with Robert Henri and George Bellows in New York City. A social realist, he achieved fame through political and social cartoons.

12/18/1998 to 04/04/1999   WORKS BY MADELINE DENARO
Brilliant large canvases possessing a powerful presence.

12/18/1998 to 05/23/1999   INTIMATE GLACKENS
Glackens was a fastidious artist and perfectionist. Fifty seminal paintings although small are fully realized..

02/06/1999 to 05/02/1999   HERB RITTS: WORK
A chronicler of the chic worlds of fashion celebrity and popular culture, he is an image maker fir our time.

04/10/1999 to 06/06/1999   FORGOTTEN FACES: VINTAGE PHOTOGRAPHIC IMAGES AND TECHNIQUES
Daguerreotypes were phenomena of the nineteenth C.

Museum of Art, Fort Lauderdale - continued

05/15/1999 to 07/04/1999   ART AND NATURE: THE HUDSON RIVER SCHOOL
Beginning with Thomas Cole and the following three generations of artists, the Hudson River School painters were known for their dramatic depictions of nature. Among the artists in this exhibition are Cole, Durand, Church, Cropsey, Hart, Kensett, Martin, Johnson Castilear and Inness who illustrate how the meaning and importance of the Hudson River School has changed over time. *Will Travel*

05/15/1999 to 08/15/1999   JAVIER MARIN: SCULPTURES
This 35 year old Mexican sculptor is considered a prodigy today.

06/05/1999 to 09/12/1999   1999 SOUTH FLORIDA CULTURAL CONSORTIUM EXHIBITION
An outstanding juried exhibition. Out of state jurors chose 7 artists from the 350 submitted.

07/11/1999 to 11/15/1999   GEOMETRY AND ABSTRACTION: A PERFECT MATCH

GAINESVILLE

Samuel P. Harn Museum of Art

Affiliate Institution: Univ. of Florida
SW 34th St. & Hull Rd., Gainesville, FL 32611-2700
📞: 352-392-9826   ◙   www.arts.ufl.edu/harn
Open: 11-5 Tu-Fr, 10-5 Sa, 1-5 Su (last adm. is 4:45)   **Closed:** Mo, LEG/HOL!
Vol/Cont
& Ⓟ   **Museum Shop   Group Tours   Drop-In Tours:** 2:00 Sa, Su, 12:30 We; Family tours 1:15 2nd Su of mo.
Permanent Collection: AM: ptgs, gr, sculp; EU: ptgs, gr, sculp; P/COL; AF; OC; IND: ptgs, sculp; JAP: gr ; CONT

The Samuel P. Harn Museum of Art provides the most advanced facilities for the exhibition, study and preservation of works of art. The Harn offers approximately 15 changing exhibitions per year. The museum's collection includes the arts of the Americas, Africa, Asia as well as contemporary international works of art. Exciting performance art, lectures and films are also featured. **NOT TO BE MISSED:** African art collection; A Distant View: Florida Paintings by Herman Herzog; MOSAIC, the new art related video, & CD-ROM study center of the permanent collection.

ON EXHIBIT 1999

03/01/1998 to 02/28/1999   BUDDHIST SCULPTURE: ALONG THE TRADE ROUTES
This thematic installation of 16 Buddhist sculptures explores the spread of Buddhism, and the evolution of Buddhist sculpture along ancient Asian trade routes. *Will Travel*

03/22/1998 to 01/03/1999   INNER EYE: CONTEMPORARY ART FROM THE MARC AND LIVIA STRAUS COLLECTION

04/19/1998 to 04/1999   ASIAN ART FROM THE PERMANENT COLLECTION

05/31/1998 to 05/1999   BUILDING THE AMERICAN COLLECTIONS: SELECTED ACQUISITIONS SINCE 1995

09/13/1998 to 01/03/99   FRANCISCO GOYA Y LUCIENTES: THE CAPRICHOS ETCHINGS AND AQUATINTS

11/01/1998 to 01/03/1999   CONSUELO KANAGA: AN AMERICAN PHOTOGRAPHER
Drawn from the Brooklyn Museum of Art's vast collection of her works will be more than 100 silver gelatin photographic images of still-lifes, urban and rural views, and portraits. Kanaga's subject matter focused primarily on portraying African-Americans with a beauty and sensitivity unique for the period in which they were taken. *Catalog Will Travel*

12/20/1998 to 03/14/1999   MASTERWORKS OF EUROPEAN DRAWING: 16TH-19TH CENTURIES FROM THE ARKANSAS ART CENTER *Catalog Will Travel*

09/1999 to 12/1999   EQUAL PARTNERS

09/05/1999 to 11/28/1999   INTIMATE EXPRESSIONS: TWO CENTURIES OF AMERICAN DRAWINGS *Catalog Will Travel*

09/13/1999 to 01/03/2000   AMERICAN IMPRESSIONISM FROM THE SHELDON MEMORIAL ART GALLERY
Significant figures in this movement are Hassam, Weir, Glackens, Metcalf. Artists working in parallel styles such as Pene du Bois and Melchers are all represented here as well.

Cummer Museum of Art & Gardens

829 Riverside Ave., Jacksonville, FL 32204

📞: 904-356-6857   ▣ www.cummer.org

Open: 10-9 Tu & Th; 10-5 We, Fr, Sa; 12-5 Su   **Closed:** Mo, 1/1, EASTER, 7/4, THGV, 12/25

ADM   Adult: $5.00   **Children:** $1.00 (5 & under)   **Students:** $3.00   **Seniors:** $3.00

& ℗ **Museum Shop**

Group Tours: 904-355-0630   **Drop-In Tours:** 10-3 Tu-Fr (by appt); 3 Su (w/o appt); 7 Th

Historic Building Gardens founded in 1901 and 1931   **Sculpture Garden**

Permanent Collection: AM: ptgs; EU: ptgs; OR; sculp; CER; DEC/ART; AN/GRK; AN/R; P/COL; IT/REN

The Cummer Museum of Art & Gardens is located on the picturesque bank of the St. Johns River. Adjacent to the river are two-and-one-half acres of formal gardens. The museum's permanent collection ranges in date from 2,000 BC to the present, with particular strength in 18th and 19th-century American and European paintings. The Wark collection of 18th-century Meissen porcelain is one of the two finest collections in the world. Art Connections, a nationally-acclaimed interactive education center, also schedules an impressive array of activities for children through adults. **NOT TO BE MISSED:** One of the earliest and rarest collections of Early Meissen Porcelain in the world

ON EXHIBIT 1999

12/03/1998 to 03/28/1999   SLEEPING BEAUTIES: AFRICAN HEADRESTS FROM THE JEROME L. JOSS COLLECTION AT UCLA

05/06/1999 to 08/29/1999   GODS, PROPHETS, AND HEROES: THE SCULPTURE OF DONALD DE LUE

07/01/1999 to 09/26/1999   THE HASKELL COLLECTION OF CONTEMPORARY ART

09/23/1999 to 12/05/1999   THE AUTOBIOGRAPHY OF A BOOK

11/26/1999 to 01/23/2000   INTERACTION OF CULTURES: INDIAN AND WESTERN PAINTING (1710-1910) FROM THE EHRENFELD COLLECTION

This exhibition highlights the art created in India by Indian and Western artists between 1780 and 1910. The 95 works, primarily paintings on canvas have been drawn from this outstanding private collections. It will be the first exhibit in North America to consider the artistic interaction between these two cultures. *Catalog Will Travel*

Jacksonville Museum of Contemporary Art

4160 Boulevard Center Dr., Jacksonville, FL 32207

📞: 904-398-8336

Open: 10-4 Tu, We, Fr; 10-10 Th; 1-5 Sa, Su   **Closed:** Mo, LEG/HOL

ADM

& ℗ **Museum Shop**

Group Tours   Drop-In Tours   Sculpture Garden

Permanent Collection: CONT; P/COL

The finest art from classic to contemporary is offered in the Jacksonville Museum, the oldest museum in the city. PLEASE NOTE: There is a nominal admission fee for non-museum member visitors. **NOT TO BE MISSED:** Collection of Pre-Columbian art on permanent display

LAKELAND

Polk Museum of Art

800 E. Palmetto St., Lakeland, FL 33801-5529
☎: 941-688-7743
Open: 9-5 Tu-Fr, 10-5 Sa, 1-5 Su   **Closed:** Mo, LEG/HOL!
♿ ℗ **Museum Shop   Group Tours   Drop-In Tours   Sculpture Garden**
Permanent Collection: P/COL; REG; AS: cer, gr; EU: cer, glass, silver 15-19: AM: 20; PHOT

Located in central Florida about 40 miles east of Tampa, the 37,000 square foot Polk Art Museum, built in 1988, offers a complete visual and educational experience to visitors and residents alike. The Pre-Columbian Gallery, with its self-activated slide presentation and hands-on display for the visually handicapped, is but one of the innovative aspects of this vital community museum and cultural center. **NOT TO BE MISSED:** "El Encuentro" by Gilberto Ruiz; Jaguar Effigy Vessel from the Nicoya Region of Costa Rica (middle polychrome period, circa A.D. 800-1200)

ON EXHIBIT 1999

10/17/1998 to 01/03/1999   THE ARTIST, HER COMMUNITY AND MANKIND: KABUYA PAMELA BOWENS

10/24/1998 to 01/24/1999   THE TRUE SOUL OF THE ARTISTIC EXPERIENCE IN FLORIDA: 1997-98 VISUAL ARTIST FELLOWSHIP AWARDS

10/24/1998 to 01/24/1999   REFLECTIONS OF A GOLDEN AGE: CHINESE TANG POTTERY: FROM THE COLLECTION OF ALAN AND SIMONE HARTMAN

11/07/1998 to 02/07/1999   THE SAMUEL AND KAREN BLATT COLLECTION

01/09/1999 to 03/21/1999   TRANSFORMATIONS: LESLIE NEWMANN IN FLORIDA

01/30/1999 to 04/11/1999   HALLMARK FOR LAKELAND

03/27/1999 to 06/13/1999   LANDSCAPE PHOTOGRAPHY

04/17/1999 to 06/27/1999   INNUENDO NON TROPPO: THE WORK OF GREGORY BARSAMIAN
Spinning constructions and strobe lights are employed in the creation of Barsamian's works of optical illusion some of which produce the appearance of vertical motion.

MAITLAND

Maitland Art Center

231 W. Packwood Ave., Maitland, FL 32751-5596
☎: 407-539-2181   ▣ www.ci.maitland.fl.us
Open: 9-4:30 Mo-Fr; Noon-4:30 Sa, Su   **Closed:** LEG/HOL!
Vol/Cont
♿ ℗ **Museum Shop**
Group Tours   Drop-In Tours: Upon request if available   **Historic Building** State of Florida Historic Site
Permanent Collection: REG: past & present

The stucco buildings of the Maitland Center are so highly decorated with murals, bas reliefs, and carvings done in the Aztec-Mayan motif, that they are a "must-see" work of art in themselves. One of the few surviving examples of "Fantastic" Architecture remaining in the southeastern U.S., the Center is listed in the NRHP **NOT TO BE MISSED:** Works of Jules Andre Smith, (1890 - 1959), artist and founder of the art center

FLORIDA

Maitland Art Center - continued

ON EXHIBIT 1999

01/08/1999 to 02/25/1999   SHAKER LEGACY, SHAKER BASKETS
Marion Wetherbee is the author and authority on Shaker Baskets and crafts. She is allowing her collection to be shown at this time.

03/05/1999 to 04/25/1999   THE ANTHROPOMORPHIC ALPHABET
James A Cogswell is an artist whose alphabet began with a series of photographs which led to a series of drypoints and now experiments in paint on canvas. Both the drypoints and painted canvases will be exhibited here. *Will Travel*

04/30/1999 to 07/04/1999   THESE ARE MY STORIES: IRA WEISSMAN
A self-taught "outsider" who started carving in wood in 1976, Weissman uses his life-experiences of traveling around the world to create his subject matter. *Will Travel*

07/19/1999 to 08/29/1999   FLORIDA ILLUSTRATORS, ART FROM CHILDREN'S BOOKS
A showcase of original illustrations for children's books by Florida artists. The exhibit features all manner of illustrative styles and media as well as the manuscript and story board leading the viewer through the development of an illustration from author's pen to artist's brush.

09/11/1999 to 10/31/1999   ART THREE BY.
A juried competition held every three years for Florida artists.

MELBOURNE

Brevard Museum of Art and Science
1463 Highland Ave., Melbourne, FL 32935

☎: 407-242-0737
Open: 10-5 Tu-Sa, 1-5 Su   **Closed:** Mo, LEG/HOL!
Free Day: 1-5 Th   **ADM   Adult:** $5.00   **Children:** $2.00   **Students:** $2.00   **Seniors:** $3.00
 ⚊ ⓟ **Museum Shop   Group Tours:** 407-254-7782   **Drop-In Tours:** 2-4 Tu-Fr; 12:30-2:30 Sa; 1-5 Su
Permanent Collection: OR; REG: works on paper

Features changing exhibitions of work by regional, national and international artists in four galleries. The Children's Science Center features more than 30 hands-on exhibits teaching concepts of physical science.

ON EXHIBIT 1999

02/13/1999 to 03/14/1999   BREVARD WATERCOLOR SOCIETY EXHIBITION

02/13/1999 to 04/18/1999   FEAST FOR THE EYES: CONTEMPORARY STILL-LIFES
Four contemporary artists including Gary Bukovnick, Jean Wetta, Dennis Wojtkewitz, and Thomas Woodruff, who create unique interpretations of classic still-life scenes.

04/24/1999 to 06/13/1999   SOUTHEAST ASIAN BRONZES FROM THE PERMANENT COLLECTION
50 bronzes, some devotional and others functional or decorative with an emphasis on iconography and function as well as the metalwork techniques in Southeast Asia.

04/24/1999 to 06/13/1999   MAGIC CARPET: PERSIAN WEAVING 1800-1920
A private collection of Persian textiles created between 1800 and 1920 all featuring narratives and the narrative tradition in Persian weaving

06/19/1999 to 07/31/1999   FLORIDA CRAFTS INVITATIONAL

06/19/1999 to 07/31/1999   NEW WORKS BY JOYCE KOZLOFF
Recent paintings and collages.

12/05/1999 to 02/07/1999   OBJECTS OF DEVOTION: ICONS AND SANTOS
Devotional art of Europe and Latin America placing images of the Catholic saints and the Virgin Mary in the context of their folkloric legends. There will also be Greek and Russian icons and Puerto Rican santos from private collectors and other museums.

Art Museum at Florida International University

University Park, PC 110, Miami, FL 33199
📞: 305-348-2762 ◙ www.fiu.edu/~museum/
Open: 10-9 Mo, 10-5 Tu-Fr, Noon-4 Sa **Closed:** ACAD!, MEM/DAY, 7/4
Ⓟ **Museum Shop Group Tours Sculpture Garden**
Permanent Collection: GR:20; P/COL; CONT/HISPANIC (CINTAS FOUNDATION COLL); ARTPARK AT FIU

Major collections acquired recently by this fast growing institution include the Coral Gable's Metropolitan Museum and Art Center's holdings of African, Oriental, Pre-Columbian, 18-20th century American & Latin American Art, and a long-term loan of the Cintas Fellowship Foundation's Collection of contemporary Hispanic art. **NOT TO BE MISSED:** "Museum Without Walls" Art Park featuring the Martin Z. Margulies Sculpture Collection including works by Calder, Serra, deKooning, DiSuvero, Flannigan, Caro, Barofsky, and Dubuffet.

ON EXHIBIT 1999

01/08/1999 to 02/13/1999   AMERICAN ART TODAY: CONTEMPORARY PHOTOGRAPHS FROM THE MARTIN Z. MARGULIES COLLECTION
An exhibit exploring contemporary artists of the Americas

02/26/1999 to 04/03/1999   JOSE BEDIA: A RETROSPECTIVE
Internationally renowned Cuban-American Artist Jose Bedia's works in paintings, sculpture and drawings will illustrate his use of myth.

Miami Art Museum

101 W. Flagler St., Miami, FL 33130
📞: 305-375-3000 ◙ mamiami@dc.seflin.org
Open: 10-5 Tu-Fr; till 9 third Th; Noon-5 Sa, Su **Closed:** Mo, 1/1, THGV, 12/25
Free Day: 5-9 3rd Th; by contrib Tu **ADM Adult:** $5.00 **Children:** F (under 12) **Students:** $2.50 **Seniors:** $2.50
ե Ⓟ **Museum Shop Group Tours:** 305-375-4073 **Drop-In Tours:** by res
Historic Building Designed by Philip Johnson 1983 **Sculpture Garden**
Permanent Collection: The acquisition of a permanent collection is now underway with the first gifts of works including those by Adolph Gottlieb, Robert Rauschenberg, Helen Frankenthaler and Jean Dubuffet

Exhibiting and collecting post-war international art, with a focus on art of the Western Hemisphere, is the primary mission of this museum. The stunning facility, formerly called the Center for the Fine Arts, was designed and built in 1983 by noted American architect Philip Johnson. It changed its name to the Miami Art Museum in October 1996. PLEASE NOTE: There is a special program or performance at the center the 3rd Thursday night of each month from 5 to 9. The second Saturday of the month from 1-4 is free for families; on Tuesdays, visitors are admitted for a contribution of their choice. **NOT TO BE MISSED:** The Dream Collection, featuring the first gifts to the permanent collection.

ON EXHIBIT 1999

10/30/1998 to 01/10/1999   NEW WORK: MIRALDA

11/11/1998 to 04/25/1999   DREAM COLLECTION PART FOUR

12/17/1998 to 03/07/1999   GEORGE SEGAL, A RETROSPECTIVE: SCULPTURES, PAINTINGS, DRAWINGS
20 monumental sculptures in a variety of media reflecting the evolution of this American artist who was indirectly linked to Pop. Segal is known for his often solitary figures placed in an environment reflecting the banality of everyday life. *Catalog Will Travel*

01/29/1999 to 04/04/1999   NEW WORK: NANCY RUBINS

FLORIDA

Miami Art Museum - continued

03/25/1999 to 05/30/1999   RE-ALIGNING VISIONS: SOUTH AMERICAN DRAWING (1960-1990)
90 drawings by 75 leading Latin American artists will be on loan from public and private sources in an exhibition of works ranging from the contemporary interpretation of 16th & 17th century old master techniques, to photographic realism, expressive figuration and abstraction.

04/23/1999 to 07/04/1999   NEW WORK: LIISA ROBERTS

06/16/1999 to 08/29/1999   BEADS, BODY AND SOUL: ART AND LIGHT IN THE YORUBA UNIVERSE
The extraordinary variety and complexity of Yoruba beaded arts which have a documented history of over 1000 years is revealed in this exhibition. This is the first exhibition that considers the Yoruba aesthetic universe over time and in the African Diaspora of the Yoruba world.

Miami-Dade Community College Kendall Campus Art Gallery
11011 Southwest 104th St., Miami, FL 33176-3393
☎: 305-237-2322
Open: 8-4 Mo, Th, Fr; Noon-7:30 Tu, We   **Closed:** Sa, Su, LEG/HOL!, ACAD!, first 3 weeks of Aug
  & Ⓟ **Museum Shop** ⊪ **Group Tours   Drop-In Tours**
Permanent Collection: CONT: ptgs, gr, sculp, phot; GR: 15-19

With nearly 600 works in its collection, the South Campus Art Gallery is home to original prints by such renowned artists of the past as Whistler, Tissot, Ensor, Corot, Goya, in addition to those of a more contemporary ilk by Hockney, Dine, Lichtenstein, Warhol and others. **NOT TO BE MISSED:** "The Four Angels Holding The Wings", woodcut by Albrecht Dürer, 1511

MIAMI BEACH

Bass Museum of Art
2121 Park Ave., Miami Beach, FL 33139
☎: 305-673-7530   ◉   http://ci.miami-beach.fl.us/culture/bass/bass/html
Open: 10-5 Tu-Sa, 1-5 S, 1-9 2nd & 4th We of the month   **Closed:** Mo, LEG/HOL!
ADM   Adult: $5.00   **Children:** F (under 6)   **Students:** $3.00   **Seniors:** $3.00
  & Ⓟ **Museum Shop   Group Tours   Drop-In Tours   Sculpture Garden**
Permanent Collection: PTGS, SCULP, GR 19-20; REN: ptgs, sculp; MED; sculp, ptgs; PHOT; OR: bronzes

Just one block from the beach in Miami, in the middle of a 9 acre park, is one of the great cultural treasures of Florida. Located in a stunning 1930 Art Deco building, the Museum is home to more than 6 centuries of artworks including a superb 500 piece collection of European art donated by the Bass family for whom the museum is named. Expansion and renovation plans are underway which will result in the addition of state-of-the-art gallery space, a café and new museum shop. PLEASE NOTE: On occasion there are additional admission fees for some special exhibitions. **NOT TO BE MISSED:** "Samson Fighting the Lion", woodcut by Albrecht Dürer

Wolfsonian-Florida International University
1001 Washington Ave., Miami Beach, FL 33139
☎: 305-531-1001
Open: 10-6 Mo, Tu, Fr, Sa, 'til 9 Th, Noon-5 Su   **Closed:** We
Free Day: Th 6-9   **ADM   Adult:** $5.00   **Children:** F (under 6)   **Students:** $3.50   **Seniors:** $3.50
Ⓟ **Museum Shop   Group Tours   Drop-In Tours**
Permanent Collection: AM & EU: furn, glass, cer, metalwork, books, ptgs, sculp, works on paper, indust. design 1885-1945

Recently opened, The Wolfsonian, which contains the 70,000 object Mitchell Wolfson, Jr. collection of American and European art and design dating from 1885-1945, was established to demonstrate how art and design are used in cultural, social and political contexts. It is interesting to note that the museum is located in the heart of the lively newly redeveloped South Beach area.

Wolfsonian-Florida International University - continued

ON EXHIBIT 1999

Ongoing ART AND DESIGN IN THE MODERN AGE: SELECTIONS FROM THE WOFSONIAN COLLECTION

11/19/1998 to 02/1999   TALK OF THE TOWN: REA IRVIN OF THE NEW YORKER

11/19/1998 to 02/1999   MAIN STREET FIVE-AND DIMES: THE ARCHITECTURAL HERITAGE OF S. H. KRESS & CO.

MID/1999 to 07/1999   DEPEROFUTURISTA ROME-PARIS-NEW YORK

10/1999 to 03/2000   LEADING 'THE SIMPLE LIFE': THE ARTS AND CRAFTS MOVEMENT IN BRITAIN 1880-1910

From the Wolfsonian collection, this superb selection of Arts and Crafts objects is presented in an exhibition designed to trace the evolution of this art form.

NAPLES

Philharmonic Center for the Arts

5833 Pelican Bay Blvd., Naples, FL 34108
☎: 941-597-1111   ◉ www.naplesphilcenter.org
Open: OCT MAY: 10-4 Mo Fr, (10-4 Sa theater schedule permitting)   **Closed:** Su, LEG/HOL!
ADM   Adult: $4.00   **Children:** $2.00   **Students:** $2.00
& ℗   **Museum Shop   Group Tours:** ex 279   **Drop-In Tours:** Oct & May: 11 Th & Sa; Nov-Apr: 11 Mo-Sa

Four art galleries, two sculpture gardens, and spacious lobbies where sculpture is displayed are located within the confines of the beautiful Philharmonic Center. Museum quality temporary exhibitions are presented from October through May of each year. PLEASE NOTE: Free Family Days where gallery admissions and the 11am docent tour are offered free of charge are scheduled for Saturdays: 1/9, 2/13, 3/13, 4/17, 5/8

ON EXHIBIT 1999

12/11/1998 to 01/30/1999   TWENTIETH CENTURY AMERICAN DRAWINGS FROM THE ARKANSAS CENTER FOUNDATION COLLECTION
A great diversity of drawing styles and techniques spanning the greater part of the 20th c. of American art includes in their definition pencil, pen and ink, watercolor, silverpoint to acrylic and oil on paper. Among the artists represented in the 100 works are Avery, Brady, Burchfield, Cottingham, Curry, Davis, Dove, Frankenthaler, Francis, Guston, Hopper, Marsh, Pollock, Sheeler and Toby. *Catalog Will Travel*

NORTH MIAMI

Joan Lehman Museum of Contemporary Art

770 NE 125th St., North Miami, FL 33161
☎: 305-893-6211
Open: 115 Tu-Sa, 12-5 Su   **Closed:** Mo, 1THGV, 12/25
Free Day: Donation Day Tu   **ADM   Adult:** $4.00   **Children:** F (under 12)   **Students:** $2.00   **Seniors:** $2.00
& ℗   **Museum Shop   Group Tours:** 305-893-6211, ex 25   **Drop-In Tours:** 2pm Tu & Su, 1pm Sa
Permanent Collection: CONT

The Museum of Contemporary Art (MoCA) opened its new state-of-the-art building, designed by acclaimed architect Charles Gwathmey of Gwathmey Siegel, New York, to the public in February 1996. MoCA, Miami's newest art-collecting institution, is known for its provocative and innovative exhibitions, and for seeking a fresh approach to examine the art of our time. MoCA maintains an active schedule, presenting national traveling and curated exhibitions of emerging and contemporary artists. Among the artists in the permanent collection are: John Baldessari, Dan Flavin, Dennis Oppenheim, Alex Katz, Uta Barth, Teresita Fernandez, Garry Simmons, and Jose Bedia

FLORIDA

Joan Lehman Museum of Contemporary Art - continued
ON EXHIBIT 1999

10/27/1998 to 01/03/1999   PABLO CANO: CAVALETTI'S DREAM
Pablo Cano's marionette theatrical production mixes 14th c. Italian chivalry and Greek mythological tales through a fabulous assortment of characters, all composed of found objects and discarded materials.

12/18/1998 to 02/07/1999   DAVID SMITH: STOP ACTION
Smith's career as one of the most important American sculptors of the 20th c. is traced through important masterworks. His mastery at depicting figures in movement and at rest will be shown in welded bronzes, painted and unpainted steelwork, and monumental abstractions from the 1930's-1069's..

OCALA

Appleton Museum of Art
4333 NE Silver Springs Blvd., Ocala, FL 34470-5000
☎: 352-236-7100   ◉   www.fsu.edu/~svad/Appleton/AppletonMuseum.html
Open: 10-4:30 Tu-Sa, 1-5 Su   **Closed:** Mo, 1/1, LEG/HOL!
ADM   Adult: $5.00   **Children:** F (under 18)   **Students:** $2.00   **Seniors:** $3.00
  ♿ ℗   **Museum Shop   Group Tours**: 352-236-7100 x109   **Drop-In Tours**: 1:15 Tu-Fr
Permanent Collection: EU; PR/COL; AF; OR; DEC/ART; ISLAMIC CERAMICS; ANTIQUITIES

The Appleton Museum of Art in central Florida, home to one of the finest art collections in the Southeast, recently opened the Edith-Marie Appleton wing which allows for the display of major traveling exhibitions. Situated among acres of tall pines and magnolias, the dramatic building sets the tone for the many treasures that await the visitor within its walls. With the addition of The Edith-Marie Appleton Wing in 1/97, the museum became one of the largest art institutions in Florida. **NOT TO BE MISSED:** Rodin's "Thinker", Bouguereau's "The Young Shepherdess" and "The Knitter"; 8th-century Chinese Tang Horse

ON EXHIBIT 1999

04/06/1998 to 05/16/1999   SALLY ROGERS
Sculptures which combine metals, glass, stone and wood in visually appealing and movement oriented forms.

12/02/1998 to 03/21/1999   COMBINED TALENTS: THE FLORIDA NATIONAL 1998
A National juried competition

12/02/1998 to 03/21/1999   GLADYS KASHDIN
Works which deal with abstractions of natural landscapes and forms.

04/06/1999 to 05/16/1999   THE SIXTH ANNUAL SHOEBOX SCULPTURE EXHIBITION
The only limitation on sculptors is that the work must fit in a standard shoebox.

06/01/1999 to 07/25/1999   FLORIDIANS IN FLORENCE

ORLANDO

Orlando Museum of Art
2416 North Mills Ave., Orlando, FL 32803-1483
☎: 407-896-4231   ◉   www.OMArt.org
Open: 9-5 Mo-Sa, Noon-5 Su   **Closed:** Mo, LEG/HOL!
Free Day: Orange, Osceola and Seminole county residents are admitted free 12-5 Th
ADM   Adult: $4.00   **Children:** $2.00 (4-11)   **Students:** $4.00   **Seniors:** $4.00
  ♿ ℗   **Museum Shop   Group Tours**: ex 260   **Drop-In Tours**: 2:00 Th & Su
Permanent Collection: P/COL; AM; 19-20; AM: gr 20; AF

Orlando Museum of Art - continued

Designated by the state of Florida as a "Major Cultural Institution", the Orlando Museum, established in 1924, recently completed its major expansion and construction project making it the only museum in the nine-county area of Central Florida capable of providing residents and tourists with "world class" art exhibits. **NOT TO BE MISSED:** Permanent collection of Pre-Columbian artifacts (1200 BC to 1500 AD) complete with "hands-on" exhibit; Art Encounter

ON EXHIBIT 1999

ONGOING   18TH,19TH AND 20TH-CENTURY AMERICAN PORTRAITS & LANDSCAPES ON LONG-TERM LOAN FROM MARTIN AND GRACIA ANDERSON

On view are works by Thomas Moran, Rembrandt Peale, John Henry Twatchman and others whose paintings reflect the many forces that shaped American art from the Colonial period to the early 20th century.

ONGOING   CONTEMPORARY AMERICAN ART FROM THE PERMANENT COLLECTION

ONGOING   19TH AND EARLY 20TH-CENTURY AMERICAN ART FROM THE PERMANENT COLLECTION

ONGOING   ART OF THE ANCIENT AMERICAS: THE ORLANDO MUSEUM OF ART'S PRE-COLUMBIAN COLLECTION

150 Pre-Columbian artifacts (1200 BC to 1500 AD)

ONGOING   ART ENCOUNTER

This hands-on art exhibition for young children and families is included in the general admission fee.

12/11/1998 to 02/14/1999   KERRY JAMES MARSHALL

04/20/1999 to 07/11/1999   SHAMANS, GODS AND MYTHIC BEASTS: COLUMBIAN GOLD AND CERAMICS IN ANTIQUITY

Presented for the first time to the American public new finds from the southwest and north coastal regions of Columbia focus on the important ceramic sculpture of ancient Columbia, the fabled land of gold "El Dorado" and the artistic qualities and themes found there. Also included are 44 exceptional gold masterpieces that share design motifs found in the ceramic figure. *Catalog Will Travel*

PALM BEACH

Hibel Museum of Art

150 Royal Poinciana Plaza, Palm Beach, FL 33480
☎: 561-833-6870   ◉ www.hibel.com
Open: 10-5 Tu-Sa, 1-5 Su   **Closed:** Mo, 1/1, 7/4, THGV, 12/25
& ℗   **Museum Shop   Group Tours   Drop-In Tours:** Upon request if available
Permanent Collection: EDNA HIBEL: all media

The 22 year old Hibel Museum is the world's only publicly owned non profit museum dedicated to the art of a single living American woman.

Society of the Four Arts

Four Arts Plaza, Palm Beach, FL 33480
☎: 561-655-7226
Open: 12/2-4/24: 10-5 Mo-Sa, 2-5 Su   **Closed:** Museum closed May-Oct
Sugg/Cont   Adult: $3.00
& ℗   **Museum Shop   Group Tours   Drop-In Tours   Sculpture Garden**
Permanent Collection: SCULP

FLORIDA

Society of the Four Arts - continued

Rain or shine, this museum provides welcome relief from the elements for all vacationing art fanciers by presenting monthly exhibitions of paintings or decorative arts. **NOT TO BE MISSED:** Philip Hulitar Sculpture Garden

ON EXHIBIT 1999

09/30/1998 to 01/30/1999   LAND OF WONDERS: HIGHLIGHTS OF THE RUTGERS COLLECTION OF ORIGINAL ILLUSTRATIONS FOR CHILDREN'S LITERATURE

12/05/1998 to 01/03/1999   60TH ANNUAL NATIONAL EXHIBITION OF CONTEMPORARY AMERICAN PAINTINGS

01/09/1999 to 02/07/1999   NORTHWEST PASSAGE
During a 3500 mile voyage on the first private yacht to cross the Northwest Passage, Robert Glenn Ketchum took the breathtaking photos of the beauty and grandeur of the natural world on view in this exhibition.

02/13/1999 to 04/07/1999   THE CECIL FAMILY COLLECTS: FOUR CENTURIES OF DECORATIVE ARTS FROM BURGHLEY HOUSE
Burghley House is one of the oldest and grandest Elizabethan houses in England. The 120 crafted works from its collection will document the evolution of taste and collecting in Britain in the course of four centuries. *Catalog Will Travel*

03/06/1999 to 04/04/1999   MEMORY IS A PAINTER: THE ART OF GRANDMA MOSES

PENSACOLA

Pensacola Museum of Art

407 S. Jefferson St., Pensacola, FL 32501
☎: 850-432-6247   ◙   www.artsnwfl.org/pma
Open: 10-5 Tu-Fr, 10-4 Sa   **Closed:** Mo, LEG/HOL!
Free Day: Tu   **ADM   Adult:** $2.00   **Students:** $1.00   **Seniors:** $2.00
  ♿ ℗   **Museum Shop   Group Tours   Drop-In Tours**: check for availability   **Historic Building**
Permanent Collection: CONT/AM: ptgs, gr, works on paper; Glass:19, 20

Now renovated and occupied by the Pensacola Museum of Art, this building was in active use as the city jail from 1906 - 1954.

ON EXHIBIT 1999

10/27/1998 to 01/09/1999   PENSACOLA TODAY

10/27/1998 to 01/09/1999   JAILHOUSE ART: 90 YEARS BEHIND BARS

01/08/1999 to 02/20/1999   WORLD EXPLORATION: THE MARY EWING TEXTILE COLLECTION
Because of her extensive world travels and passion for art from all cultures, this is an intriguing collection of Asian, Central Asian, and South African garments and accessories. *Will Travel*

01/15/1999 to 02/24/1999   QUIETLY SEEING: PHOTOGRAPHS BY KAY DUVERNET
These photographic abstractions are almost exclusively taken from the heavily metallic utilitarian world - sections of barges, boxcars, 18 wheel highway haulers and shrimp beats.

03/01/1999 to 04/16/1999   YOUTH ART FOCUS

03/02/1999 to 04/16/1999   CHINESE CHILDREN'S HATS
Elaborate ornamentation and bright colors invoke images of festive whimsical occasions. These played an important role in traditional Chinese society.

Pensacola Museum of Art - continued

03/02/1999 to 05/29/1999   THE GOOD EARTH: CHINESE FOLK ART & ARTIFACTS
A collection of Chinese peasant paintings and artifacts from Huxian. One of the ancient capitols of China, and the cradle of the revolution with a distinct culture, the works have a vigor and simplicity.

06/08/1999 to 08/14/1999   EARTH, FIRE, AND WATER: CONTEMPORARY FORGED METAL
Works of 16 contemporary artists who create objects of hand forged metal using blacksmithing techniques. *Catalog Will Travel*

06/12/1999 to 07/25/1999   FULL DECK ART QUILTS

SARASOTA

John and Mable Ringling Museum of Art
5401 Bay Shore Rd., Sarasota, FL 34243
☎: 941-359-5700
Open: 10-5:30 Daily   **Closed:** 1/1,THGV, 12/25
ADM   Adult: $9.50   **Children:** F (12 & under)   **Seniors:** $8.50
&   ℗   **Museum Shop**   ‖ Banyan Café 11-4 daily
Group Tours   Drop-In Tours: call 813-351-1660 (recorded message)
Historic Building Ca'D'Zan was the winter mansion of John & Mable Ringling   **Sculpture Garden**
Permanent Collection: AM: ptgs, sculp, EU: ptgs, sculp 15-20; DRGS; GR; DEC/ART; CIRCUS MEMORABILIA

Sharing the grounds of the museum is Ca'd'Zan, the winter mansion of circus impresario John Ringling and his wife Mable. Their personal collection of fine art in the museum features one of the country's premier collections of European, Old Master, and 17th century Italian Baroque paintings. **NOT TO BE MISSED:** The Rubens Gallery - a splendid group of paintings by Peter Paul Rubens.

ON EXHIBIT 1999

ONGOING   ALEXANDER SERIES TAPESTRIES

ONGOING   DUTCH BAROQUE PAINTINGS

01/30/1999 to 05/02/1999   BLURRING THE BOUNDARIES: INSTALLATION ART 1970-1996
A study of installation art through the collections and exhibition record of the Museum of Contemporary Art, San Diego which has a unique heritage of such art dating back to the 60's

---

ST. PETERSBURG

Florida International Museum
100 Second St. North, St. Petersburg, FL 33701
☎: 813-822-3693
Open: 9am - 8pm daily (last tour starts at 6pm)
ADM   Adult: $13.95   **Students:** $5.95   **Seniors:** $12.95
&   ℗   **Museum Shop   Group Tours**: Call for reservations and information   **Drop-In Tours**
Permanent Collection:

Created to host a single grand-scale traveling exhibition annually, Florida International Museum this year features "TITANIC: The Exhibition", a presentation that includes more than 300 objects recovered from the ill-fated and supposedly unsinkable luxury liner that, in fact, sank on its trans-Atlantic maiden voyage in 1912. PLEASE NOTE: 1. Tickets may be purchased in advance by calling (800) 777-9882. They are also available at the museum box office. 2. Season passes and discounted group rates are available! 3. Admission includes an individual audio guide. 4. The museum will be closed on 11/27 & 12/25.

FLORIDA

Museum of Fine Arts-St. Petersburg Florida

255 Beach Dr., N.E., St. Petersburg, FL 33701-3498

☎: 813-896-2667   ◙ www.fine-arts.org

Open: 10-5 Tu-Sa, 1-5 Su, till 9pm 3rd Th except in summer   **Closed:** Mo, THGV,12/25, 1/1

ADM   Adult: $6.00 ($4 for groups of 10 or more)   **Children:** F (6 & under)   **Students:** $2.00   **Seniors:** $5.00

& ℗ **Museum Shop**

Group Tours   Drop-In Tours: 10,11, 1 & 2 Tu-Fr; 11 & 1 Sa; 1 & 2 Su   **Sculpture Garden**

Permanent Collection: AM: ptgs, sculp, drgs, gr; EU: ptgs, sculp, drgs, gr; P/COL; DEC/ART; P/COL; OR; STEUBEN GLASS; NAT/AM; AS: art; AF/ART

With the addition in 1989 of 10 new galleries, the Museum of Fine Arts, considered one of the premier museums in the southeast, is truly an elegant showcase for its many treasures that run the gamut from Dutch and Old Master paintings to one of the finest collections of photography in the state. The strengths are nineteenth century European, including French Impressionist paintings and nineteenth and early twentieth century American Art. PLEASE NOTE: Spanish language tours are available by advance appointment. **NOT TO BE MISSED:** Paintings by Monet, Gauguin, Cézanne, Morisot, Renoir, and O'KEEFFE

ON EXHIBIT 1999

ONGOING   RODIN BRONZES: FROM THE IRIS AND B. GERALD CANTOR FOUNDATION

01/24/1999 to 03/07/1999   HENRI MATISSE: FLORILEGE DES AMOURS DE RONSARD, A CELEBRATION OF FRENCH RENAISSANCE POETRY

Never before exhibited in a museum setting, this collection of lithographs created by Matisse for the Swiss publisher Albert Skira illustrates an anthology of love poems by the 16th century French poet Pierre Ronsard. Created nearly four centuries apart, Ronsard's language finds a perfect partner in Matisse's lyrical style. *Catalog*

03/21/1999 to 06/13/1999   AMERICAN PAINTINGS FROM THE LAWRENCE COLLECTION

45 late 19th and early 20th century American paintings including Hassam, Inness, Robinson, Henri, Bellows, Shinn, and Prendergast *Catalog*

03/21/1999 to 06/13/1999   ART GLASS OF THIS CENTURY

The works date from the 1950s, roughly beginning with the rise of the studio glass movement, to the present.

01/24/1999 to 05/30/1999   TREASURES OF CHINESE GLASS WORKSHOPS: PEKING GLASS FROM THE GADIENT COLLECTION

This exhibit contains exquisite examples of Chinese glass from the Qing Dynasty. The 60 works included reveal the brilliant range of glass-making abilities found in Peking and the surrounding region. *Will Travel*

Salvador Dali Museum

100 Third St. South, St. Petersburg, FL 33701

☎: 813-823-3767   ◙ www.daliweb.com

Open: 9:30-5:30 Mo-Sa, Noon-5:30 Su   **Closed:** THGV, 12/25

ADM   Adult: $8.00   **Children:** F (10 & under)   **Students:** $4.00   **Seniors:** $7.00

& ℗ **Museum Shop**

Group Tours: tours 9:30-3:30 M-Sa   **Drop-In Tours:** Call for daily schedule

Permanent Collection: SALVADOR DALI: ptgs, sculp, drgs, gr

Unquestionably the largest and most comprehensive collection of Dali's works in the world, the museum holdings amassed by Dali's friends A. Reynolds and Eleanor Morse include 95 original oils, 100 watercolors and drawings, 1,300 graphics, sculpture, and other objects d'art that span his entire career. **NOT TO BE MISSED:** Outstanding docent tours that are offered many times daily.

Florida State University Museum of Fine Arts

Fine Arts Bldg., Copeland & W. Tenn. Sts., Tallahassee, FL 32306-1140

☎: 850-644-6836   ▣ www.fsu.edu/~svad/FSUMuseum/FSU-Museum.html

Open: 10-4 Mo-Fr; 1-4 Sa, Su (closed weekends during Summer Semester)   **Closed:** LEG/HOL! Acad!

   ⅁   ℗   **Museum Shop**   **Group Tours**: 850-644-1299   **Drop-In Tours**: upon request if available

Permanent Collection: EU; OR; CONT; PHOT; GR; P/COL: Peruvian artifacts; JAP: gr

With 7 gallery spaces, this is the largest art museum within 2 hours driving distance of Tallahassee. **NOT TO BE MISSED:** Works by Judy Chicago

ON EXHIBIT 1999

01/08/1999 to 02/14/1999   INSIDER TRADING

01/08/1999 to 02/14/1999   THE FACULTY ANNUAL SCHOOL OF VISUAL ARTS & DANCE

02/12/1999 to 04/04/1999   THE JUDY CHICAGO RETROSPECTIVE: WORKS ON PAPER *Catalog Will Travel*

04/09/1999 to 04/23/1999   GRADUATING ARTISTS

05/14/1999 to 06/11/1999   "WHAT I DID LAST SUMMER"

Lemoyne Art Foundation, Inc.

125 N. Gadsden, Tallahassee, FL 32301

☎: 850-222-8800

Open: 10-5 Tu-Sa, 1-5 Su   **Closed:** Mo, 1/1, 7/4, 12/25 (may be closed during parts of Aug!)

ADM   Adult: $1.00   **Children:** F (12 & under)   **Students:** $1.00   **Seniors:** $1.00

   ⅁   ℗   **Museum Shop**   **Group Tours**   **Drop-In Tours**: when requested   **Historic Building**   **Sculpture Garden**

Permanent Collection: CONT/ART; sculp

Located in an 1852 structure in the heart of Tallahassee's historic district, the Lemoyne is named for the first artist known to have visited North America. Aside from offering a wide range of changing exhibitions annually, the museum provides the visitor with a sculpture garden that serves as a setting for beauty and quiet contemplation. **NOT TO BE MISSED:** Three recently acquired copper sculptures by George Frederick Holschuh

Tampa Museum of Art

600 North Ashley Dr., Tampa, FL 33602

☎: 813-274-8130

Open: 10-5 Mo-Sa, 10-9 W, 1-5 Su   **Closed:** 1/1, 7/4, 12/25

Vol/Cont   ADM   Adult: $5.00   **Children:** 6-18 $3.00;F under 6   **Students:** $4.00   **Seniors:** $4.00

   ⅁   ℗   **Museum Shop**   **Group Tours**   **Drop-In Tours:** 1:00 We & Sa, 2:00 Su   **Sculpture Garden**

Permanent Collection: PTGS: 19-20; GR: 19-20; AN/GRK; AN/R; PHOT

A superb 400 piece collection of Greek and Roman antiquities dating from 3,000 BC to the 3rd century A.D. is one of the highlights of this comprehensive and vital art museum. The Tampa Museum has recently installed a vast new sculpture garden, part of an exterior expansion program completed in 1995. **NOT TO BE MISSED:** Joseph V. Noble Collection of Greek & Southern Italian antiquities on view in the new Barbara & Costas Lemonopoulos Gallery.

FLORIDA

USF Contemporary Art Museum
Affiliate Institution: College of Fine Arts
4202 E. Fowler Ave., Tampa, FL 33620
☎: 813-974-4133
Open: 10-5 Mo-Fr, 1-4 Sa   **Closed:** Su, STATE & LEG/HOL!
 ♿ **Museum Shop** **Group Tours** **Drop-In Tours**
Permanent Collection: CONT: phot, gr

Located in a new building on the Tampa campus, the USF Contemporary Art Museum houses one of the largest selections of contemporary prints in the Southeast. PLEASE NOTE: The museum is occasionally closed between exhibitions!

ON EXHIBIT 1999

08/1999 to 09/1999   LESLIE LERNER: THE IMAGINED CITY
Multi media installation with narratives on the travels from Delft to Venice of the 'Man With Wooden Arm'. *Will Travel*

VERO BEACH

Center for the Arts, Inc.
3001 Riverside Park Dr., Vero Beach, FL 32963-1807
☎: 561-231-0707
Open: 10-9 Mon-Sa; 12-6 Su   **Closed:** Mo!
Sugg/Cont
 ♿ **Museum Shop**
Group Tours: ex 25   **Drop-In Tours:** 1:30-3:30 Sa, Su July-Oct; We-Su Nov-June **Sculpture Garden**
Permanent Collection: AM/ART 20

Considered the premier visual arts facility within a 160 mile radius on Florida's east coast, The Center, which offers national, international and regional art exhibitions throughout the year, maintains a leadership role in nurturing the cultural life of the region. **NOT TO BE MISSED:** "Royal Tide V" by Louise Nevelson; "Watson and the Shark" by Sharron Quasius; "Transpassage T.L.S.", 20 ft. aluminum sculpture by Ralph F. Buckley

ON EXHIBIT 1999
During 1999 exhibitions will be shown at the Arts' Off Center Gallery, Indian River Mall, State Road 60, Vero Beach

11/28/1998 to 01/03/1999   VITREOGRAPHS: COLLABORATIVE WORKS FROM THE LITTLETON STUDIO
In 1976 Harvey Littleton, already world renowned for the beauty of his glass decided to explore the possibilities of glass as a printmaking medium. He invited artists to participate and Vitreography was born. The exhibition features all forms of artistic statement from lyrical works to hard edged geometry.

01/15/1999 to 02/28/1999   ROBERT CHAMBERS: SITE SPECIFIC INSTALLATION (title to be announced)
Chambers uses both visual elements as well as motion and sound to create a gallery experience like no other.

05/14/1999 to 06/27/1999   A STUDY IN LIGHT: CONTEMPORARY AMERICAN WORKS IN GLASS
Featuring three dimensional works from the permanent collection with works from Florida collections and galleries including the greatest names working in glass. .

07/16/1999 to 09/12/1999   SHADOWS OF THE AMERICAN DREAM
Becky Beerenson in ink washes and Susan Martin in acrylic paint choose as their theme the man made abundance and its by-products, of the American way of life.

WEST PALM BEACH

Norton Museum of Art
1451 S. Olive Ave., West Palm Beach, FL 33401
☎: 561-832-5196　**◼** www.norton.org
Open: 10-5 Tu-Sa, 1-5 Su　**Closed:** Mo, 1/1, MEM/DAY, 7/4, THGV, 12/25
Sugg/Cont　**Adult:** $5.00　**Children:** F (12 & under)　**Students:** $2.00 (13-21)
&　**ⓟ**　**Museum Shop**　‖ Open 11:30-2:30 M-Sa & 1-3 S, M from Feb-April!
Group Tours　**Drop-In Tours:** Noon-12:30 weekdays　Free tours of permanent collection- ARTventure-daily 2-3pm
Permanent Collection: AM: ptgs, sculp 19-20; FR: ptgs, sculp 19-20; OR: sculp, cer

Started in 1940 with a core collection of French Impressionist and modern masterpieces, as well as fine works of American painting, the newly-renovated and expanded Norton's holdings also include major pieces of contemporary sculpture, and a noteworthy collection of Asian art. It is no wonder that the Norton enjoys the reputation of being one of the finest small museums in the United States. PLEASE NOTE: An admission fee may be charged for certain exhibitions. **NOT TO BE MISSED:** Paul Manship's frieze across the main facade of the museum flanked by his sculptures of Diana and Actaeon

ON EXHIBIT 1999
09/26/1998 to 01/10/1999　DYNASTIES: MASTERPIECES FROM THE CHINESE COLLECTION OF THE NORTON MUSEUM OF ART
Select pieces from the collection will include archaic jades and bronzes, dating as far back as 1000 BC, highly prized ceramics from the Han, Wei, Tang, Ming and Song dynasties and later examples dating to the early modern era, etc.

11/07/1998 to 01/07/1999　THE SEGEL COLLECTION OF ART NOUVEAU DECORATIVE ARTS
An exhibition of European and American art nouveau, Tiffany and furniture from a local private collection showing the international style from which artists such as Mucha and the young Picasso drew inspiration.

11/14/1998 to 01/03/1999　RED GROOMS: MOBY DICK MEETS THE NEW YORK PUBLIC LIBRARY
Grooms work is graphic, quirky, almost cartoon like in style. This monumental installation work starts with an enormous representation of the New York Public Library. One of the various scenes is Herman Melville who worked on his masterpiece in the Library and was the inspiration for this piece. The entire piece is 180 x 340 x 540.

01/23/1999 to 04/04/1999　THE INVISIBLE MADE VISIBLE: ANGELS FROM THE VATICAN
A truly remarkable exhibition of angels from the extensive collection of the Vatican Museums. It will examine the representation of angels from 1000 B.C. to the present. Rare and precious objects in all media by Fabiano, Fra Angelico, Masolino, Carraci, Reni, Veronese and Raphael as well as non-biblical and pre-Christian cultures are included. Adm: Their will be a special price for admission to this exhibition. *Catalog Will Travel*　◠

03/27/1999 to 06/06/1999　RAOUL DUFY: LAST OF THE FAUVES
Dufy was an artist who rose to prominence in the early 1900's and remained popular till his death in 1953. Since then he has been largely ignored by museums. This exhibition aims to restore his reputation as one of the most original and talented artists of the first half of this century. *Catalog Will Travel*

04/10/1999 to 06/20/1999　LYNNE BUTLER: PHOTOGRAPHS
Butler takes color photographs from horseback. As a result her photographs are very impressionistic and she manipulates color so that it becomes particularly bright.

10/28/1999 to 01/09/2000　HALF PAST AUTUMN: THE ART OF GORDON PARKS
A retrospective of Park's extraordinary career as a photojournalist, filmmaker, novelist poet and musician. *Catalog Will Travel*

119

FLORIDA

Charles Hosmer Morse Museum of American Art

445 Park Avenue North, Winter Park, FL 32789

☎: 407-645-5311
Open: 9:30-4 Tu-A, 1-4 Su   **Closed:** Mo, 1/1, MEM/DAY, LAB/DAY, THGV, 12/25
Free Day: Open House Easter weekend, July 4, Christmas Eve   **Adult:** $3.00   **Children:** F (under 12)   **Students:** $1.00
& Ⓟ **Museum Shop   Group Tours   Drop-In Tours**: available during regular hours
Permanent Collection: Tiffany Glass; AM: ptgs (19 and early 20); AM: art pottery 19-20

Late 19th and early 20th century works of Louis Comfort Tiffany glass were rescued in 1957 from the ruins of Laurelton Hall, Tiffany's Long Island home, by Hugh and Jeannette McKean. These form the basis of the collection at this unique little-known gem of a museum which has recently moved into new and larger quarters. The Museum also houses a major collection of American art pottery, superb works by late 19th and early 20th century artists, including Martin Johnson Heade, Robert Henri, Maxfield Parrish, George Innis, and others. **NOT TO BE MISSED:** Tiffany chapel for the 1893 Chicago World's Columbian Exposition; the "Electrolier", elaborate 10' high chandelier, centerpiece of the Chapel; the Baptismal Font of the Chapel, which paved the way for Tiffany's leaded glass lamps; 2 marble, concrete and Favrile glass columns designed by Tiffany for his Long Island mansion.

ON EXHIBIT 1999

03/1999   GRAND OPENING OF LOUIS COMFORT TIFFANY'S CHAPEL DESIGNED FOR THE 1893 COLUMBIAN EXPOSITION

12/02/1999 to 12/02/1999   CHRISTMAS IN THE PARK

George D. and Harriet W. Cornell Fine Arts Museum

Affiliate Institution: Rollins College
1000 Holt Ave., Winter Park, FL 32789-4499

☎: 407-646-2526   ◙ www.rollins.edu/cfam
Open: 10-5 Tu-Fr; 1-5 A, Su   **Closed:** Mo, 1/1, 7/4, LAB/DAY, THGV, 12/25
Vol/Cont   & Ⓟ **Museum Shop   Group Tours   Drop-In Tours**
Permanent Collection: EU: ptgs, Ren-20; SCULP; DEC/ART; AM: ptgs, sculp 19-20; PHOT; SP: Ren/sculp

Considered one of the most outstanding museums in Central Florida, the Cornell, located on the campus of Rollins College, houses fine examples in many areas of art including American landscape painting, French portraiture, works of Renaissance and Baroque masters, and contemporary prints. **NOT TO BE MISSED:** Paintings from the Kress Collection; "Christ With the Symbols of the Passion", by Lavinia Fontana

ON EXHIBIT 1999

11/06/1998 to 01/03/1999   THE SCULPTOR'S LINE: HENRY MOORE PRINTS
Prints and maquettes by Moore will be displayed with several of his full-size sculptures.

11/06/1998 to 01/03/1999   JASPER JOHNS: "THE SEASONS"

01/16/1999 to 02/28/1999   "BEYOND THE VEIL": THE ART OF THE AFRICAN-AMERICAN ARTISTS AT CENTURY'S END
A major exhibition surveying the art of 30 important African-American artists from the well established such as Lawrence and Gilliam to emerging including Lane and Carter.

03/12/1999 to 05/01/1999   DEGAS TO DELAUNAY: MASTERWORKS FROM THE ROBERT AND MAURINE ROTHSCHILD FAMILY COLLECTION
From this outstanding collection of Post Impressionist and early Modernist paintings, sculpture, drawings and prints the exhibition reveals the creative process of many important artists including Degas, Vuillard, Cezanne, Picasso, Braque, Matisse and others. *Catalog Will Travel*

05/28/1999 to 09/12/1999   TREASURES OF THE CORNELL FINE ARTS MUSEUM
A selection of the 150 best European and American objects (1485-1996) from the permanent collection accompanied by the 'Treasure Handbook'. *Catalog*

120

Albany Museum of Art

311 Meadowlark Dr., Albany, GA 31707
☎: 912-439-8400   ■ www.albanymuseum.com
Open: 10-5 Tu-A, till 7pm W, 1-4 Su   **Closed:** Mo, LEG/HOL!
Sugg/Cont
& Ⓟ   **Museum Shop**   **Group Tours**: 912-439-8400   **Drop-In Tours:** by appointment
Permanent Collection: AM: all media 19- 20; EU: all media 19-20; AF: 19-20

With one of the largest museum collections in the south of Sub-Saharan African art, the Albany Museum, started in 1964, is dedicated to serving the people of the region by providing exposure to the visual arts through a focused collection, diversified programs and other activities. PLEASE NOTE: The museum will reopen after renovations on November 12, 1998. **NOT TO BE MISSED:** A 1500 piece collection of African art that includes works from 18 different cultures.

ON EXHIBIT 1999

11/12/1998 to 05/16/1999   SOUTHERN EXPOSURE: SPORTING SCENES BY AIDEN LASSELL RIPLEY

06/24/1998 to 08/01/1999   WITNESS TO OUR CENTURY: AN ARTISTIC BIOGRAPHY OF FRITZ EICHENBERG
Previously unexhibited works from the artist's personal collection are shown here. They include poignant images published in "The Catholic Worker", childhood caricatures from 1912, advertising posters from 1920, and political cartoons from the 20s and 30s published in Berlin and New York.

11/12/1998 to 11/14/1999   THIS WORLD AND THE NEXT: AFRICAN ART AND THE SCULPTURE OF WILLIAM EDMONDSON
Six of this African-American sculptor's work will be displayed among the Museum's collection of sub-Saharan African Art. In doing so, a bridge will be built between the cultural creative basis and beliefs shared by differing peoples exploring the intersections and modes of inspiration, spirituality and creativity.

11/12/1998 to 12/31/1999   THE MAGIC OF A FACE: HIGHLIGHTS FROM THE PERMANENT COLLECTION
On the occasion of the Museum's face-lift, the exhibition will introduce viewers to the many ways in which artists can capture a sitter's likeness.

01/12/1999 to 03/21/1999   JACOB LAWRENCE: THE FREDERICK DOUGLAS AND HARRIET TUBMAN SERIES
The artistic, cultural and historical significance of these narrative works about the struggle against slavery during the Civil War are explored in 63 paintings.

Georgia Museum of Art

Affiliate Institution: The University of Georgia
90 Carlton St., Athens, GA 30602-1719
☎: 706-542-4662   ■ www.budgets.uga.edu/gma
Open: 10-5 Tu-Th & A, 10-9 Fr, 1-5 Su   **Closed:** Mo, LEG/HOL!
Sugg/Cont$1.00
& Ⓟ   **Museum Shop**   ⅋ On Display Café open 10-2:30 M-F   **Group Tours**   **Drop-In Tours**: by appt.
Permanent Collection: AM: sculp, gr; EU: gr; JAP: gr; IT/REN: ptgs (Kress Collection); AM: ptgs 19-20

The Georgia Museum of art, which moved to a new facility on Carlton St., on the east campus of the University of Georgia in September of '96, has grown from its modest beginnings, in 1945, of a 100 piece collection donated by Alfred Holbrook, to more than 7,000 works now included in its permanent holdings. PLEASE NOTE: Public tours are often offered on Sundays (call for information). **NOT TO BE MISSED:** American paintings from the permanent collection on view continually in the C.L. Moorhead Jr. Wing.

GEORGIA

Georgia Museum of Art - continued

ON EXHIBIT 1999

07/01/1998 to 06/01/1999 50TH ANNIVERSARY GALA: ART MUSEUM/ART DEPARTMENT

11/07/1998 to 01/10/1999 REMBRANDT: TREASURES FROM THE REMBRANDT HOUSE, AMSTERDAM

01/15/1999 to 03/14/1999 BEFORE 1948: MASTERPIECES OF AMERICAN PAINTING FROM GEORGIA COLLECTIONS

01/16/1999 to 03/21/1999 WITH THESE HANDS

01/30/1999 to 03/28/1999 HERITAGE OF THE BRUSH "THE ROY AND MARILYN PAPP COLLECTION OF CHINESE PAINTING"

ATLANTA

Hammonds House Galleries and Resource Center

503 Peoples St., Atlanta, GA 31310-1815
☎: 404-752-8730
Open: 10-6 Tu-Fr; 1-5 A, Su   **Closed:** Mo, LEG/HOL!
ADM   Adult: $2.00   **Children:** $1.00   **Students:** $1.00   **Seniors:** $1.00
  Ⓟ **Museum Shop   Group Tours   Drop-In Tours**: Upon request
Historic Building 1857 East Lake Victorian House restored in 1984 by Dr. Otis T. Hammonds
Permanent Collection: AF/AM: mid 19-20; HAITIAN: ptgs; AF: sculp

As the only fine art museum in the Southeast dedicated to the promotion of art by peoples of African descent, Hammonds House features changing exhibitions of nationally known African-American artists. Works by Romare Bearden, Sam Gilliam, Benny Andrews, James Van Der Zee and others are included in the 125 piece collection. **NOT TO BE MISSED:** Romare Bearden Collection of post 60's serigraphs; Collection of Premier Contemporary Haitian Artists

High Museum of Art

1280 Peachtree St., N.E., Atlanta, GA 30309
☎: 404-733-HIGH
Open: 10-5 Tu-A, Noon-5 Su, till 9 pm 4th Fr of the month   **Closed:** Mo, 1/1, THGV, 12/25
ADM   Adult: $6.00   **Children:** $2.00 6-17;F under 6   **Students:** $4.00   **Seniors:** $4.00
  Ⓟ **Museum Shop**   ‖: Y
Group Tours: 404-733-4550   **Drop-In Tours**: ! by appt   **Historic Building** Designed by Richard Meier, 1983
Permanent Collection: AM: dec/art 18-20; EU: cer 18; AM: ptgs, sculp 19; EU: ptgs, sculp, cer, gr, REN- 20; PHOT 19-20; AM; cont (since 1970); self taught and folk

The beauty of the building, designed in 1987 by architect Richard Meier, is a perfect foil for the outstanding collection of art within the walls of the High Museum of Art itself. Part of the Robert W. Woofruff Art Center, this museum is a "must see" for every art lover who visits Atlanta. PLEASE NOTE: Admission entry fees vary according to the exhibitions being presented. **NOT TO BE MISSED:** The Virginia Carroll Crawford Collection of American Decorative Arts; The Frances and Emory Cocke Collection of English Ceramics: T. Marshall Hahn collection of Folk Art

ON EXHIBIT 1999

10/24/1998 to 01/17/1999 POP ART: SELECTIONS FROM THE MUSEUM OF MODERN ART
The exhibition focuses on the 1960's, the defining decade for this movement and features Roy Lichtenstein, Claes Oldenburg, James Rosenquist and Andy Warhol among others. It includes many rarely seen works. *Catalog Admission Fee Will Travel*

High Museum of Art - continued

02/26/1999 to 05/21/1999   JOHN HENRY TWACHTMAN: AN AMERICAN IMPRESSIONIST
The first retrospective in more than 30 years featuring over 50 oils and pastels covering four periods of the artist's production-Early Works, European Period, Connecticut Years, and Gloucester, late Period. *Catalog Admission Fee Will Travel*

02/27/1999 to 05/16/1999   IMPRESSIONISM: PAINTINGS COLLECTED BY EUROPEAN MUSEUMS
An overview of the movement offering insight into acceptance by European dealers, museums and collectors. They turned it from objects of scandal to highly prized masterworks. Included are works by Gauguin, Manet, Sisley, Monet, Morisot, Pissarro, Renoir and Van Gogh. *Catalog Will Travel*

06/12/1999 to 08/15/1999   ELLSWORTH KELLEY: THE EARLY DRAWINGS, 1948-1955
Bold colors, geometric tensions, contradictions and the principles of chance govern the creations of Kelly, a major contributor to the development of American Abstract art. 222 works on paper from 1948-1955 are featured here and many come from the artist and private collections which predate his first critical acclaim in the solo exhibition in 1956. *Catalog Will Travel*

06/12/1999 to 09/26/1999   ART AND ENTERPRISE: THE VIRGINIA CARROLL CRAWFORD COLLECTION OF AMERICAN DECORATIVE ARTS, 1825-1917
This exceptional collection is recognized as one of the leading public collections of its kind in the US. *Catalog Will Travel*

High Museum of Folk Art & Photography Galleries at Georgia-Pacific Center

133 Peachtree Street, Atlanta, GA 30303
☎: 404-577-6940   ▣ www.high.org
Open: 10-5 Mo-A   **Closed:** Su, LEG/HOL!
& ℗ **Museum Shop**
Group Tours: 404-733-4550
Drop-In Tours: call 404-733-4468
Permanent Collection: Occasional exhibits along with traveling exhibitions are drawn from permanent collection.

Folk art and photography are the main focus in the 4,5000 square foot exhibition space of this Atlanta facility located in the Georgia-Pacific Center.

ON EXHIBIT 1999

10/03/1998 to 02/27/1999   COLLECTING FOLK ART AT THE HIGH: RECENT ACQUISITIONS IN SOUTHERN DECORATIVE ART
The examples shown in this part of the collection include mostly 19th c works including brightly colored painted furniture and Germanic pottery and African American pottery and baskets.

10/09/1998 to 01/02/1999   COLLECTING FOLK ART AT THE HIGH: THE LAST 40 YEARS OF COLLECTING
Included in the wide spectrum of American Folk Art are portraits, furniture, ceramics, basketry and textiles, as well as contemporary paintings, works on paper and sculpture. Also included will be works by major folk artists not currently in the High's collection

03/06/1999 to 05/29/1999   TED GORDON
Known for his compulsive style and singular theme of the human face in infinite variety, Gordon began drawing his compulsive "doodles". Later works include fishes, birds, cats, flowers, mandalas, and designs. He uses felt markers, colored pencils, and pens on pieces of cardboard, fabric, back of posters and paper.

05/16/1999 to 07/31/1999   "I MADE THIS JAR..." THE LIFE AND WORKS OF THE ENSLAVED AFRICAN-AMERICAN POTTER, DAVE
Pots turned out by Dave and a few other potters during the antebellum period . It shows his work in the context of religious, political and cultural climate of the period, 1810-1870.

GEORGIA

Michael C. Carlos Museum

Affiliate Institution: Emory University
571 South Kilgo St., Atlanta, GA 30322
☎: 404-727-4282 ◉ www.cc.emory.edu/CARLOS/carlos.html
Open: 10-5 Mo-A, Noon-5 Su **Closed:** 1/1, THGV, 12/25
Sugg/Cont Adult: $3.00
& ℗ **Museum Shop** ‖ Caffé Antico
Group Tours: 404-727-0519 **Drop-In Tours:** 2:30 A, Su
Historic Building
Permanent Collection: AN/EGT; AN/GRK; AN/R; P/COL; AS; AF; OC; WORKS ON PAPER 14-20

Founded on the campus of Emory University in 1919 (making it the oldest art museum in Atlanta), this distinguished institution changed its name in 1991 to the Michael C. Carlos Museum in honor of its long time benefactor. Its dramatic 35,000 square foot building, opened in the spring of 1993, is a masterful addition to the original Beaux-Arts edifice. The museum recently acquired one of the largest (1,000 pieces) collections of Sub-Saharan African art in America. **NOT TO BE MISSED:** Carlos Collection of Ancient Greek Art; Thibadeau Collection of pre-Columbian Art; recent acquisition of rare 4th c Volute-Krater by the Underworld painter of Apulia

ON EXHIBIT 1999

10/31/1998 to 01/10/1999 SHAMANS, GODS AND MYTHIC BEASTS: COLUMBIAN GOLD AND CERAMICS IN ANTIQUITY
Presented for the first time to the American public new finds from the southwest and north coastal regions of Columbia focus on the important ceramic sculpture of ancient Columbia, the fabled land of gold "El Dorado" and the artistic qualities and themes found there. Also included are 44 exceptional gold masterpieces that share design motifs found in the ceramic figure. *Catalog Will Travel*

05/08/1999 to 07/11/1999 MASTER DRAWINGS FROM THE WORCESTER ART MUSEUM
More than 100 works including watercolors, pastels and illuminated manuscripts by European and American artists from 1275 to 1975 representing major trends of style and content. *Catalog Will Travel*

Ogelthorpe University Museum

Affiliate Institution: Ogelthorpe University
4484 Peachtree Road, NE, Atlanta, GA 30319
☎: 404-364-8555 ◉ www.oglethorpe.edu
Open: 12-5 Tu-Fr, till 7 PM Th **Closed:** Mo, LEG/HOL!
& ℗ **Museum Shop**
Group Tours: 404-364-8552 **Drop-In Tours:** Upon request if available
Permanent Collection: Realistic figurative art, historical, metaphysical and international art

Established just recently, this museum, dedicated to showing realistic art, has already instituted many "firsts" for this area including the opening of each new exhibition with a free public lecture, the creation of an artist-in-residence program, and a regular series of chamber music concerts. In addition, the museum is devoted to creating and sponsoring its own series of original and innovative special exhibitions instead of relying on traveling exhibitions from other sources. **NOT TO BE MISSED:** 14th century Kamakura Buddha from Japan; "The Three Ages of Man" by Giorgione (on extended loan); 18th century engravings illustrating Shakespeare's plays

Morris Museum of Art
One 10th Street, Augusta, GA 30901-1134

📞: 706-724-7501   ◼ www.themorris.org
Open: 10-5:30 Tu-A, 12:30-5:30 Su   **Closed:** Mo, 1/1, THGV, 12/25
ADM   Adult: $3.00   **Children:** F (under 6)   **Students:** $2.00   **Seniors:** $2.00
🚹 ℗   **Museum Shop   Group Tours**: 706-828-3892   **Drop-In Tours**
Permanent Collection: REG: portraiture (antebellum to contemporary), still lifes, Impr, cont; AF/AM

Rich Southern architecture and decorative appointments installed in a contemporary office building present a delightful surprise to the first time visitor. Included in this setting are masterworks from antebellum portraiture to vivid contemporary creations that represent a broad-based survey of 250 years of panting in the South. **NOT TO BE MISSED:** The Southern Landscape Gallery

ON EXHIBIT 1999

12/03/1998 to 01/17/1999   HAUNTER OF RUINS: THE PHOTOGRAPHY OF CLARENCE JOHN LAUGHLIN
65 of Laughlin's photographs of the decaying monuments and Southern landscape images that made him famous, will be on exhibit with a selection of his writings and letters from the archives of The Historic New Orleans Collection.

02/18/1999 to 05/02/1999   FINE EYE, FINE ART: REALISM IN CURRENT DUTCH PAINTING
Seven contemporary Dutch artists who work in the clearest sharpest tradition of realistic representation.

02/18/1999 to 05/09/1999   WOLF KAHN
A painting commissioned by the Morris Museum of Art forms the centerpiece of a show spotlighting pastel sketches and large works done in the South by this noted American landscape artist and colorist.

02/18/1999 to 05/09/1999   ROBERT GWATHMEY, 1903-88
Approximately 60 paintings and graphics surveying the life and career of this noted social realist. There is special emphasis on images of African-American life and the Southern Scene. *Catalog Will Travel*

05/20/1999 to 08/22/1999   ROBERT STACKHOUSE: THEN AND NOW
A noted sculptor, painter and teacher, Stackhouse is usually associated with New York although he has strong ties to the south.

08/20/1999 to 10/31/1999   FREEMAN AND CORA SCHOOLCRAFT: A TRIBUTE
Selected works highlight the careers of these artists who died in 1997.

09/09/1999 to 11/07/1999   THE CHARLESTON RENAISSANCE
During the first half of the 20th C the city of Charleston became the subject of a cultural renewal. Works by Alfred Hutty, Elizabeth O'Neill Verner and Alice Ravenal Huger Smith attracted Child Hassam, Edward Hopper and George Biddle to the city. These 50 works of art were produced then. *Catalog Will Travel*

11/18/1999 to 01/30/2000   SUBDUED HUES: LANDSCAPE PAINTING IN THE SOUTH 1865-1925
Southern expression of the totalist style inspired by the Barbizon School. Included are works by Brenner, Dangerfield, Inness, Jefferson, Meeker and Tanner.

Columbus Museum
1251 Wynnton Rd., Columbus, GA 31906

📞: 706-649-0713
Open: 10-5 Tu-A, 1-5 Su   **Closed:** Mo, LEG/HOL!
🚹 ℗   **Museum Shop**   🍽 11:30-2 Tu-F   **Group Tours   Drop-In Tours**: 3:00 Su
Permanent Collection: PTGS; SCULP; GR 19-20; DEC/ART; REG; FOLK

The Columbus Museum is unique in the Southeast for its dual presentation of American art and regional history. The Museum features changing art exhibitions and two permanent galleries, Chattahoochee Legacy (the history of the Chattahoochee Valley) and Transformations (a hands-on children's discovery gallery). **NOT TO BE MISSED:** "Fergus, Boy in Blue" by Robert Henri; A hands-on discovery gallery for children.

GEORGIA

Columbus Museum - continued

ON EXHIBIT 1999

Fall 1999/ FROM EARTH AND FIRE: AMERICAN ART POTTERY AND ART GLASS FROM THE CHRYSLER MUSEUM

05/10/1998 to 05/31/1999   LOCK, STOCK AND BARREL: HISTORICAL FIREARMS FROM THE C. DEXTER JORDAN, SR. COLLECTION
Drawn from the Museum's array of weapons, this is an amazingly diverse selection ranging from 17th c. cannons to a World War ll machine gun.

10/18/1998 to 01/10/1999   ROBERT GWATHMEY: WORKS FROM THE SOUTHERN COLLECTIONS
A small exhibition focusing on this 20th c. 'American Scene' realist

01/10/1999 to 03/07/1999   LARGE DRAWINGS FROM THE ARKANSAS ARTS CENTER FOUNDATION COLLECTION
Contemporary work by artists who prefer to work in a very large format. Drawings are often the most immediate expression of an artist's inspiration and have a freshness that does not translate as well to paintings, prints and sculpture. *Will Travel*

02/08/1999 to 04/25/1999   IMPRESSIONS IN PRINT: ETCHINGS AND LITHOGRAPHS BY CHILDE HASSAM

03/28/1999 to 06/20/1999   A ROOM WITH A VIEW: THE ART OF DANIEL GARBER AND RICHARD MILLER
These two second generation American Impressionists will be the focus of this exhibition.

04/18/1999 to 07/11/1999   AMERICAN IMPRESSIONISM FROM THE SHELDON MEMORIAL ART GALLERY
Significant figures in this movement are Hassam, Weir, Glackens, Metcalf. Artists working in parallel styles such as Pene du Bois and Melchers are all represented here, as well.

05/23/1999 to 08/25/1999   LASTING IMPRESSIONS: NEW ACQUISITIONS IN THE GRAPHIC ARTS (working title)

06/1999 to 06/2000   AFTER THE TRAIL OF TEARS: OBJECTS FROM THE YUCHI COLLECTION

07/25/1999 to 09/26/1999   JURIED EXHIBITION OF LOCAL ARTISTS

10/17/1999 to 01/09/2000   ALMA THOMAS: A RETROSPECTIVE OF THE PAINTINGS
Spanning the artistic career of DC based Thomas (1891-1978), this exhibition of 60 paintings and studies ranges from examples of her early representational works of the 50's, through the development of her signature vibrant mosaic-like abstractions.

10/31/1999 to 01/23/2000   THE FINE ARTS IN ANTEBELLUM SOUTH
The artistic environment available to citizens of Columbus, 1828-1860 will be surveyed including paintings, prints, panoramas, sculpture and architectural decoration.

SAVANNAH

Telfair Museum of Art
121 Barnard St., Savannah, GA 31401
☎: 912-232-1177
Open: 12-5 M, 10-5 Tu-A, 1-5 Su   **Closed:** Mo, LEG/HOL!
Free Day: Su   **ADM   Adult:** $6.00   **Children:** $1.00 (6-12)   **Students:** $2.00   **Seniors:** $5.00
 ⅏ ℙ **Museum Shop   Group Tours   Drop-In Tours:** 2 PM daily
Historic Building 1819 Regency Mansion designed by William Jay (National Historic Landmark)
Permanent Collection: AM: Impr & Ashcan ptgs; AM: dec/art; BRIT: dec/art; FR: dec/art

Named for its founding family, and housed in a Regency mansion designed in 1818 by architect William Jay, this museum features traveling exhibitions from all over the world. The Telfair, which is the oldest public art museum in the Southeast, also has major works by many of the artists who have contributed so brilliantly to the history of American art. The Telfair will break ground in late 1999 for a new building on Telfair Square.
NOT TO BE MISSED: American Impressionist collection; Original Duncan Phyfe furniture; casts of the Elgin Marbles

Telfair Museum of Art - continued

ON EXHIBIT 1999

11/17/1998 to 01/14/1999   MASTERS OF THE WALKING STICK: FOUR SAVANNAH CARVERS

03/1999   DECORATIVE ARTS AND RECENT ACQUISITIONS FROM THE TELFAIR MUSEUM OF ART COLLECTION

04/10/1999 to 06/06/1999   INTERACTION OF CULTURES: INDIAN AND WESTERN PAINTING (1710-1910) FROM THE EHRENFELD COLLECTION
This exhibition highlights the art created in India by Indian and Western artists between 1780 and 1910.The 95 works, primarily paintings on canvas have been drawn from this outstanding private collections. It will be the first exhibit in North America to consider the artistic interaction between these two cultures. *Catalog Will Travel*

06/22/1999 to 08/29/1999   CELEBRATING THE CREATIVE SPIRIT: CONTEMPORARY SOUTHEASTERN FURNITURE *Will Travel*

09/14/1999 to 11/07/1999   HOLOCAUST COLLAGES BY IRWIN KREMEN

09/14/1999 to 11/28/1999   CRAFTING A JEWISH STYLE: THE ART OF THE BEZALEL ACADEMY, 1906-1996 *Will Travel*

12/07/1999 to 03/2000   VOJTECH BLAU TAPESTRIES

HAWAII

Contemporary Museum
2411 Makiki Heights Drive, Honolulu, HI 96822
☎: 808-526-1322   ◙ www.tcmhi.org
Open: 10-4 Tu-A, Noon-4 Su   **Closed:** Mo, LEG/HOL
ADM   Adult: $5.00   **Children:** F (under 12)   **Students:** $3.00   **Seniors:** $3.00
  ॐ   ℗   **Museum Shop**   ⁂ Café   **Group Tours   Drop-In Tours:** 1:30 Tu-Su   **Sculpture Garden**
Permanent Collection: AM: cont; REG

Terraced gardens with stone benches overlooking exquisite vistas compliment this museum's structure which is situated in a perfect hillside setting. Inside are modernized galleries in which the permanent collection of art since 1940 is displayed. PLEASE NOTE: The museum's other gallery location where exhibitions are presented is: The Contemporary Museum at First Hawaiian Center, 999 Bishop St., Honolulu, HI 96813 (open 8:30-3 Mo-Th, 8:30-6 Fr), which mainly features works by artists of Hawaii. **NOT TO BE MISSED:** David Hockney's permanent environmental installation "L'Enfant et les Sortileges" built for a Ravel opera stage set.

Honolulu Academy of Arts
900 S. Beretania St., Honolulu, HI 96814-1495
☎: 808-532-8700   ◙ www.honoluluacademy.org
Open: 10-4:30 Tu-A, 1-5 Su   **Closed:** Mo, LEG/HOL!
Vol/Cont   Adult: $5.00   **Children:** F (under 12)   **Students:** $3.00   **Seniors:** $3.00
  ॐ   ℗   **Museum Shop**   ⁂ 11:30-2:00 Tu-A; (808-532-8734)
Group Tours: 808-532-8726   **Drop-In Tours:** 11:00 & 1 Tu-A; 1:15 Su
Historic Building 1927 Building Designed By Bertram G. Goodhue Assoc.   **Sculpture Garden**
Permanent Collection: OR: all media; AM: all media; EU: all media; HAWAIIANA COLLECTION

Thirty galleries grouped around a series of garden courts form the basis of Hawaii's only general art museum. This internationally respected institution, 70 years old in '97, features extensive notable collections that span the history of art and come from nearly every corner of the world. PLEASE NOTE: Exhibitions may be seen in the main museum and in the Museum's Academy Art Center, 1111 Victoria St. (808-532-8741). **NOT TO BE MISSED:** James A. Michener collection of Japanese Ukiyo-e Woodblock prints; Kress Collection of Italian Renaissance Paintings

ON EXHIBIT 1999
08/06/1998 to 01/17/1999   HAWAII AND ITS PEOPLE
The first of several parts of this presentation of Hawaii's finest artists.

09/24/1998 to 01/17/1999   ART OF THE GOLDSMITH: MASTERWORKS FROM BUCCELLATI
Some of the finest pieces from the Buccellati private collection dating from the mid-18th c. to today

02/25/1999 to 05/07/1999   ART AND LIFE IN COLONIAL AMERICA

03/11/1999 to 05/02/1999   FRUITS AND FLOWERS: BOTANICAL PAINTINGS BY GERALDINE KING TAM

05/11/1999 to 07/11/1999   JUNE SCHWARTZ: FORTY YEARS/FORTY PIECES
Works by enamelist Schwartz will be on exhibit.

07/20/1999 to 01/16/2000   HAWAII AND ITS PEOPLE
With the finest collection of paintings, works on paper, and decorative arts, several exhibitions will be devoted to presentation of selected works from this collection.

07/22/1999 to 08/22/1999   ARTISTS OF HAWAII 1999

09/16/1999 to 11/07/1999   INTERACTION OF CULTURES: INDIAN AND WESTERN PAINTING (1710-1910) FROM THE EHRENFELD COLLECTION
This exhibition highlights the art created in India by Indian and Western artists between 1780 and 1910. The 95 works, primarily paintings on canvas have been drawn from this outstanding private collections. It will be the first exhibit in North America to consider the artistic interaction between these two cultures. *Catalog Will Travel*

Boise Art Museum

670 S. Julia Davis Dr., Boise, ID 83702
☎: 208-345-8330   ◉ ♪◉ www.boisiartmuseum.org
Open: 10-5 Tu-Fr; Noon-5 A, Su; Open 10-5 M JUNE & AUG   **Closed:** Mo, LEG/HOL!
ADM   Adult: $3.00   **Children:** $1.00 (grades 1-12)   **Students:** $2.00   **Seniors:** $2.00
&   ℗   **Museum Shop**
Group Tours   Drop-In Tours: 12:15 Tu, 1:00 A
Permanent Collection: REG; GR; OR; AM: (Janss Collection of American Realism)

Home of the famed Glenn C. Janss Collection of American Realism, the Boise Art Museum, in its parkland setting, is considered the finest art museum in the state of Idaho. New Permanent Collection galleries and an atrium sculpture court have recently been added to the museum. **NOT TO BE MISSED:** "Art in the Park", held every September, is one of the largest art and crafts festivals in the region.

ON EXHIBIT 1999

11/27/1998 to 02/21/1999   STEPHANIE WILDE
Poetic art that explores a broad emotional range of the human condition including illness, AIDS, and social injustice.

12/05/1998 to 01/31/1999   MOUNTAIN MAJESTY: THE ART OF JOHN FERY
Born in Austria in 1859, Fery was one of the many artists drawn to the rugged splendor of America's Rocky Mountains. For four decades he devoted his life and artistic talent to grand mountain vistas. *Will Travel*

02/13/1999 to 04/25/1999   TRASHFORMATIONS: RECYCLED MATERIALS IN CONTEMPORARY AMERICAN ART AND DESIGN
Works in various media featuring the varied and inventive use of recycled materials in American art and design. *Will Travel*

05/08/1999 to 05/23/1999   PRIMARY COLORS
Featured will be a collaborative exhibition between Gallery 825/LA Art Association, Watts Towers Art Center, and SITE, all non-profit arts organizations.

05/22/1999 to 08/15/1999   ORIGINAL NATURE: THE ART OF BRAD RUDE
A multi-media artist who creates pastels, paintings, and bronze sculptures combining images and forms of animals and objects, stacked in a teetering balance.

12/04/1999 to 02/13/2000   JACK DOLLHAUSEN: DATE FOR A MILLENNIUM
Electrical and computer technology creates lively sculptures that engage the viewer through light, sound, and sensory perception. *Will Travel*

ILLINOIS

CARBONDALE

University Museum
Affiliate Institution: Southern Illinois University at Carbondale
Carbondale, IL 62901-4508
📞: 618-453-7409   📧 www.museum@siu.edu
Open: 9-3 Tu-A, 1:30-4:30 Su   **Closed:** Mo, ACAD & LEG/HOL!
⅋ ℗ **Museum Shop   Group Tours:** 618-453-5388   **Drop-In Tours:** upon request if available
Sculpture Garden
Permanent Collection: AM: ptgs, drgs, gr; EU: ptgs, drgs, gr, 13-20; PHOT 20; SCULP 20; CER; OC; DEC/ART

Continually rotating exhibitions feature the fine and decorative arts as well as those based on science related themes of anthropology, geology, natural history, and archaeology. **NOT TO BE MISSED:** In the sculpture garden, two works by Ernert Trova, "AV-A-7 and AV-YELLOW LOZENGER", and a sculpture entitled "Starwalk" by Richard Hunt.

ON EXHIBIT 1999

01/19/1999 to 03/12/1999   TOM WALSH SCULPTURE RETROSPECTIVE

01/19/1999 to 03/12/1999   COMBINED FACULTY EXHIBITION

01/24/1999 to 03/12/1999   PEOPLE'S CHOICE EXHIBITION

03/23/1999 to 04/25/1999   RICKERT/ZIEBOLD TRUST AWARDS EXHIBIT

03/23/1999 to 05/15/1999   CLAY CUP EXHIBIT

03/28/1999 to 05/15/1999   ILLINOIS OZARK CRAFT GUILD EXHIBIT

06/15/1999 to 08/07/1999   MFA EXHIBITS

08/1999 to 10/1999   CEDRIC CHATTERLEY PHOTOGRAPHS

08/1999 to 10/1999   RICHARD MAWDSLEY - SILVER AND GOLDSMITH

08/1999 to 10/1999   MIDWEST PHOTO X EXHIBITION

11/02/1999 to 12/11/1999   CHUCK SWEDLUND - PHOTO RETROSPECTIVE

CHAMPAIGN

Krannert Art Museum
Affiliate Institution: University of Illinois
500 E. Peabody Dr., Champaign, IL 61820
📞: 217-333-1860   📧 www.art.uiuc.edu/kam/
Open: 9-5 Tu-Fr, till 8pm We (SEPT-MAY), 10-5 A, 2-5 Su   **Closed:** Mo, LEG/HOL!
Vol/Cont
⅋ ℗ **Museum Shop** 🍴 Café/bookstore
Group Tours: 217-333-8642 Dorothy Fuller, Ed. Coord.   **Drop-In Tours:** !
Permanent Collection: P/COL; AM: ptgs; DEC/ART; OR; GR; PHOT; EU: ptgs; AS; AF; P/COL; ANT

Located on the campus of the University of Illinois, Krannert Art Museum is the second largest public art museum in the state. Among its 8,000, works ranging in date from the 4th millennium B.C. to the present, is the highly acclaimed Krannert collection of Old Master paintings. **NOT TO BE MISSED:** "Christ After the Flagellation" by Murillo; "Portrait of Cornelius Guldewagen, Mayor of Haarlem" by Frans Hals; Reinstalled Gallery of Asian Art

Art Institute of Chicago

111 So. Michigan Ave., Chicago, IL 60603-6110
☎: 312-443-3600   ◉ www.artic.edu
Open: 10:30-4:30 Mo, We-Fr; 10:30-8 Tu; 10-5 A; Noon-5 Su   **Closed:** 12/25, THGV
Sugg/Cont   Adult: $8.00   **Children:** $5.00   **Students:** $5.00   **Seniors:** $5.00
&   ℗   **Museum Shop**   ‖ Cafeteria & The Restaurant on the Park
Group Tours: 312-443-3933   **Drop-In Tours**: !   **Historic Building   Sculpture Garden**
Permanent Collection: AM: all media; EU: all media; CH; Korean; JAP; IND; EU: MED; AF; PHOT; architecture + textiles;
South American

Spend "Sunday in the park with George" while standing before Seurat's "Sunday on La Grande Jatte - 1884," or any of the other magnificent examples of the school of French Impressionism, just one of the many superb collections housed in this world-class museum. Renowned for its collection of post-World War II art, the museum also features the Galleries of Contemporary Art, featuring 50 of the strongest works of American and European art (1950's-1980). **NOT TO BE MISSED:** "American Gothic" by Grant Wood; "Paris Street; Rainy Day" by Gustave Caillebotte

ON EXHIBIT 1999

09/19/1998 to 01/10/1999   JULIA MARGARET CAMERON'S WOMEN
Cameron photographed many prominent figures of Victorian intellectual society in the 1860's and 70s. Her remarkable portraits of women constitute the bulk of her work. Her methods were unconventional for her time because they sought the "inner spirit" of the sitter. *Catalog Will Travel*

10/13/1998 to 01/10/1999   MARY CASSATT: MODERN WOMAN
Some 125 of Cassatt's most beautiful and compelling portraits, pastels, drawings and prints, are brought together here to place her at the heart of one of the most important Artistic movements in Western History and at the forefront of emerging modernism. *Catalog Will Travel*

10/17/1998 to 01/03/1999   JAPAN 2000: KISHO KUROKAWA
The finale of the Art Institutes " Japan 2000" celebration examines the work of one of Japans most distinguished architects and his influence on Japanese design. *Will Travel*

12/19/1998 to 03/14/1999   MASTERPIECES FROM CENTRAL AFRICA: SELECTIONS FROM THE BELGIAN ROYAL MUSEUM FOR CENTRAL AFRICA, TERVUREN
125 of the finest objects in this extraordinary collection are being brought to the US, many for the first time. The works range from awesome to sublime and include figures, masks, seats, neckrests, staffs, bowls, cups, etc, in metal, wood,, ivory and mixed media. *Will Travel*

02/13/1999 to 04/25/1999   GUSTAVE MOREAU
This major exhibition celebrating the 100th anniversary of his death will feature works from every phase of this French Symbolist painter's career. Much admired during his time, he had a profound influence on the work of Magritte and Matisse among others. *Catalog Will Travel*

05/1999 to 09/1999   THE PRITZKER ARCHITECTURE PRIZE: 1979-1999
Established in 1979, this price annually recognizes a living architect whose built work has made a commitment to the environment and to humanity. On view will be original works by some of the winners representing some of the finest examples of contemporary architecture throughout the world.

06/05/1999 to 09/06/1999   LAND OF THE WINGED HORSEMEN: ART IN POLAND, 1571-1764
In the first major display in America of works in all media from Poland during the 16th-18th c. Paintings, ceramics, glass, furniture, weaponry, metalworks, and textiles including a captured Turkish tent) will be shown. *Catalog Will Travel*

09/11/1999 to 12/05/1999   ELLSWORTH KELLEY: THE EARLY DRAWINGS, 1948-1955
Bold colors, geometric tensions, contradictions and the principles of chance govern the creations of Kelly, a major contributor to the development of American Abstract art. 222 works on paper from 1948-1955 are featured here and many come from the artist and private collections which predate his first critical acclaim in the solo exhibition in 1956. *Catalog Will Travel*

ILLINOIS

Art Institute of Chicago - continued

09/30/1999 to 01/09/2000   IKAT: SPLENDID SILKS FROM CENTRAL ASIA
Examples of Ikat textiles, created by a method of weaving in which warp threads are tie-dyed before being set up on a loom, will be on loan from one of the most significant private collections of its kind. Traditionally woven and used by nomadic Uzbek peoples, the manufacture of these textiles has influenced contemporary fashion designer Oscar de la Renta, textile manufacturer Brunschwig et Fils and others. *Catalog Will Travel*

10/16/1999 to 01/16/2000   BILL VIOLA
More than a dozen major highly theatrical installations from the 1970's to the present are included in this exhibition of works by video art pioneer Viola. Considered one of the most important and influential figures in contemporary art, Viola's emotional, powerful and visually challenging images stem from his ongoing fascination with digital computer and other modern-day technological advances. *Catalog Will Travel*

Chicago Cultural Center

78 East Washington St., Chicago, IL 60602
☎: 312-744-6630   ▣ www.ci.chi.il.us/Tourism/See/CulturalCenter/
Open: 10-7 Mo-We, 10-9 Th, 10-6 Fr, 10-5 A, 11-5 Su   **Closed:** LEG/HOL!
& **Museum Shop** ‖corner bakery   **Group Tours:** 312-744-8032   **Drop-In Tours:** 2pm Tu-A   **Historic Building**

Located in the renovated 1897 historic landmark building originally built to serve as the city's central library, this vital cultural center, affectionately called the "People's Place", consists of 8 exhibition spaces, two concert halls, two theaters and a dance studio. The facility, which serves as Chicago's architectural showplace for the lively and visual arts, offers guided architectural tours of the building at 2 PM Tu-A

ON EXHIBIT 1999

11/28/1998 to 01/1999   CITIES BY THE LAKE: PHOTOGRAPHS BY MICHELLE KEIM
Lengthy time exposures are used here to produce eerie and atmospheric color photographs at night at steel plants in Gary, Indiana and Chicago

11/28/1998 to 01/1999   DANA GARNER: PAINTINGS
Garner's most recent work is a continuing exploration of her interest in the landscape as metaphor. Her recent series focuses on more elemental qualitites-earth. Fire, water, air.

10/30/1999 to 12/30/1999   INDIA: A CELEBRATION OF INDEPENDENCE, 1947-1997 *Catalog Will Travel*

12/05/1998 to 01/31/1999   URSULA VAN RYDINGSVARD: SCULPTURE AND DRAWINGS
Large scale wood sculpture in highly abstract forms.

David and Alfred Smart Museum of Art

Affiliate Institution: The University of Chicago
5550 S. Greenwood Ave., Chicago, IL 60637
☎: 773-702-0200   ▣ http://smartmuseum@chicago.edu
Open: 10-4 Tu-Fr; Noon-6 A, Su; till 9pm Th   **Closed:** Mo, LEG/HOL!
& Ⓟ **Museum Shop** ‖ Museum Café
Group Tours: 773-702-4540   **Drop-In Tours:** 1:30 Su during special exhibitions   **Sculpture Garden**
Permanent Collection: AN/GRK: Vases (Tarbell Coll); MED/SCULP; O/M: ptgs, sculp (Kress Coll); OM: gr (Epstein Coll); SCULP:20

Among the holdings of the Smart Museum of Art are Medieval sculpture from the French Romanesque church of Cluny III, outstanding Old Master prints by Dürer, Rembrandt, and Delacroix from the Kress Collection, sculpture by such greats as Degas, Matisse, Moore and Rodin, and furniture by Frank Lloyd Wright from the world famous Robie House. **PLEASE NOTE:** The Museum will be closed after April 18, 1999 for remodeling and installation. It will reopen in the fall of 1999.

David and Alfred Smart Museum of Art - continued

ON EXHIBIT 1999

11/04/1998 to 01/10/1999   WEIMAR BODIES: FANTASIES ABOUT THE SEXUALIZED BODY IN WEIMAR ART, SCIENCE, AND MEDICINE

This exhibition addresses the relationship between "high art" images of the sexualized human body and avant-garde German culture and parallel representations of the body in scientific texts and medical illustration. *Will Travel*

11/19/1998 to 01/19/1999   SPACE/SIGHT/SELF

Contemporary portraiture is examined here as sight, space and identity.

02/18/1999 to 04/18/1999   TRANSIENCE: CHINESE ART AT THE END OF THE 20TH CENTURY

An exhibition of contemporary Chinese art since 1990. *Catalog Will Travel*

Martin D'Arcy Gallery of Art

Affiliate Institution: The Loyola Univ. Museum of Medieval, Renaissance and Baroque Art
6525 N. Sheridan Rd., Chicago, IL 60626
☎: 773-508-2679
Open: 12-5 Mo-Fr during the school year; Closed Summers   **Closed:** A, Su, ACAD!, LEG/HOL! & SUMMER
& ℗ **Museum Shop   Group Tours   Drop-In Tours**: often available upon request
Permanent Collection: MED & REN; ptgs, sculp, dec/art

Sometimes called the "Cloisters of the Midwest", The Martin D'Arcy Gallery of Art is the only museum in the Chicago area focusing on Medieval and Renaissance art. Fine examples of Medieval, Renaissance, and Baroque ivories, liturgical vessels, textiles, sculpture, paintings and secular decorative art of these periods are included in the collection. **NOT TO BE MISSED:** A pair of octagonal paintings on verona marble by Bassano; A German Renaissance Collectors Chest by Wenzel Jamitzer; A silver lapis lazuli & ebony tableau of the Flagellation of Christ that once belonged to Queen Christina of Sweden

Mexican Fine Arts Center Museum

1852 W. 19th St., Chicago, IL 60608-2706
☎: 312-738 1503   ■ www.mfacmchicago.org
Open: 10-5 Tu-Su   **Closed:** Mo, LEG/HOL!
& **Museum Shop   Group Tours**: ex 16   **Drop-In Tours**
Permanent Collection: MEX; folk; PHOT; GR; CONT

Mexican art is the central focus of this museum, the first of its kind in the Midwest, and the largest in the nation. Founded in 1982, the center seeks to promote the works of local Mexican artists and acts as a cultural focus for the entire Mexican community residing in Chicago. A new expansion project is underway that will triple the size of the museum. **NOT TO BE MISSED:** Nation's largest Day of the Dead exhibit and 2 annual performing arts festivals. There are many special shows throughout the year. Please call for specific details on solo exhibitions and on "Dia de los Muertos", which are exhibitions held annually from the beginning of October through the end of November.

ON EXHIBIT 1999

01/08/1999 to 04/11/1999   CALENDARIO EXHIBIT

02/05/1999 to 06/06/1999   JEFF MALDONADO

05/07/1999 to 08/29/1999   THE MEXICAN FINE ARTS CENTER MUSEUM'S PERMANENT COLLECTION

ILLINOIS

Mexican Fine Arts Center Museum - continued
05/21/1999 to 08/29/1999 IMAGES OF THE SPIRIT: PHOTOGRAPHS BY GRACIELA ITURBIDE
A first retrospective of a range of Iturbide's work shown in the US, it is comprised of a range of her images of religious and cultural traditions of her native Mexico. *Will Travel*

06/18/1999 to 10/03/1999 YOLLOCALLI YOUTH MUSEUM EXHIBITION

09/24/1999 to 01/15/2000 CAMINO A MICTLAN

09/25/1999 to 12/06/1999 THE 12TH ANNUAL DAY OF THE DEAD

10/08/1999 to 01/15/2000 ESPERANZA GAMA

Museum of Contemporary Art
220 East Chicago Ave., Chicago, IL 60611-2604
☎: 312-280-2660 ▣ www.mcachicago.org
Open: 11-6 Tu, Th, Fr; 11-8 We; 10-6 A, Su **Closed:** Mo, 1,1, THGV, 12/25
Free Day: 1st Tu of month **ADM Adult:** $6.50 **Children:** F (12 & under) **Students:** $4.00 **Seniors:** $4.00
  Ġ ℗ **Museum Shop** ‖ M-Café 11-5 Tu, Th, Fr; 11-8 W; 10-5 Sa, Su
Group Tours: 312-397-3898 **Drop-In Tours:** several times daily!
Historic Building Josef Paul Kleihues building opened July 1996. **Sculpture Garden**
Permanent Collection: CONTINUALLY CHANGING EXHIBITIONS OF CONTEMPORARY ART

Some of the finest and most provocative cutting-edge art by both established and emerging talents may be seen in the new $46.5 million dollar building and sculpture garden, located on a prime 2 acre site overlooking Lake Michigan. Brilliantly designed, the building is the first American project for noted Berlin architect Josef Paul Kleihues. Among its many features is the restaurant on the second floor where visitors can enjoy a spectacular view of the sculpture garden and lakefront while dining on contemporary fusion cuisine. **NOT TO BE MISSED:** An entire room devoted to sculptures by Alexander Calder, overlooks lake Michigan.

ON EXHIBIT 1999
ONGOING JACOB HASHIMOTO: AN INFINITE EXPANSE OF SKY (10,000 KITES)
An installation in the M Café which hang in a cloudlike formation from the ceiling.

04/30/1998 to SPRING 1999 ENVISIONING THE CONTEMPORARY: SELECTIONS FROM THE MCA COLLECTION
The return to the galleries of some of the best loved works in the collection - including 125 works which represent major historical developments in art making from 1945 to the present.

10/10/1998 to 01/03/1999 JANA STERBAK
A major mid career survey of sculptures, installations, photographs and videos by this artist best known for a dress made of flank steak. *Catalog Will Travel*

10/10/1998 to 01/03/1999 ARTIST/AUTHOR: THE BOOK AS ART SINCE 1980
A survey of the entire spectrum of contemporary artists' book production including the fashion world, exhibition catalogs, 'fanzine' assemblies sketchbooks, etc.

10/10/1998 to 03/14/1999 MARIKO MORI
Since the early 1990's Mori has emerged as a most imaginative and intriguing artist working today. Her large, photographs and video installations present fantastic and futuristic scenarios in which she is frequently a star in a masquerade. *Catalog*

10/10/1998 to 05/1999 DAMIEN HIRST, PHARMACEUTIC WALL PAINTING, FIVE BLACKS
Best known for his large sculptures of dead animals in formaldehyde filled vitrines, these are "spot paintings", and consist of 150 arbitrarily colored spots of the same size.

Museum of Contemporary Art - continued

01/16/1999 to 04/11/1999   JIM HODGES

Delicate everyday objects are used such as silver coins, cloth flowers, and fragments from shattered mirrors to evoke memories, longing, nostalgia and loss.

01/16/1999 to 04/18/1999   TRANSMUTE: A COLLECTION EXHIBITION GUEST CURATED BY JOSHUA DECTER

This is the second of four multimedia projects in two parts. One is an exhibition of artworks and also two touch screen computers which act as interactive interpretation of the exhibit.

01/23/1999 to 04/14/1999   RECENT ACQUISITIONS

04/10/1999 to 05/30/1999   KATHARINA FRITSCH

Works by Fritsch, a young German sculptor selected to represent her country in the summer 1995 Venice Bienniale, will be featured in the first solo museum survey of her work.

04/24/1999 to 07/11/1999   SARAH SZE

This site specific work is part of the Projects Series. It is the artists first solo exhibition in the US. She uses found objects like aspirins, plants, lights, electrical appliances, etc.

06/19/1999 to Fall 1999/1999   CHARLES RAY

Included in the first major one person mid-career survey, examples from each significant body of Ray's work will be on exhibit with new work not shown prior to this presentation. *Will Travel*

Fall 1999   ROBERT HEINECKEN

Although thought of as a photographer, he has never used a camera. He is an image scavenger and has been an important influence on a group of artists who create art by manipulating photographic images. *Catalog*

Museum of Contemporary Photography of Columbia College Chicago

600 South Michigan Ave., Chicago, IL 60605-1996

☎: 312-663-5554   ◉ www.gallery-guide.com
Open: 10-5 Mo-We, Fr; 10-8 Th, 12-5 A   **Closed:** Su, LEG/HOL! AUG
Vol/Cont
 ċ ℗ **Museum Shop**
Group Tours   Drop-In Tours: !
Permanent Collection: CONT/PHOT

Contemporary photography, after 1959, by American artists forms the basis of the permanent collection of this college museum facility.

ON EXHIBIT 1999

11/14/1998 to 01/09/1999   ART, DOCUMENT, MARKET, SCIENCE: PHOTOGRAPHY'S MULTIPLE ROLES

01/23/1999 to 03/20/1999   READING THE MEADOW: SOUTHERN STORIES

04/03/1999 to 05/29/1999   EAST OF EDEN

06/12/1999 to 07/31/1999   SOUL IN ACTION

ILLINOIS

Oriental Institute Museum
Affiliate Institution: University of Chicago
1155 E. 58th St., Chicago, IL 60637-1569
☎: 773-702-9520   ◉ www.oi.uchicago.edu/OI/MUS
Open: 10-4 Tu-A, Noon-4 Su, till 8:30pm We   **Closed:** Mo, 1/1, 7/4, THGV, 12/25
  ఉ ℗ **Museum Shop Group Tours:** 773-702-9507 **Drop-In Tours:** 2:30 Su **Historic Building**
Permanent Collection: AN: Mid/East

Hundreds of ancient objects are included in the impressive comprehensive collection of the Oriental Institute. Artifacts from the ancient Near East, dating from earliest times to the birth of Christ, provide the visitor with a detailed glimpse into the ritual ceremonies and daily lives of ancient civilized man. **NOT TO BE MISSED:** Ancient Assyrian 40 ton winged bull; 17' tall statue of King Tut; Colossal Ancient Persian winged bulls. The Egyptian Gallery of the Oriental Institute Museum reopens Dec. 12, 1998 after 2 years of renovation. Other galleries featuring artifacts from other regions will open over the next three years.

Polish Museum of America
984 North Milwaukee Ave., Chicago, IL 60622
☎: 773-384-3352
Open: 11-4 Mo-Su
Sugg/Cont Adult: $2.00 **Children:** $1.00 ఉ ℗ **Museum Shop Group Tours Drop-In Tours**
Permanent Collection: ETH: ptgs, sculp, drgs, gr

The promotion of Polish heritage is the primary goal of this museum founded in 1935. One of the oldest and largest ethnic museums in the U.S., their holdings range from the fine arts to costumes, jewelry, and a broad ranging scholarly library featuring resource information on all areas of Polish life and culture. **NOT TO BE MISSED:** Polonia stained glass by Mieczyslaw Jurgielewicz

Terra Museum of American Art
664 N. Michigan Ave., Chicago, IL 60611
☎: 312-664-3939
Open: 10-7 Tu-A, 12-5 Su **Closed:** Mo, 1/1, 7/4, THGV, 12/25
Sugg/Cont Adult: $5.00 **Children:** F (under 14) **Students:** $1.00 **Seniors:** $2.50
  ఉ **Museum Shop Group Tours Drop-In Tours:** 12:00 weekdays; 12 & 2 weekends
Permanent Collection: AM: 17-20

With over 800 plus examples of some of the finest American art ever created, the Terra, located in the heart of Chicago's "Magnificent Mile", reigns supreme as an important repository of a glorious artistic heritage. **NOT TO BE MISSED:** "Gallery at the Louvre" by Samuel Morse; Maurice Prendergast paintings and monotypes

EDWARDSVILLE

University Museum, Southern Illinois University
Affiliate Institution: So. Illinois Univ. at Edwardsville
Box 1150, Edwardsville, IL 62026-1150
☎: 618-650-2996
Open: 9-3 Tu-Sa, 1:30-4:30 Su **Closed:** Sa, Su, Mo, LEG/HOL
  ఉ ℗ **Museum Shop Group Tours Drop-In Tours Sculpture Garden**
Permanent Collection: DRGS; FOLK; CER; NAT/AM

Works in many media from old masters to young contemporary artists are included in the permanent collection and available on a rotating basis for public viewing. The museum is located in the western part of the state near St. Louis, Missouri. **NOT TO BE MISSED:** Louis Sullivan Architectural Ornament Collection

Mary and Leigh Block Gallery
Affiliate Institution: Northwestern University
1967 South Campus Drive, On the Arts Circle, Evanston, IL 60208-2410
☎: 847-491-4000   ◙ www.nwu..edu/museum
Open: Noon-5 Tu-We, Noon-8pm Th-Su (Gallery closed summer; S/G open year round)
Closed: Mo, LEG/HOL! SUMMER (Gallery only)
ᕷ   **Museum Shop**
Group Tours: 847-491-4852   **Drop-In Tours   Sculpture Garden**
Permanent Collection: EU: gr, drgs 15-19; CONT: gr, phot; architectural drgs (Griffin Collection)

In addition to its collection of works on paper, this fine university museum features an outdoor sculpture garden (open free of charge year round) which includes outstanding examples of 20th-century works by such artistic luminaries as Joan Miro, Barbara Hepworth, Henry Moore, Jean Arp and others. **NOT TO BE MISSED:** The sculpture garden with works by Henry Moore, Jean Arp, Barbara Hepworth, and Jean Miro (to name but a few) is one of the major sculpture collections in the region.

Freeport Arts Center
121 No. Harlem Ave, Freeport, IL 61032
☎: 815-235-9755
Open: 10-6 Tu, 10-5 We-Su   **Closed:** Mo, 1/1, EASTER. 7/4, THGV, 12/25
Free Day: We   **ADM   Adult:** $1.00   **Students:** $0.50   **Seniors:** $0.50
ᕷ   ℗   **Museum Shop**
Group Tours   Drop-In Tours: any time, if scheduled 2 weeks in advance
Permanent Collection: EU: 15-20; AM: 19-20; CONT: ptgs, sculp; P/COL; AN/R; NAT/AM; AN/EGT; AS; AF; OC

The Freeport Arts Center, located in north western Illinois, has six permanent galleries of paintings, sculpture, prints, and ancient artifacts, as well as temporary exhibitions featuring the work of noted regional artists. It houses one of the largest Florentine mosaic collections in the world. **NOT TO BE MISSED:** Especially popular with children of all ages are the museum's classical and the Native American galleries.

ON EXHIBIT 1999

11/22/1998 to 01/10/1999   JUSTICE SHEPRO: TRAVEL PHOTOGRAPHS

11/22/1998 to 01/10/1999   NEW POTS FROM THE RILLING COLLECTION

01/15/1999 to 03/05/1999   TOM LYNCH: WATERCOLORS

01/15/1999 to 03/05/1999   BRUCE BURRIS: MULTI-MEDIA MURALS

04/16/1999 to 06/13/1999   CONTEMPORARY BASKETS

04/16/1999 to 06/13/1999   LYNN BROOKS-KORN
Large abstract paintings on unstretched canvas.

06/18/1999 to 08/08/1999   MICHAEL JOHNSON: A PORTRAIT OF NORTHWEST ILLINOIS

ILLINOIS

Mitchell Museum

Richview Rd., Mount Vernon, IL 62864-0923
📞: 618-242-1236
Open: 10-5 Tu-Sa, 1-5 Su   **Closed:** Mo, LEG/HOL!
Vol/Cont
  🚻   Ⓟ   **Museum Shop   Group Tours   Drop-In Tours   Sculpture Garden**
Permanent Collection: AM: ptgs, sculp (late 19- early 20)

Works from the "Ashcan School", with paintings by Davies, Glackens, Henri, Luks, and Maurice Prendergast, comprise one of the highlights of the Mitchell, a museum, located in south central Illinois, which also features significant holdings of late 19th and early 20th century American art. **NOT TO BE MISSED:** Sculpture park

ON EXHIBIT 1999

11/07/1998 to 01/03/1999   REFLECTIONS OF A JOURNEY: ENGRAVINGS AFTER KARL BODMER
In 1833-34 Prince Maximilian a German Naturalist and explorer and Karl Bodmer, a Swiss Painter and illustrator, made an historic journey up the Missouri River. Works produced by both are considered a primary resource on the rich cultures of the North Plains Indians.

11/07/1998 to 01/03/1999   BARB SAVAN: SCOVILLE'S CAFÉ

12/12/1998 to 01/17/1999   ARTISTS OF THE AMERICAN WEST

01/02/1999 to 02/14/1999   COLLECTORS CLUB: RECENT ACQUISITIONS

02/25/1999 to 10/31/1999   SONJA HOROSHKO: CONTEMPORARY NAVAJO ART

02/27/1999 to 04/11/1999   LISA DESHAN: WOODBLOCK PRINTS

04/17/1999 to 05/09/1999   SIU-C FACULTY PHOTO SHOW

04/17/1999 to 06/13/1999   DIVERSITY: STUDIO ART QUILTS

05/22/1999 to 07/05/1999   25TH ANNIVERSARY INVITATIONAL

06/19/1999 to 08/29/1999   SOUTHERN ILLINOIS ARTISTS OPEN COMPETITION

11/06/1999 to 12/26/1999   WASHINGTON UNIVERSITY ART FACULTY SHOW

Lakeview Museum of Arts and Sciences

1125 West Lake Ave., Peoria, IL 61614
📞: 309-686-7000
Open: 10-5 Tu-Sa, 1-5 Su, till 8pm We   **Closed:** Mo, LEG/HOL!
ADM   Adult: $2.50   **Children:** $1.50   **Students:** $1.50   **Seniors:** $1.50
  🚻   Ⓟ   **Museum Shop   Group Tours   Drop-In Tours   Sculpture Garden**
Permanent Collection: DEC/ART; AM: 19-20; EU:19

A multi-faceted museum that combines the arts and sciences, the Lakeview offers approximately 6 touring exhibitions per year. PLEASE NOTE: Prices of admission may change during special exhibitions! **NOT TO BE MISSED:** Discovery Center and Planetarium, a particular favorite with children.

Quincy Art Center

1515 Jersey St., Quincy, IL 62301
☎: 217-223-5900
Open: 1-4 Tu-Su   **Closed:** Mo, LEG/HOL
Vol/Cont ⅟ Ⓟ   **Museum Shop   Group Tours:** 217-223-6900   **Drop-In Tours:** Often available upon request
Historic Building 1887 building known as the Lorenzo Bull Carriage House
Permanent Collection: PTGS; SCULP; GR

The Quincy Art Center is housed in an 1887 carriage house designed by architect Joseph Silsbee who was a mentor and great inspiration to Frank Lloyd Wright. A modern wing added in 1990 features gallery, studio, and gift shop space. The museum and its historic district, with architecture ranging from Greek Revival to Prairie Style, is located in the middle of the state, not far from the Missouri border. **NOT TO BE MISSED:** The Quincy Art Center, located in an historic district that 'Newsweek' magazine called one of the most architecturally significant corners in the country, is composed of various buildings that run the gamut from Greek Revival to Prairie Style architecture.

ON EXHIBIT 1999

01/15/1999 to 02/26/1999   JAMES BUTLER: TWENTY FIVE YEARS OF PRINTMAKING
Old Master and Modern Prints from The Lutheran Brotherhood Collection of Religious Art.

03/12/1999 to 04/16/1999   RON KOVATCH - A TEN YEAR SURVEY
Metaphorical Animals: Miniature works on paper by Robert Sites

07/09/1999 to 08/13/1999   RECENT (FIGURATIVE) WORK BY RONALD M. COHEN

07/09/1999 to 08/13/1999   RECENT WORK: MARIE DUTKA (PRINTS/PAINTINGS)

08/20/1999 to 09/03/1999   SELECTIONS FROM THE PERMANENT COLLECTION

Augustana College Gallery of Art

7th Ave. & 38th St., Art & Art History Dept., Rock Island, IL 61201-2296
☎: 309-794-7469
Open: Noon-4 Tu-Sa (SEPT-MAY)   **Closed:** Su, Mo, ACAD! & SUMMER
⅟ Ⓟ   **Museum Shop   Group Tours   Drop-In Tours**
Permanent Collection: SWEDISH AM: all media

Swedish American art is the primary focus of this college art gallery.

Rockford Art Museum

711 N. Main St., Rockford, IL 61103
☎: 815-968-2787   ▣   RAM-artmuseum.rockford.org
Open: 11-5 Tu-Fr, 10-5 Sa, 12-5 Su   **Closed:** Mo, LEG/HOL!
Vol/Cont
⅟ Ⓟ   **Museum Shop   Group Tours   Drop-In Tours:** by res   **Sculpture Garden**
Permanent Collection: AM: ptgs, sculp, gr, dec/art 19-20; EU: ptgs, sculp, gr, dec/art 19-20; AM/IMPR; TAOS ART, GILBERT COLL: phot; AF/AM; self-taught; contemporary glass

Rockford Art Museum - continued

With 17,000 square feet of exhibition space, this is one of the largest arts institutions in the state of Illinois. Up to 12 exhibitions are presented annually, as are works from the over 1,200 piece permanent collection of 20th century American art. **NOT TO BE MISSED:** "The Morning Sun" by Pauline Palmer, 1920; ink drawings and watercolors by Reginald Marsh (available for viewing only upon request); plaster casts by Lorado Taft, c. 1900

ON EXHIBIT 1999

12/23/1998 to 03/07/1999 THE "BIG" SHOW: WORKS OF SCALE FROM THE PERMANENT COLLECTION
Regional artists in various media from the permanent collection

02/12/1999 to 04/25/1999 JOSH GARBER
An abstract Canadian sculptor a variety of media including steel rod, sheet metal, cast iron, brass and bronze.

02/12/1999 to 04/25/1999 AND EVERYTHING NICE
Artwork from a variety of women artists who depict or comment on the cultural definitions of femininity

05/14/1999 to 07/18/1999 WPA COLLECTION FROM THE ILLINOIS STATE MUSEUM
The history and diversity of art that came out of the WPA of the 1930's.

05/14/1999 to 07/18/1999 MARTINA LOPEZ, LOUISE GONZALES PALMA, VICTOR VAZQUEZ
Photography and digital media *Will Travel*

06/04/1999 to 08/22/1999 BY POPULAR DEMAND: AUDIENCE FAVORITES FROM THE PERMANENT COLLECTION
Sculpture by Loraado Taft, paintings by Belle Emerson Keith, Pauline Palmer, and others.

08/06/1999 to 10/17/1999 CARL MILLES: SWEDISH SCULPTOR
Milles, at one time Director of the Department of Sculpture at Cranbrook Academy, is represented in many cities.

08/06/1999 to 10/17/1999 LINES IN THE SAND: CURRENT TRENDS IN CONTEMPORARY GLASS
Works from the permanent collection plus others from collectors and galleries surveys the artists and the medium which is bringing this to the forefront of the visual arts.

09/11/1999 to 11/28/1999 SOLO SERIES: BEN MAHMOUD RETROSPECTIVE
Mr. Mahmoud's development will be shown in work from the collection and from regional collectors and current paintings from the artist during the past 30 years.

11/05/1999 to 01/16/2000 THIRTY ONE SHOPPING DAYS 'TIL ARMAGEDDON: AMERICAN POP CULTURE IN ART AT THE END OF THE MILLENNIUM
Works from artists who have brought issues and images of popular culture into the realm of visual arts. The path of our culture from the 1960's to the end of the 20th c. as witnessed through painting, print, sculpture and video.

11/05/1999 to 01/16/2000 BELLE EMERSON KEITH

12/29/1999 to 03/05/2000 LL PERMANENT COLLECTION EXHIBITION: KLAWANS GIFT
This gift has two prominent focus groups: French graphics including Dubuffet, Arp, Lasanskoy, Derain and others, and Prints from Chicago and regional artists including Brown, Paschke, Florsheim, Colescott and others.

Rockford College Art Gallery / Clark Arts Center

5050 E. State, Rockford, IL 61108
☎: 815-226-4034
Open: ACAD: 2-5 Daily **Closed:** ACAD! & SUMMER
Vol/Cont
♿ Ⓟ **Museum Shop Group Tours Drop-In Tours**
Permanent Collection: PTGS, GR, PHOT, CER 20; ETH; REG

Located on a beautiful wooded site in a contemporary building, this museum presents a stimulating array of exhibitions that look at historic as well as contemporary artwork from around the country. **NOT TO BE MISSED:** African sculpture

Springfield Art Association

700 North Fourth St., Springfield, IL 62702

☎: 217-523-2631

Open: 9-4 Mo-Fr, 10-3 Sa   **Closed:** SU, LEG/HOL! (including Lincoln's birthday)

  ⅃ Ⓟ **Museum Shop**

Group Tours: 217-523-3507   **Drop-In Tours**: 1-3 We-Su   **Historic Building**

Permanent Collection: AM: ptgs, gr, cer, dec/art; EU: ptgs; CH; JAP

Fanciful is the proper word to describe the architecture of the 1833 Victorian structure that houses the Springfield Art Association, a fine arts facility that has been important to the cultural life of the city for more than a century.

ON EXHIBIT 1999

01/09/1999 to 01/23/1999   FROM THE GROUND UP: PHOTOGRAPHS OF THE GETTY CENTER

01/30/1999 to 02/27/1999   STORYTELLERS

03/13/1999 to 04/24/1999   THROUGH EASTERN EYES: EASTERN EXPERIENCES, WESTERN EXPRESSIONS

05/01/1999 to 06/19/1999   MIDWESTERN LANDSCAPES: EIGHT WOMEN'S PERSPECTIVES
The richness of work done by contemporary Midwestern women in the landscape genre . *Catalog Will Travel*

06/25/1999 to 07/27/1999   THE ART OF BONSAI

INDIANA

Anderson Fine Arts Center

32 West 10th Street, Anderson, IN 46016

☎: 765-649-0199 ▣ www.andersonart.org

Open: 10-5 Tu-Sa, till 8:30 Th, 12-5 Su **Closed:** Mo, LEG/HOL! AUG

Free Day: Tu & First Su of month **Adult:** $2.50 **Family** $6.50 **Children:** $1.25 **Students:** $1.25 **Seniors:** $2.00

& ⓟ **Museum Shop** **Group Tours:** $2.00 each call: 765-920-2649 **Drop-In Tours** **Historic Building**

Permanent Collection: REG: all media; AM: all media 20

With an emphasis on education, this museum presents 2 children's exhibitions annually; one in Dec.-Jan., and the other from May to the end of June.

Indiana University Art Museum

Affiliate Institution: Indiana University

Bloomington, IN 47405

☎: 812-855-IUAM ▣ www.indiana.edu/~iuam

Open: 10-5 We-Sa, Noon-5 Su **Closed:** Mo, Tu, LEG/HOL!

Vol/Cont

& ⓟ **Museum Shop** ⑪: Coffee Shop

Group Tours: 812-855-1045 **Drop-In Tours:** 2:00 Sa **Historic Building** Designed by I. M. Pei **Sculpture Garden**

Permanent Collection: AF; AN/EGT; AN/R; AN/GRK; AM: all media; EU: all media 14-20; OC; P/COL; JAP; CH; OR

Masterpieces in every category of its collection, from ancient to modern, make this one of the finest university museums to be found anywhere. Among its many treasures is the best university collection of African art in the United States. **NOT TO BE MISSED:** The stunning museum building itself designed in 1982 by noted architect I. M. Pei.

ON EXHIBIT 1999

01/22/1999 to 03/14/1999 **HENRY RADFORD HOPE SCHOOL OF FINE ARTS: BIENNIAL FACULTY SHOW**

03/31/1999 to 05/09/1999 **FROM THE DESERT SANDS: TEXTILE MASTERWORKS FROM COPTIC EGYPT**

09/01/1999 to 10/31/1999 **THE JUDY CHICAGO RETROSPECTIVE: WORKS ON PAPER** *Catalog Will Travel*

Indianapolis Museum of Art - Columbus Gallery

390 The Commons, Columbus, IN 47201-6764

☎: 812-376-2597

Open: 10-5 Tu-Th & Sa, 10-8 F, Noon-4 Su **Closed:** Mo, LEG/HOL!

Vol/Cont

& ⓟ **Museum Shop**

Group Tours **Drop-In Tours**

In an unusual arrangement with its parent museum in Indianapolis, four exhibitions are presented annually in this satellite gallery, the oldest continuously operating satellite gallery in the country. The Gallery is uniquely situated inside a shopping mall in an area designated by the city as an "indoor park".

Indianapolis Museum of Art - Columbus Gallery - continued
ON EXHIBIT 1999

02/06/1999 to 03/21/1999   FULL DECK ART QUILTS
54 American art quilters creative interpretation of a full deck of cards. These feature both hand and machine stitching, piecework, two and three dimensional applique and hand and specially dyed fabrics. *Catalog Will Travel*

07/17/1999 to 09/26/1999   HOOSIER ARTISTS IN MUNICH: DRAWINGS AND PAINTINGS BY ADAMS, FORSYTH , RICHARDS AND STEELE
These artists all went to study in the early 1880's at the Royal Academy in Munich. The 30 works on paper and 20 paintings done at this critical moment in their career include portraits, figure studies, landscape renderings and sketchbooks. *Will Travel*

10/10/1999 to 01/02/2000   DALE CHIHULY: SEAFORMS
Drawn from several series of his 30 year career this important exhibition of blown glass objects by Chihuly, America's foremost contemporary glass master, will be presented in room-size installations that are contrived to explore the space for which they are designed. *Will Travel*

ELKHART

Midwest Museum of American Art
429 S. Main St., Elkhart, IN 46515
☏: 219-293-6660
Open: 11-5 Tu-Fr; 1-4 Sa, Su   **Closed:** Mo, LEG/HOL!
ADM   Adult: $3.00   **Children:** F (under 5)   **Students:** $1.00   **Seniors:** $4.00
 ♿   &#9physical;   **Museum Shop   Group Tours   Drop-In Tours:** 12:20-12:40 Th (Noontime talks- free)
Permanent Collection: AM/IMPR; CONT; REG; SCULP; PHOT

Chronologically arranged, the permanent collection of 19th and 20th century paintings, sculptures, photographs, and works on paper, traces 150 years of American art history with outstanding examples ranging from American Primitives to contemporary works by Chicago Imagists. The museum is located in the heart of the mid-west Amish country. **NOT TO BE MISSED:** Original paintings by Grandma Moses, Norman Rockwell, and Grant Wood; The Vault Gallery (gallery in the vault of this former bank building.)

EVANSVILLE

Evansville Museum of Arts & Science
411 S.E Riverside Dr., Evansville, IN 47713
☏: 812-425-2406
Open: 10-5 Tu-Sa, Noon-5 Su   **Closed:** Mo, 1/1, 7/4, LAB/DAY, THGV, 12/25
 ♿   &#9physical;   **Museum Shop   Group Tours   Drop-In Tours   Sculpture Garden**
Permanent Collection: PTGS; SCULP; GR; DRGS; DEC/ART

Broad ranging in every aspect of its varied collections, the Evansville Museum will open its newly renovated permanent collection galleries and two changing exhibition galleries in the winter of '98. **NOT TO BE MISSED:** "Madonna and Child" by Murillo

ON EXHIBIT 1999

02/19/1999 to 04/09/1999   FOUR OBJECTS; FOUR ARTISTS; TEN YEARS
In 1986 four American still-life painters – Janet Fish, Sondra Freckelton, Nancy Hagin, and Harriet Shorr – agreed that each would select an object that they would all include in a painting. Ten years later they decided to repeat the project. The results of their efforts reveal the wide spectrum of choices which artists make during the creative process. *Catalog Will Travel*

INDIANA

Fort Wayne Museum of Art

311 E. Main St., Fort Wayne, IN 46802-1997
☎: 219-422-6467 ◙ www.art-museum-ftwayne.org
Open: 10-5 Tu-Sa, Noon-5 Su **Closed:** Mo, 1/1, 7/4, THGV, 12/25
ADM Adult: $3.00 **Children:** $2.00 (K-college) **Students:** $2.00 **Seniors:** $3.00
& ℗ **Museum Shop Group Tours:** 219-422-6467 x319 **Drop-In Tours Sculpture Garden**
Permanent Collection: AM: ptgs, sculp, gr 19-20; EU: ptgs, sculp, gr 19-20; CONT

Since the dedication of the new state-of-the-art building in its downtown location in 1984, the Fort Wayne Museum, established more than 75 years ago, has enhanced its reputation as a major vital community and nationwide asset for the fine arts. Important masterworks from Dürer to de Kooning are included in this institution's 1,300 piece collection. **NOT TO BE MISSED:** Etchings by Albrecht Dürer on the theme of Adam and Eve.

ON EXHIBIT 1999

11/21/1998 to 02/14/1999 NATURAL AFFINITIES

12/04/1998 to 01/2001 IN FOCUS: THE ART AND SCIENCE OF PHOTOGRAPHY

12/05/1998 to 02/14/1999 SHELDON HINE: 75 YEARS BEHIND THE LENS

01/16/1999 to 03/14/1999 FOCUS EXHIBITION

02/20/1999 to 04/18/1999 TWENTIETH CENTURY AMERICAN DRAWINGS FROM THE ARKANSAS CENTER FOUNDATION COLLECTION
A great diversity of drawing styles and techniques spanning the greater part of the 20th c. of American art includes in their definition pencil, pen and ink, watercolor, silverpoint to acrylic and oil on paper. Among the artists represented in the 100 works are Avery, Brady, Burchfield, Cottingham, Curry, Davis, Dove, Frankenthaler, Francis, Guston, Hopper, Marsh, Pollock, Sheeler and Toby. *Catalog Will Travel*

02/20/1999 to 04/18/1999 HOMER DAVISSON: A FORT WAYNE IMPRESSIONIST

03/20/1999 to 05/16/1999 FOCUS EXHIBITION

03/27/1999 to 05/09/1999 A GAME OF CHANCE

05/01/1999 to 06/27/1999 ARTISTS IN FRANCE: FROM MERYON TO PICASSO

05/22/1999 to 08/22/1999 FOCUS EXHIBITION

07/03/1999 to 09/05/1999 MATTER MIND SPIRIT: A SELECTION OF 12 CONTEMPORARY INDIANA WOMEN ARTISTS

Eiteljorg Museum of American Indians and Western Art

500 W. Washington St., White River State Park, Indianapolis, IN 46204
☎: 317-636-9378 ◙ www.eiteljorg.org
Open: 10-5 Tu-Sa, Noon-5 Su; (Open 10-5 M JUNE-AUG) **Closed:** Mo, 1/1, THGV, 12/25
ADM Adult: $5.00 **Children:** F (4 & under) **Students:** $2.00 **Seniors:** $4.00
& ℗ **Museum Shop Group Tours:** 317-636-9378 **Drop-In Tours:** 2:00 daily
Historic Building Landmark building featuring interior and exterior SW motif design
Permanent Collection: NAT/AM & WESTERN: ptgs, sculp, drgs, gr, dec/art

The Eiteljorg, one of only two museums east of the Mississippi to combine the fine arts of the American West with Native American artifacts, is housed in a Southwestern style building faced with 8,000 individually cut pieces of honey-colored Minnesota stone. **NOT TO BE MISSED:** Works by members of the original Taos Artists Colony; 4 major outdoor sculptures including a 38' totem pole by 5th generation Heida carver Lee Wallace and George Carlson's 12-foot bronze entitled "The Greeting".

Eiteljorg Museum of American Indians and Western Art - continued
ON EXHIBIT 1999
09/26/1998 to 01/03/1999   POWERFUL IMAGES: PORTRAYALS OF NATIVE AMERICA
Pop and Native American cultures blend in the contemporary works on view.

10/24/1998 to 10/03/1999 SPLENDID HERITAGE: MASTERPIECES OF NATIVE AMERICAN ART FROM THE MASCO COLLECTION
45 rare Native American masterpieces including apparel, ceremonial objects, paintings, weapons, and adornments will be on view providing the viewer with an opportunity to savor exceptional expressions of Indian aesthetic genius. *Will Travel*

02/06/1999 to 05/16/1999   AFRICAN-AMERICAN WEST
Most American are familiar with stories of the settlement of the west. Less well know is the cultural diversity and rich heritage of African Americans in the West. The exhibition focuses on three experiences; the soldiers, the cowboy, and the settler.

06/12/1999 to 09/06/1999   NATIVE VISIONS: NORTHWEST COAST ART 18TH CENTURY TO THE PRESENT
Examples of Northwest Coast art demonstrating how that tradition is constantly evolving by the inclusion of individual artists' contributions and inspirations.

10/02/1999 to 01/02/2000   GARY SMITH LANDSCAPES
Ploughed and unplowed, burnt and wet, golden and snow white fields became meaningful symbols to this well known artist. They prompted him to break from his successful and well known approach to painting.

Indianapolis Museum of Art
1200 W. 38th St., Indianapolis, IN 46208-4196
☎: 317-923-1331   ◉   WWW.IMA-ART.ORG
Open: 10-5 Tu-Sa, till 8:30pm Th, Noon-5 Su   **Closed:** Mo, LEG/HOL!
Vol/Cont
  ♿ ℗   **Museum Shop**   ⅋ 11am-1:45pm Tu-S; (Brunch S- by reservation 926-2628); Café
Group Tours: 317-920-2649   **Drop-In Tours**: 12 & 2 Tu-Su; 7pm Th (other!)
Permanent Collection: AM: ptgs; EU/OM: ptgs EU/REN:ptgs; CONT; OR; AF; DEC/ART; TEXTILES

Situated in a 52 acre park as part of a cultural complex, the Indianapolis Museum is home to many outstanding collections including a large group of works on paper by Turner, and world class collections of Impressionist, Chinese, and African art. PLEASE NOTE: 1. There is an admission fee for most special exhibitions. 2. The museum IS OPEN on 7/4.

ON EXHIBIT 1999
09/19/1998 to 01/10/1999   FRANCISCO CLEMENTE: INDIAN WATERCOLORS *Will Travel*

09/19/1998 to 03/28/1999   KASHMIR SHAWLS

04/11/1999 to 06/27/1999   ART OF THE AMERICAS
Native American objects from the United States as well as pre-Columbian objects from Central and South Americas from the Museum's collection.

05/1999 to 04/2000   URSULA VON RYDINGSVARD
Large scale wood sculpture by this American artist whose work is highly abstract, recalling organic forms, the landscape, or man made objects. *Catalog Will Travel*

05/19/1999 to 08/08/1999   VISIONS OF HOME

10/10/1999 to 01/02/2000   DALE CHIHULY: SEAFORMS
Drawn from several series of his 30 year career this important exhibition of blown glass objects by Chihuly, America's foremost contemporary glass master, will be presented in room-size installations that are contrived to explore the space for which they are designed. *Will Travel*

10/17/1999 to 09/26/1999   HOOSIER ARTISTS IN MUNICH: DRAWINGS AND PAINTINGS BY ADAMS, FORSYTH, RICHARDS, AND STEELE
In the early 1880's these artists went to study at the Royal Academy in Munich. The exhibition features te 30 works on paper and 20 paintings done during this period of their career.

INDIANA

Greater Lafayette Museum of Art

101 South Ninth St., Lafayette, IN 47901
📞: 765-742-1128   ◙ www.dcwi.com/~glma
Open: 11-4 Tu-Su   **Closed:** Mo, LEG/HOL!
🚻 ℗ **Museum Shop**
Group Tours   Drop-In Tours: 11-4 Tu-Su
Permanent Collection: AM: ptgs, gr, drgs, art pottery 19-20; REG: ptgs, works on paper; LAT/AM: gr

Art by regional Indiana artists, contemporary works by national artists of note, and a fine collection of art pottery are but three of several important collections to be found at the Greater Lafayette Museum of Art. **NOT TO BE MISSED:** Arts and craft items by Hoosier artists at museum store; Baber Collection of contemporary art

ON EXHIBIT 1999

11/21/1998 to 01/03/1999   A PASSION FOR PRINTS: THE PRUITT COLLECTION
An outstanding print and photography collection featuring Grant Wood, Ansel Adams, and many other great artists.

01/16/1999 to 02/28/1999   CHICAGO SOLILOQUY
Five women artists visually express their relationships, attitudes and feelings toward their city.

01/31/1999 to 03/07/1999   THE ARTISTS OF LILLY: WORK BY EMPLOYEES OF ELI LILY & COMPANY

03/13/1999 to 04/11/1999   INDIANA NOW!
A state-wide juried exhibition from which works are then sold for the next two years.

03/13/1999 to 04/11/1999   SCOTT FRANKENBURGER AT FIFTY
A fiftieth birthday retrospective for this acclaimed local ceramicist.

04/24/1999 to 05/30/1999   THE CHILDREN'S BOOK ILLUSTRATIONS OF AUTHOR PATRICIA PALACCO

06/05/1999 to 08/08/1999   KONRAD JUESTEL
A pupil of Oscar Kokoschka, Juestel is a printmaker.

06/05/1999 to 08/08/1999   GEORGE WINTER: THE MAN AND HIS ART
An exhibition of 80 works by Winter, a 19th century artist best known for his watercolor depictions of the American frontier in the mid 19th century.

08/21/1999 to 10/07/1999   MISCH KOHN: A RETROSPECTIVE

10/30/1999 to 11/28/1999   ANNUAL DAY OF THE DEAD DISPLAY

10/30/1999 to 01/02/2000   MATTER MIND SPIRIT: THIRTEEN CONTEMPORARY WOMEN ARTISTS
Indiana's best contemporary women artists are featured here. *Will Travel*

Ball State University Museum of Art

2000 University Ave., Muncie, IN 47306
📞: 765-285-5242
Open: 9-4:30 Tu-Fr; 1:30-4:30 Sa, Su   **Closed:** 1/1, EASTER, 7/4, THGV, 12/25
🚻 ℗ **Museum Shop   Group Tours   Drop-In Tours   Sculpture Garden**
Permanent Collection: IT/REN; EU: ptgs 17-19; AM: ptgs, gr, drgs 19-20; DEC/ART; AS; AF; OC; P/COL

5000 years of art history are represented in the 9,500 piece collection of the Ball State University Museum of Art. In addition to wonderful explanatory wall plaques, there is a fully cataloged Art Reference Terminal of the permanent collection.

NOTRE DAME

Snite Museum of Art

Affiliate Institution: University of Notre Dame
Notre Dame, IN 46556

☎: 219-631-5466　▣　www.nd.edu/~sniteart
Open: 10-4 Tu, We, 10-5 Th-Sa, 1-5 Su　**Closed:** Mo, LEG/HOL!
Vol/Cont
  ♿　℗　**Museum Shop　Group Tours**: 219-631-4717
Drop-In Tours　Sculpture Garden
Permanent Collection: IT/REN; FR: ptgs 19; EU: phot 19; AM: ptgs, phot; P/COL: sculp; DU: ptgs 17-18

With 17,000 objects in its permanent collection spanning the history of art from antiquity to the present, this premier university museum is a "must see" for all serious art lovers. **NOT TO BE MISSED:** AF; PR/COL & NAT/AM Collections

ON EXHIBIT 1999

01/17/1999 to 02/28/1999　MAPPING THE WEST

01/17/1999 to 03/14/1999　FRITZ KAESER: A LIFE IN PHOTOGRAPHY

08/22/1999 to 11/14/1999　ART PATRONAGE IN TAOS, NEW MEXICO

RICHMOND

Richmond Art Museum

Affiliate Institution: The Art Association of Richmond
350 Hub Etchison Pkwy, Richmond, IN 47374

☎: 765-966-0256
Open: 10-4 Tu-Fr, 1-4 Sa, Su　**Closed:** Mo, LEG/HOL!
  ♿　℗　**Museum Shop**
Group Tours　Drop-In Tours: !
Permanent Collection: AM: Impr/ptgs; REG

Aside from its outstanding collection of American Impressionist works, the Richmond Art Museum, which celebrated its 100th birthday in 1998, has the unique distinction of being housed in an operating high school. **NOT TO BE MISSED:** Self portrait by William Merritt Chase, considered to be his most famous work

ON EXHIBIT 1999

01/16/1999 to 02/21/1999　THE RENAISSANCE OF RUSSIAN ART

03/01/1999 to 02/28/1999　HISTORY OF WOMEN IN PHILADELPHIA ART
An ambitious survey using works from the collection as well as loans, of the work of women artists throughout the history of Philadelphia. *Catalog*

03/06/1999 to 04/11/1999　METALISTS EXHIBIT

06/1999 to 07/1999　T.C. STEELE EXHIBIT

11/1999 to 12/1999　101ST ANNUAL EXHIBITION BY RICHMOND AND AREA ARTISTS

INDIANA

South Bend Regional Museum of Art

120 S. St. Joseph St., South Bend, IN 46601
📞: 219-235-9102   ◙   www.sbt.infi.net/~sbrma
Open: 11-5 Tu-Fr; Noon-5 Sa, Su   **Closed:** Mo, LEG/HOL!
Sugg/Cont   Adult: $3.00
& ℗ **Museum Shop**   ∥Café   **Group Tours   Drop-In Tours**
Permanent Collection: AM: ptgs 19-20; EU: ptgs 19-20; CONT: reg

Since 1947, the South Bend Regional Museum of Art has been serving the artistic needs of its community by providing a wide variety of regional and national exhibitions year-round. This growing institution recently completed a reconstruction and expansion project adding, among other things, a Permanent Collections Gallery and a café. **NOT TO BE MISSED:** Permanent site-specific sculptures are situated on the grounds of Century Center of which the museum is a part.

Sheldon Swope Art Museum

25 S. 7th St., Terre Haute, IN 47807
📞: 812-238-1676
Open: 10-5 Th-Fr; Noon-5 Sa, Su; till 8pm Th   **Closed:** Mo , LEG/HOL
Vol/Cont
& ℗ **Museum Shop   Group Tours Drop-In Tours   Historic Building**
Permanent Collection: AM: ptgs, sculp, drgs 19-20;

The Sheldon Swope, opened in 1942 as a museum devoted to contemporary American art, and has expanded from the original core collection to Wabash Valley artist past and present. **NOT TO BE MISSED:** Painting by Grant Wood, Thomas Hart Benton, Edward Hopper NOTE: ALL SPECIAL EXHIBITIONS FOR 1999 HAVE BEEN SUSPENDED BECAUSE OF BUILDING RENOVATION

Purdue University Galleries

Affiliate Institution: Creative Arts Bldg., #1
West Lafayette, IN 47907
📞: 765-494-3061
Open: STEWART CENTER:10-5 & 7-9 Tu-Th, 10-5 Fr, 1-4 Su; UNION GALLERY:10-5 Tu-Fr,1-4 Su
Closed: Sa, ACAD!
& ℗ **Museum Shop**
Group Tours   Drop-In Tours
Permanent Collection: AM: ptgs, drgs, gr; EU: ptgs, gr, drgs; AM: cont/cer

In addition to a regular schedule of special exhibitions, this facility presents many student and faculty shows.

CEDAR FALLS

James & Meryl Hearst Center for the Arts
304 W. Seerly Blvd., Cedar Falls, IA 50613
☎: 319-273-8641
Open: 10-9 Tu, Th; 10-5 We, Fr; 1-4 Sa, Su   **Closed:** Mo, 1/1, 7/4, THGV, 12/25
& ℗ **Museum Shop** **Group Tours**: 319-268-5504 **Drop-In Tours**
Historic Building Located in the former home of well-known farmer poet James Hearst
Permanent Collection: REG

Besides showcasing works by the region's best current artists, the Hearst Center's permanent holdings include examples of works by such well knowns as Grant Wood, Mauricio Lasansky, and Gary Kelley. **NOT TO BE MISSED:** "Man is a Shaper, a Maker", pastel by Gary Kelley; "Honorary Degree", lithograph by Grant Wood

ON EXHIBIT 1999
01/05/1999 to 02/21/1999   ON THE LAND; THREE CENTURIES OF AMERICAN FARMLIFE

CEDAR RAPIDS

Cedar Rapids Museum of Art
410 Third Ave., S.E., Cedar Rapids, IA 52401
☎: 319-366-7503 ▣ www.crma.org
Open: 10-4 Tu-We & Fr-Sa, 10am-7pm Th, Noon-4 Su   **Closed:** Mo, LEG/HOL!
ADM Adult: $4.00 **Children:** F (under 7) **Students:** $3.00 **Seniors:** $3.00
& ℗ **Museum Shop**
Group Tours: education office **Drop-In Tours**: ! **Historic Building** Carnegie Library Wing
Permanent Collection: REG: ptgs 20; PTGS, SCULP, GR, DEC/ART, PHOT 19-20

Spanning a city block, the Cedar Rapids Museum of Art Houses 16 galleries in one wing and a Museum Shop, art library and multi-media center in another. A regionally focused museum, it was observed that by The Other Museums that, "No museum of art in this country is more deeply rooted in its own community." **NOT TO BE MISSED:** Museum includes restored 1905 Beaux Art building, formerly the Carnegie Library (free to the public); collections of Grand Wood & Marvin Cone paintings, Malvina Hoffman sculptures, & Mauricio Lasansky prints and drawings

ON EXHIBIT 1999
12/12/1998 to 02/14/1999   IN SHAPE - SIX SCULPTORS
Six contemporary sculptors with ties to the Midwest, with a very different voice.

04/10/1999 to 06/13/1999   CONTEMPORARY EXPRESSIONS IN CLAY
13 artists give one a chance to see the very best ceramic artwork currently produced in the Midwest. *Catalog*

06/26/1999 to 09/05/1999   FIBER (working title)
A survey of some of the best fiber artists working in the US today.

06/26/1999 to 09/05/1999   FRED EASKER
Easker is a local landscape painter beginning to establish a national reputation for his horizontal views.

09/11/1999 to 11/07/1999   LARGE DRAWINGS FROM THE ARKANSAS ARTS CENTER FOUNDATION COLLECTION
Contemporary work by artists who prefer to work in a very large format. Drawings are often the most immediate expression of an artist's inspiration and have a freshness that does not translate as well to paintings, prints and sculpture. *Will Travel*

11/19/1999 to 01/30/2000   MAURICIO LASANSKY AND THE IOWA PRINT GROUP
Celebrating the Museum's ten year anniversary in the new building, Lasansky's work and works by artists trained with this Group are surveyed as is their collective contribution to American printmaking. *Catalog*

IOWA

Davenport Museum of Art

1737 W. Twelfth St., Davenport, IA 52804
☎: 319-326-7804
Open: 10-4:30 Tu-Sa, 1-4:30 Su, till 8pm Th   **Closed:** Mo, LEG/HOL!
Sugg/Cont
  ❤ ℗ **Museum Shop**
Group Tours   Drop-In Tours   Sculpture Garden
Permanent Collection: AM/REG; AM: 19-20; EU: 16-18; OM; MEXICAN COLONIAL; HATIAN NAIVE

Works by Grant Wood and other American Regionalists are on permanent display at the Davenport Museum, the first public art museum established in the state of Iowa (1925). **NOT TO BE MISSED:** Grant Wood's "Self Portrait"

ON EXHIBIT 1999

11/15/1998 to 01/10/1999   OUR NATION'S COLORS: A CELEBRATION OF AMERICAN PAINTING, SELECTIONS FROM THE WICHITA ART MUSEUM
Portraits, genre scenes and landscapes from the permanent collection of the Wichita Art Museum, are among the more than 70 paintings and works on paper by George Bellows, Charles Burchfield, Stuart Davis, Thomas Eakins and other icons of American art featured in a thematic exploration of early 20th century American art. *Will Travel*

02/07/1999 to 04/11/1999   MASTER DRAWINGS FROM THE WORCESTER ART MUSEUM
More than 100 works including watercolors, pastels and illuminated manuscripts by European and American artists from 1275 to 1975 representing major trends of style and content. *Catalog Will Travel*

04/18/1999 to 06/13/1999   AFRICA! A SENSE OF WONDER: THE FALETTI FAMILY COLLECTION
Wood carvings, masks, figural pieces, beaded objects and textiles are among the 75 16th to early 20th century sub-Saharan works displayed in this exhibition. Focusing on the sublime and the fantastic in African art, these stunning works, on loan from the renowned Faletti Collection, represent the range and depth of African artistic sensibility. *Will Travel*

06/17/1999 to 09/12/1999   DAVENPORT MUSEUM OF ART BI-STATE INVITATIONAL EXHIBITION

12/26/1999 to 03/12/2000   EDOUARD DUVAL-CARRIE: THE MIGRATION OF THE SPIRIT
One of the premiere artists working in the US, this is the first major retrospective of his work to travel here.

Des Moines Art Center

4700 Grand Ave., Des Moines, IA 50312-2099
☎: 515-277-4405
Open: 11,-4 Daily, Noon-5 Su, 11-9 Th & 1st Fr of the month   **Closed:** Mo, LEG/HOL!
ADM   Adult: $4.00   **Children:** F (under 12)   **Students:** $2.00   **Seniors:** $2.00
  ❤ ℗ **Museum Shop**   ❚❙ 11-2 lunch Tu-Sa; dinner 5;30-9 T (by reserv.), 5-8 1ST F (light dining)
Group Tours: ex. 15   **Drop-In Tours**
Permanent Collection: AM: ptgs, sculp, gr 19-20; EU: ptgs, sculp, gr 19-20; AF

Its parklike setting is a perfect compliment to the magnificent structure of the Des Moines Art Center building, designed originally by Eliel Saarinen in 1948, with a south wing by the noted I. M. Pei & Partners added in 1968. Another spectacular wing, recognized as a masterpiece of contemporary architecture, was designed and built, in 1985, by Richard Meier & Partners. **NOT TO BE MISSED:** "Maiastra" by Constantin Brancusi; Frank Stella's "Interlagos"

Hoyt Sherman Place

1501 Woodland Ave., Des Moines, IA 50309
☎: 515-243-0913
Open: 8-4 Mo, Tu, Th, Fr; Closed on We from OCT.1-end of MAY   **Closed:** Sa, Su, LEG/HOL!
 ♿ Ⓟ   **Museum Shop**
Group Tours
Drop-In Tours: often available upon request
Historic Building Complex of 1877 House, 1907 Art Museum, 1923 Theater
Permanent Collection: PTGS; SCULP; DEC/ART 19; EU; sculp; B.C. ARTIFACTS

A jewel from the Victorian Era, the Hoyt Sherman Art Galleries offer an outstanding permanent collection of 19th century American and European art, complimented by antique decorative arts objects that fill its surroundings. Listed NRHP **NOT TO BE MISSED:** Major works by 19th century American masters including Church, Inness, Moran, Frieseke and others

---

DUBUQUE

Dubuque Museum of Art

8th & Central, Dubuque, IA 52001
☎: 319-557-1851
Open: 10-5 Tu-Fr; 1-5 Sa, Su   **Closed:** Mo, 1/1, EASTER, 7/4, THGV, 12/25
 ♿ Ⓟ   **Museum Shop**
Group Tours
Drop-In Tours: daily upon request
Historic Building Housed in 1857 Egyptian Revivalist Jail
Permanent Collection: REG

Located in a rare 1857 Egyptian Revivalist style building that formerly served as a jail, the Dubuque Museum has the added distinction of being the only National Landmark building in the city. Exhibitions from the permanent collection are displayed on a rotating basis.

FORT DODGE

Blanden Memorial Art Museum

920 Third Ave. South, Fort Dodge, IA 50501
☎: 515-573-2316
Open: 10-5 Tu-Fr, till 8:30 Th, 1-5 Sa & Su   **Closed:** Mo
 ♿ Ⓟ   **Museum Shop**
Group Tours
Drop-In Tours
Permanent Collection: AM: ptgs, sculp, gr 19-20; EU: ptgs, sculp, drgs, gr 15-20; OR: 16-20; P/COL

Established in 1930 as the first permanent art facility in the state, the Blanden's neo-classic building was based on the already existing design of the Butler Institute of American Art in Youngstown, Ohio. Listed NRHP **NOT TO BE MISSED:** "Central Park" by Maurice Prendergast, 1901; "Self-Portrait in Cap & Scarf" by Rembrandt (etching, 1663)

IOWA

Grinnell College Print & Drawing Study Room

Affiliate Institution: Grinnell College
Burling Library, Grinnell, IA 50112-0806
☏: 515-269-3371
Open: 1-5 Su-Fr during the academic year   **Closed:** Sa, 7/4, THGV, 12/25 THROUGH 1/1
 ♿ Ⓢ   **Museum Shop**
Group Tours   Drop-In Tours
Permanent Collection: WORKS ON PAPER (available for study in the Print & Drawing Study Room)

1,400 works on paper, ranging from illuminated manuscripts to 16th century European prints and drawings to 20th century American lithographs, are all part of the Grinnell College Collection that started in 1908 with an original bequest of 28 etchings by J. M. W. Turner. A new gallery, designed by Cesar Pelli, opened in the spring of 1998. **NOT TO BE MISSED:** Etching: "The Artist's Mother Seated at a Table" by Rembrandt

University of Iowa Museum of Art

150 North Riverside Dr., 112 Museum of Art, Iowa City, IA 52242-1789
☏: 319-335-1727   Ⓢ   www.uiowa.edu/~artmus
Open: 10-5 Tu-Sa, Noon-5 Su   **Closed:** Mo, 1/1, THGV, 12/25
 ♿ Ⓢ   **Museum Shop**
Group Tours   Drop-In Tours
Sculpture Garden
Permanent Collection: AM: ptgs, sculp 19-20; EU: ptgs, sculp 19-20; AF; WORKS ON PAPER

Over nine thousand objects form the basis of the collection at this 30 year old university museum that features, among its many strengths, 19th & 20th century American and European art, and the largest group of African art in any university museum collection. **NOT TO BE MISSED:** "Karneval" by Max Beckman: "Mural, 1943" by Jackson Pollock

Central Iowa Art Association

Affiliate Institution: Fisher Community College
Marshalltown, IA 50158
☏: 515-753-9013
Open: 11-5 Mo-Fr; 1-5 Sa, Su (APR 15-OCT 15)   **Closed:** Sa, Su, LEG/HOL!
Vol/Cont
 ♿ Ⓢ   **Museum Shop**
Group Tours   Drop-In Tours
Sculpture Garden
Permanent Collection: FR/IMPR: ptgs; PTGS; CER

You don't have to be a scholar to enjoy the ceramic study center of the Central Iowa Art Association, one of the highlights of this institution. 20th century paintings and sculpture at the associated Fisher Art Gallery round out the collection. **NOT TO BE MISSED:** The Ceramic Study Collection

MASON CITY

Charles H. MacNider Museum

303 2nd St., S.E., Mason City, IA 50401-3988

☎: 515-421-3666

Open: 10-9 Tu, Th; 10-5 We, Fr, Sa; 1-5 Su   **Closed:** Mo, LEG/HOL!, PM 12/24, PM 12/31

♿ ℗   **Museum Shop   Group Tours   Drop-In Tours**: available upon advance request during museum hours

Permanent Collection: AM: ptgs, gr, drgs, cer; REG: ptgs, gr, drgs, cer; the "Bill Baird World of Puppets"

A lovely English Tudor mansion built in 1921, complete with modern additions, is the repository of an ever growing collection that documents American art and life. Though only a short two block walk from the heart of Mason City, the MacNider sits dramatically atop a limestone ravine surrounded by trees and other beauties of nature. **NOT TO BE MISSED:** For young and old alike, a wonderful collection of Bill Baird Marionettes; "Gateways to the Sea", by Alfred T. Bricher; "Spring Tryout," by Thomas Hart Benton; "The Clay Wagon," by Arthur Dove

ON EXHIBIT 1999

12/17/1998 to 01/24/1999   **A BAIRD CHRISTMAS**

01/21/1999 to 03/14/1999   **AMERICA SEEN: PEOPLE AND PLACE**

The images on view by Grant Wood, Norman Rockwell, John Stuart Curry, Thomas Hart Benton and other giants of American art working between the 1920's through the 1950's, document two world wars, the Great Depression, the New Deal, the growth of the American city and the nostalgia for simple rural life.

01/28/1999 to 02/28/1999   **NAVAJO WEAVING, JEWELRY, AND POTTERY**

03/04/1999 to 04/11/1999   **IMAGINE - DISCOVER - CREATE**

03/14/1999 to 07/03/1999   **34TH ANNUAL AREA SHOW**

03/19/1999 to 05/09/1999   **SCULPTURE: CLAY AS MEDIUM** *Will Travel*

05/27/1999 to 07/11/1999   **RECENT ACQUISITIONS**

07/08/1999 to 08/29/1999   **WALTER BURLEY GRIFFIN IN AMERICA**

07/16/1999 to 09/05/1999   **19TH ANNUAL CERRO GORDO PHOTO SHOW**

09/01/1999 to 10/03/1999   **BIENNIAL STAFF SHOW**

09/09/1999 to 10/24/1999   **LARGE PRINTS/SMALL PRINTS**

10/06/1999 to 11/14/1999   **CONNIE HERRING: THE CLEARING**

10/29/1999 to 12/29/1999   **NEW IN SALES/RENTAL**

11/21/1999 to 01/09/2000   **IOWA CRAFTS: 32**

MUSCATINE

Muscatine Art Center

1314 Mulberry Ave., Muscatine, IA 52761

☎: 319-263-8282

Open: 10-5 Tu, We, Fr; 10-5 & 7-9 Th; 1-5 Sa, Su   **Closed:** Mo, LEG/HOL!

♿ ℗   **Museum Shop**

Group Tours   Drop-In Tours: daily when possible!   **Historic Building**1908 Edwardian Musser Mansion

Permanent Collection: AM: ptgs, sculp, gr, drgs, dec/art 19-20; NAT/AM: ptgs

IOWA

Muscatine Art Center - continued

The original Musser Family Mansion built in Edwardian Style in 1908, has been joined since 1976 by the contemporary 3 level Stanley Gallery to form the Muscatine Art Center. In addition to its fine collection of regional and national American art, the center has recently received a bequest of 27 works by 19 important European artists including Boudin, Braque, Pissarro, Degas, Matisse and others. **NOT TO BE MISSED:** The "Great River Collection" of artworks illustrating facets of the Mississippi River from its source in Lake Itasca to its southernmost point in New Orleans.

ON EXHIBIT 1999

04/11/1999 to 06/27/1999 THE STONEWARES OF CHARLES FERGUS BINNS: FATHER OF AMERICAN STUDIO CERAMICS
60 rarely seen works by a pioneer, potter, teacher and author who laid the foundation for the studio ceramics movement in this country. This ground breaking survey is the most comprehensive collection of his work ever assembled for a traveling exhibition. It includes the earliest documented stoneware vase signed and dated 1905. *Catalog Will Travel*

SIOUX CITY

Sioux City Art Center

225 Nebraska St., Sioux City, IA 51101-1712
☎: 712-279-6272 ◙ www.sc-artcenter.com
Open: 10-5 Tu, We, Fr, Sa, 12-9 Th, 1-5 Su **Closed:** Mo, LEG/HOL
♿ ⓟ **Museum Shop Group Tours**: 712-279-6272 ext. 200 **Drop-In Tours**: By reservation
Permanent Collection: NAT/AM; 19-20; CONT/REG; PTGS, WORKS ON PAPER; PHOT

Begun as a WPA project in 1938, the Center features a 900 piece permanent collection that includes regional art. A stunning new $9 million Art Center building, designed by the renowned architectural firm of Skidmore, Owings and Merrill, features a three-story glass atrium, and a state-of-the-art Hands-On Gallery for children. **NOT TO BE MISSED:** In the new facility, a hands-on gallery for children featuring creative activity stations.

ON EXHIBIT 1999

10/21/1998 to 02/07/1999 FORM, SHAPE AND SUBSTANCE
Three dimensional works from the Permanent collection.

11/21/1998 to 01/14/1999 LOCAL PERSPECTIVES
An opportunity to see the work of local artists and artisans.

12/05/1998 to 01/20/1999 MARILYN ANNIN: GARMENTS AS METAPHOR
Sculptured garments as a metaphor for a specific attitude or custom of American culture, with garments acting as portraiture, commentary or satire.

12/05/1998 to 01/24/1999 CERAMICS AND DRAWINGS BY MARY CARROLL
Polychrome ceramics and botanically inspired drawings by a Sioux City native.

01/30/1999 to 04/04/1999 UPPER MIDWEST JURIED EXHIBITION
100 works in all media except film by artists from the Upper Midwest.

01/30/1999 to 04/04/1999 UMEX: UPPER MIDWEST EXHIBITION
Formerly called the Annual Juried Exhibition, this multi-state regional features works in all media by established and emerging artists.

03/06/1999 to 03/31/1999 YOUTH ART MONTH: A JURIED EXHIBITION OF LOCAL HIGH SCHOOL STUDENTS WORK

04/16/1999 to 05/30/1999 ART FOR THE PARKS
A major national and traveling competition depicting subjects from the over 370 US parks and monuments including artists from Japan, Europe and South America as well as the US..

Sioux City Art Center - continued

04/22/1999 to 07/02/2000 MIDWESTERN GLASS

04/27/1999 to 07/06/2000 DAVID WEST RETROSPECTIVE

06/12/1999 to 08/15/1999 WATERCOLORS BY PEGGY FLORA ZALUCHA
Large scaled drawings by one of Americas premier watercolor artists known for her floral and musical still lifes.

06/28/1999 to 07/25/1999 IOWA WATERCOLOR SOCIETY

08/07/1999 to 09/25/1999 NEW QUILTS FROM OLD FAVORITES: PINEAPPLE QUILTS
18 contemporary quilts in an innovative, contemporary interpretation of the traditional pineapple pattern. *Will Travel*

09/03/1999 to 11/14/1999 AMERICAN CONTEMPORARY GRAPHICS: SELECTIONS FROM THE SHELDON MEMORIAL GALLERY
Spanning the years from 1961-1992 this exhibition offers a broad survey of the most significant achievements in the graphic arts in these thirty years. Included are works by Chuck Close, Baldesarri, Diebenkorn, Haring, Kruger, Motherwell, etc.

09/25/1999 to 10/30/1999 COMPUTER ANIMATION AND PRINTS BY JAMES D. GIBSON

09/25/1999 to 12/05/1999 SARA BELL: BOX OF STARS
Paintings based on the familiar constellations of stars.

11/11/1999 to 02/20/2000 MARK L. MOSEMAN: NEO-REGIONALIST

12/02/1999 to 01/30/2000 MIDWESTERN CERAMICS

WATERLOO

Waterloo Museum of Art
225 Commercial St., Waterloo, IA 50701
☎: 319-291-4491 ▣ www.wplwloo.lib.ia.us/waterloo/wrac.html
Open: 10-5 Mo-Fr; 1-4 Sa, Su **Closed:** LEG/HOL!
  Ⓟ **Museum Shop**
Group Tours Drop-In Tours
Permanent Collection: REG: ptgs, gr, sculp; HAITIAN: ptgs, sculp; AM: dec/art

This museum notes as its strengths its collection of Midwest art including works by Grant Wood and Marvin Cone, an outstanding collection of Haitian paintings, metal sculpture and sequined banners, and an American decorative arts collection with particular emphasis on pottery. **NOT TO BE MISSED:** Small collection of Grant Wood paintings, lithographs, and drawings

ON EXHIBIT 1999
12/11/1998 to 02/13/1999 WORKS BY FRED WOODARD

02/25/1999 to 04/23/1999 CAROL PRUSA & JEFFREY BYRD: MIXED MEDIA & PERFORMANCE

05/05/1999 to 07/02/1999 PHOTOGRAPHS BY WOODY WALTERS

07/14/1999 to 09/10/1999 DECORATIVE ARTS FROM THE COLLECTION OF THE ZANESVILLE ART CENTER

09/22/1999 to 11/16/1999 INSTALLATION BY STEVE GERBERICH

12/10/1999 to 02/13/2000 PAINTINGS BY BURTON CHENET

KANSAS

GARNETT

Walker Art Collection of the Garnett Public Library

125 W. 4th Ave., Garnett, KS 66032

☎: 913-448-3388 ▣ www.kanza.net/garnett

Open: 10-8 Mo, Tu, Th; 10-5:30 We, Fr; 10-4 Sa   **Closed:** Su, 1/1, MEM/DAY, 7/4, THGV, 12/25

Vol/Cont

Ⓕ Ⓟ **Museum Shop**

Group Tours   Drop-In Tours: upon request if available

Permanent Collection: AM: ptgs: 20; REG

Considered one of the most outstanding collections in the state, the Walker was started with a 110 piece bequest in 1951 by its namesake, Maynard Walker, a prominent art dealer in New York during the 1930's & 40's. Brilliantly conserved works by such early 20th century American artists as John Stuart Curry, Robert Henri, and Luigi Lucioni are displayed alongside European and Midwest Regional paintings and sculpture. All works in the collection have undergone conservation in the past few years and are in pristine condition. **NOT TO BE MISSED:** "Lake in the Forest (Sunrise)" by Corot; "Girl in Red Tights" by Walt Kuhn; "Tobacco Plant" by John Stuart Curry

LAWRENCE

Spencer Museum of Art

Affiliate Institution: University of Kansas

1301 Mississippi St., Lawrence, KS 66045

☎: 785-864-4710 ▣ www.ukans.edu/~sma

Open: 10-5 Tu-Sa, Noon-5 Su, till 9pm Th   **Closed:** Mo, 1/1, 7/4, THGV & FOLLOWING DAY, 12/24, 12/25

Ⓕ Ⓟ **Museum Shop**

Group Tours: School year only 785-864-4710   **Drop-In Tours**

Permanent Collection: EU: ptgs, sculp, gr 17-18; AM: phot; JAP: gr; CH: ptgs; MED: sculp

The broad and diverse collection of the Spencer Museum of Art, located in the eastern part of the state between Topeka and Kansas City, features particular strengths in the areas of European painting and sculpture of the 17th & 18th centuries, American photographs, Japanese and Chinese works of art, and Medieval sculpture. **NOT TO BE MISSED:** "La Pia de Tolommei" by Rossetti; "The Ballad of the Jealous Lover of Lone Green Valley" by Thomas Hart Benton

LINDSBORG

Birger Sandzen Memorial Gallery

401 N. 1st St., Lindsborg, KS 67456-0348

☎: 785-227-2220

Open: 1-5 We-Su   **Closed:** Mo, Tu, LEG/HOL!

ADM   Adult: $2.00   **Children:** $.50 grades 1-12   **Seniors:** $2.00

Ⓕ Ⓟ **Museum Shop**

Group Tours   Drop-In Tours

Permanent Collection: REG: ptgs, gr, cer, sculp; JAP: sculp

Opened since 1957 on the campus of a small college in central Kansas, about 20 miles south of Salina, this facility is an important cultural resource for the state. Named after Birger Sandzen, an artist who taught at the College for 52 years, the gallery is the repository of many of his paintings. PLEASE NOTE: There is reduced rate of $5.00 for families of 5 or more people. **NOT TO BE MISSED:** "The Little Triton" fountain by sculptor Carl Milles of Sweden located in the courtyard.

Birger Sandzen Memorial Gallery - continued

ON EXHIBIT 1999

01/06/1999 to 02/22/1999   PAINTINGS BY MARILYN RUSSEL BOGLE

03/03/1999 to 05/02/1999   100TH ANNUAL MIDWEST ART EXHIBITION

06/02/1999 to 07/28/1999   FRENCH PHOTOGRAPHERS IN DALARNA IN 1910

06/02/1999 to 09/26/1999   LITHOGRAPHY, A STUDY OF A PRINTMAKING TECHNIQUE AND ART

08/04/1999 to 09/26/1999   JOSEPH L. SMITH, DONNA BRIGMAN, AND BIRGER SANDZEN

09/01/1999 to 10/31/1999   MARY KAY AND BIRGER SANDZEN

LOGAN

Dane G. Hansen Memorial Museum

110 W. Main, Logan, KS 67646

☎: 785-689-4846

Open: 9-Noon & 1-4 Mo-Fr, 9-Noon & 1-5 Sa, 1-5 Su & Holidays   **Closed:** 1/1, THGV, 12/25

& ⓟ   **Museum Shop**   **Group Tours:** 785-689-4846   **Drop-In Tours**

Permanent Collection: OR; REG

Part of a cultural complex completed in 1973 in the heart of downtown Logan, the Hansen Memorial Museum, a member of the Smithsonian Associates, also presents regional artists. Also, Annual Labor Day Celebration, Labor Day Sunday. Car show, live entertainment, fireworks at dark, volleyball tournament and much, much more. All Free. **NOT TO BE MISSED:** Annual Hansen Arts & Craft Fair (3rd Sa of Sept) where judges select 12 artists to exhibit in the Hansen's artist corner, one for each month of the year.

ON EXHIBIT 1999

02/03/1999 to 03/10/1999   APRON STRINGS: TIES TO THE PAST

05/09/1999 to 06/27/1999   CROSSING BOUNDARIES: CONTEMPORARY ART QUILTS

Created by members of the Art quilt Network in America, the 39 contemporary quilts on view represent a departure from the traditional by the inclusion of innovative techniques and the incorporation of painting, photography and printmaking within the works. *Catalog Will Travel*

07/02/1999 to 09/12/1999   CURATORS FOCUS: TURNING IN CONTEXT *Will Travel*

11/12/1999 to 01/09/2000   "HOPI KATSINAS" *Will Travel*

OVERLAND PARK

Johnson County Community College Gallery of Art

Affiliate Institution: Johnson County Community College

12345 College Blvd., Overland Park, KS 66210

☎: 913-469-8500

Open: 10-5 Mo, Th, Fr; 10-7 Tu, We; 1-5 Sa, Su   **Closed:** Su, LEG/HOL!

& ⓟ   **Museum Shop**   ⅼ⅃: Yes

Group Tours: 913-469-8500 x3789   **Drop-In Tours**

Permanent Collection: AM/ CONT: ptgs, cer, phot, works on paper

The geometric spareness of the buildings set among the gently rolling hills of the campus is a perfect foil for the rapidly growing permanent collection of contemporary American art. Sculptures by Jonathan Borofsky, Barry Flanagan, Judith Shea, Louise Bourgeois, and Magdalena Abakanowicz are joined by other contemporary works in the Oppenheimer-Stein Sculpture Collection sited over the 234-acre campus. Seven exhibitions of contemporary art are presented annually.

KANSAS

Salina Art Center

242 S. Santa Fe, Salina, KS 67401
☎: 785-827-1431
Open: Noon-5 Tu-Sa, 1-5 Su, till 7pm Th **Closed:** Mo, LEG/HOL!
  ♿ Ⓟ **Museum Shop** **Group Tours**: available school year only **Drop-In Tours**: 9-5 Tu-Fr; call to schedule
Permanent Collection:

Recognized across the Midwest for bringing together art, artists, and audiences in innovative ways, the Salina Art Center specializes in exhibiting and interpreting contemporary American art. Rotating high quality original multi-cultural exhibitions, traveling exhibitions (often featuring works by international artists), and a permanent Discovery Area hands-on laboratory for children are its main features. **NOT TO BE MISSED:** A state of the art movie facility, Art Center Cinema, one block from the gallery, features the best current international and American film. Open Th-Su weekly. Cinema phone: 785-452-9868

ON EXHIBIT 1999

11/22/1998 to 02/07/1999 20TH ANNUAL JURIED EXHIBITION
Five state Juried show.

02/20/1999 to 05/16/1999 THE BODY SHOW
An exhibition that will show the relationship between the biological and imaginary body through sculpture, installation, drawing, new imaging techniques and photography. A temporary public work on the same theme will incorporate the community in its process.

05/29/1999 to 08/07/1999 DIFFERENT VOICES: NEW ART FROM POLAND
A contemporary textile exhibition featuring the social identities and creative impulses of the artist A artist will be a participant in the program. *Will Travel*

Gallery of Fine Arts-Topeka & Shawnee County

1515 W. 10th, Topeka, KS 66604-1374
☎: 913-233-2040
Open: LAB/DAY-MEM/DAY: 9-9 Mo-Fr, 9-6 Sa, 2-6 Su **Closed:** LEG/HOL!
  ♿ Ⓟ **Museum Shop** **Group Tours** **Drop-In Tours**
Permanent Collection: REG: ptgs, gr 20; W/AF; AM: cer, glass paperweights

Although the fine art permanent collection is usually not on view, this active institution presents rotating exhibitions that are mainly regional in nature. PLEASE NOTE: The museum will be closed until the year 2000 due to a major construction project that will more than triple its exhibition space and allow for more of the permanent collection to be on display. **NOT TO BE MISSED:** Glass paperweights; Akan gold weights from Ghana and the Ivory Coast, West Africa

Mulvane Art Museum

Affiliate Institution: Washburn University
17th & Jewell, Topeka, KS 66621-1150
☎: 785-231-1124
Open: SEPT-MAY: 10-7 Tu-We, 10-4 Th& Fr, 1-4 Sa, Su; SUMMER: 10-4 Tu-Fr
Closed: Mo, LEG/HOL! & during exhibit installations
Vol/Cont
  ♿ Ⓟ **Museum Shop** **Group Tours**: 785-231-1010 x1322 **Drop-In Tours**: by appointment, 10-3 Tu-Fr
Historic Building Oldest Art Museum in State of Kansas (1924) on the campus of Washburn Univ. **Sculpture Garden**
Permanent Collection: EU: dec/art 19-20; AM: dec/art 19-20; JAP: dec/art 19-20; REG: cont ptgs; GR; SCULP; CER; PHOT

Mulvane Art Museum - continued

Opened in 1924, the Mulvane is the oldest art museum in the state of Kansas located on the campus of Washburn University. In addition to an ever growing collection of works by artists of Kansas and the Mountain-Plains region, the museum counts both an international and a Japanese print collection among its holdings.

ON EXHIBIT 1999

01/09/1999 to 02/07/1999   KENT JONES: PAINTINGS AND PRINTS

02/14/1999 to 04/11/1999   ALLURE OF THE EAST: NEAR EASTERN DECORATIVE ARTS AND EUROPEAN ORIENTALIST PAINTINGS
The Touma Collection presents a fascinating survey of textiles, metalwork, pottery, and other decorative art forms displaying the mastery of ornament which blossomed under the influence of Islam in the Near East.   A look is offered from two perspectives: one the ideology that exists within a culture; and two, views of an alien culture by outsiders. *Will Travel*

06/12/1999 to 08/01/1999   TWO VIEWS: PHOTOGRAPHS PAULA CHAMLEE/RICK DINGUS

10/16/1999 to 12/29/1999   JUBILEE SHOW

11/21/1999 to 01/03/1999   MASTER PRINTS FROM THE LUTHERAN BROTHERHOOD AND THE TOPEKA COMPETITION

WICHITA

Edwin A. Ulrich Museum of Art

Affiliate Institution: Wichita State University
1845 Fairmount St., Wichita, KS 67260-0046
📞: 316-978-3664   ◉ www.twsu.edu/~ulrich
Open: 12-5 Daily   **Closed:** 1/1, 1/18, MEM/DAY, ESTR, 7/4, 7/5, LAB/DAY, THGV, 12/24-25
& ℗ **Museum Shop**
Group Tours: 316-978-6413   **Drop-In Tours**: by appointment
Historic Building Marble & glass mosaic mural by Spanish artist Joan Miro on museum facade   **Sculpture Garden**
Permanent Collection: AM: 19 20; EU: 19 20; PRIM; AM: gr; EU: gr; PHOT

The Edwin A. Ulrich Museum of Art at Wichita State University is recognized among university museums for its outdoor sculpture collection and for the quality of its exhibition program. 19th and 20th century European and American sculpture, prints, drawings, and paintings form the core of the 7,300 object collection. A major aspect of the collection is the 64-piece outdoor sculpture collection, named in honor of the founding director of the museum, placed around the 330 acre campus of Wichita State University. The collection contains a cross-section of 19th and 20th century sculptures by artists such as Auguste Rodin, Henry Moore, Louise Nevelson, George Rickey, Lynn Chadwick, and Luis Jimenez, among others. The museum is easily recognized by the centerpiece of this outdoor collection is the mosaic, Personnages Oiseaux, by Joan Miró, commissioned by the University in 1979. Consisting of nearly one million pieces of Venetian glass and marble, the mural depicts whimsical bird characters that inhabited the imagination of the artist. The Ulrich has an outstanding exhibition program and acts as a visual laboratory for the students of the University as well as the community. Exhibitions range from established art work - often from the museum's collection - to more contemporary exhibitions highlighting prominent artists working today. **NOT TO BE MISSED:** Sculpture collection on grounds of university; Collection of marine paintings by Frederick J. Waugh

ON EXHIBIT 1999

01/17/1999 to 05/02/1999   AFRICAN SCULPTURE FROM THE HARRIS KLEIN COLLECTION

03/25/1999 to 05/02/1999   MINIMALISM FROM THE COLLECTION

05/24/1999 to 08/08/1999   HALF PAST AUTUMN: THE ART OF GORDON PARKS
All aspects of his varied career will be included in the first traveling Gordon Parks retrospective. Considered by many to be an American renaissance man, Parks, a filmmaker, novelist, poet and musician is best known as a photojournalist whose powerful images deliver messages of hope in the face of adversity. *Catalog Will Travel*

KANSAS

Indian Center Museum

650 N. Seneca, Wichita, KS 67203

☎: 316-262-5221   ▣   www2.sothwind.net/~icm/museum/museum.html
Open: 10-5 Mo-Sa, (closed Mo JAN-MAR)   **Closed:** Su, LEG/HOL!
ADM   **Adult:** $2.00   **Children:** F (6 & under)   **Students:** $1.00   **Seniors:** $1.00
℗   **Museum Shop**   ❙❙: Tu only for Indian Tacos - Seasonal hours
Group Tours   **Drop-In Tours**
Permanent Collection: NAT/AM

The artworks and artifacts in this museum preserve Native American heritage and provide non-Indian people with insight into the culture and traditions of Native Americans. In addition to the art, Native American food is served on Tuesday from 11-4. **NOT TO BE MISSED:** Blackbear Bosin's 44 foot "Keeper of the Plains" located on the grounds at the confluence of the Arkansas & Little Arkansas Rivers.

Wichita Art Museum

619 Stackman St., Wichita, KS 67203-3296

☎: 316-268-4921
Open: 10-5 Tu-Sa, Noon-5 Su   **Closed:** Mo, LEG/HOL
♿   ℗   **Museum Shop**   ❙❙ Truffles Café open 11:30-1:30 Tu-Sa & Noon-2 S
Group Tours: 316-268-4907   **Drop-In Tours**
Permanent Collection: AM: ptgs, gr, drgs; EU: gr, drgs; P/COL; CHARLES RUSSELL: ptgs, drgs, sculp; OM: gr

Outstanding in its collection of paintings that span nearly 3 centuries of American art, the Wichita is also known for its Old Master prints and pre-Columbian art. **NOT TO BE MISSED:** The Roland P. Murdock Collection of American Art

Wichita Center for the Arts

9112 East Central, Wichita, KS 67206

☎: 316-634-2787
Open: 10-5 Tu-Fr; 1-5 Sa, Su   **Closed:** Mo, LEG/HOL!
♿   ℗   **Museum Shop**
Group Tours   **Drop-In Tours**
Permanent Collection: DEC/ART: 20; OR; PTGS; SCULP; DRGS; CER; GR

Midwest arts, both historical and contemporary, are the focus of this vital multi-disciplinary facility. **NOT TO BE MISSED:** 1,000 piece Bruce Moore Collection

University of Kentucky Art Museum
Rose & Euclid Ave., Lexington, KY 40506-0241

☎: 606-257-5716

Open: Noon-5 Tu-Su **Closed:** Mo, ACAD!
Vol/Cont
  ♿ ⓟ **Museum Shop** **Group Tours:** 606-257-5716 **Drop-In Tours:** By Appointment
Permanent Collection: OM: ptgs, gr: AM: ptgs 19; EU: ptgs 19; CONT/GR; PTGS 20; AF; OR; WPA WORKS

Considered to be one of Kentucky's key cultural resources, this museum houses over 3,500 art objects that span the past 2,000 years of artistic creation.

ON EXHIBIT 1999

09/13/1998 to 03/21/1999 WAY TO GO: TRANSPORTATION THEMES IN THE COLLECTION

01/17/1999 to 03/21/1999 MARK PRIEST: THE RAILROAD SERIES

02/07/1999 to 05/23/1999 MADE IN KENTUCKY: REGIONAL ARTISTS IN THE COLLECTION

02/07/1999 to 08/08/1999 THE FLOATING WORLD
The double-ended horizontal wood figures carved by Chaim Gross in the 1930s and 1940s. *Will Travel*

04/18/1999 to 08/02/1999 BLUEGRASS COLLECTORS

06/1999 to 08/1999 PHOTOGRAPHS FROM THE COLLECTION

06/1999 to 06/2000 SOUTHERN LANDSCAPES SHOW

08/1999 to 10/31/1999 A TALE OF TWO CITIES: EUGENE ATGET'S PARIS AND BERENICE ABBOTT'S NEW YORK

08/1999 to 02/2000 PRINT SHOW

09/1999 to 03/2000 TOWN AND COUNTRY: LANDSCAPES IN THE COLLECTION

09/1999 to 03/2000 ON THE BRINK: THE MILLENNIUM NEARS

11/14/1999 to 02/27/2000 HENRY CHODOWSKI: MAVOS LABYRINTHOS SERIES, 1986-1998

J. B. Speed Art Museum
2035 S. Third St., Louisville, KY 40208

☎: 502-634-2700 ▣ www.speedmuseum.org

Open: 10:30-4 Tu-Fr, 10:30-5 Sa, Noon-5 Su, till 8pm Th **Closed:** Mo, LEG/HOL!, 1st weekend in March & 1st Sa in May
Vol/Cont **Sugg/Cont:** $4.00
  ♿ ⓟ **Museum Shop** ⌨ Café,11:30-2 Tu-Sa, (Reservations suggested 634-2723)
Group Tours: 502-634-2725 **Drop-In Tours:** 2pm Sa, 1&3pm Su, 7pm Th   **Sculpture Garden**
Permanent Collection: AM: dec/art; PTGS; SCULP: GR; PRIM; OR; DU:17; FL:17; FR: ptgs 18; CONT

Founded in 1927, and located on the main campus of the University of Louisville, the newly renovated J. B. Speed Art Museum is the largest (over 3,000 works) and the most comprehensive (spanning 6,000 years of art history) public art collection in Kentucky. Free "Especially For Children" tours are offered at 11:00 each Saturday. PLEASE NOTE: A fee is charged for selected exhibitions. **NOT TO BE MISSED:** New acquisition: "Saint Jerome in the Wilderness" by Hendrick van Somer, 1651; "Head of a Ram",a 2nd century marble Roman sculpture (recent acquisition); "Colossal Head of Medusa", polychromed fiberglass sculpture by Audry Flack (recent acquisition)

KENTUCKY

J. B. Speed Art Museum - continued
ON EXHIBIT 1999
Late October 1998 to Fall 1999   OBJECTS OF FAITH: SACRED ART FROM THE JEWISH MUSEUM

12/08/1998 to 01/31/1999   RODIN: SCULPTURE FROM THE IRIS AND B. GERALD CANTOR COLLECTION
More than 50 bronzes and related works on paper including pieces from Rodin's important large-scale compositions as well as some of his best known single motifs are on loan from the most important and extensive private collections of its kind

Photographic Archives
Affiliate Institution: University of Louisville Libraries
Ekstrom Library, University of Louisville, Louisville, KY 40292
☎: 502-852-6752   ◙ www.louisville.edu/library/ekstrom/special/pa-info.html
Open: 10-4 Mo-Fr, 10-8 Th   **Closed:** Sa, Su, LEG/HOL!
 ⮾   ℗   **Museum Shop   Group Tours   Drop-In Tours**
Permanent Collection: PHOT; GR

With 33 individual collections, and over one million items, the Photographic Archives is one of the finest photography and research facilities in the country. **NOT TO BE MISSED:** 2,000 vintage Farm Security Administration photos; more than 1500 fine prints "from Ansel Adams to Edward Weston"

ON EXHIBIT 1999
01/18/1999 to 04/01/1999   PHOTOGRAPHS BY TODD MCKINNEY-CULL

OWENSBORO

Owensboro Museum of Fine Art
901 Frederica St., Owensboro, KY 42301
☎: 502-685-3181
Open: 10-4 Tu-Fr; 1-4 Sa, Su   **Closed:** M, LEG/HOL!
Vol/Cont   Adult: $2.00   **Children:** $1.00
 ⮾   ℗   **Museum Shop   Group Tours**: 502-685-3181   **Drop-In Tours**
Historic Building 1909 Carnegie Library Building, restored pre-Civil War John Hampden Smith House (both listed NRHP)
Permanent Collection: AM: ptgs, drgs, gr, sculp 19-20; BRIT: ptgs, drgs, gr, sculp 19-20; FR: ptgs, sculp, drgs, gr 19-20; CONT/AM; DEC/ART 14-18

The collection of the Owensboro Museum, the only fine art institution in Western Kentucky, features works by important 18-20th century American, English, and French masters. Paintings by regional artists stress the strong tradition of Kentucky landscape painting. A restored Civil War era mansion, the John Hampden Smith House, serves as a decorative arts wing for objects dating from the 15th to 19th century. **NOT TO BE MISSED:** 16 turn-of-the-century stained glass windows by Emil Frei (1867-1941) permanently installed in the new wing of the museum; revolving exhibitions of the museum's collection of Appalachian folk art.

ON EXHIBIT 1999
01/24/1999 to 04/04/1999   THE JOHN A. & MARGARET HILL COLLECTION OF AMERICAN WESTERN ART
The collection concentrates on works of the 20th c. with fine examples from the Taos Society of Artists, the Santa Fe School, and the American Regionalists. These included Berninghaus, Couse and Blumenschein as well as Ufer, Benton, Curry and Grant Wood.

01/24/1999 to 04/14/1999   THE AMERICAN WEST

04/11/1999 to 07/03/1999   THE GENTEEL TRADITION IN AMERICAN PAINTING
An exhibition of works by premier American painters of the Gilded Age. *Will Travel*

Yeiser Art Center

200 Broadway, Paducah, KY 42001-0732

📞: 502-442-2453   ◙ www.yeiser.org
Open: 10-4 Tu-Sa, 1-4 Su   **Closed:** Mo, LEG/HOL! & JAN.
ADM   Adult: $1.00   **Children:** F (under 12)   **Students:** $.50
 ⚬ ℗   **Museum Shop**
Group Tours   Drop-In Tours: Usually available upon request   **Historic Building** Located in historic Market House (1905)
Permanent Collection: AM, EU, AS & AF: 19-20

The restored 1905 Market House (listed NRHP), home to the Art Center and many other community related activities, features changing exhibitions that are regional, national, and international in content. **NOT TO BE MISSED:** Annual national fiber exhibition mid Mar thru Apr (call for exact dates)

ON EXHIBIT 1999

01/31/1999 to 03/14/1999   JOHN FOLSOM: PHOTOGRAPHY

03/21/1999 to 05/02/1999   FANTASTIC FIBERS
Traditional and nontraditional fiber works by artists from across the nation will be on view in the 10th annual fiber invitational.

05/09/1999 to 06/20/1999   POOLSCAPES: KEN LANGDON BUCK

06/27/1999 to 08/08/1999   MARY BORGMAN: PORTRAITS THAT PENETRATE FIGURES

08/15/1999 to 09/26/1999   ANNELIES HEIJNEN CERAMICS: A REFLECTION OF MY EMOTIONS

10/03/1999 to 11/14/1999   YEISER '99

11/21/1999 to 12/31/1999   TEEN SPIRIT HIGH SCHOOL COMPETITION

LOUISIANA

Alexandria Museum of Art
933 Main St., Alexandria, LA 71301-1028
\: 318-443-3458 ◉ www.themuseum.org
Open: 9-5 Tu-Fr, 1-5 Sa, Su **Closed:** Mo,, LEG/HOL!
ADM Adult: $4.00 **Children:** $2.00 **Students:** $3.00 **Seniors:** $3.00
& ℗ **Museum Shop** ⅋ Catered lunch pre-arranged in atrium café.
Group Tours: 318-443-3458 ext. 18 **Drop-In Tours**: often available upon request!
Historic Building 1900 Bank Building **Sculpture Garden**
Permanent Collection: CONT: sculp, ptgs; REG; FOLK

The grand foyer of the new wing of the Alexandria Museum of Art, was constructed and opened to the public in March of 1998. The Museum was founded in 1977 and originally occupied the Historic Rapides Bank Building, circa 1898, listed on the National Historic Register. The expanded AMoA is the centerpiece of Alexandria's riverfront, situated on the entire 900 block of Main Street. **NOT TO BE MISSED:** Native expression exhibit of Louisiana art and children's gallery.

Louisiana Arts and Science Center
100 S. River Rd., Baton Rouge, LA 70802
\: 504-344-5272
Open: 10-3 Tu-Fr, 10-4 Sa, 1-4 Su **Closed:** Mo, LEG/HOL!
Free Day: First Su of month **ADM Adult:** $3.00 **Children:** $2.00 (2-12) **Students:** $2.00 **Seniors:** $2.00
& ℗ **Museum Shop Group Tours**: 504-344-9478 **Drop-In Tours**
Historic Building In reconstructed Illinois Central Railroad Station **Sculpture Garden**
Permanent Collection: SCULP; ETH; GR; DRGS; PHOT; EGT; AM: ptgs 18-20; EU: ptgs 18-20

LASC, housed in a reconstructed Illinois Central Railroad Station, offers art exhibitions, and Egyptian tomb and mummies, and a five-car train (undergoing restoration). Hands-on areas for children include Discovery Depot – an "edutainment" area – and Science Station, an interactive physical science gallery. The Challenger Learning Center is a stmulated space station and mission control center (reservations required). **NOT TO BE MISSED:** Works by John Marin, Charles Burchfield, Asher B. Durand; Baroque, Neo-Classic, & Impressionist Works; Native American totem pole; 2nd largest collection in US of sculpture by Ivan Mestrovic.

ON EXHIBIT 1999

11/21/1999 to 01/09/2000 THE JOHN A. AND MARGARET HILL COLLECTION OF AMERICAN WESTERN ART
The collection concentrates on works of the 20th c. with fine examples from the Taos Society of Artists, the Santa Fe School, and the American Regionalists. These included Berninghaus, Couse and Blumenschein as well as Ufer, Benton, Curry and Grant Wood.

Zigler Museum
411 Clara St., Jennings, LA 70546
\: 318-824-0114 ◉ www.JeffDavis.org
Open: 9-5 Tu-Sa, 1-5 Su **Closed:** Mo, LEG/HOL!
Sugg/Cont Adult: $2.00 **Children:** $1.00
& ℗ **Museum Shop Group Tours Drop-In Tours**: Usually available upon request
Permanent Collection: REG; AM; EU

Zigler Museum - continued

The gracious colonial style structure that had served as the Zigler family home since 1908, was formerly opened as a museum in 1970. Two wings added to the original building feature many works by Louisiana landscape artists in addition to those by other American and European artists. PLEASE NOTE: The museum is open every day for the Christmas festival from the first weekend in Dec. to Dec. 22. **NOT TO BE MISSED:** Largest collection of works by African-American artist, William Tolliver

ON EXHIBIT 1999

01/05/1999 to 02/17/1999	MARDI GRAS EXHIBIT
01/16/1999 to 02/20/1999	BLACK HISTORY EXHIBIT: JOHN METOYER - PHOTOGRAPHER
03/06/1999 to 04/10/1999	ACADIANS, PAST & PRESENT
04/24/1999 to 05/29/1999	ACADIANA PORCELAIN ART GUILD EXHIBIT
06/12/1999 to 07/17/1999	AH LOUISIANA-THE LAND OF THE ACADIANS
07/31/1999 to 09/04/1999	LAISSEZ LE BONS TEMP ROULER - LIFESTYLES OF THE ACADIANS
09/18/1999 to 10/09/1999	LOUISIANA-THE SPORTSMAN'S PARADISE
10/23/1999 to 11/20/1999	QUILT EXHIBIT - OLD & NEW QUILTS
12/04/1999 to 12/22/1999	FESTIVAL OF CHRISTMAS-"FRENCH CHRISTMAS TRADITIONS"

LAFAYETTE

University Art Museum

Joel L. Fletcher Hall, 2nd Floor, East Lewis & Girard Park Dr., Lafayette, LA 70504
☎: 318-482-5326
Open: 9-4 Mo-Fr, 10-4 Sa   **Closed:** Su, 1/1, MARDI GRAS, EASTER, THGV, 12/25, LEG/HOL!
♿ Ⓟ **Museum Shop**
Group Tours: 318-482-5326   **Drop-In Tours**: reservation only; Mo-Fr 9 - 11:30 and 1:30 - 3:30
Permanent Collection: AM/REG: ptgs, sculp, drgs, phot 19-20; JAP: gr; PLEASE NOTE: Selections from the permanent collection are on display approximately once a year (call for specifics)

The University Art Museum is situated on the beautiful campus of The University of Southwestern Louisiana, home of Cypress Lake. The UAM offers visitors art exhibitions of regional, national and international acclaim. The Permanent Collection is housed in an 18th century style plantation home on the corner of Girard Park Drive and St. Mary Boulevard. Permanent holdings include works by Henri Le Sidaner, Franz Marc, Sir Godfrey Kneller, G.P.A. Healy, Henry Pember Smith, and Adolph Rinck to name only a few. Overlooking Girard Park, touring exhibits can be seen in the more modern Fletcher Hall Gallery located in the Art & Architecture Building on the U.S.L. campus.

MONROE

Masur Museum of Art

1400 S. Grand, Monroe, LA 71202
☎: 318-329-2237
Open: 9-5 Tu-T, 2-5 Fr-Su   **Closed:** Mo, LEG/HOL
♿ Ⓟ **Museum Shop**   **Group Tours**: 318-329-2237   **Drop-In Tours**: scheduled in advance
Historic Building On National Register of Historic Places   **Sculpture Garden**
Permanent Collection: AM: gr 20; REG/CONT

LOUISIANA

Masur Museum of Art - continued

Twentieth century prints by American artists, and works by contemporary regional artists, form the basis of the permanent collection of this museum which is housed in a stately modified English Tudor estate situated on the tree-lined banks of the Ouachita River.

ON EXHIBIT 1999

11/15/1998 to 01/31/1999   OLD PARIS PORCELAINS FROM THE NEW ORLEANS MUSEUM OF ART

02/07/1999 to 03/21/1999   AFRICAN-AMERICAN ARTISTS IN PARIS

04/04/1999 to 05/15/1999   THE 26TH ANNUAL JURIED COMPETITION

NEW ORLEANS

Historic New Orleans Collection

533 Royal St., New Orleans, LA 70130
☎: 504-523-4662   ▣   www.hnoc.org
Open: 10-4:30 Tu-Sa   **Closed:** Su, Mo, LEG/HOL!
ADM   ♿   **Museum Shop**
Group Tours: 504-523-4662   **Drop-In Tours**: 10, 11, 2 & 3 DAILY
Historic Building 1792 Jean Francois Merieult House Located in French Quarter
Permanent Collection: REG: ptgs, drgs, phot; MAPS; RARE BOOKS, MANUSCRIPTS

Located within a complex of historic buildings, the Historic New Orleans Collection serves the public as a museum and research center for state and local history. Merieult House, one of the most historic buildings of this complex, was built in 1792 during Louisiana's Spanish Colonial period. It is one of the few structures in the French Quarter that escaped the fire of 1794. The Williams Research Center, 410 Chartres St., part of this institution, contains curatorial, manuscript and library material relating to the history and culture of Louisiana.
NOT TO BE MISSED: Tours of the LA. History Galleries and Founders Residence

ON EXHIBIT 1999

to 01/09/1999   WILLIAM AIKEN WALKER: SOJOURNER ARTIST

11/17/1998 to 05/01/1999   SEEN AND NOT HEARD: FACETS OF CHILDHOOD IN 19TH CENTURY NEW ORLEANS

05/11/1999 to 07/10/1999   THE FABRIC OF HISTORY: THE COTTON INDUSTRY IN NEW ORLEANS

07/20/1999 to 10/30/1999   INDIANS IN 19TH CENTURY NEW ORLEANS

11/02/1999 to 04/08/2000   FROM PANIC TO OCCUPATION: NEW ORLEANS IN THE AGE OF T. K. WHARTON

Louisiana State Museum

751 Chartres St., Jackson Square, New Orleans, LA 70116
☎: 800-568-6968
Open: 9-5 Tu-Su   **Closed:** Mo, LEG/HOL!
ADM   Adult: $4.00   **Children:** F (12 & under)   **Students:** $3.00   **Seniors:** $3.00
♿   **Museum Shop   Group Tours   Drop-In Tours:** Gallery talks on weekends - call for specifics   **Historic Building**
Permanent Collection: DEC/ART; FOLK; PHOT; PTGS; TEXTILES

Louisiana State Museum - continued

Several historic buildings, located in the famous New Orleans French Quarter are included in the Louisiana State Museum complex, provide the visitor with a wide array of viewing experiences that run the gamut from fine art to decorative art, textiles, Mardi Gras memorabilia, and even jazz music. The Cabildo, Presbytere, and 1850 House (all located on Jackson Square) and the Old U.S. Mint are currently open to the public. PLEASE NOTE THE FOLLOWING: (1) Although the entry fee of $4.00 is charged per building visited, a discounted rate is offered for a visit to two or more sites. (2) 1850 House features special interpretive materials for handicapped visitors. **NOT TO BE MISSED:** Considered the State Museum's crown jewel, the recently reopened Cabildo features a walk through Louisiana history from Colonial times through Reconstruction. Admission to the Arsenal, featuring changing exhibits, is included in the entry fee to the Cabildo.

New Orleans Museum of Art

1 Collins Diboll Circle, City Park, P.O Box 19123, New Orleans, LA 70119-0123
📞: 504-488-2631   ▧ www.noma.org
Open: 10-5 Tu-Su   **Closed:** Mo, LEG/HOL!
Free Day: 10-noon Th for Louisiana residents only   **ADM   Adult:** $6.00   **Children:** $3.00 (3-17)   **Seniors:** $5.00
♿ ⓟ   **Museum Shop**   ‖ Courtyard Café 10:30-4:30 Tu-S (children's menu available)
Group Tours: 504-488-2631   **Drop-In Tours**: 11:00 & 2:00 Tu-Su and by appointment for groups of 10 or more
Permanent Collection: AM; OM: ptgs; IT/REN: ptgs (Kress Collection); FR; P/COL: MEX; AF; JAP: gr; AF; OC; NAT/AM; LAT/AM; AS; DEC/ART: 1st. A.D.-20; REG; PHOT; GLASS

Located in the 1,500 acre City Park, the 75 year old New Orleans Museum recently completed a $23 million dollar expansion and renovation program that doubled its size. Serving the entire Gulf South as an invaluable artistic resource, the museum houses over one dozen major collections that cover a broad range of fine and decorative art. **NOT TO BE MISSED:** Treasures by Fabergé; Chinese Jades; French Art; Portrait Miniatures; New 3rd floor showcase for Non-Western Art; The stARTing point, a new hands-on gallery area with interactive exhibits and 2 computer stations designed to help children and adults understand the source of artists' inspiration.

ON EXHIBIT 1999

10/30/1998 to 04/04/1999   ANCIENT GOLD: THE WEALTH OF THE THRACIANS, TREASURES FROM THE REPUBLIC OF BULGARIA
More than 200 magnificent gold and silver objects, dating from 1200 to 400 B.C., will be featured in and exhibition that lends credence to the life and legends of ancient Thrace. *Will Travel* ⌣

01/30/1999 to 04/11/1999   THE ART OF EDDIE KENDRICK: A SPIRITUAL JOURNEY *Will Travel*

02/20/1999 to 04/18/1999   HOSPICE: A PHOTOGRAPHIC INQUIRY
The photographs of Jim Goldberg, Nan Goldin, Sally Mann, Jack Radcliffe and Kathy Vargas, detail the emotional and collaborative experience of living and working in hospices in different regions of the country. Their works touch upon every aspect of hospice care revealing the spiritual, emotional and physical needs of the terminally ill and their families. *Catalog Will Travel*

05/1999 to 08/29/1999   EDGAR DEGAS AND NEW ORLEANS: A FRENCH IMPRESSIONIST IN AMERICA *Will Travel*

05/08/1999 to 07/03/1999   THE CECIL FAMILY COLLECTS: FOUR CENTURIES OF DECORATIVE ARTS FROM BURGHLEY HOUSE
Burghley House is one of the oldest and grandest Elizabethan houses in England. The 120 crafted works from its collection will document the evolution of taste and collecting in Britain in the course of four centuries. *Catalog Will Travel*

10/02/1999 to 11/28/1999   RAOUL DUFY: LAST OF THE FAUVES
Dufy was an artist who rose to prominence in the early 1900's and remained popular till his death in 1953. Since then he has been largely ignored by museums. This exhibition aims to restore his reputation as one of the most original and talented artists of the first half of this century. *Catalog Will Travel*

10/02/1999 to 11/28/1999   JOHN CLEMMER: A FIFTY YEAR RETROSPECTIVE

12/1999 to 02/2000   HENRY CASSELLI: MASTER OF THE AMERICAN WATERCOLOR

LOUISIANA

Meadows Museum of Art of Centenary College

2911 Centenary Blvd., Shreveport, LA 71104-1188
☎: 318-869-5169
Open: Noon-4 Tu-Fr; 1-4 Sa, Su   **Closed:** Mo, LEG/HOL!
& ℗   **Museum Shop**
Group Tours: 318-869-5169   **Drop-In Tours**: Upon request if available
Permanent Collection: PTGS, SCULP, GR, 18-20; INDO CHINESE: ptgs, gr

This museum, opened in 1976, serves mainly as a repository for the unique collection of works in a variety of media by French artist Jean Despujols and the Centenary College collection. The Museum's galleries also boast a series of temporary exhibitions throughout the year. **NOT TO BE MISSED:** The permanent collection itself which offers a rare glimpse into the people & culture of French Indochina in 1938. Also includes American and European paintings and works on paper from the college collection.

ON EXHIBIT 1999

02/21/1999 to 05/28/1999   WALTER O. EVANS COLLECTION OF AFRICAN AMERICAN ART
Portraits, landscapes and mythological imagery will be seen in this remarkable exhibition of historical and contemporary works of art by black artists.

R. W. Norton Art Gallery

4747 Creswell Ave., Shreveport, LA 71106
☎: 318-865-4201
Open: 10-5 Tu-Fr; 1-5 Sa, Su   **Closed:** Mo, LEG/HOL!
& ℗   **Museum Shop**
Group Tours   Drop-In Tours
Permanent Collection: AM: ptgs, sculp (late 17-20); EU: ptgs, sculp 16-19; BRIT: cer

With its incomparable collections of American and European art, the Norton, situated in a 46 acre wooded park, has become one of the major cultural attractions in the region since its opening in 1966. Among its many attractions are the Bierstadt Gallery, the Bonheur Gallery, and the Corridor which features "The Prisons", a 16-part series of fantasy etchings by Piranesi. Those who visit the museum from early to mid April will experience the added treat of seeing 13,000 azalea plants that surround the building in full bloom. **NOT TO BE MISSED:** Outstanding collections of works by Frederic Remington & Charles M. Russell; The Wedgwood Gallery (one of the finest collections of its kind in the southern U.S.)

ON EXHIBIT 1999

Early Spring 1999   AMERICAN IMPRESSIONISTS IN FRANCE

Late Spring 1999   THE ROSE IN AMERICAN ART

09/05/1999 to 10/24/1999   AMERICAN LANDSCAPES FROM THE PAINE ART CENTER & ARBORETUM

BRUNSWICK

Bowdoin College Museum of Art

9400 College Station, Brunswick, ME 04011-8494
☎: 207-725-3275
Open: 10-5 Tu-Sa, 2-5 Su   **Closed:** Mo, LEG/HOL! ALSO CLOSED WEEK BETWEEN 12/25 & NEW YEARS DAY
Vol/Cont
& ℗ **Museum Shop**
Group Tours: 207-725-3276   **Drop-In Tours:** by appointment only
Historic Building 1894 Walker Art Building Designed by Charles Follen McKim
Permanent Collection: AN/GRK; AN/R; AN/EGT; AM: ptgs, sculp, drgs, gr, dec/art; EU: ptgs, sculp, gr, drgs, dec/art; AF: sculp; INTERIOR MURALS BY LAFARGE, THAYER, VEDDER, COX

From the original bequest of artworks given in 1811 by James Bowdoin III, who served as Thomas Jefferson's minister to France and Spain, the collection has grown to include important works from a broad range of nations and periods. **NOT TO BE MISSED:** Winslow Homer Collection of wood engravings, watercolors, drawings, and memorabilia (available for viewing during the summer months only).

ON EXHIBIT 1999

ONGOING   BOYD GALLERY:
14th to 20th-century European art from the permanent collection.

ONGOING   BOWDOIN GALLERY:
American art from the permanent collection.

ONGOING   SOPHIA WALKER GALLERY: ART AND LIFE IN THE ANCIENT MEDITERRANEAN
4th century BC .to 4th century A.D. Assyrian, Egyptian, Cypriot, Greek and Roman objects will be featured in an installation that highlights one of the museum's great strengths.

01/19/1999 to 03/21/1999   ANCIENT PERUVIAN ART

01/28/1999 to 03/21/1999   OCCUPYING THE STREET - WORKS FROM THE PERMANENT COLLECTION

01/28/1999 to 03/21/1999   A TALE OF TWO CITIES: EUGENE ATGET'S PARIS AND BERENICE ABBOTT'S NEW YORK

04/08/1999 to 06/06/1999   HUNG LIU: A SURVEY 1988-1998

LEWISTON

Bates College Museum of Art

Affiliate Institution: Bates College
Olin Arts Center, Bates College, Lewiston, ME 04240
☎: 207-786-6158
Open: 10-5 Tu-Sa, 1-5 Su   **Closed:** Mo, LEG/HOL!
& ℗ **Museum Shop   Group Tours   Drop-In Tours**
Permanent Collection: AM: ptgs, sculp; GR 19-20; EU: ptgs, sculp, gr; drgs:

The recently constructed building of the Museum of Art at Bates College houses a major collection of works by American artist Marsden Hartley. It also specializes in 20th-century American and European prints, drawings, and photographs, and has a small collection of 20th century American paintings. **NOT TO BE MISSED:** Collection of Marsden Hartley drawings and memorabilia

ON EXHIBIT 1999
ONGOING   HIGHLIGHTS FROM THE PERMANENT COLLECTION

MAINE

Ogunquit Museum of American Art

181 Shore Rd., Ogunquit, ME 03907
☎: 207-646-4909
Open: (open 7/1 through 9/30 ONLY) 10:30-5 Mo-Sa, 2-5 Su **Closed:** LAB/DAY
ADM Adult: $4.00 **Children:** F (under 12) **Students:** $3.00 **Seniors:** $3.00
🚫 ℗ **Museum Shop Group Tours Drop-In Tours:** upon request if available **Sculpture Garden**
Permanent Collection: AM: ptgs, sculp 20

Situated on a rocky promontory overlooking the sea, this museum has been described as the most beautiful small museum in the world! Built in 1952, the Ogunquit houses many important 20th century American paintings and works of sculpture in addition to site-specific sculptures spread throughout its three acres of land. **NOT TO BE MISSED:** "Mt. Katadhin, Winter" by Marsden Hartley; "The Bowery Drunks" by Reginald Marsh; "Pool With Four Markers" by Dozier Bell; "Sleeping Girl" by Walt Kuhn

University of Maine Museum of Art

5712 Carnegie Hall, Orono, ME 04469-5712
☎: 207-581-3255
Open: 9-4:30 Mo-Fr; Weekends by appointment **Closed:** Su, STATE & LEG/HOL!
℗ **Museum Shop Group Tours Drop-In Tours Historic Building** 1904 Library of Palladian Design
Permanent Collection: AM: gr, ptgs 18-20; EU: gr, ptgs 18-20; CONT; REG

Housed in a beautiful 1904 structure of classic Palladian design, this university art museum, located just to the north east of Bangor, Maine, features American and European art of the 18th-20th centuries, and works by Maine based artists of the past and present. The permanent collection is displayed throughout the whole university and in the main center-for-the-arts building,

Portland Museum of Art

Seven Congress Square, Portland, ME 04101
☎: 207-775-6148 ▣ www.portlandmuseum.org
Open: 10-5 Tu, We, Sa, Su; 10-9 Th, Fr; (open 10-5 Mo MEM/DAY to Columbus Day) **Closed:** Mo, 1/1, THGV, 12/25
Free Day: 5-9 Fr **ADM Adult:** $6.00 **Children:** $1.00 (6-12) **Students:** $5.00 **Seniors:** $5.00
🚫 ℗ **Museum Shop** 🍴 Museum Café **Group Tours:** 207-775-6148 **Drop-In Tours:** 2:00 daily & 6pm Fr
Permanent Collection: AM; ptgs, sculp 19-20; REG; DEC/ART; gr

The Portland Museum of Art is the oldest and largest art museum in the state of Maine. Established in 1882, the outstanding museum features Impressionist and American master works housed in an award-winning building designed by renowned architect I. M. Pei & Partners. PLEASE NOTE: Also, there is a toll free number (1-800-639-4067) for museum recorded information. **NOT TO BE MISSED:** The Charles Shipman Payson Collection of 17 works by Winslow Homer

ON EXHIBIT 1999

11/05/1998 to 01/03/1999 PORTLAND MUSEUM OF ART BIENNIAL
A juried exhibition of works in all media by Maine-based artists.

Portland Museum of Art - continued
01/21/1999 to 03/21/1999   LOUISE NEVELSON: STRUCTURE EVOLVING
Recognized as one of America's premiere sculptors, this exhibit includes 43 works and examines Nevelson's wide choice of media in both sculpture and works on paper. It will highlight her practice of recycling components of existing works to create new ones. *Will Travel*

06/24/1999 to 10/17/1999   LOVE AND THE AMERICAN DREAM: THE ART OF ROBERT INDIANA
What distinguished Indiana from his "pop" colleagues is the use of words and his keen interest in the American Dream . His 65 works include paintings, sculpture, and prints. *Will Travel*

ROCKLAND

Farnsworth Art Museum and Wyeth Center
352 Main St., Rockland, ME 04841-9975
☎: 207-596-6457   ▣   www.wyethcenter.com; www.midcoast.com/~farnsworth
Open: SUMMER: 9-5 daily; WINTER: 10-5 Tu-Sa, 1-5 Su   **Closed:** LEG/HOL!
ADM   Adult: $9.00   **Children:** F (under 17)   **Students:** $5.00   **Seniors:** $7.00
& ℗   **Museum Shop**
Group Tours: ex 104
Drop-In Tours
Historic Building 1850 Victorian Homestead and Olson House open MEM/DAY to Columbus Day.
Permanent Collection: AM: 18-20; REG; PHOT; GR

Nationally acclaimed for its collection of American Art, the Farnsworth, located in the mid coastal city of Rockland, counts among its important holdings the largest public collection of works by sculptor Louise Nevelson. The museum's 8 galleries offer a comprehensive survey of American art. Recently, the museum opened the Wyeth center, a new gallery building and study center, to house the works of Andrew, N.C. and Jamie Wyeth. **NOT TO BE MISSED:** Major works by N.C., Andrew & Jamie Wyeth, Fitz Hugh Lane, John Marin, Edward Hopper, Neil Welliver, Louise Nevelson; The Olson House, depicted by Andrew Wyeth in many of his most famous works

ON EXHIBIT 1999
11/29/1998 to 02/21/1999   FAIRFIELD PORTER FROM THE PERMANENT COLLECTION OF THE PARRISH ART MUSEUM

12/06/1998 to Ongoing   MAINE IN AMERICA
The history of American art with a special emphasis on works related to Maine will be seen in the examples on view from the permanent collection.

02/28/1999 to 05/30/1999   RECENT ACQUISITIONS FROM THE PERMANENT COLLECTION

02/28/1999 to 10/30/1999   INVENTING ACADIA: ARTISTS AND TOURISTS AT MOUNT DESERT
The contributions of landscape painters who shaped aesthetic appreciation of Mount Desert into a major recreation and resort area in Maine and the creation of Mount Desert National Park.

11/07/1999 to 02/13/2000   JOHN MCCOY

MAINE

Colby College Museum of Art
Mayflower Hill, Waterville, ME 04901
☏: 207-872-3228
Open: 10-4:30 Mo-Sa, 2-4:30 Su   **Closed:** LEG/HOL!
 ♿ &#9physical; **Museum Shop   Group Tours   Drop-In Tours**
Permanent Collection: AM: Impr/ptgs, folk, gr; Winslow Homer: watercolors; OR: cer

Located in a modernist building on a campus dominated by neo-Georgian architecture, the museum at Colby College houses a distinctive collection of several centuries of American Art. Included among its many fine holdings is a 36 piece collection of sculpture donated to the school by Maine native, Louise Nevelson. **NOT TO BE MISSED:** 25 watercolors by John Marin; "La Reina Mora" by Robert Henri (recent acquisition)

ON EXHIBIT 1999

01/24/1999 to 02/21/1999   **GARRY MITCHELL**

02/14/1999 to 03/14/1999   **BEVIN ENGMAN**

02/14/1999 to 03/21/1999   **THE CHARLES HOVEY PEPPER COLLECTION OF JAPANESE PRINTS**

04/1999 to 06/1999   **CLEVE GRAY**

07/05/1999 to 08/01/1999   **QUILT NATIONAL**

Elizabeth Myers Mitchell Art Gallery

Affiliate Institution: St. John's College

60 College Ave., Annapolis, MD 21404-2800

☎: 410-626-2556   ▣ www.sjca.edu/gallery/gallery.html

Open: Noon-5 Tu-Su, 7pm-8pm Fr; Closed for the summer 7/26 - 9/17/1999   **Closed:** Mo, LEG/HOL!

&   ℗   **Museum Shop**   ⑪ College Coffee Shop open 8:15-4

Group Tours Drop-In Tours   Historic Building

Established in 1989 primarily as a center of learning for the visual arts, this institution, though young in years, presents a rotating schedule of educational programs and high quality exhibitions containing original works by many of the greatest artists of yesterday and today.

ON EXHIBIT 1999

01/05/1999 to 02/26/1999   GEORGES ROUAULT: CIRQUE DE L'ETOILE FILANTE

Circus of the Shooting Stars brings to life scenes from the circus in a series of color etchings, aquatint, and wood engravings

03/09/1999 to 04/23/1999   SUNLIGHT AND SHADOW: AMERICAN IMPRESSIONISM, 1885-1945

78 works in oil, watercolor and pastel highlight the American Impressionists exploration of intense color oppositions in which they created an exuberant and immediate sense of color and light in the American landscape.

06/24/1999 to 07/25/1999   THE FINE ART OF CRAFT: NATIONAL CRAFT SHOW OF MARYLAND

American Visionary Art Museum

800 Key Highway & Covington in the Baltimore Inner Harbor, Baltimore, MD 21202-3940

☎: 410-244-1900

Open: 10-6 Tu-Su   **Closed:** THGV, 12/25

ADM   Adult: $6.00   **Children:** F (under 4)   **Students:** $4.00   **Seniors:** $4.00

&   ℗   **Museum Shop**   ⑪ Joy America Café open 11:30am - 10pm Tu-S, Sunday Brunch 11-4:30 (call 410-244-6500 to reserve)   **Group Tours Drop-In Tours   Historic Building** 1913 elliptical brick building   **Sculpture Garden**

Permanent Collection: Visionary art

Dedicated to intuition, The American Visionary Art Museum, designated by Congress, is the nation's official repository for original self-taught (a.k.a. "outsider") visionary art. Among the many highlights of the 4,000 piece permanent collection are Gerlad Hawkes' one-of-a-kind matchstick sculptures, 400 original pen and ink works by postman/visionary Ted Gordon, and the entire life archive of the late Otto Billig, M.D., an expert in transcultural psychiatric art who was the last psychiatrist to Zelda Fitzgerald. **NOT TO BE MISSED:** Towering whirligig by Vollis Simpson, located in outdoor central plaza, which is like a giant playwheel during the day and a colorful firefly-like sculpture when illuminated at night; Joy America Café featuring ultra organic gourmet food created by four-star chef Peter Zimmer, formerly of The Inn of the Anazazi in Santa Fe, NM.; Wildflower sculpture garden complete with woven wood wedding chapel by visionary artist Ben Wilson.

ON EXHIBIT 1999

05/16/1998 to 05/30/1999   LOVE: ERROR AND EROS

Summer 1999   SELF-MADE WORLDS

Fall 1999 to Fall 2000   WE ARE NOT ALONE: ANGELS AND ALIENS

MARYLAND

Baltimore Museum of Art
Art Museum Drive, Baltimore, MD 21218-3898
📞: 410-396-7100   📧 www.artbma.org
Open: 11-5 We-Fr; 11-6 Sa, Su; 5-9 1st Th of Mo.(except major hols.)   **Closed:** Mo, Tu, 1/1, 7/4, THGV, 12/25
ADM   Adult: $6.00   **Children:** F (18 & under)   **Students:** $4.00   **Seniors:** $4.00
  ♿ ℗   **Museum Shop**   ¶Geertrudes at the BMA 410-889-3399
Group Tours: 410-396-6320   **Drop-In Tours**   **Historic Building** 1929 building designed by John Russell Pope
Sculpture Garden
Permanent Collection: AM: ptgs 18-20; EU: ptgs, sculp 15-20; MATISSE: Cone Coll; FR: phot 19; AM: dec/art, cont; EU: dec/art, cont; P/COL; AF; OC; NAT/AM; AN/R: mosaics

One of the undisputed jewels of this important artistic institution is the Cone Collection of works by Matisse, the largest of its kind in the Western Hemisphere. The Museum recently added a new 17 gallery wing for contemporary art, making it the first and largest of its kind not only for this institution, but for the state of Maryland as well. Works by Andy Warhol, from the second largest permanent collection of paintings by the artist, are on regular display in this new wing. **NOT TO BE MISSED:** The Cone Collection; American: dec/arts; Antioch mosaics; Sculpture gardens; American: paintings 19; OM: paintings; The new installation (late spring '97) of the American Wing of American Decorative Arts and Painting.

ON EXHIBIT 1999

10/04/1998 to 01/03/1999   DEGAS AND THE LITTLE DANCER
The sculpture, one of the most celebrated of the modern age, is known to millions through the 20 or more bronze casts in collections throughout the world. It is considered a masterpiece of the artist's impressionist years. It will be shown with drawings, paintings and pastels which illustrate its beginnings in his dance repertoire.

10/14/1998 to 01/03/1999   PHOTOIMAGE: 60s-90s
Ranging from silk-screen and lithography to photogravure and ink jet prints, the 100 European and American prints in this exhibition examine the ongoing dialogue between photographic imagery and contemporary printmaking.

01/27/1999 to 04/11/1999   ELIZABETH CATLETT SCULPTURE: A RETROSPECTIVE
A first comprehensive look at the sculpture of this respected African-American artist and her prodigious accomplishments.

01/27/1999 to 04/11/1999   DANCING AT THE LOUVRE: FAITH RINGOLD'S FRENCH COLLECTION AND OTHER STORY QUILTS
The first museum exhibition of selected quilt paintings including some from the 1980s. The exhibition will focus on two history-based series, both made of acrylic on canvas with pieced fabric. The "French Connection" combines a revisionist view of the early 20th C. School of Paris with a fictional biography of an African-American artist and model who lived in Paris during the 1920s. The "American Collection" continues the story through the life of the artist's daughter who becomes an artist in America. *Catalog Will Travel*

02/17/1999 to 07/04/1999   NOUVEAU TO DECO: TEXTILES OF THE EARLY TWENTIETH CENTURY

04/07/1999 to 06/30/1999   PRINT FAIR ACQUISITIONS (print and drawing society acquisitions)
To celebrate the 10th anniversary of the Baltimore Print Fair, these prints collected by the Baltimore community since the Fair began. This is the only fair in the country dedicated to the sale of contemporary prints.

06/13/1999 to 09/05/1999   CHOKWE! ART AND INITIATION OF CHOKWE AND RELATED PEOPLES
In the first exhibition of its kind in the U.S., the 200 artifacts on view, gathered from important public and private collections here and in Europe, highlight the artistry of the Chokwe and related peoples of Angola, Zaire and Zambia. Interactive elements and innovative video techniques will be integrated into this gallery installation to provide a rich contextual setting for the items on view. *Will Travel*

10/10/1999 to 01/30/2000   IMPRESSIONIST PORTRAITS FROM AMERICAN COLLECTIONS
Impressionist artists and their progressive approach to portraiture are the focus of this ground breaking exhibition . Included for the first time are works by Cassatt, Gauguin, Cezanne, Degas, Manet, Monet, Morisot and Renoir. This is the first attempt to provide insight into the genre as it was practiced by masters of this influential movement. *Catalog Will Travel*

11/25/1999 to 03/21/1999   PHOTOGRAPHS, DRAWINGS, AND COLLAGES BY FREDERICK SOMMER
Recognized as one of the 20th C. most inventive photographers, Sommers later in his career created negatives without a camera, using smoke and paint on cellophane. He also photographed cut paper abstractions and collages of old Prints, as in the work of Surrealist Max Ernst which are removed from their original context and reassembled to suggest new meanings.

The Contemporary

601 N. Howard St., Baltimore, MD 21201

: 410-333-8600 ◙ www.softaid.net/the contemporar

Open: For administrative office only: usually 12-5 Tu-Su

Sugg/Cont

Museum Shop

Group Tours **Drop-In Tours**

Permanent Collection:

Considering itself an "un-museum" The Contemporary is not a permanent facility but rather an institution dedicated to the presentation of exhibitions at various venues throughout the city of Baltimore. It is suggested that visitors call ahead to verify the location (or locations), hours of operation, and information on their schedule of exhibitions.

Evergreen House

Affiliate Institution: The Johns Hopkins University

4545 N. Charles St., Baltimore, MD 21210-2693

: 410-516-0341

Open: 10-4 Mo-Fr, 1-4 Sa, Su **Closed:** LEG/HOL!

ADM **Adult:** $6.00 **Children:** F (under 5) **Students:** $3.00 **Seniors:** $5.00

♿ Ⓟ **Museum Shop** 🍴 Call ahead for box lunches, high tea & continental breakfast for groups

Group Tours: 410-516-0344 (Groups more than 20 $5 pp) **Drop-In Tours**: call for specifics

Historic Building 1850-1860 Evergreen House

Permanent Collection: FR: Impr, Post/Impr; EU: cer; OR: cer; JAP

Restored to its former beauty and reopened to the public in 1990, the 48 rooms of the magnificent Italianate Evergreen House © 1878), with classical revival additions, contain outstanding collections of French Impressionist and Post-Impressionist works of art collected by its founders, the Garrett family of Baltimore.. PLEASE NOTE: All visitors to Evergreen House are obliged to go on a 1 hour tour of the house with a docent. It is recommended that large groups call ahead to reserve. It should be noted that the last tour of the day begins at 3:00.S **NOT TO BE MISSED:** Japanese netsuke and inro; the only gold bathroom in Baltimore; private theatre designed by Leon Bakst.

Peale Museum

225 Holliday St., Baltimore, MD 21202

: 410-396-3525

Open: 10-5 Tu-Sa, Noon-5 Su **Closed:** Mo, LEG/HOL

ADM **Adult:** $2.00 **Children:** $1.50 (4-18) **Seniors:** $1.50

♿ Ⓟ **Museum Shop**

Group Tours **Drop-In Tours**

Historic Building First building built as a museum in U.S. by Rembrandt Peale, 1814

Sculpture Garden

Permanent Collection: REG/PHOT; SCULP; PTGS; 40 PTGS BY PEALE FAMILY ARTISTS

The Peale, erected in 1814, has the distinction of being the very first museum in the U.S. One of the several City Life Museums in Baltimore. Over 40 portraits by members of the Peale Family are displayed in an ongoing exhibition entitled "The Peales, An American Family of Artists in Baltimore". PLEASE NOTE: The museum is temporarily closed until further notice.

MARYLAND

Walters Art Gallery

600 N. Charles St., Baltimore, MD 21201
☎: 410-547-9000   ◉ www.TheWalters.org
Open: 10-4 Tu-Fr; 11-5 Sa, Su; till 8pm every first Th   **Closed:** Mo, 1/1, Thgv, 12/24, 12/25
Free Day: Sa 11 am to 1 PM   **ADM   Adult:** $6.00   **Children:** $2.00 (under 6 free)   **Students:** $3.00   **Seniors:** $4.00
丙   ℗   **Museum Shop**   ⅼⅼ: Café offering light food during museum hours
Group Tours: ex 232   **Drop-In Tours:** Noon We, 1:30pm Su
Historic Building 1904 building modeled after Ital. Ren. & Baroque palace designs
Permanent Collection: AN/EGT; AN/GRK; AN/R; MED; DEC/ART 19; OM: ptgs; EU: ptgs & sculp; DEC/ART

The Walters, considered one of America's most distinguished art museums, features a broad-ranging collection that spans more than 5,000 years of artistic achievement from Ancient Egypt to Art Nouveau. Remarkable collections of ancient, medieval, Islamic & Byzantine art, 19th century paintings and sculpture, and Old Master paintings are housed within the walls of the magnificently restored original building and in a large modern wing as well. Until Spring 2001 the 1974 building will be closed while it undergoes renovation. During the renovation period the Walter's 1904 building at the corner of N. Charles and Centre Streets and its Hackerman House Museum of Asian Art will remain open. "Highlights from the Permanent Collection" will be displayed temporarily in galleries off the Renaissance Sculpture Court. **NOT TO BE MISSED:** Hackerman House, a restored mansion adjacent to the main museum building, filled with oriental decorative arts treasures.

ON EXHIBIT 1999

ONGOING AT HACKERMAN HOUSE   JAPANESE CLOISONNÉ ENAMELS

ONGOING AT HACKERMAN HOUSE   A MEDLEY OF GERMAN DRAWINGS

11/08/1998 to 01/03/1999   THE INVISIBLE MADE VISIBLE: ANGELS FROM THE VATICAN
A truly remarkable exhibition of angels from the extensive collection of the Vatican Museums. It will examine the representation of angels from 1000 B.C. to the present. Rare and precious objects in all media by Fabiano, Fra Angelico, Masolino, Carracci, Reni, Veronese and Raphael as well as non-biblical and pre-Christian cultures are included. Adm: There will be a special price for admission to this exhibition. *Catalog Will Travel* ◠

12/16/1998 to 03/14/1999   MAKE THEM LAUGH: SLAPSTICK AND SATIRE IN JAPAN
This exhibition displays Japanese prints that inspire both smiles and belly laughs and contain touches of the fascinating and the weird.

03/03/1999 to 05/09/1999   LAND OF THE WINGED HORSEMEN: ART IN POLAND, 1571-1764
In the first major display in America of works in all media from Poland during the 16th-18th c. Paintings, ceramics, glass, furniture, weaponry, metalworks, and textiles including a captured Turkish tent) will be shown. *Catalog Will Travel*

EASTON

Academy of the Arts

106 South Sts., Easton, MD 21601
☎: 410-822-ARTS   ◉ WWW.ART-ACADEMY.ORG
Open: 10-4 Mo-Sa, till 9 We   **Closed:** Su, LEG/HOL! month of Aug
丙   ℗   **Museum Shop   Group Tours:** 410-822-5997   **Drop-In Tours**
Historic Building Housed in Old Schoolhouse
Permanent Collection: PTGS; SCULP; GR: 19-20; PHOT

Housed in two 18th century buildings, one of which was an old school house, the Academy's permanent collection contains an important group of original 19th & 20th century prints. This museum serves the artistic needs of the community with a broad range of activities including concerts, exhibitions and educational workshops. **NOT TO BE MISSED:** "Slow Dancer" sculpture by Robert Cook, located in the Academy Courtyard; Works by James McNeil Whistler, Grant Wood, Bernard Buffet, Leonard Baskin, James Rosenquist, and others.

Washington County Museum of Fine Arts

91 Key St., City Park, Box 423, Hagerstown, MD 21741

📞: 301-739-5727   ◉ www.washcomuseum.org
Open: 10-5 Tu-Sa, 1-5 Su   **Closed:** Mo, LEG/HOL
Vol/Cont
 ♿ ℗ **Museum Shop**
Group Tours   Drop-In Tours: 2 weeks notice   **Sculpture Garden**
Permanent Collection: AM: 19-20; REG; OM; 16-18; EU: ptgs 18-19; CH

In addition to the permanent collection of 19th and 20th century American art, including works donated by the founders of the museum, Mr. & Mrs. William H. Singer, Jr., the Museum has a fine collection of Oriental Art, African Art, American pressed glass, and European paintings, sculpture and decorative arts. Hudson River landscapes, Peale family paintings, and works by "The Eight", all from the permanent collection, are displayed throughout the year on an alternating basis with special temporary exhibitions. The museum is located in the northwest corner of the state just below the Pennsylvania border. **NOT TO BE MISSED:** "Sunset Hudson River" by Frederic Church

ON EXHIBIT 1999

01/10/1999 to 02/14/1999	66TH CUMBERLAND VALLEY PHOTO SESSION
01/17/1999 to 02/28/1999	VALLEY ART ASSOCIATION
01/17/1999 to 03/14/1999	CHARLES AMOS TRAIN EXHIBIT
02/21/1999 to 04/11/1999	STILL LIFE FROM THE PERMANENT COLLECTION
02/28/1999 to 04/04/1999	BALTIMORE WATERCOLOR SOCIETY
03/07/1999 to 04/04/1999	JAMES HILLEARY
04/11/1999 to 05/09/1999	PUBLIC SCHOOL ART
04/18/1999 to 06/13/1999	CHARLES WALTHER: MODERNIST AND HIS SNALLYGASTER SCHOOL
05/16/1999 to 06/27/1999	67TH ANNUAL CUMBERLAND VALLEY ARTISTS
06/20/1999 to 08/01/1999	EVELYN METZGER
07/01/1999 to 08/22/1999	WIGINTON COLLECTION
08/29/1999 to 10/17/1999	BRIAN NOVANTY
10/29/1999 to 12/26/1999	JAMES WARHOLA
11/07/1999 to 01/02/2000	GEORGE SAKKAL

MASSACHUSETTS

Mead Art Museum

Affiliate Institution: Amherst College
Amherst, MA 01002-5000
☎: 413-542-2335 ▣ www.amherst.edu/~mead
Open: SEPT-MAY: 10-4:30 Weekdays, 1-5 Weekends; Summer: 1-4 Tu-Su
Closed: LEG/HOL!; ACAD!; MEM/DAY; LAB/DAY
 ら Ⓟ **Museum Shop** **Group Tours** **Drop-In Tours**: 12:15 Tu
Permanent Collection: AM: all media; EU: all media; DU: ptgs 17; PHOT; DEC/ART; AN/GRK: cer; FR: gr 19

Surrounded by the Pelham Hills in a picture perfect New England setting, the Mead Art Museum, at Amherst College, houses a rich collection of 14,000 art objects dating from antiquity to the present. PLEASE NOTE: Summer hours are 1-4 Tu-Sun. **NOT TO BE MISSED:** American paintings and watercolors including Eakins "The Cowboy" & Homer's "The Fisher Girl"

ON EXHIBIT 1999
Due to planned renovations the exhibition schedule is uncertain for 1999-2000

University Gallery, University of Massachusetts

Affiliate Institution: Fine Arts Center
University of Massachusetts, Amherst, MA 01003
☎: 413-545-3670
Open: 11-4:30 Tu-Fr; 2-5 Sa, Su **Closed:** JAN.
 ら **Museum Shop**
Group Tours **Drop-In Tours** **Sculpture Garden**
Permanent Collection: AM: ptgs, drgs, phot 20

With a focus on the works of contemporary artists, this museum is best known as a showcase for the visual arts. It is but one of a five college complex of museums, making a trip to this area of New England a worthwhile venture for all art lovers. PLEASE NOTE: Due to construction of The Fine Arts Center's Atrium project, there will be no exhibitions after 5/5/1998. The Gallery hopes to reopen in November with an exhibition celebrating the history of the permanent collection.

Addison Gallery of American Art

Affiliate Institution: Phillips Academy
Andover, MA 01810-4166
☎: 978-749-4015 ▣ www.andover.edu/addison
Open: 10-5 Tu-Sa, 1-5 Su **Closed:** Mo, LEG/HOL!; 12/24
 ら Ⓟ **Museum Shop**
Group Tours **Drop-In Tours**: upon request **Sculpture Garden**
Permanent Collection: AM: ptgs, sculp, phot, works on paper 17-20

Since its inception in 1930, the Addison Gallery has been devoted exclusively to American art. The original benefactor, Thomas Cochran, donated both the core collection and the neo-classic building designed by noted architect Charles Platt. With a mature collection of more than 12,000 works, featuring major holdings from nearly every period of American art history, a visit to this museum should be high on every art lover's list. **NOT TO BE MISSED:** Marble fountain in Gallery rotunda by Paul Manship; "The West Wind" by Winslow Homer; R. Crosby Kemper Sculpture Courtyard

Addison Gallery of American Art - continued
ON EXHIBIT 1999
ONGOING ALL YEAR   SELECTIONS FROM THE ADDISON COLLECTION

09/09/1998 to 01/1999   SELECTIONS FROM THE PERMANENT COLLECTION

09/09/1998 to 01/04/1999   HANS HOFMANN: CONTINUING THE SEARCH FOR THE REAL

09/19/1998 to 01/01/1999   FRANK STELLA (PA 1954) AT TYLER GRAPHICS: A UNIQUE COLLABORATION

01/1999 to 03/1999   WILLEM DE KOONING: THE SEEING HAND *Will Travel*

01/1999 to 03/1999   FRAMED
The history, design and use of frames on works of art, *Will Travel*

01/1999 to 03/1999   SELECTIONS FROM THE PERMANENT COLLECTION INCLUDING PAINTINGS, PRINTS, PHOTOGRAPHY

04/1999 to 06/30/1999   PHOTOGRAPHY AND THE WEST

04/1999 to 07/1999   SELECTIONS FROM THE PERMANENT COLLECTION

04/1999 to 07/31/1999   ARTISTIC LEGACIES: A LOAN EXHIBITION INCLUDING WORKS OF JOSEF ALBERS, DAVID SMITH, GERALD SHERTZER, AND HIS STUDENTS

07/1999 to 10/1999   TO CONSERVE A LEGACY: AMERICAN ART FROM HISTORICALLY BLACK COLLEGES AND UNIVERSITIES
Both the range and importance of the collections and the need for active preservation and care will be emphasized in the 80-100 works from 5 historically Black colleges.

11/1999 to 01/2000   NATHAN LYONS: RIDING FIRST CLASS ON THE TITANIC
A 200 photograph exhibition . *Catalog Will Travel*

BOSTON

Boston Athenaeum
10 ½ Beacon St., Boston, MA 02108
☎: 617-227-0270
Open: JUNE-AUG: 9-5:30 Mo-Fr; SEPT-MAY: 9-5:30 Mo-Fr, 9-4 Sa   **Closed:** Su, LEG/HOL!
♿   **Museum Shop**
Group Tours: ex 221   **Drop-In Tours**
Historic Building National Historic Landmark Building
Permanent Collection: AM: ptgs, sculp, gr 19

The Athenaeum, one of the oldest independent libraries in America, features an art gallery established in 1827. Most of the Athenaeum building is closed to the public EXCEPT for the 1st & 2nd floors of the building (including the Gallery). In order to gain access to many of the most interesting parts of the building, including those items in the "do not miss" column, free tours are available on Tu & T at 3pm. Reservations must be made at least 24 hours in advance by calling The Circulation Desk, 617-227-0270 ex 221. **NOT TO BE MISSED:** George Washington's private library; 2 Gilbert Stuart portraits; Houdon's busts of Benjamin Franklin, George Washington, and Lafayette from the Monticello home of Thomas Jefferson.

MASSACHUSETTS

Boston Public Library

Copley Square, Boston, MA 02117-3194

☎: 617-536-5400

Open: OCT 1-MAY 22!: 5-9 Mo-Th, 9-5 Fr-Sa, 1-5 Su   **Closed:** Su, LEG/HOL! & 5/28

& **Museum Shop   Group Tours:** ex 216   **Drop-In Tours:** 2:30 Mo; 6:00 Tu, Th; 11am Fr, Sa, 2:00 Su Oct-May

Historic Building Renaissance "Palace" designed in 1895 by Charles Follen McKim

Permanent Collection: AM: ptgs, sculp; FR: gr 18-19; BRIT: gr 18-19; OM: gr, drgs; AM: phot 19, gr 19-20; GER: gr; ARCH/DRGS

Architecturally a blend of the old and the new, the building that houses the Boston Public Library, designed by Charles Follen McKim, has a facade that includes noted sculptor Augustas Saint-Gauden's head of Minerva which serves as the keystone of the central arch. A wing designed by Philip Johnson was added in 1973. There are a multitude of changing exhibitions throughout the year in the many galleries of both buildings. Call for current information. PLEASE NOTE: While restoration of the McKim Building is in progress, some points of interest may temporarily be inaccessible. **NOT TO BE MISSED:** 1500 lb. bronze entrance doors by Daniel Chester French; staircase mural painting series by Puvis de Chavannes; Dioramas of "Alice in Wonderland", "Arabian Nights" & "Dickens' London" by Louise Stimson.

Boston University Art Gallery

855 Commonwealth Ave., Boston, MA 02215

☎: 617-353-3329

Open: mid SEPT to mid DEC & mid JAN to mid MAY: 10-5 Tu-Fr; 1-5 Sa, Su   **Closed:** 12/25

& ℗ **Museum Shop   Group Tours   Drop-In Tours**

Permanent Collection:

Several shows in addition to student exhibitions are mounted annually in this 35 year old university gallery which seeks to promote under-recognized sectors of the art world by including the works of a variety of ethnic artists, women artists, and those unschooled in the traditional academic system. Additional emphasis is placed on the promotion of 20th century figurative art.

Institute of Contemporary Art

955 Boylston St., Boston, MA 02115-3194

☎: 617-266-5152   ▣ www.upenn.edu/ica

Open: 12-5 We, Fri-Sun, 12-9 Th   **Closed:** Mo, Tu

Free Day: Th after 5 PM   **ADM   Adult:** $6   **Children:** Free under 12   **Students:** $4.00   **Seniors:** $4.00

& ℗ **Museum Shop**

Group Tours: 617-927-6607   **Drop-In Tours:** We # & $, Th 3, 4, 5 & 6; Sa 12, 1 & 2   **Historic Building**

Permanent Collection: No permanent collection

The Institute of Contemporary Arts in 1936 as the first non-collecting contemporary art institution in the United States. Presenting contemporary art in a dynamic context since its inception, the ICA has showcased artists such as Andy Warhol, Roy Lichtenstein, Laurie Anderson, and Robert Rauschenberg early in their careers. The ICA's current programs remain responsive to the variable landscape of contemporary art.

ON EXHIBIT 1999

01/20/1999 to 03/14/1999   WALL PAINTINGS

01/20/1999 to 03/14/1999   TRACEY MOFFATT

03/30/1999 to 05/16/1999   COLLECTORS COLLECT CONTEMPORARY

06/09/1999 to 08/22/1999   KERRY JAMES MARSHALL

Institute of Contemporary Art - continued

09/08/1999 to 10/17/1999   RINEKE DIJKSTRA

09/08/1999 to 10/17/1999   STEVE MCQUEEN

11/10/1999 to 01/02/2000   SHIMON ATTIE

Isabella Stewart Gardner Museum

280 The Fenway, Boston, MA 02115

☎: 617-566-1401   ■ www.boston.com/gardner
Open: 11-5 Tu-Su   **Closed:** Mo, LEG/HOL!
ADM   Adult: $10.00   **Children:** F (under 18)   **Students:** $5.00   **Seniors:** $7.00
& ℗   **Museum Shop**   ¶ Café 11:30-4 Tu-Fr, 11-4 Sa ,Su
Group Tours: 617-278-5147   **Drop-In Tours:** 2:30 Fr Gallery tour   **Historic Building**   **Sculpture Garden**
Permanent Collection: PTGS; SCULP; DEC/ART; GR; OM

Located in the former home of Isabella Stewart Gardner, the collection reflects her zest for amassing this most exceptional and varied personal art treasure trove. PLEASE NOTE: 1. The admission fee of $5.00 for college students with current I.D. is $3.00 on Wed.; 2.Children under 18 admitted free of charge; 3. The galleries begin closing at 4:45pm. **NOT TO BE MISSED:** Rembrandt's "Self Portrait"; Italian Renaissance works of art

ON EXHIBIT 1999

09/18/1998 to 01/03/1999   ABELARDO MORRELL: FACE TO FACE: PHOTOGRAPHS AT THE GARDNER MUSEUM
Photographer Abelardo Morrell creates black and white photographs that examine familiar objects and environments from deceptively innocent perspectives. During the last year Morrell has worked as an artist in residence at the Gardner Museum and the eighteen resulting pictures will be on view in this exhibition.

01/22/1999 to 04/25/1999   JOSIAH MCELHENY

05/21/1999 to 09/26/1999   SARGENT: THE LATE LANDSCAPES

Museum of Fine Arts, Boston

465 Huntington Ave., Boston, MA 02115

☎: 617-267-9300   ■ www.mfa.org
Open: 10-4:45 Mo, Tu; 10-9:45 We-Fr; 10-5:45 Sa, Su   **Closed:** THGV, 12/24, 12/25
ADM   Adult: $10.00   **Children:** F (17 & under)   **Students:** $8.00   **Seniors:** $8.00
& ℗   **Museum Shop**   ¶ Café, Restaurant & Cafeteria
Group Tours: ex 368   **Drop-In Tours:** On the half hour from 10:30-2:30 Mo-Fr
Permanent Collection: AN/GRK; AN/R; AN/EGT; EU: om/ptgs; FR: Impr, post/Impr; AM: ptgs 18-20; OR: cer

A world class collection of fine art with masterpieces from every continent is yours to enjoy at this great Boston museum. Divided between two buildings the collection is housed both in the original (1918) Evans Wing, with its John Singer Sargent mural decorations above the Rotunda, and the dramatic West Wing (1981), designed by I. M. Pei. PLEASE NOTE: 1. There is a "pay as you wish" policy from 4pm-9:45 PM on Wed. and a $2.00 admission fee on T & F evenings. 2. The West Wing ONLY is open after 5pm on T & F. **NOT TO BE MISSED:** Egyptian Pectoral believed to have decorated a royal sarcophagus of the Second Intermediate Period (1784 - 1570 B.C.), part of the museum's renowned permanent collection of Egyptian art.

ON EXHIBIT 1999

to 05/1999   BEYOND THE SCREEN: CHINESE FURNITURE OF THE 16TH AND 17TH CENTURIES
Exquisite Ming period Chinese furniture will be displayed within gallery space that has been converted especially for it into rooms and courtyards of a Chinese house.

Museum of Fine Arts, Boston - continued
09/19/1998 to 01/1999 REFLECTIONS OF MONET

04/03/1999 to 06/06/1999 ANCIENT GOLD: THE WEALTH OF THE THRACIANS, TREASURES FROM THE REPUBLIC OF BULGARIA
The first exhibition of Bulgaria's cultural artistry, primarily metalwork, to be seen in the US in the post-Communist era. More than 200 magnificent gold and silver objects, dating from 1200 to 400 B.C., will be featured in an exhibition that lends credence to the life and legends of ancient Thrace.

06/23/1999 to 09/26/1999 JOHN SINGER SARGENT
This exhibition of more than 100 paintings and watercolors represents the artist's most significant and beautiful works. It will be the first time since the retrospective mounted after his death that so many works will be exhibited together. *Catalog Will Travel*

09/22/1999 to 01/16/2000 AMERICAN VISIONARY: THE PAINTINGS OF MARTIN JOHNSON HEADE *Catalog*

11/14/1999 to 02/06/2000 PHARAOHS OF THE SUN: AKHENATEN, NEFERTITI, TUTANKHAMEN
A retrospective on the culture of Amarna, a long time source of fascination to scholars and the lay public alike due to the beauty of its art and the revolutionary change in religion which influenced it. The exhibition will display key works from the classical style preceding this period to examine the contrast in stylistic change which followed. *Catalog Will Travel*

Museum of the National Center of Afro-American Artists
300 Walnut Ave., Boston, MA 02119
📞: 617-442-8614
Open: 1-5 Tu-Su **Closed:** Mo,
ADM Adult: $4.00 **Children:** F (under 5) **Students:** $3.00 **Seniors:** $3.00
Museum Shop Group Tours Drop-In Tours Historic Building 19th C
Permanent Collection: AF/AM: ptgs; sculp; GR

Art by African-American artists is highlighted along with art from the African continent itself.

BROCKTON

Fuller Museum of Art
455 Oak St., Brockton, MA 02301-1399
📞: 508-588-6000 ◙ www.art-online.com/fuller.htm
Open: Noon-5 Tu-Su **Closed:** Mo, 1/1, 7/4, LAB/DAY, THGV, 12/25
ADM Adult: $3.00 **Children:** F (under 18) **Seniors:** $2.00
♿ Ⓟ **Museum Shop** ‖ Café 11:30 - 2 Tu-F **Group Tours**: ex 125 **Drop-In Tours Sculpture Garden**
Permanent Collection: AM: 19-20; CONT: reg

A park-like setting surrounded by the beauty of nature is the ideal site for this charming museum that features works by artists of New England with particular emphasis on contemporary arts and cultural diversity.

ON EXHIBIT 1999
12/19/1998 to 02/28/1999 THE FUNCTION OF BEAUTY
An exhibition of functional and sculptural ceramics based on the vessel form by contemporary artists.

03/13/1999 to 06/06/1999 TO HONOR AND COMFORT: NATIVE QUILTING TRADITIONS
From the National Museum of the American Indian and the Michigan State University Museum this is the first in an annual series of exhibitions.

06/19/1999 to 08/22/1999 FOR THE LOVE OF NATURE
Paintings, prints and sculpture from the collections of the Massachusetts Audubon Society.

09/09/1999 to 01/02/1999 THE NINTH TRIENNIAL
A tradition since 1972, the Triennial presents a tapestry of contemporary art from New England.

Arthur M. Sackler Museum
Affiliate Institution: Harvard University
485 Broadway, Cambridge, MA 02138
☎: 617-495-9400　◉　web address for all 3 Harvard University Art Museums www.artmuseums.harvard.edu
Open: 10-5 Mo-Sa, 1-5 Su　**Closed:** LEG/HOL!
Free Day: We & Sa AM　**ADM**　**Adult:** $5.00　**Children:** F (under 18)　**Students:** $3.00　**Seniors:** $4.00
&　ⓟ　**Museum Shop**　**Group Tours:** 617-496-8576　**Drop-In Tours:** 2:00 Mo-Fr
Permanent Collection: AN/ISLAMIC; AN/OR; NAT/AM

Opened in 1985, the building and its superb collection of Ancient, Asian, and Islamic art were all the generous gift of the late Dr. Arthur M. Sackler, noted research physician, medical publisher, and art collector. **NOT TO BE MISSED:** World's finest collections of ancient Chinese jades; Korean ceramics; Japanese woodblock prints; Persian miniatures

ON EXHIBIT 1999
09/12/1998 to 07/18/1999　NATURE AS METAPHOR: PAINTINGS FROM CHINA, KOREA AND JAPAN
A selection of later Chinese, Korean and Japanese paintings that feature the details of nature, rather than its vast panorama, as their principal subject matter.

12/05/1998 to 01/31/1999　MASTERY AND ELEGANCE: TWO CENTURIES OF FRENCH DRAWING FROM THE COLLECTION OF JEFFREY E. HORVITZ
Approximately 115 works from the early seventeenth to the late eighteenth century by about seventy artists. *Catalog Will Travel*

03/06/1999 to 05/16/1999　ELLSWORTH KELLEY: THE EARLY DRAWINGS, 1948-1955
Bold colors, geometric tensions, contradictions and the principles of chance govern the creations of Kelly, a major contributor to the development of American Abstract art. 222 works on paper from 1948-1955 are featured here and many come from the artist and private collections which predate his first critical acclaim in the solo exhibition in 1956. *Catalog Will Travel*

Busch-Reisinger Museum
Affiliate Institution: Harvard University
32 Quincy St., Cambridge, MA 02138
☎: 617-495-9400　◉　www.artmuseums.harvard.edu
Open: 10-5 Mo-Sa, 1-5 Su　**Closed:** LEG/HOL!
ADM　**Adult:** $5.00　**Children:** F (under 18)　**Students:** $3.00　**Seniors:** $4.00
&　ⓟ　**Museum Shop**　**Group Tours:** 617-496-8576　**Drop-In Tours:** 1:00 Mo-Fr
Permanent Collection: GER: ptgs, sculp 20; GR; PTGS; DEC/ART; CER 18; MED/SCULP; REN/SCULP

Founded in 1901 with a collection of plaster casts of Germanic sculpture and architectural monuments, the Busch-Reisinger later acquired a group of modern "degenerate" artworks purged by the Nazi's from major German museums. All of this has been enriched over the years with gifts from artists and designers associated with the famous Bauhaus School, including the archives of artist Lyonel Feininger, and architect Walter Gropius. **NOT TO BE MISSED:** Outstanding collection of German Expressionist Art

ON EXHIBIT 1999
05/22/1999 to 08/01/1999 MULTIPLE CONFIGURATIONS: PRESENTING THE CONTEMPORARY PORTFOLIO
The art portfolio is a collection of works made in any media by an individual or group of artists. Its contents are based on a concept or theme which can range from specific to vague. Exhibiting a portfolio in a museum can be problematic. This exhibition will explore different ways of handling portfolios.

10/31/1998 to 01/10/1999　A LABORATORY OF MODERNITY: IMAGE AND SOCIETY IN THE WEIMAR REPUBLIC

02/13/1999 to 04/25/1999　W. O. SCHULZE ("WOLS") PHOTOGRAPHS
This exhibition of 1930s photographs by Wols will be the first presentation of this work in the US.

MASSACHUSETTS

Fogg Art Museum
Affiliate Institution: Harvard University
32 Quincey St., Cambridge, MA 02138
📞: 617-495-9400   🖳 www.artmuseums.harvard.edu
Open: 10-5 Mo-Sa, 1-5 Su   **Closed:** LEG/HOL!
ADM   Adult: $5.00   **Children:** F (under 18)   **Students:** $3.00   **Seniors:** $4.00
  ᕕ ⓟ **Museum Shop**
Group Tours: 617-496-8576   **Drop-In Tours**: 11:00 Mo-Fr
Permanent Collection: EU: ptgs, sculp, dec/art; AM: ptgs, sculp, dec/art; GR; PHOT, DRGS

The Fogg, the largest university museum in America, with one of the world's greatest collections, contains both European and American masterpieces from the Middle Ages to the present. Access to the galleries is off of a two story recreation of a 16th century Italian Renaissance courtyard. **NOT TO BE MISSED:** The Maurice Wertheim Collection containing many of the finest Impressionist and Post-Impressionist paintings, sculptures and drawings in the world.

ON EXHIBIT 1999

ONGOING   INVESTIGATING THE RENAISSANCE
 A reinstallation of 3 galleries of one of the most important collections of early Italian Renaissance paintings in North America.

ONGOING   FRANCE AND THE PORTRAIT, 1799-1870
Changing conventions in and practices of portraiture in France between the rise of Napoleon and the fall of the Second Empire will be examined in the individual images on view from the permanent collection.

ONGOING   CIRCA 1874: THE EMERGENCE OF IMPRESSIONISM
Works by Bazille, Boudin, Johgkind, Monet, Degas and Renoir selected from the Museum's collection reveal the variety of styles existing under the single "new painting" label of Impressionism.

ONGOING   THE PERSISTENCE OF MEMORY: CONTINUITY AND CHANGE IN AMERICAN CULTURES
From pre-contact Native American to African to Euro-American, the 60 works of art on exhibit reflect the personal immigrant histories and cultures of each of the artists who created them.

ONGOING   SUBLIMATIONS: ART AND SENSUALITY IN THE NINETEENTH CENTURY
19th century artworks chosen to convey the sensual will be seen in an exhibition that demonstrates how these often erotic images impacted on the social, personal and religious lives of the times.

ONGOING   THE ART OF IDENTITY: AFRICAN SCULPTURE FROM THE TEAL COLLECTION
A diverse group of sub-Saharan African sculptures, collected over a 35 year period, is featured in this exhibition.

01/23/1999 to 04/11/1999   BUILDING REPRESENTATION: PHOTOGRAPH AND ARCHITECTURE, CONTEMPORARY INTERACTIONS
Selected works by contemporary artists that investigate the conceptual foundation of photography through imagery of the built environment.

05/08/1999 to 07/18/1999   DEATH BY HOGARTH

06/10/1999 to 09/05/1999   SARGENT IN THE STUDIO

03/06/1999 to 05/15/1999   ELLSWORTH KELLEY: THE EARLY DRAWINGS, 1948-1955
Bold colors, geometric tensions, contradictions and the principles of chance govern the creations of Kelly, a major contributor to the development of American Abstract art. 222 works on paper from 1948-1955 are featured here and many come from the artist and private collections which predate his first critical acclaim in the solo exhibition in 1956. *Catalog Will Travel*

MIT-List Visual Arts Center
20 Ames St., Wiesner Bldg., Cambridge, MA 02142
📞: 617-253-4680 ◉ web.mit.edu/lvac/www
Open: Noon-6 Tu-Th, Sa, Su; till 8pm Fr **Closed:** Mo, LEG/HOL
Sugg/Cont Adult: $5.00
♿ ℗ **Museum Shop**
Group Tours: 617-253-4400 **Drop-In Tours** **Historic Building** 1985 I. M. Pei building **Sculpture Garden**
Permanent Collection: SCULP; PTGS; PHOT; DRGS; WORKS ON PAPER

Approximately 10 temporary exhibitions of contemporary art are mounted annually in MIT's List Visual Arts Center designed by the internationally known architect I. M. Pei, a graduate of the MIT School of Architecture with an interior mural by Kenneth Noland and seating by Scott Burton. **NOT TO BE MISSED:** Alexander Calder, "The Big Sail" (1965), MIT's first commissioned public outdoor sculpture.

ON EXHIBIT 1999
Winter 1999 ARTISTS ON AGING

Winter 1999 KIKI SMITH: NEW PHOTOGRAPHIC WORK

Spring 1999 WHAT IS NATURAL NOW

Spring 1999 EVE ANDREE LARAMEE

CHESTNUT HILL

McMullen Museum of Art Boston College
Affiliate Institution: Boston College
Devlin Hall, 140 Commonwealth Ave., Chestnut Hill, MA 02167 3809
📞: 617-552-8587 or 8100 ◉ www.bc.edu:80/bc_org/avp/cas/artmuseum/
Open: SEP-MAY: 11-4 Mo-Fr; Noon-5 Sa, Su; JUNE-AUG: 11-3 Mo-Fr **Closed:** LEG/HOL!
♿ ℗ **Museum Shop** ⅋ On campus
Group Tours Drop-In Tours Historic Building
Permanent Collection: IT: ptgs 16 & 17; AM: ptgs; JAP: gr; MED & BAROQUE TAPESTRIES 15-17

Devlin Hall, the Neo-Gothic building that houses the museum, consists of two galleries featuring a display of permanent collection works on one floor, and special exhibitions on the other. **NOT TO BE MISSED:** "Madonna with Christ Child & John the Baptist" By Ghirlandaio, 1503-1577)

ON EXHIBIT 1999
02/01/1999 to 05/25/1999 SAINTS AND SINNERS: CARAVAGGIO AND THE BAROQUE IMAGE

CONCORD

Concord Art Association
37 Lexington Rd., Concord, MA 01742
📞: 978-369-2578
Open: 10-4:30 Tu-Sa **Closed:** Mo, LEG/HOL!
♿ ℗ **Museum Shop**
Group Tours Drop-In Tours
Historic Building Housed in building dated 1720 **Sculpture Garden**
Permanent Collection: AM: ptgs, sculp, gr, dec/art

MASSACHUSETTS

Concord Art Association - continued

Historic fine art is appropriately featured within the walls of this historic (1720) building. The beautiful gardens are perfect for a bag lunch picnic during the warm weather months. **NOT TO BE MISSED:** Ask to see the secret room within the building which was formerly part of the underground railway.

ON EXHIBIT 1999

Rotating exhibits of fine art and crafts are mounted on a monthly basis.

04/16/1999 to 06/11/1999   THE PHILADELPHIA TEN: A WOMEN ARTIST GROUP 1917-1945

This unique and progressive group of painters and sculptors broke the rules of society and the art world by working and exhibiting together. Their work included urban and rural landscapes, portraiture, still life, and a variety of representational and myth inspired sculpture. This is the first time in over fifty years to examine this group and other like it who played an importune role in American culture in the first half of the century. Highlighted particularly are Isabel Cartwright, Constancy Cochrane, Marry Colton, and Lucille Howard. In addition there were Theresa Bernstein, Cora Brooks, Fern Coppedge, Nancy Ferguson, Sue Gill. Helen McCarthy , Emma MacRae, M. Elizabeth Price, Susan Schell and sculptors Harriet Frishmuth and Beatrice Fenton. *Will Travel*

COTUIT

Cahoon Museum of American Art

4676 Falsmouth Rd., Cotuit, MA 02635
☎: 508-428-7581
Open: 10-4 Tu-Sa   **Closed:** Mo, Tu, LEG/HOL!; Also closed FEB. & MAR.
Vol/Cont
  Ġ ℗ **Museum Shop   Group Tours   Drop-In Tours**: Gallery talks 11:00 Fr
Historic Building 1775 Former Cape Cod Colonial Tavern   **Sculpture Garden**
Permanent Collection: AM: ptgs 19-20; CONT/PRIM

Art by the donor artists of this facility, Ralph and Martha Cahoon, is shown along with works by prominent American Luminists and Impressionists. Located in a restored 1775 Colonial tavern on Cape Cod, the museum is approximately 9 miles west of Hyannis. **NOT TO BE MISSED:** Gallery of marine paintings

DENNIS

Cape Museum of Fine Arts

Rte. 6A, Dennis, MA 02638-5034
☎: 508-385-4477
Open: 10-5 Tu-Sa, 1-5 S, till 7:30 T, open M May-Sep   **Closed:** Mo, LEG/HOL!
ADM   Adult: $5.00   **Children:** F (16 and under)
  Ġ ℗ **Museum Shop**
Group Tours: 508-385-4477 x16   **Drop-In Tours**: !
Permanent Collection: REG

Art by outstanding Cape Cod artists, from 1900 to the present, is the focus of this rapidly growing permanent collection which is housed in the restored former summer home of the family of Davenport West, one of the original benefactors of this institution. New galleries provide wonderful new space for permanent collections and special exhibitions. On the grounds of the Cape Playhouse and Cape Cinema.

ON EXHIBIT 1999

Summer 1999   CAPE COD AND AMERICAN IMPRESSIONISM

Art Complex Museum

189 Alden St., Duxbury, MA 02331
📞: 781-934-6634
Open: 1-4 We-Su   **Closed:** Mo-Tu, LEG/HOL!
& ℗ **Museum Shop**
Group Tours   Drop-In Tours   Sculpture Garden
Permanent Collection: OR: ptgs; EU: ptgs; AM: ptgs; gr

In a magnificent sylvan setting that compliments the naturalistic wooden structure of the building, the Art Complex houses a remarkable core collection of works on paper that includes Rembrandt's "The Descent from the Cross by Torchlight". An authentic Japanese Tea House, complete with tea presentations in the summer months, is another unique feature of this fine institution. The museum is located on the eastern coast of Massachusetts just above Cape Cod. **NOT TO BE MISSED:** Shaker furniture; Tiffany stained glass window

Fitchburg Art Museum

185 Elm St., Fitchburg, MA 01420
📞: 978-345-4207
Open: 11-4:00 Tu-Sa, 1-4 Su   **Closed:** Mo, LEG/HOL!
ADM   Adult: $3.00   **Children:** F (under 18)   **Seniors:** $2.00
& ℗ **Museum Shop**
Group Tours   Drop-In Tours   Sculpture Garden
Permanent Collection: AM: ptgs 18-20 EU: ptgs 18-20; PRTS & DRGS: 15-20; PHOT 20; AN/GRK; AN/R, AS, ANT; ILLUSTRATED BOOKS & MANUSCRIPTS 14-20

Eleanor Norcross, a Fitchburg artist who lived and painted in Paris for 40 years, became impressed with the number and quality of small museums that she visited in the rural areas of northern France. This led to the bequest of her collection and personal papers, in 1925, to her native city of Fitchburg, and marked the beginning of what is now a 40,000 square foot block long museum complex. The museum is located in north central Massachusetts near the New Hampshire border. **NOT TO BE MISSED:** "Sarah Clayton" by Joseph Wright of Derby, 1770

Danforth Museum of Art

123 Union Ave., Framingham, MA 01702
📞: 508-620-0050   ▣   www.e-guide.com/sites/Danforth
Open: Noon-5 We-Su   **Closed:** Mo, Tu, LEG/HOL! AUG!
ADM   Adult: $3.00   **Children:** F (12 & under)   **Students:** $2.00   **Seniors:** $2.00
& ℗ **Museum Shop**
Group Tours   Drop-In Tours: 1:00 We (Sep-May)
Permanent Collection: PTGS; SCULP; DRGS; PHOT; GR

The Danforth, a museum that prides itself on being known as a community museum with a national reputation, offers 19th & 20th century American and European art as the main feature of its permanent collection. **NOT TO BE MISSED:** 19th & 20th century American works with a special focus on the works of New England artists

MASSACHUSETTS

Danforth Museum of Art - continued

ON EXHIBIT 1999

ONGOING   HARVEY WANG: PHOTOGRAPHS OF OLDER AMERICANS AT WORK
Taken by documentary photographer Wang on his many trips crisscrossing the U.S. since 1979, the photographs on view feature images of the hands and faces of older persons whose skills and occupations recall the nation's past and dramatize the dignity of the work ethic.

to Spring 1999   FRESHWATER

01/1999 to 03/1999   JACK WOLFE

01/1999 to 03/1999   BEYOND A VIEW: THE LANDSCAPE DRAWINGS OF TERI MALO

09/01/1999 to 11/07/1999   ANDREW STEVOVICH: PAINTINGS, DRAWINGS, AND PRINTS, 1978-1999

GLOUCESTER

Cape Ann Historical Association

27 Pleasant St., Gloucester, MA 01930
☎: 978-283-0455
Open: 10-5 Tu-Sa   **Closed:** Su, Mo, LEG/HOL!; FEB
ADM   Adult: $4.00   **Children:** F (under 6)   **Students:** $2.50   **Seniors:** $3.50
  ♿ ⓟ   **Museum Shop**
Group Tours Drop-In Tours   Historic Building 1804 Federal period home of Captain Elias Davis is part of museum
Permanent Collection: FITZ HUGH LANE: ptgs; AM: ptgs, sculp, DEC/ART 19-20; MARITIME COLL

Within the walls of this most charming New England treasure of a museum is the largest collection of paintings (39), drawings (100), and lithographs by the great American artist, Fitz Hugh Lane. A walking tour of the town takes the visitor past many charming small art studios & galleries that have a wonderful view of the harbor as does the 1849 Fitz Hugh Lane House itself. Be sure to see the famous Fisherman's Monument overlooking Gloucester Harbor. **NOT TO BE MISSED:** The only known watercolor in existence by Fitz Hugh Lane

LINCOLN

DeCordova Museum and Sculpture Park

Sandy Pond Rd., Lincoln, MA 01773-2600
☎: 781-259-8355   ⊙   www.decordova.org
Open: 11-5 Tu-Su   **Closed:** Mo, LEG/HOL!
ADM   Adult: $6.00   **Children:** F (5 & under)   **Students:** $4.00   **Seniors:** $4.00
  ♿ ⓟ   **Museum Shop** ⫽ Terrace Café open 11-4 W-Sa
Group Tours: 781-259-0505   **Drop-In Tours**: 1:00 We & 2:00 Su   **Sculpture Garden**
Permanent Collection: AM: ptgs, sculp, gr, phot 20; REG

In addition to its significant collection of modern and contemporary art, the DeCordova features the only permanent sculpture park of its kind in New England. While there is an admission charge for the museum, the sculpture park is always free and open to the public from 8am to 10pm daily. The 35 acre park features nearly 70 site-specific sculptures. PLEASE NOTE: The museum IS OPEN on SELECTED Monday holidays! **NOT TO BE MISSED:** Annual open air arts festival June 13; summer concert series from 7/11 - Labor Day

ON EXHIBIT 1999

06/13/1998 to 05/31/1999   NIKI KETCHMAN: FABRICATIONS
Her large-scale outdoor sculptures, fabricated with welded, twisted and braided metals, feature applied ornament and bright colors. In this way she seeks to merge the seemingly incommensurate domains of the monumental and the decorative. Related works on paper and small-scale indoor sculptures will be shown

DeCordova Museum and Sculpture Park - continued

06/13/1998 to 06/2000   ABSTRACT EXPRESSIONISM/FIGURATIVE EXPRESSIONISM: COMMON GROUND
This thematic exhibit will trace commonalities and differences in style and content in abstract expressionist and figurative expressionist painting in the second half of the twentieth-century. Major themes to be explored will include myth and religion, psychological states, landscape, and references to history and the history of art.

09/26/1998 to 01/03/1999   HARRIET CASDIN-SILVER: THE ART OF HOLOGRAPHY
This retrospective exhibition traces the career of Casdin-Silver, America's foremost holographic artist, and a major figure in the history of art and technology in America in the latter half of the 20th century. Holograms, multi-media installations, video and sculpture made by the artist between 1968 and 1998 will be shown. *Catalog*

09/26/1998 to 03/07/1999   CITY VIEWS: WORKS ON PAPER FROM THE PERMANENT COLLECTION
Twenty images of the city which depict its architecture, street life, and skyline.

10/13/1998 to 01/17/1999   TWO INVENTIONS AND A LAW: THE EXPLOSION OF VIDEO ACCESS
Video works by Boston artists reveal the dominant influences of two contemporary phenomena: the availability of video production equipment as inexpensive consumer items and the proliferation of legislatively mandated publicly-available production facilities at community cable television stations. During the 1980s and 90s, video art exploded as members of a new technologically savvy generation took their camcorders to the streets and studios.

03/27/1999 to 05/31/1999   NEW WORK/NEW ENGLAND
Artist(s) to be announced

03/27/1999 to 05/31/1999   MAKE YOUR MOVE: INTERACTIVE COMPUTER ART
Three cutting-edge, computer-assisted interactive installations by internationally recognized Boston area artists Christopher Dodge, Jennifer Hall, and Karl Sims. Integral to these ambitious works are visitor participation in the creation of an aesthetic and philosophical experience (without computer screen menus or keyboards) and shared content based on issues of creation, life, death, and personal responsibility.

03/27/1999 to 06/27/1999   KARL SIMS: A VIDEO RETROSPECTIVE
Presented in conjunction with "Make Your Move," this exhibition includes all the single channel video art produced by artist Karl Sims.

06/12/1999 to 09/06/1999   THE 1999 DECORDOVA ANNUAL EXHIBITION
To celebrate the tenth year of the series participants will be selected from short lists of contemporary regional artists submitted by the artists and artist teams who have been included in the series since its inception.

09/18/1999 to 01/02/2000   SCOTT PRIOR RETROSPECTIVE
A retrospective of the work of this contemporary Realist painter, nationally acclaimed for his lucid, detailed style and appealing images. Included will be his early surreal work as well as later landscapes, portraits, still lifes, and scenes of domestic life with his family in and around his home.

LOWELL

Whistler House Museum of Art and Parker Gallery

243 Worthen St., Lowell, MA 01852-1822
☎: 978-452-7641   ◙   www.valley.uml.edu/lowell/historic/museums/whistler.html
Open: May-Oct 11-4 We-Sa, 1-4 Su; Nov, Dec, Mar, Apr 11-4 We-Sa   **Closed:** Mo, Tu, LEG/HOL! JAN. & FEB.
ADM   Adult: $3.00   **Children:** F (under 5)   **Students:** $2.00   **Seniors:** $2.00
&   ℗   **Museum Shop**
Group Tours: 978-452-7641   **Drop-In Tours**: upon request   **Historic Building**   **Sculpture Garden**
Permanent Collection: AM: ptgs

Works by prominent New England artists are the highlight of this collection housed in the 1823 former home of the artist. **NOT TO BE MISSED:** Collection of prints by James A.M. Whistler

MASSACHUSETTS

Whistler House Museum of Art and Parker Gallery - continued
ON EXHIBIT 1999

03/01/1999 to 04/15/1999   WOMEN ARTISTS: A CELEBRATION OF WOMEN'S HISTORY MONTH

03/15/1999 to 06/15/1999   ALDRO HIBBARD: THE ROCKPORT MASTER

04/20/1999 to 05/31/1999   KEVIN DADOLY: RECENT WATERCOLORS

04/20/1999 to 05/31/1999   CULTURAL CONTINUUM II - THE DYNAMIC ACRE

06/01/1999 to 06/30/1999   PHOTOGRAPHY OF JIM GREENE

07/01/1999 to 08/15/1999   WHISTLER HOUSE 1999 JURIED EXHIBITION

09/05/1999 to 10/30/1999   CHILDREN'S BOOK ILLUSTRATORS

09/15/1999 to 12/31/1999   PRINTS FROM THE PERMANENT COLLECTION

11/15/1999 to 12/31/1999   REALITY RECONSIDERED: TOM GILL

MEDFORD

Tufts University Art Gallery
Affiliate Institution: Tufts University
Aidekman Arts Center, Medford, MA 02115
📞: 617-627-3518
Open: SEPT to mid DEC & mid JAN to MAY: 12-8 We-Sa, 12-5 Su   **Closed:** Mo, LEG/HOL!; ACAD!; SUMMER
♿ **Museum Shop   Group Tours   Drop-In Tours   Sculpture Garden**
Permanent Collection: PTGS, GR, DRGS, 19-20; PHOT 20; AN/R; AN/GRK; P/COL

Located just outside of Boston, most of the Tufts University Art Museum exhibitions feature works by undergraduate students and MFA candidates.

NORTH ADAMS

Massachusetts Museum of Contemporary Art
87 Marshall St., North Adams, MA 01247
📞: 413-664-4481   🔘 www.massmoca.org
Open: The museum will open in late spring, 1999. Hours and admission TBA.
♿ ℗ **Museum Shop**   🍴: Y: The Night Shift Café with jazz, blues, rock & alternative music
Group Tours: 413-664-4481   **Drop-In Tours   Historic Building** Museum is located in a late 19th-century industrial site.
Permanent Collection: The Museum has two permanent works of sound art in its collection; the majority of work shown here will be long-term loans of oversized or sited works from major museum collections.

Scheduled to open in late spring 1999, the much anticipated Massachusetts Museum of Contemporary Art (MASS MoCA), created from a 27-building historic mill complex on 13 acres in the Berkshires of western Massachusetts, promises to be an exciting multi-disciplinary center for visual and performing arts. International in scope, MASS MoCA will offer exhibitions of work on loan from the Solomon R. Guggenheim Museum in New York City and other major museum collections, as well as special exhibitions of contemporary art.

Smith College Museum of Art

Elm St. at Bedford Terrace, Northampton, MA 01063

☎: 413-585-2760   ◉ www.smith.edu/artmuseum

Open: SEPT-JUNE: 9:30-4 Tu, Fr, Sa; 12-8 Th, Noon-4 We, Su; JUL & AUG: Noon-4 Tu-Su

Closed: Mo, 1/1, 7/4, THGV, 12/25

&. ℗ **Museum Shop   Group Tours   Drop-In Tours**

Permanent Collection: AM: ptgs, sculp, gr, drgs, dec/art 17-20; EU: ptgs, gr, sculp, drgs, dec/art 17-20; PHOT; DU:17; ANCIENT ART

With in-depth emphasis on American and French 19th & 20th century art, and literally thousands of superb artworks in its permanent collection, Smith College remains one of the most highly regarded college or university repositories for fine art in the nation. PLEASE NOTE: Print Room hours are 1-4 Tu-F & 1-5 T from Sep. to May - other hours by appointment only. **NOT TO BE MISSED:** "Mrs. Edith Mahon" by Thomas Eakins; "Walking Man" by Rodin

ON EXHIBIT 1999

12/10/1998 to 03/14/1999   A RENAISSANCE TREASURY: THE FLAGG COLLECTION OF EUROPEAN DECORATIVE ARTS AND SCULPTURE

This outstanding collection of later Medieval and Renaissance decorative arts was a gift to the Milwaukee Art Museum. Approximately 80 objects of diverse media, place of origin, and social function might provide insight into the Renaissance as well as the taste of an individual collector. Highlights of this collection are a number of rare secular objects like German and Swiss clocks, Limoges platters with classical scenes, marriage boxes, etc. as well as religious objects including the polychromed sculpture of 'St. George Slaying the Dragon'. *Catalog Will Travel*

Words & Pictures Museum

140 Main St., Northampton, MA 01060

☎: 413-586-8545   ◉ wordsandpictures.org

Open: Noon-5 Tu-Th & Su, Noon-8 Fr, 10-8 Sa   **Closed:** 1/1, MEM/DAY, 7/4, LAB/DAY, THGV, 12/25

Free Day: Intl. Museum Day   **ADM   Adult:** $3.00   **Children:** $1.00 (under 18)   **Students:** $2.00   **Seniors:** $2.00

&. ℗ **Museum Shop   Group Tours   Drop-In Tours**: Upon request if available

Permanent Collection: Original contemporary sequential/comic book art & fantasy illustration, 1970's - present

Mere words cannot describe this Words & Pictures Museum, one of only three in the country. Located in a building opened 1/95, this museum, which follows the evolution of comic book art, intersperses traditional fine art settings with exhibits of pure fun. There are numerous interactive displays including entry into the museum through a maze and an exit-way through an area that demonstrates the history of the American comic. **NOT TO BE MISSED:** The entryway to the building featuring a life-size artist's studio built with a false perspective so that it appears to actually be viewed from above through a skylight.

Berkshire Museum

39 South St., Pittsfield, MA 01201

☎: 413-443-7171   ◉ www.berkshireweb.com/berkshiremuseum

Open: 10-5 Tu-Sa, 1-5 Su; Open 10-5 Mo JUL & AUG   **Closed:** Mo, LEG/HOL!

Free Day: 3-5 We and on one's birthday   **ADM   Adult:** $6.00   **Children:** $4.00(4-18), F under 3   **Seniors:** $5.00

&. ℗ **Museum Shop   ⊪** Snacks at the Vendo-Mat Café

Group Tours: 413-443-7171 x11   **Drop-In Tours:** 11 am Sa in Jun, Jul, Aug

Historic Building 1903 Italian Renaissance Revival

Permanent Collection: AM: 19-20; EU: 15-19; AN/GRK; AN/R; DEC/ART; PHOT; Natural Science; Aquarium

MASSACHUSETTS

Berkshire Museum - continued

Three Museums in one - art, natural science and history - set the stage for a varied and exciting visit to this complex in the heart of the beautiful Berkshires. In addition to its rich holdings of American art of the 19th and 20th-centuries, the Museum has an interactive aquarium and exciting changing exhibitions. **NOT TO BE MISSED:** "Giant Redwoods" by Albert Bierstadt

ON EXHIBIT 1999

11/21/1998 to 01/03/1999   14TH ANNUAL FESTIVAL OF TREES

02/06/1999 to 05/30/1999   KID STUFF: GREAT TOYS FROM OUR CHILDHOOD
More than 40 classic 20th century toys, including Mr. Potato Head, Slinky, Lincoln Logs and Barbie, will be featured in an exhibition complete with fun facts and interactive activities.

Spring 1999   DISTANT VIEWS: THE HUDSON RIVER SCHOOL COLLECTION AT THE BERKSHIRE MUSEUM

Summer 1999   ALEXANDER CALDER EXHIBITION

PROVINCETOWN

Provincetown Art Association and Museum
460 Commercial St., Provincetown, MA 02657
📞: 508-487-1750   ◙ www.CapeCodAccess.com/Gallery/PAAM.html
Open: SUMMER: 12-5 & 8-10 daily; SPRING/FALL: 12-5 Fr, Sa, Su; WINTER: 12-4 Sa, Su; Open most holidays!; open weekends only Nov-Apr
Sugg/Cont   Adult: $3.00   **Students:** $1.00   **Seniors:** $1.00
♿   ℗   **Museum Shop   Group Tours   Drop-In Tours**
Permanent Collection: PTGS; SCULP; GR; DEC/ART; REG

Works by regional artists is an important focus of the collection of this museum. **NOT TO BE MISSED:** Inexpensive works of art by young artists that are for sale in the galleries

---

SOUTH HADLEY

Mount Holyoke College Art Museum
South Hadley, MA 01075-1499
📞: 413-538-2245   ◙   www.mtholyoke.edu/offices/artmuseum
Open: 11-5 Tu-Fr, 1-5 Sa, Su   **Closed:** LEG/HOL!, ACAD!
♿   ℗   **Museum Shop**
Group Tours: 413-538-2085   **Drop-In Tours:** by appointment at least 3 weeks prior   **Sculpture Garden**
Permanent Collection: AS; P/COL; AN/EGT; IT: med/sculp; EU: ptgs; AN/GRK; AM: ptgs, dec/art, gr, phot; EU: ptgs, dec/art, gr, phot

A stop at this leading college art museum is a must for any art lover traveling in this area. Founded in 1876, it is one of the oldest college museums in the country. **NOT TO BE MISSED:** Albert Bierstadt's "Hetch Hetchy Canyon"; A Pinnacle from Duccio's "Maesta" Altarpiece; Head of Faustina the Elder, 2nd century AD, Roman

ON EXHIBIT 1999
04/06/1999 to 05/30/1999   SALLY MANN: STILL TIME
A survey of Mann's work from 1971-1991 selected by the photographer herself. *Catalog Will Travel*

SPRINGFIELD

George Walter Vincent Smith Art Museum

At the Quadrangle, Corner State & Chestnut Sts., Springfield, MA 01103

☎: 413-263-6800   ◙   www.spfldlibmus.org

Open: Noon-4 We-Su   **Closed:** Mo-We, LEG/HOL

ADM   Adult: $4.00   **Children:** $1.00 (6-18)   **Students:** $4.00   **Seniors:** $4.00

&   ℗   **Museum Shop**   ⅋ year-round café

Group Tours: 413-263-6800 x472   **Drop-In Tours:** by reservation   **Historic Building** Built in 1896

Permanent Collection: ENTIRE COLLECTION OF 19th C AMERICAN ART OF GEORGE WALTER VINCENT SMITH; OR; DEC/ART 17-19; CH: jade; JAP: bronzes, ivories, armor, tsuba 17-19; DEC/ART: cer; AM: ptgs 19

With the largest collection of Chinese cloisonné in the western world, the G. W. V. Smith Art Museum, built in 1895 in the style of an Italian villa, is part of a four museum complex that also includes The Museum of the Fine Arts. The museum reflects its founder's special passion for collecting the arts of 17th to 19th century Japan. **NOT TO BE MISSED:** Early 19th century carved 9' high wooden Shinto wheel shrine

ON EXHIBIT 1999

02/28/1999 to 04/18/1999   CROSSING BOUNDARIES: CONTEMPORARY ART QUILTS

Created by members of the Art quilt Network in America, the 39 contemporary quilts on view represent a departure from the traditional by the inclusion of innovative techniques and the incorporation of painting, photography and printmaking within the works. *Catalog Will Travel*

03/06/1999 to 05/16/1999   AMERICAN GLASS: MASTERS OF THE ART *Will Travel*

07/07/1999 to 08/22/1999   TREASURES OF DECEIT: ARCHAEOLOGY AND THE FORGER'S CRAFT

Objects representing ancient Near Eastern, Egyptian, Etruscan, Greek and Roman civilizations will be used as springboards in an exhibition designed to explain how art historians and classical archeologists determine the authenticity of antiquities. Visitors will be encouraged to examine many of the genuine, reworked and forged objects on view through a magnifying glass, enabling them to evaluate works utilizing some of the methodology of the experts. *Catalog Will Travel*

09/15/1999 to 10/31/1999   ART SCENE: JOHN ROY

11/14/1999 to 01/09/2000   ON THE ROAD WITH THOMAS HART BENTON: IMAGES OF A CHANGING AMERICA

Benton is a widely acclaimed artist who first attained prominence in the 20's and 30's as both an artist, writer and art personality. He was the first artist featured on the cover of 'Time' magazine. Drawn from the collection of his estate the exhibition demonstrates how drawing, one of his greatest talents, was combined with travel for which he had a passion, to produce some of his most significant work. *Catalog Will Travel*

Museum of Fine Arts

At the Quadrangle, Corner of State & Chestnut Sts., Springfield, MA 01103

☎: 413-263-6800   ◙   www.spfldlibmus.org

Open: 9-12 & 1-4 Mo-Fr   **Closed:** Mo-Tu, LEG/HOL!

ADM   Adult: $4.00   **Children:** $1.00 (6-18)   **Students:** $4.00   **Seniors:** $4.00

&   ℗   **Museum Shop**   ⅋

Group Tours: ex 472   **Drop-In Tours:** by reservation

Permanent Collection: AM: 19-20; FR: 19-20; IT Baroque; Dutch; Flemish

Part of a four museum complex located on The Quadrangle in Springfield, the Museum of Fine Arts, built in the 1930's Art Deco Style, offers an overview of European and American art. Single admission fee provides entry to all four museums on the Quadrangle. **NOT TO BE MISSED:** "The Historical Monument of the American Republic, 1867 & 1888 by Erastus S. Field, a monumental painting in the court of the museum

MASSACHUSETTS

Museum of Fine Arts - continued

ON EXHIBIT 1999

10/04/1998 to 01/03/1999   THE STORIES WOVEN IN: NAVAJO WEAVING IN A STORYTELLING CONTEXT

02/28/1999 to 04/18/1999   CROSSING BOUNDARIES: CONTEMPORARY ART QUILTS
Created by members of the Art quilt Network in America, the 39 contemporary quilts on view represent a departure from the traditional by the inclusion of innovative techniques and the incorporation of painting, photography and printmaking within the works. *Catalog Will Travel*

07/07/1999 to 08/22/1999   TREASURES OF DECEIT: ARCHAEOLOGY AND THE FORGER'S CRAFT
Objects representing ancient Near Eastern, Egyptian, Etruscan, Greek and Roman civilizations will be used as springboards in an exhibition designed to explain how art historians and classical archeologists determine the authenticity of antiquities. Visitors will be encouraged to examine many of the genuine, reworked and forged objects on view through a magnifying glass, enabling them to evaluate works utilizing some of the methodology of the experts. *Catalog Will Travel*

11/14/1999 to 01/09/2000   ON THE ROAD WITH THOMAS HART BENTON: IMAGES OF A CHANGING AMERICA
Benton is a widely acclaimed artist who first attained prominence in the 20's and 30's as both an artist, writer and art personality. He was the first artist featured on the cover of 'Time' magazine. Drawn from the collection of his estate the exhibition demonstrates how drawing, one of his greatest talents, was combined with travel for which he had a passion, to produce some of his most significant work. *Catalog Will Travel*

Chesterwood
Off Rte. 183, Glendale Section, Stockbridge, MA 01262-0827
☏: 413-298-3579
Open: 10-5 Daily (MAY 1-OCT 31)   **Closed:** None during open season
ADM   Adult: $7.50   **Children:** $4.00 (13-18), $2.00 (6-12)   **Students:** $2.50 (10 or more)
♿ &#9física;   **Museum Shop   Group Tours:** ex 11   **Drop-In Tours**: hourly throughout the day
Historic Building Two Buildings (1898 studio & 1901 house) of Daniel Chester French   **Sculpture Garden**
Permanent Collection: SCULP; PTGS; WORKS OF DANIEL CHESTER FRENCH; PHOT

Located on 120 wooded acres is the original studio Colonial Revival house and garden of Daniel Chester French, leading sculptor of the American Renaissance. Working models for the Lincoln Memorial and the Minute Man, his most famous works, are on view along with many other of his sculptures and preliminary models. PLEASE NOTE: There are reduced admission rates to see the grounds only, and a special family admission rate of $16.50 for the museum buildings, grounds and tour. **NOT TO BE MISSED:** Original casts and models of the seated Abraham Lincoln for the Memorial.

Norman Rockwell Museum at Stockbridge
Stockbridge, MA 01262
☏: 413-298 4100   ▣ www.nrm.org
Open: MAY-OCT: 10-5 Daily; NOV-APR: 11-4 Mo-Fr & 10-5 Sa, Su & HOL   **Closed:** 1/1, THGV, 12/25
ADM   Adult: $9.00 (Family $20 for 2 adults & children under 18)   **Children:** $2.00 (F under 5)   **Students:** $7.00
Seniors: $4.50 We Nov-April
♿ &#9física;   **Museum Shop   Group Tours**: ex 220   **Drop-In Tours**: tours daily on the hour
Historic Building 1800 Georgian House (admin. ofcs. - not open to public)
Permanent Collection: NORMAN ROCKWELL ART & ARTIFACTS

The Norman Rockwell Museum displays works from all periods of the long and distinguished career of America's most beloved artist/illustrator. In addition to Rockwell's studio, moved to the new museum site in 1986, visitors may enjoy the permanent exhibition entitled "My Adventure as an Illustrator", which contains 60 paintings that span Rockwell's entire career (1910 thru most of the 1970's). PLEASE NOTE: Rockwell's studio is open May through Oct. **NOT TO BE MISSED:** The "Four Freedoms" Gallery in the new museum building.

Norman Rockwell Museum at Stockbridge - continued
ON EXHIBIT 1999
ONGOING   A MIRROR ON AMERICA
Rockwell's images as they both influenced and depicted the American way of life is the focus of this exhibition.

ONGOING   MY BEST STUDIO YET
Business, personal and social aspects of Rockwell's daily working life are revealed in this display of archival and ephemeral material. Many of the objects on view concern his relationships with his family, friends, business colleagues and even some of the models he used for his portraits of American life.

ONGOING   MY ADVENTURES AS AN ILLUSTRATOR
More than 60 paintings that cover Rockwell's 60 year career from the 1910's to the 1970's will be included in this permanent installation of familiar and lesser-known works accompanied by autobiographical quotations.

09/05/1998 to 01/24/1999   NORMAN ROCKWELL: PICTURES FOR THE AMERICAN PEOPLE
Seventy of his oil paintings and all 322 'Saturday Evening Post' covers are featured in this always popular show. *Catalog*

11/07/1998 to 05/21/1999   VISUAL SOLUTIONS – SEVEN ILLUSTRATORS & THE CREATIVE PROCESS
This lively exhibition can be your guide to how illustrators work. Seven contemporary illustrators are taken from rough sketch to final piece.

03/1999 to 06/1999   MADE IN MASSACHUSETTS

WALTHAM

Rose Art Museum
Affiliate Institution: Brandeis University
415 South St., Waltham, MA 02254-9110
☏: 781-736-3434   ◉   www.brandeis.edu/rose
Open: 12-5 Tu-Su, 12-9 Th   **Closed:** Mo, LEG/HOL!
♿   ℗   **Museum Shop**
Group Tours   Drop-In Tours: by advance reservation
Permanent Collection: AM: ptgs, sculp 19-20; EU: ptgs, sculp 19-20; CONT; ptgs, drgs, sculp, phot. PLEASE NOTE: The permanent collection is not always on view!

The Rose Art Museum, founded in 1961, and located on the campus of Brandeis University, just outside of Boston, features one of the largest collections of contemporary art in New England. Selections from the permanent collection, and an exhibition of the works of Boston area artists are presented annually.

ON EXHIBIT 1999
01/21/1999 to 03/07/1999   BOSTON AREA ARTISTS EXHIBITION

03/25/1999 to 05/30/1999   SARAH CHARLESWORTH: A RETROSPECTIVE
With issues ranging from sexual and gender politics to mythology and religion, the 60 works on view in the first overview of the artist's 20-year career, reveal Charlesworth's innovative use of the photograph as a subject beyond its traditional role as a medium.

09/11/1999 to 11/07/1999   PAINTINGS TO LIVE BY: FEMINISM AND ABSTRACTION IN THE 70S (PART II)

MASSACHUSETTS

Davis Museum and Cultural Center
Affiliate Institution: Wellesley College
106 Central St., Wellesley, MA 02181-8257
☎: 781-283-2051 ◙ www.wellesley.edu/DavisMuseum/davismenu.html
Open: 11-5 Tu , Fr, Sa, 11-8 We, Th, 1-5 Su **Closed:** 1/1, 12/25
& ℗ **Museum Shop** ⅋ Café Collins open M-F (call 781-283-3379 for hours and info.)
Group Tours: 617-283-2081 **Drop-In Tours**
Permanent Collection: AM: ptgs, sculp, drgs, phot; EU: ptgs, sculp, drgs, phot; AN; AF; MED; REN

Established over 100 years ago, the Davis Museum and Cultural Center, formerly the Wellesley College Museum, is located in a stunning 61,000 square foot state-of-the-art museum building. One of the first encyclopedic college art collections ever assembled in the United States, the museum is home to more than 5,000 works of art. PLEASE NOTE: The museum closes at 5pm on We & Th during the month of Jan. and from 6/15 to 8/15). **NOT TO BE MISSED:** "A Jesuit Missionary in Chinese Costume", a chalk on paper work by Peter Paul Rubens (recent acquisition)

Sterling and Francine Clark Art Institute
225 South St., Williamstown, MA 01267
☎: 413-458-9545
Open: 10-5 Tu-Su; Tu until 8 July 1 - Aug 31 **Closed:** Mo, 1/1, THGV, 12/25
Free Day: Tu and daily Nov 1 - June 30 **ADM** **Adult:** $5 We-Su
& ℗ **Museum Shop** ⅋ **Group Tours**: 413-458-2303 ex 324 **Drop-In Tours**: 3:00 Tu-Fr during Jul & Aug
Permanent Collection: IT: ptgs 14-18; FL: ptgs 14-18; DU: ptgs 14-18; OM: ptgs, gr, drgs; FR: Impr/ptgs; AM: ptgs 19

More than 30 paintings by Renoir and other French Impressionist masters as well as a collection of old master paintings and a significant group of American works account for the high reputation of this recently expanded, outstanding 40 year old institution. PLEASE NOTE: Recorded tours of the permanent collection are available for a small fee. **NOT TO BE MISSED:** Impr/ptgs; works by Homer, Sargent, Remington, Cassatt; Silver coll.; Ugolino Da Siena Altarpiece; Porcelain gallery

ON EXHIBIT 1999
to Summer 1999 DRAWN INTO THE LIGHT: JEAN FRANCOIS MILLET

to Summer 2000 A MILLION AND ONE NIGHTS: ORIENTALISM IN AMERICAN CULTURE 1870-1930

09/12/1998 to 01/03/1999 FAREWELL TO THE WET NURSE: ETIENNE AUBRY AND IMAGES OF BREAST-FEEDING IN EIGHTEENTH-CENTURY FRANCE

02/06/1999 to 05/09/1999 THE PAINTED SKETCH: IMPRESSIONS FROM NATURE BY AMERICAN LANDSCAPE PAINTERS, 1830-1880

Williams College Museum of Art
Main St., Rte. #2, Williamstown, MA 01267
☎: 413-458-2429 ◙ www.wiliams.edu/wcma
Open: 10-5 Tu-Sa, 1-5 Su (open on MEM/DAY, LAB/DAY, COLUMBUS DAY) **Closed:** Mo, 1/1, THGV, 12/25
& ℗ **Museum Shop** **Group Tours**: 413-597-2038 **Drop-In Tours**: 2:00 We & Su Jul & Aug, other times by appt.
Historic Building 1846 Birch Octagon by Thomas Tefft; 1983-86 additions by Chas. Moore
Permanent Collection: AM: cont & 18-19; ASIAN & OTHER NON-WESTERN CIVILIZATIONS; BRIT: ptgs 17-19; SP: ptgs 15-18; IT/REN: ptgs ; PHOT; GR/ARTS; AN/GRK; AN/R

Williams College Museum of Art - continued

Considered one of the finest college art museums in the U.S., the Williams collection of 11,000 works that span the history of art, features particular strengths in the areas of contemporary & modern art, American art from the late 18th century to the present, and non-Western art. The original museum building of 1846, a two-story brick octagon with a neoclassic rotunda, was joined, in 1986, by a dramatic addition designed by noted architect Charles Moore. **NOT TO BE MISSED:** Works of Maurice and Charles Prendergast

ON EXHIBIT 1999

ONGOING   AN AMERICAN IDENTITY: 19TH-CENTURY AMERICAN ART FROM THE PERMANENT COLLECTION
Works by Eakins, Harnett, Homer, Inness, Kensett, LaFarge, Whistler and others examine the ways in which creative artists helped define a national image for the new republic.

ONGOING   ART OF THE ANCIENT WORLDS
From the permanent collection, a selection of ancient sculpture, vases, artifacts, and jewelry from Greece, Rome, Egypt, the Near East, Southeast Asia and the Americas.

ONGOING   OUTDOOR SCULPTURE FROM THE "KNOTS" AND "TAICHI" SERIES BY THE CHINESE ARTIST, JU MING

ONGOING   INTERNATIONAL BIRD MUSEUM
Mounted on the outside of the Museum, this unusual, elaborate structure constructed of 10,000 quarter-inch glazed bricks, is intentionally placed high enough off the ground so that only birds can visit the exhibitions.

ONGOING   INVENTING THE TWENTIETH CENTURY: SELECTIONS FROM THE PERMANENT COLLECTION (1900-1950)
Aspects of "The New" as contemporary art evolved will be explored in thematic groupings of paintings, sculpture, drawings and photographs.

ONGOING   VITAL TRADITIONS: OLD MASTER WORKS FROM THE PERMANENT COLLECTION
300 years of artistic change, from the Renaissance to the Baroque, will be highlighted in the 17 paintings by Guardi, Ribera, van Ostade and others on view from the permanent collection.

01/17/1998 to 12/1999   TRANSITION AND TRADITION – AFRICAN ART FROM THE BROOKLYN MUSEUM OF ART
Twenty functional objects used in religious or political ceremonial life.

06/27/1998 to 07/14/1999   A LEAP OF FAITH: ABSTRACT ART FROM THE ALBRIGHT-KNOX ART GALLERY
11 important works from the outstanding holdings of the Museum in Buffalo including Bontecou, Ferber, Motherwell, Smith, and Still as well as de Kooning and a 1957 oil and collage work by Rauschenberg.

07/18/1998 to 01/03/1999   TWO PORTFOLIOS FROM THE COLLECTION OF SOL LEWITT: ROBERT RYMAN AND TIM ROLLINS AND THE KIDS OF SURVIVAL

04/17/1999 to 10/1999   TONY OURSLER
This retrospective will examine Oursler's pioneering work in video projection.

07/03/1999 to 09/06/1999   WILLIAM WEGMAN PHOTOGRAPHS AND PAINTINGS (working title)

07/24/1999 to 01/2000   THE PANAMA CANAL AND THE ART OF CONSTRUCTION
A selection of paintings, prints and photographs of canal construction.

WORCESTER

Iris & B. Gerald Cantor Art Gallery

Affiliate Institution: College of Holy Cross
1 College St., Worcester, MA 01610

: 508-793-3356 ◙ www.holycross.edu/visitor/cantor/cantor/html
Open: 10-4 Mo-Fr, 2-5 Sa & S; Summer hours by appointment **Closed:** ACAD!
♿ Ⓟ **Museum Shop** **Group Tours** **Drop-In Tours**
Permanent Collection: SCULP; CONT/PHOT; 10 RODIN SCULPTURES

Five to seven exhibitions are mounted annually in this Gallery with themes that focus on contemporary art, art historical and social justice topics, and student work.

Worcester Art Museum

55 Salisbury St., Worcester, MA 01609-3196

: 508-799-4406 ◙ www.woresterart.org
Open: 11-5 We-Fr, 10-5 Sa, 11-5 Su **Closed:** Mo, Tu, 1/1, 7/4, THGV, 12/25
ADM **Adult:** $8.00 **Children:** F (under 17) **Students:** $6.00 **Seniors:** $6.00
♿ Ⓟ **Museum Shop** Café 11:30-2 W-Sa (ex. 3068)
Group Tours: ex 3061 **Drop-In Tours**: 2:00 most Su Sep-May; 2:00 Sa
Historic Building Museum recently celebrated 100th anniversary **Sculpture Garden**
Permanent Collection: AM: 17-19; JAP: gr; BRIT: 18-19; FL: 16-17; GER: 16-17; DU: 17; P/COL; AN/EGT; OR: sculp; MED: sculp; AM: dec/art

Opened to the public in 1898, the Worcester Art Museum is the second largest art museum in New England. Its exceptional 35,000-piece collection of paintings, sculpture, decorative arts, photography, prints and drawings is displayed in 36 galleries and spans 5,000 years of art and culture, ranging from Egyptian antiquities and Roman mosaics to Impressionist paintings and contemporary art. Throughout its first century, the Museum has proven itself a pioneer. Among its many "firsts," the Museum was the first American museum to purchase work by Claude Monet (1910) and Paul Gauguin (1921); the first museum to bring a medieval building to America; a sponsor of the first major excavation at Antioch, one of the four great cities of ancient Rome (1932); the first museum to organize a Members' Council (1949); and the first museum to create an Art All-State program for high school artists. **NOT TO BE MISSED:** Antiochan Mosaics ; American Portrait miniatures; New Roman Art Gallery; New Contemporary Art Gallery

ON EXHIBIT 1999

03/13/1999 to 06/27/1999 ALL THAT IS GLORIOUS AROUND US: PAINTINGS FROM THE HUDSON RIVER SCHOOL

Led by Thomas Cole, the Hudson River School painters were the first to paint American scenes rather than the then traditional custom of painting only European subjects. Many lesser known and women artists as well as William Trost Richards and others equally well known will be featured. *Will Travel*

MICHIGAN

University of Michigan Museum of Art
525 S. State St. at S. Univ., Ann Arbor, MI 48109
☎: 734-764-0395 **◙** www.umich.edu/~umma/
Open: 10-5 Tu-Sa, till 9 T, 12-5 Su; SUMMER HOURS: 11-5 Tu-Sa, till 9 Th, 12-5 Su **Closed:** Mo, 1/1, 7/4, THGV, 12/25 **Sugg/Cont:** $3.00
♿ ℗ **Museum Shop**
Group Tours Drop-In Tours: 12:10-12:30 Th; 2pm Su
Permanent Collection: CONT; gr, phot; OM; drgs 6-20; OR; AF; OC; IS

This museum, which houses the second largest art collection in the state of Michigan, also features a changing series of special exhibitions, family programs, and chamber music concerts. With over 12,000 works of art ranging from Italian Renaissance panel paintings to Han dynasty Tomb figures, this 50 year old university museum ranks among the finest in the country. **NOT TO BE MISSED:** Works on paper by J. M. W. Whistler

ON EXHIBIT 1999
ONGOING AFRICAN ARTS: OBJECTS OF POWER, KNOWLEDGE AND MEDIATION
Fascinating and rarely seen objects from the museum's impressive and growing collection of African art.

11/07/1998 to 01/17/1999 MASTER DRAWINGS FROM THE WORCESTER ART MUSEUM
More than 100 works including watercolors, pastels and illuminated manuscripts by European and American artists from 1275 to 1975 representing major trends of style and content. *Catalog Will Travel*

12/05/1998 to 01/24/1999 DRAWINGS OF EUGENE DELACROIX

01/23/1999 to 03/21/1999 BILL JACOBSEN PHOTOGRAPHS: 1992-1998
Jacobson's Photographs are haunting and evocative in exploring feelings of vulnerability and tentativeness in this age of AIDS

02/13/1999 to 05/02/1999 MAGDALENA ABAKANOVWICZ *Catalog Will Travel*

05/15/1999 to 08/29/1999 HIGHLIGHTS FROM THE 20TH CENTURY COLLECTIONS

07/26/1999 to 09/26/1999 TOUCHSTONE: 200 YEARS OF ARTIST'S LITHOGRAPHS FROM THE HARVARD UNIVERSITY MUSEUM

Art Center of Battle Creek
265 E. Emmett St., Battle Creek, MI 49017-4601
☎: 616-962-9511
Open: 10-5 Tu-Sa; Noon-4 Su, till 7pm Th **Closed:** Mo, LEG/HOL!
♿ ℗ **Museum Shop**
Group Tours Drop-In Tours
Permanent Collection: REG

The mission of the Art Center is to present quality exhibitions and programming in the visual arts for the education, enrichment and enjoyment of the southwestern Michigan region. **NOT TO BE MISSED:** KIDSPACE, a hands-on activity gallery for children.

ON EXHIBIT 1999
11/19/1998 to 01/10/1999 BREATHLESS: THE FIGURE IN CONTEMPORARY GLASS

MICHIGAN

Art Center of Battle Creek - continued
01/21/1999 to 03/21/1999   WILLIAM WEGMAN
Wegman's amusing and often poignant Polaroid photographs of his beloved Weimaraners along with his drawings, early conceptual video's etc.

05/13/1999 to 06/27/1999   CONTEMPORARY AFRICAN-AMERICAN ARTISTS
How far has today's society come in extinguishing racism ? Explore the important and often painful subject through the visions and creations of the artists in this challenging exhibition.

07/09/1999 to 08/29/1999   MICHIGAN ARTISTS COMPETITION

BLOOMFIELD HILLS

Cranbrook Art Museum
1221 North Woodward Ave., Bloomfield Hills, MI 48303-0801
☎: 248-645-3323   ◙   www.cranbrook.edu/museum
Open: 11-5 Tu-Su, till 9pm Th   **Closed:** Mo, LEG/HOL!
ADM   Adult: $5.00   **Children:** F (7 and under)   **Students:** $3.00   **Seniors:** $3.00
&   ℗   **Museum Shop**
Group Tours: 248-645-3323   **Drop-In Tours:** varies
Historic Building Designed by noted Finnish-Amer. architect, Eliel Saarinen   **Sculpture Garden**
Permanent Collection: ARCH/DRGS; CER; PTGS; SCULP; GR 19-20 ; DEC/ART 20

The newly restored Saarinen House, a building designed by noted Finnish-American architect Eliel Saarinen, is part of Cranbrook Academy, the only institution in the country solely devoted to graduate education in the arts. In addition to outdoor sculpture on the grounds surrounding the museum, the permanent collection includes important works of art that are influential on the contemporary trends of today. PLEASE NOTE: Please call ahead (248-645-3323) for specific information on tours and admission fees for Cranbrook House, Cranbrook Gardens (for the architecture & sculpture tour), Cranbrook Art Museum, and Saarinen House. **NOT TO BE MISSED:** Works by Eliel Saarinen; carpets by Loja Saarinen

---

DETROIT

Detroit Institute of Arts
5200 Woodward Ave., Detroit, MI 48202
☎: 313-833-7900   ◙   www.dia.org
Open: 11-4 We-Fr; 11-5 Sa, Su   **Closed:** Mo, Tu, Some Holidays
Sugg/Cont   Adult: $4.00   **Children:** $1.00   **Students:** $1.00
&   ℗   **Museum Shop**   ⑪ Kresge Court Café (833-1932), Gallery Grille (833-1857)
Group Tours: 313-833-7981   **Drop-In Tours:** 1:00 We-Sa; 1 & 2:30 Su
Permanent Collection: FR: Impr; GER: Exp; FL; ptgs; AS; EGT; EU: 20; AF; CONT; P/COL; NAT/AM; EU: ptgs, sculp, dec/art; AM: ptgs, sculp, dec/art

With holdings that survey the art of world cultures from ancient to modern times, The Detroit Institute of Arts, founded in 1885, ranks fifth largest among the nation's fine art museums. **NOT TO BE MISSED:** "Detroit Industry" by Diego Rivera, a 27 panel fresco located in the Rivera court.

ON EXHIBIT 1999
09/27/1998 to 02/07/1999   PRINTS BY TERRY WINTERS: A RETROSPECTIVE FROM THE COLLECTION OF ROBERT AND SUSAN SOSNICK

10/11/1998 to 02/14/1999   A PASSION FOR GLASS: THE AVIVA AND JACK A. ROBINSON COLLECTION

Detroit Institute of Arts - continued

10/17/1998 to 01/31/1999 "WHERE THE WILD THINGS ARE" ANIMALS IN ANCIENT ART AT THE DETROIT INSTITUTE OF ARTS

01/27/1999 to 05/02/1999   PERSONAL ARTIFACTS IN THE WORLD OF THE SAMURAI WARRIOR

02/07/1999 to 04/25/1999   HALF PAST AUTUMN: THE ART OF GORDON PARKS
All aspects of his varied career will be included in the first traveling Gordon Parks retrospective. Considered by many to be an American renaissance man, Parks, a filmmaker, novelist, poet and musician is best known as a photojournalist whose powerful images deliver messages of hope in the face of adversity. *Catalog Will Travel* ⌒

03/1999   BAL AFRICAIN

04/1999   DETROIT PUBLIC SCHOOLS STUDENT EXHIBITION

04/14/1999 to 06/27/1999   WALKER EVANS SIMPLE SECRETS: PHOTOGRAPHS FROM THE COLLECTION OF MARIAN AND BENJAMIN A. HILL
90 vintage photographic prints, some of which have never been published, will be featured in this career wide exhibition of works by Evans, one of the most important figures in the history of American photography.

05/19/1999 to 09/19/1999   WISDOM AND PERFECTION: LOTUS BLOSSOMS IN ASIAN ART

06/27/1999 to 08/29/1999   ANCIENT GOLD: THE WEALTH OF THE THRACIANS, TREASURES FROM THE REPUBLIC OF BULGARIA
The first exhibition of Bulgaria's cultural artistry, primarily metalwork, to be seen in the US in the post-Communist era. More than 200 magnificent gold and silver objects, dating from 1200 to 400 B.C., will be featured in an exhibition that lends credence to the life and legends of ancient Thrace. *Will Travel* ⌒

Summer 1999   FLASH BASH

07/25/1999 to 10/31/1999   COMMON MAN, MYTHIC VISION: THE PAINTINGS OF BEN SHAHN
Over 50 of the finest paintings created by Shahn between 1936-1962. It begins with the wartime shift in his work from social realism to 'personal realism' and culminates in the series of paintings, "The Lucky Dragon" inspired by the fate of a fishing crew exposed to nuclear testing in Japan. *Catalog Will Travel*

EAST LANSING

Kresge Art Museum
Affiliate Institution: Michigan State University
East Lansing, MI 48824-1119
☎: 517-355-7631   ▣ www.msu.edu/unit/kamuseum
Open: 9:30-4:30 Mo-We, Fr; Noon-8 Th; 1-4 Sa, Su; SUMMER: 11-4 Mo-Fr; 1-4 Sa, Su   **Closed:** LEG/HOL! ACAD!
Vol/Cont
  ♿ ℗   **Museum Shop**
Group Tours   Drop-In Tours
Sculpture Garden
Permanent Collection: GR 19-20; AM: cont/ab (1960'S), PHOT

Founded in 1959, the Kresge, an active teaching museum with over 4,000 works ranging from prehistoric to contemporary, is the only fine arts museum in central Michigan. **NOT TO BE MISSED:** "St. Anthony" by Francisco Zuberon; "Remorse" by Salvador Dali; Contemporary collection

MICHIGAN

Flint Institute of Arts
1120 E. Kearsley St., Flint, MI 48503-1991
\: 810-234-1695
Open: 10-5 Tu-Sa, 1-5 Su   **Closed:** Mo, LEG/HOL!
Vol/Cont
& Ⓟ **Museum Shop**
Group Tours: 810-234-1695   **Drop-In Tours**: 10-5 Tu-Sa
Permanent Collection: AM: ptgs, sculp, gr 19-20; EU: ptgs, sculp, gr 19-20; FR/REN: IT/REN: dec/art; CH; cer, sculp

The Flint Institute of Arts, founded in 1928, has grown to become the largest private museum collection of fine art in the state. In addition to the permanent collection with artworks from ancient China to modern America, visitors to this museum can enjoy the recently renovated building itself, a stunning combination of classic interior gallery space housed within the walls of a modern exterior. **NOT TO BE MISSED:** Bray Gallery of French & Italian Renaissance decorative art.

Calvin College Center Art Gallery
Affiliate Institution: Calvin College
Grand Rapids, MI 49546
\: 616-957-6271
Open: 9-9 Mo-Th, 9-5 Fr, Noon-4 Sa   **Closed:** Su, ACAD!
& Ⓟ **Museum Shop   Group Tours**: 616-957-6271   **Drop-In Tours**: Available upon request
Permanent Collection: DU: ptgs, drgs 17-19; GR, PTGS, SCULP, DRGS 20

17th & 19th century Dutch paintings are one of the highlights of the permanent collection.

ON EXHIBIT 1999
01/08/1999 to 02/11/1999   ART IN WORSHIP

02/20/1999 to 03/17/1999   ART FACULTY EXHIBITION

04/17/1999 to 04/28/1999   BACHELOR OF FINE ARTS EXHIBITION II

Grand Rapids Art Museum
155 N. Division, Grand Rapids, MI 49503
\: 616-459-4677
Open: 12-4 Tu, Sa, Su; 10-4 We, Fr; 10-9 Th   **Closed:** Mo, LEG/HOL!
ADM   Adult: $3.00   **Children:** F (under 5)   **Students:** $1.00   **Seniors:** $1.50
& Ⓟ **Museum Shop   Group Tours   Drop-In Tours   Historic Building** Beaux Arts Federal Building
Permanent Collection: REN: ptgs; FR: ptgs 19; AM: ptgs 19-20; GR; EXP/PTGS; PHOT; DEC/ART

Located in a renovated Federal Style Building, the Grand Rapids Art Museum, founded in 1911, exhibits paintings and prints by established and emerging artists, as well as photographs, sculpture, and a collection of furniture & decorative arts from the Grand Rapids area and beyond. **NOT TO BE MISSED:** "Harvest" by Karl Schmidt-Rottluff; "Ingleside" by Richard Diebenkorn, and other works by Alexander Calder, Childe Hassam, Max Pechstein, Grach Hartigan, and Christo.

Kalamazoo Institute of Arts

314 South Park St., Kalamazoo, MI 49007
☎: 616-349-7775　▣ www.kia.iserv.net
Open: 10-5 Tu, We, Fr, Sa, 10-8 Th, 12-5 Su　**Closed:** Mo, LEG/HOL!
Vol/Cont
& ℗ **Museum Shop**
Group Tours: 616-349-7775　**Drop-In Tours**　**Historic Building** architecturally significant　**Sculpture Garden**
Permanent Collection: sculp, ptgs, drgs, cer, gr, photo

The Kalamazoo Institute, established in 1924, is known for its collection of 20th century American art and European graphics, as well as for its outstanding art school. More than 3,000 objects are housed in a building that in 1979 was voted one of the most significant structures in the state and in 1998 recently underwent a significant expansion. **NOT TO BE MISSED:** The state of the art interactive gallery and permanent collection installations, including "La Clownesse Aussi (Mlle. Cha-U-Ka-O)" by Henri de Toulouse Lautrec; "Sleeping Woman" by Richard Diebenkorn; "Simone in a White Bonnet" by Mary Cassatt

ON EXHIBIT 1999

02/27/1999 to 05/09/1999　A TASTE FOR SPLENDOR: TREASURES FROM THE HILLWOOD MUSEUM
This is a rare opportunity to see the exquisite art collection of Marjorie Merriwether Post, heir to the Post cereal fortune, which never before has been seen outside her home at Hillwood. More than 160 decorative and fine arts objects created in Imperial Russia and Europe, dating from the 17th to the mid-20th c. range from 19th century French furniture to porcelains and gold boxes commissioned by Catherine The Great and treasures by Fabergé including two of the Imperial Easter Eggs.

Muskegon Museum of Art

296 W. Webster, Muskegon, MI 49440
☎: 616-720-2570
Open: 10-5 Tu-Fr; Noon-5 Sa, Su　**Closed:** Mo, LEG/HOL!
Vol/Cont & ℗ **Museum Shop**　**Group Tours**　**Drop-In Tours**
Permanent Collection: AM: ptgs, gr 19-early 20; EU: ptgs; PHOT; SCULP; OM: gr; CONT: gr

The award winning Muskegon Museum, which opened in 1912, and has recently undergone major renovation, is home to a permanent collection that includes many fine examples of American and French Impressionistic paintings, Old Master through contemporary prints, photography, sculpture and glass. **NOT TO BE MISSED:** American Art Collection

ON EXHIBIT 1999

12/06/1998 to 01/03/1999　CHRISTMAS STUFF: MINIATURE ROOMS AND THE SNOWMAN TREE

12/06/1998 to 01/17/1999　ALLEGORIES & NARRATIVES: PAINTINGS BY ED WONG-LIGDA & TIMOTHY FISHER

01/10/1999 to 03/04/1999　SPANNING 5 DECADES: SELECTIONS FROM THE PAUL FRIED GRAPHIC ARTS COLLECTION

02/07/1999 to 04/11/1999　WENDELL MINOR: ART FOR THE WRITTEN WORD

02/07/1999 to 04/11/1999　17TH ANNUAL STUDENT ART SHOW

03/28/1999 to 07/11/1999　PAUL SEIDE NEON GLASS ARTIST

MICHIGAN

Muskegon Museum of Art - continued
05/02/1999 to 07/15/1999   71ST REGIONAL JURIED ART SHOW

08/01/1999 to 09/12/1999   THE GREAT AMERICAN POP ART STORE

08/01/1999 to 09/12/1999   AARON FINK RECENT WORKS

PETOSKEY

Crooked Tree Arts Council
461 E. Mitchell St., Petoskey, MI 49770
☎: 616-347-4337
Open: 10-5 Mo-Fr, 11-4 Sa   Closed: LEG/HOL!
& ℗   Museum Shop   Group Tours Drop-In Tours   Historic Building 1890 Methodist Church
Permanent Collection: REGIONAL & FINE ART

This fine arts collection makes its home on the coast of Lake Michigan in a former Methodist church built in 1890.

ROCHESTER

Meadow Brook Art Gallery
Affiliate Institution: Oakland University
Rochester, MI 48309-4401
☎: 248-370-3005
Open: 1-5 Tu-Fr; 2-6:30 Sa, Su (7-9:30 Tu-Fr theater performance days)   Closed: Mo
& ℗   Museum Shop   Group Tours   Drop-In Tours   Sculpture Garden
Permanent Collection: AF; OC; P/COL; CONT/AM: ptgs, sculp, gr; CONT/EU: ptgs, gr, sculp

Located 30 miles north of Detroit on the campus of Oakland University, the Meadow Brook Art Gallery offers four major exhibitions annually.

ON EXHIBIT 1999
01/08/1999 to 02/21/1999   PICTURING PARIS: 19TH & 20TH CENTURY PHOTOGRAPHS FROM THE DETROIT INSTITUTE OF ARTS COLLECTION

02/28/1999 to 04/11/1999   PARALLEL VISIONS - CONTEMPORARY RUSSIAN ARTISTS

04/16/1999 to 05/16/1999   5TH ANNUAL STUDENT EXHIBITION

SAGINAW

Saginaw Art Museum
1126 N. Michigan Ave., Saginaw, MI 48602
☎: 517-754-2491   ◙   www.cris.com/~jKerman/SAM.shtml
Open: 10-5 We, Fr, Sa; 10-6:30 Tu, Th; 1-5 Su   Closed: Mo, LEG/HOL!
Vol/Cont
& ℗   Museum Shop   Group Tours: 517-754-2491 (ask for Dona)   Drop-In Tours: by appointment
Historic Building former 1904 Clark Lombard Ring Family Home
Permanent Collection: EU: ptgs, sculp 14-20; AM: ptgs sculp; OR: ptgs, gr, dec/art; JAP: GR; JOHN ROGERS SCULP; CHARLES ADAM PLATT: gr

The interesting and varied permanent collections of this museum, including an important group of John Rogers sculptures, are housed in a gracious 1904 Georgian-revival building designed by Charles Adam Platt. The former Clark Lombard Ring Family home is listed on the state & federal registers for historic homes.
NOT TO BE MISSED: T'ang Dynasty Marble Buddha

Saginaw Art Museum - continued

ON EXHIBIT 1999

01/1999 to 01/1999   ROBERT VANDERZEE

01/07/1999 to 01/31/1999   ALL AREA SHOW

02/1999 to 02/1999   MAEA STUDENTS ART EXHIBITION

02/1999 to 03/1999   PRINTS BY JAMES MCNEILL WHISTLER

03/04/1999 to 03/28/1999   PAUL COLLINS

04/1999 to 04/1999   FREDA TSCHUMY

04/1999 to 04/1999   NADLYA JINNAH

04/10/1999 to 05/02/1999   ALL AREA PHOTO SHOW

05/1999 to 05/1999   LEGEND OF JOHN BROWN BY JACOB LAWRENCE

05/06/1999 to 05/30/1999   LATINO ART EXHIBITION

06/1999 to 06/1999   RALPH WICKISER

06/1999 to 06/1999   YURAN LEE

06/08/1999 to 07/09/2000   ALMA COLLEGE PRINT SHOW

07/1999 to 08/1999   ROBERT BISSELL
Bissell is a noted illustrator of children's books whose whimsical works feature animal characters in humorous situations.

07/1999 to 08/1999   FRANCES QUINT

09/1999 to 09/1999   AMERICAN WATERCOLOR SOCIETY

10/1999 to 10/1999   CAROL COATES

11/1999 to 11/1999   HOLLYMART

ST. JOSEPH

Krasl Art Center
707 Lake Blvd., St. Joseph, MI 49085
✆: 616-983-0271   ■ www.krasl.org
Open: 10-4 M-Th & Sa, 10-1 Fr, 1-4 Su   **Closed:** Fr PM, LEG/HOL! & Sa of Blossomtime Parade in early May
& Ⓟ Museum Shop
Group Tours: 616-983-0271   **Drop-In Tours**: by appt
Permanent Collection: SCULP

Located on the shores of Lake Michigan, site-specific sculptures are placed in and around the area of the center. Maps showing locations and best positions for viewing are provided for the convenience of the visitor. The center is also noted for hosting one of the Midwest's finest art fairs each July. **NOT TO BE MISSED:** "The Heavyweight (nicknamed lotus)" by Dr. Burt Brent "Three Lines Diagonal Jointed-Wall" by George Rickey; "Allegheny Drift" by Michael Duntar

ON EXHIBIT 1999

03/04/1999 to 04/18/1999   ALL MICHIGAN ALL MEDIA

08/12/1999 to 09/15/1999   RICHARD HUNT AND ASSISTANTS

10/03/1999 to 11/21/1999   AMERICAN IMPRESSIONISM

MICHIGAN

Dennos Museum Center

Affiliate Institution: Northwestern Michigan College

1701 East Front St., Traverse City, MI 49686

📞: 616-922-1055 ◉ dmc.nmc.edu

Open: 10-5 Mo-Sa, 1-5 Su **Closed:** LEG/HOL!

ADM Adult: $2.00 **Children:** $1.00 **Students:** $1.00 **Seniors:** $2.00

♿ Ⓟ **Museum Shop**

Group Tours Drop-In Tours: by appointment **Sculpture Garden**

Permanent Collection: Inuit art; CONT: Canadian Indian graphics; AM; EU; NAT/AM

With a collection of more than 575 works, the Dennos Museum Center houses one of the largest and most historically complete collections of Inuit art from the peoples of the Canadian Arctic. The museum also features a "hands-on" Discovery Gallery. **NOT TO BE MISSED:** The Power Family Inuit Gallery with over 860 Inuit sculptures and prints; The Thomas A. Rutkowski interactive "Discovery Gallery"

Tweed Museum of Art

Affiliate Institution: Univ. of Minn.

10 University Dr., Duluth, MN 55812

☎: 218-726-8222 ◉ www.d.umn.edu/tma

Open: 9-8 Tu, 9-4:30 We-Fr, 1-5 Sa & Su **Closed:** Mo, ACAD!

Sugg/Cont Adult: $2.00 (family $5) **Children:** F (under 6) **Students:** $1.00 **Seniors:** $1.00

  Ⓖ Ⓟ **Museum Shop Group Tours:** 218-726-8222 **Drop-In Tours:** as arranged

Historic Building on campus of University of Minnesota Duluth **Sculpture Garden**

Permanent Collection: OM: ptgs; EU: ptgs 17-19; F: Barbizon ptgs 19; AM: all media 19-20; CONT; AF; JAP: cer; CONT/REG

Endowed with gifts of American and European paintings by industrialist George Tweed, for whom this museum is named, this fine institution also has an important growing permanent collection of contemporary art. One-person exhibitions by living American artists are often presented to promote national recognition of their work. PLEASE NOTE: The museum offers a reduced suggested contribution of $5.00 per family. **NOT TO BE MISSED:** "The Scourging of St. Blaise", a 16th century Italian painting by a follower of Caravaggio

ON EXHIBIT 1999

01/05/1999 to 03/07/1999 MICHAEL CHANDLER

03/20/1999 to 04/18/1999 UMD ART STUDENT EXHIBITION

05/04/1999 to 07/04/1999 CONTEMPORARY REGIONAL ARTISTS SERIES: CELEBRATE: WOMEN IN THE ARTS

07/20/1999 to 10/17/1999 BOTANICA: CONTEMPORARY ART AND THE WORLD OF PLANTS
Images, systems and/or the metaphorical potential of botany as the basis for art will be seen in the works on display by notable contemporary artists from the U.S. and abroad.

09/12/1999 to 11/07/1999 UNFOLDING LIGHT: THE EVOLUTION OF TEN HOLOGRAPHERS
Holography is a process for recording images in three dimensions in which a laser is used as a light source. Invented in the 40's, it was more fully developed in the 60's. While it has many industrial and commercial applications, it also has creative properties which can be used to make works of art. Subjects explored by artists include portraits, still lifes, landscapes, etc..
Will Travel

11/02/1999 to 04/02/2000 COMMUNITY CURATORS PROJECT

11/02/1999 to 04/02/2000 FOCUS ON TWEED COLLECTIONS / 50TH ANNIVERSARY

Frederick R. Weisman Art Museum at the University of Minnesota

Affiliate Institution: University of Minnesota

333 East River Road, Minneapolis, MN 55455

☎: 612-625-9494 ◉ hudson.acad.umn.edu

Open: 10-5 Tu, We, Fr; 10-8 Th; 11-5 Sa, Su **Closed:** Mo, ACAD!, LEG/HOL!

  Ⓖ Ⓟ **Museum Shop Group Tours:** 612-625-9656 **Drop-In Tours:** 1 PM Sa, Su

Historic Building Terra-cotta brick & stainless steel bldg. (1993) by Frank O. Ghery

Permanent Collection: AM: ptgs, sculp, gr 20; KOREAN: furniture 18-19; Worlds largest coll of works by Marsden Hartley & Alfred Maurer (plus major works by their contemporaries such as Feiningner & O'Keeffe

MINNESOTA

Frederick R. Weisman Art Museum at the University of Minnesota - continued

Housed since 1993 in a striking, sculptural stainless steel and brick building designed by architect Frank Gehry, the Weisman Art Museum offers a convenient and friendly museum experience. The museum's collection features early 20th-century American artists, such as Georgia O'Keeffe and Marsden Hartley, as well as a selection of contemporary art. A teaching museum for the University and the community, the Weisman provides a multi-disciplinary approach to the arts through an array of programs and a changing schedule of exhibitions. **NOT TO BE MISSED:** "Oriental Poppies", by Georgia O'Keeffe

ON EXHIBIT 1999

ONGOING   SELECTIONS FROM THE WEISMAN ART FOUNDATION

ONGOING   REINSTALLATION OF THE WEISMAN PERMANENT COLLECTION

12/19/1998 to 03/07/1999   IT'S THE REAL THING: SOVIET AND POST-SOVIET SOTS ART AND AMERICAN POP ART

03/27/1999 to 05/23/1999   RALPH RAPSON: SIXTY YEARS OF MODERN DESIGN AND CHARLES BIEDERMAN

04/10/1999 to 05/30/1999   BERENICE ABBOTT'S CHANGING NEW YORK 1935-1939
On view will be 125 of her New York City photographs which have come to define Depression-era New York in the popular imagination. These are from the benchmark CHANGING NEW YORK project of 1935-1939. *Will Travel*

06/19/1999 to 08/15/1999   THEATRE OF WONDER: A QUARTER-CENTURY WITH IN THE HEART OF THE BEAST

Minneapolis Institute of Arts
2400 Third Ave. So., Minneapolis, MN 55404
☎: 612-870-3000   ◼ www.mtn.org/MIA
Open: 10-5 Tu-Sa, 10-9 Th, Noon-5 Su   **Closed:** Mo, 7/4, THGV, 12/25
⟐ ℗ **Museum Shop**   ⫧ Restaurant 11:30-2:30 Tu-S
Group Tours: 612-870-3140   **Drop-In Tours:** 2:00 Tu-Su, 1:00 Sa & Su, 7pm Th
Historic Building 1915 NEO-CLASSIC BUILDING BY McKIM MEAD & WHITE
Permanent Collection: AM: ptgs, sculp; EU: ptgs, sculp; DEC/ART; OR; P/COL; AF; OC; ISLAMIC; PHOT; GR; DRGS; JAP: gr

Distinguished by a broad-ranging 80,000 object collection housed within its walls, this landmark building consists of a 1915 neo-classic structure combined with 1974 Japanese inspired additions. With the recent completion of a 50 million dollar renovation project, the museum has reinstalled its redesigned 20th-century galleries on the 1st & 2nd floors of the East Wing. PLEASE NOTE: There is a charge for some special exhibitions. **NOT TO BE MISSED:** Rembrandt's "Lucretia"

ON EXHIBIT 1999

09/05/1998 to 04/11/1999   MEMORY OF THE HAND

09/19/1998 to 01/10/1999   THE MECHANICS OF MOTION: PHOTOGRAPHS BY EADWEARD MUYBRIDGE AND DR. HAROLD E. EDGERTON

10/24/1998 to 1999   HELMUT STERN COLLECTION OF CENTRAL AFRICAN ART

11/27/1998 to 01/03/1999   HOLIDAY TRADITIONS IN THE PERIOD ROOMS
Complete with costumed docents, the Museum's period rooms, decorated to reflect 18th and 19th century holiday traditions, will be embellished with such items as period toys, sweets, works of art and an 18th century Bavarian nativity scene.

12/18/1998 to 02/09/1999   6 SCULPTORS

Minneapolis Institute of Arts - continued

12/20/1998 to 03/07/1999   ANCIENT GOLD JEWELRY FROM THE DALLAS MUSEUM OF ART
Recently acquired by the Dallas Museum from a major private collection, the more than 100 marvelous examples of Greek, Etruscan, Roman and Near Eastern gold jewelry on view highlight the skill of ancient goldsmiths in creating these small, intricate sculptural marvels.

02/13/1999 to 04/25/1999   ROY DE CARAVA: A RETROSPECTIVE
Groundbreaking pictures of everyday life in Harlem, civil rights protests, lyrical studies of nature, and photographs of jazz legends will be among the 200 black & white photographs on view in the first comprehensive survey of DeCarava's works.

04/11/1999 to 05/30/1999   FRANCIS BACON: A RETROSPECTIVE EXHIBITION *Admission Fee*

04/28/1999 to 05/01/1999   ART IN BLOOM

05/27/1999 to 06/1999   RALPH RALPHSON: MIDWEST MODERNIST

06/1999 to 10/1999   RECENT ACCESSIONS 1999

07/1999 to 10/1999   RENOIR IN ITALY

Fall 1999   PORTRAITS OF JEREMIAH GURNEY

10/1999   16TH ANNUAL ANTIQUES SHOW AND SALE

10/24/1999 to 01/16/2000   CHOKWE! ART AND INITIATION OF CHOKWE AND RELATED PEOPLES
In the first exhibition of its kind in the U.S., the 200 artifacts on view, gathered from important public and private collections here and in Europe, highlight the artistry of the Chokwe and related peoples of Angola, Zaire and Zambia. Interactive elements and innovative video techniques will be integrated into this gallery installation to provide a rich contextual setting for the items on view. *Will Travel*

11/1999 to 01/2000   HOW PRINTS ARE MADE

Walker Art Center
Vineland Place, Minneapolis, MN 55403
☎: 612-375-7622   ◉ www.walkerart.org
Open: Gallery. 10-5 Tu-Sa, 11-5 Su, till 8pm Th   **Closed:** Mo, LEG/HOL!
Free Day: Th & First Sa of month   **ADM   Adult:** $4.00   **Children:** F (under 12)   **Students:** $3.00   **Seniors:** $3.00
&   ℗   **Museum Shop**   ‖: Gallery 8 Restaurant 11:30-3
Group Tours: 612-375-7609   **Drop-In Tours:** 2pm Sa, Su; 2 & 6pm Th (Free with adm.)   **Sculpture Garden**
Permanent Collection: AM & EU CONT: ptgs, sculp; GR; DRGS

Housed in a beautifully designed building by noted architect Edward Larabee Barnes, the Walker Art Center, with its superb 8,000 piece permanent collection, is particularly well known for its major exhibitions of 20th century art. PLEASE NOTE: 1. The Sculpture Garden is open free to all from 6am to midnight daily. There is a self-guided audio tour of the Garden available for rent at the Walker lobby desk. 2. For information on a wide variety of special needs tours or accommodations call 612-375-7609. **NOT TO BE MISSED:** Minneapolis Sculpture Garden at Walker Art Center (open 6- Midnight daily; ADM F); "Standing Glass Fish" by F. Gehry at Cowles Conservatory (open 10 -8 Tu-Sa, 10-5 S; ADM F)

ON EXHIBIT 1999
12/13/1998 to 03/07/1999   LOVE FOREVER: YAYOI KUSAMA, 1958 TO 1968
Combining imagery of surrealism, abstract expressionism, pop and minimalism, the 80 paintings, collages, objects and installations by Kusama on view in her first U.S. museum show, highlight the important contribution she made on the contemporary art scene during the first 10 years that she lived in New York.

MINNESOTA

Walker Art Center - continued
02/14/1999 to 05/09/1999   ROBERT GOBER: SCULPTURE AND DRAWING
Winner of the 1996 Larry Aldrich Foundation Award, this presentation features Gober's installations, drawings, and a new major sculpture created specifically for this exhibition.

03/07/1999 to 06/13/1999   MATTHEW BARNEY, CREMASTER 2

04/11/1999 to 07/11/1999   EDWARD RUSCHA, EDITIONS 1962-1999

07/1999 to 08/1999   WING YOUNG HULE, LAKE STREET PROJECT

08/08/1999 to 11/14/1999   ANDY WARHOL DRAWINGS, 1942-1986

10/10/1999 to 01/02/2000   2000 BC: THE BRUCE CONNER STORY PART II

ST. PAUL

Minnesota Museum of American Art
Landmark Center - 75 West Fifth St., St. Paul, MN 55102-1486
\: 651-292-4355   ▣ www.mtn.org/mmaa/
Open: 11-4 Tu-Sa, 11-7:30 Th, 1-5 Su   **Closed:** Mo, LEG/HOL!
Vol/Cont
 ♿ Ⓢ   **Museum Shop**   ❯❮ 11:30-1:30 Tu-Fr; 11-1 Su
Group Tours: by appt. 651-292-4367   **Drop-In Tours**: Group tours scheduled daily, regular Museum hours
Historic Building   Sculpture Garden
Permanent Collection: AM

The Minnesota Museum of American Art is Saint Paul's only art museum, Located in historic Landmark Center, the Museum presents an ongoing installation of selections from it's collection of American art from the 19th and 20th centuries, as well as special, temporary exhibitions. The Museum's galleries are on the second floor of the Landmark Center.

ON EXHIBIT 1999
03/07/1999 to 05/23/1999   DRAWING ON THE COLLECTION

06/13/1999 to 08/22/1999   HMONG ARTISTRY: PRESERVING A CULTURE ON CLOTH

George E. Ohr Arts and Cultural Center

136 George E. Ohr St., Biloxi, MS 39530
☎: 601-374-5547   ◉ www.georgeohr.org
Open: 9-5 Mo-Sa   **Closed:** Su, 1/1, 7/4, THGV, 12/25
ADM   Adult: $2.00   **Seniors:** $1.00
& ℗ **Museum Shop   Group Tours**: 601-374-5547   **Drop-In Tours**
Permanent Collection: George Ohr pottery

In addition to a 300 piece collection of pottery by George Ohr, a man often referred to as the mad potter of Biloxi, this museum features a gallery dedicated to the promotion of local talent and another for rotating and traveling exhibitions. **NOT TO BE MISSED:** Art Activity, a program for children from 10-12 on the 2nd Saturday of the month, led each time by a different artist using a different medium.

ON EXHIBIT 1999

01/1999   A WINDING RIVER: JOURNEY OF CONTEMPORARY ART IN VIETNAM
Almost 80 paintings by 45 artists, this represents the first major cultural exchange since the diplomatic relations between the US and Vietnam were resumed. *Will Travel*

Mid 1999   THE BEST OF SOUTHERN ART POTTERY OF THE 1800S

08/1999 to 09/1999   LE TOUR DE L'ART

Mississippi Museum of Art

201 E. Pascagoula St., Jackson, MS 39201
☎: 601-960-1515   ◉ www.msmuseumart.org
Open: 10-5 Mo-Sa, Noon-5 Su   **Closed:** LEG/HOL
ADM   Adult: $3.00   **Children:** $2.00 (F under 3)   **Students:** $2.00   **Seniors:** $2.00
& ℗ **Museum Shop**   ⊪ Palette Restaurant (open for lunch 11:30-1:30 M-F)
Group Tours: 960-1515 x2242   **Drop-In Tours**: upon request if available   **Sculpture Garden**
Permanent Collection: AM: 19 20; REG: 19-20; BRIT: ptgs, dec/art mid 18-early 19; P/COL: cer; JAP: gr

Begun as art association in 1911, the Mississippi Museum now has more than 3,100 works of art in a collection that spans more than 30 centuries.

ON EXHIBIT 1999

10/24/1998 to 01/17/1999   IRWIN KREMEN: COLLAGES

10/24/1998 to 01/17/1999   LIGHT OF THE SPIRIT: PORTRAITS OF SOUTHERN OUTSIDER ARTISTS

11/07/1998 to 01/31/1999   CELEBRATING AMERICAN CRAFT: A SELECTION OF CONTEMPORARY OBJECTS FROM THE COLLECTIONS OF THE AMERICAN CRAFT MUSEUM

01/16/1999 to 02/14/1999   MISSISSIPPI REGIONAL SCHOLASTIC ART AWARDS

01/23/1999 to 03/14/1999   WORK IN PROGRESS: LEALEY DILL

01/23/1999 to 03/14/1999   RECENT ACQUISITIONS OF CONTEMPORARY ART

02/13/1999 to 04/18/1999   MISSISSIPPI INVITATIONAL
Art in all media will be seen in an exhibition of works by some of the State's most significant contemporary artists.

MISSISSIPPI

Mississippi Museum of Art - continued
05/01/1999 to 07/04/1999   BATS AND BOWLS: A CELEBRATION OF LATHE-TURNED ART
Baseball bats created by 24 North American and European wood turners will be on view with another piece by each artist indicative of his or her standard work.

08/19/1999 to 10/15/2000   SPIRIT OF THE MASK

09/04/1999 to 10/31/1999   MISSISSIPPI: THE NINETEENTH CENTURY

11/13/1999 to 02/06/2000   CROSSING THE THRESHOLD
As we approach a new millennium this exhibition reflects on the artistic milestones of women artists during the past 100 years. While striving for equality, the 31 women included here will be remembered for challenging and overcoming the traditional social mores of our American culture. Artists include Louise Bourgeois, Elizabeth Catlett, Helen Frankenthaler, Nell Blaine, Agnes Martin, Nancy Spiro, Lois Mailou Jones and others.

LAUREL

Lauren Rogers Museum of Art
5th Ave. at 7th St., Laurel, MS 39441-1108
☎: 601-649-6374
Open: 10-4:45 Tu-Sa, 1-4 Su   **Closed:** Mo, LEG/HOL!
♿ ℗ **Museum Shop**
Group Tours   Drop-In Tours: 10-12 & 1-3 Tu-Fr
Permanent Collection: AM:19-20; EU: 19-20; NAT/AM; JAP: gr 18-19; NAT/AM: baskets; ENG: silver

Located among the trees in Laurel's Historic District, the Lauren Rogers, the first museum to be established in the state, has grown rapidly since its inception in 1922. While the original Georgian Revival building still stands, the new adjoining galleries are perfect for the display of the fine art collection of American and European masterworks. **NOT TO BE MISSED:** One of the largest collections of Native American Indian baskets in the U.S.; Gibbons English Georgian Silver Collection

ON EXHIBIT 1999
01/1999 to 03/15/1999   AMERICAN PAINTINGS FROM THE CHEEKWOOD COLLECTION

03/30/1999 to 04/30/1999   MISSISSIPPI COLLEGIATE ART COMPETITION

05/18/1999 to 08/08/1999   A PAINTER'S PAINTER

08/22/1999 to 10/17/1999   ON THE ROAD WITH THOMAS HART BENTON: IMAGES OF A CHANGING AMERICA
Benton is a widely acclaimed artist who first attained prominence in the 20's and 30's as both an artist, writer and art personality. He was the first artist featured on the cover of 'Time' magazine. Drawn from the collection of his estate the exhibition demonstrates how drawing, one of his greatest talents, was combined with travel for which he had a passion, to produce some of his most significant work. *Catalog Will Travel*

10/29/1999 to 11/21/1999   MISSISSIPPI INVITATIONAL PHOTOGRAPHY EXHIBIT

12/14/1999 to 01/16/2000   LAUREN ROGERS MUSEUM OF ART COLLECTION: WORKS ON PAPER

MERIDIAN

Meridian Museum of Art

25th Ave. & 7th St., Meridian, MS 39301

☎: 601-693-1501
Open: 1-5 Tu-Su   **Closed:** Mo, LEG/HOL!
ⓟ   **Museum Shop**
Group Tours   Drop-In Tours: Upon request if available
Permanent Collection: AM: phot, sculp, dec/art; REG; WORKS ON PAPER 20; EU: portraits 19-20

Housed in the landmark Old Carnegie Library Building, built in 1912-13, the Meridian Museum, begun in 1933 as an art association, serves the cultural needs of the people of East Mississippi and Western Alabama. **NOT TO BE MISSED:** 18th century collection of European portraits

OCEAN SPRINGS

Walter Anderson Museum of Art

510 Washington Ave. P.O. Box 328, Ocean Springs, MS 39564

☎: 228-872-3164   ▣   www.motif.org
Open: 10-5 Mo-Sa, 1-5 Su   **Closed:** 1/1, EASTER, THGV, 12/25
Free Day: 1st Mo of each month   **Adult:** $4.00   **Children:** $1.50 (6-12),F under 6
Students: $3.00   **Seniors:** $3.00
♿ ⓟ   **Museum Shop**
Group Tours   Drop-In Tours
Permanent Collection: Works by Walter Inglis Anderson (1903-1965), in a variety of media and from all periods

This museum celebrates the works of Walter Inglis Anderson, whose vibrant and energetic images of plants and animals of Florida's Gulf Coast have placed him among the forefront of American painters of the 20th century. **NOT TO BE MISSED:** "The Little Room", a room with private murals seen only by Anderson until after his death when it was moved in its entirety to the museum.

ON EXHIBIT 1999

09/25/1998 to 07/07/1999   A LIVING LEGEND: SHEARWATER POTTERY AT SEVENTY

01/30/1999 to 04/04/1999   THE POETRY OF SIGHT: OLD WORLD MASTERS AND NEW WORLD VISIONS

02/13/1999 to 05/02/1999   THE DREAM LIVES: ACQUISITIONS 1990-1993

04/17/1999 to 08/15/1999   WALLS OF LIGHT: THE MURALS OF WALTER ANDERSON

09/04/1999 to 10/24/1999   CROSSCURRENTS: A BIENNIAL JURIED EXHIBITION OF CONTEMPORARY ART

09/20/1999 to 01/30/2000   NEW ACQUISITIONS 1997-1999

11/06/1999 to 01/16/2000   STILL LIFE: WALTER ANDERSON

MISSISSIPPI

Tupelo Artist Guild Gallery

211 W. Main St., Tupelo, MS 38801

☎: 601-844-ARTS

Open: 10-4 Tu-Th, 1-4 Fr   **Closed:** Mo,1/1, 7/4, THGV, 12/25

  ⑰   **Museum Shop**

Group Tours   Drop-In Tours: Upon request if available   **Historic Building**

Housed in the former original People's Bank Building (1904-05) this small but effective non-collecting institution is dedicated to bringing traveling exhibitions from all areas of the country to the people of the community and its visitors.

ON EXHIBIT 1999

11/24/1998 to 01/15/1999   **4TH TAG JURIED EXHIBIT**

01/18/1999 to 02/28/1999   **BLACK HISTORY MONTH**

03/03/1999 to 03/24/1999   **SHARED TREASURES**

03/29/1999 to 04/19/1999   **RAINBOW IMPRESSIONS**

07/01/1999 to 08/14/1999   **MISSISSIPPI ARTIST COLONY 50 YEAR RETROSPECTIVE**

MISSOURI

Museum of Art and Archaeology

Affiliate Institution: MU campus, University of Missouri

1 Pickard Hall, Columbia, MO 65211

📞: 573-882-3593   ◙ www.research.missouri.edu/museum/

Open: 9-5 Tu, We, Fr; Noon-5 Sa, Su; 9-5 & 6-9 Th   **Closed:** Mo, LEG/HOL!; 1/1, 12/25

Vol/Cont

 ♧ Ⓟ **Museum Shop   Group Tours   Drop-In Tours**

Permanent Collection: AN/EGT; AN/GRK; AN/R; AN/PER; BYZ; DRGS 15-20; GR 15-20; AF; OC; P/COL; CH; JAP; OR

Ancient art and archaeology from Egypt, Palestine, Iran, Cyprus, Greece, Etruria and Rome as well as early Christian and Byzantine art, the Kress study collection, and 15th-20th century European and American artworks are among the treasures from 6 continents and five millennia that are housed in this museum. **NOT TO BE MISSED:** "Portrait of a Musician", 1949, Thomas Hart Benton and classical archaeology, mummy shroud, "New England Landscape #8" by Charles Demuth

ON EXHIBIT 1999

ONGOING   **EXPRESSIONS OF AFRICA**

ONGOING   **TRADITION AND INNOVATION IN THE TWENTIETH CENTURY**

ONGOING   **THE SAUL AND GLADYS WEINBERG GALLERY OF ANCIENT ART**

ONGOING   **EUROPEAN AND AMERICAN GALLERY**

ONGOING   **EARLY CHRISTIAN AND BYZANTINE GALLERY**

Kemper Museum of Contemporary Art

4420 Warwick Blvd., Kansas City, MO 64111-1821

📞: 816-753 5784   ◙ www.kemperart.org

Open: 10-4 Tu-Th, 10-9 Fr, 10-5 Sa, 11-5 Su   **Closed:** Mo, 1/1, 7/4, THGV, 12/25

♧ Ⓟ **Museum Shop**   ❙❙ Café Sebastienne 11-2:30 Tu-S, 6-9pm F

Group Tours   Drop-In Tours   Sculpture Garden

Permanent Collection: WORKS BY MODERN, CONTEMPORARY, EMERGING AND ESTABLISHED ARTISTS

Designed by architect Gunnar Birkerts, the stunning Kemper Museum of Contemporary Art (a work of art in itself) houses a rapidly growing permanent collection of modern and contemporary works, and hosts temporary exhibitions and creative programs designed to both entertain and challenge. A **Museum Shop** and the lively Café Sebastienne round out the Museum's amenities. **NOT TO BE MISSED:** Louise Bourgeois's bronze "Spider" sculptures; a Waterford crystal chandelier by Dale Chihuly; Ursula Von Rydingsvaard's "Bowl with Sacks"; "Ahulani" bronze sculpture by Deborah Butterfield; Frank Stella's "The Prophet"; "The History of Art" in Café Sebastienne, a 110-painting cycle by Frederick James Brown.

ON EXHIBIT 1999

11/13/1998 to 01/10/1999   SHAHZIA SIKANDER
Mixed media works

11/13/1998 to 01/31/1999   MICHAEL SHAUGHNESSY
Hay sculptures

01/15/1999 to 03/21/1999   CATHERINE MCCARTHY

MISSOURI

Kemper Museum of Contemporary Art - continued

02/12/1999 to 04/11/1999 NEW PHOTOGRAPHY ACQUISITIONS

03/26/1999 to 05/23/1999 WENDY JACOBS: SQUEEZE CHAIRS

05/28/1999 to 08/22/1999 PERMANENT COLLECTION

07/1999 to 10/1999 KATHRYN SPENCE

08/27/1999 to 11/14/1999 TINA BARNEY

11/05/1999 to 01/28/2000 HERB RITTS: WORK
More than 200 photographs will be on view in the first full-scale exhibition devoted to the work of American photographer Ritts.

11/19/1999 to 02/11/2000 LEZLEY SAAR

Nelson-Atkins Museum of Art
4525 Oak St., Kansas City, MO 64111-1873
\: 816-751-IART ◙ www.nelson-atkins.org and www.kansascity.com
Open: 10-4 Tu-Th, 10-9 Fr, 10-5 Sa, 1-5 Su   **Closed:** Mo, 1/1, 7/4, THGV, 12/24, 12/25
ADM   Adult: $5.00   **Children:** $1 (6-18)   **Students:** $2 (with ID)
& Ⓟ **Museum Shop**   ⵌ Rozzelle Court Restaurant 10-3 Tu-Th, 10-8 Fr (closed 3-5), 10-3 Sa, 1-3 Su
Group Tours: 816-751-1238   **Drop-In Tours**: 10:30, 11, 1,& 2 Tu-Sa; 1:30, 2, 2:30, 3 Su   **Sculpture Garden**
Permanent Collection: AM: all media; EU: all media; PER/RMS; NAT/AM; OC; P/COL; OR

Among the many fine art treasures in this outstanding 65 year old museum is their world famous collection of Oriental art and artifacts that includes the Chinese Temple Room with its furnishings, a gallery displaying delicate scroll paintings, and a sculpture gallery with glazed T'ang dynasty tomb figures. **NOT TO BE MISSED:** Largest collection of works by Thomas Hart Benton; Kansas City Sculpture Park; "Shuttlecocks", a four-part sculptural installation by Claes Oldenburg and Coosje van Bruggen located in the grounds of the museum

ON EXHIBIT 1999
03/28/1999 to 06/06/1999   OLD MASTER PAINTINGS ON COPPER, 1525-1775
An exhibition of nearly 100 spectacular and best preserved 16th to 18th century masterworks on copper, gathered from public and private collections throughout the U.S. and Europe.

05/09/1998 to 03/28/1999   URSULA VON RYDINGSVARD: SCULPTURE AND DRAWINGS
Large scale wood sculpture by this American artist whose work is highly abstract, recalling organic forms, the landscape, or man made objects.

POPLAR BLUFF

Margaret Harwell Art Museum
421 N. Main St., Poplar Bluff, MO 63901
\: 573-686-8002 ◙ www.webcurrent.com/mham
Open: 1-4 We-Su   **Closed:** Mo, Tu, LEG/HOL!
Vol/Cont
& **Museum Shop   Group Tours Drop-In Tours   Historic Building** Located in 1883 mansion
Permanent Collection: DEC/ART; REG; CONT

The 1880's mansion in which this museum is housed is a perfect foil for the museum's permanent collection of contemporary art. Located in the south-eastern part of the state, just above the Arkansas border, the museum features monthly exhibitions showcasing the works of both regional and nationally known artists.

Albrecht-Kemper Museum of Art

2818 Frederick Avenue, Saint Joseph, MO 64506
☎: 816-233-7003 ◉ www.albrecht-kemper.org
Open: 10-4 Tu-Sa, till 8pm Th, 1-4 Su **Closed:** Mo, 1/1, EASTER, 7/4, THGV, 12/25, MEM/DAY, LAB/DAY
Free Day: Su **ADM Adult:** $3.00 (18 & over) **Children:** F (under 12) **Students:** $1.00 **Seniors:** $2.00
  ♿ ℗ **Museum Shop** ⑪ Special Events Only
Group Tours: 816-233-7003 **Drop-In Tours Sculpture Garden**
Permanent Collection: AM: ldscp ptgs, Impr ptgs, gr, drgs 18-20

Considered to have the region's finest collection of 18th through 20th century American art, the Albrecht-Kemper Museum of Art is housed in the expanded and transformed 1935 Georgian-style mansion of William Albrecht. **NOT TO BE MISSED:** North American Indian Portfolio by Catlin: illustrated books by Audubon; Thomas Hart Benton collection

ON EXHIBIT 1999

to 01/17/1999 REMEMBERING HARRISON HARTLEY

to 03/07/1999 AMISH QUILTS

01/21/1999 to 02/21/1999 25TH ANNUAL MEMBERSHIP EXHIBITION

03/14/1999 to 06/06/1999 HALLMARK MASTER ARTISTS

04/08/1999 to 06/06/1999 DEBE RILEY: PHOTOGRAPHS

06/13/1999 to 09/05/1999 JAMES KELLER: HISTORIC ILLUSTRATIONS

Springfield Art Museum

1111 E. Brookside Dr., Springfield, MO 65807-1899
☎: 417-837-5700
Open: 9-5 Tu, We, Fr, Sa; 1-5 Su; till 8pm Th **Closed:** Mo, LOCAL & LEG/HOL!
Vol/Cont
  ♿ ℗ **Museum Shop Group Tours Drop-In Tours**
Permanent Collection: AM: ptgs, sculp, drgs, gr, phot 18-20; EU: ptgs, sculp, gr, drgs, phot 18-20; DEC/ART; NAT/AM; OC; P/COL

Watercolor U.S A , an annual national competition is but one of the features of the Springfield Museum, the oldest cultural institution in the city. **NOT TO BE MISSED:** New Jeannette L. Musgrave Wing for the permanent collection; John Henry's "Sun Target", 1974, a painted steel sculpture situated on the grounds directly east of the museum; paintings and prints by Thomas Hart Benton

Forum for Contemporary Art

3540 Washington Avenue, St. Louis, MO 63103
☎: 314-535-4660 ◉ www.forumart.org
Open: 10-5 Tu-Sa **Closed:** Su, Mo, LEG/HOL! & INSTALLATIONS
Vol/Cont
  ♿ ℗ **Museum Shop Group Tours:** 314-535-4660 **Drop-In Tours:** By appt. during museum hours
Permanent Collection: No permanent collection. Please call for current exhibition information not listed below.

MISSOURI

Forum for Contemporary Art - continued

Experimental cutting-edge art of the new is the focus of the Forum for Contemporary Art which presents exhibitions of important recent national and international art enhanced by educational programming and public discussions.

ON EXHIBIT 1999

01/22/1999 to 03/13/1999   MATT MULLICAN: "LIVE IN YOUR HEAD"

01/22/1999 to 03/13/1999   MATTHEW ANTEZZO: PORTRAITS

03/26/1999 to 05/15/1999   CPLY: THE ART OF WILLIAM COPLEY

03/26/1999 to 05/15/1999   SUE WILLIAMS: RECENT PAINTINGS

Laumeier Sculpture Park Museum

12580 Rott Rd., St. Louis, MO 63127
☏: 314-821-1209
Open: Park: 7am-1/2 hour after sunset; Museum: 10-5 Tu-Sa & Noon-5 Su
Closed: Sculpture Park & Museum: 1/1, THGV, 12/25
 ᕗ Ⓟ **Museum Shop** †╎: Picnic Area
Group Tours: 314-821-1298 ($10 groups less than 25) **Drop-In Tours**: 1st & 3rd Su of month at 2pm (May - Oct)
Sculpture Garden
Permanent Collection: CONT/AM; sculp: NATIVE SCULP & ART; SITE SPECIFIC SCULP

More than 75 internationally acclaimed site-specific sculptures that complement their natural surroundings are the focus of this institution whose goal is to promote greater public involvement and understanding of contemporary sculpture. In addition to audio cassettes that are available for self-guided tours, there are, for the visually impaired, 12 scale models of featured works, accompanied by descriptive braille labels, that are placed near their full sized outdoor counterparts. **NOT TO BE MISSED:** Works by Alexander Liberman, Beverly Pepper, Dan Graham, Jackie Ferrara

ON EXHIBIT 1999

10/03/1998 to 01/17/1999   ROBIN MUREZ

10/25/1998 to 01/17/1999   EARTHLY PARADISE: HIRO YAMAGATA

Saint Louis Art Museum

1 Fine Arts Park, Forest Park, St. Louis, MO 63110-1380
☏: 314-721-0072
Open: 1:30-8:30 Tu, 10-5 We-Su **Closed:** Mo, 1/1, THGV, 12/25
 ᕗ Ⓟ **Museum Shop** †╎ Café 11-3:30 & 5-8 Tu; 11-3:30 W-S; 10-2 S (brunch); Snack Bar also
Group Tours: ex 484 **Drop-In Tours**: 1:30 We-Fr (30 min.); 1:30 Sa, Su (60 min.)
Historic Building Located in a 1904 World's Fair Exhibition Building **Sculpture Garden**
Permanent Collection: AN/EGT; AN/CH; JAP; IND; OC; AF; P/COL; NAT/AM; REN; PTGS:18-CONT; SCULP: 18-CONT

Just 10 minutes from the heart of downtown St. Louis, this museum is home to one of the most important permanent collections of art in the country. A global museum featuring pre-Columbian and German Expressionist works that are ranked among the best in the best in the world, this institution is also known for its Renaissance, Impressionist, American, African, Oceanic, Asian and Ancient through Contemporary art. PLEASE NOTE: Although there is an admission fee for special exhibitions, admission to these exhibitions is offered free on Tuesdays from 1:30 - 8:30 PM. **NOT TO BE MISSED:** The Sculpture Terrace with works by Anthony Caro, Pierre Auguste Renoir, Henry Moore, Alexander Calder, and Aristide Maillol; Egyptian mummy and Cartonnage on display with a full-size x-ray of the mummy.

Saint Louis Art Museum - continued

ON EXHIBIT 1999

06/16/1998 to 04/04/1999   AFRICAN TEXTILES

12/11/1998 to 02/07/1999   GABRIEL OROZCO

02/1999 to 04/1999   DIANA THATER

02/06/1999 to 05/09/1999   BECKMANN AND PARIS

02/23/1999 to 05/23/1999   REVEALING THE HOLY LAND: THE PHOTOGRAPHIC EXPLORATION OF PALESTINE

05/1999 to 12/1999   SERAPE TEXTILES FROM HISTORIC MEXICO

06/1999 to 08/1999   BEYOND PARIS: IMAGES OF RURAL FRANCE, 1800-1900

06/19/1999 to 08/15/1999   CONTEMPORARY JAPANESE TEXTILES

06/19/1999 to 08/15/1999   EARLY AMERICAN DECORATIVE ARTS FROM ST. LOUIS COLLECTIONS

10/1999 to 01/2000   KIKI SMITH

Washington University Gallery of Art, Steinberg Hall

One Brookings Drive, St. Louis, MO 63130-4899
☎: 314-935-5490   **◙**   www.proserve.wustle.edu/wugallery
Open: SEPT-MAY 10-4:30 Mo-Fr & 1-5 Sa, Su; CLOSED mid MAY-early SEPT.   **Closed:** LEG/HOL! Occasionally closed for major installations; Call (314-935-4523)
&   ℗   **Museum Shop**
Group Tours   Drop-In Tours: by rcs.
Permanent Collection: EU: ptgs, sculp 16-20; OM: 16-20; CONT/GR; AM: ptgs, sculp 19-20; DEC/ART; FR: academic; AB/EXP; CUBISTS

With a well-deserved reputation for being one of the premier university art museums in the nation, the more than 100 year old Gallery of Art at Washington University features 19th and 20th century American and European art, with outstanding examples by Dupre, Daumier, Church, and Gifford, Picasso, Ernst, Miro, de Kooning and Pollock among a host of other major artists. **NOT TO BE MISSED:** Hudson River School Collection

MONTANA

Yellowstone Art Museum
410 N. 27th St., Billings, MT 59101
☎: 406-256-6804   ▣ yellowstone.artmuseum.org
Open: 11-5 Tu-Sa, Noon-5 Su, till 8pm Th; Open one hour earlier in summer   **Closed:** Mo, LEG/HOL!
ADM   Adult: $3.00   **Children:** $1.00 6-18; F under6   **Students:** $2.00   **Seniors:** $2.00
♿ ℗ **Museum Shop   Group Tours**: 406-256-6804   **Drop-In Tours**: 10-2 Tu-Fr
Historic Building Original building built in 1884. Expansion and remodel Feb '98 added 30,000 sq. ft. to orig. structure.
Permanent Collection: CONT/HISTORICAL: ptgs, sculp, cer, phot, drgs, gr

Situated in the heart of downtown Billings, the focus of the museum is on displaying the works of contemporary regional artists and on showcasing artists who have achieved significant regional or national acclaim. With nearly 2,000 objects in its permanent collection, the museum is well-known for its "Montana Collection" dedicated to the preservation of art of the West. The museum collection includes work by notable artists such as Rudy Autio, John Buck, Deborah Butterfield, Clarice Dreyer, Peter Voulkos and Theodore Waddell. Additionally, the museum houses a collection of 90 abstract expressionist paintings from the George Poindexter family of New York and the largest private collection of work by cowboy author and illustrator Will James. The museum re-opened its doors February 28, 1998 after closing for two years to complete a 6.2 million dollar expansion and renovation project. The expansion added 30,000 square feet to the original structure. In addition to tripling the exhibition space, other visitor amenities were added including: an education classroom/studio, public meeting room, courtyard and enhanced museum store. The museum is fully accessible with ramped entrances and elevators to assist handicapped patrons. Wheel chairs are also available.

ON EXHIBIT 1999

01/22/1999 to 03/05/1999   **31ST ART AUCTION EXHIBITION**

03/12/1999 to 04/04/1999   **RECENT ACQUISITIONS**

03/12/1999 to 05/23/1999   **FOCUS: ANNE APPLEBY**

04/09/1999 to 05/23/1999   **ROY DeFOREST / GAYLEN HANSEN**

05/29/1999 to 07/25/1999   **CLARICE DREYER**

last half 1999   **FOCUS: JAUNE QUICK-TO-SEE SMITH**

08/1999 to 09/1999   **MARIO REIS**

09/1999 to 10/1999   **FOCUS: RICHARD NOTKIN**

09/1999 to 10/1999   **FOCUS: KEN LITTLE**

11/1999 to 01/2000   **HOLIDAY EXHIBITION(S)**

C. M. Russell Museum
400 13th St. North, Great Falls, MT 59401-1498
☎: 406-727-8787
Open: MAY 1-SEPT 30: 9-6 Mo-Sa & 1-5 Su; WINTER: 10-5 Tu-Sa & 1-5 Su   **Closed:** 1/1, EASTER, THGV, 12/25
Free Day: Su in Jan & Feb   **ADM   Adult:** $4.00   **Children:** F (5 and under)   **Students:** $2.00   **Seniors:** $3.00
♿ ℗ **Museum Shop**
Group Tours: 406-727-8787 ask for Education Dept.   **Drop-In Tours**: 9:15 & 1:15 Mo-Fr (June through Aug)
Historic Building
Permanent Collection: REG; CONT; CER

C. M. Russell Museum - continued

A western art museum that houses more than 7,000 works of art, capturing the flavor of the old west and its bygone way of life. The museum's permanent collection includes the most comprehensive collection of original Russell art works and personal objects in the world. Constructed mainly of telephone poles, the log cabin studio of the great cowboy artist C.M. Russell still contains the original cowboy gear and Indian artifacts that were used as the artist's models. **NOT TO BE MISSED:** Charlie's Log Cabin Studio and original residence.

ON EXHIBIT 1999

09/24/1998 to 02/14/1999   THE COWBOY: TODAY'S TRADITION EXHIBITION
Nine living artists who meet the standards set out by Charlie Russell, the original and sustaining link between the disparate realm of cowboys and art. They all make original valid statements in art that portray today's cowboy. The artists here are Joe Beeler, Fred Fellows, John Hampton, Jack Hines, Herb Mignery, Newman Myrah, Jim Norton, and R. E. Pierce.

04/01/1999 to 09/01/1999   AN EXACT VIEW EXHIBITION

07/16/1999 to 09/10/1999   C. M. RUSSELL MUSEUM "BENEFIT ART" EXHIBITION

08/1999 to 10/1999   Museum Shop EXHIBITION AND SALE

10/1999 to 10/1999   3RD ANNUAL "ART THAT GLITTERS" JEWELRY EXHIBITION AND SALE

11/09/1999 to 01/03/2000   Museum Shop HOLIDAY EXHIBITION AND SALE

Paris Gibson Square Museum of Art

1400 1st Ave., North, Great Falls, MT 59401-3299
📞: 406-727-8255
Open: 10-5 Tu-Fr, Noon-5 Sa, Su; 7-9 Th; Also open Mo MEM/DAY to LAB/DAY   **Closed:** Mo, LEG/HOL
  ♿ &#9physic;   **Museum Shop**   ‖ Lunch Tu-F
Group Tours   Drop-In Tours
Historic Building 19th C Romanesque structure built in 1895 as a high school   **Sculpture Garden**
Permanent Collection: REG: ptgs, sculp, drgs, gr

Contemporary arts are featured within the walls of this 19th century Romanesque building which was originally used as a high school.

ON EXHIBIT 1999

11/10/1998 to 01/05/1999   PHOEBE TOLAND: RECENT WORK

11/10/1998 to 01/05/1999   SELECTIONS FROM THE DENVER ART MUSEUM

01/15/1999 to 03/26/1999   WILD BEASTS! ROY DE FOREST AND GAYLEN HANSEN

04/09/1999 to 05/05/1999   GREAT FALLS PUBLIC SCHOOLS ALL-CITY ART EXHIBIT

05/14/1999 to 07/15/1999   JAY RUMMELL, A MONTANA ORIGINAL

05/14/1999 to 07/15/1999   DAN RICE: RECENT WORK

07/29/1999 to 09/30/1999   ART EQUINOX 1999

10/15/1999 to 12/13/1999   MSU FACULTY EXHIBIT

10/15/1999 to 12/13/1999   1999 PERMANENT COLLECTION EXHIBIT

12/22/1999 to 02/07/2000   RICHARD NOTKIN RETROSPECTIVE

MONTANA

Hockaday Center for the Arts

Second Ave E. & Third St, Kalispell, MT 59901

☎: 406-755-5268

Open: 10-6 Tu-Sa, 10-8 We   **Closed:** Su, Mo, LEG/HOL!

Free Day: We   **Adult:** $2.00   **Children:** F   **Students:** $1.00   **Seniors:** $1.00

& Ⓟ **Museum Shop**

Group Tours: 406-755-5268   **Drop-In Tours**: Upon request if available

Historic Building   Sculpture Garden

Permanent Collection: CONT/NORTHWEST: ptgs, sculp, gr, port, cer

The Hockaday Center for the Arts which places strong emphasis on contemporary art is housed in the renovated Carnegie Library built in 1903. A program of rotating regional, national, or international exhibitions is presented approximately every 6 weeks. **NOT TO BE MISSED:** The Hockaday permanent collection of works by NW Montana artists and our **Museum Shop** featuring fine arts and crafts.

ON EXHIBIT 1999

ONGOING   PERMANENT COLLECTION INSTALLATION: HUGH HOCKADAY

ONGOING   PERMANENT COLLECTION INSTALLATION: RUSSEL CHATHAM

01/1999   PERMANENT COLLECTION: BLACKFEET TEEPEE PORTFOLIO

01/08/1999 to 02/27/1999   BILL OHRMANN: HOW WE LIVE

01/08/1999 to 02/27/1999   WOMEN OF POMPEII

07/1999 to 09/1999   AN OLD-TIME MONTANA RODEO

Custer County Art Center

Water Plant Rd., Miles City, MT 59301

☎: 406-232-0635

Open: 1-5 Tu-Su   **Closed:** Mo, 1/1, EASTER, THGV, 12/25

Vol/Cont

& Ⓟ **Museum Shop**

Group Tours   Drop-In Tours

Historic Building   Located in the old holding tanks of the water plant (member NRHP)

Permanent Collection: CONT/REG; 126 EDWARD S. CURTIS PHOTOGRAVURES; 81 WILLIAM HENRY JACKSON PHOTOCHROMES

The old holding tanks of the water plant (c. 1914) provide an unusual location for the Custer Art Center. Situated in the southeastern part of the state in a park-land setting overlooking the Yellowstone River, this facility features 20th century Western and contemporary art. The gift shop is worthy of mention due to the emphasis placed on available works for sale by regional artists. **NOT TO BE MISSED:** Annual Western Art Roundup & Quick Draw Art Auction 3rd weekend in May

Art Museum of Missoula

335 North Pattee, Missoula, MT 59802
☎: 406-728-0447   ◙ www.artmissoula.org
Open: Noon 6 Tu Su, till 8pm Th   **Closed:** Mo, LEG/HOL!
ADM   Adult: $2.00   **Children:** F (under 18)   **Students:** $2.00   **Seniors:** $2.00 Tu Free
♿ ℗ **Museum Shop**
Group Tours Drop-In Tours   **Historic Building**
Permanent Collection: REG: 19-20

Lively community-based museum featuring international and regional contemporary art housed in an early 20th century Carnegie Library building in downtown Missoula.

ON EXHIBIT 1999

03/05/1999 to 05/08/1999   BRIDLES, BITS AND BEADS

01/08/1999 to 02/27/1999   BRAD RUDE: ORIGINAL NATURE

09/01/1999 to 11/15/1999   MIRIAM SCHAPIRO WORKS ON PAPER
From traditional watercolors to cast paper pieces, Schapiro's wide-ranging works on view include such diverse elements as collaged fabrics, lace and glitter, stenciling, and Xerox reproductions or cutouts attached to the walls with Velcro.

Museum of Fine Arts

Affiliate Institution: School of Fine Arts, University of Montana
Missoula, MT 59812
☎: 406-243-4970
Open: 9-12 & 1-4 Mo-Fr   **Closed:** Su, Mo, STATE/HOL & LEG/HOL!
♿ ℗ **Museum Shop**
Group Tours Drop-In Tours
Permanent Collection: REG

Great American artists are well represented in this University museum with special emphasis on Western painters and prints by such contemporary artists as Motherwell and Krasner. The permanent collection rotates with exhibitions of a temporary nature.

NEBRASKA

Museum of Nebraska Art

Affiliate Institution: University of Nebraska at Kearney
24th & Central, Kearney, NE 68848

☎: 308-865-8559
Open: 11-5 Tu-Sa,1-5 Su   Closed: LEG/HOL!
ꜩ ℗   Museum Shop   Group Tours   Drop-In Tours   Historic Building   Sculpture Garden
Permanent Collection: REG: Nebraskan 19-present

The museum building, listed in the National Register of Historic Places, has been remodeled and expanded with new gallery spaces and a sculpture garden. Featured is the Nebraska Art Collection-artwork by Nebraskans from the Artist-Explorers to the contemporary scene. **NOT TO BE MISSED:** 'The Bride', by Robert Henri

Great Plains Art Collection

Affiliate Institution: University of Nebraska
215 Love Library, Lincoln, NE 68588-0475

☎: 402-472-6220   ◙ www.unl.edu/plains/artcol.html
Open: 9:30-5 Mo-Fr, 10-5 Sa, 1:30-5 Su   Closed: LEG/HOL!
Vol/Cont
ꜩ ℗   Museum Shop   Group Tours   Drop-In Tours
Permanent Collection: WESTERN: ptgs, sculp 19, 20; NAT/AM

This collection of western art which emphasizes the Great Plains features sculptures by such outstanding artists as Charles Russell & Frederic Remington, and paintings by Albert Bierstadt, John Clymer, Olaf Wieghorst, Mel Gerhold and others. **NOT TO BE MISSED:** William de la Montagne Cary, (1840-1922), 'Buffalo Throwing the Hunter', bronze

ON EXHIBIT 1999

01/18/1999 to 02/26/1999   THE NORTH PLATTE PROJECT: PHOTOGRAPHING NATURE'S WORKS & THEIR TRANSFORMATIONS

03/10/1999 to 04/30/1999   MOTION TO MUSIC: IMAGES OF PLAINS AND SOUTHWEST INDIAN DANCERS

Sheldon Memorial Art Gallery and Sculpture Garden

Affiliate Institution: University of Nebraska
12th and R Sts., Lincoln, NE 68588-0300

☎: 402-472-2461   ◙ http://sheldon.unl.edu
Open: 10-5 Tu-Sa, 7-9 T-Sa, 2-9 Su   Closed: Mo, LEG/HOL!
Vol/Cont
ꜩ ℗   Museum Shop   Group Tours   Drop-In Tours   Historic Building   Sculpture Garden
Permanent Collection: AM: ptgs 19, 20,sculp, phot, w/col, drgs, gr

This highly regarded collection is housed in a beautiful Italian marble building designed by internationally acclaimed architect Philip Johnson. It is located on the University of Nebraska-Lincoln campus and surrounded by a campus-wide sculpture garden consisting of over 34 key examples by artists of renown including di Suvero, Lachaise, David Smith, Heizer, Shea and Serra. **NOT TO BE MISSED:** Recent Acquisitions: Joseph Cornell "Pipe Box" and Clyfford Still, "Untitled" c. 1946

Sheldon Memorial Art Gallery and Sculpture Garden - continued
ON EXHIBIT 1999

11/17/1998 to 01/17/1999   WORKING WITH THE GRAIN: WOODEN BOWLS AND BOXES
Works featuring the crafted skill of woodturning

12/01/1998 to 02/07/1999   PABLO PICASSO AND PEERS
Graphics and ceramics by Picasso, Braque, Metzinger, Gris, and Duchamp

12/09/1998 to 03/14/1999   SELECTED ACQUISITIONS IN PHOTOGRAPHY AND PRINTS
Recent print acquisitions including William Burroughs, Jim Dine, Starn Twins, and Louis Gonzalez Palma

12/11/1998 to 02/14/1999   ICONS OF PUBLIC MEMORY: PHOTOGRAPHS FROM THE COLLECTION OF THE COLLEGE OF JOURNALISM
80 photo-journalism images of the nearly 500 donated.

02/09/1999 to 03/21/1999   ROBERT RAUSCHENBERG

03/19/1999 to 06/27/1999   FLETCHER BENTON: NEW CONSTRUCTIVISM
Forty recent works including freestanding and pedestal sculpture, new wall reliefs, and a few recent paintings

03/23/1999 to 06/13/1999   JAM: C. S. WILSON AND JOHN GIERLACH
Original story board illustrations for underground comics

06/15/1999 to 08/22/1999   CHARLES RAIN: MAGIC REALISM
Highly detailed paintings and shadow boxes

09/24/1999 to 01/02/2000   ROBERT COLESCOTT: RECENT PAINTINGS
The 19 provocative paintings on view, created over the past decade by Arizona-based artist Colescott, contain his highly personal narrative figurative imagery blended with ironic viewpoints that address major contemporary social issues. One of the most important U.S. artists working today, Colescott was the first painter since Jasper Johns in 1988, to be included in the 47th Venice Biennale. He was also the first American ever to be given a solo exhibition at that prestigious event. *Catalog Will Travel*

OMAHA

Joslyn Art Museum
2200 Dodge St., Omaha, NE 68102-3300
☎: 402-342-3300   ◉ www.joslyn.org
Open: 10-4 Tu-Sa, 12-4 Su   **Closed:** Mo, LEG/HOL!
ADM   Adult: $5.00   **Children:** $2.50 5-17   **Students:** $3.00   **Seniors:** $3.00
&   ℗   **Museum Shop**   ¶ Y, open Tu-Sa 11-4, S 12-4
Group Tours   Drop-In Tours: We 1, Sa 10, 11   **Historic Building   Sculpture Garden**
Permanent Collection: AM: ptgs 19, 20; WESTERN ART; EU: 19, 20

Housing works from antiquity to the present the Joslyn, Nebraska's only art museum with an encyclopedic collection, has recently completed a major $16 million dollar expansion and renovation program. **NOT TO BE MISSED:** World-renowned collection of watercolors and prints by Swiss artist Karl Bodmer that document his journey to the American West 1832-34; Noted collection of American Western art including works by Catlin, Remington, and Leigh.

ON EXHIBIT 1999

01/23/1999 to 04/18/1999   DALI'S MOUSTACHE: A PHOTOGRAPHIC INTERVIEW BY SALVADOR DALI AND PHILLIPPE HALSMAN

03/27/1999 to 05/25/1999   SEARCHING FOR ANCIENT EGYPT
From the display of the interior wall of a 4,300-year-old funerary chapel to an exquisite gold-covered mummy mask, this exhibition features more than 130 extraordinary objects from every major period of ancient Egypt. Many of those included have not been on public view for 30 years. *Catalog Will Travel*

05/01/1999 to 06/27/1999   MODOTTI AND WESTON: MEXICANIDAD

07/17/1999 to 10/24/1999   RECENT ACQUISITIONS: WORKS ON PAPER

NEVADA

Nevada Museum of Art/E. L. Weigand Gallery

160 W. Liberty Street, Reno, NV 89501
☎: 702-329-3333 ◙ nevadaart.org
Open: 10-4 Tu, We, Fr; 10-7 Th, 12-4 Sa, Su   **Closed:** Mo, LEG/HOL!
Free Day: Fr   **ADM Adult:** $5.00   **Children:** $1.00 (6-12)   **Students:** $3.00   **Seniors:** $3.00
♿ Ⓟ **Museum Shop**
Group Tours: 702-329-3333   **Drop-In Tours:** Res. Req 2 weeks in advance
Permanent Collection: AM: ptgs 19, 20, NAT/AM; REG

Visit Nevada's premiere fine arts museum and enjoy world-class exhibitions ranging from historical to contemporary perspectives. PLEASE NOTE: The permanent collection is on display only during specific exhibitions. Call for specifics.

ON EXHIBIT 1999

10/11/1998 to 01/10/1999 FROM EXPLORATION TO CONSERVATION: PICTURING THE SIERRA NEVADA
The exhibition features approximately 65 paintings, photographs and works on paper by Albert Bierstadt, Thomas Hill, William Keith, Ansel Adams, Carleton Watkins, Eadweard Maybridge, Wayne Thiebaud and many others including Native American and Basque artists. *Catalog*

10/11/1998 to 01/10/1999 A COMMON THREAD

01/15/1999 to 02/21/1999 SELECTIONS FROM THE WELLS FARGO COLLECTION
Over 50 large-scale prints by American modenists and other important contemporary artists from the recent gift to the Museum.

10/07/1999 to 12/05/1999 THE ALTERED LANDSCAPE: A FOCUS COLLECTION OF THE NEVADA MUSEUM OF ART
The focus of the work is the aesthetic articulation of the landscape and man's interaction with the environment.

06/09/1999 to 09/26/1999 ALPHONSE MUCHA: THE FLOWERING OF ART NOUVEAU
The first major exhibition of the work of this artist since 1921 will feature about 150 0f his most important paintings, posters, jewelry, sculpture, decorative panels, pastels and illustrations from collections all over the world. *Catalog Will Travel*

CORNISH

Saint-Gaudens
St. Gaudens Rd, Cornish, NH 03745-9704
☎: 603-675-2175   ◉ www.sgnhs.org or www.nps.gov/saga
Open: 9:00-4:30 Daily last weekend May-Oct
Free Day: Aug 25   **ADM   Adult:** $4.00   **Children:** F
ⓟ   **Museum Shop   Group Tours**: 603-675-2175   **Drop-In Tours**: adv res req   **Historic Building   Sculpture Garden**
Permanent Collection: AUGUSTUS SAINT GAUDENS: sculp

The house, the studios, and 150 acres of the gardens of Augustus Saint-Gaudens (1848-1907), one of America's greatest sculptors.

DURHAM

Art Gallery, University of New Hampshire
Paul Creative Arts Center, 30 College Road, Durham, NH 03824-3538
☎: 603-862-3712
Open: 10-4 Mo-We, 10-8 Th, 1-5 Sa, Su (Sep-May)   **Closed:** Fr, ACAD!
♿ ⓟ **Museum Shop   Group Tours   Drop-In Tours**
Permanent Collection: JAP: gr 19; EU & AM: drgs 17-20; PHOT; EU: works on paper 19, 20

Each academic year The Art Gallery of the University of New Hampshire presents exhibitions of historical to contemporary art in a variety of media. Exhibitions also include work by the University art faculty, alumni, senior art students and selections from the permanent collection.

ON EXHIBIT 1999
01/26/1999 to 04/11/1999   ALONG THE WATER'S EDGE; SEASCAPES FROM THE PERMANENT COLLECTION
Seascapes by A.T. Bricher, M.F.H. deHaas, Thomas Moran, and Herbert Waters.

01/26/1999 to 04/11/1999   WORLDVIEWS: MAYA CERAMICS FROM THE PALMER COLLECTION
56 objects of ceramics, jade and stone, from the classic Maya period (A.D. 250-900). They provide insight into the complex Maya civilization-its technological development, social structure, and intellectual achievements.

01/26/1999 to 04/11/1999   ART FACULTY COLLECTORS: STUDENT CURATORS
Works from collections of faculty members researched and curated by students.

HANOVER

Hood Museum Of Art
Affiliate Institution: Dartmouth College
Wheelock Street, Hanover, NH 03755
☎: 603-646-2808
Open: 10-5 Tu, Th-Sa, 10-9 We, 12-5 Su   **Closed:** Mo, LEG/HOL!
♿ ⓟ **Museum Shop**   ♟: Y
Group Tours   Drop-In Tours
Permanent Collection: AM: ptgs 19, 20; GR; PICASSO; EU: ptgs

The Museum houses one of the oldest and finest college collections in the country in an award-winning post-modern building designed by Charles Moore and Chad Floyd. **NOT TO BE MISSED:** Panathenaic Amphora by the Berlin Painter 5th C. BC.

NEW HAMPSHIRE

Thorne-Sagendorph Art Gallery
Affiliate Institution: Keene State College
Wyman Way, Keene, NH 03435-3501
☎: 603-358-2720   ◙ www.keene.edu/FACILITIES/TSAG
Open: 12-4 Mo-We, 12-7 Th, Fr, 12-4 Sa, Su   **Closed:** ACAD!
Vol/Cont
&   Ⓟ   **Museum Shop**
Group Tours   Drop-In Tours: by appt
Permanent Collection: REG: 19; AM & EU: cont, gr

Changing exhibitions as well as selections from the permanent collection are featured in the contemporary space of this art gallery.

ON EXHIBIT 1999
02/1999 to 03/1999   1999 REGIONAL JURORS' CHOICE COMPETITION

02/1999 to 03/1999   PAINTINGS BY JOSEPH LYNDON SMITH: EGYPT AT THE THORNE

04/1999 to 05/1999   SELECTIONS FROM THE THORNE COLLECTION

Currier Gallery of Art
201 Myrtle Way, Manchester, NH 03104
☎: 603-669-6144   ◙ www.currier.org
Open: 11-5 Mo, We, Th, Su, 11-8 Fr, 10-5 Sa   **Closed:** Tu, LEG/HOL!
Free Day: 10-1 Sa, 5-8 Fr   **ADM   Adult:** $5.00   **Children:** F (under 18)   **Students:** $4.00   **Seniors:** $4.00
&   Ⓟ   **Museum Shop**   ⅰ: Y
Group Tours: 603-626-4154   **Drop-In Tours**
Historic Building Registered in National Landmark of historic places (Circa 1929)
Permanent Collection: AM & EU: sculp 13-20; AM: furniture, dec/art

Set on beautifully landscaped grounds, The Gallery is housed in a elegant, newly renovated 1929 Beaux Arts building reminiscent of an Italian Renaissance villa. **NOT TO BE MISSED:** Zimmerman House (separate admission: Adults $7, Seniors and Students $5) designed in 1950 by Frank Lloyd Wright. It is one of five Wright houses in the Northeast and the only Wright designed residence in New England that is open to the public.

ON EXHIBIT 1999
10/17/1998 to 01/04/1999   MOMENTS IN TIME: MASTER PHOTOGRAPHS FROM THE CURRIER

01/16/1999 to 02/22/1999   NEW HAMPSHIRE ART ASSOCIATION 52ND ANNUAL EXHIBITION

03/06/1999 to 05/03/1999   PRINTS BY JOHN JAMES AUDUBON

03/13/1999 to 06/13/1999   HENRY MELVILLE FULLER COLLECTION OF PAPERWEIGHTS

11/26/1999 to 01/23/2000   MAXFIELD PARRISH, 1870-1966
A major retrospective of the work of one of the Academy's most distinguished alumni exploring the artistic influences, his work as one of the century's most popular illustrators and as a painter. Also to be explored are the qualities of his work which have led to his "rediscovery" by many contemporary artists. *Catalog Will Travel*

CAMDEN

Stedman Art Gallery

Affiliate Institution: The State Univ of NJ

Rutgers Fine Arts Center, Camden, NJ 08102

☎: 609-225-6245   ■ arts@camden-rutgers.edu

Open: 10-4 Mo-Sa   **Closed:** Su, MEM/DAY, 7/4, LAB/DAY, THGV, 12/24-1/2

  ♿ Ⓟ   **Museum Shop   Group Tours   Drop-In Tours**

Permanent Collection: AM & EU: Cont works on paper

Located in southern New Jersey, the gallery brings visual arts into focus as an integral part of the human story.

JERSEY CITY

Jersey City Museum

472 Jersey Ave, Jersey City, NJ 07302

☎: 201-547-4514

Open: 10:30-5 Tu, Th-Sa, 10:30-8 We, closed Sa in summer   **Closed:** Su, Mo, LEG/HOL!, 12/24, 12/31

  ♿ Ⓟ   **Museum Shop   Group Tours**: 201-547-4380   **Drop-In Tours   Historic Building**

Permanent Collection: AUGUST WILL COLLECTION: views of Jersey City, 19; AM: ptgs, drgs, gr, phot; HIST: dec/art; JERSEY CITY INDUSTRIAL DESIGN

Established in 1901, the museum is located in the historic Van Vorst Park neighborhood of Jersey City in the 100-year old public library building. In addition to showcasing the works of established and emerging contemporary regional artists, the museum presents exhibitions from the permanent collection documenting regional history.

ON EXHIBIT 1999

10/07/1998 to 03/1999   FROM THE COLLECTION: THE TWENTIETH CENTURY

Highlights from the growing print collection with emphasis on social and urban realism and contemporary art that reflects urban diversity.

10/07/1998 to 03/1999   FROM THE COLLECTION: THE NINETEENTH CENTURY

Paintings, works on paper, and decorative artifacts, some making direct references to Jersey City and Hudson County.

12/02/1998 to 03/1999   JUAN SANCHEZ: PRINTED CONVICTIONS-PRINTS AND RELATED DRAWINGS

A survey show of prints and related drawings that reflect the artist's political and spiritual commitments as a Nuyorican artist.

04/1999 to 06/1999   PAUL GARDERE: RECENT WORK

04/1999 to 06/1999   GWEN FABRICANT: RECENT PAINTINGS

04/1999 to 06/1999   PHOTOGRAPHY FROM THE COLLECTION

MILLVILLE

Museum of American Glass at Wheaton Village

Affiliate Institution: 998-4552

1501 Glasstown Road, Millville, NJ 08332-1566

☎: 609-825-6800 or 800-998-4552   ■ www.wheatonvillage.org

Open: 10-5 daily(Apr-Dec), 10-5 We-Su (Jan-Mar)   **Closed:** 1/1, Easter, THGV, 12/25

ADM   Adult: $6.50   **Children:** F under 5   **Students:** $3.50   **Seniors:** $5.50

  ♿ Ⓟ   **Museum Shop**   ¶ 7am-9pm, PaperWaiter Restaurant and Pub, adjacent to Village

Group Tours: 800-998-4552, ext. 2730   **Drop-In Tours:** by appt   **Historic Building**   **Sculpture Garden**

Permanent Collection: AM/GLASS

Museum of American Glass at Wheaton Village - continued

The Museum of American Glass has one of the finest, and largest, collections of American glass in the country. The collection features more than 6,500 objects ranging from paperweights to fiber optics, mason jars to Tiffany masterpieces. **NOT TO BE MISSED:** Featured in addition to the Museum are a fully operational glass factory with daily narrated demonstrations as well as demonstrations in pottery, woodworking, and glass lampworking. Also, Stained Glass Studio, Down Jersey Folklife Center, Tinsmith Shop, Museum stores, 122 year-old schoolhouse, train ride and more.

ON EXHIBIT 1999
04/10/1999 to 11/24/1999 AMERICAN PERFUME BOTTLES

MONTCLAIR

Montclair Art Museum
3 South Mountain Ave, Montclair, NJ 07042
📞: 973-746-5555　◙　www.montclair-art.com
Open: 11-5 Tu, We, Fr, Sa, 1-5 Th, Su, Summer hours 12-5 We-Su 7/4-LAB/DAY　**Closed:** Mo, LEG/HOL!
Free Day: Sa, 11-2　**ADM**　**Adult:** $5.00　**Children:** F (under 12)　**Students:** $4.00　**Seniors:** $4.00
  ⍻　℗　**Museum Shop**　**Group Tours**: 973-746-5555 x221　**Drop-In Tours**: by appointment
Permanent Collection: NAT/AM: art 18-20; AM: ldscp, portraits 19; AM; Hudson River School: Am Impressionists

Located just 12 miles west of midtown Manhattan and housed in a Greek Revival style building, this museum, founded in 1914, features an impressive American art collection of a quality not usually expected in a small suburb.

ON EXHIBIT 1999
09/13/1998 to 01/10/1999 MASTERWORKS ON PAPER FROM THE COLLECTION OF THE MONTCLAIR ART MUSEUM
Watercolors, gouaches, pastels and drawings by George Inness, Winslow Homer, Childe Hassam, Everett Shinn, Jackson Pollock, Robert Motherwell and many others.

09/13/1998 to 01/10/1999 WILLIAM B. JOHNSON: TRUTH BE TOLD
Nearly 50 works by this African-American artist also including photographs of him and ephemera relating to him.

09/13/1998 to 01/10/1999 DAN NAMINGHA
Recent work including paintings and sculpture by this contemporary Native-American artist. Raised at Hopi, in the village of Polaccca, AZ, his paintings, works on paper, and statuary all relate to his cultural background and reflect the architecture, landscape and spiritual imagery of his people.

01/19/1999 to 04/18/1999 CONSUELO KANAGA: AN AMERICAN PHOTOGRAPHER
Drawn from the Brooklyn Museum of Art's vast collection of her works will be more than 100 silver gelatin photographic images of still-lifes, urban and rural views, and portraits. Kanaga's subject matter focused primarily on portraying African-Americans with a beauty and sensitivity unique for the period in which they were taken. *Catalog Will Travel*

01/31/1999 to 05/02/1999 THE MOVING PANORAMA OF BUNYAN'S "PILGRIM PROGRESS"(1851)
An exhibition of a work of art that was presumed lost by art historians for more than a century. Known only during the 19th century as the Bunyan Tableaux, this is one of only a handful of moving panoramas and the only one to feature enormous, posed figures.

05/23/1999 to 08/15/1999 SELECTIONS FROM THE PERMANENT COLLECTION
Selections from the Museum's growing photography collection including works from 1850 to the present by Haynes, Evans, Nixon, Frank, Oppenheim, Siskind and many others.

05/23/1999 to 08/15/1999 WAXING POETIC: ENCAUSTIC ART IN AMERICA

05/23/1999 to 08/15/1999 HIGHLIGHTS FROM THE NATIVE AMERICAN COLLECTION
Focusing on the original Native American collection given to the Montclair Museum in 1914, the exhibition will highlight objects from California as well as other cultures.

Montclair Art Museum - continued

09/28/1999 to 01/19/2000   PARIS 1900: THE"AMERICAN SCHOOL" AT THE UNIVERSAL EXPOSITION
A millennial recreation of the American display at the Paris Exposition featuring the major artists of the 19th century. It was the first time that the existence of a uniquely "American School" was established in parity with the European Schools.

09/28/1999 to 01/19/2000   AMERICAN TONALISM: SELECTIONS FROM THE METROPOLITAN MUSEUM OF ART AND THE MONTCLAIR ART MUSEUM
An outstanding selection of turn-of-the-century masterpieces with muted hues and misty effects by Inness, Whistler, Ryder, Steichen, Twachtman, Davies and many others.

NEW BRUNSWICK

Jane Voorhees Zimmerli Art Museum

Affiliate Institution: Rutgers, The State University of New Jersey
Corner George & Hamilton Streets, New Brunswick, NJ 08903
☎: 732-932-7237
Open: 10-4:30 Tu-Fr, Noon-5 Sa, Su   **Closed:** Mo, LEG/HOL! 12/25 thru 1/1; Month of August, Mo, Tu in July
Free Day: 1st Su ea month   **ADM   Adult:** $3.00   **Children:** F   **Students:** $3.00   **Seniors:** $3.00
♿ ℗   **Museum Shop   Group Tours   Drop-In Tours:** res req   **Historic Building**
Permanent Collection: FR: gr 19; AM: 20; EU: 15-20; P/COL; cer; CONT/AM: gr; THE NORTON AND NANCY DODGE COLLECTION OF NONCONFORMIST ART FROM THE SOVIET UNION

Housing the Rutgers University Collection of more than 50,000 works, this museum also incorporates the International Center for Japonisme which features related art in the Kusakabe-Griffis Japonisme Gallery. **NOT TO BE MISSED:** The George Riabov Collection of Russian Art; The Norton and Nancy Dodge Collection of Nonconformist Russian Art from the Soviet Union.

NEWARK

Newark Museum

49 Washington Street,, Newark, NJ 07101-0540
☎: 973-596-6550
Open: 12-5 We-Sa   **Closed:** Mo, Tu, 1/1, 7/4, THGV, 12/25
♿ ℗   **Museum Shop**   ⅋ Café in Engelhard Court noon-3:30 W-S (wheelchair accessible)
Group Tours: 973-596-6615   **Drop-In Tours:** 12:30-3:30 w-s   **Historic Building** Ballantine House, schoolhouse
Permanent Collection: AM: ptgs 17-20; AM: folk; AF/AM; DEC/ARTS; GLASS; JAP; CONT; AM: Hudson River School ptgs; AF; AN/GRK; AN/R; EGT

Established in 1909 as a museum of art and science, The Newark Museum features one of the finest collection of Tibetan art in the world. The museum encompasses 80 galleries and includes the historic 1885 Ballantine House, a landmark Victorian mansion; New Jersey's first planetarium; a Mini Zoo; and an 18th-century one-room schoolhouse. **NOT TO BE MISSED:** Joseph Stella's 5-panel mural "The Voice of the City of New York Interpreted," 1920-22; the Tibetan Altar, consecrated in 1990 by His Holiness the 14th Dalai Lama.

ON EXHIBIT 1999

ONGOING   HOUSE AND HOME: BALLANTINE HOUSE EXHIBITION
The Victorian origins of today's concept of "home" through the restored rooms and new thematic galleries that showcase the Museum's extensive decorative arts collection. This 1885 national landmark building is the only urban Victorian mansion open to the public in the Tri-state area. Included is an interactive computer game allowing the players to chose items for their own fantasy house.

02/1999 to 06/1999   OFF LIMITS: RUTGERS UNIVERSITY & AVANT-GARDE ART

09/1999 to 01/2000   MOUNTAINS AND VALLEYS, CASTLES AND TENTS: TIBETAN ART FROM THE NEWARK MUSEUM COLLECTION

NEW JERSEY

Newark Public Library
5 Washington Street, Newark, NJ 07101
☏: 973-733-7745
Open: 9-5:30 Mo, Fr, Sa, 9-8:30 Tu, We, Th   **Closed:** LEG/HOL!
♿ **Museum Shop**
Group Tours Drop-In Tours
Historic Building
Permanent Collection: AM & EU: gr

Since 1903 the library can be counted on for exhibitions which are of rare quality and well documented.

OCEANVILLE

Noyes Museum
Lily Lake Rd, Oceanville, NJ 08231
☏: 609-652-8848   ✉ users.jerseyscape.com/thenoyes
Open: 11-4 We-Su   **Closed:** Mo, Tu, LEG/HOL! 12/24-1/2
Free Day: Fr   **ADM   Adult:** $3.00   **Children:** F, under 18   **Students:** $2.00   **Seniors:** $2.00
♿ ⓒ **Museum Shop**
Group Tours: 800-669-2203   **Drop-In Tours**: on req, 6 or more
Permanent Collection: AM: cont, craft, folk; NJ: reg; VINTAGE BIRD DECOYS

Nestled in a peaceful lakeside setting, the Museum displays rotating exhibitions of American art and craft. Southern New Jersey's only fine art museum, it is a hidden treasure worth discovering and is located only 15 minutes from Atlantic City. **NOT TO BE MISSED:** Purple Martin Palace, view of Lily Lake

ON EXHIBIT 1999

01/02/1999 to 03/31/1999   "do it"
This installation at museums throughout New Jersey features thought-provoking perspective-challenging activities. The activities here are "The Square Meter Boundary Marker", "Do It Now", and "Wish Piece"(designed by Yoko Ono).

01/10/1999 to 05/02/1999   RITA BERNSTEIN: DOMESTIC LANDSCAPES
Black and white interior photographs.

01/17/1999 to 05/02/1999   CONNIE JOST: A RETROSPECTIVE
A South Jersey artist and environmental activist, her works indicate her love for nature and her incisive and satirical wit.

01/24/1999 to 06/30/1999   BRUSHES WITH SPIRITUALITY: ETHEREAL PAINTINGS BY BERNARD MAISNER, BRUCE POLLOCK, ROBERT STRAIGHT, RICHARD TSAO AND DARREN WATERSTON

05/16/1999 to 09/12/1999   STACY LEVY: ARTIST IN RESIDENCE
Levy will create a full-gallery installation.

06/20/1999 to 10/03/1999   JUSTIN MCCARTHY: A RETROSPECTIVE
A look at the life and work of this untrained artist.

09/26/1999 to 12/19/1999   THE FUTURE IS NOW
Science fiction illustrations.

10/17/1999 to 01/16/2000   AMBIENCE AND ENERGY: EXPRESSIONIST PAINTERS GIVE LIFE TO SPACES
Three emerging expressionists: David Brewster, Jeff Epstein, and William Smith.

10/17/1999 to 01/19/2000   BRIAN MEUNIER
Whimsical sculptures based on nature.

ORADELL

Hiram Blauvelt Art Museum

705 Kinderkamack Road, Oradell, NJ 07649
☎: 201-261-0012
Open: 10-4 We-Fr, 2-5 Sa, Su **Closed:** Mo, Tu, LEG/HOL!
Vol/Cont
⌖ ℗ **Museum Shop**
Group Tours Drop-In Tours: by appt **Historic Building Sculpture Garden**
Permanent Collection: WILDLIFE ART; AUDUBON FOLIO; IVORY GALLERY; BIG GAME ANIMALS, EXTINCT BIRDS, REPTILES

Founded in 1957 the museum is dedicated to bringing awareness to issues facing the natural world and to showcasing the artists who are inspired by it. It is located in an 1893 shingle and turret style carriage house. The 1679 Demarest House in River Edge, NJ is also owned by the Blauvelt-Demarest Foundation. **NOT TO BE MISSED:** Carl Rungius oil

PRINCETON

Art Museum

Affiliate Institution: Princeton University
Nassau Street, Princeton, NJ 08544-1018
☎: 609-258-3788 ▣ www.princeton, edu
Open: 10-5 Th-Sa, 1-5 Su **Closed:** Mo, LEG/HOL!
⌖ ℗ **Museum Shop**
Group Tours: 609-258-3043 **Drop-In Tours**: 2:00 Sa
Historic Building original 1890 Romanesque revival building designed by A. Page Brown
Permanent Collection: AN/GRK; AN/R+Mosaics; EU: sculp, ptgs 15-20; CH: sculp, ptgs; GR; P/COL; OM: ptgs, drgs; AF

An outstanding collection of Greek and Roman antiquities including Roman mosaics from Princeton University's excavations in Antioch is but one of the features of this highly regarded eclectic collection housed in a modern building on the lovely Princeton University campus. **NOT TO BE MISSED:** Picasso sculpture, ' Head of a Woman'

ON EXHIBIT 1999

10/03/1998 to 01/03/1999 PHOTOGRAPHY AT PRINCETON: CELEBRATING TWENTY-FIVE YEARS OF COLLECTING AND TEACHING THE HISTORY OF PHOTOGRAPHY
An exhibition of historic breadth and international scope with works ranging from the 1840s to the present. All fields will be included: from landscape to portraiture, still-life, genre scenes, and social documentary. *Catalog*

11/24/1998 to 01/03/1999 CONTEMPORARY PHOTOGRAPHY

Gallery at Bristol-Myers Squibb

Route 206 and Provinceline Road, Princeton, NJ 08540
☎: 609-252-6275
Open: 9-5 Mo-Fr, 9-7 T, 1-5 Sa, Su, Holidays
⌖ ℗ **Museum Shop**
Group Tours Drop-In Tours
Permanent Collection: Non collecting gallery

A corporate gallery with noteworthy changing exhibitions including professional and employee shows.

NEW JERSEY

New Jersey Center For Visual Arts

68 Elm Street, Summit, NJ 07901
☎: 908-273-9121   ▣ www.njmuseums.com/njcva/index.htm
Open: 12-4 Mo-Fr, 7:30-10 Th, 2-4 Sa, Su   **Closed:** LEG/HOL! & last 2 weeks in August
ADM   Adult: $1.00   **Children:** F (under 12)   **Students:** $1.00
& ℗   **Museum Shop   Group Tours   Drop-In Tours**: !   **Sculpture Garden**

The Center presents exhibitions of contemporary art by artists of national and international reputation as well as classes for people of all ages and levels of ability.

ON EXHIBIT 1999

11/13/1998 to 01/17/1999   NJCVA FACULTY EXHIBITION, PORTRAITS

01/31/1999 to 03/10/1999   INTERNATIONAL JURIED EXHIBITION

03/21/1999 to 05/02/1999   FOOD FOR THOUGHT

05/09/1999 to 06/20/1999   CONTEMPORARY PHOTOGRAPHY

06/25/1999 to 07/16/1999   MEMBERS EXHIBITION

African Art Museum of the S.M.A. Fathers

23 Bliss Ave, Tenafly, NJ 07670
☎: 201-894-8611   ▣ www.smafathers.org
Open: 10-5 Daily   **Closed:** Mo, LEG/HOL!
& ℗   **Museum Shop   Group Tours   Drop-In Tours**: by appt
Permanent Collection: AF; sculp, dec/art

Located in a cloistered monastery with beautiful gardens in the gracious old town of Tenafly, this museum features changing collection and loan exhibitions.

ON EXHIBIT 1999

04/19/1998 to 01/03/1999   CLAY, FIBER, WOOD AND METAL: FROM THE COLLECTION OF THE AFRICAN ART MUSEUM OF THE S.M.A. FATHERS (SMA: SOCIETY OF AFRICAN MISSIONS)
Works from South Africa, Tanzania, Burkina Faso, Ivory Coast, Nigeria, Cameroon, Ethiopia, and many others including the Tuareg of the Sahara Desert.

10/04/1998 to 12/31/1999   IN SPIRIT: SCULPTURE AND TEXTILES FROM THE COLLECTION OF THE AFRICAN ART MUSEUM OF THE S.M.A. FATHERS
Works from Liberia, Mali, Ivory Coast, Ghana, Nigeria, Zaire,/Democratic republic of the Congo, Tanzania, Kenya, Zambia and South Africa with several new acquisitions.

New Jersey State Museum

205 West State Street, CN530, Trenton, NJ 08625-0530
☎: 609-292-6464   ▣ www.state.nj.us/state/museum/usidx.html
Open: 9-4:45 Tu-Sa, 12-5 Su   **Closed:** Mo, LEG/HOL!
Adult: Planetarium $1.00   **Children:** Planetarium $1.00   **Students:** $1.00   **Seniors:** $1.00
& ℗   **Museum Shop   Group Tours   Drop-In Tours**
Permanent Collection: AM: cont, gr; AF/AM

The museum is located in the Capitol Complex in downtown Trenton. The fine art collections cover broad areas of interest with a special focus on New Jersey and culturally diverse artists. **NOT TO BE MISSED:** Ben Shahn Graphics Collection

Georgia O'Keeffe Home and Studio
Affiliate Institution: The Georgia O'Keeffe Foundation
Abiquiu, NM 87510
☎: 505-685-4539
Open: open by reservation only! 1 hr Tours seasonally on Tu, Th, Fr **Closed:** Mo, We, Sa, Su, LEG/HOL
ADM **Adult:** $20 interior $15 ext **Students:** $15.00 **Seniors:** $15.00
   ♿ ⓒ **Museum Shop** **Group Tours Drop-In Tours** **Historic Building**
Permanent Collection: Home and studio of artist Georgia O'Keeffe

To the extent possible the house remains as it was left by O'Keeffe in 1984 when she moved to Santa Fe. O'Keeffe Foundation President, Elizabeth Glassman says "Few places exist in America where one can see how an artist lived and worked. To experience the spaces created by O'Keeffe and to see the places she so often painted allows the visitor a new glimpse of the artist." No photographs or tape recorders are permitted. Visitors are required to wear soft rubber-soled shoes to protect the traditional adobe floors.

University Art Museum and Jonson Gallery
Affiliate Institution: The University of New Mexico
Fine Arts Center, Albuquerque, NM 87131-1416
☎: 505-277-4001
Open: 9-4 Tu-Fr, 5-8 Tu, 1-4 Su, Jonson Gallery closed on weekends **Closed:** Mo, Sa, LEG/HOL!
  ♿ ⓒ **Museum Shop**
Group Tours: 505-277-4001 **Drop-In Tours** **Sculpture Garden**
Permanent Collection: CONT; 19, 20; GR; PHOT; SP/COL; OM

In addition to changing exhibitions of work drawn from the permanent collection the Museum features significant New Mexico and regional artists working in all media. There is a branch gallery – 5-1-6 University Art Gallery Downtown. call 505-242-8244. Open from 10-4 Tu-Sa the downtown gallery offers a sampling of the rich diversity and strengths of the Museum's collection. **NOT TO BE MISSED:** Photography exhibitions

ON EXHIBIT 1999
08/25/1998 to 04/19/1999 RAYMOND JONSON: SEVEN DECADES
Jonson, a pioneer American Modernist painter moved to New Mexico to pursue his work in an atmosphere removed from urban life. The works here demonstrate his seventy years of work and progression into abstract interpretations of the landscape..

Art Center at Fuller Lodge
2132 Central Avenue, Los Alamos, NM 87544
☎: 505-662-9331 □ www.losalamos.org/flac.htm
Open: 10-4 Mo-Sa **Closed:** S, LEG/HOL!
  ♿ ⓒ **Museum Shop**
Group Tours Drop-In Tours: by res. **Historic Building**
Permanent Collection:

Located in historic Fuller Lodge, this art center presents monthly changing exhibitions of local and regional fine arts and crafts.

NEW MEXICO

ROSWELL

Roswell Museum and Art Center
100 West 11th, Roswell, NM 88201

\: 505-624-6744   www.roswellmuseum.org
Open: 9-5 Mo-Sa, 1-5 S & HOL   **Closed:** 1/1, THGV, 12/25
Vol/Cont
& Ⓟ   **Museum Shop**
Group Tours
Drop-In Tours: 1 week adv. notice
Permanent Collection: SW/ART; HISTORY; SCIENCE; NM/ART; NAT/AM

16 galleries featuring works by Santa Fe and Taos masters and a wide range of historic and contemporary art in its impressive permanent collection make this museum one of the premier cultural attractions of the Southwest. Temporary exhibitions of Native American, Hispanic, and Anglo art are often featured. **NOT TO BE MISSED:** Rogers Aston Collection of Native American and Western Art

SANTA FE

Institute of American Indian Arts Museum
108 Cathedral Place, Santa Fe, NM 87504

\: 505-988-6281   www.iaiamcad.org
Open: 9-5 daily June - Sept; 10-5 Mo-Sa, 12-5 Su Oct-May   **Closed:** 1/1, 7/4, 12/25
ADM   Adult: $4.00; F NAT/AM   **Children:** F under 16   **Students:** $2.00   **Seniors:** $2.00
& Ⓟ   **Museum Shop**
Group Tours Drop-In Tours   Sculpture Garden
Permanent Collection: Home of the National Collection of Contemporary Indian Art and Alaskan native arts

The Institute of American Indian Arts Museum is the home of a unique collection of art derived from ancient traditions and realized in contemporary forms, representing the vanguard of indigenous creativity for the new millennium. Exhibitions focus on the works of alumni, students and faculty of the Institute of American Indian Arts, as well as new art forms from Indian Country.   Admission to Allan Houser Art Park with Museum adm

ON EXHIBIT 1999
08/20/1998 to 02/01/1999   SWIAI MONUMENTAL SCULPTURE
An annual presentation and competition of monumental works by the Southwestern Association for Indian Arts, Inc presented in Allan Houser Art Park

12/11/1998 to 03/21/1999   NATIVE AMERICAN QUILTS
A presentation of current trends in the visual and traditional artwork embodied in Native American quilts. The regional focus includes western Oklahoma, Texas, New Mexico, Arizona, southern Colorado, and Southern Utah.

03/26/1999 to 07/18/1999   SEASONS OF THE WOODLAND PEOPLES
Seasons of the year and Native connections to the earth through the animal world and ceremonies will be the focus of this exhibition from the Great Lakes and eastern areas of North America.

07/30/1999 to 11/26/1999   EEWDOOWATA'W AG'E: DID THEY ROB YOU
An exhibition in 1995 in Bellingham, WA made clear the similarity of themes in contemporary Native American, Alaskan Native and Native Hawaiian themes. The focus of this new exhibition is the appropriation of spiritual elements and cultural life by Western mainstream media and academia.

07/30/1999 to 11/26/1999   CONTEMPORARY CERAMICS OF THE PEOPLE
An examination of contemporary trends and influences developed at the Institute.

Museum of New Mexico
113 Lincoln Ave., Santa Fe, NM 87501

📞: 505-827-6451 ◉ www.nmculture.org
Open: All Museums 10-5 Tu-Su!, Monuments, 8:30-5 daily **Closed:** Mo, 1/1, EASTER ,THGV, 12/25
ADM Adult: $10, 4 day pass all **Children:** F (under 17) **Seniors:** F, W
♿ ℗ **Museum Shop**
Group Tours: 505-827-6452 **Drop-In Tours**: ! each Museum **Historic Building**
Permanent Collection: (5 Museums with varied collections): TAOS & SANTA FE MASTERS; PHOT; SW/REG ;NAT/AM; FOLK; 5 State Monuments

In 1917 when it opened, the Museum of Fine Arts set the Santa Fe standard in pueblo-revival architecture. The Palace of the Governors, built by Spanish Colonial and Mexican governors, has the distinction of being the oldest public building in the US. Its period rooms and exhibitions of life in New Mexico during the Colonial Period are unique. Also included in the Museum is the Museum of Indian Arts and culture and the Museum of International Folk Art. The new Georgia O'Keeffe Museum is America's first museum dedicated to the work of a woman artist of international stature. Although it is a private, non-profit museum, it is in close partnership with the Museum of New Mexico. It is included in the 4 day pass. **NOT TO BE MISSED:** The entire complex

ON EXHIBIT 1999

PALACE OF THE GOVERNORS ON THE PLAZA
ART OF ANCIENT AMERICA
ANOTHER MEXICO: SPANISH LIFE ON THE UPPER RIO GRANDE
SEGESSER HIDE PAINTINGS
PERIOD ROOMS

MUSEUM OF FINE ARTS ON THE PLAZA

MUSEUM OF INDIAN ARTS AND CULTURE
HERE NOW AND ALWAYS
THE BUCHSBAUM GALLERY OF SOUTHWESTERN POTTERY

MUSEUM OF INTERNATIONAL FOLK ART
MULTIPLE VISIONS: A COMMON BOND
FAMILIA Y FE: FAMILY AND FAITH

THE GEORGIA O'KEEFFE MUSEUM

NEW MEXICO STATE MONUMENTS: CALL FOR ADMISSION COST
　　FORT SELDEN STATE MONUMENT
　　FORT SUMNER STATE MONUMENT
　　JEMEZ STATE MONUMENT
　　LINCOLN STATE MONUMENT
　　CORONADO STATE MONUMENT

to 01/03/1999 Museum of International Folk Art LAS OBRAS DE UN SANTERO (THE WORKS OF A SANTERO) RAMON JOSE LOPEZ

to 03/14/1999 Museum of International Folk Art AT HOME AWAY FROM HOME: TIBETAN CULTURE IN EXILE

08/29/1998 to 11/1999 Museum of International Folk Art THE EXTRAORDINARY IN THE ORDINARY FROM THE COLLECTIONS OF LLOYD COTSEN AND NEUTROGENA CORPORATION

09/04/1998 to 01/04/1999 Museum of Fine Arts STONY SILENCE: EXPERIMENTAL PRINTS BY FREDERICK O'HARA

09/04/1998 to 03/08/1999 Museum of Fine Arts I SAW WHOLE PAINTINGS RIGHT BEFORE MY EYES: THE FOUNDING OF THE TAOS ART COLONY

NEW MEXICO

Museum of New Mexico - continued

09/25/1998 to 03/22/1999   Museum of Fine Arts   PUEBLO ARCHITECTURE AND MODERN ADOBES: THE RESIDENTIAL DESIGNS OF WILLIAM LUMPKINS

10/12/1998 to 01/1999   Museum of Indian Arts and Culture   A CRITICAL CENTURY: ANCESTRAL ROCK ART BEFORE AND AFTER AD 1300

10/16/1998 to 01/25/1999   Museum of Fine Arts   THE POWER OF PLACE

01/24/1999 to 06/27/1999   Museum of International Folk Art   LA ESCULTERIA DE DON JOSE ARAGON (working title)

02/1999 to 05/1999   Museum of Indian Arts and Crafts   CHANGING TRADITIONS, THREE GENERATIONS: PABLITA VALARDE, HELEN HARDIN, MARGARET BAGSHAW-TINDEL

02/19/1999 to 05/24/1999   Museum of Fine Arts   ANCIENT IRANIAN CERAMICS FROM THE ARTHUR M. SACKLER COLLECTIONS

03/05/1999 to 05/24/1999   Museum of Fine Arts   SUSAN ROTHENBERG: DRAWINGS AND PRINTS

04/09/1999 to 06/27/1999   Museum of Fine Arts   MILTON AVERY: PAINTINGS FROM THE COLLECTION OF THE NEUBERGER MUSEUM OF ART

06/06/1999 to 12/31/1999   Museum of International Folk Art   CASA COLONIAL

06/06/1999 to 09/05/2000   Museum of International Folk Art   ANTECEDENTES: HISPANA AND HISPANO ARTISTS OF THE EARLY TWENTIETH CENTURY

06/13/1999 to 12/1999   WEAVING AT THE MARGINS: NAVAJO MEN AS WEAVERS

06/18/1999 to 09/20/1999   Museum of Fine Arts   JOHN CANDELARIA: PHOTOGRAPHIC MODERNIST

06/27/1999 to 05/2000   Museum of American Indian Arts and Crafts   OF STONES AND STORIES: VOICES FROM THE DINETAH

SANTA FE

Wheelwright Museum of the American Indian

704 Camino Lejo, Santa Fe, NM 87502
✆: 505-982-4636   ◙ www.collectorsguide.com
Open: 10-5 Mo-Sa, 1-5 S   **Closed:** 1/1, 12/25, THGV
& Ⓟ   **Museum Shop   Group Tours   Drop-In Tours**: 2pm Tu, Fr   **Historic Building**   **Sculpture Garden**
Permanent Collection: NAT/AM, Navajo; SW Ind (not always on view)

Inside this eight sided building, shaped like a Navajo 'hooghan' or home, on a hillside with vast views, you will find breathtaking American Indian art. **NOT TO BE MISSED:** Case Trading Post **Museum Shop**.

ON EXHIBIT 1999
SKYLIGHT GALLERY: CHANGING EXHIBITS OF EMERGING NATIVE AMERICAN ARTISTS

05/15/1999 to 10/27/1999   CLAY PEOPLE: THE HUMAN FIGURE IN PUEBLO ART
Contemporary and historic Pueblo figurative ceramics with emphasis on artists of the Pueblo communities close to Santa Fe will be featured in this important exhibition. Included are historic examples from Cochiti made from 1880-1920, works from Tesuque and Cochiti 1920-1980 including Helen Cordero and work of recent artists, some emerging. *Catalog*

11/07/1999 to 04/28/1999   LEGACY: TREASURES OF THE SCHOOL OF AMERICAN RESEARCH
Because the School of American Research has no exhibition space this is a rare opportunity to see 90 of the most notable objects of traditional Native American arts. *Catalog*

11/09/1999 to 04/2000   PAINTINGS BY JUDITH LOWRY (Mountain Maidu/Hammawi-Pit River) (working title)
Judith Lowery's heritage is of California Native Peoples. Figuration and accessability are most important to her. She uses ideas from stories she has heard from family and other images from her family history.

TAOS

Harwood Museum of the University of New Mexico
Affiliate Institution: University of New Mexico
238 Ledoux St, Taos, NM 87571
📞: 505-758-9826   ▣ www.laplaza.org/a-l/art/harwood/
Open: 10-5 Tu-Sa, 12-5 S   **Closed:** Mo, LEG/HOL!
ADM   Adult: $4.00   **Children:** $2.00 under 12   **Seniors:** $4.00
& ℗ **Museum Shop**
Group Tours: 505-788-9826   **Drop-In Tours**
Historic Building
Permanent Collection: HISPANIC: 19; TAOS ARTISTS: 20

Many of the finest artists who have worked in Taos are represented in this collection. The building housing the museum is one of the first twentieth-century buildings that set the Pueblo Revival architectural style which became popular in northern New Mexico. **NOT TO BE MISSED:** 'Winter Funeral' by Victor Higgins, Agnes Martin Gallery

ON EXHIBIT 1999
THREE PERSON EXHIBITION (each for about 2 months, artists to be announced)

12/13/1998 to 02/14/1999   75TH ANNIVERSARY GROUP EXHIBITION

02/21/1999 to 05/02/1999   MADE FROM SCRATCH: FIVE PERSON SHOW

05/09/1999 to 07/04/1999   CHARLES STRONG

07/11/1999 to 09/19/1999   REALISM

09/26/1999 to 11/28/1999   MARX/COLBY?/ZINK?

12/05/1999 to 02/2000   BURTON PHILLIPS: ARTIST AND COLLECTOR

Millicent Rogers Museum
Museum Road, 4 miles N of Taos, Taos, NM 87571
📞: 505-758-2462
Open: 10-5 Daily Apr-Oct, closed Mo Nov-Mar   **Closed:** Mo Nov Mar, 1/1, EASTER, SAN GERONIMO DAY 9/30, THGV, 12/25
Free Day: Su   **ADM   Adult:** $6.00   **Children:** 6-16 $1.00   **Students:** $5.00   **Seniors:** $5.00
& ℗ **Museum Shop**
Group Tours   Drop-In Tours   Historic Building   Sculpture Garden
Permanent Collection: NAT/AM & HISP: textiles, basketry, pottery, jewelry; REG

Dedicated to the display and interpretation of the art and material of the Southwest, the Millicent Rogers Museum places particular focus on New Mexican cultures. **NOT TO BE MISSED:** Extensive collection of pottery by Maria Martinez, as well as Native American and Hispanic jewelry.

NEW YORK

Albany Institute of History and Art

125 Washington Ave, Albany, NY 12210
☎: 518-463-4478   ▣ www.albanyinstitute.org
Open: 12-5 We-Su   **Closed:** Mo, Tu, LEG/HOL!
Free Day: We   **ADM**   **Adult:** $3.00   **Children:** F, under 12
♿   Ⓟ   **Museum Shop**   **Group Tours**   **Drop-In Tours**   **Historic Building**
Permanent Collection: PTGS: Hudson River School & Limner; AM: portraits 19; CAST IRON STOVES; DEC/ARTS: 19

Founded in 1791, this museums, one of the oldest in the nation, presents permanent displays and changing exhibitions throughout the year. There are over 20,000 objects in the permanent collection. The Museum will be under construction and renovation beginning in April 1999 and reopening in 2001. Please call ahead for exhibition information. **NOT TO BE MISSED:** Hudson River School Ptgs by Cole, Durand, Church, Kensett, Casilear and the Hart Brothers

University Art Museum

Affiliate Institution: University At Albany, State University of NY
1400 Washington Ave,, Albany, NY 12222
☎: 518-442-4035   ▣ www.albany.edu/museum
Open: 10-5 Tu-F, 12-4 Sa, Su   **Closed:** Mo, LEG/HOL!
♿   Ⓟ   **Museum Shop**   🍴: In Campus Center   **Group Tours**   **Drop-In Tours**
Permanent Collection: AM: gr, ptng, dr 20

This museum, the largest of its kind among the State University campuses and one of the major galleries of the Capitol District, features work from student and mid-career to established artists of national reputation. **NOT TO BE MISSED:** Richard Diebenkorn, 'Seated Woman', 1966, (drawing)

ON EXHIBIT 1999

The Museum will be closed summer 1999 for Collections inventory and Research and Self-Study/Strategic Planning.

01/26/1999 to 03/07/1999   CROSSING THE THRESHOLD
As we approach a new millennium this exhibition reflects on the artistic milestones of women artists during the past 100 years. While striving for equality, the 31 women included here will be remembered for challenging and overcoming the traditional social mores of our American culture. Artists include Louise Bourgeois, Elizabeth Catlett, Helen Frankenthaler, Nell Blaine, Agnes Martin, Nancy Spiro, Lois Mailou Jones and others.

03/19/1999 to 04/18/1999   TWO SCULPTORS: RECENT WORK (working title)

09/22/1999 to 11/14/1999   WILLIAM B. SHADE-A 25 YEAR RETROSPECTIVE
An examination of the total oeuvre of paintings, sculpture, drawings and prints by this exceptionally creative and energetic artist. *Catalog*

Center for Curatorial Studies and Art in Contemporary Culture

Bard College, Annandale on Hudson, NY 12504
☎: 914-758-7598   ▣ www.bard.edu/ccs
Open: 1-5 We-Su   **Closed:** Mo, Tu, 12/31, 1/1, MEM/DAY, 7/4, THGV, 12/25
♿   Ⓟ   **Museum Shop**   **Group Tours**   **Drop-In Tours**
Permanent Collection: CONT: all media; VIDEO: installation 1960-present

Housed in a facility which opened in 1992, the CCS Museum changing exhibition of contemporary art is curated by internationally renowned guest curators and graduate thesis candidates.

ASTORIA

American Museum of the Moving Image
35th Ave at 36th St, Astoria, NY 11106
☎: 718-784-0077 ◉ www.ammi.org
Open: 12-5 Tu-F, 11-6 Sa, Su **Closed:** Mo, 12/25
ADM Adult: $8.00 **Children:** $4.00 (5-18) under 4 F **Students:** $5.00 **Seniors:** $5.00
♿ &#9physics; **Museum Shop** 🍽: café
Group Tours: 718-784-4520 **Drop-In Tours**
Historic Building
Permanent Collection: BEHIND THE SCREEN, combination of artifacts, interactive experiences, live demonstrations and video screenings to tell the story of the making, marketing and exhibiting of film, television and digital media. Especially popular are Automated Dialogue Replacement where visitors can dub their own voices into a scene from a movie and Video Flipbook where visitors can create a flipbook of themselves that they can pick up at the gift shop as a memento.

The only Museum in the US devoted exclusively to film, television, video and interactive media and their impact on 20th century American life. **NOT TO BE MISSED:** 'Tut's Fever Movie Palace', Red Grooms and Lysiane Luongs interpretation of a 1920's neo-Egyptian movie palace showing screenings of classic movie serials daily.

AUBURN

Schweinfurth Memorial Art Center
205 Genesee St, Auburn, NY 13021
☎: 315-255-1553
Open: 10-5 Tu-Sa, 1-5 S (extended hours during Quilt Show) **Closed:** Mo, THGV, 12/25
ADM Adult: $3.00 **Children:** F (under 12) **Seniors:** $3.00
♿ &#9physics; **Museum Shop**
Group Tours Drop-In Tours
Permanent Collection: Non collecting institution

Regional fine art, folk art and crafts are featured in changing exhibitions at this cultural center located in central New York State. **NOT TO BE MISSED:** Made in New York gift shop featuring regional fine arts and crafts.

BAYSIDE

QCC Art Gallery
Affiliate Institution: Queensborough Community College
222-05 56th Ave., Bayside, NY 11364-1497
☎: 718-631-6396
Open: 9-5 Mo-Fr and by appt. **Closed:** Sa, Su, ACAD!
♿ **Museum Shop** 🍽: 9am-2pm
Group Tours Drop-In Tours
Historic Building
Permanent Collection: AM: after 1950; WOMEN ARTISTS

The Gallery which reflects the ethnic diversity of Queensborough Community College and its regional residents also highlights the role art plays in the cultural history of people.

NEW YORK

BINGHAMTON

Roberson Museum Science Center
30 Front St., Binghamton, NY 13905-4779
☎: 607-772-0660 ◉ www.roberson.org
Open: 10-5 Mo-Th, Sa, 10-9 Fr, 12-5 Su; 10-9 last Fr of month   **Closed:** Mo, LEG/HOL!
ADM Adult: $5.00 **Children:** F under 4 **Students:** $3.00 **Seniors:** $3.00
& ℗ **Museum Shop**
Group Tours   Drop-In Tours
Historic Building
Permanent Collection: Reg: TEXTILES; PHOT; PTGS; DEC/ART: late 19, 20; historical agricultural tools, cameras, ceramics, and household accessories, natural history & archeological materials

A regional museum featuring 19th and 20th c art, history, folklife, natural history and technology. It includes a 1907 mansion, a museum, a Planetarium, and the off-site Kopernik Observatory. Also the site for the Binghamton Visitor Center, a state-sponsored facility which includes an orientation film and changing exhibits. **NOT TO BE MISSED:** 'Blue Box' trainer circa 1942 by Edwin Link; mammoth tusk and mammoth tooth c.9000 B.C.

ON EXHIBIT 1999

10/12/1998 to 04/11/1999   I SPY
Explore a variety of engaging and challenging environments filled with interesting objects from the museum and play the game based on the original I Spy.

01/25/1999 to 06/30/1999   1000 FACES
Contemporary portraits can be fun, funky, quirky, and touching. See how four artists interpret their subjects in sculptures, oil paintings, caricatures, and public murals.

05/08/1999 to 08/08/1999   DINOS! FROM THE INSIDE OUT

Mid September 1999 to Mid-November 1999   REFUGE: THE NEWEST NEW YORKERS

BLUE MOUNTAIN LAKE

Adirondack Museum
Blue Mountain Lake, NY 12812
☎: 518-352-7311 ◉ www.adkmuseum.org
Open: 9:30-5:30 Mo-Su, MEM/DAY weekend to Columbus day weekend
ADM Adult: $10.00 **Children:** 7-16 $6.00 **Seniors:** $9.00
& ℗ **Museum Shop** ⅱ: Y
Group Tours Drop-In Tours
Historic Building
Permanent Collection: AM: Pntgs, GR, Drgs, 1850-present

The Museum tells the stories of how people lived, moved, worked and played in the Adirondacks. There are 23 indoor and outdoor exhibit areas featuring special events and programs. Just an hour from Lake Placid and Lake George, the museum has a cafeteria overlooking Blue Mountain Lake.

ON EXHIBIT 1999
THE AMERICAN CHRISTMAS TREE: AN EVERGREEN TRADITION

BRONX

Bronx Museum of the Arts
1040 Grand Concourse, Bronx, NY 10456

☎: 718-681-6000

Open: 3-9 We; 10-5 Th, Fr; 1-6 Sa, Su   **Closed:** Mo, Tu, THGV, 12/25
Free Day: We   **ADM   Adult:** $3.00   **Children:** F (under 12)   **Students:** $2.00   **Seniors:** $1.00
  ᚼ   ℗   **Museum Shop   Group Tours**: 718-681-6000 x132   **Drop-In Tours**
Permanent Collection: AF: LAT/AM: SE/ASIAN: works on paper 20; CONT/AM: eth

Noted for its reflection of the ethnically diverse NYC metro area it is the only fine arts museum in the Bronx. The collection and exhibitions are a fresh perspective on the urban experience.

ON EXHIBIT 1999

03/11/1999 to 08/22/1999   URBAN MYTHOLOGIES: THE BRONX REPRESENTED SINCE THE 1960S
An examination of the shifting image of the Bronx as represented in contemporary visual art, street culture, and the mass media, in relation to significant historical events and urban issues from 1960 to the present. Works shown from the Museum collection.

07/1999 to 09/1999   ARTIST IN THE MARKETPLACE: NINETEENTH ANNUAL EXHIBITION
Works from the collection in a broad range of media by 36 artists from the New York metropolitan area. The program provides artists with the opportunity to develop important career management skills.

The Hall of Fame for Great Americans
Affiliate Institution: Bronx Community College
University Ave and W. 181 St, Bronx, NY 10453

☎: 718-289-5161   ◉   www.bcc.cuny.edu

Open: 10-5 Daily   **Closed:** None
  ᚼ   ℗   **Museum Shop**   ⊮: Y
Group Tours   Drop-In Tours: by appt   **Historic Building**   **Sculpture Garden**
Permanent Collection: COLONNADE OF 98 BRONZE BUSTS OF AMERICANS ELECTED TO THE HALL OF FAME SINCE 1900 (includes works by Daniel Chester French, James Earle Fraser, Frederick MacMonnies, August Saint-Gaudens

Overlooking the Bronx & Harlem Rivers, this beautiful Beaux arts style architectural complex, once a Revolutionary War fort, contains a Stanford White designed library modeled after the Pantheon in Rome. 98 recently restored bronze portrait busts of famous Americans elected to the Hall of Fame since 1900 and placed within the niches of the 'Men of Renown' classical colonnade allow the visitor to come face-to-face with history through art.

BROOKLYN

The Brooklyn Museum of Art
200 Eastern Parkway, Brooklyn, NY 11238

☎: 718-638-5000   ◉   wwwq.brooklynart.org

Open: 10-5 We-Fr, 11-9 Sa, 11-5 Su   **Closed:** Mo, Tu, THGV, 12/25, 1/1
Sugg/Cont   Adult: $4.00   **Children:** F (under 12)   **Students:** $2.00   **Seniors:** $1.50
  ᚼ   ℗   **Museum Shop**   ⊮: open until 4 weekdays, till 5 Weekends & holidays, coffee/wine bar Sa eve
Group Tours: 718-638-5000, ext 221   **Drop-In Tours**: !Th, Fr 1pm, Sa, Su, 1 & 3pm
Historic Building   **Sculpture Garden**
Permanent Collection: EGT; AM-EU ptgs, sculp, dec/art 18-20; AS; AF; OC; NW/AM; W/COL

The Brooklyn Museum of Art is one of the nation's premier art institutions. Housed in a Beaux-Arts structure designed in 1893 by McKim, Mead & White, its collections represent virtually the entire history of art from Egyptian artifacts to modern American paintings. **NOT TO BE MISSED:** Newly renovated and brilliantly installed Charles A. Wilbour Egyptian Collection

NEW YORK

The Brooklyn Museum of Art - continued
ON EXHIBIT 1999

10/17/1998 to 09/1999   THE SLOAN COLLECTION: BARD SECOND YEAR
A small but choice group of fine eighteenth century American furniture recently given to the Museum.

11/13/1998 to 04/04/1999   LEWIS WICKES HINE: THE FINAL YEARS
These 169 photographs were given to the Museum in 1979 and have never been shown to the public. They show the oeuvre for the first time of the last years of one of America's most important photographers.

12/18/1998 to 03/14/1999   JAPONISME IN FASHION
An astonishing assemblage of costumes and textiles dating from the 17th century to the present. It was organized to illustrate and "clarify the emergence of Japonism in European fashion". The major focus is on material produced from mid 19th century to the 1990s.

12/20/1998 to 03/14/1999   WORKING IN BROOKLYN: DOMESTIC TRANSFORMATIONS
Four Brooklyn artists, Ann Agee, Ron Baron, Jean Blackburn, and Andy Yoder present two or three common objects transformed into sculpture. They explore materials and subject matter.

02/04/1999 to 04/30/2000   DECADE: THE BROOKLYN MUSEUM OF ART'S TWENTY-SIXTH PRINT NATIONAL REVIEWS PRINTS OF THE PAST TEN YEARS
The Print National originated at the Brooklyn Museum of Art in 1947. The last one was held in 1989. The Annual will examine the developments of collaborative printmaking and technological advances focusing on different regions of the United States *Catalog*

04/09/1999 to 06/14/1999   FROM HIP TO HIP-HOP: BLACK: FASHION AND A CULTURE OF INFLUENCE
An exploration of the complex and often controversial elements that constitute contemporary fashion within the urban African-American community and its subsequent influence on mainstream fashion both in the United States and abroad. Belle Epoch gowns and European couture creations will be juxtaposed with continental African objects.

04/23/1999 to 08/15/1999   JACK LEVINE PRINT RETROSPECTIVE
Jack Levine, born in 1915, has been living and working in New York since the 1930s. He is known for his caustic wit and commentary on American political life. 72 of the prints included here have never before been the focus of an exhibit. He did not devote himself to printmaking until the 1960s and often returns to images painted years ago for inspiration for his etchings.

09/03/1999 to 01/23/2000   VIVIAN CHERRY: A WORKING STREET PHOTOGRAPHER, 1940s-1990s
Cherry is one of the few women who had street assignments given to her. The quintessential New York photographer she made photographs evocative of the period when Manhattan was at its most vigorous. In addition she went on assignments to the rural south and southwest. Many of her works are an important record of New York City history.

10/29/1999 to 02/06/2000   EASTMAN JOHNSON
Johnson is one of the most important American artists of the 19th Century. Famous for images of American life including rural genre subjects, Civil War scenes, interior scenes, and portraiture. The exhibition is a comprehensive exploration of the entire range of his work. *Catalog*

Rotunda Gallery
33 Clinton Street, Brooklyn, NY 11201
☏: 718-875-4047
Open: 12-5 Tu-Fr, 11-4 Sa   **Closed:** Su, Mo, LEG/HOL!
♿ Ⓟ   **Museum Shop**
Group Tours Drop-In Tours: 10-11:30 am Mo-Fr
Permanent Collection: non-collecting institution

The Gallery's facility is an architecturally distinguished space designed for exhibition of all forms of contemporary art. It is located in Brooklyn Heights which is well known for its shops, restaurants and historic brownstones.

Rotunda Gallery - continued

ON EXHIBIT 1999

12/10/1998 to 01/23/1999   SEEING MONEY
A group exhibition selected from the Rotunda slide registry of 850 artists treating the subject of money, exploring its physical presence, social connotations and symbolic implications.

02/04/1999 to 03/27/1999   ZONE OF RISIBILITY
Wit and Humor are common strategies employed by many visual artists. They are nevertheless critical tools which artists employ.

04/08/1999 to 05/22/1999   UNTITLED GROUP EXHIBITION ON THE SUBJECT OF SPIRITUALITY

Rubelle & Norman Schafler Gallery
Affiliate Institution: Pratt Institute
200 Willoughby Ave, Brooklyn, NY 11205
☎: 718-636-3517
Open: 9-5 Mo-Fr   **Closed:** Sa, Su, LEG/HOL!
& ℗ **Museum Shop**
Group Tours Drop-In Tours
Permanent Collection: Currently building a collection of Art and Design Works by Pratt Alumni, Faculty and Students

Varied programs of thematic, solo, and group exhibitions of contemporary art, design and architecture are presented in this gallery.

BUFFALO

Albright Knox Art Gallery
1285 Elmwood Ave, Buffalo, NY 14222
☎: 716-882-8700   ◙   www.albrightknox.org
Open: 11-5 Tu-Sa, 12-5 Su   **Closed:** Mo, THGV, 12/25, 1/1
Free Day: 11-1 Sa   **ADM   Adult:** $4.00   **Children:** F (under 12)   **Students:** $3.00   **Seniors:** $3.00
& ℗ **Museum Shop**   ⅋: Y
Group Tours Drop-In Tours: 12:15 We-Th, 1:30 Sa-Su   **Historic Building**   **Sculpture Garden**
Permanent Collection: AB/EXP; CONT: 70's & 80's; POST/IMPR, POP, OP, CUBIST, AM & EU: 18-19

With one of the world's top international surveys of twentieth-century painting and sculpture, the Albright-Knox is especially rich in American and European art of the past fifty years. The permanent collection which also offers a panorama of art through the centuries dating from 3000 BC., is housed in a 1905 Greek Revival style building designed by Edward B. Green with a 1962 addition by Gordon Bunshaft of Skidmore, Owings and Merrill.

ON EXHIBIT 1999

Please note that during 1998 some sections of the Museum will be closed for renovation. The permanent collection and selected special exhibitions will remain open. During this time additional special exhibitions will be presented at the Anderson Gallery, Martha Jackson Place, Buffalo.

05/23/1999 to 08/29/1999   MONET AT GIVERNY: MASTERPIECES FROM THE MUSÉE MARMOTTAN
22 paintings on loan from the distinguished Musée Marmotton in Paris offer an overview of Monet's late works, considered by the artist to be the finest of his career. *Catalog Will Travel*

NEW YORK

Burchfield Penney Art Center
Affiliate Institution: Buffalo State College
1300 Elmwood Ave, Buffalo, NY 14222-6003
☎: 716-878-6011
Open: 10-5 Tu, Th-Sa, 10-7:30 We, 1-5 Su   **Closed:** Mo, LEG/HOL!
Vol/Cont
  ⑤ ℙ **Museum Shop** ⑪: on college grounds **Group Tours**: **Drop-In Tours:** by appt **Historic Building**
Permanent Collection: AM; WEST/NY: 19, 20: CHARLES A BURCHFIELD; CHARLES CARY RAMSEY, Roycroft, Photo,

The Burchfield-Penney Art Center is dedicated to the art and artists of Western New York. Particular emphasis is given to the works of renowned American watercolorist Charles E. Burchfield. The museum holds the largest archives and collection in the world of his works. **NOT TO BE MISSED:** Burchfield's' Appalachian Evening'; 'Oncoming Spring', 'Fireflies and Lightening' hand crafted objects by Roycroft Arts and Crafts community artists, sculpture by Charles Cary Rumsey. Hands-on gallery-USEUM.

ON EXHIBIT 1999
01/16/1999 REINSTALLED   THE ROYCROFT LEGACY

ONGOING:/   CHARLES BURCHFIELD'S STUDIO
A recreation of a corner of Burchfield's Gardenville, NY studio will present for the first time objects which have been in storage at the Center since 1971. Many of the artmaking tools and supplies he used as well as inspirational objects etc will also be shown/

10/24/1998 to 01/03/1999   MY MR. BURCHFIELD
Growing up next to the Burchfields, Jackie Albarellla was influenced in ways she did not recognize until adulthood. This exhibition of her landscape photography utilizes video projections and other contemporary technology to learn how she appreciated the natural world through his sensitivity.

10/24/1998 to 03/21/1999   HOW BURCHFIELD PAINTED
An interpretive presentation of paintings, drawings and unfinished works will illustrate his unique watercolor painting techniques.

11/21/1998 to 01/31/1999   BURCHFIELD IN CONTEXT
American painting from the Albright-Knox Art Gallery, Art Gallery of Hamilton, and the Burchfield-Penney Art Center.

12/12/1998 to 02/21/1999   WORKS FROM THE COLLECTION

12/12/1998 to 04/11/1999   CRAFT ART

02/13/1999 to 04/18/1999   THE FILMIC ART OF PAUL SHARITS
A first retrospective exhibition to include both the films and two dimensional works of this filmmaker who has been recognized internationally as a pioneering experimental filmmaker who was trained as a painter.

05/01/1999 to 07/11/1999   CATHERINE PARKER
Work of the past ten years by watercolorist Parker, whose interpretation of landscape is characterized by bold brushwork and rich color contrasts.

CANAJOHARIE

Canajoharie Library and Art Gallery
2 Erie Blvd, Canajoharie, NY 13317
☎: 518-673-2314
Open: 10-4:45 Mo-We, Fr, 10-8:30 Th, 10-1:30 Sa   **Closed:** Su, LEG/HOL!
  ⑤ ℙ **Museum Shop** **Group Tours Drop-In Tours** **Sculpture Garden**
Permanent Collection: WINSLOW HOMER; AMERICAN IMPRESSIONISTS; 'The Eight'

Located in downtown Canajoharie, the gallery's collection includes 21 Winslow Homers.

CLINTON

Emerson Gallery

Affiliate Institution: Hamilton College
198 College Hill Road, Clinton, NY 13323
☎: 315-859-4396
Open: 12-5 Mo-Fr, 1-5 Sa, Su during exhibitions, closed weekends June, Jul & Aug **Closed:** LEG/HOL!
 Ⓟ **Museum Shop Group Tours Drop-In Tours**
Permanent Collection: NAT/AM; AM & EU: ptgs, gr 19, 20; WEST INDIES ART

While its ultimate purpose is to increase the educational scope and opportunity for appreciation of the fine arts by Hamilton students, the gallery also seeks to enrich campus cultural life in general, as well as to contribute to the cultural enrichment of the surrounding community.

ON EXHIBIT 1999

01/18/1999 to 02/21/1999 MAKING IT REAL
A thematic exhibit of photographic works by contemporary artists who explore and challenge commonly-held assumptions about photography's relation to truth, thus raising important questions about how we understand reality at the end of the 20th century.

CORNING

Corning Museum of Glass

1 Museum Way, Corning, NY 14830-2253
☎: 800-732-6945, 607-937-5371 ▣ www.corningglasscenter.com
Open: 9-5 daily, 9-8 July & Aug **Closed:** 1/1, THGV, 12/24, 12/25!
ADM Adult: $7.00, family $16 **Children:** $5 (6-17) **Students:** $6.00 **Seniors:** $6.00
 Ⓟ **Museum Shop** ⅱ: **Group Tours:** 607-974-2000 **Drop-In Tours:** by reservation
Permanent Collection: GLASS: worldwide 1500 BC - present

The Museum houses the world's premier glass collection – more than 30,000 objects representing 3500 years of achievements in glass design and craftsmanship. It is part of the Corning Glass Center complex. New hot-glass studio presents workshops, classes and demonstrations. In June 1999, the New Glass Innovation Center and the Glass Sculpture Gallery open. **NOT TO BE MISSED:** The Hot Glass show where visitors can watch artisans make glass objects.

Rockwell Museum

111 Cedar St at Denison Parkway,, Corning, NY 14830
☎: 607-937-5386 ▣ www.stny.lrun.com/RockwellMuseum
Open: 9-5 Mo-Sa, 12-5 S **Closed:** 1/1, THGV, 12/24, 12/25
Free Day: 12-5 Su (Nov - Apr), Int'l Museum Day in May (usually 18th) **ADM Adult:** $5.00, family $12.50 **Children:** $2.50 (6-17)F under 6 **Seniors:** $4.50
 Ⓟ **Museum Shop**
Group Tours Drop-In Tours: 10am & 2pm weekdays (Jun - Sep), other times by appointment and extra fee **Historic Building** 1893 City Hall, Corning, NY
Permanent Collection: PTGS & SCULP: by Western Artists including Bierstadt, Remington and Russell 1830-1920; FREDERICK CARDER STEUBEN GLASS; ANT: toys

Located in the 1893 City Hall of Corning, NY, and nestled in the lovely Finger Lake Region of NY State is the finest collection of American Western Art in the Eastern U.S. The museum building is in a Romanesque revival style and served as a City Hall, firehouse and jail until the 1970s. It is also home to the worlds most comprehensive collection of Frederick Carder Steuben glass. **NOT TO BE MISSED:** Model of Cyrus E. Dallin's famous image, 'Appeal to the Great Spirit'.

NEW YORK

Rockwell Museum - continued

ON EXHIBIT 1999

11/19/1998 to 03/14/1999 ONCE UPON A PAGE: THE ART OF CHILDREN'S BOOKS
71 works by some of the most distinguished American and international illustrators of children's books all from the Dr. and Mrs. August C. Mazza collection. The diverse collection includes art from the 19th century to the present.

06/20/1999 to 08/08/1999 A WALK THROUGH THE PAPER FOREST
Latino prints and drawings from El Museo del Barrio, New York City.

09/09/1999 to 01/25/2000 MASTER OF GLASS: FREDERICK CARDER (1863-1963)
A comprehensive, critical survey of the achievements of Carder, co-founder of Steuben Glass Works, tracing his American career in the context of contemporary decorative arts. *Catalog Will Travel*

CORTLAND

Dowd Fine Arts Gallery
Affiliate Institution: State University of New York College at Cortland
Suny Cortland, Cortland, NY 13045
☎: 607-753-4216
Open: 11-4 Tu-Sa **Closed:** Su, Mo, ACAD!
Vol/Cont
 ♿ Ⓟ **Museum Shop Group Tours**: 607-753-4816 **Drop-In Tours**: scheduled by request **Sculpture Garden**
Permanent Collection: Am & EU: gr, drgs 20; CONT: art books

Temporary exhibitions of contemporary and historic art which are treated thematically are presented in this university gallery.

EAST HAMPTON

Guild Hall Museum
158 Main Street, East Hampton, NY 11937
☎: 516-324-0806 ◉ thehamptons.com/guild-hall
Open: 11-5 daily (Summer), 11-5 We-Sa, 12-5 Su (Winter) **Closed:** THGV, 12/25, 1/1, LEG/HOL!
Sugg/Cont $3
 ♿ Ⓟ **Museum Shop Group Tours**: 516-324-0806 Drop-In Tours **Historic Building Sculpture Garden**
Permanent Collection: AM: 19, 20

Located in one of America's foremost art colonies this cultural center combines a fine art museum and a 400 seat professional theater.

EAST ISLIP

Islip Art Museum
50 Irish Lane, East Islip, NY 11730
☎: 516-224-5402
Open: 10-4 We-Sa, 2-4:30 Su **Closed:** Mo, Tue, LEG/HOL!
Vol/Cont
 ♿ Ⓟ **Museum Shop Group Tours**: 516-224-5402 **Drop-In Tours**: by request **Historic Building**
Permanent Collection: AM/REG: ptgs, sculp, cont

The Islip Museum is the leading exhibition space for contemporary and Avant Garde Art on LI. The Carnegie House Project Space, open in the summer and fall, features cutting-edge installations and site-specific work. A satellite gallery called the Anthony Giordamo Gallery is at Dowling College in Oakdale, LI.

Arnot Art Museum

235 Lake St, Elmira, NY 14901-3191
☎: 607-734-3697
Open: 10-5 Tu-Sa, 1-5 Su **Closed:** Mo, THGV, 12/25, 1/1
ADM Adult: $2.00 **Children:** $.50 (6-12) **Students:** $1.00 **Seniors:** $1.00
♿ Ⓟ **Museum Shop Group Tours Drop-In Tours Historic Building**
Permanent Collection: AM: salon ptgs 19, 20; AM: sculp 19

The original building is a neo-classical mansion built in 1833 in downtown Elmira. The museum modern addition was designed by Graham Gund. **NOT TO BE MISSED:** Matthias Arnot Collection; one of last extant private collections housed intact in its original showcase

Godwin-Ternbach Museum

Affiliate Institution: Queens College
65-30 Kissena Blvd, Flushing, NY 11367
☎: 718-997-4734
Open: 11-7 Mo-Th Call! **Closed:** Sa, Su, ACAD!
♿ Ⓟ **Museum Shop Group Tours Drop-In Tours**
Permanent Collection: GR: 20; ANT: glass; AN/EGT; AN/GRK; PTGS; SCULP

This is the only museum in Queens with a broad and comprehensive permanent collection which includes a large collection of WPA/FAP prints.

Hyde Collection

161 Warren St,, Glens Falls, NY 12801
☎: 518-792-1761
Open: 12-5 We-Su 1/1-4/30, 10-5 Tu-Su 5/1-12/31 **Closed:** Mo, Tu, LEG/HOL!
♿ Ⓟ **Museum Shop**
Group Tours Drop-In Tours: 1-4pm **Historic Building Sculpture Garden**
Permanent Collection: O/M: ptgs; AM: ptgs; ANT; IT/REN, FR. 18

A world-class permanent collection spanning western art from 4th c. BC - 2nd c. containing significant works by European Old Masters as well as modern European and American artists. The fine art is displayed among an important selection of European antiques, housed in an Italianate Renaissance-style villa built in 1912. An Education Wing offers year round programming including temporary exhibitions in three gallery spaces, concerts, lectures, family activities and a **Museum Shop**. **NOT TO BE MISSED:** 'Portrait of a Young Man' by Raphael; 'Portrait of Christ' by Rembrandt; 'Coco' by Renoir; 'Boy Holding a Blue Vase' by Picasso; 'Geraniums' by Childe Hassam

ON EXHIBIT 1999

11/14/1998 to 02/21/1999	**PERMANENT COLLECTION DRAWINGS**
01/17/1999 to 04/11/1999	**JOHN VAN ALSTINE**
05/22/1999 to 08/22/1999	**GEORGE MCNEIL: THE LATE PAINTINGS**
07/31/1999 to 09/25/1999	**A LOADED BRUSH: NANCY BRETT: RECENT PAINTINGS**
09/25/1999 to 11/28/1999	**WARP AND WEFT: NAVAJO WEAVING**
10/09/1999 to 11/28/1999	**MELLISA MEYER**

HAMILTON

Picker Art Gallery

Affiliate Institution: Colgate University
Charles A Dana Center for the Creative Arts, Hamilton, NY 13346-1398
: 315-824-7634 http://picker.colgate.edu
Open: 10-5 Daily **Closed:** ACAD!; (also open by request!)
Museum Shop **Group Tours** **Drop-In Tours**
Permanent Collection: ANT; PTGS & SCULP 20; AS; AF

Located on the Colgate University campus, the setting of the Charles A. Dana Art Center is one of expansive lawns and tranquility. Exhibition information: 315-824-7746

ON EXHIBIT 1999

01/23/1999 to 04/04/1999 SALUTING THE SPIRITS: VOODOO FLAGS OF HAITI

03/07/1999 to 05/09/1999 "COMPANY SCHOOL PAINTINGS" AND "DEITIES" FROM THE COLLECTION OF CHANDRIKA AND RANJAN TANDON

04/04/1999 to 06/06/1999 ALAN PAULSON OUTDOOR SCULPTURE

HEMPSTEAD

Hofstra Museum

Affiliate Institution: Hofstra University
112 Hofstra University, Hempstead, NY 11549
: 516-463-5672
Open: 10-9 Tu, 10-5 We-Fr, 1-5 Sa, Su !varying hours in galleries **Closed:** Mo, Easter Wknd, Thgv Wknd, LEG/HOL
Vol/Cont **Museum Shop** **Group Tours** **Drop-In Tours** **Sculpture Garden**
Permanent Collection: SCULP: Henry Moore, H. J. Seward Johnson, Jr, Tony Rosenthal, Paul Manship, Greg Wyatt

Hofstra University is a living museum. Five exhibition areas are located throughout the 238-acre campus, which is also a national arboretum. **NOT TO BE MISSED:** Sondra Rudin Mack Garden designed by Oehme, Van Sweden and Assoc. Henry Moore's 'Upright Motive No. 9', and 'Hitchhiker', and Tony Rosenthal's 'T's, Greg Wyatt's "Hofstra Victory Eagle", Paul Manships's "Three Bears"

ON EXHIBIT 1999

01/31/1999 to 03/28/1999 UNFOLDING LIGHT: THE EVOLUTION OF TEN HOLOGRAPHERS
Holography is a process for recording images in three dimensions using a laser as a light source. Invented in the 40's, it was more fully developed in the 60's. While it has many industrial and commercial applications, it also has creative properties which can be used to make works of art. Subjects explored by artists include portraits, still lifes, landscapes, etc.. *Will Travel*

HOWES CAVE

Iroquois Indian Museum

Caverns Road, Howes Cave, NY 12092
: 518-296-8949 www.iroquoismuseum.org
Open: 10-5 daily April 1-12/31; Mo: Columbus Day, Mem/Day & 7/1-Lab/Day **Closed:** Mo, Easter, THGV, 12/24, 12/25
ADM **Adult:** $7.00 **Children:** $4 **Students:** $5.50 **Seniors:** $5.50
Museum Shop
Group Tours **Drop-In Tours** **Historic Building** two 1840's Iroquois log homes from Six Nations Reservation
Permanent Collection: Cont IROQUOIS art; local archeology; history

The Museum sees Iroquois arts as a window into the Iroquois culture. Exhibits and demonstrations focus on the visual and performing arts of contemporary Iroquois people and the creativity and tradition of their ancestors as expressed in historic and archeological artifacts. **NOT TO BE MISSED:** 'Corn Spirit' by Stanley Hill

HUDSON

Olana State Historic Site
State Route 9G, Hudson, NY 12534

📞: 518-828-0135
Open: 10-4 We-Su 4/1-11/1
Closed: Mo, Tu, open MEM/DAY, 7/4, LAB/DAY, Columbus Day (open Mo Holidays), closed Nov-Mar
ADM   Adult: $3.00   **Children:** $1.00(5-12)   **Seniors:** $2.00
  ♿ &#9physical; Ⓟ   **Museum Shop   Group Tours**: 518-828-0135   Drop-In Tours
Historic Building
Permanent Collection: FREDERIC CHURCH: ptgs, drgs; PHOT COLL; CORRESPONDENCE

Olana, the magnificent home of Hudson River School artist Frederic Edwin Church, was designed by him in the Persian style, and furnished in the Aesthetic style. He also designed the picturesque landscaped grounds. Many of Church's paintings are on view throughout the house. The house is only open by guided tour. Visitor's Center and grounds are open 7 days a week.

HUNTINGTON

Heckscher Museum of Art
2 Prime Ave, Huntington, NY 11743

📞: 516-351-3250
Open: 10-5 Tu-Fr, 1-5 Sa, Su, 1st Fr till 8:30   **Closed:** Mo
Adult: $3.00   **Children:** $1.00   **Students:** $1.00   **Seniors:** $1.00
   Ⓟ   **Museum Shop   Group Tours**: 516-357-3250   **Drop-In Tours**: 2:30, 3:30 Sa, Su; 1, 3 We   **Historic Building**
Permanent Collection: AM: ldscp ptg 19; AM: Modernist ptgs, drgs, works on paper

Located in a 18.5 acre park, the museum, whose collection numbers more than 900 works, was presented as a gift to the people of Huntington by philanthropist August Heckscher. The Museum closes for several days for installation of an exhibition. Call! **NOT TO BE MISSED:** 'Eclipse of the Sun', by George Grosz (not always on view!)

ON EXHIBIT 1999

11/21/1998 to 01/31/1999   MODERN AMERICAN REALISM: THE SARA ROBY FOUNDATION COLLECTION FROM THE NATIONAL MUSEUM OF AMERICAN ART
60 works drawn from one of the premiere collections of American figurative art including Raphael Soyer, Edward Hopper, Paul Cadmus, George Tooker and others. *Catalog Will Travel*

02/06/1999 to 04/18/1999   BETTY PARSONS: HER ART AND HER ARTISTS
Although best known for the artists she represented, art dealer Betty Parsons was also a talented artist. Featured are her works as well as those of Barnett Newman, Jackson Pollock, Mark Rothko and others.

05/15/1999 to 06/13/1999   ALLI'S 44TH ANNUAL LONG ISLAND ARTISTS EXHIBITION
The annual contemporary juried exhibition of the Art League of Long Island.

06/19/1999 to 08/29/1999   MAURICE PRENDERGAST IN THE WILLIAMS COLLEGE MUSEUM OF ART: THE STATE OF THE ESTATE
Works drawn from this large collection of the American Impressionists' oeuvre including early work and many of his personal favorites.

Fall 99 to Winter 00   MILLENNIUM MESSAGES
Approximately 40 major artists, architects and designers will create individual time capsules filled with either existing or newly made objects to identify significant aspects of the 20th C and to speak to people of future generations.

NEW YORK

Herbert F. Johnson Museum of Art

Affiliate Institution: Cornell University
Cornell University, Ithaca, NY 14853-4001
📞: 607-255-6464   📵 www.museum.cornell.edu
Open: 10-5 Tu-Su   **Closed:** Mo, MEM/DAY, 7/4, THGV + Fr
 👍 Ⓟ   **Museum Shop**   **Group Tours:** 607-255-6464   **Drop-In Tours:** 12 noon every other Th; 1 Sa, Su!
Historic Building IM Pei built in 1973   **Sculpture Garden**
Permanent Collection: AS; AM: gr 19, 20

The Gallery, in an I. M. Pei building with a view of Cayuga Lake, is located on the Cornell Campus in Ithaca, NY. **NOT TO BE MISSED:** 'Fields in the Month of June', by Daubigny

ON EXHIBIT 1999

08/28/1998 to 10/17/1999   **SEEING THE UNSEEN: DR. HAROLD EDGERTON AND THE WONDERS OF STROBE ALLEY**
Edgerton as a photographer was first of all a scientist and electrical engineer who investigated, measured and sought new facts about natural phenomenon. His photographic genius which he always downplayed, captured bullets in flight, athletes in motion, the flutter of hummingbird's wings and produced the picture of a drop of milk as it splashed into a saucer.

01/16/1999 to 03/07/1999   **SYLVIA MANGOLD PAINTINGS**

01/23/1999 to 03/14/1999   **RUBELL COLLECTION: CONTEMPORARY AMERICAN PAINTINGS**

01/23/1999 to 03/14/1999   **WOMEN PHOTOGRAPHERS**

03/27/1999 to 06/13/1999   **LIVINGSTON COLLECTION**

03/27/1999 to 06/13/1999   **STRONG HEARTS: NATIVE AMERICAN PHOTOGRAPHY**

05/01/1999 to 08/01/1999   **CORNELL'S ATTICS: COLLECTIONS AT CORNELL**

06/19/1999 to 08/18/1999   **VERHOEVEN COLLECTION**

08/1999 to 10/1999   **FAKES AND FORGERIES**

08/1999 to 10/1999   **NETSUKE**

08/1999 to 10/1999   **BYRD COLLECTION**

08/1999 to 10/1999   **DEHOOGHE WORKS FROM DALLETT COLLECTION**

08/28/1999 to 10/17/1999   **EDGERTON PHOTOS**

11/1999 to 01/2000   **CORNELL ART FACULTY**

Caramoor Center for Music and the Arts

149 Girdle Ridge Road, Katonah, NY 10536
📞: 914-232-5035   📵 www.caramoor.com
Open: 11-4 Tu-Sa, 1-4 S Jun-Sep, 11-4 We-Su Oct-May, by appt Mo-Fr Nov-May   **Closed:** Mo, Tu, LEG/HOL!
ADM   Adult: $6.00   **Children:** F under 16   **Students:** $6.00   **Seniors:** $6.00
 👍 Ⓟ   **Museum Shop**   🍴: Picnic facilities
Group Tours: 914-232-8076   **Drop-In Tours**: 1-3 We-Sun May-Oct, other times by appt.   **Historic Building**
Sculpture Garden
Permanent Collection: FURNITURE; PTGS; SCULP; DEC/ART; REN; OR: all media

Caramoor Center for Music and the Arts - continued

Built in the 1930s by Walter Rosen as a country home, this 54 room Mediterranean style mansion is a treasure trove of splendid collections spanning 2000 years. There are six unusual gardens including the Marjorie Carr Sense Circle (for sight-impaired individuals). Tours of the gardens are by appt spring and fall. Caramoor also presents a festival of outstanding concerts each summer and many other programs throughout the year. At 11 Wed Apr-Nov a short recital in the music room is followed by a tour of the house. High teas in the summer dining room. Reservations Required. Two exhibitions relating to Caramoor are mounted each year **NOT TO BE MISSED:** Extraordinary house-museum with entire rooms from European villas and palaces

Katonah Museum of Art

Route 22 at Jay Street, Katonah, NY 10536
☎: 914-232-9555 ▣ www.katonah-museum.org
Open: 1-5 Tu-Fr, Su, 10-5 Sa **Closed:** Mo, 1/1, MEM/DAY; PRESIDENTS/DAY, 7/4, THGV, 12/25
ADM Adult: $2.00 **Children:** $2.00 over 12 **Students:** $2.00 **Seniors:** $2.00
& ⓟ **Museum Shop** ❢: Snack bar
Group Tours: 914-232-3128 **Drop-In Tours:** 2:30pm
Sculpture Garden
Permanent Collection: No Permanent Collection

Moved to a building designed by Edward Larabee Barnes in 1990, the museum has a commitment to outstanding special exhibitions which bring to the community art of all periods, cultures and mediums.

ON EXHIBIT 1999

10/04/1998 to 02/28/1999 JAMES HORN: ANTHROPOMORPHIC SCULPTURE
Steel sculptures that pair iconic architecture with animal and human forms. A walk in the Sculpture Garden among these captivating pieces offers a thought-provoking lesson about man's relationship to his environment.

12/13/1998 to 02/28/1999 PRIVATE WORLDS: CLASSIC OUTSIDER ARTISTS FROM EUROPE
Works by the most compelling self-taught artists of the 20th C. -spiritualists, mediums, visionaries, and the institutionalized. Private worlds will offer proof that emotional imbalance need not mean mental deficiency.

03/14/1999 to 05/16/1999 RE-RIGHTING HISTORY: WORK BY CONTEMPORARY AFRICAN-AMERICAN ARTISTS
Artists include Robert Colescott, Beverly Buchanan, Carrie Mae Williams, Kara Walker, Lezley Saar, Radcliff Bailey and Adrien Piper.

07/18/1999 to 10/03/1999 MAZES

10/17/1999 to 01/02/2000 REFLECTIONS OF TIME AND PLACE: LATIN AMERICAN STILL LIFE IN THE 20TH CENTURY

LONG ISLAND CITY

Isamu Noguchi Garden Museum

32-37 Vernon Blvd, Long Island City, NY 11106
☎: 718-721-1932 ▣ www.noguchi.org
Open: 10-5, We-Fr,11-6 Sa, Su (Apr-Oct only)
Sugg/Cont Adult: $4.00 **Children:** $2.00 **Students:** $2.00 **Seniors:** $2.00
& ⓟ **Museum Shop**
Group Tours: 718-721-1932 x203 **Drop-In Tours:** 2 PM daily
Historic Building   Sculpture Garden
Permanent Collection: WORKS OF ISAMU NOGUCHI

Isamu Noguchi Garden Museum - continued

Designed by Isamu Noguchi,(1904-1988), this museum offers visitors the opportunity to explore the work of the artist on the site of his Long Island City studio. The centerpiece of the collection is a tranquil outdoor sculpture garden. PLEASE NOTE: A shuttle bus runs to the museum on Sat. & Sun. every hour on the half hour starting at 11:30am from the corner of Park Ave. & 70th St, NYC, and returns on the hour every hour till 5pm. The round trip fare is $5.00 and DOES NOT include the price of museum admission. **NOT TO BE MISSED:** Permanent exhibition of over 250 sculptures as well as models, drawings, and photo-documentation of works of Noguchi; stage sets designed for Martha Graham; paper light sculptures called Akari

P.S.1 Contemporary Arts Center

2225 Jackson Avenue, Long Island City, NY 11101
☎: 718-784-2084   ◙ www.ps1.com
Open: 12-6 We-Su   **Closed:** Mo, Tu, MEM/DAY, 7/4, LAB/DAY, THGV, 12/25
ADM   Adult: $4.00   **Children:** $2.00   **Students:** $2.00   **Seniors:** $2.00
♿ Ⓟ **Museum Shop**   �ⵏcoffee shop   **Group Tours   Drop-In Tours   Sculpture Garden**
Permanent Collection: CONT, AM

P.S.1 recognizes and introduces the work of emerging and lesser known artists. **NOT TO BE MISSED:** 'Meeting' by James Turrell, 1986

MOUNTAINVILLE

Storm King Art Center

Old Pleasant Hill Rd, Mountainville, NY 10953
☎: 914-534-3115
Open: 11-5:30 Daily (Apr-Nov.14), Special eve hours Sa, June, July, Aug   **Closed:** closed 11/15-3/31
ADM   Adult: $7.00   **Children:** F (under 5)   **Students:** $3.00   **Seniors:** $5.00
♿ Ⓟ **Museum Shop**
Group Tours: 914-534-3115 x110   **Drop-In Tours:** 2pm daily   **Historic Building   Sculpture Garden**
Permanent Collection: SCULP: Alice Aycock, Alexander Calder, Mark di Suvero, Andy Goldsworthy, Louise Nevelson, Isamu Noguchi, Richard Serra, David Smith, Kenneth Snelson

America's leading open-air sculpture museum features over 120 masterworks on view amid 500 acres of lawns, fields and woodlands. Works are also on view in a 1935 Normandy style building that has been converted to museum galleries. **NOT TO BE MISSED:** "Momo Taro," a 40 ton, nine-part sculpture by Isamu Noguchi designed for seating and based on Japanese Folk tale.

MUMFORD

Genesee Country Village & Museum

Flint Hill Road, Mumford, NY 14511
☎: 716-538-6822   ◙ www.history.rochester.edu/gcmuseum
Open: 10-5 Tu-Su July, Aug,10-4 Tu-F,10-5 Sa, Su Spring and Fall, season May-Oct   **Closed:** Mo
ADM   Adult: $10   **Children:** 4-10 $4.00 under 4 F   **Seniors:** $8.50
♿ **Museum Shop**   ⵏ   **Group Tours Drop-In Tours**
Permanent Collection: AM:Ptgs, sculp; AM/SW; late 19; NAT/AM; sculp;WILDLIFE art; EU&AM sport art 17-20

The outstanding J. F. Wehle collection of sporting art is housed in the only museum in New York specializing in sport, hunting and wildlife subjects. The collection and carriage museum are part of an assembled village of 19th century shops, homes and farm buildings.

College Art Gallery

Affiliate Institution: State University of New York at New Paltz
New Paltz, NY 12561

☎: 914-257-3844   ◙ www.newpaltz.edu/artgallery
Open: 11-4 Th, Fr, 2-4 Sa, Su, Tue eve 7-9   **Closed:** Mo, 1/1, EASTER, THGV & Fr, 12/24, 12/25, ACAD!
Ġ   Ⓟ   **Museum Shop**
Group Tours   Drop-In Tours
Permanent Collection: AM; gr, ptgs 19, 20; JAP: gr; CH: gr; P/COL; CONT: phot, P/Col artifacts, Anc. Grk & Rom artifacts, AF art & artifacts

A major cultural resource for the mid-Hudson Valley region., the College Art Gallery will be closed for most of 1999 for renovation and expansion. It will reopen in late 1999 as the Samuel Dorsky Museum of Art. **NOT TO BE MISSED:** The opening of the new Samuel Dorsky Museum of Art and the new installation of the museum's permanent collection which spans over 4,000 years.

See Astoria, Bayside, Bronx, Brooklyn, Flushing, Long Island City, New York, Queens and Staten Island

Alternative Museum

594 Broadway, New York, NY 10012

☎: 212-966-4444   ◙   www.alternativemuseum.org
Open: 11-6 We-Sa   **Closed:** Su, Mo, Tu, August, 12/24-1/2
Sugg/Cont   Adult: $3.00
Ġ   Ⓟ   **Museum Shop**
Group Tours Drop-In Tours
Permanent Collection: CONT

This contemporary arts institution is devoted to the exploration and dissemination of new avenues of thought on contemporary art and culture.

ON EXHIBIT 1999

02/12/1999 to 04/03/1999   LIFE, LIBERTY AND OUR PURSUIT OF HAPPINESS
A timely and important photography project focusing on current world-wide human rights movements. It will document key global struggles being enacted today. *Will Travel*

04/14/1999 to 05/29/1999   EXPANSION ARTS: ARTISTS OF OUR TIMES III
An annual exhibition highlighting the work of emerging artistes from diverse ethnic, racial and national backgrounds who in some manner incorporate the use of technology to convey issues such as gender, cultural icons, ethnicity, violence and national dislocation.

06/10/1999 to 07/24/1999   SHOWCASE 99
Emerging artists from all regions of the country who have been under-represented in the New York area.

NEW YORK

Americas Society

680 Park Avenue, New York, NY 10021

☎: 212-249-8950   ◙ www.americas-society.org
Open: 12-6 Tu-Su   **Closed:** Mo, 7/4,THGV,12/24,12/25
♿ ℗ **Museum Shop   Group Tours** Drop-In Tours   **Historic Building**
Permanent Collection: No permanent collection

Located in a historic neo federal townhouse built in 1909, the goal of the Americas Society is to increase public awareness of the rich cultural heritage of our geographic neighbors.

ON EXHIBIT 1999

02/09/1999 to 04/18/1999   GERARDO SUTER
A Mid career retrospective of the Argentine artist living in Mexico, whose work includes monumentally scaled photographs, videos, and installation.

Fall 1999   GONZALO FONSECA
Fonseca passed away in June 1997. This memorial exhibition will trace his career as on of the most accomplished Latin American sculptors and will be an in depth examination of his achievements. *Catalog*

Asia Society

725 Park Ave, New York, NY 10021

☎: 212-517-ASIA   ◙ www.asiasociety.org
Open: 11-6 Tu-Sa, 11-8 Th, 12-5 Su   **Closed:** Mo, LEG/HOL!
Free Day: Th 6-8pm   **ADM   Adult:** $4.00   **Children:** $2.00, F under 12   **Students:** $2.00   **Seniors:** $2.00
♿ ℗ **Museum Shop   Group Tours:** 212-288-6400   **Drop-In Tours:** 12:30 Tu-Sa, 6:30 Th, 2:30 Su
Permanent Collection: The Mr. and Mrs. John D. Rockefeller 3rd Collection of Asian Art

The Asia Society is America's leading institution dedicated to fostering understanding of Asia and communication between Americans and the peoples of Asia and the Pacific.

ON EXHIBIT 1999

09/15/1998 to 01/17/1999   INSIDE OUT: NEW CHINESE ART
Concepts of "modernity" and "identity" are undergoing rapid transformation in the Chinese world as Asian societies evolve in the post-1980s climate of radical social, economic and political change. This major exhibition is the first to bring together more than 100 works from various parts of the Chinese world including Taiwan, Hong Kong and outside of Asia. The political and economic change will be traced in the work of artists who worked in Asia before Tiananmen and outside after. Some of the works will be at the P.S. 1 Contemporary Art Center in Long Island City, New York *Catalog Will Travel*

Spring 99   JAPANESE BASKETS AS SCULPTURE
Woven bamboo baskets and related types are shown to reveal the sculptural quality of the medium usually appreciated for its functional beauty. Types shown will illustrate the relationship of styles to different tea and flower-arranging schools, the development of signed baskets, and hereditary lineages among basket makers.

Chaim Gross Studio Museum

526 LaGuardia Place, New York, NY 10012

☎: 212-529-4906
Open: 12-6 Tu-Sa.   **Closed:** Su, Mo,, LEG/HOL
♿ ℗ **Museum Shop   Group Tours   Drop-In Tours:** by appt   **Historic Building**
Permanent Collection: Sculp, wood, stone, bronze; sketches, w/c, prints

A seventy year sculpture collection of several hundred Chaim Gross (1904-1991) works housed on three floors of the Greenwich Village building which was the artist's home and studio for thirty-five years. The studio is left intact and is also open to the public. **NOT TO BE MISSED:** "Roosevelt and Hoover in a Fistfight" 1932, Mahogany 72x20x1 ½. The 1932 cubist inspired wood sculptures were done in the only year when Gross submitted to modernist influences. Also "The Lindbergh Family-Charles A."; 2 Totemic columns

China Institute Gallery, China Institute in America
125 East 65th Street, New York, NY 10021-7088

☎: 212-744-8181 ▣ www.chinainstitute.org

Open: 10-5 Mo, We-Sa, 1-5 Su, 10-8 Tu **Closed:** LEG/HOL!, CHINESE NEW YEAR

Adult: $5.00 **Children:** F **Students:** $3.00 **Seniors:** $3.00

& ℗ **Museum Shop** **Group Tours Drop-In Tours**: Varies **Historic Building**

Permanent Collection: Non-collecting institution

The only museum in New York and one of five in the entire country specializing in exhibitions of Chinese art and civilization. The Gallery reaches out to people interested in learning about and staying connected to China.

ON EXHIBIT 1999

01/07/1999 to 02/24/1999 CHINESE LITERATI IN THE TWENTIETH CENTURY: CHINESE PAINTINGS AND CALLIGRAPHY FROM THE WANG FANGYU COLLECTION

03/26/1999 to 06/20/1999 EARLY CHINESE CERAMICS FROM THE MEIYINTANG COLLECTION

The Cloisters
Affiliate Institution: The Metropolitan Museum of Art

Fort Tryon Park, New York, NY 10040

☎: 212-923-3700

Open: 9:30-5:15 Tu-Su (3/1-10/30), 9:30-4:45 Tu-Su (11/1-2/28) **Closed:** Mo, 1/1, THGV, 12/25

Sugg/Cont Adult: $8 inc Met Museum **Children:** F (under12) **Students:** $4.00 **Seniors:** $4.00

& ℗ **Museum Shop** **Group Tours Drop-In Tours**: !

Historic Building 1938 bldg resembling med monastery, incorporates actual med arch elements

Permanent Collection: ARCH: Med/Eu; TAPESTRIES; ILLUMINATED MANUSCRIPTS; STAINED GLASS; SCULP; LITURGICAL OBJECTS

This unique 1938 building set on a high bluff in a tranquil park overlooking the Hudson River recreates a medieval monastery in both architecture and atmosphere. Actual 12th - 15th century medieval architectural elements are incorporated within various elements of the structure which is filled with impressive art and artifacts of the era. **NOT TO BE MISSED:** 'The Unicorn Tapestries'; 'The Campin Room'; Gardens; Treasury; the 'Belles Heures' illuminated manuscript of Jean, Duke of Breey

Cooper-Hewitt, National Design Museum, Smithsonian Institution
2 East 91st Street, New York, NY 10128

☎: 212 849 8300 ▣ www.si.edu/ndm

Open: 10-9 Tu, 10-5 We-Sa, Noon-5 Su **Closed:** Mo, LEG/HOL!

Free Day: Th 5-9 **ADM Adult:** $5.00 **Children:** F, under 12 **Students:** $3.00 **Seniors:** $3.00

& ℗ **Museum Shop**

Group Tours: 212-849-8389 **Drop-In Tours**: times vary; call 212-849-8389 **Historic Building** **Sculpture Garden**

Permanent Collection: DRGS; TEXTILES; DEC/ART; CER

Cooper Hewitt, housed in the landmark Andrew Carnegie Mansion, has more than 250,000 objects which represent 3000 years of design history from cultures around the world. It is the only museum on Museum Mile with an outdoor planted garden and lawn open during regular museum hours-weather permitting.

ON EXHIBIT 1999

10/06/1998 to 01/10/1999 THE ARCHITECTURE OF REASSURANCE: DESIGNING THE DISNEY THEME PARKS

Uniquely American in its origins, the Disney theme park, whether admired or reviled, has become an international phenomenon. For the first time the intentions and methods of the Imagineers (as the design team for the parks is called) will be investigated. Approximately 300 objects, most never before available for public viewing, will be shown. *Catalog Will Travel*

Cooper-Hewitt, National Design Museum, Smithsonian Institution - continued
11/17/1998 to 03/21/1999   UNLIMITED BY DESIGN
The first major exhibition of products, services and environments designed to meet the needs of all people throughout their lifespan. Included will be the familiar, kitchens, bathroom, playground and public signage, as well as interactive computer technologies. The Museum conviction is that design can and does affect the quality of life for all people.

02/09/1999 to 05/30/1999   GRAPHIC DESIGN IN THE MECHANICAL AGE: SELECTIONS FROM THE MERRILL C. BERMAN COLLECTION
200 works of international graphic design drawn from one of the world's premier private collections including posters, paintings, drawings, collages etc. created between the two World Wars. *Will Travel*

04/27/1999 to 08/08/1999   THE HUGUENOT LEGACY: ENGLISH SILVER, 1680-1760
Featured will be special pieces from grand ambassadorial services, works by Paul de Lamerie and David Willaume and elaborately decorated tureens, etc. by silversmiths trained in the fashion of the French courts.

06/29/1999 to 09/12/1999   EL NUEVO MUNDO/THE NEW WORLD: THE LANDSCAPE OF LATINO L.A.
In approximately 130 color photographs by Camilo Jose Vergara, the profound changes in the physical character and social texture of Los Angeles as its population has become increasingly Latino.

09/14/1999 to 02/06/2000   CONTEMPORARY JEWELRY: SELECTIONS FROM THE HELEN WILLIAMS DRUTT COLLECTION
The field of art jewelry, individual pieces created as one-of-a-kind objects or in small limited editions, has influenced the most creative and provocative work in jewelry design over the past 30 years. This outstanding collection including works by artists from North America, Europe, Australia, New Zealand and Japan will be presented in its only New York showing.

10/12/1999 to 01/02/2000   THE WORK OF CHARLES AND RAY EAMES: A LEGACY OF INVENTION
The first posthumous retrospective of the work of the American husband and wife team considered among the greatest designers of the 20th C will present more than 500 objects created between the 1940s and 1970s.

Dahesh Museum
601 Fifth Avenue, New York, NY 10017
☎: 212-759-0606
Open: 11-6 Tu-Sa   **Closed:** Su, M, LEG/HOL!
Vol/Cont   ♿   ⓟ   **Museum Shop   Group Tours   Drop-In Tours**: lunchtime daily
Permanent Collection: Acad pntg;19, 20

More than 3,000 works collected by writer, philosopher Salim Achi who was known as Dr. Dahesh form the collection of this relatively new museum housed on the second floor of a commercial building built in 1911. Included are works by Auguste Bonheur, Luc-Olivier Merson, Henri Picou, Constant Troyon.

ON EXHIBIT 1999
09/22/1998 to 01/02/1999   FRENCH OIL SKETCHES AND THE ACADEMIC TRADITION
This exhibition draws on one of the great private collections of oil sketches and reveals the importance and range of such paintings. The works shown have not been previously seen in New York and will not travel. Included are examples by Jouet, Boucheer and Gerome. *Catalog*

01/19/1999 to 04/17/1999   A VICTORIAN SALON: PAINTINGS FROM THE RUSSELL-COTES ART GALLERY AND MUSEUM, BOURNEMOUTH, ENGLAND
The 50 important paintings from this exceptional collection are being shown in the US because of the renovation of their home. Included are works by Moore, Long, Rossetti and Godward. *Will Travel*

06/08/1999 to 08/28/1999   REVEALING THE HOLY LAND: THE PHOTOGRAPHIC EXPLORATIONS OF PALESTINE
Rare and exquisite 19th C photographs which document the most historic area in the Middle East. Beginning with Maxime Du Camp in the 1840s and 50s and including Saltzmann's images from 1856, the exhibition includes copies of the original stereoscopic cards. *Catalog Will Travel*

09/14/1999 to 01/2000   THE WOMEN OF THE ACADEMIE JULIAN
The Julian was particularly important because it was the principal atelier which accepted women until the end of the 19th C. Among the Americans who studied there were Anna Klumpke, Elizabeth Gardner Bouguereau and Celia Beaux. Early in the 20th C Louise Bourgeouis studied there.

Dia Center for the Arts
548 West 22nd Street, New York, NY 10011
☏: 212-989-5566 ◉ www.diacenter.org
Open: 12-6 Th-Su Sep-Jun **Closed:** Mo-We, LEG/HOL!
Adult: $4.00 **Children:** F under 10 **Students:** $2.00 **Seniors:** $2.00
⚅ ℗ **Museum Shop** ❢❢: Rooftop café and video lounge **Group Tours Drop-In Tours**
Permanent Collection: not permanently on view

With several facilities and collaborations Dia has committed itself to working with artists to determine optimum environments for their most ambitious and uncompromising works which are usually on view for extended exhibition periods. **NOT TO BE MISSED:** Two Walter De Maria extended exhibitions, THE NEW YORK EARTH ROOM at the gallery at 141 Wooster Street and THE BROKEN KILOMETER at 393 Broadway. Both are open 12-6 W-Sa, closed July and August, adm F

ON EXHIBIT 1999
09/10/1998 to 06/13/1999 JOSEPH BUEYS: DRAWINGS AFTER THE CODICES MADRID OF LEONARDO DA VINCI, AND SCULPTURE
Bueys executed this suite of 96 pencil drawings which he did in 1974 for a book, a multiple, inspired by the lost manuscript of Codices Madrid.

09/10/1998 to 06/13/1999 ROBERT IRWIN: EXCURSUS: HOMAGE TO THE SQUARE
An array of brightly colored lights into the eighteen chambers identified by scrims, which he created for the first part of the exhibition.

09/24/1998 to 06/13/1999 THOMAS SHUTTE: SCENEWRIGHT
Dia will explore in detail works created over the past 20 years by this mid-career German artist.

11/1998 to 06/13/1999 ANDY WARHOL: SHADOWS
Andy Warhol's series of 102 paintings will constitute the second exhibition at Dia's new facility at 545 West 22nd St.

Drawing Center
35 Wooster Street, New York, NY 10013
☏: 212-219-2166
Open: 10-6 Tu-Fr,11-6 Sa **Closed:** Su, Mo, 1/1, 12/25, AUGUST
Vol/Cont ⚅ ℗ **Museum Shop Group Tours** Drop-In Tours **Historic Building**

Featured at The Drawing Center are contemporary and historical drawings and works on paper both by internationally known and emerging artists.

ON EXHIBIT 1999
01/09/1999 to 02/06/1999 SELECTIONS WINTER '99

04/1999 to 06/1999 CONTEMPORARY IRISH DRAWING (working title)

04/1999 to 06/1999 ARTISTS COLLECT (working title)
Works on paper from the collections of Jasper Johns, Sol Lewitt, Helen and Brice Marden, and Ellsworth Kelly.

El Museo del Barrio
1230 Fifth Ave, New York, NY 10029-4496
☏: 212-831-7272 ◉ www.elmuseo.org
Open: 11-5 We-Su **Closed:** Mo-Tu, LEG/HOL!
Adult: $4.00 **Children:** F (under 12) **Students:** $2.00 **Seniors:** $2.00
⚅ ℗ **Museum Shop Group Tours Drop-In Tours**
Permanent Collection: LAT/AM: P/COL; CONT: drgs, phot, sculp

One of the foremost Latin American cultural institutions in the United States, this museum is also the only one in the country that specializes in the arts and culture of Puerto Rico. **NOT TO BE MISSED:** Santos: Sculptures Between Heaven and Earth

NEW YORK

Equitable Gallery

787 Seventh Avenue, New York, NY 10019

☎: 212-554-4818
Open: 11-6 Mo-Fr, 12-5 Sa   **Closed:** Su, LEG/HOL, 12/24
♿ ℗ **Museum Shop** ⊪: 3 fine restaurants located in the space overlooking the Galleria
Group Tours Drop-In Tours
Permanent Collection: Public art in lobby of Equitable Tower: Roy Lichtenstein's Mural with Blue Brushstroke

The gallery presents works from all fields of the visual arts that would not otherwise have a presence in New York City.

Frick Collection

1 East 70th Street, New York, NY 10021

☎: 212-288-0700   ◙ www.frick.org
Open: 10-6 Tu-Sa, 1-6 Su, also open 2/12, Election Day, 11/11   **Closed:** Mo, 1/1, 7/4, THGV, 12/24, 12/25
ADM Adult: $7.00   **Children:** under 10 not adm   **Students:** $5.00   **Seniors:** $5.00
♿ ℗ **Museum Shop Group Tours** Drop-In Tours   **Historic Building   Sculpture Garden**
Permanent Collection: PTGS; SCULP; FURNITURE; DEC/ART; Eur, Or, PORCELAINS

The beautiful Henry Clay Frick mansion built in 1913-14, houses this exceptional collection while preserving the ambiance of the original house. In addition to the many treasures to be found here, the interior of the house offers the visitor a tranquil respite from the busy pace of city life outside of its doors. Beginning Fall 1998 free Acoustiguide INFORM tour will be available in English, Spanish, French, German, Japanese PLEASE NOTE: Children under 10 are not permitted in the museum and those from 11-16 must be accompanied by an adult. **NOT TO BE MISSED:** Boucher Room; Fragonard Room; Paintings by Rembrandt, El Greco, Holbein and Van Dyck; 3 works by Vermeer.

ON EXHIBIT 1999

10/14/1998 to 01/17/1999   VICTORIAN FAIRY PAINTING
Critically and commercially popular during the 19th C. this distinctly British genre of Fairy Painting signal the public's avid and continuing absorption with this subject. Drawn from public and private collections, the works include Richard Dadd, John Amster Fitzgerald, Daniel Maclise, and Sir Joseph Noel Paton. Also included are surprises such as Sir Edwin Landseer, Sir John Everett Millais, and J.M.W. Turner. *Catalog Will Travel*

01/26/1999 to 04/25/1999   DROUHAIS' PORTRAIT OF MADAME DE POMPADOUR FROM THE NATIONAL GALLERY, LONDON
By special arrangement, the full length portrait of Madame de Pompadour will be on public view in the US for the first time. The portrait was painted in 1763, the last year of her life. She is surrounded by objects which reflect her taste as a great patron of the arts and letters, *Brochure Will Travel*

02/08/1999 to 04/26/1999   FRENCH AND ENGLISH DRAWINGS OF THE EIGHTEENTH AND NINETEENTH CENTURIES FROM THE NATIONAL GALLERY OF CANADA
A stunning collection of old master and nineteenth century drawings seldom travels. For the first time in more than a decade, American audiences will have an opportunity to view these 68 exceptional works. The British works which represent the largest portion of the drawings include Burne-Jones, Constable, Hogarth, Rossetti, Turner and West. The French artists include, Bonnard, Boucher, Courbet, David, Degas, Delacroix, Fragonard, Ingres and Watteau. *Catalog Will Travel*

05/11/1999 to 07/08/1999   THE MEDIEVAL HOUSEBOOK
This is a compendium of secular texts and illustrations providing a remarkable look at the princely court at the end of the late middle ages. The manuscript which has only been exhibited twice in this century and for the first time, all the illustrations can be viewed. The pages and drawings in each venue take a different form. The catalog will be available in the shop. *Catalog Will Travel*

10/18/1999 to 01/09/2000   WATTEAU AND HIS WORLD: FRENCH DRAWINGS FROM 1700-1750
The drawings of Watteau are an unrivaled achievement of observation and imagination, a window onto the lost world, and a glimpse into the creative mind that came to define his age. *Catalog Will Travel*

260

George Gustav Heye Center of the National Museum of the American Indian
Affiliate Institution: Smithsonian Institution
One Bowling Green, New York, NY 10004

☎: 212-668-6624 ◉ www.si.edu/nmai
Open: 10-5 daily, 10-8 Th **Closed:** 12/25
&. Ⓟ **Museum Shop Group Tours**: 212-825-8096 **Drop-In Tours**: daily! **Historic Building**
Permanent Collection: NAT/AM; Iroq silver, jewelry, NW Coast masks

The Heye Foundation collection contains more than 1,000,000 works which span the entire Western Hemisphere and present a new look at Native American peoples and cultures. Newly opened in the historic Alexander Hamilton Customs House, it presents masterworks from the collection and contemporary Indian art.

ON EXHIBIT 1999

ONGOING CREATION'S JOURNEY: MASTERWORKS OF NATIVE AMERICAN IDENTITY AND BELIEF
Objects of beauty and historical significance, representing numerous cultures throughout the Americas, ranging from 3200 B.C. to the present will be on display. CAT

ONGOING ALL ROADS ARE GOOD: NATIVE VOICES ON LIFE AND CULTURE
Artifacts chosen by 23 Indian selectors. CAT

ONGOING THIS PATH WE TRAVEL: CELEBRATIONS OF CONTEMPORARY NATIVE AMERICAN CREATIVITY
Collaborative exhibition featuring works by 15 contemporary Indian artists. CAT

03/28/1999 to 07/25/1999 POMO INDIAN BASKET WEAVERS
This exhibition of 110 baskets and 100 Historical photos examines the effect of the art market on the lives of 50 Pomo women, their families, community and basketry during 1900-1915.

05/02/1999 to 08/15/1999 INSTRUMENTS OF CHANGE: JAMES SCHOPPERT RETROSPECTIVE, 1947-TO 1992
Tlinget artist Schoppert is showcased against 50 objects which include, pottery, carvings, masks and jewelry. Schoppert challenged the traditional norms which may have contributed to the norms of Tlinget art while serving as a spokesperson for all Alaskan Native artists.

06/26/1999 to indefinite/ SPIRIT CAPTURE: NATIVE AMERICANS AND THE PHOTOGRAPHIC IMAGE.
Photographs which will reveal new and deeper images in the development of cultural Stereotypes.

10/17/1999 to 03/2000 RESERVATION X
Installation pieces by native artists

Grey Art Gallery and Study Center
Affiliate Institution: New York University Art Collection
100 Washington Square East, New York, NY 10003-6619

☎: 212-998-6780 ◉ www.nyu.edu/greyart
Open: 11-6 Tu, Th, Fri, 11-8 We, 11-6 Sa **Closed:** Su, Mo,, LEG/HOL!
Adult: $2.00
&. Ⓟ **Museum Shop**
Group Tours Drop-In Tours
Permanent Collection: AM: ptgs 1940-present; CONT; AS; MID/EAST

Located at Washington Square Park and adjacent to Soho, the Grey Art Gallery occupies the site of the first academic fine arts department in America established by Samuel F. B. Morse in 1835.

NEW YORK

Grey Art Gallery and Study Center - continued
ON EXHIBIT 1999

11/17/1998 to 01/16/1999   COUNTER CULTURE; PARISIAN CABARETS AND THE AVANT-GARDE, 1875-1905
The first truly avant-garde communities of artists, composers, and performers congregated in Montmartre, Using humor and non-traditional media these forerunners of Dada and Surrealism created ephemeral and conceptual performances, satires, and parodies that challenged the academic worlds of art, literature and politics.

01/27/1999 to 02/20/1999   FIRST STEPS II: EMERGING ARTISTS FROM JAPAN
This biennial competition was established to discover, nurture, and support young artists in Japan and stimulate recognition for their work. Cutting edge works in diverse media by seven emerging artists will be presented. They were also awarded a stipend.

03/09/1999 to 05/08/1999   PROJECTED SELVES: CAHUN, DEREN, SHERMAN AND PHOTOGRAPHIC TRANSFORMATION
Self-projection has been central to photographic portraiture since the invention of the medium. This exhibition explores the diverse expressive means through which these three artists enact their creative self-transformations. By placing Cindy Sherman in the context of the extraordinary women who preceded her the curators strive to re-evaluate not only her post-modern work but also the feminist and modernist history of which she is a part.,

06/25/1999 to 07/31/1999   WHEN TIME BEGAN TO RANT AND RAGE: TWENTIETH CENTURY FIGURATIVE PAINTING FROM IRELAND
Taking its title from a poem by William Butler Yeats, this is the most significant examination of modern Irish art ever to be held in the United States. It traces the development of a distinctly Irish identity in the visual arts from the 1890s to the present as well as the great independence movement from its beginning to the present day. The approximately 70 works include those by Sir John Lavery, Jack B. Yeats and contemporary artists. *Catalog Will Travel*

Guggenheim Museum Soho
575 Broadway at Prince St, New York, NY 10012
☎: 212-423-3500   ▣ www.guggenheim.org
Open: 11-6 S, We-Fr, 11-8 Sa   **Closed:** Mo, Tu, 1/1, 12/25
ADM   Adult: $8.00   **Children:** F (under 12)   **Students:** $5.00   **Seniors:** $5.00
 よ Ⓟ **Museum Shop** ¶¶ **Group Tours**: 212-423-3652   Drop-In Tours   **Historic Building**
Permanent Collection: INTERNATIONAL CONT ART

As a branch of the main museum uptown, this facility, located in a historic building in Soho, was designed as a museum by Arata Isozaki. There is a special 7 day pass to the Museum and the Solomon R. Guggenheim Museum. The cost is Adults $16, Stu/Sen $10

ON EXHIBIT 1999

ONGOING   ENEL Electronic reading room

ONGOING   ENEL Virtual Reality Gallery

10/14/1998 to 01/1999   PREMISES: INVESTED SPACES IN VISUAL ARTS AND ARCHITECTURE FROM FRANCE

Spring 1999   JOSEPH BUEYS

Summer 1999   DAKIS JOANNOW COLLECTION

Fall 1999   1900: PART AT THE CROSSROADS

Hispanic Society of America

155th Street and Broadway, New York, NY 10032

☎: 212-926-2234   ◙ www.hispanicsociety.org
Open: 10-4:30 Tu-Sa, 1-4 Su   **Closed:** Mo, LEG/HOL!
Vol/Cont
  Ⓟ   **Museum Shop   Group Tours** x254   Drop-In Tours   **Historic Building   Sculpture Garden**
Permanent Collection: SP: ptgs, sculp; arch; HISPANIC

Representing the culture of Hispanic peoples from prehistory to the present, this facility is one of several diverse museums located within the same complex on Audubon Terrace in NYC. **NOT TO BE MISSED:** Paintings by El Greco, Goya, Velazquez , Sorolla, Renaissance tomb sculptures

International Center of Photography

1130 Fifth Avenue,& Midtown, 1133 Avenue of the Americas, 10036, New York, NY 10128

☎: 212-860-1777   ◙ www.icp.org
Open: 11-8 Tu, 11-6 We-Su   **Closed:** Mo, 1/1, 7/4, THGV, 12/25
Vol/Cont: 6-8PM Tu   **ADM   Adult:** $5.50   **Students:** $4.00   **Seniors:** $4.00
  Ⓟ   **Museum Shop**   ⅈ: Nearby   **Group Tours:** 212-860-1777 x154   Drop-In Tours   **Historic Building**
Permanent Collection: DOCUMENTARY PHOT: 20

ICP was established in 1974 to present exhibitions of photography, to promote photographic education at all levels, and to study 20th century images, primarily documentary. The uptown museum is housed in a 1915 Neo-Georgian building designed by Delano and Aldrich.

ON EXHIBIT 1999

03/12/1999 to 06/06/1999   NEWMAN'S GIFT: 50 YEARS OF PHOTOGRAPHY

06/12/1999 to 09/16/1999   SEA CHANGE: THE SEASCAPE IN CONTEMPORARY PHOTOGRAPHY
The vast expanse of the sea is most often seen in paintings, poetry and literature. The 19 artists shown here share their preoccupation with the sea and the extraordinary possibilities of the seascape. *Will Travel*

Japan Society Gallery

333 E. 47th Street, New York, NY 10017

☎: 212-832-1155
Open: 11-5 Tu-Su   **Closed:** Mo, LEG/HOL!
Sugg/Cont   Adult: $3.00   **Children:** $3.00   **Students:** $3.00   **Seniors:** $3.00
  Ⓟ   **Museum Shop**
Group Tours: 212-715-1253   Drop-In Tours   **Historic Building   Sculpture Garden**
Permanent Collection: JAPANESE ART

Exhibitions of the fine arts of Japan are presented along with performing and film arts at the Japan Society Gallery which attempts to promote better understanding and cultural enlightenment between the peoples of the U.S. and Japan.

ON EXHIBIT 1999

01/19/1998 to 01/10/1999   THE ART OF TWENTIETH CENTURY ZEN
The first exhibition in America to present a survey of painting and calligraphy by Japan's greatest Zen masters of the 20th C. *Catalog Will Travel*

NEW YORK

Jewish Museum

1109 5th Ave., New York, NY 10128

☎: 212-423-3200   ◙ www.thejewishmuseum.org
Open: 11-5:45 Su, Mo, We & Th, 11-8 Tu   **Closed:** Fr, Sa, JEWISH/HOL, Martin Luther King Day, THGV
Free Day: Tu after 5   **ADM**   **Adult:** $7.00   **Children:** F (under 12)   **Students:** $5.00   **Seniors:** $5.00
 ੬ ℗ **Museum Shop**   ⵊ: Café Weissman, kosher cuisine
Group Tours: 212-423-3225   **Drop-In Tours:** Noon & 2:30 Mo-Th   **Historic Building**
Permanent Collection: JUDAICA: ptgs by Jewish and Israeli artists; ARCH; ARTIFACTS

27,000 works of art and artifacts covering 4000 years of Jewish history created by Jewish artists or illuminating the Jewish experience are displayed in the original building (the 1907 Felix Warburg Mansion), and in the new addition added in 1993. The collection is the largest of its kind outside of Israel. CULTURE AND CONTINUITY: THE JEWISH JOURNEY The centerpiece of the Museum is a core exhibition on the Jewish experience that conveys the essence of Jewish identity – the basic ideas, values and culture developed over 4000 years. **NOT TO BE MISSED:** 'Vilna Nights' by Eleanor Antin

ON EXHIBIT 1999

11/08/1998 to 03/07/1999   COMMON MAN, MYTHIC VISION: THE PAINTINGS OF BEN SHAHN
Over 50 of the finest paintings created by Shahn between 1936-1962. It begins with the wartime shift in his work from social realism to 'personal realism' and culminates in the series of paintings, "The Lucky Dragon" inspired by the fate of a fishing crew exposed to nuclear testing in Japan. *Catalog Will Travel*

02/07/1999 to 05/16/1999   IKAT: SPLENDID SILKS FROM CENTRAL ASIA
Examples of Ikat textiles, created by a method of weaving in which warp threads are tie-dyed before being set up on a loom, will be on loan from one of the most significant private collections of its kind. Traditionally woven and used by nomadic Uzbek peoples, the manufacture of these textiles has influenced contemporary fashion designer Oscar de la Renta , textile manufacturer Brunschwig et Fils and others. *Catalog Will Travel*

04/18/1999 to 09/09/1999   SIGMUND FREUD: CULTURE AND CONFLICT

06/20/1999 to 10/17/1999   FACING WEST: ORIENTAL JEWS OF CENTRAL ASIA AND THE CAUCASUS

The Metropolitan Museum of Art

5th Ave at 82nd Street, New York, NY 10028

☎: 212-879-5500   ◙ www.metmuseum.org
Open: 9:30-5:15 Tu-Th, Su, 9:30-9pm Fr, Sa   **Closed:** Mo, THGV,12/25, 1/1
Sugg/Cont   Adult: $8.00   **Children:** F (under 12)   **Students:** $4.00   **Seniors:** $4.00
 ੬ ℗ **Museum Shop**   ⵊ: Y
Group Tours: 212-570-3711   Drop-In Tours   **Historic Building**   **Sculpture Garden**
Permanent Collection: EU: all media; GR & DRGS: Ren-20; MED; GR; PHOT; AM: all media; DEC/ART: all media; AS: all media; AF; ISLAMIC; CONT; AN/EGT; AN/R; AN/AGR; AN/ASSYRIAN

The Metropolitan is the largest world class museum of art in the Western Hemisphere. Its comprehensive collections includes more than 2 million works from the earliest historical artworks through those of modern times and from all areas of the world. Just recently, the museum opened the Florence & Herbert Irving Galleries for the Arts of South & Southeast Asia, one of the best and largest collections of its kind in the world. **NOT TO BE MISSED:** Temple of Dendur; The 19th century European Paintings & Sculpture galleries (21 in all), designed to present the permanent collection in chronological order and to accommodate the promised Walter Annenberg collection now on view approximately 6 months annually.

The Metropolitan Museum of Art - continued
ON EXHIBIT 1999

New and Recently Opened Installations:
SCULPTURE AND DECORATIVE ARTS OF THE QUATTROCENTO
NEW CHINESE GALLERIES
THE NEW AMARNA GALLERIES: EGYPTIAN ART 1353-1295 B.C.
PHASE 1 OF THE NEW GREEK AND ROMAN ART GALLERIES: THE ROBERT & RENEE BELFER COURT
STUDIOLO FROM THE PALACE OF DUKE FEDERICO DE MONTEFELTRO AT GUBBIO
THE AFRICAN GALLERY
ANTONIO RATTI TEXTILE CENTER

07/23/1998 to 01/31/1999   LOUIS COMFORT TIFFANY AT THE METROPOLITAN MUSEUM OF ART
Drawn exclusively from the Museum's holdings the exhibition celebrates the 150th anniversary of Tiffany's birth. Examples of his decorative art objects, as well as some drawings, will be on view. A Museum Bulletin on the subject will be published.

09/10/1998 to 01/10/1999   THE NATURE OF ISLAMIC ORNAMENT, PART II: VEGETAL DESIGN
This the second in a four part series of exhibitions which explore in various media from the Museum's permanent collection, the vegetal and floral patterns used in the ornamentation of Islamic art.

09/16/1998 to 02/28/1999   JADE IN ANCIENT COSTA RICA
Costa Rica was one of only two regions in pre-Columbian America which used jade extensively in ancient times. The distinct, personal ornaments combined human and animal imagery with the shape of a functional tool or celt. The objects shown, dating from 300 B.C. to A.D. 700, are drawn primarily from museum collections in Costa Rica. *Catalog*

09/22/1998 to 01/03/1999   FROM VAN EYCK TO BREUGEL: EARLY NETHERLANDISH PAINTINGS IN THE METROPOLITAN MUSEUM OF ART
The Museum's comprehensive collection of early Netherlandish painting will be shown here for the first time. More than 100 paintings from various collections in the Museum will be brought together and organized thematically to shed new light on this important period in European painting. A number of loan works will also be shown. *Catalog Will Travel*

10/06/1998 to 01/17/1999   SACRED VISIONS: EARLY PAINTING FROM TIBET
This is the first exhibition to concentrate solely on early Tibetan painting. It brings together approximately 60 of the finest Tibetan thankas and painted objects known from the mid-11th to the mid-15th century. *Catalog*

10/08/1998 to 01/17/1999   HEROIC ARMOR OF THE ITALIAN RENAISSANCE: FILIPPO NEGROLI AND HIS CONTEMPORARIES
Created in Milan in 1530-1550, Negrolli and his workshop displayed a virtuoso skill at modeling in high relief. The exhibition includes all the signed or firmly attributed armors by him and his atelier as well as works by contemporary armorers and a number of paintings, drawings, and engravings illustrating the history of antique-style armor in Renaissance Italy. *Catalog*

10/14/1998 to 01/03/1999   EDGAR DEGAS, PHOTOGRAPHER
35 rare photographs accompanied by some paintings, pastels, and monotypes reveal the artist's restless creativity in a medium in which he has gone largely unrecognized. This is the first time all the surviving major photographs have been brought together. Most of the images are figure studies, self portraits or portraits of the artist's circle of friends and family in intimate settings. They have a powerful, intensely expressive presence. *Catalog Will Travel*

10/20/1998 to 01/24/1999   MARY CASSATT: DRAWINGS AND PRINTS IN THE METROPOLITAN MUSEUM OF ART
Included in this exhibition are most of the Museum's drawings and prints by Cassatt, many fragile or light sensitive works which are rarely shown, works in pastel, and many of the more than 200 sheets she executed in drypoint, soft-ground etching, aquatint, or a combination of all three techniques. She depicted women in and around Paris attending theater and opera, at tea, visiting parks and tending to children.

10/24/1998 to 05/30/1999   CONTEMPORARY CERAMICS
After World War II artists working in ceramics were keenly aware of and worked side by side with the Abstract Expressionists, Pop Artists, and Color Field painters. The leading artists shown, all works from the Museum collection, include Peter Voulkos, John Mason, and Rudy Autio. Also included are examples by today's younger ceramists. *Catalog*

NEW YORK

The Metropolitan Museum of Art - continued

10/27/1998 to 01/31/1999 DONATO CRETI
Creti was the last and most exquisite exponent of the classical-idealist painting emanating from Bologna. He is little known in America because of the rarity of his paintings. Included in the exhibition is his greatest achievement: a series of 18 paintings carried out for his most enthusiastic patron. *Catalog*

10/27/1998 to 02/1999 CHARLES BURCHFIELD FROM THE COLLECTION
20 watercolors, oil paintings, and prints created between 1915 and 1963 and illustrating the two opposing aspects of Burchfield's oeuvre: first, his mystical and romantic fascination with nature, and second his ability to record with objective realism the mundane details of life in small-town America.

11/28/1998 to 01/03/1999 ANNUAL CHRISTMAS TREE AND NEAPOLITAN BAROQUE CRECHE
The continuation of a long and beloved tradition is the presentation of the 18th century Neapolitan Nativity adorning a candle-lit spruce. Lighting ceremony Friday and Saturday at 7 PM.

12/1998 to 03/1999 SELECTIONS FROM THE BERGGRUEN KLEE COLLECTION
The thematic selection of works from this collection will be continued.

12/10/1998 to 03/14/1999 CHESSY RAYNOR: NEW YORK STYLE
The fashion biography of one of New York's most elegant women of style.

12/15/1998 to 03/21/1999 ANSELM KIEFER: WORKS ON PAPER, 1969-1987
The 54 works in the exhibition are all from the Museum collection and range in date from 1969-1987. They constitute a rich overview of the ideas and themes of the first two decades of the artist's career. Included are mixed media drawings predominantly in watercolor, works in acrylic and graphite pencil, and gouache and acrylic over photographs staged and shot by the artist.

01/14/1999 to 03/28/1999 DOSSO DOSSI
Dossi was court painter to the dukes of Ferrara from 1514-1542 . A generation following Giorgione, he reinterpreted the Venetian artist's poetic visions of painting. *Catalog Will Travel*

02/1999 to 05/1999 AMERICAN FOLK PAINTINGS AND DRAWINGS IN THE METROPOLITAN MUSEUM OF ART
Works by Rufus Hathaway, Edward Hicks, Joshua Johnson, Ammi Phillips and others working within naïve and provincial traditions in the United States during the 18th and 19th centuries include oil paintings, drawings, watercolors and portrait miniatures.

02/02/1999 to 04/25/1999 EIGHTEENTH-CENTURY FRENCH DRAWINGS IN NEW YORK COLLECTIONS
Ranging from Watteau and the early Rococo to the Neoclassicism of David and his followers, this exhibition surveys the many accomplishments of a much admired period of French art. *Catalog*

03/1999 to 07/1999 THE NATURE OF ISLAMIC ORNAMENT, PART III: GEOMETRIC DESIGN
Ornamental motifs based on geometric patterns that developed from simple figures such as circles, triangles, or polygons and were subsequently combined, duplicated, interlaced, and arranged in complex manners represent one of the most distinctive characteristics of Islamic art. The exhibition examines this usage of these motifs in Islamic ornamentation.

03/1999 to 07/1999 PICASSO: PAINTER AND SCULPTOR IN CLAY
Picasso is the most documented artist of our time. However, his significant production as a sculptor and painter in clay has not been previously surveyed. He created about 1000 pieces and each is unique. Some 200 are featured in this exhibition. *Catalog*

03/09/1999 to 06/1999 MIRROR OF THE MEDIEVAL WORLD
The acquisition of 300 works of art by the Department of Medieval Art and The Cloisters from late 1977 to the present dramatically broadened what was already considered the finest medieval collection in the Western Hemisphere. Many of these works are exhibited ranging from simple Bronze Age jewelry to Byzantine silver and enamels, panels of stained glass, and exceptional sculpture. *Catalog*

The Metropolitan Museum of Art - continued
03/25/1999 to 08/15/1999   CUBISM AND FASHION
The cubist revolution in fashion ca. 1908-1920 witnessed the cylindrical silhouette, faceting, flattening and the pastiche of modern elements – and its consequences.

04/1999 to 2000   HANS HOFFMAN AT THE METROPOLITAN MUSEUM OF ART
Nine paintings by Hofmann executed in 1965 as a tribute to his sequin wife and known as "The Renate Series" demonstrates Hofmann's synthesis of Cubism and general abstraction. It reflects his experiences with artistic developments in Paris and Munich between the early 1900s and 1930s and his response to a younger generation of painters in New York – the Abstract Expressionists. Also included are drawings and three paintings belonging to the Museum. *Catalog*

06/07/1999 to 09/05/1999   GUSTAVE MOREAU
This major exhibition celebrating the 100th anniversary of his death will feature works from every phase of this French Symbolist painter's career. Much admired during his time, he had a profound influence on the work of Magritte and Matisse among others. *Catalog Will Travel*

Miriam and Ira D. Wallach Art Gallery
Affiliate Institution: Columbia University
Schermerhorn Hall, 8th Fl.116th St. and Broadway, New York, NY 10027
☎: 212-854-7288
Open: 1-5 We-Sa The gallery is open only when there is an exhibition!
Closed: Su, Mo, Tu, 1/1, week of THGV, 12/25, 6/3-10/10, Mem Day weekend
 ♿ Ⓟ **Museum Shop   Group Tours**: 212-854-7288   **Drop-In Tours**: call 212-854-7288   **Historic Building**
Permanent Collection: non-collecting institution

Operated under the auspices of Columbia University and situated on its wonderful campus, the gallery functions to complement the educational goals of the University.

ON EXHIBIT 1999
01/26/1999 to 03/20/1999   PIRANESI/RAPHAEL: PRINTS FROM THE AVERY LIBRARY

10/05/1999 to 12/04/1999   ALLAN KAPROW, ROBERT WATTS, 1956-1966

Morgan Library
29 East 36th Street, New York, NY 10016-3490
☎: 212-685 0610
Open: 10:30-5 Tu-F, 10:30-6 Sa, noon-6 S   **Closed:** Mo, LEG/HOL!
Sugg/Cont Adult: $6.00   **Children:** F under 12   **Students:** $4.00   **Seniors:** $4.00
 ♿ Ⓟ **Museum Shop**
🍴: Café open daily for luncheon and afternoon tea 212-685-0008, ext 401
Group Tours: 212-695-0008, ext. 390   **Drop-In Tours**: daily ! ext 390
Historic Building
Permanent Collection: MED & REN: drgs, books, ptgs, manuscripts, obj d'art

Both a museum and a center for scholarly research, the Morgan Library is an extraordinary complex of buildings, occupying half a block in the heart of NYC. Among the greatest treasures of seminal artistic, literary, musical, and historical works, the Library's renowned collection of rare books, manuscripts, and drawings have as their principal focus the history, art, and literature of Western Civilization from the Middle Ages to the twentieth Century. **NOT TO BE MISSED:** The historic East Room, Pierpont Morgan's library, and the West Room, Morgan's private study, which still contain many of his favorite objects. The Stavelot Triptych, a jeweled 12th century reliquary regarded as one of the finest medieval objects in America. Three copies of the Gutenberg Bible, one rare copy on vellum, and two on paper.

Morgan Library - continued

ON EXHIBIT 1999

09/1998 to 01/1999 RUSSIAN ILLUSTRATED BOOKS AND BINDINGS
25 works including the only known copy in America of the Moscow 1663 Bible in Church Slavonic, the first Bible printed in Russia, colorful children's books illustrated by major pre-Revolutionary artists, and examples of the avant-garde during the early Soviet era.

09/25/1998 to 01/08/1999 MASTER DRAWINGS FROM THE HERMITAGE AND PUSHKIN MUSEUMS
A landmark exhibition providing Americans with their first opportunity to see 120 western European drawings dating from the 15th to the 20th C and including works never before seen outside of Russia. There is particular emphasis on Rubens, Greuze, Matisse, and Picasso. Evening hours will be extended for this exhibition 5-8, F. *Only Venue Catalog*

11/1998 to 01/1999 CHARLES DICKENS: A CHRISTMAS CAROL
The author's manuscript will be the centerpiece of this holiday exhibition.

01/27/1999 to 05/02/1999 THE WORMSLEY LIBRARY: A PERSONAL SELECTION BY SIR PAUL GETTY, K.B.E.
More than 100 works from this extraordinary library of illuminated manuscripts, early printed books, historical bookbindings, later illustrated books, calligraphic material, and drawings and paintings.

05/19/1999 to 08/29/1999 NEW YORK COLLECTS: DRAWINGS AND WATERCOLORS, 1900-1950
A major survey exhibition of European and American draughtsmanship from 1900-1950. Every major artistic current will be explored with major works by Gorky, Kandinsky, Klee, de Kooning, Matisse, Mondrian, Picasso, Pollock, and many others. Many of the drawings are little known and have seldom been exhibited. *Catalog Will Travel*

Spring 99 PIERPONT MORGAN: AN AMERICAN LIFE
The life and times of Pierpont Morgan whose collection is the basis of the Library, based on letters, manuscripts, photographs, and other documents.

09/16/1999 to 01/02/2000 THE GREAT EXPERIMENT: GEORGE WASHINGTON AND THE AMERICAN REPUBLIC
Using Washington's career and the 200th anniversary of his death as a vehicle, the exhibition will present the creation of the American republic as a genuinely revolutionary process, which produced the first successful republican nation in the modern world. *Catalog Will Travel*

Museum for African Art

593 Broadway, New York, NY 10012
☎: 212-966-1313
Open: 10:30-5:30 Tu-F, 12-6 Sa, Su **Closed:** Mo, LEG/HOL!
ADM Adult: $5.00 **Children:** $2.50 **Students:** $2.50 **Seniors:** $2.50
♿ Ⓟ **Museum Shop Group Tours Drop-In Tours**: call for specifics **Historic Building**
Permanent Collection: AF: all media

This new facility in a historic building with a cast iron facade was designed by Maya Lin, architect of the Vietnam Memorial in Washington, D.C. Her conception of the space is 'less institutional, more personal and idiosyncratic'. She is using 'color in ways that other museums do not, there will be no white walls here'.
NOT TO BE MISSED: Sub-Saharan art

ON EXHIBIT 1999

09/11/1998 to 01/1999 VIEWING THE UNVIEWABLE: THE MUSEUM FOR AFRICAN ART REVEALS THE PRIVATE ART OF THE BAULE PEOPLE OF THE IVORY COAST
Imagine an exhibition of art designed to be unseen? Through unique installation that contrasts the distinctive ways the Baule intended these pieces to be seen, with the traditional western manner of display, the exhibit takes a novel approach to examining art. The result is a deeper understanding of how cultural differences in how art is approached, viewed and appreciated

02/1999 to 08/1999 LIBERATED VOICES: CONTEMPORARY SOUTH AFRICAN ART SINCE MANDELA
Works dating from 1994 , the end of apartheid. A landmark exhibition it is the first to show the works of young African artists rather than South Africans of European decent.

Museum of American Folk Art

Two Lincoln Square, New York, NY 10023-6214
☎: 212-595-9533 ◙ www.folkartmus.org
Open: 11:30-7:30 Tu-Su **Closed:** Mo, LEG/HOL!
Vol/Cont ♿ ℗ **Museum Shop Group Tours Drop-In Tours**
Permanent Collection: FOLK: ptgs, sculp, quilts, textiles, dec/art

The museum is known both nationally and internationally for its leading role in bringing quilts and other folk art to a broad public audience. **NOT TO BE MISSED:** 'Girl in Red with Cat and Dog', by Ammi Phillips; major works in all areas of folk art

ON EXHIBIT 1999

ONGOING   AMERICA'S HERITAGE
Major works from the permanent collection shown on a rotating basis.

10/03/1998 to 01/10/1999   MASTERPIECES IN WOOD: AMERICAN FOLK MARQUETRY FROM THE HIRSCHHORN FOUNDATION

01/16/1999 to 05/16/1999   NELLIE MAE ROWE: NINETY-NINE-AND-A-HALF WON'T DO IT
A painter as well as a sculptor, Rowe's oeuvre includes color-saturated, energetic works on paper, enigmatic chewing gum sculpture, whimsical dolls, installations of found objects, and photographic collages.

05/22/1999 to 09/12/1999   UKRAINIAN FOLK ART

Museum of Modern Art

11 West 53rd Street, New York, NY 10019-5498
☎: 212-708-9400 ◙ www.moma.org
Open: 10:30-6 Sa-Tu, Th, 10:30-8:30 Fr   **Closed:** We, THGV12/25
Free Day: Fr 4:30-8:30 vol cont   **Adult:** $9.50   **Children:** F under 16 with adult   **Students:** $6.50   **Seniors:** $6.50
♿ ℗ **Museum Shop** ǁ: Garden Café and Sette Moma (open for dinner exc W & S)
Group Tours: 212-708-9685   **Drop-In Tours:** ! 212-708-9795 Weekdays, Sa, Su 1 & 3p
Historic Building 1939 Bldg by Goodwin & Stone considered one of first examples of Int. Style   **Sculpture Garden**
Permanent Collection: WORKS BY PICASSO, MATISSE, VAN GOGH, WARHOL AND MONET, DESIGN 20

The MOMA offers the world's most comprehensive survey of 20th century art in all media as well as an exceptional film library. MOMA Bookstore hours: 10-6:30 Sa-T, 10-9 F MOMA Design Store: 10-6:00 Sa-T, 10-8 F Garden Café: 11-5 Sa-Tu, T, 11-7:45 F Sette MOMA: 12-3, 5-10:30 daily exc. www.ticketweb.com for advance adm. tickets (service fee on ticketweb) **NOT TO BE MISSED:** Outstanding collection of 20th century photography, film and design.

ON EXHIBIT 1999

11/01/1998 to 02/02/1999   JACKSON POLLOCK
This is the first full survey in the US of the artist's career since 1967, and comprises nearly 200 paintings, works on paper, and sculptures. *Catalog Will Travel* ◖

11/07/1998 to 01/26/1999   STRUCTURE AND SURFACE: CONTEMPORARY JAPANESE TEXTILES
A selection of about 100 works by two dozen of the most influential fiber artists, textile designers, and fashion designers currently working in Japan.

11/19/1998 to 02/02/1999   MIRO'S BLACK AND RED SERIES : A NEW ACQUISITION IN CONTEXT
About 150 prints, photographs drawings, posters and paintings, demonstrate how this work of art created in 1938, was affected by a variety of complex forces.

winter 1999/1999 to 05/04/1999   JULIA MARGARET CAMERON'S WOMEN
Cameron photographed many prominent figures of Victorian intellectual society in the 1860's and 70s. Her remarkable portraits of women constitute the bulk of her work. Her methods were unconventional for her time because they sought the "inner spirit" of the sitter. *Catalog Will Travel*

Museum of Modern Art - continued

03/11/1999 to 06/01/1999   THE MUSEUM AS MUSE: ARTISTS OBSERVE
Paintings, sculptures, photographs, drawings, prints, video's and installations by some 60 artists illustrate how they address the concept, function , and nature of the museum. *Will Travel*

03/31/1999 to 06/01/1999   SIGMAR POLKE: WORKS ON PAPER, 1963-1974
One of the most interesting artists of his generation, some 200 gouaches, drawings, and sketchbooks emphasize the spontaneous, subversive, and experimental nature of his work.

10/1999 to 08/2000   END OF CENTURY
Three cycles of exhibitions celebrate the multiplicity of modernism's that comprise the visual arts since the 1880's and provide an unparalleled overview of some of the century's most powerful art.

Museum of the City of New York

Fifth Ave. at 103rd Street, New York, NY 10029
☎: 212-534-1672   ◉ www.mcny.org
Open: 10-5 We-Sa, 1-5 Su   **Closed:** Mo, Tu, LEG/HOL!
ADM   Adult: $5.00, Family $10   **Children:** $4.00   **Students:** $4.00   **Seniors:** $4.00
&   ℗   **Museum Shop   Group Tours**: 212-534-1672 ext 206   **Drop-In Tours**: !   **Historic Building**
Permanent Collection: NEW YORK: silver 1678-1910; INTERIORS: 17-20; THE ALEXANDER HAMILTON COLLECTION; PORT OF THE NEW WORLD MARINE GALLERY

Founded in 1933 this was the first American museum dedicated to the history of a major city. The Museum's collections encompass the City's heritage, from its exploration and settlement to the NY of today. **NOT TO BE MISSED:** Period Rooms

ON EXHIBIT 1999

ONGOING   BROADWAY
A survey of the magical Broadway comedies, dramas and musicals from 1866 to the present.

ONGOING   BROADWAY CAVALCADE
The history of the street known as Broadway from its origins as a footpath in Colonial New York to its development into the City's most dynamic, diverse and renowned boulevard.

ONGOING   FAMILY TREASURES: TOYS AND THEIR TALES
Toys from the Museum's renowned collection present a history of New York City through their individual stories.

ONGOING   ISADORA DUNCAN
A display focusing on the provocative life of the dancer who transformed the concept of dance into an art form.

National Academy Museum and School of Fine Arts

1083 Fifth Avenue, New York, NY 10128
☎: 212-369-4880
Open: 12-5 We-Su, 12-8 Fr   **Closed:** Mo, Tu, LEG/HOL!
Free Day: Fr, 5-8 pay-as-you-wish   **ADM   Adult:** $5.00   **Students:** $3.50   **Seniors:** $3.50
&   ℗   **Museum Shop   Group Tours   Drop-In Tours**
Permanent Collection: AM: all media 19-20

With outstanding special exhibitions as well as rotating exhibits of the permanent collection, this facility is a school as well as a resource for American Art.   **NOT TO BE MISSED:** The oldest juried annual art exhibition in the nation is held in spring or summer with National Academy members only exhibiting in the odd-numbered years and works by all U.S. artists considered for inclusion in even-numbered years.

ON EXHIBIT 1999

04/14/1999 to 09/12/1999   ALL THAT IS GLORIOUS AROUND US: PAINTINGS FROM THE HUDSON RIVER SCHOOL
Led by Thomas Cole, the Hudson River School painters were the first to paint American scenes rather than the then traditional custom of painting only European subjects. Many lesser known and women artists as well as William Trost Richards and others equally well known will be featured. *Will Travel*

National Arts Club

15 Gramercy Park South, New York, NY 10024

☎: 212-475-3424

Open: 1-6 daily   **Closed:** LEG/HOL!

& Ⓟ **Museum Shop** ⅋: For members   **Group Tours** Drop-In Tours   **Historic Building**

Permanent Collection: AM: ptgs, sculp, works on paper, dec/art 19, 20; Ch: dec/art

The building which houses this private club and collection was the 1840's mansion of former Governor Samuel Tilden. The personal library of Robert Henri which is housed here is available for study on request.

New Museum of Contemporary Art

583 Broadway, New York, NY 10012

☎: 212-219-1222   ⊙ www.newmuseum.org

Open: 12-6 We, Su, 12-8 Th-Sa   **Closed:** Mo, Tu, 1/1, 12/25

Free Day: 6-8 Th   **ADM   Adult:** $5.00, ARTISTS $3.00   **Children:** F (18 & under)   **Students:** $3.00   **Seniors:** $3.00

& Ⓟ **Museum Shop   Group Tours Drop-In Tours   Historic Building** Astor Building

Permanent Collection: Semi-permanent collection

The New Museum has been reopened to the public after an extensive renovation and expansion of its landmark building. The $3 million project has created new second-floor and mezzanine galleries, an airy, multi-level lobby, a new bookstore, and a new public-access level which houses exhibitions free to the public.

ON EXHIBIT 1999

10/08/1998 to 01/05/1999   ANN PRADA

A young sculptor from Spain, Prada creates intimate, site-specific works creating repetitive patterns with objects like rubber bands or wooden ice cream spoons within very contained spaces so that they first appear to the viewer as conventional paintings of sculptures.

10/08/1998 to 01/05/1999   MARCEL ODENBACH

German photographer/figurative sculptor Odenbach has created for the past 20 years one of the most provocative bodies of work being produced in Europe. Although less familiar to New York audiences he addresses many of the same social and political themes that have been associated with the most compelling American art of the last few years. *Catalog*

10/08/1998 to 01/12/1999   XU BING: AN INTRODUCTION TO SQUARE WORD CALLIGRAPHY

The newest installation by this highly respected artist of the group which left China in the late 1980s is based on a classroom setting where traditional Chinese calligraphy is taught. Visitors will be supplied with a brush, ink and practice pads and invited to learn the fundamentals of calligraphy from an instructional video. As the lesson proceeds, participants realize that the characters they are forming are actually English words written in the style of ancient calligraphic ideograms.

New-York Historical Society

2 W. 77th St. at Central Park West, New York, NY 10024

☎: 212-873-3400

Open: 11-5 Tu-Su, Library 11-5 Tu-Sa   **Closed:** Mo, LEG/HOL!

ADM   Adult: $5.00   **Students:** $3.00   **Seniors:** $3.00

& Ⓟ **Museum Shop   Group Tours**: 212-501-9233   **Drop-In Tours**: 1pm & 3pm   **Historic Building**

Permanent Collection: AM: Ptgs 17-20; HUDSON RIVER SCHOOL; AM: gr, phot 18-20; TIFFANY GLASS; CIRCUS & THEATER: post early 20; COLONIAL: portraits (includes Governor of NY dressed as a woman)

Housed in an elegant turn of the century neoclassical building is a collection of all but 2 of the 435 'Birds of America' watercolors by John James Audubon. In addition there are 150 works from Tiffany Studios. **NOT TO BE MISSED:** 435 original W/COl by John James Audubon

NEW YORK

New-York Historical Society - continued
ON EXHIBIT 1999

10/06/1998 to 01/10/1999   19TH CENTURY ETCHINGS FROM THE COLLECTION OF DAVE AND REBA WILLIAMS
Prints from the etching revival of 1890-1900, many by New York artists and published by New York firms

10/13/1998 to 01/10/1999   GEORGE POST, ARCHITECT
Architectural drawings by the architect of City College, the Williamsburgh Savings Bank and the New York Stock Exchange.

11/25/1998 to 03/21/1999   NEW YORK'S FINEST: THE HISTORY OF THE NEW YORK POLICE DEPARTMENT
The story of the development of law enforcement in New York with emphasis on the changing relationship of the police department and the community.

12/15/1998 to 05/09/1999   A PREVIEW OF THE HENRY LUCE III CENTER FOR THE STUDY OF AMERICAN CULTURE
A look at a work in progress: the computerization and design plan for the study/storage center opening in 2000 to house some 60,000 objects from the museum collection.

02/03/1999 to 05/30/1999   REFUGE: THE NEWEST NEW YORKERS
Photographs by Mel Rosenthal of recently arrived refugees which reveal the hopes and aspirations of thousands who have found safe havens and new lives in New York.

04/20/1999 to 08/15/1999   DANCE IN THE CITY: FIFTY YEARS OF THE NEW YORK CITY BALLET
The story of George Ballanchine's Foundation and its climb to international renown.

09/14/1999 to 01/23/2000   CASS GILBERT: TEN PROJECTS
Ten renowned structures by Gilbert are followed from drawings through completion. Included are the Woolworth Building, the Custom House at Bowling Green and the New York Life Insurance Building.

Pratt Manhattan Gallery
295 Lafayette Street, 2nd floor, New York, NY 10012
☎: 718-636-3517
Open: 10-5 Mo-Sa   **Closed:** Su, LEG/HOL!
& Ⓟ **Museum Shop**
Group Tours Drop-In Tours   Historic Building Puck Building
Permanent Collection: Not continuously on view.

Pratt Manhattan and Schaffler Galleries in Brooklyn present a program of exhibitions of contemporary art, design, and architecture in thematic exhibitions as well as solo and group shows of work by faculty, students and alumni.

Salmagundi Museum of American Art
47 Fifth Avenue, New York, NY 10003
☎: 212-255-7740
Open: 1-5 daily   **Closed:** LEG/HOL!
& Ⓟ **Museum Shop** ⑪: Members Only
Group Tours: 212-255-7740 **Drop-In Tours**: can be arranged   **Historic Building**
Permanent Collection: AM: Realist ptgs 19, 20

An organization of artists and art lovers in a splendid landmark building on lower 5th Avenue.

Sidney Mishkin Gallery of Baruch College

135 East 22nd Street, New York, NY 10010

☎: 212-387-1006
Open: 12-5 Mo-We, Fr, 12-7 Th ACAD **Closed:** Sa, Su, ACAD!
ょ ℗ **Museum Shop Group Tours Drop-In Tours Historic Building**
Permanent Collection: GR; PHOT 20

The building housing this gallery was a 1939 Federal Courthouse erected under the auspices of the WPA.
NOT TO BE MISSED: Marsden Hartley's 'Mount Katadin, Snowstorm', 1942

Society of Illustrators Museum of American Illustration

128 East 63rd St, New York, NY 10021

☎: 212-838-2560
Open: 10-5 We-Fr, 10-8 Tu, 12-4 Sa **Closed:** Su, Mo, LEG/HOL!
ょ ℗ **Museum Shop** ⑪: by membership @ $125/Yr
Group Tours Drop-In Tours **Historic Building**
Permanent Collection: NORMAN ROCKWELL AND OTHERS, 2,500 TOTAL

A very specialized collection of illustrations familiar to everyone.

Solomon R. Guggenheim Museum

1071 Fifth Ave, New York, NY 10128

☎: 212-423-3500 ◉ www.guggenheim.org
Open: 10-6 Su-We, 10-8 Fr, Sa **Closed:** Th, 12/25,1/1
ADM Adult: $12.00 **Children:** F under 12 w/adult **Students:** $7.00 **Seniors:** $7.00
ょ ℗ **Museum Shop** ⑪ **Group Tours:** 212-423-3652 Drop-In Tours
Historic Building Sculpture Garden
Permanent Collection: AM & EU: ptgs, sculp; PEGGY GUGGENHEIM COLL: cubist, surrealist, & ab/exp artworks;
PANZA diBIUMO COLL: minimalist art 1960's -70's

Designed by Frank Lloyd Wright in 1950, and designated a landmark building by New York City, the
museum was recently restored and expanded. Originally called the Museum of Non-Objective Painting, the
Guggenheim houses one of the world's largest collections of paintings by Kandinsky as well as prime
examples of works by such modern masters as Picasso, Giacometti, Mondrian and others. There is a special
7 day combined admission to the Museum and the Guggenheim Museum Soho. The cost is Adults $16,
Stu/Sen $10. **NOT TO BE MISSED:** Kandinsky's 'Blue Mountain'

ON EXHIBIT 1999

**10/16/1998 to 01/31/1999 RENDEZVOUS: MASTERPIECES FROM CENTRE GEORGES POMPIDOU SNF THE
GUGGENHEIM MUSEUMS**
An unprecedented partnership to exhibit jointly masterworks from their permanent collections. This exhibition will form a
trans-Atlantic dialogue between the two museums and create an exceptional display of the history of modern art from the turn
of the century to 1970.

Spring 99 JIM DINE

Summer 1999 PICASSO AND THE WARS

Fall 1999 FRANCESCO CLEMENTE

Fall 1999 PRIVATE EYES: SURREALISM AND FILIPACCI COLLECTION

NEW YORK

Studio Museum in Harlem

144 West 125th Street, New York, NY 10027

☎: 212-864-4500   ▣ WWW.STUDIOMUSEUMINHARLEM.ORG
Open: 10-5 We-Fr, 1-6 Sa, Su   **Closed:** Mo, Tu, LEG/HOL!
Adult: $5.00   **Children:** $1.00 (under 12)   **Students:** $3.00   **Seniors:** $3.00
♿   Ⓟ   **Museum Shop**
Group Tours   Drop-In Tours
Sculpture Garden
Permanent Collection: AF/AM; CARIBBEAN; LATINO

This is the premier center for the collection, interpretation and exhibition of the art of Black America and the African Diaspora. The five-story building is located on 125th Street, Harlem's busiest thorofare and hub of it's commercial rebirth and redevelopment.

ON EXHIBIT 1999

03/10/1999 to 06/27/1999   TO CONSERVE A LEGACY AMERICAN ART FROM HISTORICALLY BLACK COLLEGES AND UNIVERSITIES
The collections of 6 historically Black colleges will be showcased in a exhibition of over 150 artworks. *Will Travel*

07/14/1999 to 09/19/1999   FROM THE STUDIO: ARTISTS IN RESIDENCE, 1998-1999
This year's Participants in this program are featured here.

07/14/1999 to 09/19/1999   WRIGHTS OF PASSAGE: CONTEMPORARY AFRICAN-AMERICAN ARTISTS IN TRANSITION
This exhibition celebrates the 30th anniversary of the Studio Museum.

10/06/1999 to 02/28/2000   AFRICAN-AMERICAN ARTISTS AND AMERICAN MODERNISM
In the 20th C many African-American artists experimented with modernism to express the black experience or reflect the constant changing characteristics of mainstream American art.

Whitney Museum of American Art

945 Madison Ave, New York, NY 10021

☎: 212-570-3676   ▣ www.echony.com/nwhitney
Open: 11-6 We, 1-8 Th, 11-6 Fr-Su   **Closed:** Mo, Tu, 1/1, THGV, 12/25
Free Day: 6-8 Th   **ADM   Adult:** $8.00   **Children:** F (under 12)   **Students:** $7.00   **Seniors:** $7.00
♿   Ⓟ   **Museum Shop**   ⅋: Y
Group Tours: 212-570-7720   **Drop-In Tours**: We-Su, & Th eve 212-570-3676   **Historic Building   Sculpture Garden**
Permanent Collection: AM: all media, 20

Founded by leading American art patron Gertrude Vanderbilt Whitney in 1930, the Whitney is housed in an award winning building designed by Marcel Breuer. The museum's mandate, to devote itself solely to the art of the US, is reflected in its significant holdings of the works of Edward Hopper (2,500 in all), Georgia O'Keeffe, and more than 850 works by Reginald Marsh. New directions and developments in American art are featured every 2 years in the often cutting edge and controversial 'Whitney Biennial'. **NOT TO BE MISSED:** Alexander Calder's 'Circus'

Satellite Galleries:
Whitney Museum of American Art at Philip Morris,120 Park Ave, NYC

Whitney Museum of American Art at Champion, Stamford, CT

Yeshiva University Museum

2520 Amsterdam Avenue, New York, NY 10033
☎: 212-960-5390 ◉ www.yu.edu/museum
Open: 10:30-5 Tu-Th, 12-6 Su **Closed:** Fr, Sa, Mo, LEG/HOL!, JEWISH/HOL!
ADM Adult: $3.00 **Children:** $2.00, 4-16 **Students:** $2.00 **Seniors:** $2.00
& ℗ **Museum Shop** ⵏ: Cafeteria on campus **Group Tours Drop-In Tours**
Permanent Collection: JEWISH: ptgs, gr, textiles, ritual objects, cer

Major historical and contemporary exhibitions of Jewish life and ceremony are featured in this museum. **NOT TO BE MISSED:** Architectural models of historic synagogues

ON EXHIBIT 1999

to July 1999 THEODOR HERZL: "IF YOU WILL IT, IT IS NOT A DREAM"
Celebrating the 100th anniversary of Herzl's book, features photographs, medals, coins, stamps, busts, and carpets all bearing the likeness of Herzl.

09/13/1998 to 01/15/1999 HATYSAD M'RAKDIM: VARIETIES OF JEWISH DANCE : FABRIC COLLAGE TAPESTRIES BY BAT-ZVI
The tapestries display Bat-Zvi's virtuoso technique of literally painting with fabric.

09/13/1998 to 01/15/1999 THE LEGENDS OF THE BAAL SHEM TOY: LITHOGRAPHS BY FERENCE FLAMM
Flamm's lithographs illustrate the history of Hassidism in the 16th C.

09/13/1998 to 01/15/1999 THE GROWTH OF A VINEYARD IN THE LAND OF THE BIBLE: SILK PAINTINGS BY CHAIM KIRKELL
Kirkell document life in Beit Yatir Mosha, a religious settlement in the high plateau's of the Negev desert, known for its vineyards.

09/13/1998 to 01/15/1999 COVER THEM: OUTLINE FOR THE FRENCH CHILDREN OF THE HOLOCAUST BY RACHEL BRUMMER
Brummer created a series of art quilts, made up of various images.

09/13/1998 to 01/15/1999 A MEMORIAL PARK AT NAHARIM: SEVEN GIRLS, SEVEN DREAMS A MULTI MEDIA INSTALLATION BY GIGI MCKENDRIC; IN COLLABORATION WITH RANDALL L. GASKINS AND VIA GRABILL
Dedicated to the seven Israeli girls killed by Jordanian fire in 1997, this installation calls for a memorial park to be built.

09/13/1998 to 01/15/1999 WINGS OF WITNESS: A HOLOCAUST MEMORIAL WORK IN PROGRESS
Shreier conceived of teaching students in the US about the holocaust by involving them in collecting 11 million pull tabs from soda cans into feathers of angels wings.

09/13/1998 to 01/15/1999 ILLUSTRATED TALES: ORIGINAL ART FROM CHILDREN'S BOOKS BY JEFFREY ALLON
Original works in gouache on paper by this internationally known illustrator of Talmudic tales and Jewish folklore

---

NIAGARA FALLS

Castellani Art Museum-Niagara University

Niagara Falls, NY 14109
☎: 716-286-8200 ◉ www:/niagara.edu/~cam
Open: 11-5 We-Sa, 1-5 Su **Closed:** Mo, Tu, ACAD!
& ℗ **Museum Shop Group Tours Drop-In Tours**
Permanent Collection: AM: ldscp 19; CONT: all media; WORKS ON PAPER: 19-20; PHOT: 20

Castellani Art Museum-Niagara University - continued

Minutes away from Niagara Falls, Artpark, and the New York State Power Vista, the Castellani Art Museum features an exciting collection of contemporary art and a permanent folk arts program in a beautiful grey marble facility. **NOT TO BE MISSED:** 'Begonia', 1982, by Joan Mitchell

ON EXHIBIT 1999

10/04/1998 to 01/10/1999   THE PUERTO RICAN YEAR:
An exhibition documenting the role of community celebration in the expression and maintenance of Puerto Rican identity.

11/07/1998 to 02/09/1999   20TH ANNIVERSARY EXHIBITION:
Recent additions to the collection as well as installations by Michelle Stuart and Chrisanne Stathacos.

11/22/1998 to 01/10/1999   LILLIAN MENDEZ:
Room installation featuring traditional art in a contemporary framework.

04/18/1999 to 07/18/1999   MINDS EYE: THE CREELEY COLLABORATIONS:
40 years of Robert Creeley's collaborations with visual artists.

SUMMER 1999   RIPARIAN NIAGARA

10/31/1999 to 01/16/1999   ARAB AMERICAN:10

NORTH SALEM

Hammond Museum

Deveau Rd. Off Route 124, North Salem, NY 10560
☏: 914-669-5033   ▣ www.hammondmuseum.org.com
Open: 12-4 We-Sa   **Closed:** Su, Mo, Tu, 12/25, 1/1
ADM   Adult: $4.00   **Children:** F (under12)   **Students:** $3.00   **Seniors:** $3.00
 ♿   Ⓟ   **Museum Shop**   ⊢: Apr through Oct   **Group Tours   Drop-In Tours**: Res
Permanent Collection: Changing exhibitions

The Hammond Museum and Japanese Stroll Garden provide a place of natural beauty and tranquility to delight the senses and refresh the spirit.

OGDENSBURG

Frederic Remington Art Museum

303/311 Washington Street, Ogdensburg, NY 13669
☏: 315-393-2425
Open: 10-5 Mo-Sa,1-5 Su (5/1-10/31), 10-5 Tu-Sa (11/1-4/30)   **Closed:** LEG/HOL!
ADM   Adult: $3.00   **Children:** F (under 13)   **Students:** $2.00   **Seniors:** $2.00
 ♿   Ⓟ   **Museum Shop   Group Tours**   Drop-In Tours   **Historic Building**
Permanent Collection: REMINGTON: ptgs, w/col, sculp, works on paper

The library, memorabilia, and finest single collections of Frederic Remington originals are housed in a 1809-10 mansion with a modern gallery addition. **NOT TO BE MISSED:** 'Charge of the Rough Riders at San Juan Hill'

ONEONTA

Yager Museum
Affiliate Institution: Hartwick College
Oneonta, NY 13820
☎: 607-431-4480
Open: 11-5 Tu-Sa, 1-4 Su **Closed:** Mo, LEG/HOL!
& ℗ **Museum Shop Group Tours Drop-In Tours**
Permanent Collection: NAT/AM: artifacts; P/COL: pottery; VAN ESS COLLECTION OF REN, BAROQUE & AM ptgs 19; masks; shells; botanical specimens

The Yager Museum has a permanent and changing exhibition schedule which reflects its unique collections ranging from the fine art of the Renaissance, 19th century American paintings, Upper Susquehanna area archeology, ethnographic material from the Americas, American Indian Artifacts, to folk and contemporary art.

PLATTSBURGH

S.U.N.Y. Plattsburgh Art Museum
Affiliate Institution: State University Of New York
State University of New York, Plattsburgh, NY 12901
☎: 518-564-2474 ■ www.plattsburgh.edu/museum
Open: 12-4 daily **Closed:** LEG/HOL!
& ℗ **Museum Shop** ⅃⅃: on campus across from museum
Group Tours: 518-564-2813 **Drop-In Tours:** by appt **Sculpture Garden**
Permanent Collection: ROCKWELL KENT: ptgs, gr, cer; LARGEST COLLECTION OF NINA WINKEL SCULPTURE

This University Museum features a 'museum without walls' with late 19th and 20th century sculptures, paintings, and graphics displayed throughout its campus and in four secure galleries. **NOT TO BE MISSED:** Largest collection of Rockwell Kent works

ON EXHIBIT 1999
12/04/1998 to 02/07/1999 HOLIDAYS AT KENT
A special exhibition of prints donated by Morris Schuster through the London Arts Gallery, Detroit; prints from Moonkosh Press, a gift from the Norton family and student Association acquisitions.

02/12/1999 to 04/05/1999 MAJOR SPRING EXHIBITION

03/1999 to 04/1999 UNDERGRADUATE JURIED EXHIBITION

04/10/1999 to 04/18/1999 MOUNTAIN LAKE AUCTION EXHIBITION

POTSDAM

Roland Gibson Gallery
Affiliate Institution: State University College
State University College at Potsdam, Potsdam, NY 13676-2294
☎: 315-267-2250
Open: 12-5 Mo-Fr, 12-4 Sa, Su, 7-9:30 Mo-Th eve **Closed:** LEG/HOL!
& ℗ **Museum Shop Group Tours Drop-In Tours Sculpture Garden**
Permanent Collection: CONT: sculp; WORKS ON PAPER; JAP: ptgs

Based on the New York State University campus in Potsdam, this is the only museum in northern New York that presents a regular schedule of exhibitions. **NOT TO BE MISSED:** 'Untitled', by Miro

NEW YORK

Frances Lehman Loeb Art Center at Vassar College
Affiliate Institution: Vassar College
124 Raymond Ave., Poughkeepsie, NY 12601
☎: 914-437-5235
Open: 10-5 Tu-Sa, 1-5 Su **Closed:** Mo, EASTER, THGV, 12/25-1/1
& ℗ **Museum Shop Group Tours Drop-In Tours**
Permanent Collection: AM, EU: ptgs, sculp; AN/GR & AN/R: sculp; GR: old Master to modern

Housed in a newly built facility, this is the only museum between Westchester County and Albany exhibiting art of all periods. **NOT TO BE MISSED:** Magoon Collection of Hudson River Paintings

ON EXHIBIT 1999
01/15/1999 to 03/07/1999 APPEAL TO THIS AGE: PHOTOGRAPHY OF THE CIVIL RIGHTS ERA, 1954-1968
A survey of the photography of the black-led freedom movement of the middle of our century, these are among the most inspiring images of 20th century America. Included are 75 powerful and moving images by Gordon Parks, James Karales, Sandra Weiner, Charles Moore and others.

04/23/1999 to 09/19/1999 REFINING THE IMAGINATION: TRADITION, COLLECTING, AND THE VASSAR EDUCATION

10/15/1999 to 12/19/1999 LANDSCAPES OF RETROSPECTION: THE MAGOON COLLECTION OF BRITISH PRINTS & DRAWINGS, 1760-1860

Donald M. Kendall Sculpture Gardens at Pepsico
700 Anderson Hill Road, Purchase, NY 10577
☎: 914-253-2890
Open: 9-5 daily **Closed:** LEG/HOL!
& ℗ **Museum Shop Group Tours Drop-In Tours Sculpture Garden**
Permanent Collection: 44 SITE-SPECIFIC SCULPTURES BY 20TH CENTURY ARTISTS

42 site-specific sculptures are located throughout the 168 magnificently planted acres that house the headquarters of PepsiCo, designed in 1970 by noted architect Edward Durell Stone. A large man-made lake and wandering ribbons of pathway invite the visitor to enjoy the sculptures within the ever-changing seasonal nature of the landscape. The garden, located in Westchester County about 30 miles outside of NYC, is an art lover's delight.

Neuberger Museum of Art
Affiliate Institution: Purchase College, SUNY
735 Anderson Hill Rd, Purchase, NY 10577-1400
☎: 914-251-6100 ◙ www.neuberger.org
Open: 10-4 Tu-Fr, 11-5 Sa, Su **Closed:** Mo, LEG/HOL
ADM Adult: $4.00 **Children:** F, under 12 **Students:** $2.00 **Seniors:** $2.00
& ℗ **Museum Shop** ℍ: Museum Café 11:30-2:30 Tu-F, 12-4 Sa, Su
Group Tours: 914-251-6110 **Drop-In Tours**: 1pm, Tu-Fr; 2 and 3pm, Su
Permanent Collection: PTGS, SCULP, DRGS 20; ROY R. NEUBERGER COLLECTION; EDITH AND GEORGE RICKEY COLLECTION OF CONSTRUCTIVIST ART; AIMEE HIRSHBERG COLLECTION OF AFRICAN ART; HANS RICHTER BEQUEST OF DADA AND SURREALIST OBJECTS; ANC GRK, ETR VASES GIFT OF NELSON A. ROCKEFELLER

On the campus of Purchase College, SUNY, the Neuberger Museum of Art houses a prestigious collection of 20th century art. **NOT TO BE MISSED:** Selections from the Roy R. Neuberger Collection of 20th century American art

Neuberger Museum of Art - continued
ON EXHIBIT 1999

ONGOING   ROY R. NEUBERGER COLLECTION
More than sixty works from the permanent collection displayed on a rotating basis form the heart and soul of the Museum's collection and include major works by Romare Bearden, Jackson Pollock, Edward Hopper, Georgia O'Keeffe and others.

ONGOING   OBJECT AND INTELLECT: AFRICAN ART FROM THE PERMANENT COLLECTION
Over forty objects created in the 19th and 20th century reflect African tradition, rites and religious beliefs. The exhibition presents the African view of the universe as being composed of two inseparable realms: a visible, tangible world of the living and an invisible world of the sacred.

ONGOING   INTERACTIVE LEARNING CENTER
Interactive video program enables visitors to delve into the style, history and artistic vocabulary of 200 works of art from the Roy R. Neuberger Collection of 20th century paintings and sculpture.

09/06/1998 to 01/24/1999   FOUR WORKS BY FOUR WOMEN
One large work each from the collection by Mary Frank, Yayoi Kusana, Joan Snyder, and Pat Steir.

09/06/1998 to 01/24/1999   REVELATIONS
A series of single-artist exhibitions revealing new and evolving talent in the visual arts. Artists from various cultural heritages working in all media, styles, and content will be included.

09/13/1998 to 01/03/1999   MAURICE PRENDERGAST
Paintings by this Modernist painter who was noted for his agitated silhouettes and rich color. He interpreted the urban and suburban life of this century *Will Travel*

09/20/1998 to 01/31/1999   THE NEXT WORD
An interdisciplinary exhibition of work of the 1990s drawing on a wide variety of works exploring the visual properties of text as image in new and traditional media.

09/27/1998 to 01/24/1999   AL LOVING: COLOR CONSTRUCTS
Representative paintings from the African-American painter done from the late 60s to the present. His colorful curvilinear work breaks away from traditional rectangular form.

01/17/1999 to 03/21/1999   THE BOBCAT: KAY MILLER
Brightly colored, heavily painted works by this Native American painter that deal with her study of her culture's animal mythology.

02/07/1999 to 04/25/1999   FIVE DECADES IN PRINT: ED COLKER
Woodcuts, lithographs, etchings and limited editions by this printmaker, teacher, and publisher. *Catalog Will Travel*

04/04/1999 to 05/30/1999   CLEVE GREY, PAINTER: A QUARTER OF A CENTURY
19 paintings tracing the artist's fascination with the painted line over the past 25 years and also celebrating abstract painting itself. *Catalog Will Travel*

05/09/1999 to 08/15/1999   THE DOG SHOW: PAINTINGS BY CYNTHIA CARLSON
Paintings capturing the idiosyncratic gestures and attitudes of our canine pets.

06/13/1999 to 08/22/1999   CAROL SUN
Icons of daily life are used by this Asian American artist, including dishes, wallpaper, etc, to identify and restore affinities between private and public life.

06/27/1999 to 10/24/1999   BIENNIAL EXHIBITION OF PUBLIC ART
The second Biennial is a major national showcase of contemporary artists who work in the areas of public art. Juried works in all media, are presented throughout the public spaces of Purchase College.

09/13/1999 to 01/10/2000   KILENGI: THE BAREISS COLLECTION OF AFRICAN ART
Selections from a world renowned collection depict the creation of new art forms that meet the changing needs of the people who use them.

NEW YORK

Queens Museum of Art

New York City Building, Flushing Meadows Corona Park, Queens, NY 11368-3393
☎: 718-592-9700   ◙ www.queensmuse.org
Open: 10-5 We-Fr, 12-5 Sa, Su, Tu; groups by appt   **Closed:** Mo, Tu, 1/1, THGV, 12/25
Sugg/Cont   Adult: $4.00   **Children:** F (under 5)   **Students:** $2.00   **Seniors:** $2.00
 ♿ Ⓟ   **Museum Shop   Group Tours   Drop-In Tours   Historic Building**
Permanent Collection: CHANGING EXHIBITIONS OF 20TH CENTURY ART AND CONTEMPORARY ART

The Panorama is where all of NYC fits inside one city block. You will feel like Gulliver when you experience it for the first time. The building was built for the 1939 World's Fair and was later used for United Nations meetings. Satellite Gallery at Bulova Corporate Center, Jackson Heights, Queens. **NOT TO BE MISSED:** 'The Panorama of NYC', largest architectural scale model of an Urban Area. "Tiffany in Queens: Selections from the Neustadt Museum Collection". Lamps, desk objects and a window on long term loan.

ON EXHIBIT 1999

01/26/1999 to 03/21/1999   LIFE CYCLES: THE CHARLES E. BURCHFIELD COLLECTION
62 paintings by Burchfield (1893-1967), a man whose highly original style helped to inspire several generations of artists, reflect his strong concerns for the dwindling of America's virginal landscape, the passage of time, and memories of childhood.

04/29/1999 to 08/22/1999   CONCEPTUALIST ART: POINTS OF ORIGIN

10/05/1999 to 01/02/2000   MODERN ODYSSEYS: GREEK AMERICAN ARTISTS OF THE 20TH CENTURY

George Eastman House, International Museum of Photography and Film

900 East Ave, Rochester, NY 14607
☎: 716-271-3361   ◙ www.eastman.org
Open: 10-4:30 Tu-Sa, 1-4:30 Su   **Closed:** Mo, LEG/HOL!
ADM   Adult: $6.50   **Children:** $2.50 (5-12)   **Students:** $5.00   **Seniors:** $5.00
 ♿ Ⓟ   **Museum Shop**   🍴
Group Tours: 716-271-3361, ext 238   **Drop-In Tours:** 10:30 & 2, Tu-Sa, 2, Su   **Historic Building**
Permanent Collection: PHOT: prints; MOTION PICTURES; MOTION PICTURE STILLS; CAMERAS; BOOKS

The historic home of George Eastman, founder of Eastman Kodak Co. includes a museum that contains an enormous and comprehensive collection of over 400,000 photographic prints, 21,000 motion pictures, 25,000 cameras, 41,000 books and 5,000,000 motion picture stills. **NOT TO BE MISSED:** Discovery room for children

ON EXHIBIT 1999

SEMI PERMANENT:
THROUGH THE LENS: SELECTIONS FROM THE PERMANENT COLLECTION

AN HISTORICAL TIMELINE OF PHOTO IMAGING

A PICTURE-PERFECT RESTORATION: GEORGE EASTMAN'S HOUSE AND GARDEN

ENHANCING THE ILLUSION: THE ORIGINS AND PROGRESS OF PHOTOGRAPHY

GEORGE EASTMAN IN FOCUS

10/18/1998 to 01/31/1999   PHOTOPLAY: WORKS FROM THE CHASE MANHATTAN COLLECTION
Included here are many international artists who have extended the material boundaries and conceptual range of photography in the last 30 years. They were not trained as photographers, but have changed the parameters of the medium. These include Hockney, Warhol, Kruger, Barney and Baldessari

07/25/1999 to 11/01/1999   THE RISE OF A LANDMARK: LEWIS HINE AND THE EMPIRE STATE BUILDING

Memorial Art Gallery
Affiliate Institution: University of Rochester
500 University Ave, Rochester, NY 14607
☎: 716-473-7720 ◙ www.rochester.edu/MAG
Open: 12-9 Tu, 10-4 We-Fr, 10-5 Sa, 12-5 Su **Closed:** Mo, LEG/HOL
ADM Adult: $5.00, $2 Tu 5-9 **Children:** 6-8 $3.00, F (5 and under) **Students:** $4.00 **Seniors:** $4.00
 🚻 ℗ **Museum Shop** 🍴 **Group Tours Drop-In Tours:** 2pm, Fr, Su; 7:30 PM Tu
Historic Building Sculpture Garden
Permanent Collection: MED; DU: 17; FR: 19; AM: ptgs, sculp 19, 20; FOLK

The Gallery's permanent collection of 10,000 works spans 50 centuries of world art and includes masterworks by artists such as Monet, Cezanne, Matisse, Homer and Cassatt. An interactive learning center focuses on Learning to Look. Also included is an interactive CD-ROM "tour" of the Gallery. **NOT TO BE MISSED:** 'Waterloo Bridge, Veiled Sun' 1903, by Monet

ON EXHIBIT 1999
11/22/1998 to 01/17/1999 LIVING WITH ART: ROCHESTER COLLECTS
This special holiday exhibit gives artists a rare opportunity to see art that is usually "behind closed doors".

05/16/1999 to 08/08/1999 57TH ROCHESTER-FINGER LAKES EXHIBITION
Since 1938, this has been a juried biennial showcase for area artists who have gone on to national recognition.

08/28/1999 to 04/14/1999 THE FRAME IN AMERICA: 1860-1960
The study of the frame and what it reveals as an enclosure and as a work of art in its own right is a new area of study. Many of these are from the Gallery's own collection of works including Eakins, Benton and Cassatt.

12/12/1999 to 01/30/2000 CIRCA 1900
A dazzling array of objects in all media created at the turn of the last century, greets the millennium. The works come from the Upstate Museum Consortium (Albany, Buffalo, Ithaca, Rochester, Syracuse and Utica)

ROSLYN HARBOR

Nassau County Museum of Fine Art
Northern Blvd & Museum Dr, Roslyn Harbor, NY 11576
☎: 516-484-9338 ◙ www.nassaumuseum.org
Open: 11-5 Tu-Su **Closed:** Mo, LEG/HOL
ADM Adult: $4.00 **Children:** $2.00 **Students:** $2.00 **Seniors:** $3.00
 🚻 ℗ **Museum Shop** 🍴 **Group Tours Drop-In Tours:** 2pm Tu-Sa **Historic Building Sculpture Garden**
Permanent Collection: AM: gr, sculp

Situated on 145 acres of formal gardens, rolling lawns and meadows, the museum presents four major exhibitions a year and is home to one of the east coasts' largest publicly accessible outdoor sculpture gardens.

SARATOGA SPRINGS

Schick Art Gallery
Affiliate Institution: Skidmore College
Skidmore Campus North Broadway, Saratoga Springs, NY 12866-1632
☎: 518-584-5000
Open: 9-5 Mo-Fr, 1-3:30 Sa, Su **Closed:** LEG/HOL!, ACAD!
 🚻 ℗ **Museum Shop** 🍴 **Group Tours Drop-In Tours**
Permanent Collection: non-collecting institution

Theme oriented or one person exhibitions that are often historically significant are featured in this gallery located on the beautiful Skidmore Campus.

NEW YORK

Parrish Art Museum

25 Job's Lane, Southampton, NY 11968
☎: 516-283-2118
Open: 11-5 Mo, Th, Fri, Sa, 1-5 Su; Open Daily Jun 1 - Sep 15   **Closed:** 1/1, EASTER, 7/4, THGV, 12/25
Sugg/Cont   Adult: $2.00   **Students:** F (with valid ID)   **Seniors:** $1.00
♿ ℗ **Museum Shop**
Group Tours   Drop-In Tours
Historic Building   Sculpture Garden
Permanent Collection: AM: ptgs, gr 19; WILLIAM MERRITT CHASE; FAIRFIELD PORTER

Situated in a fashionable summer community. this Museum is a 'don't miss' when one is near the Eastern tip of Long Island. It is located in an 1898 building designed by Grosvenor Atterbury.

ON EXHIBIT 1999

04/11/1999 to 06/20/1999   MARSDEN HARTLEY: AMERICAN MODERN
A part of the influential avant garde surrounding Alfred Steiglitz, which included John Marin, Georgia O'Keeffe, and Arthur Dove. He originally advocated American transcendentalists, then reversed to "real art come from the soul" and then returned to the belief in the subjective self. *Will Travel*

Jacques Marchais Museum of Tibetan Art

338 Lighthouse Ave., Staten Island, NY 10306
☎: 718-987-3500
Open: 1-5 We-Su (Apr-mid Nov or by appt. Dec-Mar)   **Closed:** Mo, Tu, EASTER, 7/4, LAB/DAY, THGV & day after
ADM   Adult: $3.00   **Children:** $1.00 (under 12)   **Students:** $3.00   **Seniors:** $2.50
♿ **Museum Shop**
Group Tours Drop-In Tours   Sculpture Garden
Permanent Collection: TIBET; OR: arch; GARDEN, BUDDHIST, HIMALAYAN

This unique museum of Himalayan art within a Tibetan setting consists of two stone buildings resembling a Buddhist temple. A quiet garden and a goldfish pond help to create an atmosphere of serenity and beauty. It is the only museum in this country devoted primarily to Tibetan art.

John A. Noble Collection at Snug Harbor

Affiliate Institution: Snug Harbor Cultural Center
270 Richmond Terrace, Staten Island, NY 10301
☎: 718-447-6490
Open: by appt.   **Closed:** LEG/HOL!
♿ ℗ **Museum Shop   Group Tours**: 718-447-6490   Drop-In Tours   **Historic Building**
Permanent Collection: PTGS; LITHOGRAPHS; DOCUMENTS AND ARTIFACTS; SALOON HOUSEBOAT OF JOHN A. NOBLE

John Noble wrote 'My life's work is to make a rounded picture of American Maritime endeavor of modern times'. He is widely regarded as America's premier marine lithographer. The collection, in a new site at historic Snug Harbor Cultural Center, is only partially on view as renovation continues.

Snug Harbor Cultural Center
Affiliate Institution: Newhouse Center for Contemporary Art
1000 Richmond Terrace, Staten Island, NY 10301
☎: 718-448-2500
Open: 12-5 We-Su **Closed:** Mo, LEG/HOL!
Adult: $2.00
  ⑤ Ⓟ **Museum Shop** ❘❘
Group Tours **Drop-In Tours**
Historic Building   **Sculpture Garden**
Permanent Collection: Non-collecting institution

Once a 19th century home for retired sailors Snug Harbor is a landmarked 83 acre, 28 building complex being preserved and adapted for the visual and performing arts. The Newhouse Center for Contemporary art provides a forum for regional and international design and art. **NOT TO BE MISSED:** The award winning newly restored 1884 fresco ceiling in the Main Hall.

ON EXHIBIT 1999
11/08/1998 to 03/28/1999 NEW ISLAND VIEWS

05/02/1999 to 09/26/1999 THROUGH THE LOOKING GLASS: VISIONS OF CHILDHOOD

Staten Island Institute of Arts and Sciences
75 Stuyvesant Place, Staten Island, NY 10301
☎: 718-727-1135
Open: 9-5 Mo-Sa, 1-5 S **Closed:** LEG/HOL!
Sugg/Cont Adult: $2.50 **Students:** $1.50 **Seniors:** $1.50
  ⑤ Ⓟ **Museum Shop**
Group Tours Drop-In Tours
Permanent Collection: PTGS; DEC/ART; SCULP; STATEN ISLAND: arch

One of Staten Island's oldest and most diverse cultural institutions, this facility explores and interprets the art, natural resources and cultural history of Staten Island. **NOT TO BE MISSED:** Ferry Collection on permanent exhibition. This exhibition on the history of the world-famous ferry service is located in the Staten Island Ferry terminal.

ON EXHIBIT 1999
ONGOING THE STATEN ISLAND FERRY COLLECTION OF SIIAS
The history of the world's most famous Ferry Line is explored in an exhibition in the Staten Island Ferry waiting room, St. George. open daily 9-2 Suggested donation: adults $1.00; children under 12 $.25

01/12/1999 to 02/12/1999 RACHEL FRIEDBERG

03/01/1999 to 07/02/1999 MICROSCOPES

03/26/1999 to 05/26/1999 JOAN GIORDANO SHOW (working title)

06/10/1999 to 09/05/1999 JACQUES REICH AND HERMAN ZAAGE PRINTS

07/23/1999 to 01/09/2000 1999 JURIED STATEN ISLAND CRAFTS EXHIBITION

09/24/1999 to 03/05/2000 A HISTORY OF STATEN ISLAND FROM CITY TO BOROUGH

NEW YORK

Museums at Stony Brook

1208 Rte. 25A, Stony Brook, NY 11790-1992
☎: 516-751-0066   ◙ www.museumsatstonybrook.org
Open: 10-5 We-Sa, 12-5 Su, July, Aug 10-5 Mo-Sa, 12-5 S   **Closed:** Mo, Tu, 1/1, THGV, 12/24, 12/25
Free Day: We, for Students   **ADM**   **Adult:** $4.00   **Children:** $2.00 (6-17)under6 F   **Students:** $2.00   **Seniors:** $3.00
& ℗   **Museum Shop**
Group Tours: EXT.248   **Drop-In Tours**: !
Permanent Collection: AM: ptgs; HORSE DRAWN CARRIAGES; MINIATURE ROOMS; ANT: decoys; COSTUMES; TOYS

A museum complex on a nine acre site with art, history, and carriage museums, blacksmith shop, 19th century one room schoolhouse, carriage shed and 1794 barn. **NOT TO BE MISSED:** Paintings by William Sidney Mount (1807-1868), 100 horse drawn carriages.

ON EXHIBIT 1999

08/1998 to Spring 1999/   WILLIAM SIDNEY MOUNT: PAINTER OF AMERICAN LIFE
At a time when other American Artists portrayed European models, Mount successfully transferred these images into imagery specific to American life. His scenes of everyday life included stories and jokes about rural life. Farmer, boys and musicians were regulars in his cast of characters. He struck a sympathetic chord with public and critics and was zoom pronounced the most talented artist of his time. 50 paintings and works on paper will be featured here. *Catalog Will Travel*

11/14/1998 to 01/03/1999   HOLIDAY CELEBRATIONS '98!
More than 150 decorations by artists and craftspeople will be on display.

01/16/1999 to 05/22/1999   THE HOLOCAUST WALL HANGINGS OF JUDITH LIBERMAN
American fabric artist Judith Liberman documents the events and acts against humanity during the Holocaust.

06/06/1999 to 05/31/1999   GEORGE WASHINGTON, AMERICAN SYMBOL
To coincide with the 200th Anniversary of George Washington's death, this exhibition will analyze the changing image of our nation's celebrated Revolutionary War Commander and first President.

07/08/1999 to 09/10/1999   NEW YORK IN THE CARRIAGE ERA
The Museum's Carriage collection will be shown at the Paine-Webber Gallery in New York City.

Everson Museum of Art

401 Harrison Street, Syracuse, NY 13202
☎: 315-474-6064   ◙   www.everson.org
Open: 12-5 Tu-Fr, 10-5 Sa, 12-5 Su   **Closed:** Mo, LEG/HOL
Sugg/Cont   Adult: $2.00
& ℗   **Museum Shop**   ‼
Group Tours   **Drop-In Tours**   **Historic Building**   **Sculpture Garden**
Permanent Collection: AM: cer; AM: ptgs 19, 20; AM: Arts/Crafts Movement Objects

When it was built in 1968, the first museum building designed by I. M. Pei was called 'a work of art for works of art'. The museum houses American art including paintings spanning two centuries, the most comprehensive holding of American ceramic art in the nation, and significant collections of sculpture, video, photography, and decorative arts. **NOT TO BE MISSED:** The Syracuse China Center for the Study of Ceramics with a permanent exhibition of American and world ceramics.

Everson Museum of Art - continued

ON EXHIBIT 1999

ONGOING   ONE HUNDRED FIFTY YEARS OF AMERICAN ART
An overview of American art featuring turn of the century portraits and genre paintings, late 19th century landscapes and American modernism through the 1950s, including American Scene painting by some of America's best known artists.

ONGOING   INTERNATIONAL CONTEMPORARY CERAMICS

ONGOING   SYRACUSE CHINA CENTER FOR THE STUDY OF AMERICAN CERAMICS

to 02/14/1999   CARRIE MAE WEEMS

03/05/1999 to 05/23/1999   MODERN AMERICAN REALISM: THE SARA ROBY FOUNDATION COLLECTION FROM THE NATIONAL MUSEUM OF AMERICAN ART
60 works drawn from one of the premiere collections of American figurative art including Raphael Soyer, Edward Hopper, Paul Cadmus, George Tooker and others. Modern American Realism: The Sara Roby Foundation Collection from the National Museum of American Art *Catalog Will Travel*

06/11/1999 to 08/08/1999   THE UNEXPECTED: ARTISTS' CERAMICS OF THE 20TH CENTURY

09/1999 to 12/1999   FRANK GILETTE

TARRYTOWN

Kykuit

Affiliate Institution: Historic Hudson Valley,
150 White Plains Road, Tarrytown, NY 10591
☎: 914-631-9491
Open: Closed: Tu, Open mid-April through October
ADM   Adult: $18.00   **Children:** not rec under 12   **Seniors:** $16.00
♿ ⓟ **Museum Shop**
Group Tours   Drop-In Tours
Sculpture Garden
Permanent Collection:

The six story stone house which was the Rockefeller home for four generations is filled with English and American furnishings, portraits and extraordinary collections of Asian ceramics. In the art galleries are paintings and sculpture by Andy Warhol, George Segal, Alexander Calder, Robert Motherwell and many others. Visitors also view the enclosed gardens and terraces with their collections of classical and 20th century sculpture and stunning river views. The Coach Barn contains horse-drawn carriages and classic automobiles. The Beaux-Arts gardens were designed by William Welles Bosworth and are filled with an extraordinary collection of modern sculpture.
www.hudsonvalley.org

ON EXHIBIT 1999

Reservations are strongly recommended. Reservations are assigned to groups of 18. There will be two tours in 1997: the House and Galleries Tour and the new Garden and Sculpture Tour which includes areas of the estate never before open to the public. Tours are 1-1 ½ hours. There is also a N.Y. Waterway Tour which leaves NYC or NJ for a cruise to Tarrytown and then boards a bus to the Philipsburg Manor Visitors Center which is the point of departure for all tours. For reservations via the ferry call 1-800-53-ferry.

NEW YORK

Munson-Williams Proctor Institute Museum of Art

310 Genesee Street, Utica, NY 13502
☎: 315-797-0000   ◉ www.mwpi.edu
Open: 10-5 Tu-Sa, 1-5 Su   **Closed:** Mo, LEG/HOL
Sugg/Cont
& ℗ **Museum Shop**
Group Tours: 315-797-0000, ext 2170   **Drop-In Tours**: by appt   **Historic Building**   **Sculpture Garden**
Permanent Collection: AM: ptgs, dec/art; EU: manuscripts, gr, drgs

The Museum is a combination of the first art museum designed by renowned architect Philip Johnson (1960) and Fountain Elms, an 1850 historic house museum which was the home of the museum's founders.

ON EXHIBIT 1999

09/05/1998 to 01/31/1999   JAWS, CLAWS AND PAWS

11/21/1998 to 12/31/1999   THE GILDED EDGE: FRAMES IN THE PERMANENT COLLECTION

02/13/1999 to 05/09/1999   PIUOS PAGES: GOTHIC AND RENAISSANCE BOOK ART FROM THE MUNSON-WILLIAMS-PROCTOR INSTITUTE COLLECTION

05/02/1999 to 10/31/1999   MASTERPIECES OF AMERICAN FURNITURE FROM THE MUNSON-WILLIAMS-PROCTOR INSTITUTE COLLECTION

06/05/1999 to 09/12/1999   SATORU TAKAHASHI: THE SCULPTURE COURT PROJECT

Hudson River Museum

511 Warburton Ave, Yonkers, NY 10701-1899
☎: 914-963-4550   ◉ www.hrm.org
Open: 12-5 We-Su, (Oct-Apr), 12-5 We, Th, Sa, Su, 12-9 Fr (May-Sept)   **Closed:** Mo, Tu, LEG/HOL!
ADM   Adult: $3.00   **Children:** $1.50 (under 12)   **Seniors:** $1.50
& ℗ **Museum Shop**   ¶: The Hudson River Café overlooking the Hudson River
Group Tours: 914-963-4550 ext 40   **Drop-In Tours**: by appt   **Historic Building**   **Sculpture Garden**
Permanent Collection: AM: ldscp/ptgs 19, 20; DEC/ART; GR: 19, 20; COSTUMES; PHOT: 19, 20.

The Hudson River Museum overlooking the Palisades, provides a dramatic setting for changing exhibitions of art, architecture, design, history and science - many designed for families. Discover the Hudson River's special place in American life as you enjoy the art. The Museum Shop was designed by Pop artist Red Grooms. There are Planetarium Star Shows in the Andrus Planetarium at 1:30, 2:30, 3:30 Sa, Su. **NOT TO BE MISSED:** Hiram Powers ''Eve Disconsolate', marble statue, 1871, (gift of Berol family in memory of Mrs. Gella Berolzheimer, 1951). Also, woodwork and stencils in the decorated period rooms of the 1876 Glenview Mansion.

ON EXHIBIT 1999

ONGOING   GLENVIEW MANSION
Completed in 1877 and overlooking the Hudson and the Palisades, four period rooms of the Mansion have been restored to reflect the lifestyle of its turn-of-the-century inhabitants, the John Trevor Bond family. This building is considered one of the finest examples of an Eastlake interior open to the public.

ONGOING   THE ANDRUS PLANETARIUM
Star shows Sa, Su 1:30, 2:30 and 3:30 PM; Fr 7

Hudson River Museum - continued

09/25/1998 to 01/17/1999   RELATIVELY SPEAKING: PAINTINGS BY KATHERINE HU FAN

Shanghai born and American university educated, Katherine Fan's provocative mixed media, multi paneled paintings comment on myriad social views. Her colorist sensibilities and unique brushwork reflect the Western influence of Abstract Expressionism and her Eastern heritage is evident in the Chinese characters and rice paper collage.

10/02/1998 to 01/24/1999   GETTING FROM HERE TO THERE

Paintings, drawings, prints, photographs, building plans and historical artifacts as well as specially fabricated interactive stations enabling visitors to assemble bridges based on professional design principles and engineering standards. 11 bridges in the New York Metropolitan area will be examined from the perspective of art, history and technology. Central to the show's theme and organization is how artists have rendered and interpreted bridges.

10/02/1998 to 01/24/1999   THE LITTLE RED LIGHTHOUSE AND THE GREAT GRAY BRIDGE

40 original illustrations from the Lynd Ward and Hildegarde children's story will be shown to compliment, for children, the exhibition 'Getting From Here To There'. Labels will be written from the "big brother" bridge's point of view.

10/09/1998 to 01/03/1999   STONE AND STEEL: BRIDGES BY BASCOVE

Bascove began painting bridges in the late 70s in Paris and has continued to do so. Her pencil drawings and oil paintings offer a unique perspective on New York City's bridges.

10/16/1998 to 01/10/1999   MAKING WAVES: SCULPTURE BY SARAH HAVILAND

Each sculpture by this artist begins with a female figure and a gesture or pose that carries emotional and symbolic meaning for her. She then simplifies the form to almost geometric clarity. The result is a delicate balance between abstract sculpture and female identity. Materials used include wire mesh, plaster, cement, steel, bronze, plywood and mirrors.

11/27/1998 to 01/03/1999   VISIONS OF SUGARPLUMS

A display of Victorian Christmas ornaments and holiday decorations as well as an opportunity for visitors to create their own ornaments during specially scheduled gallery activities.

01/15/1999 to 05/09/1999   FAMILY TIES: WORKS BY DENISE ALLEN

Folk artist Allen has been using needlework to address social and historical themes. She fabricates powerful wall hangings exploring slavery in 19th century America also using hand-sown dolls and found objects in her three dimensional works.

02/12/1999 to 06/20/1999   DRIP, BLOW, BURN

The work of contemporary artists who employ wind, water and fire as integral components of their art is shown here. They vary in scope and media to include sculpture, photography, installation, performance. Video and conceptual art.

07/02/1999 to 09/19/1999   ANDY WARHOL: ENDANGERED SPECIES

In 1983 Warhol produced this series of 10 silk screen images of animals which were facing extinction at that time. The many screens used to print each image is an exciting opportunity for various color combinations. *Will Travel*

07/02/1999 to 01/09/2000   HUNTERS OF THE SKY

For hundreds of years birds of prey have maintained a fierce grip on the human imagination. The ways in which they have adapted to their ecological niches is examined through their use as symbols in art, literature, and religions of the world from ancient times to the present day.

10/15/1999 to 12/19/1999   ART AND NATURE: THE HUDSON RIVER SCHOOL

Beginning with Thomas Cole and the following three generations of artists the Hudson River School painters were known for their dramatic depictions of nature. Among the artists in this exhibition are Cole, Durand, Church, Cropsey, Hart, Kensett, Martin, Johnson Castilear and Inness who illustrate how the meaning and importance of the Hudson River School has changed over time. *Will Travel*

NORTH CAROLINA

ASHEVILLE

Asheville Art Museum
2 S. Pack Square, Asheville, NC 28801
☎: 828-253-3227
Open: 10-5 Tu-Fr, Summer hours June-Oct also 1-5 Sa, Su, and until 8 Fr
Closed: Mo, 1/1,MEM/DAY,7/4,LAB/DAY,THGV,12/25
Free Day: 1st We 3-5pm **Sugg/Cont:** for special exh $2.00
Adult: $3.00 **Children:** 4-14 $2.50 **Students:** $2.50 **Seniors:** $2.50
♿ ⓖ **Museum Shop Group Tours:** 800-935-0204 **Drop-In Tours Historic Building**
Permanent Collection: AM/REG: ptgs, sculp, crafts 20

The Museum collection of more than 1,200 objects in all media is housed in the splendidly restored Old Pack Memorial Library, a 1920's Beaux Arts Building. 14 special exhibitions are mounted annually.

CHAPEL HILL

Ackland Art Museum
Columbia & Franklin Sts-Univ. Of North Carolina, Chapel Hill, NC 27599
☎: 919-966-5736 ▣ www.unc.edu/depts/ackland/
Open: 10-5 We-Sa, 1-5 Su **Closed:** Mo, Tu, 12/25
Sugg/Cont: $3.00
♿ ⓖ Museum Shop **Group Tours**: 919-962-3342 **Drop-In Tours**
Permanent Collection: EU & AM: ptgs, gr 15-20; PHOT; REG

The Ackland, with a collection of more than 12,000 works of art ranging from ancient times to the present, includes a wide variety of categories conveying the breadth of mankind's achievements.

ON EXHIBIT 1999
09/19/1998 to 07/28/1999 HUNG LIU: PAINTINGS 1988-1998

10/24/1998 to 01/04/1999 THE SYMBOLIST PRINTS OF EDWARD MUNCH
A rare opportunity to see one of the finest collections of Munch prints in the world representing the full spectrum of his emotions and his unique contribution to Expressionism at the end of the 19th C.

12/06/1998 to 01/04/1999 TRADITION AND TRANSFORMATION: CONTEMPORARY INUIT ART FROM NUNAVUT
60 Prints and sculptures representing the inauguration of the Inuit homeland of Nunavut as an independent Canadian territory.

12/03/1999 to 01/02/2000 DUTCH LANDSCAPE DRAWINGS FROM THE PECK COLLECTION

12/19/1999 to 03/26/2000 TRANSATLANTIC DIALOGUES : AFRICAN/AFRICAN-AMERICAN ART

CHARLOTTE

Mint Museum of Art
2730 Randolph Road, Charlotte, NC 28207-2031
☎: 704-337-2000 ▣ www.mintmuseum.org
Open: 10-10 Tu, 10-5 We-Sa, 12-5 Su **Closed:** Mo, LEG/HOL
Free Day: Tu 5-10, 2nd Su of mo ADM: **Adult:** $4.00 **Children:** under 12 F **Students:** $2.00 **Seniors:** $3.00
♿ ⓖ **Museum Shop Group Tours**: 704-337-2032 **Drop-In Tours**: 2 PM daily **Historic Building**
Permanent Collection: EU &AM: ptgs; REN; CONT; CH; DEC/ART; AM: pottery, glass; BRIT: cer

Mint Museum of Art - continued
The building, erected in 1836 as the first branch of the US Mint, produced 5 million dollars in gold coins before the Civil war. In 1936 it opened as the first art museum in North Carolina. When the museum was moved to its present parkland setting the facade of the original building was integrated into the design of the new building. **NOT TO BE MISSED:** Extensive Delhom collection of English pottery beautifully displayed

The Mint Museum of Craft and Design will open Spring 1999
Exhibitions scheduled:
Spring 1999   THE WHITE HOUSE COLLECTION OF AMERICAN CRAFT   *Catalog   Will Travel*

Spring 1999   HARVEY LITTLETON REFLECTIONS, 1946-1994

06/1999-12/1999   DALE CHIHULY: INSTALLATIONS (glass)

ON EXHIBIT 1999
08/01/1998 to 02/14/1999   EARTH FIRE AND SPIRIT: AFRICAN POTTERY AND SCULPTURE
A newly acquired collection of West African ceramic vessels and sculpture including a Yoruba shrine fertility vessel and a Dakakari ceramic grave marker in the form of a goat. *Will Travel*

09/05/1998 to 03/14/1999   WILLIAM LITTLER: AN 18TH CENTURY ENGLISH POTTER
Littler was a pioneer in the refinement of English soft paste porcelain and salt glazes. The exhibition focuses on his innovations in stoneware and glazes.

10/31/1998 to 01/03/1999   LOIS MAILOU JONES AND HER STUDENTS
A tribute to this artist and teach. The work of 38 of her students represent the struggles and triumphs of artists of color during this century.

07/24/1999 to 12/05/1999   FROM SHIP TO SHORE: MARINE PAINTING
Over 60 paintings, ranging from ship portraiture to ocean views, highlight the general fascination with marine culture since colonial times. *Will Travel*

DALLAS

Gaston County Museum of Art and History
131 W. Main Street, Dallas, NC 28034
☎: 704-922-7681 INFO-LINE (events) 704 852-6025
Open: 10-5 Tu-Fr, 1-5 Sa, 2-5 4th Su of month   **Closed:** Mo, Su other than 4th of month, LEG/HOL!
  Ⓟ   **Museum Shop   Group Tours**: 704-923-8103   **Drop-In Tours   Historic Building   Sculpture Garden**

The museum, housed in the 1852 Hoffman Hotel located on the historic Court Square, features including a new hands-on parlor on the newly renovated third floor. Changing exhibits alternate regional, national and international art topics with history of Gaston County from 1840's on. **NOT TO BE MISSED:** Sleighs, drays, and buggies, the largest public collection of carriages in the Southeast.

DAVIDSON

William H. Van Every Gallery and Edward M. Smith Gallery
Davidson College, Visual Arts Center, 315 N. Main Street, Davidson, NC 28036
☎: 704-892-2519
Open: 10-6 Mo-Fr, 10-2 Sa, Su (Sep-June)   **Closed:** LEG/HOL! ACAD
Vol/Cont: Yes
  Ⓟ   **Museum Shop   Group Tours   Drop-In Tours   Historic Building** Designed by Graham Gund
Permanent Collection: WORKS ON PAPER, PTGS Hist, Cont

In the fall of 1993 the Gallery moved to a new building designed by Graham Gund where selections from the 2,500 piece permanent collection are displayed at least once during the year. The Gallery also presents a varied roster of contemporary and historical exhibitions. **NOT TO BE MISSED:** Auguste Rodin's 'Jean d'Aire, bronze

NORTH CAROLINA

DURHAM

Duke University Museum of Art

Affiliate Institution: Duke University
Buchanan Blvd at Trinity, Durham, NC 27701
☎: 919-684-5135
Open: 9-5 Tu-Fr, 11-2 Sa, 2-5 Su **Closed:** Mo, LEG/HOL!
♿ Ⓟ Museum Shop
Group Tours **Drop-In Tours**
Permanent Collection: MED: sculp; DEC/ART; AF: sculp; AM & EU: all media

Duke University Art Museum, with its impressive collection ranging from ancient to modern works includes the Breumner collection of Medieval art, widely regarded as a one of a kind in the US, and a large pre-Columbian collection from Central and South America as well as a collection of contemporary Russian art.

ON EXHIBIT 1999

01/14/1999 to 02/28/1999 CATALINA AROCENA

01/22/1999 to 03/21/1999 A CELEBRATION OF BARRIER ISLANDS: RESTLESS RIBBONS OF SAND

01/31/1999 to 02/21/1999 AN ELIZABETHAN BESTIARY RETOLD

04/09/1999 to 06/06/1999 STUDENT CURATED EXHIBITION XI: ART IN LA

04/11/1999 to 04/25/1999 NUNAVUT: AN INTUIT HOMELAND *Catalog Will Travel*

04/15/1999 to 06/16/1999 CRITIC'S CHOICE: MICHELE NATALE

05/28/1999 to 06/13/1999 3RD ANNUAL DUMA/DURHAM MAGNET SCHOOL EXHIBITION

06/25/1999 to 08/08/1999 NEW ART IN THE TRIANGLE

FAYETTEVILLE

Fayetteville Museum of Art

839 Stamper Road, Fayetteville, NC 28303
☎: 910-485-5121 ◙ www.fayetteville.com/community/fmaster
Open: 10-5 Mo-Fr, 1-5 Sa, Su **Closed:** Mo, 1/1, EASTER, 7/4, THGV, 12/23-12/31
♿ Ⓟ Museum Shop
Group Tours: 910-485-0548 **Drop-In Tours** **Sculpture Garden**
Permanent Collection: CONT: North Carolina art; PTGS, SCULP, CER, AF artifacts

The museum, whose building was the first in the state designed and built as an art museum, also features an impressive collection of outdoor sculpture on its landscaped grounds.

ON EXHIBIT 1999

11/21/1998 to 01/17/1999 AMERICAN LANDSCAPE PAINTING
An exploration of landscape painting ranging from the Hudson River School period to the present.

01/23/1999 to 03/07/1999 THE ARTISTS OF WILMINGTON
This is the first in a series of exhibitions showcasing leading contemporary artists from metro areas of the state.

Fayetteville Museum of Art - continued

03/14/1999 to 05/02/1999   TWENTY-SEVENTH ANNUAL COMPETITION FOR NORTH CAROLINA ARTISTS
A distinguished and professional juried competition.

05/08/1999 to 07/04/1999   KEEPING THE CIRCLE
Visual arts, music, stories and videotape of the Native Americans of eastern North Carolina.

07/10/1999 to 09/05/1999   SELECTIONS FROM THE PERMANENT COLLECTION
Works by North Carolina artists including David Loren Bass, George Bireline, Joe Cox, Maud Gatewood, Ruth Shaw and others.

09/11/1999 to 11/07/1999   THE ART OF COLLAGE
Contemporary North Carolina artists working in the medium.

11/13/1999 to 12/18/1999   A SURVEY OF CONTEMPORARY NORTH CAROLINA PRINTS
Current explorations in printmaking.

GREENSBORO

Weatherspoon Art Gallery

Affiliate Institution: The University of North Carolina
Spring Garden & Tate Street, Greensboro, NC 27412-5001
☎: 910-334-5770   ◙   www.uncg.edu/wag/
Open: 10-5 Tu, Th, Fr, 1-5 Sa, Su, 10-8 We   **Closed:** Mo, ACAD! and vacations
&.   ℗   **Museum Shop   Group Tours Drop-In Tours:** 1st Su 2pm !   **Historic Building   Sculpture Garden**
Permanent Collection: AM: 20; MATISSE PRINTS AND BRONZE SCULPTURES; OR

Designed by renowned architect, Romaldo Giurgola, the Weatherspoon Art Gallery features six galleries showcasing special exhibitions and a predominantly 20th century collection of American art with works by Willem de Kooning, Alex Katz, Louise Nevelson, David Smith, and Robert Rauschenberg. **NOT TO BE MISSED:** The Cone Collection of Matisse prints and bronzes

GREENVILLE

Greenville Museum of Art Inc

802 Evans Street, Greenville, NC 27834
☎: 919-758-1946   ◙   GMA.greenvillenc.com
Open: 10-4:30 Th, Fr, 1-4 Su   **Closed:** LEG/HOL!
&.   ℗   **Museum Shop   Group Tours Drop-In Tours**
Permanent Collection: AM: all media 20

Founded in 1939 as a WPA Gallery, the Greenville Museum of Art focuses primarily on the achievements of 20th century American art. Many North Carolina artists are represented in its collection which also includes works by George Bellows, Thomas Hart Benton, Robert Henri, Louise Nevelson, and George Segal, to name but a few. **NOT TO BE MISSED:** Major collection of Jugtown pottery

Wellington B. Gray Gallery

Affiliate Institution: East Carolina University
Jenkins Fine Arts Center, Greenville, NC 27858
☎: 919-757-6336   ◙   www.ecu.edu/art/home.html
Open: 10-5 Mo-We, Fr 10-8 Th, 10-3 Sa   **Closed:** Su, LEG/HOL!,ACAD/HOL
&.   ℗   **Museum Shop   Group Tours Drop-In Tours   Sculpture Garden**
Permanent Collection: CONT; AF

One of the largest contemporary art galleries in North Carolina. **NOT TO BE MISSED:** Print portfolio, Larry Rivers 'The Boston Massacre'; African Art Collection

NORTH CAROLINA

Hickory Museum of Art

243 Third Ave. NE, Hickory, NC 28601
☎: 828-327-8576
Open: 10-5 Tu-Fr, 10-4 Sa, 1-4 S **Closed:** Mo, LEG/HOL!
Vol/Cont: **Adult:** $2.00 **Children:** $1.00 over 12 **Students:** $1.00 **Seniors:** $1.00
& ℗ **Museum Shop Group Tours:** 828-327-8576 **Drop-In Tours Historic Building**
Permanent Collection: AM: all media 19, 20 ; ART POTTERY; AM: Impr

The second oldest art museum in North Carolina and the first in the southeast US to collect American art, it is located in one of Hickory's finest examples of neo-classic revival architecture. **NOT TO BE MISSED:** William Merritt Chase painting (untitled)

ON EXHIBIT 1999

01/16/1999 to 04/04/1999 PULP FICTION: AN EXAMINATION OF WORKS ON PAPER FROM THE PERMANENT COLLECTION
The diversity of art and medium applied to paper *Brochure*

01/24/1999 to 04/11/1999 UN DIALOGO VISUAL A TRAVES EN LAS AMERICAS: WORKS FROM THE ART MUSEUM OF THE AMERICAS
Art from across North and South America to continue the dialog of building a better understanding of cultures. *Catalog Admission Fee*

02/26/1999 to 09/12/1999 ART ENTWINED: A FIBER INVITATIONAL
Whether woven, painted, plaited, or worked with a needle, Fibers have always been carriers of meaning.

04/10/1999 to 06/27/1999 PEOPLE AT WORK: A CELEBRATION OF AMERICAN LABOR

08/29/1999 to 11/08/1999 GRAPHICS BY 20TH CENTURY MASTERS
56 works by artists including Calder, Chagall, Lichtenstein, Stella, Rauschenberg, Stela, and Wesselman . *Catalog*

11/07/1999 to 01/02/2000 THE UNIFOUR COLLECTION *Catalog*

Wilkes Art Gallery

800 Elizabeth Street, North Wilkesboro, NC 28659
☎: 910-667-2841
Open: 10-5 Tu-Fr, 12-4 Sa **Closed:** Su, Mo,1/1, EASTER, EASTER MONDAY, 7/4, 12/25
& ℗ **Museum Shop Group Tours Drop-In Tours**
Permanent Collection: REG & CONT: all media

This 80 year old neighborhood facility which was formerly the Black Cat Restaurant presents monthly changing exhibitions often featuring minority artists.

North Carolina Museum of Art

2110 Blue Ridge Road, Raleigh, NC 27607-6494
☎: 919-839-6262 ▣ www2.ncsu.edu/ncma
Open: 9-5 Tu-Th, Sa, 9-9 Fr, 11-6 Su **Closed:** Mo, LEG/HOL!
& ℗ **Museum Shop** ‖: Café serves lunch daily & dinner Fri 5:30-8:45
Group Tours: 919-839-6262, ext. 2145 **Drop-In Tours:** 1:30 daily **Sculpture Garden**
Permanent Collection: EU/OM: ptgs; AM: ptgs 19; ANCIENT ART; AF; REG; JEWISH CEREMONIAL ART

North Carolina Museum of Art - continued

The Kress Foundation, in 1960, added to the museum's existing permanent collection of 139 prime examples of American and European artworks, a donation of 71 masterworks. This gift was second in scope and importance only to the Kress bequest to the National Gallery in Washington, D.C. **NOT TO BE MISSED:** Kress Collection

ON EXHIBIT 1999

10/18/1998 to 02/14/1999 SELECTIONS FROM THE FRANCES M. AND WILLIAM R. ROBERSON, JR. COLLECTION

01/31/1999 to 03/28/1999 ALPHONSE MUCHA: THE FLOWERING OF ART NOUVEAU
The first major exhibition of the work of this artist since 1921 will feature about 150 0f his most important paintings, posters, jewelry, sculpture, decorative panels, pastels and illustrations from collections all over the world. *Catalog Will Travel*

03/21/1999 to 06/27/1999 THE HASKELL COLLECTION OF CONTEMPORARY ART

04/17/1999 to 09/26/1999 TOGETHER FOREVER: PORTRAIT PENDANTS FROM THE NORTH CAROLINA MUSEUM OF ART

06/13/1999 to 09/19/1999 NORTH CAROLINA ARTISTS EXHIBITION 1999

09/19/1999 to 12/05/1999 THE NEWBY COLLECTION OF CONTEMPORARY ART

North Carolina State University Gallery of Art & Design

Cates Ave.,University Student Center, Raleigh, NC 27695-7306
☎: 919-515-3503   █ www2.acs.ncsu.edu/visualart
Open: 12-8 We-Fr, 2-8 Sa, Su   **Closed:** Mo, Tu, ACAD!
♿ Ⓟ **Museum Shop** ۱۱
Group Tours: 919-515-3503   **Drop-In Tours**
Permanent Collection: AM: cont, dec/art, phot, outsider art, textiles, ceramics, paintings

The Center hosts exhibitions of contemporary arts and design of regional and national significance and houses research collections of photography, historical and contemporary ceramics, textiles, glass and furniture.

ON EXHIBIT 1999

01/28/1999 to 03/07/1999 STEVEN ASSAEL: ORDINARY/EXTRAORDINARY FIGURES

01/28/1999 to 03/07/1999 BUILDING ON A SMALL SCALE

04/08/1999 to 06/06/1999 FRIENDS OF THE GALLERY COLLECT

04/08/1999 to 06/06/1999 PHOTOGRAPHS FROM THE ESTATE OF RICK HORTON

08/08/1999 to 09/26/1999 APPLIQUÉS: THE INTERNATIONAL COLLECTION OF NELL SONNEMAN

10/21/1999 to 12/12/1999 MODERNIST EYE: THE ART AND DESIGN OF NATHAN LERNER

10/21/1999 to 12/12/1999 CHAIRS

Blount Bridgers House/Hobson Pittman Memorial Gallery

130 Bridgers Street, Tarboro, NC 27886
☎: 919-823-4159 ▣ www2.coastalnet.com/ng3f3w5rm
Open: 10-4 Mo-Fr, 2-4 Sa, Su **Closed:** LEG/HOL!, Good Fri, Easter
Vol/Cont: **ADM:** **Adult:** $2.00
♿ Ⓝ **Museum Shop**
Group Tours: 252-823-4159 **Drop-In Tours**: Mo-Fr 10-4, Sa, Su, 2-4
Historic Building
Permanent Collection: AM: 20; DEC/ART:19

In a beautiful North Carolina town, the 1808 Plantation House and former home of Thomas Blount houses decorative arts of the 19th Century and the Hobson Pittman (American, 1899-1972) Collections of paintings and memorabilia. **NOT TO BE MISSED:** 'The Roses',oil, by Hobson Pittman

ON EXHIBIT 1999

01/14/1999 to 02/28/1999 HOBSON PITTMAN-THE EARLY YEARS-1899-1930

03/05/1999 to 04/25/1999 HOBSON PITTMAN EARLY STILL LIFES-1927-1950

05/01/1999 to 06/27/1999 HOBSON PITMAN INTERIORS-1930-1970

07/06/1999 to 08/29/1999 HOBSON PITTMAN EXTERIORS -1918-1970

09/14/1999 to 10/24/1999 HOBSON PITTMAN LATE STILL LIFES-1950-1972

11/04/1999 to 11/14/1999 GREAT TARBORO ART BAZAAR

11/18/1999 to 12/31/1999 WORKS FROM THE PERMANENT COLLECTION
Including Frank London, Leon Stacks, Ralph Feichter, Helene Stephanson, Hiram Williams, Elliot Dangerfield, H.C.Ahl, Barclay Sheaks.

St. John's Museum of Art

114 Orange Street, Wilmington, NC 28401
☎: 910-763-0281 ▣ www.wilmington.org/stjohnsart
Open: 10-5 Tu-Sa, 12-4 Su **Closed:** Mo, LEG/HOL!
Free Day: 1st Su of month **Vol/Cont:** Yes ADM: **Adult:** $2.00 **Children:** $1.00 under 18
♿ Ⓝ **Museum Shop**
Group Tours Drop-In Tours
Historic Building
Permanent Collection: AM: ptgs, sculp

Housed in three architecturally distinctive buildings dating back to 1804, St. John's Museum of Art is the primary visual arts center in Southeastern North Carolina. The Museum highlights two centuries of North Carolina and American masters. **NOT TO BE MISSED:** Mary Cassatt color prints

Reynolda House, Museum of American Art

Reynolda Road, Winston-Salem, NC 27106
☎: 336-725-5325 ▣ www.reynoldahouse.org
Open: 9:30-4:30 Tu-Sa, 1:30-4:30 Su **Closed:** Mo, 1/1, THGV, 12/25
ADM: Adult: $6.00 **Children:** $3.00 **Students:** $3.00 **Seniors:** $5.00
& ℗ **Museum Shop Group Tours:** 336-725-5325 **Drop-In Tours Historic Building**
Permanent Collection: AM: ptgs 18-present; HUDSON RIVER SCHOOL; DOUGHTY BIRDS

Reynolda House, an historic home designed by Charles Barton Keen, was built between 1914 and 1917 by Richard Joshua Reynolds, founder of R.J. Reynolds Tobacco Company, and his wife, Katharine Smith Reynolds **NOT TO BE MISSED:** Costume Collection

Southeastern Center for Contemporary Art

750 Marguerite Drive, Winston-Salem, NC 27106
☎: 336-725-1904
Open: 10-5 Tu-Sa, 2-5 Su **Closed:** Mo, LEG/HOL!
ADM: Adult: $3.00 **Children:** F (under 12) **Students:** $2.00 **Seniors:** $2.00
& ℗ **Museum Shop**
Group Tours: 336-725-1904, EXT 14 **Drop-In Tours Historic Building Sculpture Garden**
Permanent Collection: Non-collecting institution

Outstanding contemporary art being produced throughout the nation is showcased at the Southeastern Center for Contemporary Art, a cultural resource for the community and its visitors.

ON EXHIBIT 1999

10/24/1998 to 02/07/1999 IN SEQUENCE: SELECTIONS FROM THE METROPOLITAN SAVINGS BANK COLLECTIONS
This group exhibition explores the work of contemporary photographers who work sequentially.

10/24/1998 to 02/07/1999 THE ART GUYS
A Houston based collaborative team including Michael Galbreth and Jack Massing. They draw from Dadaism, Fluzuz, and Conceptual Art to highlight the accidental and ephemeral aspects of making art. They make serious art in a humorous vein.

02/20/1999 to 05/30/1999 ACCOUNTS SOUTHEAST
A group exhibition of artists who live and work in the Southeast. They have made significant contributions to art of the religious and the nation.

02/20/1999 to 05/30/1999 CE SCOTT
Ce Scott delves into racial and feminist concerns in mixed-media sculptures and installations. She uses traditional feminist enterprises including knitting, wrapping, sewing, etc. to create suggestive and highly charged assemblages including human hair, fetishes, copper wire, plastics, and other found, industrial materials to allude to emotional and gender based barriers.

02/20/1999 to 05/30/1999 SLIDING SCALE
Artwork from the infinitesimal to the oversized in a variety of media. The artists exploit or exaggerate scale to enhance or call into question our perceptions about the art and the world around us.

06/10/1999 to 09/29/1999 ARTIST AND THE COMMUNITY: MR. IMAGINATION
Gregory Warmack, a self-taught artist, will be the 9th artist featured in SEECA's artist and the Community series. Among the self-taught artists his work stands out as highly imaginative and visually engaging.

10/1999 to 02/2000 MILLENNIUM
Significant moments of the last 20th C. as interpreted by a select group of contemporary artists, roughly 25 years, the lifespan of "contemporary" art. Artists considered for inclusion include Baird, Bedia, Durham, Fury, Noland, Rath, Spero, Wall and Warhol.

NORTH DAKOTA

Plains Art Museum
704 First Avenue North, Fargo, ND 58102-2338
📞: 702-232-3821
Open: 10-5 Mo, 10-8 Tu & Th, 10-6 We, Fr, Sa, 12-6 Su   **Closed:** Mo, LEG/HOL!
Free Day: 2nd & 4th Tu of month   **ADM:**   **Adult:** $3.00   **Children:** $2.00   **Students:** $2.50   **Seniors:** $2.50
♿ ℗ **Museum Shop** 🍽: Y
Group Tours: ext. 126   **Drop-In Tours**   **Historic Building** Renovated turn-of-the-century warehouse
Permanent Collection: AM/REG;NAT/AM;AF;PHOT 20

The new home of the museum, moved from Moorhead, Minnesota to Fargo, North Dakota, is a historically significant warehouse which has been turned into a state of the art facility. It blends the old with the new with a result that is both stunning and functional.

ON EXHIBIT 1999

09/01/1998 to 06/30/1999   2000 AD: COLLECTION REDEFINED II
Part of Permanent Collection Series

North Dakota Museum of Art
Affiliate Institution: University of North Dakota
Centennial Drive, Grand Forks, ND 58202
📞: 701-777-4195   ◉ www.ndmoa.com
Open: 9-5 Mo-Fr, 1-5 Sa, Su   **Closed:** 7/4, THGV, 12/25
♿ ℗ **Museum Shop** 🍽: Coffee bar
Group Tours   Drop-In Tours   Historic Building   Sculpture Garden
Permanent Collection: CONT: Nat/Am; CONT: reg ptgs, sculp; REG HIST (not always on display)

In ARTPAPER 1991 Patrice Clark Koelsch said of this museum 'In the sparsely populated state that was the very last of all the US to build an art museum,...(The North Dakota Museum of Art) is a jewel of a museum that presents serious contemporary art, produces shows that travel internationally, and succeeds in engaging the people of North Dakota'.

BUILDING FOR THE 21ST CENTURY: The Museum in cooperation with 2 local architectural firms, will sponsor a year long series of lectures and seminars addressing the building or re-building of urban spaces from a global perspective.

AKRON

Akron Art Museum

70 East Market Street, Akron, OH 44308-2084
📞: 330-376-9185 ◙ www.akronartmuseum.org
Open: 11-5 daily; 11-9 Th 6/24 - 8/26 **Closed:** Mo, LEG/HOL
♿ Ⓟ Museum Shop
Group Tours: 330-376-9185, ext 229 **Drop-In Tours:** Museum hours, free guided tour 2:30 Su
Historic Building 1899 Italian Renaissance Revival structure, listed NRHP **Sculpture Garden**
Permanent Collection: EDWIN C. SHAW COLLECTION; AM: ptgs, sculp, phot

Conveniently located in the heart of downtown Akron, the Museum offers a distinctive look at some of the finest regional, national and international art from 1850 to the present, with a special focus on contemporary art and photography. **NOT TO BE MISSED:** Claus Oldenburg's ' Soft Inverted Q', 1976; The Myers Sculpture Courtyard

ON EXHIBIT 1999

12/05/1998 to 02/28/1999 DALE CHIHULY: THE GEORGE R. STROEPLE COLLECTION AND CHIHULY OVER VENICE
This collection by contemporary glassmaster Dale Chihuly offers a survey of his remarkable career.

03/20/1999 to 06/06/1999 OHIO PERSPECTIVES

ATHENS

Kennedy Museum of Art

Affiliate Institution: Ohio University
Lin Hall, Athens, OH 45701-2979
📞: 740-593-1304 ◙ www.cats.ohiou.edu.kenmus
Open: 12-5 Tu, We, Fr; 12-8 Th; Sa, Su, 1-5 **Closed:** Sa, Su, Mo, LEG/HOL!
♿ Ⓟ **Museum Shop**
Group Tours Drop-In Tours Historic Building
Permanent Collection: NAT/AM; AM art

Housed in the recently renovated 19th century Lin Hall, the Museum collections include the Edwin L and Ruth Kennedy Southwest Native American, American textiles and jewelry, and the Martha and Foster Harmon Collection which is on long term loan.

CANTON

Canton Museum of Art

1001 Market Ave. N., Canton, OH 44702
📞: 330-453-7666 ◙ http://204.210.221.2/Canton_Museum_of_Art
Open: 10-5 & 7-9 Tu-Th, 10-5 Fr, Sa, 1-5 Su **Closed:** Mo, 1/1, THGV, 12/25
♿ Ⓟ **Museum Shop**
Group Tours Drop-In Tours Sculpture Garden
Permanent Collection: WORKS ON PAPER; AM & EU: ptgs 19-20; CER: after 1950

Located in the Cultural Center for the Arts, the Canton Museum of Art is the only visual arts museum in Stark County. A mix of permanent with traveling exhibitions creates a showcase for a spectrum of visual art. **NOT TO BE MISSED:** Painting by Frank Duveneck 'Canal Scene with Washer Women, Venice'

OHIO

Canton Museum of Art - continued

ON EXHIBIT 1999

11/27/1998 to 02/26/1999 THE WATERCOLORS OF JOSEPH RAFFAEL AND CAROLYN BRADY11

11/27/1998 to 02/26/1999 ALEXANDRA NECHITA EXHIBITION

01/23/1999 to 02/26/1999 TIMKIN 100TH ANNIVERSARY

04/25/1999 to 07/25/1999 A MATTER OF TIME: FROM THE PERMANENT COLLECTION

06/06/1999 to 07/25/1999 OHIO CERAMIC SHOWCASE

11/27/1999 to 01/23/2000 UNFOLDING LIGHT: THE EVOLUTION OF TEN HOLOGRAPHERS
Holography is a process for recording images in three dimensions in which a laser is used as a light source. Invented in the 40's, it was more fully developed in the 60's. While it has many industrial and commercial applications, it also has creative properties which can be used to make works of art. Subjects explored by artists include portraits, still lifes, landscapes, etc.. *Will Travel*

CINCINNATI

Cincinnati Art Museum

Eden Park, Cincinnati, OH 45202-1596
☎: 513-721-5204 ◼ www.cincinattiartmuseum.org
Open: 10-5 Tu-Sa, 12-6 Su **Closed:** Mo, THGV, 12/25
Free Day: Sa ADM: **Adult:** $5.00 **Children:** F (under 9) $3.00 10-17 **Students:** $4.00 **Seniors:** $4.00
& ℗ **Museum Shop** ¶ **Group Tours**: 513-721-5204, x 291 **Drop-In Tours** **Sculpture Garden**
Permanent Collection: AS; AF; NAT/AM: costumes, textiles; AM & EU: ptgs, dec/art, gr, drgs, phot

One of the oldest museums west of the Alleghenies, The Cincinnati Art Museum's collection includes the visual arts of the past 5,000 years from almost every major civilization in the world. **NOT TO BE MISSED:** 'Undergrowth with Two Figures,' Vincent van Gogh, 1890

ON EXHIBIT 1999

10/10/1998 to 01/10/1999 ROYALS, ROGUES AND RUINS
60 Prints from the Museum's collection in conjunction with "British Elegance: Decorative arts from Burghley House". These feature royal personalities and contrasting lifestyles of the lower and middle classes.

10/10/1998 to 01/10/1999 WHAT I REALLY LIKE IS MUSIC: PHOTOGRAPHS BY MICHAEL WILSON
An in depth look at Wilson who has designed album covers for the last several years.

01/30/1999 to 03/27/1999 AMERICAN ART POSTERS OF THE 1890S
During the 1890s printing technology was characterized by rapid change as a result of rapid change and technological advancement and experimentation. The focus will be on those which were meant to educate and sell ideas. .

02/21/1999 to 05/02/1999 AN EXPRESSIONIST IN PARIS: THE PAINTINGS OF CHAIM SOUTINE
A major retrospective of focusing on the years between his arrival in Paris to his death. The works by this great French painter include 50 of his most important canvases, known for his highly expressive gestural and thickly painted work. *Will Travel*

04/17/1999 to 06/13/1999 TRAINS THAT PASSED IN THE NIGHT: THE RAILROAD PHOTOS OF O. WINSTON LINK
The largest exhibition of Link's railroad photos ever mounted . The 75 prints serve as a complete document of the Norfolk and Western Railway, its equipment and the people who ran it as well as life along the line. These photos are remarkable records of a vanished culture.

06/06/1999 to 09/05/1999 JOHN HENRY TWACHTMAN: AN AMERICAN IMPRESSIONIST
The first retrospective in more than 30 years featuring over 50 oils and pastels covering four periods of the artist's production- Early Works, European Period, Connecticut Years, and Gloucester, late Period. *Catalog Will Travel*

Contemporary Arts Center

115 E. 5th St., Cincinnati, OH 45202-3998
✆: 513-721-0390 ▣ www.spiral.org
Open: 10-6 Mo-Sa, 12-5 Su **Closed:** LEG/HOL!
Free Day: Mo ADM: **Adult:** $3.50 **Children:** F (under 12) **Students:** $2.00 **Seniors:** $2.00
& ℗ **Museum Shop Group Tours:** 513-345-8400 **Drop-In Tours**
Permanent Collection: Non-collecting Institution

This is one of the first contemporary art museums in the United States, founded in 1939. Art of today in all media including video is presented.

ON EXHIBIT 1999

11/21/1998 to 01/17/1999 THEATER OF EXCESS: AN INSTALLATION BY DAVID MACH
Since the early 80's Mach has been creating grand, dramatic spectacles from ordinary and recycled materials. This series of site specific works will encompass the entire 10,000 square feet of the CAC's exhibition space and use a minimum of 40 tons of material. His undulating sculptures of thousands of pounds of stacked periodicals are littered with everything from the kitchen sink to stuffed exotic African wildlife.

11/21/1998 to 01/17/1999 HENRY GWIAZDA: BUZZING REYNOLD'S DREAMLAND
Gwiazda is a composer, arranger, instrumentalist and sound experimenter who is the first person to create works in virtual audio. He uses various software programs to create a one-of-a-kind audio experience.

01/30/1999 to 03/28/1999 THE PHOTOGRAPHY OF JIM DINE
Dine constructs and reassembles the iconic object in pictorial space using two distinctly different photographic processes – photogravure and computer-manipulated ink jet printing. The images are vibrant and bear the distinct mark of this artist. *Catalog Will Travel*

04/03/1999 to 06/06/1999 THE AMERICAN LAWN: SURFACE OF EVERYDAY LIFE
Several in depth approaches are taken in examining the American obsession with the lawn, including gender roles, compulsive domestic habits and critical reflections on the landscape and suburbia. *Catalog Will Travel*

06/18/1999 to 08/22/1999 JOEP VAN LIESHOUT
Working under the name of Atelier van Lieshout, this artist produces in plastic, fiberglass and wood veneer, useful sculptural objects in the shape of tables, shelving units, washbasins, kitchens, furniture and mobile units for living. His work straddles the borderline between art, design and function. *Catalog Will Travel*

06/19/1999 to 08/29/1999 IN THE KITCHEN WITH LIZA LOU
"The Kitchen" is a self-contained, room-sized installation where everything that can possibly be used in a culinary workplace is covered with multi-colored beads.

06/19/1999 to 08/29/1999 MARTIN PURYEAR
Puryear's sculptures of wood, tar and metal show the vitality of the materials and bear his distinct mark. His work is almost spiritual or visionary but seem comfortable and familiar.

Taft Museum

316 Pike Street, Cincinnati, OH 45202-4293
✆: 513-241-0343
Open: 10-5 Mo-Sa, 1-5 Su & Hol! **Closed:** 1/1, THGV, 12/25
Free Day: We ADM: **Adult:** $4.00 **Children:** F (under 8) **Students:** $2.00 **Seniors:** $2.00
& ℗ **Museum Shop Group Tours Drop-In Tours:** by appt **Historic Building**
Permanent Collection: PTGS; CH: Kangzi-period cer; FR/REN: Limoges enamels; EU & AM: furniture 19

Collections include masterpieces by Rembrandt, Hals, Gainsborough, Turner and Corot, arranged within the intimate atmosphere of the 1820 Baum-Taft house, a restored Federal-period residence. **NOT TO BE MISSED:** 'At The Piano' 1858-59 by James A. McNeill Whistler; French Gothic ivory Virgin and Child from the Abbey Church of St. Denis, ca. 1260.

OHIO

Cleveland Museum of Art

11150 East Blvd, Cleveland, OH 44106
☏: 216-421-7340　◉　www.clemusart.com
Open: 10-5 Tu, Th, Sa, Su, 10-9 We, Fr　**Closed:** Mo, 1/1, 7/4, THGV, 12/25
&　Ⓟ　**Museum Shop**　⑪: Y
Group Tours: 216-421-7340, ex6t 380　**Drop-In Tours:** by appt　**Historic Building**　**Sculpture Garden**
Permanent Collection: ANCIENT: Med, Egt, Gr, R; EU; AM; AF; P/COL; OR; phot, gr, text, drgs

One of the world's major art museums, The Cleveland Museum of Art is known for the exceptional quality of its collections with exquisite examples of art spanning 5000 years. Especially noteworthy are the collections of Asian and Medieval European art and the renovated 18th-20th c galleries. A portion of the museum includes a wing designed in 1970 by Marcel Breuer. Some special exhibitions have admission fees. **NOT TO BE MISSED:** Guelph Treasure, especially the Portable Altar of Countess Gertrude (Germany, Lower Saxony, Brunswick, c 1040; gold, red porphyry, cloisonné, enamel, niello, gems, glass, pearls; 'La Vie' by Picasso; 'Burning of the Houses of Parliament' by J. M. W. Turner; works by Fabergé.

ON EXHIBIT 1999

10/24/1998 to 01/06/1999　THOMAS JOSHUA COOPER PHOTOGRAPHS (working title)
An American expatriate living in Scotland, Cooper is best known in Europe. His extremely detailed depictions of remote European and North American geography have a sense of timelessness and the presence of their ancient inhabitants.

11/08/1998 to 01/10/1999　CLEVELAND COLLECTS CONTEMPORARY ART
A survey of key artists and trends that have defined contemporary art in the past 16 years drawn entirely from Cleveland-area private and corporate collections. This is a wonderful local resource not usually available for public viewing.

12/13/1998 to 02/21/1999　MEDITERRANEAN: PHOTOGRAPHS BY MIMMO JODICE
The first one-person museum exhibition in the U.S. devoted to this Neapolitan photographer. The hand-toned unique black-and-white photographs chart a modern artist's five year voyage through classical space and time. He traveled through Italy, France, Greece, Macedonia, Turkey, Tunisia, Syria, and Jordan to record classical ruins and take photographs in museums.

02/21/1999 to 05/02/1999　DIEGO RIVERA: ART AND REVOLUTION (working title)
A major retrospective featuring 120 works exploring the artist's contribution to symbolism, cubism, the neoclassical revival of the 1910s-1920s, social realism, surrealism, and muralism. Included are 2 murals in true fresco and other masterworks never before exhibited in the US.

03/14/1999 to 05/23/1999　MEXICAN PRINTS FROM THE COLLECTION OF REBA AND DAVE WILLIAMS
These prints are primarily etchings, woodcuts, linocut and lithograph. The explore the important contribution of Mexican artists to the art of printmaking. Included are works by Charlot, Rivera, Orozco, Siqueiros and Tamayo, Aguilar, and others. *Will Travel*

03/14/1999 to 05/23/1999　PAINTING IN FOCUS: JEAN-BERNARD RESTOUT'S 'SOMNUS' AND THE FRENCH ROYAL ACADEMY
The Royal Academy of Painting and Sculpture in Paris was the training ground for almost every important French artist of the 18th century. It's influence is examined here by focusing on one of the Museum's finest paintings from this period-'Somnus' painted in 1771 by Jean Bernard Restout.

06/13/1999 to 08/29/1999　TWENTIETH-CENTURY WORKS ON PAPER FROM THE ISRAEL MUSEUM, JERUSALEM (working title)
The highlight of the Israel Museum's collection of 45,000 works on paper is the group from the 20th century. These works have not previously been exhibited elsewhere and represent a major survey of the artistic trends of the last 100 years. Included are works by Nolde, Schiele, Klimt, Grosz, Kollwitz, Matisse, Kandinsky, Klee, Chagall and Picasso as well as American artists Marin, Pollock, de Kooning, and others. *Will Travel*

Cleveland Museum of Art - continued

07/18/1999 to 09/19/1999 BUGATTI
Three generations of the Bugatti family will be featured: Carlo (1856-1940) was primarily a designer of furniture in Milan and later moved to Paris creating mostly silver; Rembrandt (1885-1916) worked as a sculptor mostly of animals and chiefly in bronze; Ettore (1881-1947) created automobiles; Jean (1909-1939) designed automobiles.

09/19/1999 to 11/28/1999 EDWARD WESTON AND MODERNISM
A chronological survey of the key themes of this American photographer's landmark career. Included are early constructivist-inspired portraits, views of the Armco Steel Plant in Middletown, Ohio, and examples of several of his best-known images-close-up depictions of peppers, nudes and ordinary objects. Also included are selections from his abstract studies of trees, dunes, and rocks. *Catalog Will Travel*

10/31/1999 to 01/09/2000 STILL-LIFE PAINTINGS FROM THE NETHERLANDS, 1550-1720
In a cooperative project with the Rjksmuseum, Amsterdam this survey will look at the accomplishments of Dutch and Flemish still-life painters of the 17th century emphasizing the connections between still-lifes and contemporary life. Principal artists include Aertsen, Peeters, Heda, Rembrandt, Snyders, and de Heem.

11/14/1999 to 01/23/2000 A PAINTING IN FOCUS: NICHOLAS POUSSIN'S 'HOLY FAMILY ON THE STEPS'
This exhibition will bring together the painting of this subject purchased by the Cleveland Museum in 1981 and the one in the collection of the National Gallery of Art, Washington, D.C. There has been much discussion as to which is the Poussin and which a later copy. X-radiograms, preparatory drawings and prints and other paintings relating to this work will also be shown.

12/19/1999 to 02/27/2000 THE JEANNE MILES BLACKBURN COLLECTION OF ILLUMINATED MANUSCRIPTS.
The 70 single leaves in this collection range in date from the 13th through the 16th centuries. Included are works by de Brailles, the Master of the Queen Mary Psalter, the Gold Scrolls Group, Guilebeert de Mets, the Limbourg Circle, and a humanistic leaf by Benedetto Bordone.

COLUMBUS

Columbus Museum of Art

480 East Broad Street, Columbus, OH 43215
☏: 614-221-6801   ▣ www.columbusart.mus.oh.us
Open: 10-5:30 Tu, We, Fr-S, 10-8:30 Th   **Closed:** Mo, LEG/HOL!
Free Day: Th 5:30-8:30 **Sugg/Cont: Adult:** $4.00 **Children:** $2.00, F, under 5 **Students:** $2.00 **Seniors:** $2.00
& ℗ **Museum Shop** ǁ: Palette Café **Group Tours:** reservations required 614-221-6801, x236
Drop-In Tours: Fr noon, Su 2 **Historic Building   Sculpture Garden**
Permanent Collection: EU & AM: ptgs 20

Located in downtown Columbus in a Renaissance-revival building, the Museum is an educational and cultural center for the people of central Ohio and its visitors.

ON EXHIBIT 1999

09/26/1998 to 01/03/1999 CHIHULY OVER VENICE

10/03/1998 to 01/10/1999 SHADOWS AND LIGHT: MAN RAY AND HIS LEGACY

11/14/1998 to ongoing/ EYE SPY: ADVENTURES IN ART
This interactive exhibition for children and families will be the premiere exhibition in the Children's Education Center. Visitors will learn about the carvings of Elijah Pierce, sculpture from the Tang Dynasty in China, ancient treasures from Mexico, and Dutch painting of the 1600s.

01/16/1999 to 03/21/1999 EDWARD EBERLE, CONTEMPORARY CERAMICS

01/22/1999 to 03/28/1999 A BASKETMAKER IN RURAL JAPAN

01/22/1999 to 03/28/1999 ANDREAS GURSKY

01/22/1999 to 03/28/1999 PHOTOGRAPHIC TABLEAUX: TINA BARNEY'S FAMILY ALBUM

Columbus Museum of Art - continued
03/27/1999 to 07/18/1999   JOSEPH MARIONI

04/03/1999 to 06/06/1999   WILLIAM LITTLE, COLUMBUS PICTORIALIST, 1850-1937

04/23/1999 to 10/24/1999   FROM THE AGE OF SPLENDOR TO THE AGE OF ENLIGHTENMENT: 18TH CENTURY PAINTINGS FROM THE OLD MASTERS PICTURE GALLERY IN DRESDEN

07/24/1999 to 10/31/1999   JULIAN STANCZAK

10/23/1999 to 01/02/2000   THIS LAND IS YOUR LAND/MARILYN BRIDGES

11/19/1999 to 01/30/2000   SPECTACULAR ST. PETERSBURG: 100 YEARS OF RUSSIAN THEATRE DESIGN

Schumacher Gallery
Affiliate Institution: Capital University
2199 East Main Street, Columbus, OH 43209-2394
☎: 614-236-6319
Open: 1-5 Mo-Fr, 2-5 Sa Closed May through August   **Closed:** Su LEG/HOL!; ACAD!
 ♿ Ⓜ **Museum Shop   Group Tours   Drop-In Tours**
Permanent Collection: ETH; AS; REG; CONT; PTGS, SCULP, GR 16-19

In addition to its diverse 1600 object collection, the gallery, located on the 4th floor of the University's library building, hosts exhibitions which bring to the area artworks of historical and contemporary significance.

ON EXHIBIT 1999
01/15/1999 to 02/18/1999   AFRICAN ART REVEALED, 1999
The rich artistic and religious traditions of Africa are visible in this collection on loan to a Chicago Collector.

03/07/1999 to 03/27/1999   CONTEMPORARY WORKS OF FAITH "99"
A biennial exhibition of the Liturgical Art Guild of Ohio draws together liturgical, religious and spiritual works in an international competition. Included are a variety of works of spiritual content.

Wexner Center for the Arts
Affiliate Institution: The Ohio State University
1871 N. High Street, Columbus, OH 43210-1393
☎: 614-292-3535 ◉ www.wexarts.org
Open: 10-6 Tu, We, Fr-Sa, 10-9 Th,12-6 Su   **Closed:** Mo, LEG/HOL!
Free Day: 5-9 Th   **ADM: Adult:** $3.00   **Children:** F under 12   **Students:** $2.00   **Seniors:** $2.00
 ♿ Ⓜ **Museum Shop** ⛶ **Group Tours:** 614-292-6982   **Drop-In Tours:** 1:00 Sa, Su   **Historic Building**
Permanent Collection: ART OF THE 70's

The Wexner Center, a "national laboratory for the arts," is a contemporary arts center dedicated to the visual, performing, and media arts with a strong commitment to new work. Its home, designed by Peter Eisenmann and the late Richard Trott has been acclaimed as a landmark of postmodern architecture. Sine its opening in November 198, the Wexner Center has presented an ambitious program of exhibitions, performances, films, and video screenings.

ON EXHIBIT 1999
09/18/1998 to 01/03/1999   BODY MECANIQUE: ARTISTIC EXPLORATIONS OF DIGITAL REALMS
The human body is one of the oldest themes in art. This exhibition brings it together with recent technological developments in digital and electronic media. Variously using technology as subject, artistic medium, or vehicle for presentation, the 14 artists or collaborating teams investigate new ways of thinking about technology, the human form, and relationships between the two, while moving beyond the novelty and dazzle of techno-gadgetry. Artists include Laurie Anderson, Jim Cambell, Toni Dove, Greg Marker, Beth Stryker/Sawad Brooks, and others. *Catalog*

Wexner Center for the Arts - continued

01/30/1999 to 04/18/1999   ON THE TABLE: A SUCCESSION OF COLLECTIONS 3
A survey of the shift from heavily ornamented to more abstract forms in 20th century American design through a focused selection of table and place settings. *Catalog*

01/30/1999 to 04/18/1999   RIRKRIT TIRAVANIJA
Tiravanija is a conceptual installation know for creating environments in which visitors are both viewers and interactive participants. His work transforms museum and gallery spaces into the site of everyday occurrences where people have been invited to eat, play, make art or simply engage in conversation. Collaboration with others and intimate awareness of the surrounding community are central to his working process. *Catalog*

05/15/1999 to 08/15/1999   SELF-TAUGHT ARTISTS OF THE 20th CENTURY: AN AMERICAN ANTHOLOGY
Regarded as among the most vital and intriguing spheres of 20th century art, with an ever growing popular appeal, the work of self-taught artists continues to elude categorization. These artists work outside the mainstream art world with little or no access to galleries, museums, or other mechanisms for broad exposure. The works exhibited here span more than a century and encompass all media. Included are established artists such as Grandma Moses, Horace Pippin and Martin Ramirez as well as younger artists Purvis Young, and Ken Grimes. *Catalog Will Travel*

05/15/1999 to 08/15/1999   WILLEM DE KOONING: DRAWING SEEING/SEEING DRAWING
The four series of de Kooning's drawings shown here provide a close-up view of his working process and his constant reinvention of mark making. The works created between 1958 and the late 1970s range from lush charcoals to spare, calligraphic pen and ink drawings. The final of the four series has never before been exhibited . It comprises large scale drawings on vellum of paintings in process. They began as studio aids, but were constantly added to and eventually became complete works in their own right. *Catalog Will Travel*

DAYTON

Dayton Art Institute

456 Belmonte Park North, Dayton, OH 45405
☎: 937-223-5277   ■ www.daytonartinstitute.org
Open: 10-5 daily
  ♿ ℗ **Museum Shop** ¶
Group Tours: 937-223-5277, ext 337   **Drop-In Tours:** by appt
Historic Building   Sculpture Garden
Permanent Collection: AM; EU; AS; OCEANIC; AF; CONT; PRE/COL

The Dayton Art Institute is located at the corner of Riverview Avenue and Belmonte Park North in a Edward B. Green designed Italian Renaissance style building built in 1930. A $17 million renovation/expansion project completed in June 1997 added 40% to gallery space and remodeled all 90,000 square feet of existing galleries. **NOT TO BE MISSED:** 'Water Lilies', by Monet; 'Two Study Heads of an Old Man'' by Rubens; 'St. Catherine of Alexandria in Prison', by Preti; 'High Noon', by Hopper; 'Watch Tower' Han Dynasty in China

ON EXHIBIT 1999

11/21/1998 to 01/03/1999   ARNOLD NEWMAN'S GIFT: 50 YEARS OF PHOTOGRAPHY
Newman's own visual instinct and inspirations have been honed and tempered by his friendships with many of the world's leading artists, writers, poets, politicians, etc. His portraits of these many personal friends include Picasso, O'Keeffe, Kennedy, Copeland and others and have appeared in all the leading magazines. Included in this exhibition are rare, vintage prints. ADM: Adults, $5.00; SR, STU; $3.00; under 12, F *Admission Fee*

01/16/1999 to 03/21/1999   STILL-LIFE PAINTINGS FROM THE PHILLIPS COLLECTION
Oil paintings by European and American artists reflecting more than half-a-century of changing attitudes toward style and subject. Artists include Avery, Davis, Bonnard, Graves, Hartley, O'Keeffe, Picasso and Roualt. ADM: Adults, $6.00; SR, ST $4.00; under 12 F *Catalog Admission Fee Will Travel*

OHIO

Dayton Art Institute - continued

01/16/1999 to 03/21/1999   TWENTIETH CENTURY STILL LIFE PAINTINGS FROM THE PHILLIPS COLLECTION

This exhibition brings together for the first time some of the wonderful still-life paintings in its collection and focuses on Duncan and Marjorie Philips collecting tastes and purchases of modern still-lifes. The approximately 75 works by 46 artists chronicles the evolution of the modern still-life tradition in the US and reflects the broad range of still life painting. Artists include Man Ray, Bonnard, Tamayo, Braque, Davis Picasso, Knaths, Tomlin and Graham. In the Cubist idiom are also Milton Avery, Ben Shahn, Roualt, Merandi and Nicholson.

05/08/1999 to 07/18/1999   SINNERS AND SAINTS, DARKNESS AND LIGHT: CARAVAGGIO AND HIS DUTCH AND FLEMISH FOLLOWERS IN AMERICA

A showcase of more than 35 paintings directly or indirectly influenced by the powerful works of Caravaggio, this exhibition will also address the history of how these paintings were acquired by museums in the US and Canada..ADM: Adults, $5.00; SR, STU, 3.00; under 12 F *Catalog Admission Fee Will Travel*

08/07/1999 to 10/03/1999   WHEN THE SPIRIT MOVES: THE AFRICANIZATION OF AMERICAN DANCE

From its earliest presence in this country, at first slowly and later explosively, African-American dance has profoundly influenced American culture. This exhibition chronicles that story and its far-reaching effects on music, dance, language, clothing design and professional entertainment. The components of the exhibition include historical, art historical, original music composition, video and multi media. More than 100 paintings and sculptures will be shown. ADM:(includes "Modotti and Weston" Exh) Adult,$6.00; SR, STU, $4.00; under 12 F *Catalog Admission Fee Will Travel*

08/07/1999 to 10/03/1999   MODOTTI AND WESTON: MEXICANIDAD

Vintage silver gelatin prints dating from the 1920s and documenting the period during which Modotti and Weston lived and worked in Mexico. ADM: (includes "When the Spirit Moves") Adult, $6.00; SR, STU, $4.00; under 12 F. *Admission Fee*

10/30/1999 to 01/30/2000   IN PRAISE OF NATURE: ANSEL ADAMS AND PHOTOGRAPHERS OF THE AMERICAN WEST

An eclectic and varied photographic record of the American West during the first century of photography (1850-1950). In addition to Adams, the 150 works will include images by Jackson, Watkins, Muybridge and Fiske as well as Lange, Evans, Rothstein and Cunningham. ADM: Adults, $6.00; SR, STU $4.00; under 12 F *Admission Fee Will Travel*

Wright State University Galleries

Affiliate Institution: Wright State University
A 128 CAC Colonel Glenn Highway, Dayton, OH 45435
☎: 937-775-2978
Open: 10-4 Tu-Fr, 12-5 Sa, Su   **Closed:** ACAD!
♿ Ⓟ **Museum Shop**
Group Tours Drop-In Tours
Permanent Collection: PTGS, WORKS ON PAPER, SCULP 20

The Museum is located on the Wright State University campus. **NOT TO BE MISSED:** Aimee Rankin Morgana's 'The Dream', 1988

GRANVILLE

Denison University Gallery

Burke Hall of Music & Art, Granville, OH 43023
☎: 740-587-6610
Open: 1-4 daily   **Closed:** ACAD!
♿ Ⓟ **Museum Shop**
Group Tours Drop-In Tours
Permanent Collection: BURMESE & SE/ASIAN; EU & AM: 19; NAT/AM

Located on the Denison University Campus

KENT

Kent State University Art Galleries
Affiliate Institution: Kent State University
Kent State University, School of Art, Kent, OH 44242
☎: 330-672-7853
Open: 10-4 Mo-Fr; 2-5 Su   **Closed:** Sa, ACAD!
&   **Museum Shop   Group Tours   Drop-In Tours**
Permanent Collection: GR & PTGS: Michener coll; IGE COLL: Olson photographs; GROPPER PRINTS: (political prints)

Operated by the School of Art Gallery at Kent State University since its establishment in 1972, the gallery consists of two exhibition spaces both exhibiting Western and non-Western 20th century art and craft.

LAKEWOOD

Beck Center for the Cultural Arts
17801 Detroit Ave, Lakewood, OH 44107
☎: 216-521-2540   ▣   www.beckcenter.org
Open: 12-6 Th-Sa   **Closed:** Su, Mo, LEG/HOL!
&   ℗   **Museum Shop   Group Tours   Drop-In Tours**
Permanent Collection: KENNETH BECK WATERCOLORS

A multi arts facility featuring an Art Gallery, Main Stage Theater, Studio Theater, and rental and conference spaces. The Art Gallery is now home to the Cleveland Artists Foundation (CAF), a non-profit organization dedicated to the preservation, exhibition, and research of the visual arts of Northeast Ohio. Throughout the year the CAF provides free exhibits highlighting works from over 350 items in their permanent collection and other special shows.

OBERLIN

Allen Memorial Art Museum
Affiliate Institution: Oberlin College
87 North Main Street, Oberlin, OH 44074
☎: 440-775-8665   ▣   www.oberlin.edu/-allenart
Open: 10-5 Tu-Sa, 1-5 Su   **Closed:** Mo, LEG/HOL!
Vol/Cont: Yes
&   ℗   **Museum Shop   Group Tours**: 440-775-8048   **Drop-In Tours   Historic Building   Sculpture Garden**
Permanent Collection: DU & FL: ptgs; CONT/AM: gr; JAP: gr; ISLAMIC: carpets

Long ranked as one of the finest college or university art collections in the nation, the Allen continues to grow in size and distinction. The museum's landmark building designed by Cass Gilbert was opened in 1917. The **Museum Shop** and Gallery "Uncommon Objects" is a combined effort with the Firelands Association of Visual Arts New Union Center for the Visual Arts- 39 S Main St. Oberlin, OH. PLEASE NOTE: The Weitzheimer/Johnson House, one of Frank Lloyd Wright's Usonian designs, was recently opened. It is open on the first Sunday and third Saturday of the month from 1-5pm with tours on the hour. Admission is $5.00 pp with tickets available at the Museum. **NOT TO BE MISSED:** Hendrick Terbrugghen's 'St. Sebastian Attended by Irene', 1625; Modigliani 'Nude With Coral Necklace'.

ON EXHIBIT 1999
10/02/1998 to 01/03/1999   NOW TOMORROW
Multi-media installation by Diana Thater

OHIO

Allen Memorial Art Museum - continued
10/30/1998 to 01/10/1999   MINI-MODERN MASTERS

01/26/1999 to 03/21/1999   NATIVE AMERICAN ART AND PRE-COLUMBIAN ART FROM THE PERMANENT COLLECTION

01/26/1999 to 05/30/1999   KUNIYOSHI'S KISOKAIDO ROAD SERIES

02/04/1999 to 05/30/1999   TALL SHIPS AND LEARNING CURVE
Two video installations by Gary Hill

04/09/1999 to 06/06/1999   MASAMI TERAOKA: FROM TRADITION TO TECHNOLOGY, THE FLOATING WORLD COMES OF AGE
Watercolors that mimic the style and conventions of the 19th c Japanese woodblock prints as they satirize the clash between Eastern and Western cultures. *Will Travel*

06/22/1999 to 08/09/1999   DECORATIVE ARTS FROM THE PERMANENT COLLECTION

10/26/1999 to 12/19/1999   PHOTOGRAPHS FROM THE PERMANENT COLLECTION

OXFORD

Miami University Art Museum
Affiliate Institution: Miami University
Patterson Ave, Oxford, OH 45056
☎: 513-529-2232
Open: 11-5 Tu-Su   **Closed:** Mo, LEG/HOL! ACAD!
  ⅊   **Museum Shop**
Group Tours Drop-In Tours
Permanent Collection: AM: ptgs, sculp; FR: 16-20; NAT/AM; Ghandharan, sculp

Designed by Walter A. Netsch, the museum building is located in an outstanding natural setting featuring outdoor sculpture.

PORTSMOUTH

Southern Ohio Museum and Cultural Center
825 Gallia Street, Portsmouth, OH 45662
☎: 614-354-5629
Open: 10-5 Tu-Fr, 1-5 Sa, Su   **Closed:** Mo, LEG/HOL!
Free Day: Fr   **ADM:**   **Adult:** $1.00   **Children:** $0.75   **Students:** $0.75   **Seniors:** $1.00
  ⅊   **Museum Shop**
Group Tours: 740-354-5629   **Drop-In Tours**: by arrangement   **Historic Building**
Permanent Collection: PORTSMOUTH NATIVE ARTIST CLARENCE CARTER; ANT: doll heads

Constructed in 1918, this beaux art design building is located in the heart of Portsmouth.

ON EXHIBIT 1999
03/02/1999 to 04/10/1999   WATERCOLOR MASTERS OF NORTHEAST OHIO, 1903-1958

04/17/1999 to 06/20/1999   PAPER ROUTES

SPRINGFIELD

Springfield Museum of Art
107 Cliff Park Road, Springfield, OH 45501
📞: 937-325-4673   ▣ www.spfld-museum-of-art.com
Open: 9-5 Tu, Th, Fr, 9-9 We, 9-3 Sa, 2-4 Su   **Closed:** Mo, MEM/DAY, 7/4, LAB/DAY, THGV WEEKEND, 12/24-1/1
♿ ℗ **Museum Shop**
Group Tours: 937-324-3729   **Drop-In Tours**: by appt
Permanent Collection: AM & EU: 19, 20; ROOKWOOD POTTERY; REG: ptgs, works on paper

Located in Cliff Park along Buck Creek in downtown Springfield, this 51 year old institution is a major and growing arts resource for the people or Southwest Ohio. Its 1,400 piece permanent collection attempts to provide a comprehensive survey of American art enhanced by works that represent all of the key movements in the development of Western art during the past two centuries. **NOT TO BE MISSED:** Gilbert Stuart's 'Portrait of William Miller',1795

ON EXHIBIT 1999
01/16/1999 to 02/28/1999   **PURVIS YOUNG: ART AS A MATTER OF LIFE AND DEATH**

03/13/1999 to 05/09/1999   **LANDFALL PRESS: 25 YEARS**

05/22/1999 to 06/27/1999   **BRETT ANGELL**

05/22/1999 to 06/27/1999   **LEONARD KOSCIANSKI**

07/11/1999 to 08/25/1999   **ANNUAL MEMBERS JURIED EXHIBITION**

08/28/1999 to 10/10/1999   **DENNIS WOJTKIEWRCZ**

10/16/1999 to 11/28/1999   **OUR OHIO**

10/16/1999 to 11/28/1999   **ROBERT KNIPSCHILD**

12/04/1999 to 01/09/2000   **THE WESTERN OHIO WATERCOLOR SOCIETY JURIED EXHIBITION**

TOLEDO

Toledo Museum of Art
2445 Monroe Street, Toledo, OH 43697
📞: 419-255-8000   ▣ www.toledomuseum.org
Open: 10-4 Tu-Th, Sa, 10-10 Fr, 11-5 Su   **Closed:** Mo, 1/1, 7/4, THGV, 12/25
♿ ℗ **Museum Shop**   ⑂: Y
Group Tours: 419-255-8000, x 352   **Drop-In Tours**: by appt
Historic Building   **Sculpture Garden**
Permanent Collection: EU: glass, ptgs, sculp, dec/art; AM: ptgs; AF;IND;OR

Founded in 1901 by Edward Drummond Libbey who founded Libbey Glass, the Museum is internationally known for the quality and depth of its collections. Housed in a perfectly proportioned neo-classical marble building designed by Edward Green, the Museum features American, European, African, Chinese, and Indian art, along with strength is glass and decorative arts. Award winning architect Frank Gehry designed the adjacent Center for the Visual Arts which opened in 1993. **NOT TO BE MISSED:** 'The Crowning of St. Catherine" Peter Paul Rubens, 1633; "The Architect's Dream" Thomas Cole, 1840

OHIO

Toledo Museum of Art - continued

ON EXHIBIT 1999

Spring 1999   JEWELRY FROM THE PERMANENT COLLECTION: RECENT JEWELRY ACQUISITIONS

10/25/1998 to 01/03/1999   SOUL OF AFRICA : AFRICAN ART FROM THE HAN CORAY COLLECTION
This collection is from one of the finest and most important in Europe at the turn of the century. It includes masks, sculptures, textiles and musical instruments illustrating the rich customs and religions of the many tribes of Africa. *Will Travel*

01/22/1999 to 05/16/1999   PHOTOGRAPHY FROM THE PERMANENT COLLECTION

02/12/1999 to 05/16/1999   SANDY SKOGLUND: REALITY UNDER SIEGE
Four life sized installation rooms, numerous prints, photographs, drawings and paintings by Skoglund, known for his large-scale, mixed media creations. His work has been described as dream-like, conceptual, and even surreal. *Catalog Will Travel*

07/1999 to 08/1999   TOLEDO AREA ARTISTS 81ST ANNUAL EXHIBITION
One of the most important Ohio exhibitions.

09/27/1999 to 01/03/1999   DERRIERE LE MIROIR

10/1999 to 01/2000   AN AMERICAN TREASURY: MASTER QUILTS FROM THE MUSEUM OF AMERICAN FOLK ART

11/1999 to 01/2000   PHILIPPE HALSMAN: PHOTOGRAPHS (1906-1979) *Will Travel*

11/07/1999 to 01/16/2000 PICASSO: GRAPHIC MAGICIAN – PRINTS FROM THE NORTON SIMON MUSEUM
The 120 drawings shown here look at Picasso's career over three-quarters of a century providing insight into the artist, his career, his family, friends and loves. *Will Travel*

YOUNGSTOWN

Butler Institute of American Art
524 Wick Ave, Youngstown, OH 44502

☎: 330-743-1711   ◙ www.butlerart.com
Open: 11-4 Tu, Th, Sa, 11-8 We, 12-4 Su   **Closed:** Mo, 1/1, EASTER, 7/4, THGV, 12/25
&. ℗ **Museum Shop** ¶: adjacent
Group Tours: 330-743-1711, ext 114   **Drop-In Tours**: by appt   **Historic Building**   **Sculpture Garden**
Permanent Collection: AM: ptgs 19, 20; EARLY/AM: marine coll; AM/IMPR; WESTERN ART; AM: sports art

Dedicated exclusively to American Art, this exceptional museum, containing numerous national artistic treasures is often referred to as 'America's Museum'. It is housed in a McKim, Mead and White building that was the first structure erected in the United States to house a collection of American art. **NOT TO BE MISSED:** Winslow Homer's 'Snap the Whip',1872, oil on canvass

BUTLER INSTITUTE OF AMERICAN ART/SALEM
343 East State St. Salem, Oh 44460
330-332-8213

BUTLER INSTITUTE OF AMERICAN ART/TRUMBULL
9350 East Market Street Howland, OH 44484
330-609-9900

Both satellite museums have hours 11-4 Th, Fr; 10-3 Sa; 12-4 Su, Closed Leg/Hols

Butler Institute of American Art - continued

ON EXHIBIT 1999

09/12/1999 to 11/02/1999   **THE STONEWARES OF CHARLES FERGUS BINNS: FATHER OF AMERICAN STUDIO CERAMICS**

60 rarely seen works by a pioneer, potter, teacher and author who laid the foundation for the studio ceramics movement in this country. This ground breaking survey is the most comprehensive collection of his work ever assembled for a traveling exhibition. It includes the earliest documented stoneware vase signed and dated 1905. *Catalog Will Travel*

ZANESVILLE

Zanesville Art Center

620 Military Road, Zanesville, OH 43701

☎: 614-452-0741

Open: 10-5 Tu, We, Fr, 10-8:30 Th, 1-5 Sa, Su   **Closed:** Mo, LEG/HOL!

 ♿ Ⓟ **Museum Shop**

Group Tours Drop-In Tours

Permanent Collection: ZANESVILLE: cer; HAND BLOWN EARLY GLASS; CONT; EU

In addition to the largest public display of Zanesville art pottery (Weller, Roseville & J.B. Owens), the Art Center also has a generally eclectic collection including Old and Modern Masters, African, Oriental and European, Indian, Pre-Columbian, Mexican and regional art. **NOT TO BE MISSED:** Rare areas (unique) hand blown glass & art pottery; 300 year old panel room from Charron Garden, London

OKLAHOMA

ARDMORE

Charles B. Goddard Center for Visual and Performing Arts

First Ave & D Street SW, Ardmore, OK 73401

☎: 405-226-0909

Open: 9-4 Mo-Fr, 1-4 Sa, Su **Closed:** LEG/HOL!

♿ Ⓟ **Museum Shop** **Group Tours** **Drop-In Tours**

Permanent Collection: PTGS, SCULP, GR, CONT 20; AM: West/art; NAT/AM

Works of art by Oklahoma artists as well as those from across the United States & Europe are featured in this multi-cultural center.

BARTLESVILLE

Woolaroc Museum

Affiliate Institution: The Frank Phillips Foundation, Inc

State Highway, 123, Bartlesville, OK 74003

☎: 918-336-0307

Open: 10-5 Tu-Su, Mem day-Lab day 10-5 daily **Closed:** Mo, THGV, 12/25

ADM: **Adult:** $4.00 **Children:** F (under 16) **Seniors:** $3.00

♿ Ⓟ **Museum Shop** 🍴: Snack bar w/sandwiches, etc. **Group Tours** **Drop-In Tours** **Historic Building**

Permanent Collection: WEST: ptgs; sculp

Brilliant mosaics surround the doors of this museum situated in a wildlife preserve. The large Western art collection includes Remington, Russell, Leigh and others. The original country home of oilman Frank Phillips called his Lodge (built in 1926-27) is completely restored. On the upper level is the Woolaroc monoplane, winner of the 1927 race across the Pacific to Hawaii.

MUSKOGEE

Five Civilized Tribes Museum

Agency Hill, Honor Heights Drive, Muskogee, OK 74401

☎: 918-683-1701

Open: 10-5 Mo-Sa, 1-5 Su **Closed:** 1/1, THGV, 12/25

ADM: **Adult:** $2.00 **Children:** F (under 6) **Students:** $1.00 **Seniors:** $1.75

♿ Ⓟ **Museum Shop** **Group Tours** **Drop-In Tours** **Historic Building**

Permanent Collection: NAT/AM

Built in 1875 by the US Government as the Union Indian Agency, this museum was the first structure ever erected to house the Superintendency of the Cherokee, Chickasaw, Choctaw, Creek and Seminole Tribes.

NORMAN

Fred Jones Jr. Museum of Art

Affiliate Institution: University of Oklahoma

410 West Boyd Street, Norman, OK 73019-0525

☎: 405-325-3272 ◙ www.ou.edu/fjjma

Open: 10-4:30 Tu, We, Fr, 10-9 Th, 1-4:30 Sa, Su, Summer 12-4:30 Tu-Su **Closed:** Mo, LEG/HOL!; ACAD!; HOME FOOTBALL GAMES 10-kickoff

♿ Ⓟ **Museum Shop** **Group Tours** **Drop-In Tours**: 10 days advance notice req.

Permanent Collection: AM: ptgs 20; NAT/AM; PHOTO; cont cer; GR 16-present

Fred Jones Jr. Museum of Art - continued

Considered one of the finest art museums in the region, the strength of the permanent collection includes twentieth century American painting and sculpture, contemporary art, traditional and contemporary Native American art of the Southwest, ceramics, Asian art, and European graphics from the sixteenth century to the present. Several temporary exhibitions are mounted annually which explore the art of various periods and cultures. **NOT TO BE MISSED:** State Department Collection

ON EXHIBIT 1999

01/22/1999 to 03/22/1999   MARSDEN HARTLEY: AMERICAN MODERN

A part of the influential avant garde surrounding Alfred Steiglitz, which included John Marin, Georgia O'Keeffe, and Arthur Dove. He originally advocated American transcendentalists, then reversed to "real art come from the soul" and then returned to the belief in the subjective self. *Will Travel*

05/02/1999 to 08/15/1999   LUIS JIMENEZ: WORKING CLASS HEROES

OKLAHOMA CITY

National Cowboy Hall of Fame and Western Heritage Center

1700 N.E. 63rd Street, Oklahoma City, OK 73111

☎: 405-478-2250   ◙ www.cowboyhalloffame.com

Open: 9-5 daily (Lab/Day-Mem/Day), 8:30-6 daily (Mem/Day-Lab/Day)   **Closed:** 1/1, THGV, 12/25

ADM: Adult: $6.50   **Children:** 6-12 $3.25   **Seniors:** $5.50

 ⟐   ℗   **Museum Shop**   ❙❙: overlooking gardens

Group Tours: 405-478-2250, ext 277   **Drop-In Tours:** by res   **Sculpture Garden**

Permanent Collection: WEST/ART

Housing the largest collection of contemporary Western art available for public view, this unusual and unique museum features work by Frederic Remington, Charles M. Russell, Charles Schreyvogel, Nicolai Fechin, and examples from the Taos School. Cowboy and Native historical exhibits from the Museum's impressive holdings are on display. New galleries are opening as expansion continues. **NOT TO BE MISSED:** Gerald Balclair's 18' Colorado yule marble "Canyon Princess"; Wilson Hurley's 5 majestic landscape paintings, 7 ft bronze of former President Ronald Reagan

Oklahoma City Art Museum

3113 Pershing Blvd, Oklahoma City, OK 73107

☎: 405-946-4477   ◙ www.oakhartmuseum.com

Open: 10-5 Tu-Sa, 10-9 Th, 1-5 Su, Fairgrounds 10-8 Th   **Closed:** Mo, LEG/HOL!

ADM: Adult: $3.50   **Children:** F (under 12)   **Students:** $2.50   **Seniors:** $2.50

 ⟐   ℗   **Museum Shop   Group Tours   Drop-In Tours:** by appointment   **Sculpture Garden**

Permanent Collection: AM: ptgs, gr 19, 20; ASHCAN SCHOOL COLLECTION

The Museum complex includes the Oklahoma City Art Museum at the Fairgrounds built in 1958 (where the design of the building is a perfect circle with the sculpture court in the middle), **NOT TO BE MISSED:** Works by Washington color school painters and area figurative artists are included in the collection of modern art from the former Washington Gallery.

ON EXHIBIT 1999

12/10/1998 to 03/14/1999   AGE OF OPULENCE: ARTS OF THE BAROQUE

The exhibit is designed to impart a basic understanding of the nature of the arts in the period between 1660 -1750 and to provide a context for understanding the Baroque in the history of art.

OKLAHOMA

Oklahoma City Art Museum - continued

03/25/1999 to 05/23/1999   WITNESS AND LEGACY: CONTEMPORARY ART ABOUT THE HOLOCAUST
Recent paintings, photography, sculpture, video and installations by 22 artists from around the US who explore the visual legacy of the holocaust in their work. Included are Mauricio Lasansky, Jerome Witkin, Mindy Weisel, Joyce Lyon, and others, some of whom are survivors.

06/03/1999 to 08/16/1999   CORNERSTONES: COLLECTING OKLAHOMA
The art of collecting both from the standpoint of the public museum and the private collector. Collecting will be examined as an aspect of the Museum's Mission and its role in preserving the artistic heritage of the state.

OMNIPLEX

2100 NE 52nd, Oklahoma City, OK 73111
☎: 405-427-5461
Open: 9-6 Mo-Sa, 11-6 Su (Mem/Day-Lab/Day), 9:00-5 Mo-Fr, 9-6 Sa, 11-6 Su (Winter months)   **Closed:** THGV, 12/25
ADM: **Adult:** $6.50 + tax   **Children:** 3-12,$4.00 + tax   **Students:** $6.50   **Seniors:** $4.00
& ℗   **Museum Shop**   ❙❙: Limited   **Group Tours**: 405-424-0066   **Drop-In Tours**
Permanent Collection: VARIED; REG; AF; AS

The former Kirkpatrick center is now Omniplex and includes the Kirkpatrick Science and Air Space Museum; the International Photography Hall of Fame and Museum; Red Earth Indian Center as well as the Kirkpatrick Planetarium; Conservatory and Botanical Garden as well as numerous galleries. **NOT TO BE MISSED:** Sections of the Berlin Wall

---

SHAWNEE

Mabee-Gerrer Museum of Art

1900 West MacArthur Drive, Shawnee, OK 74801
☎: 405-878-5300
Open: 10-4 Tu-Sa, 1-5 Su   **Closed:** 1/1, GOOD FRI, HOLY SAT, EASTER, THGV, 12/25
Sugg/Cont: Yes   **Adult:** $3.00   **Children:** $1.00   **Students:** $3.00   **Seniors:** $3.00
& ℗   **Museum Shop**
Group Tours Drop-In Tours   Sculpture Garden
Permanent Collection: EU: ptgs (Med-20); AN/EGT; NAT/AM; GRECO/ROMAN; AM: ptgs

The oldest museum collection in Oklahoma. **NOT TO BE MISSED:** Egyptian mummy 32nd Dynasty and associated funerary and utilitarian objects.

TULSA

Gilcrease Museum

1400 Gilcrease Museum Road, Tulsa, OK 74127-2100
☎: 918-596-2700   ▣ www.gilcrease.org
Open: 9-5 Tu-Sa, 1-5 Su and Holidays, Mem Day-Lab Day open Mo   **Closed:** Mo, 12/25
Sugg/Cont: Yes   **Adult:** $3.00 (Fam $5)   **Children:** F (under 18)
& ℗   **Museum Shop**   ❙❙: Rendezvous Restaurant open 11-2 Tu-S, Res.918-596-2720
Group Tours: 918-596-2712   **Drop-In Tours**: 2pm daily
Permanent Collection: THOMAS MORAN, FREDERIC REMINGTON, C.M. RUSSELL, ALBERT BIERSTADT, ALFRED JACOB MILLER, GEORGE CATLIN, THOMAS EAKINS

Virtually every item in the Gilcrease Collection relates to the discovery, expansion and settlement of North America, with special emphasis on the Old West and the American Indian. The Museum's 440 acre grounds include historic theme gardens. **NOT TO BE MISSED:** 'Acoma', by Thomas Moran

Gilcrease Museum - continued

ON EXHIBIT 1999

ONGOING   LAS ARTES DE MEXICO
The story of Mexico from pre-Columbian times to the present in a permanent, hands-on installation.

ONGOING   DECLARING A NATION
Historical documents and art focused on the formative years of our nation. On display is the only surviving certified copy of the Declaration of Independence signed by John Hancock, Benjamin Franklin, Charles Thomson and Silas Deane.

01/22/1999 to 04/25/1999   SYMBOLS OF FAITH AND BELIEF: ART OF THE NATIVE AMERICAN CHURCH

02/19/1999 to 05/16/1999   NORMAN ROCKWELL - AN AMERICAN PORTRAIT

04/30/1999 to 07/04/1999   GILCREASE RENDEZVOUS 1999

05/16/1999 to 07/18/1999   ART PATRONAGE IN TAOS, NEW MEXICO

08/20/1999 to 11/07/1999   DOWN FROM THE SHIMMERING SKY: MASKS OF THE NORTHWEST COAST

11/05/1999 to 12/05/1999   AMERICAN ART IN MINIATURE 1999

Philbrook Museum of Art Inc

2727 South Rockford Road, Tulsa, OK 74114
📞: 918-749-7941 or 800-324-7941   ◙ www.philbrook.org
Open: 10-5 Tu-Sa, 10-8 Th, 11-5 Su   **Closed:** Mo, 1/1, THGV, 12/25
Free Day: Twice each year in May & Oct   **Adult:** $5.00   **Children:** F (12 & under)   **Students:** $3.00   **Seniors:** $3.00
   ♿ ℗ **Museum Shop**   ❙❙: 11-2 Tu-S, Sunday Brunch, Cocktails 5-7 T
Group Tours: 918-749-5309   **Drop-In Tours:** upon request   **Historic Building**   **Sculpture Garden**
Permanent Collection: NAT/AM; IT/REN: ptgs, sculp; EU & AM: ptgs 19-20;

An Italian Renaissance style villa built in 1927 on 23 acres of formal and informal gardens and grounds. The collections, more than 6000 works, are from around the world, more than half of which are by Native-Americans. Visitors enter a 75,000 square foot addition via a striking rotunda which was completed in 1990 and is used for special exhibitions, a shop, a restaurant, and Oklahoma's only Museum school.

ON EXHIBIT 1999

09/20/1998 to 01/03/1999   PUEBLO PEOPLE: ANCIENT TRADITIONS, MODERN LIVES

09/27/1998 to 01/10/1999   CELEBRATING 200 YEARS OF LITHOGRAPHY: PRINTS FROM THE PERMANENT COLLECTION

01/31/1999 to 03/14/1999   PURE VISION: AMERICAN BEAD ARTISTS
From intimate necklace forms to large wall constructions, this exhibition of works by 28 artists demonstrates the broad range of individual creativity and artistic expression possible through beadwork, a medium that is enjoying a renaissance among contemporary American artists.

01/31/1999 to 03/14/1999   BEADS: A CROSS-CULTURAL MEDIUM

04/24/1999 to 06/20/1999   ALPHONSE MUCHA: THE FLOWERING OF ART NOUVEAU
The first major exhibition of the work of this artist since 1921 will feature about 150 0f his most important paintings, posters, jewelry, sculpture, decorative panels, pastels and illustrations from collections all over the world. *Catalog Will Travel*

07/11/1999 to 08/29/1999   MILTON AVERY PAINTINGS FROM THE COLLECTION OF THE NEUBERGER MUSEUM OF ART
Milton Avery's stature as one of America's foremost artists and colorists has been internationally recognized, as well as his profound influence on a generation of American artists. 29 of his finest paintings will be presented here.

09/12/1999 to 11/07/1999   CONTEMPORARY AMERICAN LANDSCAPE

11/21/1999 to 12/05/1999   FESTIVAL OF TREES

OREGON

Coos Art Museum
235 Anderson, Coos Bay, OR 97420
☎: 541-267-3901
Open: 11-5 Tu-Fr, 1-4 Sa   **Closed:** Su, Mo, LEG/HOL!
& ℗ Museum Shop
Group Tours   Drop-In Tours   Historic Building
Permanent Collection: CONT: ptgs, sculp, gr; AM; REG

This cultural center of Southwestern Oregon is the only art museum on the Oregon coast. It's collection includes work by Robert Rauschenberg, Red Grooms, Larry Rivers, Frank Boyden, Henk Pander and Manuel Izquierdo. Newly added is the Prefontaine Room, a special memorial to the late Olympic track star who was a native of Coos Bay. **NOT TO BE MISSED:** 'Mango, Mango', by Red Grooms

University of Oregon Museum of Art
Affiliate Institution: University of Oregon
1430 Johnson Lane, Eugene, OR 97403
☎: 541-346-3027   ▣ www.uoma.uoregon.edu
Open: 12-5 Th-Su, 12-8 We   **Closed:** Mo, Tu, ACAD!, 1/1, 7/4, THGV, 12/25
Free Day: We 5-8   **ADM:**   **Adult:** $3.00
& Museum Shop
Group Tours: 541-346-0968   **Drop-In Tours**: !   **Historic Building**   **Sculpture Garden**
Permanent Collection: CONT: ptgs, phot, gr, cer; NAT/AM

Enjoy one of the premier visual art experiences in the Pacific Northwest. The second largest museum of in the state, the museum collection features more than 12,500 objects from throughout the world as well as contemporary Northwest art and photography. **NOT TO BE MISSED:** Museum Fountain Courtyard

ON EXHIBIT 1999
01/15/1998 to 03/07/1999   POWER AND PLACE
Contemporary photographers examine various issues of power and place.

10/23/1998 to 01/03/1999   C.S. PRICE: LANDSCAPE, IMAGE, SPIRIT
Paintings by this American artist exploring the work of one of the Northwest's most unique and pioneering modern painters. "Changing Perspectives on Modernism " will be an exhibit of paintings from the collection and private collections by contemporaries of Price. Also the museum will present an interactive gallery for visitors to explore issues related to Northwest art and aesthetics.

10/30/1998 to 01/03/1999   ELEMENTS OF ART DISCOVERY ROOM

03/26/1999 to 05/02/1999   MASAMI TERAOKO
Contemporary work by one of Japan's most preeminent artists including works from his two major series: 'Tradition and Technologies: Floating world comes of Age' and 'Ascending Chaos'.

07/1999 to 09/1999   TRANSIENCE: CHINESE ART AT THE END OF THE 20TH CENTURY
An exhibition of contemporary Chinese art since 1990. *Catalog Will Travel*

314

KLAMATH FALLS

Favell Museum of Western Art and Indian Artifacts

125 West Main Street, Klamath Falls, OR 97601

📞: 541-882-9996

Open: 9:30-5:30 Mo-Sa   **Closed:** Su, LEG/HOL!

ADM: **Adult:** $4.00   **Children:** $2.00 (6-16)   **Seniors:** $3.00

 ♭ Ⓟ **Museum Shop   Group Tours   Drop-In Tours**

Permanent Collection: CONT/WEST: art; NAT/AM; ARTIFACTS; MINI FIREARMS

The museum is built on an historic campsite of the Klamath Indians. There are numerous artifacts – some of which have been incorporated into the stone walls of the museum building itself.

PORTLAND

Douglas F. Cooley Memorial Art Gallery

Affiliate Institution: Reed College

3203 S.E. Woodstock Blvd., Portland, OR 97202-8199

📞: 503-777-7790   ▣ www.reed.edu/resources/gallery

Open: 12-5 Tu-Su   **Closed:** M, LEG/HOL!

♭ Ⓟ Museum Shop

Group Tours   Drop-In Tours

Permanent Collection: AM: 20; EU: 19

The gallery is committed to a program that fosters a spirit of inquiry and questions the status quo.

ON EXHIBIT 1999

01/08/1999 to 03/21/1999   DAVID SMITH

Fall 1999   CHINESE TOMB ART

Portland Art Museum

1219 S.W. Park Ave., Portland, OR 97205

📞: 503-226-2811   ▣ www.pam.org/pam/

Open: 10-5 Tu-Su, 10-9 W e(begin Oct thru winter) & 1st Th   **Closed:** Mo, LEG/HOL

ADM: **Adult:** $6.00   **Children:** under 5, F,   **Students:** $2.50   **Seniors:** $4.50

♭ Museum Shop

Group Tours: 503-226-2811 ext 889   **Drop-In Tours   Historic Building**

Permanent Collection: NAT/AM; P/COL; AS; GR; EU & AM: ptgs; CONT: ptgs

Designed by Pietro Belluschi, the Portland Art Museum has a permanent collection that spans 35 centuries of international art. It is the region's oldest and largest visual arts and media center. The museum also hosts a Jazz series, Museum After Hours. Note: Some exhibitions may have extended hours and/or admission fees.

ON EXHIBIT 1999

09/18/1998   ESSAY ON IMPRESSIONISM AND THE OTHER 19TH CENTURY

To provide context for 'Late Paintings' this supporting exhibition delves into the Museum's fine permanent collection of 19th c painting for an understanding of the visual tenets of Impressionism. Works shown include Degas, Pissarro, Renoir and others. In contrast 'The Other 19th Century' shows the other movements which flourished at the same time. Monticelli, Sargent, Tissot, Courbet and others are represented here.

OREGON

Portland Art Museum - continued

09/18/1998 to 01/03/1999   AFTER IMPRESSIONISM: PRINTMAKERS IN PARIS
While many great artists made Paris their home, most are known for their paintings. The Vivian and Gordon Gilkey Collection of Graphic Art contains many examples of their works on paper. This exhibit will present an overview of all the major post-impressionist movements that were prevalent in Paris during this century including works by Chagall, Arp, Matisse, Picasso, Braque and many others.

09/18/1998 to 01/03/1999   MONET: PAINTINGS OF GIVERNY FROM THE MUSÉE MARMITTON
22 paintings on loan from the distinguished Musée Marmatton in Paris offer an overview of Monet's late works, considered by the artist to be the finest of his career. *Catalog Will Travel*

10/01/1998 to 01/24/1999   CONTEMPORARY ART FROM THE PORTLAND ART MUSEUM PERMANENT COLLECTION (working title)
The Museum has a strong commitment to the collection and exhibition of contemporary art. For the first time several exciting new acquisitions including Robert Irwin's untitled disk (1966-67), Gwynn Murrill's Coyote VI (1986), and Mary Corse's Light Painting (1970)

01/15/1999 to 03/21/1999   ROBERT COLESCOTT: RECENT PAINTINGS
The 19 provocative paintings on view, created over the past decade by Arizona-based artist Colescott, contain his highly personal narrative figurative imagery blended with ironic viewpoints that address major contemporary social issues. One of the most important U.S. artists working today, Colescott was the first painter since Jasper Johns, in 1988, to be included in the 47th Venice Biennale. He was also the first American ever to be given a solo exhibition at that prestigious event. *Catalog Will Travel*

01/15/1999 to 03/28/1999   AN ESCHER CELEBRATION
In celebration of the hundredth anniversary of the birth of Escher this exhibition provides an opportunity to examine his creative genius and vast subject matter. Included in the exhibition is his famous 'Metamorphosis Scroll' which measures more that 12 feet in length. Primarily from his own estate, the collection includes rare drawing, woodcuts, engravings, lithographs and original plates. Ticket through Ticketmaster and the Museum box office. *Admission Fee*

02/04/1999 to 04/25/1999   CONTEMPORARY ART TODAY (working title)
Recent work from many of today's most important artists. The exhibit explores the possibilities of art at the end of the century as these artists use a range of new materials from photo-based to new media.

02/23/1999   GLIMPSES OF IMMORTALITY: EARLY CHINESE ART FROM THE PAMPLIN COLLECTION
For the first major rotation of this outstanding collection, some 30 works have been chosen. They include a pair of extraordinarily well preserved black jars (hu) from the late Warring States period (4th-3rd c BCE) and an unusually large horse from the Han Dynasty.

04/11/1999 to 07/11/1999   DOWN FROM THE SHIMMERING SKY: MASKS OF THE NORTHWEST COAST
Some 150 masks from First Nations artists on to closely linked thematic units: the human face mask, the celestial world, the mortal world, the undersea world, the spirit world and the contemporary non-traditional mask. *Catalog Will Travel*

04/11/1999 to 07/11/1999   PHOTOGRAPHS OF EDWARD S CURTIS
Curtis is well known for his pioneering work in all areas of Native-American life and lore. His documentation, 'The North American Indian' begun in 1898 the exceptional example of this work. The photographs show here are drawn from the Portland's collection.

05/06/1999 to 07/18/1999   OTTO FRIED: SPHERES AND ATMOSPHERES
Fried's work of the past 15 years is shown here including paintings, sculptures, and assemblages, illustrating his preoccupation with geometric volumes: spheres, cylinders, and cones

05/14/1999 to 07/11/1999   RODIN'S MONUMENT TO VICTOR HUGO
The second in a series of focus exhibitions addressing specific issues in the sculpture of Auguste Rodin is a product of the Iris and Gerald B. Cantor Foundation's mission to bring the work of a great sculptor to a broader audience.

WARM SPRINGS

Museum at Warm Springs Oregon
Affiliate Institution: Confederated Tribes of the Warm Springs Reservation
Warm Springs, OR 97761

☎: 541-553-3331
Open: 10-5 daily   **Closed:** 12/25, 1/1, THGV
ADM: **Adult:** $6.00   **Children:** $3.00 5-12 ; Free under 5   **Seniors:** $5.00
  ♿ ℗   Museum Shop
Group Tours Drop-In Tours
Permanent Collection: NAT/AM: art, phot, artifacts

The Museum at Warm Springs draws from a rich collection of native artwork, photographs and stories that tell the long history of the three tribes (Wasco, Warm Springs and Paiute) that comprise the Confederate Tribes of Warm Springs. It is architecturally designed to evoke a creekside encampment among a stand of cottonwoods. **NOT TO BE MISSED:** A trio of traditional buildings built by tribal members; the tule mat wickiup, or house of the Paiutes, the Warm Springs summer teepee, and the Wasco wooden plank house.

PENNSYLVANIA

ALLENTOWN

Allentown Art Museum

Fifth & Court Street, Allentown, PA 18105

☎: 610-432-4333 ◙ www.allentownartmuseum.org
Open: 11-5 Tu-Sa, 12-5 Su **Closed:** Mo, LEG/HOL!
ADM: **Adult:** $4.00 **Children:** F (under 12) **Students:** $2.00 **Seniors:** $3.00
♿ Ⓟ **Museum Shop** ⑂: small café **Group Tours:** 610-432-4333,ext. 32 **Drop-In Tours:** by appt
Permanent Collection: EU: Kress Coll; AM; FRANK LLOYD WRIGHT: library; OM: gr; gem collection

Discover the intricate and visual riches of one of the finest small art museums in the country. **NOT TO BE MISSED:** John Clem Clarke: Comforts, Near Disasters, and Pentimenti October 11, 1998 - January 3, 1999

ON EXHIBIT 1999

10/11/1998 to 01/03/1999 JOHN CLEM CLARKE: COMFORTS, NEAR DISASTERS, AND PENTIMENTI
Clarke makes his finished paintings by enlarging a maquette using an opaque projector to make sets of stencils through which the finished paintings are brushed. *Catalog*

01/10/1999 to 03/14/1999 PICASSO, ROUALT, BECKMANN: PORTFOLIO
These three outstanding print projects of the 1920's will be installed including Picasso's illustrations for Victor Hugo's 'Chef D'Oeuvre Inconnu", Roualt's monumental 'Miserere' and Beckmann's 'The Berlin Trip'.

01/10/1999 to 03/14/1999 ALL THAT JAZZ: PRINTED FASHION SILKS OF THE 20'S AND 30'S
Fashion is as telling about the tenor of the times as newspaper headlines. The flamboyance of the 20's and the sober quality of the depression era of the 30's can be found in these designs.

01/31/1999 to 04/25/1999 AMERICAN CLASSICS: PHOTOGRAPHS FROM THE MUSEUM COLLECTION
The photographs of Edward Weston, Ansel Adams, and Weegee have greatly influenced how we understand ourselves as America. Those shown here present this most vividly.

03/28/1999 to 06/27/1999 COMMON MAN, MYTHIC VISION: THE PAINTINGS OF BEN SHAHN
Over 50 of the finest paintings created by Shahn between 1936-1962. It begins with the wartime shift in his work from social realism to 'personal realism' and culminates in the series of paintings, "The Lucky Dragon" inspired by the fate of a fishing crew exposed to nuclear testing in Japan. *Catalog Will Travel*

05/02/1999 to 07/11/1999 INDUSTRIAL PENNSYLVANIA
The Museum continues to acquire images of the steel, coal and mining industries of Pennsylvania despite the Depression. These will be shown as a part of the artistic heritage of the state.

07/11/1999 to 09/05/1999 TINA BARNEY: THE THEATER OF MANNERS (working title)
Monumental photographs of an elitist way of life which Barney feels is threatened with extinction. *Will Travel*

10/1999 to 01/2000 VINCENT DESIDERIO
Desiderio emerged as a leader of the new "History Painting" in the mid-1980's making monumental paintings with subjects generated by personal tragedy and hope.

AUDUBON

Mill Grove, The Audubon Wildlife Sanctuary

Paulings and Audubon Roads, Audubon, PA 19407-7125

☎: 610-666-5593
Open: 10-4 Tu-Sa, 1-4 S, grounds open dawn to dusk Tu-Su **Closed:** M, 1/1, EASTER, 7/4, THGV, 12/24, 12/25, 12/31
Vol/Cont: Yes
♿ Ⓟ **Museum Shop** **Group Tours:** by appt **Drop-In Tours** **Historic Building**
Permanent Collection: JOHN JAMES AUDUBON: all major published artwork, (complete 19th C editions) & related items

Mill Grove, The Audubon Wildlife Sanctuary - continued

Housed in the 1762 National Historic Landmark building which was the first American home of John James Audubon, artist/naturalist. This site is also a wildlife sanctuary complete with nature trails and feeding stations. Grounds self-guide map Free.

BETHLEHEM

Lehigh University Art Galleries

Affiliate Institution: Zoellner Arts Center

420 East Packer Ave, Bethlehem, PA 18015-3007

☎: 610-758-3615

Open: Call for hours!   **Closed:** Mo, Tu, LEG/HOL!

& Ⓟ **Museum Shop** ⌟: In Iacocca Bldg. open until 2 PM

Group Tours: by Appt. only   **Drop-In Tours:** Openings and by special arrangement

Sculpture Garden

Permanent Collection: EU & AM: ptgs; JAP: gr; PHOT

The Galleries do not permanently exhibit all the important works in its collections. Call to inquire. More than 20 temporary exhibitions a year in five campus galleries introduce students and the community to current topics in art, architecture, history, science and technology **NOT TO BE MISSED:** Outdoor sculpture throughout 3 Campuses, including work by Henry Moore, David Cerulli and Menash Kadishman

ON EXHIBIT 1999

01/13/1999 to 03/14/1999   QUIET LIGHT: ISAMU NOGUCHI

"Akari"light sculpture including the sculptural use of illumination in Noguchi's cultural heritage. *Will Travel*

04/07/1999 to 06/06/1999   SHOUTS FROM THE WALL: POSTERS AND PHOTOGRAPHS BROUGHT HOME FROM THE SPANISH CIVIL WAR BY AMERICAN VOLUNTEERS

These posters appeared throughout Spain in the late 1930's giving people information, building morale and focusing debate. *Will Travel*

06/23/1999 to 08/01/1999   GLENN HANSEN: OIL PAINTINGS

Paintings done in the last ten years.

BRYN ATHYN

Glencairn Museum: Academy of the New Church

1001 Cathedral Road, Bryn Athyn, PA 19009

☎: 215-947-9919

Open: 9-5 Mo-Fr by appt, 2-5 second Su each month (except July & Aug)   **Closed:** Sa, LEG/HOL!

ADM: **Adult:** $4.00   **Children:** $2.00   **Students:** $2.00   **Seniors:** $3.00

& Ⓟ **Museum Shop**

Group Tours   Drop-In Tours

Permanent Collection: MED, GOTHIC & ROMANESQUE: sculp; STAINED GLASS; EGT, GRK & ROMAN: cer, sculp; NAT/AM

Glencairn is a unique structure built in the Romanesque style using building processes unknown since the middle ages. It is the former home of Raymond and Mildred Pitcairn. **NOT TO BE MISSED:** French Medieval stained glass and sculpture

PENNSYLVANIA

CARLISLE

Trout Gallery, Weiss Center for the Arts
Affiliate Institution: Dickinson College
High Street, Carlisle, PA 17013
☎: 717-245-1344
Open: 10-4 Tu-Su **Closed:** LEG/HOL!; ACAD!
& ℗ **Museum Shop**
Group Tours: 717-245-1492 **Drop-In Tours**
Permanent Collection: GR; 19, 20; AF

The exhibitions and collections here emphasize all periods of art history. **NOT TO BE MISSED:** Gerofsky Collection of African Art and the Carnegie Collection of prints. Rodin's 'St. John the Baptist' and other gifts from Meyer P. and Vivian Potamkin.

ON EXHIBIT 1999
02/19/1999 to 04/09/1999 FOUR OBJECTS; FOUR ARTISTS; TEN YEARS
In 1986 four American still-life painters – Janet Fish, Sondra Freckelton, Nancy Hagin, and Harriet Shorr – agreed that each would select an object that they would all include in a painting. Ten years later they decided to repeat the project. The results of their efforts reveal the wide spectrum of choices which artists make during the creative process. *Catalog Will Travel*

CHADDS FORD

Brandywine River Museum
U.S. Route 1, Chadds Ford, PA 19317
☎: 610-388-2700 ◙ www.brandywinemuseum.org
Open: 9:30-4:30 Daily **Closed:** 12/25
ADM: **Adult:** $5.00 **Children:** F (under 6) **Students:** $2.50 **Seniors:** $2.50
& ℗ **Museum Shop** ⵏ: 11-3 (Closed M and Tu Jan through Mar)
Group Tours Drop-In Tours Historic Building
Permanent Collection: AM: ptgs by three generations of the Wyeth Family

Situated in a pastoral setting in a charming converted 19th century grist mill, this museum is devoted to displaying the works of three generations of the Wyeth family and other Brandywine River School artists. Particular focus is also placed on 19th c American still-life & landscape paintings and on works of American illustration. The restored studio of N.C. Wyeth has reopened for public tours W-S 10-3:15. Timed tickets must be purchased at the Museum. There is a shuttle bus.

ON EXHIBIT 1999
Ongoing BRANDYWINE HERITAGE GALLERIES
Works by Pyle, his students and other artists of the period.

Ongoing ANDREW WYETH GALLERY
Works from various stages of his career

01/23/1999 to 03/21/1999 POLITICAL SATIRE OF THOMAS NAST
Nast, one of America's early illustrators in pen and ink, was also a great political cartoonist. He is credited with creating the mascots for the Republican and Democratic Parties, the elephant and the donkey.

CHESTER

Widener University Art Museum
Affiliate Institution: Widener University
1300 Potter Street, Chester, PA 19013
☎: 610-499-1189
Open: 10-4:30 We-Sa, 10-7 Tu **Closed:** Su, Mo, LEG/HOL
& ℗ **Museum Shop Group Tours Drop-In Tours**
Permanent Collection: AM & EU: ptgs 19, 20

The Museum is located in the new University Center on 14th St on the main campus. It includes in its holdings the Widener University Collection of American Impressionist paintings, the Alfred O. Deshong Collection of 19th and 20th c European and American painting, and 19th c Asian art and Pre-Columbian pottery. PLEASE NOTE: Children under 16 must be accompanied by an adult.

ON EXHIBIT 1999
01/19/1999 to 02/20/1999 PAINTINGS BY DANE TILGHMAN

03/02/1999 to 04/01/1999 PASTELS AND PAINTINGS BY WILLIAM KNIGHT

04/20/1999 to 05/22/1999 JURIED PHOTOGRAPHY SHOW: WIDENER UNIVERSITY FACULTY AND STAFF

05/07/1999 to 08/19/1999 SELECTIONS FROM THE PERMANENT COLLECTION

COLLEGEVILLE

Philip and Muriel Berman Museum of Art at Ursinus College
Main Street, Collegeville, PA 19426-1000
☎: 610-409-3500 ◉ www.ursinus.edu
Open: 10-4 Tu-Fr, Noon-4:30 Sa, Su **Closed:** Mo, LEG/HOL!
Vol/Cont: Yes
& ℗ **Museum Shop Group Tours Drop-In Tours**: by appt **Historic Building Sculpture Garden**
Permanent Collection: AM: ptgs 19, 20; EU: ptgs 18; JAP: ptgs; PENNSYLVANIA GERMAN ART: cont outdoor sculp

With 145 works from 1956-1986, the Berman Museum of Art holds the largest private collection of sculpture by Lynn Chadwick in a U.S. museum, housed in the original Georgian Style stone facade college library built in 1921. **NOT TO BE MISSED:** 'Seated Couple on a Bench' (1986 bronze), by Lynn Chadwick (English b. 1914)

ON EXHIBIT 1999
11/17/1998 to 01/31/1999 ART FROM WITHIN: INMATE EXPRESSIONS FROM GRATERFORD PRISON

12/08/1998 to 03/28/1999 IN HER VOICE: SELF PORTRAITS BY WOMEN
Self portraits by contemporary women artists are set in context with their counterparts in history who painted their reflections in a more traditional format. Legacy artists are Henriette Wyeth, Angelica Kauffman, Dorothea Lange, Käthe Kollwitz, and Alice Neal. Contemporary expressions by Mary Frank, Carol May, Dianne Edison, Jan Baltzell, Syd Carpenter and Anna B. McCoy.

03/1999 to 04/1999 MACLAS CONFERENCE/EXHIBITION

05/1999 to 08/1999 ARTISTS' EQUITY 50TH ANNIVERSARY JURIED EXHIBITION

09/1999 to 10/1999 PETER SCULTHORPE: PAINTINGS, PRINTS, AND WATERCOLORS

10/1999 to 01/2000 STEVEN QUILLER WATERCOLORS

11/12/1999 to 01/23/2000 FOUR OBJECTS; FOUR ARTISTS; TEN YEARS
In 1986 four American still-life painters – Janet Fish, Sondra Freckelton, Nancy Hagin, and Harriet Shorr – agreed that each would select an object that they would all include in a painting. Ten years later they decided to repeat the project. The results of their efforts reveal the wide spectrum of choices which artists make during the creative process. *Catalog Will Travel*

PENNSYLVANIA

DOYLESTOWN

James A. Michener Art Museum
138 South Pine Street, Doylestown, PA 18901
📞: 215-340-9800 　■ www.michener-artmuseum.org
Open: 10-4:30 Tu-Fr, 10-5 Sa, Su 　**Closed:** Mo, LEG/HOL
ADM: 　**Adult:** $5.00 　**Children:** F (under 12) 　**Students:** $1.50 　**Seniors:** $4.50
 ᕕ 　ⓟ 　**Museum Shop** 　🍴: Expresso Café
Group Tours ext 126 　**Drop-In Tours:** 2pm, Sa, Su, & by appt 　**Historic Building** 　**Sculpture Garden**
Permanent Collection: AM: Impr/ptgs 19-20; BUCKS CO: 18-20; AM: Exp 20; SCULP 20; NAKASHIMA READING ROOM; CREATIVE BUCKS COUNTY

Situated in the handsomely reconstructed buildings of the antiquated Bucks County prison, the Museum, with its recently opened addition, provides an invigorating environment for viewing a wonderful collection of 19th and 20th century American art. **NOT TO BE MISSED:** Redfield, Garber & New Hope School

ON EXHIBIT 1999
PERMANENT INSTALLATIONS　CREATIVE BUCKS COUNTY: A CELEBRATION OF ART AND ARTISTS
A multi-media exhibition in the new Mari Sabusawa Michener Wing which tells the story of Bucks County's rich artistic tradition. Included are individual displays on 12 of the country's best known artists, a video theater, and a comprehensive database containing information on hundreds of Bucks County artists, both living and deceased. The featured artists are Pearl S. Buck, Daniel Garber, Oscar Hammerstein II, Moss Hart, Edward Hicks, George S. Kaufman, Henry Chapman Mercer, Dorothy Parker, S.J. Perelman, Charles Sheeler, Edward Redfield, and Jean Toomer.

PERMANENT INSTALLATIONS　JAMES A MICHENER: A LIVING LEGACY
Michener's Bucks County office is installed at the Museum and included are a video, the Presidential Medal of Freedom and the original manuscript of 'The Novel'.

PERMANENT INSTALLATIONS　NAKASHIMA READING ROOM
Classic furniture from the studio of internationally known woodworker George Nakashima.

PERMANENT INSTALLATIONS　VISUAL HERITAGE OF BUCKS COUNTY
A comprehensive exhibition based on the permanent collection which traces art in the region from Colonial times through to the present.

PERMANENT INSTALLATIONS　INSIDE OUR VAULT: SELECTIONS FROM THE COLLECTION
A small-scale exhibition of delights and surprises in the Museum's rapidly expanding collection.

ONGOING　SCULPTURE PROGRAM
Using the grass covered field between the Museum and the adjacent library, this program highlights both regional and national artists who explore the remarkable variety of styles and materials employed by today's sculptors.

09/12/1998 to 01/17/1999　"MACHINERY CAN'T MAKE ART": THE POTTERY AND TILES OF HENRY CHAPMAN MERCER
A major exhibition celebrating the 100th anniversary of the Moravian Pottery and Tile Works featuring a full range of tiles, mosaics and art pottery made by Mercer juxtaposed with many of the historical works which served as sources for his designs.

09/26/1998 to 03/07/1999　A LEGACY PRESERVED: THE FIRST DECADE OF COLLECTING AT THE MICHENER ART MUSEUM
A exhibition featuring some if the most significant objects acquired including work by many of the county's best-known historic and contemporary artists

01/03/1999 to 05/23/1999　FROM ARTIST TO CHILD: THE BUCKS COUNTY INTERMEDIATE UNIT COLLECTION
Highlights of this fine collection by Pennsylvania Impressionist and related artists.

03/20/1999 to 06/27/1999　BUCKS COUNTY INVITATIONAL III
Small solo exhibitions by six contemporary Bucks County artists working in a variety of media.

06/05/1999 to 09/05/1999　FROM SOUP CANS TO NUTS: PRINTS BY ANDY WARHOL
Some of Warhol's most celebrated images drawn from the collection of the Andy Warhol Museum in Pittsburgh will be featured here.

James A. Michener Art Museum - continued

07/17/1999 to 10/03/1999 THE PHILADELPHIA TEN: A WOMEN ARTIST GROUP 1917-1945

This unique and progressive group of painters and sculptors broke the rules of society and the art world by working and exhibiting together. Their work included urban and rural landscapes, portraiture, still life, and a variety of representational and myth inspired sculpture. This is the first time in over fifty years to examine this group and other like it who played an importune role in American culture in the first half of the century. Highlighted particularly are Isabel Cartwright, Constancy Cochrane, Marry Colton, and Lucille Howard. In addition there were Theresa Bernstein, Cora Brooks, Fern Coppedge, Nancy Ferguson, Sue Gill. Helen McCarthy , Emma MacRae, M. Elizabeth Price, Susan Schell and sculptors Harriet Frishmuth and Beatrice Fenton. *Will Travel*

EASTON

Lafayette College Art Gallery, Williams Center for the Arts

Hamilton and High Streets, Easton, PA 18042-1768

: 610-250-5361 ◙ www.lafayette.edu

Open: 10-5 Tu, Th, Fr; 10-8 We; 2-5 We Sep-May **Closed:** Mo, ACAD!

♿ Ⓟ **Museum Shop**

Group Tours **Drop-In Tours**

Permanent Collection: AM: ptgs, portraits, gr

Located in Easton, Pennsylvania, on the Delaware River, the collection is spread throughout the campus. **NOT TO BE MISSED:** 19th c American history paintings and portraits

ERIE

Erie Art Museum

411 State Street, Erie, PA 16501

: 814-459-5477 ◙ www.erie.net/~erieartm/

Open: 11-5 Tu-Sa, 1-5 Su **Closed:** Mo, LEG/HOL!

Free Day: We ADM: **Adult:** $1.50 **Children:** $.50 (under 12) **Students:** $0.75 **Seniors:** $0.75

♿ Ⓟ **Museum Shop**

Group Tours **Drop-In Tours**: Fr **Historic Building**

Permanent Collection: IND: sculp; OR; AM & EU: ptgs, drgs, sculp gr; PHOT

The museum is located in the 1839 Greek Revival Old Customs House built as the U. S. Bank of PA. Building plans are underway to provide more gallery space in order to exhibit works from the 4,000 piece permanent collection. **NOT TO BE MISSED:** Soft Sculpture installation ' The Avalon Restaurant'

ON EXHIBIT 1999

12/08/1998 to 01/30/1999 JACK HANRAHAN: PHOTOGRAPHS

04/24/1999 to 06/20/1999 THE 76TH ANNUAL SPRING SHOW

06/26/1999 to 09/26/1999 ART OF THE ANIMATED FILM

AN exhibition exploring the art, history and process of the animated film.

12/31/1999 to 04/2000 MARC BROWN

Works by beloved the children's book illustrator and creator of Arthur the Aardvark

PENNSYLVANIA

GREENSBURG

Westmoreland Museum of American Art
221 North Main Street, Greensburg, PA 15601-1898

📞: 724-837-1500   ◉ www.wmuseumaa.org
Open: 11-5 We-Su, 11-9 Th   **Closed:** Mo, Tu, LEG/HOL!
Sugg/Cont: $3.00; children under 12 free
♿ ⓟ **Museum Shop**
Group Tours   **Drop-In Tours:** by appt
Permanent Collection: AM: ptgs (18-20), sculp, drgs, gr, furniture, dec/art

This important collection of American art is located in a beautiful Georgian style building situated on a hill overlooking the city. PLEASE NOTE: the Museum will be closed for renovations until June 6, 1999 **NOT TO BE MISSED:** Portraits by William Merritt Chase and Cecilia Beaux; Largest known collection of paintings by 19th century southwestern Pennsylvania artists.

ON EXHIBIT 1999
05/06/1999 to 08/08/1999   INVITATIONAL EXHIBITION OF SOUTHWESTERN PENNSYLVANIA ARTISTS
In honor of their 40th anniversary of the Westmoreland will show a selection of 40 years of painting and Sculpture in Southwestern Pennsylvania.

06/06/1999 to 08/08/1999   MAKING THE WESTMORELAND MUSEUM OF ART
In celebration of the reopening of the Museum, this exhibition of architectural drawings, models, etc. describes the design process involved in creating the building and grounds, 1959 to the present.

11/26/1999 to 01/16/2000   HOLIDAY TOY AND TRAIN EXHIBITION: CHRISTMAS: PAST, PRESENT AND FUTURE
The Museum collection will be supplemented by loans from private collections, representing toys highlighted and manufactured during each decade of the 20th century.

HARRISBURG

State Museum of Pennsylvania
3rd and North Streets, Harrisburg, PA 17108-1026

📞: 717-787-7789   ◉ www.statemuseumpa.com
Open: 9-5 Tu-Sa, 12-5 Su   **Closed:** Mo, LEG/HOL!
Vol/Cont:
♿ **Museum Shop**
Group Tours: 717-772-6997   **Drop-In Tours:** !
Permanent Collection: VIOLET OAKLEY COLL; PETER ROTHERMEL MILITARY SERIES; PA: cont

A newly renovated 5,000 squar foot Art Gallery within the State Museum of Pennsylvania is host to changing exhibitions of both contemporary and historical art. The art collection is composed of 5,000 paintings, works on paper, photographs or art crafts dating from 1650 to the present, which relate specifically to the history of art and artists of Pennsylvania **NOT TO BE MISSED:** The 16' X 32' 'Battle of Gettysburg: Pickett's Charge', by P.F. Rothermel (the largest battle scene on canvas in North America)

ON EXHIBIT 1999
04/1999 to 05/1999   EXHIBIT FROM PERMANENT COLLECTION

05/1999 to 09/1999   ART OF THE STATE: Pa 99

10/1999 to 04/2000   THE MILLENNIUM MAZE

University Museum

Affiliate Institution: Indiana University
John Sutton Hall, Indiana University of Penn, Indiana, PA 15705-1087

☎: 724-357-7930 ▣ www.iup.edu/fa/museum
Open: 11-4 Tu-Fr, 7-9 Th, 1-4 Sa, Su **Closed:** Mo, ACAD!
♿ ⓟ **Museum Shop**
Group Tours   Drop-In Tours
Permanent Collection: AM: 19, 20; NAT/AM; MILTON BANCROFT: ptgs & drgs; INUIT: sculp

The museum collection includes photography by Wilbur Loffman, and an American graphics general collection **NOT TO BE MISSED:** 1875 period dormitory room for girls

Center Gallery of Bucknell University

Affiliate Institution: Bucknell University
Seventh Street and Moore Ave, Lewisburg, PA 17837

☎: 717-524-3792
Open: 11-5 Mo-Fr, 1-4 Sa, Su **Closed:** LEG/HOL!
♿ ⓟ **Museum Shop** ⵊⵊ: Not in museum but in bldg.
Group Tours   Drop-In Tours
Permanent Collection: IT/REN: ptgs; AM: ptgs 19, 20; JAP

NOT TO BE MISSED: 'Cupid Apollo', by Pontormo

Southern Alleghenies Museum of Art

Affiliate Institution: Saint Francis College
Saint Francis College Mall, P.O. Box 9, Loretto, PA 15940

☎: 814-472-3920 ▣ www.sama-sfc.org
Open: 10-4 Mo-Fr, 1:30-4:30 Sa, Su **Closed:** Leg/Hols
♿ ⓟ **Museum Shop** ⵊⵊ: Nearby and on college campus
Group Tours: by appt   **Drop-In Tours:** by appt
Sculpture Garden
Permanent Collection: AM: ptgs 19, 20; sculp; drgs; gr

The museum was founded to bring museum services to this geographically isolated rural region and to provide the audience with an opportunity to view important trends in American Art. Also: Southern Alleghenies Museum of Art, Brett Bldg, 1210 11th Ave, Altoona, PA 16602 814-946-4464, Southern Alleghenies Museum of Art at Pasquerilla Performing Arts Center, University of Pittsburgh at Johnstown, PA 15904 814-946-4464. Southern Alleghenies Museum of Art at Ligonier Valley, One Boucher Lane, Route 711S, Ligonier, PA 15658 724-238-6015 **NOT TO BE MISSED:** John Sloan's 'Bright Rocks'

PENNSYLVANIA

MERION STATION

Barnes Foundation

300 North Latch's Lane, Merion Station, PA 19066

☎: 610-667-0290 ◙ www.thebarnes.org/

Open: 9:30-5, Fr, Sa; 12:30 - 5 Su (subject to change !) **Closed:** Mo-Th (subject to change), 12/25

ADM: **Adult:** $5.00, $5.00 for audio tour

& ℗ **Museum Shop**

Group Tours: 610-664-5191 **Drop-In Tours**

Permanent Collection: FR: Impr, post/Impr; EARLY FR MODERN; AF; AM: ptgs, sculp 20

The core of the collection includes a great many works by Renoir, Cezanne, and Matisse, but also contains works by Picasso, van Gogh, Seurat, Braque, Modigliani, Soutine, Monet and Manet. Various traditions are displayed in works by El Greco, Titian, Courbet, Corot, Delacroix and others. Works are displayed among American antique furniture, ironwork, ceramics and crafts. The building has just undergone a 3 year, $12 million renovation. **NOT TO BE MISSED:** This outstanding collection should not be missed.

MILL RUN

Fallingwater

Rt. 381, Mill Run, PA 15464

☎: 724-329-8501

Open: 11/21-12/20, 2/27-3/14, weekends only, Xmas week 10-4 Tu-Su, Closed Jan/Feb **Closed:** Mo, Some LEG/HOLS!

ADM: **Adult:** $8.00 Tu-F;$12 wknds

& ℗ **Museum Shop** ᶧᶦ: Open 5/1 - 11/1

Group Tours **Drop-In Tours** **Historic Building** National Historic Landmark **Sculpture Garden**

Permanent Collection: ARCH; PTGS; JAP: gr; SCULP; NAT/AM

Magnificent is the word for this structure, one of Frank Lloyd Wrights most widely acclaimed works. The key to the setting of the house is the waterfall over which it is built. Fallingwater is undergoing some renovation. Special hours are listed. 3/15-11/15 hours will be 10-4 Tu-S, 11/1-4/1 weekends only. **NOT TO BE MISSED:** The Frank Lloyd Wright designed building.

PAOLI

Wharton Esherick Museum

Horseshoe Trail, Paoli, PA 19301

☎: 610-644-5822

Open: 10-4 Mo-Fr, 10-5 Sa, 1-5 Su, (Mar-Dec) **Closed:** LEG/HOL!

ADM: **Adult:** $6.00 **Children:** $3.00 under 12 **Seniors:** $6.00

& ℗ **Museum Shop**

Group Tours **Drop-In Tours**: Hourly, (reservations required) **Historic Building**

Permanent Collection: WOOD SCULP; FURNITURE; WOODCUTS; PTGS

Over 200 works in all media, produced between 1920-1970 which display the progression of Esherick's work are housed in his historic studio and residence. **NOT TO BE MISSED:** Oak spiral stairs

ON EXHIBIT 1999

09/1999 to 12/31/1999 ANNUAL THEMATIC WOODWORKING COMPETITION EXHIBITION

Afro-American Historical and Cultural Museum

701 Arch Street, Philadelphia, PA 19106

☎: 215-574-0380
Open: 10-5 Tu-Sa, 12-5 Su   **Closed:** Mo, LEG/HOL!
ADM: **Adult:** $6.00   **Children:** $4.00   **Students:** $4.00   **Seniors:** $4.00
 ⚅ ⓟ   **Museum Shop**   **Group Tours:** 215-574-0380 x228   **Drop-In Tours**
Permanent Collection: JACK FRANK COLL: phot; PEARL JONES COLL: phot drgs, dec/art: JOSEPH C. COLEMAN personal papers, photos and awards

A diverse and unique showplace, this is the first museum built by a major city to house and interpret collections of African-American art, history, and culture primarily in, but not limited to the Commonwealth of Pennsylvania. The museum contains over 300,000 objects.

ON EXHIBIT 1999

ONGOING   INTRODUCTION TO THE MUSEUM AND ITS COLLECTION

12/03/1998 to 02/28/1999   INVOKING THE SPIRIT

03/10/1999 to 04/22/1999   THE CHILDREN'S HOUR

04/13/1999 to 09/30/1999   OBJECTS TO BEHOLD: SELECTIONS FROM THE PERMANENT COLLECTION

05/14/1999 to 11/30/1999   CALL TO ORDER: BLACKS IN THE LAW

10/09/1999 to 04/20/2000   OBJECTS TO BEHOLD: PART II

12/12/1999 to 02/28/2000   TUSKEGEE AIRMEN

Institute of Contemporary Art

Affiliate Institution: University of Pennsylvania

118 South 36th Street at Sansom, Philadelphia, PA 19104-3289

☎: 215-898-7108   ▣   www.upenn.edu/ica
Open: 12-8 We- Fr, 11-5 Sa-Su   **Closed:** Mo, Tue, 1/1, Easter, THGV, 12/25
Free Day: Su, 11-1   **Adult:** $3.00   **Children:** $2.00, F under 12   **Students:** $2.00   **Seniors:** $2.00.
 ⚅ ⓟ   **Museum Shop**   **Group Tours:** 215-898-7108   **Drop-In Tours:** Hours to be announced
Historic Building Contemporary building designed by Adele Naude Santos
Permanent Collection: non-collecting institution

The Museum was founded in 1963 and is one of the premier institutions solely dedicated to the art of our time.

ON EXHIBIT 1999

11/14/1998 to 01/03/1999   TACITA DEAN

01/16/1999 to 03/07/1999   STICKER SHOCK: ARTISTS STICKERS

01/16/1999 to 03/07/1999   THREE STANZAS ON MELANCHOLY: MIROSLAW BALKA, ROBERT GOBER, & SEAMUS HEANEY

03/20/1999 to 04/25/1999   BIOGRAPHIES: PHILADELPHIA NARRATIVES
ICA'S commitment to showing works by artists who deal with biography and autobiography underscores the depth and range of the visual arts community in Philadelphia.

03/20/1999 to 05/02/1999   TERESITA FERNANDEZ

05/14/1999 to 07/03/1999   PENN COLLECTS: FOUR ALUMNI COLLECTIONS
The second in a series of exhibitions which were begun in 1993. This showcases the contemporary art collections of Penn alumni.

PENNSYLVANIA

La Salle University Art Museum
Affiliate Institution: LaSalle University
20th and Olney Ave, Philadelphia, PA 19141
📞: 215-951-1221
Open: 11-4 Tu-Fr, 2-4 Su, Sep-July   **Closed:** Sa, ACAD!
♿   Ⓟ   **Museum Shop**   **Group Tours**   **Drop-In Tours**
Permanent Collection: EU: ptgs, sculp, gr 15-20; AM: ptgs

Many of the major themes and styles of Western art since the Middle ages are documented in the comprehensive collection of paintings, prints, drawings and sculpture at this museum.

Pennsylvania Academy of the Fine Arts
Broad Street and Cherry Street, Philadelphia, PA 19102
📞: 215-972-7600 ◙ www.pafa.org
Open: 10-5 Mo-Sa, 11-5 Su   **Closed:** LEG/HOL!
Free Day: 3-5 Su   **ADM: Adult:** $5.00   **Children:** $2.00 F under 5   **Students:** $4.00   **Seniors:** $4.00
♿   Ⓟ   **Museum Shop** ❙❙ **Group Tours:** 215-972-1667   **Drop-In Tours:** Sa, Su 12:30 & 2   **Historic Building**
Permanent Collection: AM: ptgs, sculp 18-20

The Museum is housed in a Victorian Gothic masterpiece designed by Frank Furness and George Hewitt located in the heart of downtown Philadelphia. Its roster of past students includes some of the most renowned artists of the 19th & 20th centuries.

ON EXHIBIT 1999

09/12/1998 to 01/03/1999   ARTISTS' SKETCHES
Sketchbooks and oil studies from the permanent collection including Thomas Anshutz, Cecilia Beaux, Thomas Eakins, William Glackens and others.

09/12/1998 to 01/03/1999   NOTHING PERSONAL: IDA APPLEBROOG, 1987-1997
A site-specific installation including approximately 50 paintings by this contemporary New York artist, whose work explores the conflict between the real and ideal view of human relationships with irony and macabre humor.

09/19/1998 to 11/29/1998   JUDITH SCHAECHTER
The work of a noted contemporary stained glass artist is featured.

12/05/1998 to 01/03/1999   SEASON'S GREETINGS: ARTISTS' HOLIDAY CARDS
Greeting cards by historical and contemporary artists from private local collections are featured.

01/1999 to 04/1999   I'LL MAKE ME A WORLD
Coinciding with a city-wide celebration of African-American culture, the Museum is presenting selected graphics from the permanent collection by African-American artists.

01/09/1999 to 03/07/1999   PARKS AND PORTRAITS: DONA NELSON, 1983-88
Featured is the "Park Series" by this noted contemporary painter.

03/1999 to 05/1999   POSTWAR PRINTS: RECENT ACQUISITIONS

06/19/1999 to 09/26/1999   MAXFIELD PARRISH, 1870-1966
A major retrospective of the work of one of the Academy's most distinguished alumni exploring the artistic influences, his work as one of the century's most popular illustrators and as a painter. Also to be explored are the qualities of his work which have led to his "rediscovery" by many contemporary artists. *Catalog Will Travel*

10/09/1999 to 01/02/2000   JOHN HENRY TWACHTMAN: AN AMERICAN IMPRESSIONIST
The first retrospective in more than 30 years featuring over 50 oils and pastels covering four periods of the artist's production- Early Works, European Period, Connecticut Years, and Gloucester, late Period. *Catalog Will Travel*

12/1999 to 02/2000   BARRY GOLDBERG
Work from this recent Pennsylvania Academy Graduate.

Philadelphia Museum of Art

26th Street & Benjamin Franklin Parkway, Philadelphia, PA 19130

☎: 215-763-8100   ▣ www.philamuseum.org

Open: 10-5 Tu, Th-Su, 10-8:45 We   **Closed:** Mo, LEG/HOL!

Free Day: Su, 10-1   **ADM:**   **Adult:** $8.00   **Children:** $5.00   **Students:** $5.00   **Seniors:** $5.00

&   ⓟ   **Museum Shop**   ¶: Tu-Sa 11:30-2:30, W 5-7, S 11-3:30

Group Tours   **Drop-In Tours:** on the hour 10-3   **Historic Building**   **Sculpture Garden**

Permanent Collection: EU: ptgs 19-20; CONT; DEC/ART; GR; AM: ptgs, sculp 17-20

With more than 400,000 works in the permanent collection the Philadelphia Art Museum is the 3rd largest art museum in the country. Housed within its more than 200 galleries are a myriad of artistic treasures from many continents and cultures. **NOT TO BE MISSED:** Van Gogh's 'Sunflowers"; A Ceremonial Japanese Teahouse; Medieval & Early Renaissance Galleries (25 in all) which include a Romanesque cloister, a Gothic chapel, and a world-class collection of early Italian & Northern paintings.

ON EXHIBIT 1999

Spring/summer 19999   HON'AMI KOETSU: JAPANESE RENAISSANCE MASTER

An in-depth exhibition of 60 works from Japanese, American, and European collections celebrating this central figure in the early 17th C. artistic world in Japan. He is universally acknowledged as a master whose wide-ranging talents influenced numerous areas of Japanese art. *Catalog*

Fall 1999   PENNSYLVANIA BAROQUE: 1695-1755

The first comprehensive examination of the important developments in the lifestyles and traditions of decorative and fine arts that evolved in Philadelphia and the surrounding colony during its early and pre-Revolutionary period. Included are the distinct styles of furniture, painting, ceramics, textiles, prints, maps, books, silver and metalwork.

Fall 1999   THE KINGDOMS OF EDWARD HICKS

The first retrospective devoted to the life and work of Bucks County, Pennsylvania artist Edward Hicks. Included are paintings, decorated objects and important manuscripts which illustrate his deep spirituality and talent as an artist and his involvement in the doctrinal controversies that divided the Quakers in the early 19th C. *Catalog Will Travel*

09/16/1998 to 01/03/1999   DELACROIX: THE LATE WORK

Some 70 paintings and 40 works on paper have been assembled from public and private collections around the world in celebration of the bicentennial of the birth of Delacroix. This will be the first exhibition in a decade to examine his great genius. Renoir, Cezanne, Picasso, and Matisse were profoundly influenced by his work *Catalog*

10/03/1998 to 12/06/1998   JOSEPH CORNELL/MARCEL DUCHAMP: IN RESONANCE

An exploration of the influences and collaborations of these two artists. Cornell's "Duchamp Dossier" will be shown. This collection of 117 items ranging from Mona Lisa postcards, dry cleaning receipts, correspondence, and a study by Duchamp for his "Allegory de Genre". Included will be about 40 works by each artist examining their shared interests including film, optics, glass, games, the "portable museum" . *Catalog Will Travel*

Spring 1999   RAYMOND PETTIBON

This first major museum presentation of Pettibon's drawings and books will include some 600 drawings chosen from the thousands he has made in the last two decades. These are done in a distinctive style and broad emotional spectrum, often elegiac, ironic or disturbing. Also on view will be a selection of his unique handmade books and watercolor drawings. *Catalog Will Travel*

01/1999 to 02/1999   JASPER JOHNS: PROCESS AND PRINTMAKING

The 125 proofs and edition prints shown are draw almost entirely from the artists' personal collection. Thirty finished works are shown with a series of proofs leading up to each print. These give a revealing view of John's often esoteric works as well as insight into the working process of this unusually reclusive artist. *Will Travel*

Spring 99/1999 to 05/16/1999   A PASSION FOR PICASSO: AN ARTIST COLLECTS MODERN ART

Artist Earl Horter collected art between the New York Armory Show and the beginning of World War II. That now dispersed collection included European and American modern art, African sculpture, and Native American artifacts. Reconstructed here will be 50-60 paintings, drawings, sculptures and prints by European and American artists as well as some 20 African sculptures and Native American artifacts. Also included are some 25 works by Horter himself. Artists represented include Picasso, Brancusi, Braque, Matisse, Sheeler, Marin and Benton. *Catalog*

PENNSYLVANIA

Rodin Museum

Benjamin Franklin Parkway at 22nd Street, Philadelphia, PA 19101

☎: 215-763-8100   ◙ www.rodinmuseum.org
Open: 10-5 Tu-Su   **Closed:** Mo, LEG/HOL!
Sugg/Cont: Yes   **Adult:** $3.00   **Students:** $3.00   **Seniors:** $3.00
& Ⓟ **Museum Shop**
Group Tours   Drop-In Tours   Historic Building   Sculpture Garden
Permanent Collection: RODIN: sculp, drgs

The largest collection of Rodin's sculptures and drawings outside of Paris is located in a charming and intimate building designed by architects Paul Cret and Jacques Greber. **NOT TO BE MISSED:** 'The Thinker', by Rodin

Rosenbach Museum & Library

2010 DeLancey Place, Philadelphia, PA 19103

☎: 215-732-1600   ◙ www.rosenbach.org
Open: 11-4 Tu-Su   **Closed:** Mo, LEG/HOL! August thru 2nd Tu after Labor Day
Free Day: Bloomsday, June 16th   ADM: **Adult:** $5.00 incl guide   **Children:** $3.00   **Students:** $3.00   **Seniors:** $3.00
& **Museum Shop   Group Tours   Drop-In Tours   Historic Building**
Permanent Collection: BRIT & AM: ptgs; MINI SCALE DEC/ARTS; BOOK ILLUSTRATIONS; Rare books and Manuscripts

In the warm and intimate setting of a 19th-century townhouse, the Rosenbach Museum & Library retains an atmosphere of an age when great collectors lived among their treasures. It is the only collection of its kind open to the public in Philadelphia. **NOT TO BE MISSED:** Maurice Sendak drawings

ON EXHIBIT 1999

11/22/1998 to 03/07/1999   LEWIS CARRROLL, ALICE AND THE RISE OF CHILDREN'S LITERATURE. A CENTENNIAL EXHIBITION
With the publication of "Alice's Adventures" in 1865 Lewis Carroll ushered in a new era of literature written especially for children. Dr. Rosenbach was one of the world's great collectors of Carrolliana. The exhibition will draw from those collections as well as selected loans.

04/08/1999 to 07/31/1999   BEHIND THE FIRST PRESIDENCY. THE LIFE AND LETTERS OF GEORGE WASHINGTON, 1732-1799 (working title)
Behind George Washington the icon there is evidence of Washington the man: a father and husband, a surveyor, a farmer, a lawyer, etc. In more than 100 autograph letters this aspect of Washington will be examined from a unique personal perspective. Included also is the longest surviving portion of a manuscript biography written by his aide-de-camp and friend David Humphrey in 1788 containing a sketch of his character and habits. *Will Travel*

09/1999 to 11/1999   "DRIFTING TO THE SOUTHEAST" THE AUTOBIOGRAPHY OF MANJIRO, A NINETEENTH-CENTURY JAPANESE ACCOUNT OF AMERICA
After being shipwrecked in 1841 Nakahama Manjiro was rescued by a whaling ship out of Fairhaven, Massachusetts and became the first Japanese man to visit America. After a decade in and around Massachusetts he returned to Japan as "John Mung" and commissioned a lavish autobiography (Hyoson Kiryaku) "Drifting to the Southeast". It is illustrated with more than 50 drawings of America. The Rosenbach Manjiro manuscript is the most complete of the six known copies. *Catalog*

11/1999 to 03/2000   TERRA NOVA: THE OREGON COLLECTION (working title)
The Museum preserves the largest surviving collection of documents and early imprints relating to the discovery and settlement of the Oregon Territory. Virtually unknown and completely unpublished, the collection offers new territory for the new millennium.

Rosenwald-Wolf Gallery, The University of the Arts

Broad and Pine Streets, Philadelphia, PA 19102
📞: 215-875-1116   ▣ www.uarts.edu
Open: 10-5 Mo, Tu, Th, Fr, 10-9 We, 12-5 Sa, Su, (10-5 weekdays Jun & July)   **Closed:** ACAD!
⅊   ℗   **Museum Shop   Group Tours   Drop-In Tours**
Permanent Collection: non-collecting institution

This is the only university in the nation devoted exclusively to education and professional training in the visual and performing arts. The gallery presents temporary exhibitions of contemporary art.

ON EXHIBIT 1999

01/08/1999 to 02/26/1999   VITO ACCONCI: PUBLIC ART
Since 1969 Vito Acconci has embraced poetry, body art, performance, video, and, since the eighties has focused primarily on sculpture and installations for public sites in cities, galleries, and museums. He has continued to explore the terrain of public spaces and social interaction. Represented here will be a selection of proposed and realized public art projects.

03/15/1999 to 04/04/1999   GRAPHIC DESIGN RETROSPECTIVE

04/16/1999 to 05/09/1999   BOOK ARTS RETROSPECTIVE
Book Arts will mark its 10th anniversary at the Philadelphia College of Art and Design with an alumni Invitational exhibition.

University of Pennsylvania Museum of Archaeology and Anthropology

Affiliate Institution: University of Pennsylvania
33rd and Spruce Streets, Philadelphia, PA 19104
📞: 215-898-4000   ▣ www.upenn.edu/mus
Open: 10-4:30 Tu-Sa, 1-5 Su, closed Su Mem day-Lab day   **Closed:** Mo, LEG/HOL!
Free Day: Su through May 16, 1999 **Vol/Cont** **Adult:** $5.00 **Children:** F (under 6)   **Students:** $2.50   **Seniors:** $2.50
⅊   ℗   **Museum Shop**   ⅋: Y
Group Tours: 215-898-4015   **Drop-In Tours**: 1:30 Sa, Su (mid Sep-mid May)!   **Sculpture Garden**
Permanent Collection: GRECO/ROMAN; AF; AN/EGT; ASIA; MESOPOTAMIA; MESOAMERICAN; POLYNESIAN; AMERICAS

Dedicated to the understanding of the history and cultural heritage of humankind, the museum's galleries include objects from China, Ancient Egypt, Mesoamerica, Polynesia, Africa, the Bible Lands, the Americas, and the Greco Roman world. **NOT TO BE MISSED:** Twelve ton sphinx and palatial remnants from Memphis, Egypt, circa 1200 BC

ON EXHIBIT 1999

LONG TERM EXHIBITIONS:

   TIME AND RULERS AT TIKAL: ARCHITECTURAL SCULPTURE OF THE MAYA

   ANCIENT MESOPOTAMIA: THE ROYAL TOMBS OF UR

   THE EGYPTIAN MUMMY: SECRETS AND SCIENCE

   RAVEN'S JOURNEY: THE WORLD OF ALASKA'S NATIVE PEOPLE

   BUDDHISM: HISTORY AND DIVERSITY OF A GREAT TRADITION

09/27/1997 to 05/1999   ROMAN GLASS: REFLECTIONS ON CULTURAL CHANGE
More than 200 spectacular examples of Roman glass and associated materials from the 1st C. B.C. through the 6th C.A.D. illustrate how cultural change, technical innovation, and social aspects of wealth and taste were constant influences on Roman glass making.

PENNSYLVANIA

University of Pennsylvania Museum of Archaeology and Anthropology - continued
03/14/1998 to 01/03/1999   TREASURES OF THE CHINESE SCHOLAR
"Scholar Art" including calligraphy, painting, works of art in wood, lacquer, ivory, stone, horn and metal from the early Zhou Dynasty (770-256 B.C.) through the Qing Dynasty (1644-1911 A.D.). Traditional scholars spent years studying the ancient classics and philosophical treatises while steeping himself in Confucianism in hopes of passing the Civil Service Examination allowing him to enter a life of privilege.

09/17/1998 to 12/1998   AN ITALIAN JOURNEY
33 black and white photographs by Liana Miuccio exploring the journey of her family as they emigrated from Sicily to the US. It is at the same time a highly personal journey and a look at the common experience of all immigrants.

10/18/1998   CANAAN AND ANCIENT ISRAEL
This long term exhibition is the first in North America dedicated to the archaeology of ancient Israel and neighboring lands.

01/23/1999 to 03/28/1999   LAYERS THROUGH THE MIST
More than 40 color photographs of Vietnamese life taken by Ellen Kaplowitz during the 1994 New Year celebration known as "Tet".

Woodmere Art Museum
9201 Germantown Ave, Philadelphia, PA 19118
☎: 215-247-0476
Open: 10-5 Tu-Sa, 1-5 Su   **Closed:** Mo, 1/1, EASTER, 7/4, THGV, 12/25
Sugg/Cont: Yes   **ADM:**   **Adult:** $3.00   **Children:** F under 12   **Students:** $3.00   **Seniors:** $3.00
& Ⓟ   **Museum Shop**   **Group Tours**: 215-247-0476   **Drop-In Tours**
Permanent Collection: AM: ptgs 19, 20, prints, gr, drgs; EU (not always on view()

The Woodmere Art Museum, located in a mid 1850's Victorian eclectic house, includes a large rotunda gallery The collection of local, Philadelphia area and Pennsylvania Impressionist art is outstanding. **NOT TO BE MISSED:** Benjamin West's 'The Death of Sir Phillip Sydney'

ON EXHIBIT 1999
10/18/1998 to 01/03/1999   WILLIAM H. CAMPBELL AND HAROLD KIMMELMAN: PATHS TO ABSTRACT ART
The works shown will demonstrate that both realism and abstract art require study of nature and solid training.

10/18/1998 to 11/29/1999   THE AMERICAN COLOR PRINT SOCIETY
This show was founded when color prints were viewed as a novelty. It will be full of assorted images and vibrant palettes

11/10/1998 to 02/28/1999   WILLIAM TROST RICHARDS: REDISCOVERED, OILS, WATERCOLORS AND DRAWINGS FROM THE ARTIST'S FAMILY
This monographic exhibition brings together more than 80 superb works by one of America's leading watercolorists, draughtsmen, and marine painters. Many of these works have belonged to the family of the artist and have been little seen.

12/13/1998 to 03/28/1999 · TREASURES FROM THE WESTMORELAND MUSEUM OF AMERICAN ART
Due to a major renovation of the galleries at the Westmoreland, more than 20 of its treasures will be seen here. Featured will be artists with close Philadelphia ties including Mary Cassatt, Robert Henri, William Harnett, Rembrandt Peale and Gilbert Stuart.

02/21/1999 to 04/25/1999   WOODMERE ART MUSEUM 58TH ANNUAL JURIED EXHIBITION
One of the longest running exhibitions of its kind in the Philadelphia region shows a spectrum of artistic styles and technique.

04/11/1999 to 06/27/1999   THE HEROIC OBSESSION: GRAPHIC WORK BY JACOB LANDAU
A retrospective exhibition of prints by this Philadelphia native documenting his long and distinguished career.

Woodmere Art Museum - continued

07/11/1999 to 08/29/1999 ANNUAL MEMBER'S EXHIBITION
A museum tradition since 1940, each member is invited to submit a work of art made during the last year. Hundreds participate!

07/11/1999 to 08/29/1999 A FERTILE FELLOWSHIP: CELEBRATING 125 YEARS OF THE SALMAGUNDI CLUB
A major show which has been assembled to give a retrospective look at one of the grandest artist societies in the history of America. Included are Howard Chandler Christy, Edward Redfield, Will Low and works from the collection.

12/1999 to 02/2000 PHILADELPHIA WATER COLOR CLUB ANNUAL
The year 2000 is the 100th anniversary of the Club.

PITTSBURGH

Andy Warhol Museum
417 Sandusky Street, Pittsburgh, PA 15212-5890
☎: 412-237-8300   ◉ www.warhol.org/warhol
Open: 11-6 We, Su, 11-8 Th-Sa   **Closed:** Mo, Tu
ADM: **Adult:** $6.00   **Children:** $4.00   **Students:** $4.00   **Seniors:** $5.00
♿ ⓟ **Museum Shop** ‖: Café
Group Tours Drop-In Tours Historic Building Former Volkwein building renovated by Richard Gluckman Architects
Permanent Collection: ANDY WARHOL ARTWORKS

The most comprehensive single-artist museum in the world, this 7 story museum with over 40,000 square feet of exhibition space permanently highlights artworks spanning every aspect of Warhol's career. A unique feature of this museum is a photo booth where visitors can take cheap multiple pictures of themselves in keeping with the Warhol tradition. **NOT TO BE MISSED:** Rain Machine, a 'daisy waterfall' measuring 132'by 240'; 'Last Supper' paintings; 10' tall 'Big Sculls' series

Carnegie Museum of Art
4400 Forbes Ave, Pittsburgh, PA 15213
☎: 412-622-3131   ◉ www.clpgh.org
Open: 10-5 Tu-Sa, 1-5 Su, 10-5 Mo, 10-9 Fr July/Aug only   **Closed:** Mo, LEG/HOL!
ADM: **Adult:** $6.00   **Children:** $4.00   **Students:** $4.00   **Seniors:** $5.00
♿ ⓟ **Museum Shop** ‖: café open weekdays; coffee bar daily
Group Tours: 412-622-3289   **Drop-In Tours**: 1:30, Tu-Sa, 3, Su   **Historic Building**   **Sculpture Garden**
Permanent Collection: FR/IMPR: ptgs; POST/IMPR: ptgs; AM: ptgs 19, 20; AB/IMPR; VIDEO ART

The original 1895 Carnegie Institute, created in the spirit of opulence by architects Longfellow, Alden and Harlowe, was designed to house a library with art galleries, the museum itself, and a concert hall. A stunning light filled modern addition offers a spare purity that enhances the enjoyment of the art on the walls. **NOT TO BE MISSED:** Claude Monet's 'Nympheas' (Water Lilies)

Frick Art Museum
7227 Reynolds Street, Pittsburgh, PA 1520821
☎: 412-371-0600
Open: 10-5:30 Tu-Sa, 12-6 Su   **Closed:** Mo, LEG/HOL!
♿ ⓟ **Museum Shop Group Tours**: 412-371-0600, ext. 158   **Drop-In Tours**: We, Sa, Su 2pm
Permanent Collection: EARLY IT/REN: ptgs; FR & FLEM: 17; BRIT: ptgs; DEC/ART

Frick Art Museum - continued
The Frick Art Museum features a permanent collection of European paintings, sculptures and decorative objects and temporary exhibitions from around the world. Clayton House: Admission, Adults $6.00, Seniors $5.00, Students $4.00 Car and Carriage Museum: Adults $4.00, Seniors $3.00, Students $2.00 Combination admission   Adults $7.00, Seniors $6.00, Students $5.00

ON EXHIBIT 1999
11/13/1998 to 01/10/1999   WILLIAM SIDNEY MOUNT: PAINTER OF AMERICAN LIFE
At a time when other American Artists portrayed European models, Mount successfully transferred these images into imagery specific to American life. His scenes of everyday life included stories and jokes about rural life. Farmer, boys and musicians were regulars in his cast of characters. He struck a sympathetic chord with public and critics and was zoom pronounced the most talented artist of his time. 50 paintings and works on paper will be featured here. *Catalog Will Travel*

Hunt Institute for Botanical Documentation
Affiliate Institution: Carnegie Mellon University
Pittsburgh, PA 15213-3890
☎: 412-268-2434   ◙   www.huntbot.andrew.cmu.edu/HIBD
Open: 9-12 & 1-5 Mo-Fr   **Closed:** Sa, S, LEG/HOL!,12/24-1/1
♿   ℗   **Museum Shop**
Group Tours   Drop-In Tours
Permanent Collection: BOTANICAL W/COL 15-20; DRGS; GR

30,000 botanical watercolors, drawings and prints from the Renaissance onward represented in this collection.

ON EXHIBIT 1999
10/12/1998 to 02/26/1999   9TH INTERNATIONAL EXHIBITION OF BOTANICAL ART AND ILLUSTRATION
The works in this comprehensive exhibition prove that in the world of art the infinite variety of plant forms and colors still holds special fascination and offers undiminished challenge and delight. 76 artists from Brazil, Canada, England, India, Italy, Mexico, New Zealand, Japan, South Africa, The People's Republic of China, and the US are represented. *Catalog Will Travel*

Spring 1999   ARUNDHATI VARTAK
Working in Mumbai and Pune, Vartak has devoted herself to painting portraits of common Indian trees in a most distinctive style.

Fall 1999   JAMES SAIN
Last shown in the 6th International, Sain has continued to develop as an exceptional botanical artist.

Mattress Factory Ltd
500 Sampsonia Way, satellite bldg at 1414 Monterey, Pittsburgh, PA 15212
☎: 412-231-3169   ◙   www.mattress.org
Open: 10-5 Tu-Sa, 1-5 Su (Sep-July or by appt)   **Closed:** Mo, 1/1, EASTER, MEM/DAY, THGV, 12/25
Free Day: Th   **Sugg/Cont:** Yes   **Adult:** $4.00   **Children:** Free   **Students:** $3.00   **Seniors:** $3.00
♿   ℗   **Museum Shop   Group Tours   Drop-In Tours   Historic Building   Sculpture Garden**
Permanent Collection: Site-specific art installations completed in residency

A museum of contemporary art that commissions, collects and exhibits site-specific art installations. Founded in 1977 in a six story warehouse in the historic Mexican War Streets of Pittsburgh's North Side. **NOT TO BE MISSED:** Yayoi Kusama, "Repetitive Vision" 1997

READING

Freedman Gallery
Affiliate Institution: Albright College
Center for the Arts, 13th and Bern Streets, Reading, PA 19604
☎: 610-921-2381
Open: 12-8 Tu; 12 6 We-Fr, 12-4 Sa, Su; Summer 12-4 We-Su **Closed:** M, LEG/HOL!, ACAD! Summer Mon, Tu
& ℗ **Museum Shop**
Group Tours: 610-921-7541 **Drop-In Tours**
Permanent Collection: CONT: gr, ptgs

An education and exhibition center in Southeastern Pennsylvania that presents an on-going program of provocative work by today's leading artists. **NOT TO BE MISSED:** Mary Miss Sculpture creates an outdoor plaza which is part of the building

SCRANTON

Everhart Museum
1901 Mulberry Street, Nay Aug Park, Scranton, PA 18510
☎: 717-346-7186
Open: 12-5 daily, 12-8 T 4/1-10/12, 12-5 We Su 12 8 T 10/13-3/30 **Closed:** THGV, 12/25
Sugg/Cont: Yes **Adult:** $3.00 **Children:** $1.00, F under 6 **Seniors:** $2.00
& ℗ **Museum Shop**
Group Tours **Drop-In Tours**: by appt
Permanent Collection: AM: early 19, 20; WORKS ON PAPER; AM: folk, gr; AF; Glass; Nat/Hist

This art, science, and natural history museum is the only wide-ranging museum of its type in Northeastern Pennsylvania.

UNIVERSITY PARK

Palmer Museum of Art
Affiliate Institution: The Pennsylvania State University
Curtin Road, University Park, PA 16802-2507
☎: 814-865-7672
Open: 10-4:30 Tu-Sa, 12-4 Su **Closed:** Mo, LEG/HOL!, 12/25-1/1
& ℗ **Museum Shop**
Group Tours **Drop-In Tours**: ! **Sculpture Garden**
Permanent Collection: AM; EU; AS; S/AM: ptgs, sculp, works on paper, ceramics

A dramatic and exciting facility for this collection of 35 centuries of artworks. **NOT TO BE MISSED:** The building by Charles Moore, a fine example of post-modern architecture

ON EXHIBIT 1999
01/19/1999 to 05/23/1999 PICTORIALISM INTO MODERNISM: THE CLARENCE H. WHITES SCHOOL OF PHOTOGRAPHY
This exhibition of more than 117 images by 58 photographers are the first comprehensive study of this School and in addition to White himself, include some of photography's greatest artists. These include Dorothea Lange, Paul Outerbridge, Margaret Bourke White, Ralph Steiner and Laura Gilpin. *Will Travel*

PENNSYLVANIA

Palmer Museum of Art - continued
01/19/1999 to 05/30/1999   SHADOWS AND REFLECTIONS: PICTORIAL PHOTOGRAPHY BY WILBUR H. PORTERFIELD
A selection of landscape photographs by one of the guiding spirits of the Photo-Pictorialists of Buffalo.

02/02/1999 to 06/27/1999   DRAWINGS BY JOHN BIGGERS *Catalog Will Travel*

06/22/1999 to 09/12/1999   DALE CHIHULY: SEAFORMS
Drawn from several series of his 30 year career this important exhibition of blown glass objects by Chihuly, America's foremost contemporary glass master, will be presented in room-size installations that are contrived to explore the space for which they are designed. *Will Travel*

10/1999 to 01/2000   SEYMOUR LIPTON (1903-1983): A RETROSPECTIVE

WILKES-BARRE

Sordoni Art Gallery
Affiliate Institution: Wilkes University
150 S. River Street, Wilkes-Barre, PA 18766-0001
☎: 717-408-4325
Open: 12-5 daily   **Closed:** LEG/HOL!
⛓ ⓟ **Museum Shop**
Group Tours   Drop-In Tours
Permanent Collection: AM: ptgs 19, 20; WORKS ON PAPER

Located on the grounds of Wilkes University, in the historic district of downtown Wilkes-Barre, this facility is best known for mounting both historical and contemporary exhibitions.

Fine Arts Center Galleries, University of Rhode Island

105 Upper College Road, Suite 1, Kingston, RI 02881-0820
☎: 401-874-2775 or 2131
Open: Main Gallery 12-4 & 7:30-9:30 Tu-Fr,1-4 Sa, Su, Phot Gallery 12-4 Tu-F, 1-4 Sa, Su   **Closed:** LEG/HOL!; ACAD!
Vol/Cont:
 ♿ Ⓟ **Museum Shop**
Group Tours   Drop-In Tours: !
Permanent Collection: non-collecting institution

A university affiliated 'kunsthalle' distinguished for the activity of their programming (20-25 exhibitions annually) and in generating that programming internally. Contemporary exhibitions in all media are shown as well as film and video showings. The Corridor Gallery is open from 9-9 daily.

ON EXHIBIT 1999

01/22/1999 to 02/28/1999   UNLOCKING THE GRID (CONCERNING THE GRID IN CONTEMPORARY ART)

03/09/1999 to 04/18/1999   INSTALLATION BY FRED SANDBACK

03/25/1999 to 05/02/1999   RHODE ISLAND MILLS OF THE 19TH CENTURY

Newport Art Museum

76 Bellevue Avenue, Newport, RI 02840
☎: 401-848-8200
Open: 10-4 Tu-Sa,12-4 Su   **Closed:** Mo, THGV, 12/25, 1/1
ADM: Adult: $5.00   **Children:** F (under 12)   **Students:** $4.00   **Seniors:** $4.00
♿ Ⓟ **Museum Shop**
Group Tours   Drop-In Tours   Historic Building
Permanent Collection: AM: w/col 19, 20

Historic J.N.A. Griswold House in which the museum is located was designed by Richard Morris Hunt in 1862-1864.

Redwood Library and Athenaeum

50 Bellevue Avenue, Newport, RI 02840
☎: 401-847-0292   ▣ www.redwood1747.org
Open: 9:30-5:30 daily   **Closed:** Su, LEG/HOL!
Vol/Cont:
♿ Ⓟ **Museum Shop**
Group Tours   Drop-In Tours   Historic Building
Permanent Collection: AM: gr, drgs, phot, portraits, furniture, dec/art 18,19

Established in 1747, this facility serves as the oldest circulating library in the country. Designed by Peter Harrison, considered America's first architect, it is the most significant surviving public building from the Colonial period. **NOT TO BE MISSED:** Paintings by Gilbert Stuart and Charles Bird King

RHODE ISLAND

David Winton Bell Gallery

Affiliate Institution: Brown University

List Art Center, 64 College Street, Providence, RI 02912

📞: 401-863-2932

Open: 11-4 Mo-Fr & 1-4 Sa, Su (Sept-May)   **Closed:** 1/1, THGV, 12/25

 ♿ Ⓟ **Museum Shop   Group Tours   Drop-In Tours**

Permanent Collection: GR & PHOT 20; WORKS ON PAPER 16-20; CONT: ptgs

Located in the List Art Center, an imposing modern structure designed by Philip Johnson, the Gallery presents exhibitions which focus on the arts and issues of our time.

ON EXHIBIT 1999

01/23/1999 to 03/07/1999   MASAMI TERAOKA: FROM TRADITION TO TECHNOLOGY, THE FLOATING WORLD COMES OF AGE

Watercolors that mimic the style and conventions of the 19th c Japanese woodblock prints as they satirize the clash between Eastern and Western cultures. *Will Travel*

Rhode Island Black Heritage Society

202 Washington Street, Providence, RI 02903

📞: 401-751-3490

Open: 10-5 Mo-Fr, 10-2 Sa & by appt   **Closed:** LEG/HOL!

 ♿ Ⓟ **Museum Shop   Group Tours   Drop-In Tours**

Permanent Collection: PHOT; AF: historical collection

The Society collects documents and preserves the history of African-Americans in the state of Rhode Island with an archival collection which includes photos, rare books, and records dating back to the 18th century. Ongoing Permanent Exhibition – CREATIVE SURVIVAL **NOT TO BE MISSED:** Polychrome relief wood carvings by Elizabeth N. Prophet

Rhode Island School of Design Museum

Affiliate Institution: Rhode Island School Of Design

224 Benefit Street, Providence, RI 02903

📞: 401-454-6500   □ www.risd.edu

Open: 10-5 We-Su, 10-8 Fr   **Closed:** LEG/HOL!

Free Day: Sa   **ADM:**   **Adult:** $5.00   **Children:** $1.00 (5-18)   **Students:** $2.00   **Seniors:** $4.00

 ♿ Ⓟ **Museum Shop   Group Tours   Drop-In Tours   Sculpture Garden**

Permanent Collection: AM: ptgs, dec/art; JAP: gr, cer; LAT/AM

The museum's outstanding collections are housed on three levels: in a Georgian style building completed in 1926, in Pendleton House, completed in 1906, and in The Daphne Farago Wing, a center dedicated to the display and interpretation of contemporary art in all media. **NOT TO BE MISSED:** "Mantled Figure" 1993

ON EXHIBIT 1999

12/09/1998 to 03/07/1999   NINETEENTH-CENTURY JAPANESE PRINTMAKING

12/23/1998 to 04/04/1999   TRADITION AND INNOVATION IN AMERICAN WATERCOLORS

01/20/1999 to 04/04/1999   TACTILE TECHNOLOGY: CONTEMPORARY JAPANESE TEXTILE DESIGN

03/10/1999 to 06/06/1999   SPRING BLOSSOMS: SEASONAL JAPANESE PRINTS

CHARLESTON

City Hall Council Chamber Gallery

Broad & Meeting Streets, Charleston, SC 29401

☏: 803-724-3799

Open: 9-5 Mo-Fr, closed 12-1 **Closed:** Sa, Su, LEG/HOL!

Vol/Cont: Yes

♿ **Museum Shop** **Group Tours** **Drop-In Tours**: 9-5 (closed 12-1) **Historic Building**

Permanent Collection: AM: ptgs 18,19

What is today Charleston's City Hall was erected in 1801 in Adamsesque style to be the Charleston branch of the First Bank of the United States. **NOT TO BE MISSED:** 'George Washington', by John Trumbull is unlike any other and is considered one of the best portraits ever done of him.

Gibbes Museum of Art

135 Meeting Street, Charleston, SC 29401

☏: 843-722-2706 ◙ www.gibbes.com

Open: 10-5 Tu-Sa, 1-5 Su **Closed:** M, LEG/HOL!

ADM: **Adult:** $5.00 **Children:** $3.00 **Students:** $4.00 **Seniors:** $4.00

♿ Ⓟ **Museum Shop** **Group Tours** **Drop-In Tours**: 1st We of mo at 2:30pm **Sculpture Garden**

Permanent Collection: AM: reg portraits, miniature portraits; JAP: gr

Charleston's only fine arts museum offers a nationally significant collection of American art, American Renaissance period (1920's-40's) room interiors done in miniature scale, and a miniature portrait collection, the oldest and finest in the country. **NOT TO BE MISSED:** 'John Moultie and Family' ca 1782 by John, Francis Rigaud

ON EXHIBIT 1999

09/05/1998 to 01/31/1999 THE ROMAN REMAINS: JOHN IZARD MIDDLETON'S VISUAL SOUVENIRS OF 1820-1823

Pencil, pen and wash works executed by American expatriate Middleton who dedicated his life to the study of antiquity and classical ruins.

09/12/1998 to 09/06/1999 THE CHARLESTON RENAISSANCE: ANNA HEYWARD TAYLOR

Anna Heyward Taylor illustrated for 'This is Our Land' as well as an exhibition at the opening of 'Porgy and Bess' in Milan Italy.

09/19/1998 to 10/10/1999 AN INSIDE LOOK: CONSERVING MINIATURE PORTRAITS

Small landscapes and images of Charleston are combined with miniature portraits which launches a new look for the Gallery. Conservation practices will be examined and a closed-captioned video presentation for the hearing impaired will be featured.

11/04/1998 to 01/07/1999 BEARING WITNESS: CONTEMPORARY WORKS BY AFRICAN AMERICAN WOMEN ARTISTS

History, ethnicity, gender, marginalization and invisibility are some of the issues addressed by these 25 prominent artists. Included are Howardina Pindell, Betye and Alison Saar, Faith Ringold, Carrie Mae Weems, and Lorna Simpson.

11/21/1998 to 11/28/1999 EMBRACING THE FAR EAST: THE HUME COLLECTION

The third in a series of exhibits focusing on the development of the Gibbes Japanese Print Collection and the local artists influenced by these works of art.

01/21/1999 to 03/14/1999 EDWARD RICE: SELECTED ARCHITECTURAL PAINTINGS, 1978-1998

Rice had a broad range of intellectual and visual statements, shown here.

SOUTH CAROLINA

Gibbes Museum of Art - continued

04/09/1999 to 07/03/1999   IN PURSUIT OF REFINEMENT: CHARLESTON ABROAD, 1740-1860
The cultural interaction existing between Charleston and Europe before, during and after the Revolutionary War.

07/13/1999 to 09/19/1999   TRAINS THAT PASS IN THE NIGHT: THE RAILROAD PHOTOGRAPHS OF O. WINSTON LINK
70 primarily black and white photographs that chronicle the history of the Norfolk and Western Railway in Virginia, West Virginia, and part of North Carolina. These are miracles of innovation capturing the images of the last steam engines of the century. *Will Travel*

COLUMBIA

Columbia Museum of Arts

Main at Hampton, Columbia, SC 29202

☎: 803-799-2810   ◉   www.colmusart.org
Open: 10-5 Tu-Fr, 10-9 We, 10-5 Sa, 1-5 Su   **Closed:** Mo, 1/1, Mem/Day, 7/4, LAB/DAY, THGV, 12/24, 12/25
Free Day: 1st Sa each mo   ADM: **Adult:** $4.00   **Children:** F under 6   **Students:** $2.00   **Seniors:** $2.00
♿   Ⓟ   **Museum Shop**
Group Tours   **Drop-In Tours:** Sun, 2-3, We eve, Th, 12:15-1
Permanent Collection: KRESS COLL OF MED, BAROQUE & REN; AS; REG

The museum emphasizes a broad spectrum of European and American fine arts dating from the 14th C to the present. It also has one of the Southeast's most important collections of Italian Renaissance and Baroque paintings, sculpture and decorative art by the Old Masters.

ON EXHIBIT 1999

07/18/1998-07/02/1999   MAJOLICA FROM THE WILLIAM CLARK COLLECTION, CORCORAN GALLERY OF ART

01/16/1999 to 03/21/1999   19TH-CENTURY DUTCH WATERCOLORS AND DRAWINGS FROM THE MUSEUM BOYMANS-VAN BEUNINGEN, ROTTERDAM
80 works will present an overview of the development of Dutch drawing between 1800 and 1900. Included are works by Hendrik Voogd whose work reflect his time's fascination with Italian antiquities; Vincent van Gogh, and Willem Arnold Witsen, whose works show the influences of modernism. *Catalog Bilingual Will Travel*

04/03/1999 to 06/06/1999   THE CHARLESTON RENAISSANCE
During the first half of the 20th C the city of Charleston became the subject of a cultural renewal. Works by Alfred Hutty, Elizabeth O'Neill Verner and Alice Ravenal Huger Smith attracted Child Hassam, Edward Hopper and George Biddle to the city. These 50 works of art were produced then. *Catalog Will Travel*

04/03/1999 to 06/06/1999   COSTA MANOS: AMERICAN COLOR
Costa Manos is a photojournalist and fine arts photographer.

06/19/1999 to 09/05/1999   THE WALTER O. EVANS COLLECTION OF AFRICAN-AMERICAN ART
One of the finest privately owned collections of African-American art this features a comprehensive look at the work of some of the most important artists of the 19th and 20th centuries. Included are works by Bannister, Tanner, Lewis, Duncanson, Bearden, White, Catlett and Lawrence. *Catalog Will Travel*

09/18/1999 to 12/12/1999   100 MASTERPIECES FROM THE VITRA DESIGN MUSEUM
One of the worlds most important collections of modern furniture examines furniture through a selection of 100 chairs and related works. Each portrays a unique vision of the challenge in creating furniture as both a functional and sculptural object. *Will Travel*

FLORENCE

Florence Museum of Art, Science & History

558 Spruce Street, Florence, SC 29501

: 803-662-3351

Open: 10-5 Tu-Sa, 2-5 Su **Closed:** Mo, LEG/HOL!

♿ Ⓟ **Museum Shop** **Group Tours** **Drop-In Tours** **Historic Building**

Permanent Collection: AM/REG: ptgs; SW NAT/AM; pottery; CER

Founded to promote the arts and sciences, this museum, located in a 1939 art deco style building originally constructed as a private home, is surrounded by the grounds of Timrod Park. **NOT TO BE MISSED:** 'Francis Marion Crossing to Pee Dee', by Edward Arnold

GREENVILLE

Bob Jones University Museum & Gallery, Inc.

1700 Wade Hampton Blvd., Greenville, SC 29609-5735

: 864-242-5100 ◙ www.bju.edu/artgallery/

Open: 2-5 Tu-Su **Closed:** 1/1, 7/4, 12/20 thru 12/25, Commencement Day (early May)

♿ Ⓟ **Museum Shop** **Group Tours**: ext. 4206 **Drop-In Tours**

Permanent Collection: EU: ptgs including Rembrandt, Tintoretto, Titian Veronese, Sebastiano del Piombo

One of the finest collections of religious art in America.

Greenville County Museum of Art

420 College Street, Greenville, SC 29601

: 864-271-7570 ◙ www.greenvillemuseum.org

Open: 10-5 Tu-Sa, 1-5 Su **Closed:** Mo, LEG/HOL!

Vol/Cont: Yes

♿ Ⓟ **Museum Shop** **Group Tours** **Drop-In Tours**: 2pm Su

Permanent Collection: AM: ptgs, sculp, gr; REG

The Southern Collection is nationally recognized as one of the countries best regional collections. It provides a survey of American art history from 1726 to the present through works of art that relate to the South. The Museum recently acquired 24 watercolors by Andrew Wyeth.

ON EXHIBIT 1999

10/30/1998 to 01/10/1999 BARBARA COONEY: THE YEAR OF THE PERFECT CHRISTMAS TREE

11/04/1998 to 01/10/1999 COLORPRINT USA

One printmaker from each state was selected to submit a print to this prestigious exhibition. The works will be shown in all fifty states.

11/06/1998 to 01/17/1999 AFRICAN-AMERICAN ART FROM THE PERMANENT COLLECTION

11/18/1998 to 01/17/1999 BETYE SAAR

In this new body of work, Betye Saar continues her satirical commentary on today's African American experience..

12/02/1998 to 03/07/1999 THE CHARLESTON RENAISSANCE

During the first half of the 20th C the city of Charleston became the subject of a cultural renewal. Works by Alfred Hutty, Elizabeth O'Neill Verner and Alice Ravenal Huger Smith attracted Child Hassam, Edward Hopper and George Biddle to the city. These 50 works of art were produced then. *Catalog Will Travel*

02/03/1999 to 04/04/1999 SHAMAN'S FIRE: THE LATE PAINTINGS OF DAVID HARE

Hare was known primarily as a sculptor, but in the last decade of his career devoted himself to painting. This exhibition is the first opportunity to examine these paintings.

SOUTH CAROLINA

Greenville County Museum of Art - continued
02/03/1999 to 04/18/1999   JOHN ACORN

02/13/1999 to 05/23/1999   MORRIS GRAVES: THE EARLY WORKS

05/05/1999 to 07/03/1999   WILLIAM HALSEY

MURRELLS INLET

Brookgreen Gardens
1931 Brookgreen Gardens Drive, Murrells Inlet, SC 29576
☎: 843-237-4218
Open: 9:30-4:45 daily, ! for summer hours   **Closed:** 12/25
ADM: **Adult:** $7.50   **Children:** $3.00 6-12   **Students:** $7.50   **Seniors:** $7.50
& ℗ **Museum Shop**   ⫙: Terrace Café open year round
Group Tours: 800-849-1931   **Drop-In Tours:** ! seasonal   **Historic Building**   **Sculpture Garden**
Permanent Collection: AM: sculp 19, 20

The first public sculpture garden created in America is located on the grounds of a 200-year old rice plantation. It is the largest permanent outdoor collection of American Figurative Sculpture in the world with more than 750 works by 250 American sculptors on permanent display. **NOT TO BE MISSED:** 'Fountain of the Muses', by Carl Milles

---

SPARTANBURG

Spartanburg County Museum of Art
385 South Spring Street, Spartanburg, SC 29306
☎: 864-582-7616
Open: 9-5 Mo-Fr, 10-2 Sa, 2-5 Su   **Closed:** LEG/HOL!, EASTER, 12/24
& ℗ **Museum Shop**   **Group Tours**   **Drop-In Tours**
Permanent Collection: AM/REG: ptgs, gr, dec/art

A multi-cultural Arts Center that presents 20 exhibits of local, regional, and national art each year. **NOT TO BE MISSED:** 'Girl With The Red Hair', by Robert Henri

ON EXHIBIT 1999
01/11/1999 to 02/28/1999   ESCAPE FROM THE VAULT
All of the permanent collection of the Museum.

03/08/1999 to 04/25/1999   SCENT OF PAINT: SOUL OF A WOMEN
Figurative sculpture and paintings-Kathleen Engler, Harriet Goode

05/03/1999 to 06/20/1999   ARTISTS GUILD- JURIED SHOW

06/28/1999 to 07/15/1999   PERMANENT COLLECTION - ANNUAL GROUP AND STUDENT SHOW

08/23/1999 to 07/28/1999   SOUTH CAROLINA WATERCOLOR SOCIETY TRAVELING SHOW
A Juried watercolor show and Printmaker Steve LeWinter and Kit Loney's weaving w/drawings

10/04/1999 to 11/21/1999   MARGARET M. LAW: RETROSPECTIVE

11/29/1999 to 01/02/2000   GROUP LANDSCAPE SHOW
Stephen Chesley, William Jamison, Marshall McCall. Margaret McCann (oils with Roman theme), holiday invitational of local artists.

South Dakota Art Museum

Medary Ave at Harvey Dunn Street, Brookings, SD 57007-0899
☎: 605-688-5423
Open: 8-5 Mo-Fr, 10-5 Sa, 1-5 Su, Holidays   **Closed:** 1/1, THGV, 12/25
& Ⓟ **Museum Shop**
Group Tours   Drop-In Tours
Sculpture Garden
Permanent Collection: HARVEY DUNN: ptgs; OSCAR HOWE: ptgs; NAT/AM; REG 19, 20

Many of the state's art treasures including the paintings by Harvey Dunn of pioneer life on the prairie, a complete set of Marghab embroidery from Madeira, outstanding paintings by regional artist Oscar Howe, and masterpieces from all the Sioux tribes are displayed in the 6 galleries of this museum established in 1970. The Museum will be closing for renovation sometime in 1998 !.

Middle Border Museum of American Indian and Pioneer Life

1311 S. Duff St., PO Box 1071, Mitchell, SD 57301
☎: 605-996-2122
Open: 8-6 Mo-Sa & 10-6 S (Jun-Aug), 9-5 Mo-Fr & 1-5 Sa, Su (May-Sep), by appt(Oct-Apr)   **Closed:** 1/1, THGV, 12/25
Free Day: 1st weekend in May   ADM: **Adult:** $3.00   **Children:** F (under 12)   **Students:** $1.25   **Seniors:** $2.00
& Ⓟ **Museum Shop**
Group Tours   Drop-In Tours
Historic Building   Sculpture Garden
Permanent Collection: AM: ptgs 19, 20; NAT/AM

This Museum of American Indian and Pioneer life also has an eclectic art collection in the Case Art Gallery, the oldest regional art gallery including works by Harvey Dunn, James Earle Fraser, Gutzon Borglum, Oscar Howe, Charles Hargens, Anna Hyatt Huntington and many others. **NOT TO BE MISSED:** Fraser's 'End of the Trail' and Lewis and Clark Statues

Oscar Howe Art Center

119 W. Third, Mitchell, SD 57301
☎: 605-996-4111
Open: 9-5 Mo-Sa   **Closed:** Su, LEG/HOL!
Vol/Cont: Adult: $2.50   **Children:** $1.00   **Seniors:** $2.00
& Ⓟ **Museum Shop**
Group Tours: 605-996-4111   **Drop-In Tours:** upon request
Historic Building
Permanent Collection: OSCAR HOWE: ptgs, gr

Housed in a beautifully restored 1902 Carnegie Library, the Oscar Howe Art Center displays both a collection of work by Yanktonai Sioux artist Oscar How and rotating exhibits of work by regional artists. **NOT TO BE MISSED:** 'Sun and Rain Clouds Over Hills', dome mural painted by Oscar Howe in 1940 as a WPA project (Works Progress Administration)

SOUTH DAKOTA

Heritage Center Inc

Affiliate Institution: Red Cloud Indian School
, Pine Ridge, SD 57770
☎: 605-867-5491 ▣ www.basic.net/rcheritaqe
Open: 9-5 Mo-Fr **Closed:** Sa, Su, EASTER, THGV, 12/25
& Ⓟ **Museum Shop**
Group Tours   Drop-In Tours   Historic Building
Permanent Collection: CONT NAT/AM; GR; NW COAST; ESKIMO: 19, 20

The Center is located on the Red Cloud Indian school campus in an historic 1888 building built by the Sioux and operated by them with the Franciscan sisters. The Holy Rosary Mission church built in 1998 has stained glass windows designed by the students.

ON EXHIBIT 1999

01/1999 to 03/1999   READ MY CHEST
Tee-shirts designed by Native Americans

Dahl Fine Arts Center

713 Seventh Street, Rapid City, SD 57701
☎: 605-394-4101
Open: 9-5 Mo-Sa, 1-5 Su (winter), 9-7 Mo-Th, 9-5 Fr. Sa, 1-5 Su (summer)   **Closed:** LEG/HOL!
Sugg/Cont: $1.00 per person
& Ⓟ **Museum Shop**
Group Tours   Drop-In Tours
Permanent Collection: CONT; REG: ptgs; gr 20

The Dahl presents a forum for all types of fine arts: visual, theatre, and music, that serve the Black Hills region, eastern Wyoming, Montana, and Western Nebraska. **NOT TO BE MISSED:** 200 foot cyclorama depicting the history of the US.

ON EXHIBIT 1999

01/10/1999 to 03/14/1999   BURTON SILVERMAN

01/17/1999 to 02/28/1999   STEPHEN GRABER

01/31/1999 to 02/28/1999   JAY BOLOTIN

03/07/1999 to 04/18/1999   AL WEBER AND KEITH MUSCOTT

03/07/1999 to 04/18/1999   NORMAN BLUHM

03/14/1999 to 04/25/1999   GREGORY STRACHOV

04/02/1999 to 04/30/1999   TRIUMPHANT SPIRIT

04/04/1999 to 05/30/1999   LARGE DRAWINGS FROM THE ARKANSAS ARTS CENTER FOUNDATION COLLECTION
Contemporary work by artists who prefer to work in a very large format. Drawings are often the most immediate expression of an artist's inspiration and have a freshness that does not translate as well to paintings, prints and sculpture. *Will Travel*

Dahl Fine Arts Center - continued

04/25/1999 to 06/27/1999   JIM MOOSE – MOOSEWOOD FURNITURE

05/02/1999 to 06/27/1999   PAT STEIR

05/09/1999 to 06/13/1999   SUSAN GRAYSON

06/27/1999 to 08/22/1999   63RD NATIONAL MIDYEAR EXHIBITION

07/08/1999 to 08/29/1999   DAVID ROTHERMEL

07/11/1999 to 08/29/1999   BEM SHONZEIT

09/02/1999 to 10/31/1999   JOHN RAIMONDI

09/12/1999 to 11/02/1999   THE STONEWARES OF CHARLES FERGUS BINNS: FATHER OF AMERICAN STUDIO CERAMICS
60 rarely seen works by a pioneer, potter, teacher and author who laid the foundation for the studio ceramics movement in this country. This ground breaking survey is the most comprehensive collection of his work ever assembled for a traveling exhibition. It includes the earliest documented stoneware vase signed and dated 1905. *Catalog Will Travel*

09/15/1999 to 10/17/1999   ROBERT GWATHMEY

10/31/1999 to 11/21/1999   ELBRIDGE AYER BURBANK

Sioux Indian Museum

222 New York Street, Rapid City, SD 57701
📞: 605-394-2381   ◉   www.sdsmt.edu/journey
Open: 9-8 daily summer; 10-4 Mo-Sa, 11-4 Su winter   **Closed:** 1/1, THGV, 12/25
Vol/Cont: Yes   **Adult:** $5.00   **Children:** $2.00 (7-17)   **Seniors:** $5.00
♿ Ⓟ **Museum Shop**
Group Tours: 605-394-6923   **Drop-In Tours**
Permanent Collection: SIOUX ARTS

The rich diversity of historic and contemporary Sioux art may be enjoyed in the Journey Museum, location of the Sioux Indian Museum. This museum and native crafts center with rotating exhibitions, and interactive displays which dramatically reveal the geography, people and historical events that shaped the history and heritage of the Black Hills area. **NOT TO BE MISSED:** THE JOURNEY, Black Hills History thru sight, sound and touch

SIOUX FALLS

Civic Fine Arts Center

235 West Tenth Street, Sioux Falls, SD 57102
📞: 605-336-1167   ◉   www.siouxfalls.org/members/cfa
Open: 8-5 Mo-Fr, 10-5 Sa, 1-5 Su & Hol   **Closed:** 1/1, EASTER, THGV, 12/25
♿ Ⓟ **Museum Shop**
Group Tours   **Drop-In Tours**   **Historic Building**
Permanent Collection: REG/ART: all media

The building was originally the 1902 Carnegie Library. It will close in February or March 1999. Opening in June 1999 is the 250,000 square foot Washington Pavilion of Arts and Science.

SOUTH DAKOTA

SISSETON

Tekakwitha Fine Arts Center
401 South 8th Street W., Sisseton, SD 57262
\: 605-698-7058
Open: 10-4 daily (Mem day-Lab day),10-4 Tu-Fr & 12:30-4 Sa, Su (mid Sep-mid May)   **Closed:** LEG/HOL!
 ♿ ⓒ **Museum Shop**
Group Tours   Drop-In Tours
Permanent Collection: TWO DIMENSIONAL ART OF LAKE TRAVERSE DAKOTA SIOUX RESERVATION

VERMILLION

University Art Galleries
Affiliate Institution: University of South Dakota
Warren M. Lee Center, 414 E. Clark Street, Vermillion, SD 57069-2390
\: 605-677-5481   ▪   www.usd.edu/cfa/art/gallery.html
Open: 10-4 Mo-Fr, 1-5 Sa, Su   **Closed:** ACAD!
 ♿ ⓒ **Museum Shop**
Group Tours   Drop-In Tours
Permanent Collection: Sioux artist OSCAR HOWE; HIST REG/ART

CHATTANOOGA

Hunter Museum of American Art

10 Bluff View, Chattanooga, TN 37403-1197

☎: 423-267-0968   ◉ www.huntermuseum.org

Open: 10-4:30 Tu-Sa, 1-4:30 Su   **Closed:** Mo, LEG/HOL!

Free Day: 1st Fr of month   ADM: **Adult:** $5.00   **Children:** 3-12, $2.50   **Students:** $3.00   **Seniors:** $4.00

♿ Ⓟ **Museum Shop**

Group Tours   Drop-In Tours

Historic Building   Sculpture Garden

Permanent Collection: AM: ptgs, gr, sculp, 18-20

Blending the old and the new, the Hunter Museum consists of a recently restored 1904 mansion with a 1975 contemporary addition opened 7/20/97.

ON EXHIBIT 1999

12/05/1998 to 01/01/1999   WILLIAM CHRISTENBERRY: THE EARLY YEARS 1954-1968

Included in the exhibition is a full range of works including paintings, drawings, constructions and photographs. Many of the largest and most important works, restored and reframed will be shown as well as "constructions" which have never been previously exhibited.

01/16/1999 to 03/14/1999   VIRGINIA DUDLEY

03/30/1999 to 05/09/1999   TOM FARNAM

06/09/1999 to 06/13/1999   PULITZER PRIZE CARTOONIST SHOW

12/11/1999 to 02/06/2000   LARGE DRAWINGS

40 of the best examples in the collection are divided in two sections: "Structural Foundations of Clarity" and "Expressive Voices of the Meaningful".In addition to the traditional drawing media works on paper represent acrylic and oil and incorporate collage, photography and printmaking. Artists include Barnet, Stackhouse, Sultan and Wesselmann.

KNOXVILLE

Knoxville Museum of Art

1050 World's Fair Park Drive, Knoxville, TN 37916-1653

☎: 615-525-6101   ◉ www.esper.com/kma

Open: 10-5 Tu-Th, S, 10-9 F, 12-5 Su   **Closed:** Mo, LEG/HOL!

Sugg/Cont: Yes   **Adult:** $4.00   **Children:** $1 under 12, $2,13-17   **Seniors:** $3.00

♿ Ⓟ **Museum Shop**   ⁌⁍

Group Tours

Drop-In Tours: 3pm Su for focus exh.

Permanent Collection: CONT; GR ; AM: 19

Begun in 1961 as the Dulin Gallery of art, located in a ante bellum mansion, the Museum because of its rapidly expanding collection of contemporary American art then moved to the historic Candy Factory. It now occupies a building designed in 1990 by Edward Larabee Barnes. PLEASE NOTE: Some exhibitions have admission charges. **NOT TO BE MISSED:** Historic Candy Factory next door; the nearby Sunsphere, trademark building of the Knoxville Worlds Fair

TENNESSEE

Dixon Gallery & Gardens
4339 Park Ave, Memphis, TN 38117
☎: 901-761-5250   ▣ www.dixon.org
Open: 10-5 Tu-Sa, 1-5 Su, Gardens only Mo ½ price   **Closed:** Mo, LEG/HOL!
Free Day: Th, Seniors only   **ADM:**   **Adult:** $5.00   **Children:** $1.00 under 12   **Students:** $3.00   **Seniors:** $4.00
& ℗ **Museum Shop**
Group Tours   Drop-In Tours: !   **Historic Building   Sculpture Garden**
Permanent Collection: FR: Impr, 19; GER: cer

Located on 17 acres of woodlands and formal gardens, the Dixon was formerly the home of Hugo and Margaret Dixon, collectors and philanthropists.

ON EXHIBIT 1999
02/07/1999 to 04/18/1999   CELEBRATING AMERICA: PAINTINGS FROM THE MANOOGIAN COLLECTION

06/27/1999 to 09/05/1999   RAOUL DUFY: LAST OF THE FAUVES
Dufy was an artist who rose to prominence in the early 1900's and remained popular till his death in 1953. Since then he has been largely ignored by museums. This exhibition aims to restore his reputation as one of the most original and talented artists of the first half of this century. *Catalog Will Travel*

10/18/1998 to 01/24/1999   ALL THINGS BRIGHT AND BEAUTIFUL: CALIFORNIA IMPRESSIONIST PAINTINGS FROM THE IRVINE MUSEUM
This is the first important exhibition of American Impressionists from California to be held on the east coast. It includes masterworks by leading artists, including Franz Bischoff, Alison Clark, Colin Campbell Cooper, Guy Rose and George Gardner Symons, all National Academicians. *Catalog Will Travel*

09/19/1999 to 11/28/1999   A TASTE FOR SPLENDOR: RUSSIAN IMPERIAL AND EUROPEAN TREASURES FROM THE HILLWOOD MUSEUM *Will Travel*

Memphis Brooks Museum of Art
Overton Park, 1934 Poplar Ave., Memphis, TN 38104-2765
☎: 901-722-3500   ▣ www.brooksmuseum.org
Open: 9-4 Tu-Fr, 9-8 We during Art in the Evenings, 9-5 Sa, 11:30-5 Su   **Closed:** Mo, 1/1, 7/4, THGV (open 10-1), 12/25
Free Day: We (except during "Ancient Gold: Wealth of the Thracians"
ADM: **Adult:** $5.00   **Children:** $2.00, (7-17)   **Students:** $2.00   **Seniors:** $4.00
& ℗ **Museum Shop**   ⅇ: Brushmark Restaurant; Lunch 11:30-2:30; Cocktails and dinner 5-8, W
Group Tours: 901-722-3515   **Drop-In Tours:** 10:30, 1:30 Sa; 1:30 Su   **Historic Building**
Permanent Collection: IT/REN, NORTHERN/REN, & BAROQUE: ptgs; BRIT & AM: portraits 18,19; FR/IMPR; AM: modernist

Founded in 1916, this is the mid-south's largest and most encyclopedic fine arts museum. Works in the collection range from those of antiquity to present day creations. **NOT TO BE MISSED:** Global Survey Galleries

ON EXHIBIT 1999
11/26/1998 to 01/17/1999   TREASURES OF DECEIT: ARCHAEOLOGY AND THE FORGER'S CRAFT
Objects representing ancient Near Eastern, Egyptian, Etruscan, Greek and Roman civilizations will be used as springboards in an exhibition designed to explain how art historians and classical archeologists determine the authenticity of antiquities. Visitors will be encouraged to examine many of the genuine, reworked and forged objects on view through a magnifying glass, enabling them to evaluate works utilizing some of the methodology of the experts. *Catalog Will Travel*

Memphis Brooks Museum of Art - continued

01/17/1999 to 03/14/1999   ANCIENT GOLD: THE WEALTH OF THE THRACIANS, TREASURES FROM THE REPUBLIC OF BULGARIA
The first exhibition of Bulgaria's cultural artistry, primarily metalwork, to be seen in the US in the post-Communist era. More than 200 magnificent gold and silver objects, dating from 1200 to 400 B.C., will be featured in an exhibition that lends credence to the life and legends of ancient Thrace.   *Will Travel*

04/18/1999 to 06/13/1999   DUANE HANSON RETROSPECTIVE
Hanson' sculptures ranged from early expressionistic statements against war, crime, and violence in general to later "familiar lower and middle-class American types"

07/11/1999 to 09/12/1999   A RENAISSANCE TREASURY: THE FLAGG COLLECTION OF EUROPEAN DECORATIVE ARTS AND SCULPTURE
This outstanding collection of later Medieval and Renaissance decorative arts was a gift to the Milwaukee Art Museum. Approximately 80 objects of diverse media, place of origin, and social function might provide insight into the Renaissance as well as the taste of an individual collector. Highlights of this collection are a number of rare secular objects like German and Swiss clocks, Limoges platters with classical scenes, marriage boxes, etc. as well as religious objects including the polychromed sculpture of 'St. George Slaying the Dragon'. *Catalog Will Travel*

08/15/1999 to 11/21/1999   MARSDEN HARTLEY: AMERICAN MODERN
A part of the influential avant garde surrounding Alfred Steiglitz, which included John Marin, Georgia O'Keeffe, and Arthur Dove. He originally advocated American transcendentalists, then reversed to "real art come from the soul" and then returned to the belief in the subjective self. *Will Travel*

10/03/1999 to 11/28/1999   THE ALLURE OF THE EAST: ISLAMIC DECORATIVE ARTS AND EUROPEAN ORIENTALIST PAINTINGS
Paintings, textiles, furniture, decorative arts objects and two beautifully embellished copies of the Koran all with the exquisite ornamentation which became an almost natural element under the consuming influence of Islam in these cultures *Catalog Will Travel*

12/12/1999 to 02/13/2000   THE PRINTED WORLD OF PIETER BREUGEL THE ELDER
Although he himself etched only one print (The Rabbit Hunt, 1566) Pieter Breugel the Elder was an artist whose work was transferred into print often in the 16th century. This exhibition presents a remarkable selection of prints that illustrate the rich and varied imagery of his world. *Catalog Will Travel*

MURFREESBORO

Baldwin Photographic Gallery
Affiliate Institution: Middle Tennessee State University
Learning Resources Center, Murfreesboro, TN 37132
\: 615-898-5628
Open: 8-4:30 Mo-Fr, 8-noon Sa, 6-10pm Su   **Closed:** EASTER, THGV, 12/25
 ⓖ ⓟ **Museum Shop   Group Tours   Drop-In Tours**
Permanent Collection: CONT: phot

A college museum with major rotating photographic exhibitions.

NASHVILLE

Cheekwood - Nashville's Home of Art and Gardens
1200 Forrest Park Drive, Nashville, TN 37205-4242
\: 615-356-8000   ▣ www.cheekwood.org
Open: 9-5 Mo-Sa, 12-5 Su (Grounds open 11-5 Su)   **Closed:** 1/1, THGV, 12/24, 12/25, 12/31
ADM: **Adult:** $5.00   **Children:** $2.00 (7-17)   **Students:** $4.00   **Seniors:** $4.00
 ⓖ ⓟ **Museum Shop Group Tours:** 615-353-2155   **Drop-In Tours   Historic Building   Sculpture Garden**
Permanent Collection: AM: ptgs, sculp, dec/art 19-20

One of the leading cultural centers in the South, the Museum of Art is a former mansion built in the 1920s. Located in a luxuriant botanical garden, it retains a charming homelike quality.

TENNESSEE

The Parthenon
Centennial Park, Nashville, TN 37201
✆: 615-862-8431 ◙ www.parthenon.org
Open: 9-4:30 Tu-Sa, (April-Sept) 12:30-4:30 Su **Closed:** Mo, LEG/HOL!
ADM: **Adult:** $2.50 **Children:** $1.25, 4-17 **Seniors:** $1.25
&. Ⓟ **Museum Shop**
Group Tours Drop-In Tours: !
Historic Building
Permanent Collection: AM: 19, 20; The Cowan Collection

First constructed as the Art Pavilion for the Tennessee Centennial Exposition, in 1897, The Parthenon is the world's only full size reproduction of the 5th century B.C. Greek original complete with the 42 foot statue of Athena Parthenos. **NOT TO BE MISSED:** 'Mt. Tamalpais', by Albert Bierstadt; 'Autumn in the Catskills' by Sanford Green

ON EXHIBIT 1999

10/31/1998 to 01/02/1999 TENNESSEE ALL-STATE EXHIBITION
An annual juried exhibition for Tennessee artists.

01/16/1999 to 03/13/1999 VAN VECHTEN/FISK COLLECTION
An African-American collection

03/20/1999 to 05/15/1999 GREGORY MYOFIS
This Russian painter creates works reminiscent of Rembrandt and Michelangelo using the figure in both a modern and historical presentation which is beautiful and emotional.

05/22/1999 to 07/17/1999 DR. MESSIER/ARCHEOLOGY

07/17/1999 to 09/11/1999 SIMIN VAFAIE/PHOTOGRAPHY

07/24/1999 to 09/18/1999 ROBERT EVANS/PHOTOGRAPHY

09/25/1999 to 11/27/1999 DIANE BURKO
A Philadelphia artist with a long career of painting the landscape.

12/04/1999 to 01/29/2000 VISUAL ARTISTS ALLIANCE OF NASHVILLE

University Galleries
Affiliate Institution: Fisk University
1000 17th Avenue North, Nashville, TN 37208-3051
✆: 615-329-8720
Open: 9-5 Tu-Fr, 1-5 Sa, Su, summer closed Su **Closed:** Mo, ACAD!
Vol/Cont: Yes
&. Ⓟ **Museum Shop**
Group Tours Drop-In Tours
Historic Building
Permanent Collection: EU; AM; AF/AM: ptgs; AF: sculp

The Museum is housed in an historic (1888) building and in the University library. **NOT TO BE MISSED:** The Alfred Steiglitz Collection of Modern Art

Vanderbilt University Fine Arts Gallery

23rd at West End Ave, Nashville, TN 37203

☎: 615-322-0605 ◉ www.vanderbilt.edu/AnS/finearts/gallery.html

Open: 12-4 Mo-Fr, 1-5 Sa, Su, Summer 1-4 Mo-Fr **Closed:** ACAD!

& Ⓟ **Museum Shop**

Group Tours   Drop-In Tours   Historic Building

Permanent Collection: OR: Harold P. Stern Coll; OM & MODERN: gr (Anna C. Hoyt Coll); CONTINI-VOLTERRA PHOT ARCHIVE; EU: om/ptgs (Kress Study Coll)

The history of world art may be seen in the more than 7,000 works from over 40 countries and cultures housed in this museum. Rich in contemporary prints and Oriental art, this historical collection is the only one of its kind in the immediate region. **NOT TO BE MISSED:** 'St. Sebastian', 15th century Central Italian tempera on wood

ON EXHIBIT 1999

01/14/1999 to 02/07/1999   HENRY HUFFNAGLE: THE 1997 MARGARET STONEWALL WOOLDRIDGE HAMBLET AWARD WINNER EXHIBITION

02/11/1999 to 03/21/1999   BYZANTIUM: ART AND RITUAL
Zdenko Zivkovik is a world renown fresco copyist and restorer. The works featured here, drawn from the Gallery collection, are a series of full-scale fresco copies of medieval wall paintings which still decorate Byzantine churches in Serbia and Macedonia.

03/27/1999 to 05/09/1999   DIVERSE VISIONS 1999
A broad range of work in different media by members of the faculty.

05/27/1999 to 08/20/1999   ADGFAD: CONTEMPORARY GRAPHIC ARTS FROM THE ASSOCIATION OF ART DIRECTORS, GRAPHIC DESIGNERS AND ILLUSTRATORS, BARCELONA, SPAIN
Works drawn from a collection of posters in the Gallery collection.

10/24/1999 to 12/12/1999   SPACE WALK: FRONTIERS IN ART AND SCIENCE
These selections from the NASA Art Collection were commissioned by NASA to document America's major accomplishments in aeronautics and space. Artists include Robert Rauschenberg, Andy Warhol, Vija Celmins, Charles Ross and the Starn Twins. They go beyond mere record, looking to the future and the efforts of science to impact and shape it.

OAK RIDGE

Oak Ridge Art Center

201 Badger Avenue, Oak Ridge, TN 37830

☎: 423-482-1441

Open: 9-5 Tu-Fr, 1-4 Sa-Mo **Closed:** LEG/HOL!

& Ⓟ **Museum Shop**

Group Tours   Drop-In Tours: !

Permanent Collection: AB/EXP: Post WW II

Two galleries with monthly changing exhibitions, educational programs, and art lectures. Call for exhibit schedule.

TEXAS

Museums of Abilene, Inc.
102 Cypress, Abilene, TX 79601
☎: 915-673-4587
Open: 10-5 Tu, We, Fr, Sa, 5-8:30 Th, 1-5 Su   **Closed:** Mo, LEG/HOL!
Free Day: Th-Eve   ADM: **Adult:** $2.00   **Children:** $1.00 (3-12)   **Students:** $2.00   **Seniors:** $2.00
& ℗   **Museum Shop   Group Tours   Drop-In Tours   Historic Building**
Permanent Collection: TEXAS/REG; AM: gr, CONT: gr; ABILENE, TX, & PACIFIC RAILWAY: 18-20

The museums are housed in the 1909 'Mission Revival Style' Railroad Hotel.

ON EXHIBIT 1999

01/24/1999 to 03/14/1999   ULTRA-REALISTIC SCULPTURE BY MARK SIJAN
Sijan's incredibly lifelike polyester resin sculptures of ordinary people include such specific attention to the details of tiny hairs, veins, pours and blemishes, that the works on view appear to be real human beings whose actions are suspended for a moment in time.

03/14/1999 to 05/02/1999   THE INTIMATE COLLABORATION: PRINTS FROM THE TEABERRY PRESS
Timothy Teaberry, an artist and printer, established a unique printmaking workshop over the past 19 years by specializing in one medium-etching. His intimate setting and studio atmosphere have attracted some of the most important contemporary artists . *Will Travel*

Old Jail Art Center
Hwy 6 South, Albany, TX 76430
☎: 915-762-2269   ◙ www.albanytexas.com
Open: 10-5 Tu-Sa, 2-5 Su   **Closed:** Mo, LEG/HOL!
& ℗   **Museum Shop   Group Tours   Drop-In Tours   Historic Building   Sculpture Garden**
Permanent Collection: AS, EU, BRIT cont, Mod, P/COL

The Old Jail Art Center is housed partly in a restored 1878 historic jail building with a small annex which opened in 1980 and new wings added in 1984 and 1998 featuring a courtyard, sculpture garden and educational center. **NOT TO BE MISSED:** 'Young Girl With Braids', by Modigliani; 37 Chinese terra cotta tomb figures

ON EXHIBIT 1999

11/28/1997 to 01/17/1999   TEXAS FOLK ART
Selected Self-Taught artists from Texas

01/23/1999 to 03/20/1999   THE PHILADELPHIA TEN: A WOMEN ARTIST GROUP 1917-1945
This unique and progressive group of painters and sculptors broke the rules of society and the art world by working and exhibiting together. Their work included urban and rural landscapes, portraiture, still life, and a variety of representational and myth inspired sculpture. This is the first time in over fifty years to examine this group and other like it who played an importune role in American culture in the first half of the century. Highlighted particularly are Isabel Cartwright, Constancy Cochrane, Marry Colton, and Lucille Howard. In addition there were Theresa Bernstein, Cora Brooks, Fern Coppedge, Nancy Ferguson, Sue Gill. Helen McCarthy, Emma MacRae, M. Elizabeth Price, Susan Schell and sculptors Harriet Frishmuth and Beatrice Fenton. *Will Travel*

03/27/1999 to 05/30/1999   CITY FOCUS: HOUSTON ARTISTS

06/05/1999 to 08/01/1999   ANNE WALLACE: DRAWINGS AND SCULPTURES, JEANNE NORSWORTHY: PAINTINGS: (title unconfirmed)

Old Jail Art Center - continued

08/07/1999 to 09/26/1999 DONELD VOGEL: RETROSPECTIVE

10/02/1999 to 11/21/1999 BILL BOMAR: THE COLLECTOR AND THE ARTIST
Selections from the permanent collection.

11/27/1999 to 01/16/2000 JEAN CARRUTHERS WETTA: A SURVEY, 1883-98

AMARILLO

Amarillo Museum of Art

2200 S. Van Buren, Amarillo, TX 79109
☎: 806-371-5050
Open: 10-5 Tu-F, 1-5 Sa, Su **Closed:** Mo, LEG/HOL!
  ᚷ ⓟ **Museum Shop**
Group Tours **Drop-In Tours**: by appt **Sculpture Garden**
Permanent Collection: CONT AM; ptgs, gr, phot, sculp; JAP gr; SE ASIA sculp, textiles

Opened in 1972, the Amarillo Museum of Art is a visual arts museum featuring exhibitions, art classes, tours and educational programs. The building was designed by Edward Durell Stone.

ON EXHIBIT 1999
07/04/1999 to 08/22/1999 THE JOHN A. AND MARGARET HILL COLLECTION OF AMERICAN WESTERN ART
The collection concentrates on works of the 20th c. with fine examples from the Taos Society of Artists, the Santa Fe School, and the American Regionalists. These included Berninghaus, Couse and Blumenschein as well as Ufer, Benton, Curry and Grant Wood.

ARLINGTON

Arlington Museum of Art

201 West Main St., Arlington, TX 76010
☎: 817-275-4600
Open: 10-5 We-Sa **Closed:** Su, Mo, Tu, LEG/HOLS, 12/25 1/2!
Vol/Cont: Yes
  ᚷ **Museum Shop**
Group Tours **Drop-In Tours**: Occasional
Permanent Collection: Non-collecting institution

Texas contemporary art by both emerging and mature talents is featured in this North Texas museum located between the art-rich cities of Fort Worth and Dallas. It has gained a solid reputation for showcasing contemporary art in the six exhibitions it presents annually.

ON EXHIBIT 1999
11/07/1998 to 01/02/1999 TEXAS ROOTS & GERMAN FIGURES

01/16/1999 to 02/06/1999 THE BEAUTY SHOW

04/03/1999 to 06/05/1999 TRUE STORIES: PHOTOGRAPHY AND VIDEO

06/19/1999 to 08/07/1999 A HOT SHOW: ABSTRACT PAINTINGS

TEXAS

CRCA: The Gallery at UTA
Affiliate Institution: University of Texas at Arlington
Fine Arts Bldg, Cooper Street, Arlington, TX 76019-0089
☎: 817-272-3143
Open: 10-5 Mo-Th, 12-5 Sa   **Closed:** ACAD!
Free Day: Su
  ᕹ ℗ **Museum Shop   Group Tours   Drop-In Tours**
Permanent Collection: Non-collecting institution

A University gallery with varied special exhibitions.

ON EXHIBIT 1999
01/22/1999 to 03/02/1999   DAVID MCGEE/BENITO HUERTA

03/10/1999 to 04/24/1999   TRACY HICKS: PRESERVING AND COLLECTING

AUSTIN

Austin Museum of Art-Downtown
823 Congress Avenue, Austin, TX 78701
☎: 512-495-9224
Open: 11-7 Tu-Sa, 11-9 Th, 1-5 Su   **Closed:** LEG/HOL
ADM: **Adult:** $3.00, $1 day T   **Children:** under 12 F   **Students:** $2.00   **Seniors:** $2.00
  ᕹ **Museum Shop**
Group Tours   Drop-In Tours
Permanent Collection: AM: ptgs 19, 20; WORKS ON PAPER

An additional facility for the Museum

Austin Museum of Art-Laguna Gloria
3809 W. 35th Street, Austin, TX 78703
☎: 512-458-8191   ◙ www.amoa.org
Open: 10-5 Tu-Sa, 10-9 T, 1-5 Su   **Closed:** Mo, LEG/HOL!
ADM: **Adult:** $2.00, $1 T   **Children:** F (under 16)   **Students:** $1.00   **Seniors:** $1.00
  ᕹ ℗ **Museum Shop**
Group Tours   Drop-In Tours   Historic Building   Sculpture Garden
Permanent Collection: AM: ptgs 19, 20; WORKS ON PAPER

The Museum is Located on the 1916 Driscoll Estate which is listed in the National Register of Historic Places.
Also see Austin Museum of Art-Downtown

Jack S. Blanton Museum of Art
Affiliate Institution: University of Texas at Austin
Art Bldg, 23rd&San Jacinto & Harry Ransom Center, 24th & Guadalupe, Austin, TX 78712-1205
☎: 512-471-7324   ◙ www.utexas.edu/cofa/hag
Open: 9-5 M, Tu, W, F, 9-9 T, 1-5 Sa, Su   **Closed:** MEM/DAY, LAB/DAY, THGV, XMAS WEEK
  ᕹ ℗ **Museum Shop**
Group Tours: 512-471-5025   **Drop-In Tours**: !
Permanent Collection: LAT/AM; CONT; GR; DRGS,

Jack S. Blanton Museum of Art - continued

One of the foremost university art museums in the country and the leading art museum serving the city of Austin, the Blanton Museum of Art features a collection of nearly 12,000 works of art that span the history of Western civilization. Selections from the permanent collection are shown at the Harry Ransom Humanities Research Center while temporary exhibitions and the Clark Print Room are in the Art Building. There is a second location for the gallery in the Harry Ransom Center at 21st and Guadalupe. A current ongoing search for a architectural firm to create a new state of the art building to open in 2002 has reached its final stages. **NOT TO BE MISSED:** The Mari and James A. Michener Collection of 20th c. American Art; C.R. Smith Collection of Western American Art; Contemporary Latin American Collection

ON EXHIBIT 1999

01/16/1999 to 03/07/1999 CANTOS PARALELOS: VISUAL PARODY IN CONTEMPORARY ARGENTINE ART
Post World War II painting, sculpture and assemblage that parody Argentine middle class ideas of good taste. Large scale works by Berni, de la Vega, Grippo and Heredia are included. *Catalog Will Travel*

BEAUMONT

Art Museum of Southeast Texas
500 Main Street, Beaumont, TX 77701
☎: 409-832-3432   ◉ www.amsct.org
Open: 9-5 Mo-Sa, 12-5 Su   **Closed:** LEG/HOL!
Sugg/Cont: **Adult:** $5.00   **Children:** $2.00
  ⓖ   ⓟ   **Museum Shop**   ⑪   **Group Tours**   **Drop-In Tours**: We, noon   **Sculpture Garden**
Permanent Collection: AM: ptgs, sculp, dec/art, FOLK: 19, 20

This new spacious art museum with 4 major galleries and 2 sculpture courtyards is located in downtown Beaumont. **NOT TO BE MISSED:** Putt Modernism - 18 Hole Miniature Golf Course

---

COLLEGE STATION

MSC Forsyth Center Galleries
Affiliate Institution: Texas A & M University
Memorial Student Center, Joe Routt Blvd, College Station, TX 77844-9081
☎: 409-845-9251   ◉ www.charlotte.tamu.edu/services/forsyth
Open: 9-8 Mo-Fr, 12-6 Sa, Su, 10-4:30 Mo-Fr, 12-4:30 Sa, Su May-Aug   **Closed:** 7/4, THGV, 12/25-1/2
  ⓖ   ⓟ   **Museum Shop**   **Group Tours**   **Drop-In Tours**: by appt
Permanent Collection: EU, BRIT,& AM; glass; AM: western ptgs

The Gallery is particularly rich in its collection of American Art glass, and has one of the finest collections of English Cameo Glass in the world. **NOT TO BE MISSED:** Works by Grandma Moses

Texas A&M University/J. Wayne Stark University Center Galleries
Mem Student Ctr. Joe Routt Blvd, College Station, TX 77844-9083
☎: 409-845-8501   ◉ stark.tamu.edu
Open: 9-8 Tu-Fr, 12-6 Sa, Su   **Closed:** Mo, ACAD!
  ⓖ   ⓟ   **Museum Shop**   **Group Tours**   **Drop-In Tours**
Permanent Collection: REG; GER 19

A University gallery featuring works by 20th century Texas artists

TEXAS

Texas A&M University/J. Wayne Stark University Center Galleries - *continued*

ON EXHIBIT 1999

01/21/1999 to 03/16/1999   THE FRAME IN AMERICA

03/18/1999 to 04/30/1999   EARTH, FIRE, WATER

07/29/1999 to 09/12/1999   WEIFONG INTERNATIONAL KITE FESTIVAL

CORPUS CHRISTI

Art Museum of South Texas

1902 N. Shoreline, Corpus Christi, TX 78401

☎: 512-884-3844

Open: 10-5 Tu-Sa, 1-5 Su   **Closed:** Mo, 1/1, 7/4, THGV, 12/25

Free Day: Th   ADM: **Adult:** $3.00   **Children:** $1.00 (2-12)   **Students:** $2.00   **Seniors:** $2.00

& ℗   **Museum Shop**   ⚏ **Group Tours**   **Drop-In Tours**   **Sculpture Garden**

Permanent Collection: AM; REG

The award winning building designed by Philip Johnson, has vast expanses of glass which provide natural light for objects of art and breathtaking views of Corpus Christi Bay.

ON EXHIBIT 1999

09/12/1999 to 10/31/1999   THE JOHN A. AND MARGARET HILL COLLECTION OF AMERICAN WESTERN ART

The collection concentrates on works of the 20th c. with fine examples from the Taos Society of Artists, the Santa Fe School, and the American Regionalists. These included Berninghaus, Couse and Blumenschein as well as Ufer, Benton, Curry and Grant Wood.

Asian Cultures Museum and Educational Center

1809 North Chaparral, Corpus Christi, TX 78412

☎: 512-882-2641

Open: 12-5 Tu-Sa   **Closed:** Su, Mo, LEG/HOL!, EASTER

Vol/Cont: Yes   **Adult:** $4.00   **Children:** $2.50, 6-15   **Students:** $3.50   **Seniors:** $3.50

& ℗   **Museum Shop**   **Group Tours**   **Drop-In Tours**: by request

Permanent Collection: JAP,CH,IND,AS CUL

An oasis of peace and tranquility as well as a resource of Asian history and information for the Corpus Christi Community. **NOT TO BE MISSED:** Cast bronze Buddha weighing over 1500 lb

---

DALLAS

African American Museum

3536 Grand Avenue, Dallas, TX 75210

☎: 214-565-9026

Open: 12-5 Th-Fr, 10-5 Sa, 1-5 Su   **Closed:** M, LEG/HOL!

& ℗   **Museum Shop**   ⚏

Group Tours: 214-565-9026, ext 328   **Drop-In Tours**: by appt   **Historic Building**   **Sculpture Garden**

Permanent Collection: AF/AM: folk

The African American Museum collects, preserves, exhibits and researches artistic expressions and historic documents which represent the African-American heritage. Its mission is to educate and give a truer understanding of African-American culture to all.

African American Museum - continued
ON EXHIBIT 1999
09/18/1998 to 06/30/1999   THE LAYTON REVEL NEGRO LEAGUES COLLECTION: NEGRO LEAGUES BASEBALL

10/09/1998 to 01/08/1999   RELIGIOUS SCENES AND MEMORY PAINTINGS BY REV. JOHNNIE SWEARINGER

Biblical Arts Center
7500 Park Lane, Dallas, TX 75225
☎: 214-691-4661   ◉ www.biblicalarts.org
Open: 10-5 Tu-Sa, 10-9 T, 1-5 Su   **Closed:** Mo, 1/1, THGV, 12/24, 12/25
ADM: **Adult:** $4.00   **Children:** $2.50 (6-12)   **Students:** $3.00 (13-18)   **Seniors:** $3.50
♿ ℗ Museum Shop Group Tours   Drop-In Tours
Permanent Collection: BIBLICAL ART

The sole purpose of this museum is to utilize the arts as a means of helping people of all faiths to more clearly envision the places, events, and people of the Bible. The building, in the Romanesque style, features early Christian era architectural details. **NOT TO BE MISSED:** 'Miracle at Pentecost', painting with light and sound presentation

Dallas Museum of Art
1717 N. Harwood, Dallas, TX 75201
☎: 214-922-1200   ◉ www.dma-art.org
Open: 11-4 Tu, We, Fr, 11-9 Th, 11-5 Sa, Su   **Closed:** Mo, 1/1, THGV, 12/25
Free Day: Th after 5, spec exh
♿ ℗ **Museum Shop** ❙❙
Group Tours: 214-922-1217   **Drop-In Tours:** Tu, Fr 1pm, Sa Su 2pm, Th 7PM   **Sculpture Garden**
Permanent Collection: P/COL; AF; AM: furniture; EUR: ptgs, sculp, Post War AM; AF; AS; CONT

Designed by Edward Larabee Barnes, the 370,000 square foot limestone building houses a broad and eclectic permanent collection. The art of the Americas from the pre-contact period (which includes a spectacular pre-Columbian gold Treasury of more than 1,000 works) through the mid-20th century is outstanding. **NOT TO BE MISSED:** 'The Icebergs' by Frederick Church; Claes Oldenburg's pop art 'Stake Hitch in the Barrel Vault'; Colonial and post-Colonial decorative arts: early and late paintings by Piet Mondrian; Reves Collection of Impressionist paintings and decorative arts installed in a setting reminiscent of the Reves' villa on the Riviera

ON EXHIBIT 1999
The J.E.R. Chilton Galleries (Special Exhibition Galleries) have an admission charge: Adults $8.00; Students/Seniors $6.00; Children under 12 $2.00. Audio tour is included. Thursday after 5 adm is free-audio tour $4.00.

ONGOING   ETERNAL EGYPT
A three part installation on long term loan containing funerary art, sculptures of kings and gods, and other objects from tombs and temples in ancient Egypt. Views of everyday life and the afterlife are seen through vessels, jewelry and religious objects. Art of Nubia includes fine examples of blue faience vessels, weapons, lamps, etc., as well as a large group of 'shabti' tomb figures.

ONGOING   SOUTH ASIAN SCULPTURE
Exceptionally fine sculptures representing the artistic traditions of India, Nepal, Tibet, Thailand and Indonesia.

10/11/1998 to 02/07/1999   QUILTS, OFF THE BED AND ON THE WALL
From the collection, outstanding quilts spanning the last two centuries.

TEXAS

Dallas Museum of Art - continued

02/14/1999 to 04/15/1999   BILL VIOLA: THE CROSSING *Catalog Will Travel*

02/14/1999 to 04/25/1999   BRICE MARDEN: WORK OF THE 1990'S PAINTINGS, DRAWINGS AND PRINTS
A survey of Marden's work featurying 24 paintings and 24 drawings and prints drawn from public and private collections demonstrating the richness and variety of his work of the last decade. Adm: Adults: $5.00

05/30/1999 to 09/05/1999   GOLDEN TREASURES FROM THE ANCIENT WORLD
One of two exhibitions depicting wonders from ancient western civilization will be on display. Adm: Adults $8.00, Stu/Sen $5.00, Child und 12 $3.00 F, after 5 TH

05/30/1999 to 09/05/1999   TREASURES FROM THE ROYAL TOMBS OF UR
Mid-third millennium BC gold & silver jewels, cups, bowls and other ancient objects excavated from the royal burial tombs of Ur will be on exhibit. *Catalog Will Travel*

07/11/1999 to 10/03/1999   FABULOUS FORMS: PRESTIGE ART OF THE EDOINDA OF ZAIRE

09/12/1999 to 11/28/1999   DIEGO RIVERA: ART AND REVOLUTION

Meadows Museum

Affiliate Institution: SMU School of the Arts
Bishop Blvd. at Binkley Ave., Dallas, TX 75275-0356
📞: 214-768-2516   ◉ www.smu.edu/meadows/museum
Open: 10-5 Mo, Tu, Fr, Sa, 10-8 Th, 1-5 Su   **Closed:** We, 1/1, EASTER, 7/4, THGV, 12/25
Vol/Cont: Yes
 ♿ Ⓟ   **Museum Shop   Group Tours**: 214-823-7644   **Drop-In Tours**: 2pm, Su, Sept-May   **Sculpture Garden**
Permanent Collection: SP; ptgs, sculp, gr, drgs; AM: sculp 20,

The collection of Spanish Art is the most comprehensive in the US with works from the last years of the 10th century through the 20th century. **NOT TO BE MISSED:** 'Sibyl With Tabula Rasa' by Diego Rodriquez de Silva y Velazquez, Spanish, 1599-1660

EL PASO

El Paso Museum of Art

One Arts Festival Plaza, El Paso, TX 79901
📞: 915-532-1707
Open: 9-6 Tu-Sa, 9-9 Th, 12-5 Su   **Closed:** Mo, LEG/HOL!
♿ Ⓟ   **Museum Shop   Group Tours   Drop-In Tours**
Permanent Collection: EU: Kress Coll 13-18; AM; MEX: 18,19; MEX SANTOS: 20; REG

Newly constructed, contemporary building in the heart of downtown El Paso. **NOT TO BE MISSED:** American Impressionists, Spanish Colonial, Contemporary Collection - American and Mexican, Works on Paper, American Southwest Moderns 1900-1950

ON EXHIBIT 1999

01/06/1999 to 03/14/1999   TWENTY FIVE YEARS OF PHOTOGRAPHY: IMAGES FROM TEXAS MONTHLY

01/22/1999 to 03/21/1999   REFOCUS II/CONTEMPORARIES OF THE GREAT SOUTHWEST

05/21/1999 to 08/01/1999   NELSON-ATKINS - SELECTED ASIAN WORKS

04/09/1999 to 05/30/1999   OIL PATCH DREAMS: IMAGES OF THE PETROLEUM INDUSTRY
Over 50 works in a variety of media emphasizing the importance and impact of the oil industry on American life and culture. Artists include Benton, George Grosz, Rackstraw Downs, Jerry Bywaters and Andy Warhol, among others. *Will Travel*

Amon Carter Museum

3501 Camp Bowie Blvd, Fort Worth, TX 76107-2631
✆: 817-738-1933 ▣ www.cartermuseum.org
Open: 10-5 Tu-Sa, 12-5 Su **Closed:** Mo, 1/1, 7/4, THGV,12/25
& ℗ **Museum Shop Group Tours**: 817-738-1933, ext.222   **Drop-In Tours**: 2pm daily !
Permanent Collection: AM: ptgs, sculp, gr, phot 19, 20

One of the foremost museums of American Art, the Amon Carter is located in Fort Worth's cultural district. It represents the Western experience and embraces the history of 19th and 20th century American Art. **NOT TO BE MISSED:** 'Swimming', by Thomas Eakins

ON EXHIBIT 1999

10/31/1998 to 01/24/1999 SELF-TAUGHT ARTISTS OF THE 20th CENTURY: AN AMERICAN ANTHOLOGY
Regarded as among the most vital and intriguing spheres of 20th century art, with an ever growing popular appeal, the work of self-taught artists continues to elude categorization. These artists work outside the mainstream art world with little or no access to galleries, museums, or other mechanisms for broad exposure. The works exhibited here span more than a century and encompass all media. Included are established artists such as Grandma Moses, Horace Pippin and Martin Ramirez as well as younger artists Purvis Young, and Ken Grimes. *Catalog Will Travel*

02/05/1999 to 04/04/1999 WILLIAM SIDNEY MOUNT: PAINTER OF AMERICAN LIFE
At a time when other American Artists portrayed European models, Mount successfully transferred these images into imagery specific to American life. His scenes of everyday life included stories and jokes about rural life. Farmer, boys and musicians were regulars in his cast of characters. He struck a sympathetic chord with public and critics and was zoom pronounced the most talented artist of his time. 50 paintings and works on paper will be featured here. *Catalog Will Travel*

Kimbell Art Museum

3333 Camp Bowie Blvd, Fort Worth, TX 76107-2792
✆: 817-332-8451 ▣ www.kimbellart.org
Open: 10-5 Tu-Th, Sa, 12-8 Fr, 12-5 Su **Closed:** Mo, 1/1, 7/4, THGV, 12/25
Free Day: Perm Coll Free daily, Adm is for Special exhibitions ADM: **Adult:** charges depend on exhibition: $6.00 - $10.00 **Children:** 6-12 $2.00 - $6.00 **Students:** $4.00 - $8.00 **Seniors:** $4.00 - $8.00
& ℗ **Museum Shop** ⊨
Group Tours: ext. 249 for school grps ext. 229 other   **Drop-In Tours**: 2pm Tu-Fr, Su, exh tours 2pm Su, 3:00 Su
Sculpture Garden
Permanent Collection: EU: ptgs, sculp 14-20; AS; AF; Med/Ant

Designed by Louis I. Kahn, this classic museum building is perhaps his finest creation and a work of art in its own right. It was the last building completed under his personal supervision It is often called 'America's best small museum'. The permanent collection of the Museum is free. Admission is for Special exhibitions **NOT TO BE MISSED:** "The Cardsharps" by Caravaggio

Modern Art Museum of Fort Worth

1309 Montgomery Street, Fort Worth, TX 76107
✆: 817-738-9215 ▣ www.mamfw.org
Open: 10-5 Tu-Fr, 11-5 Sa, 12-5 Su **Closed:** Mo, LEG/HOL!
& ℗ **Museum Shop**
Group Tours   Drop-In Tours: !   **Sculpture Garden**
Permanent Collection: AM; EU; CONT; ptgs, sculp, works on paper, photo, 14 new works by Modern and Contemporary photographers and artists.

Modern Art Museum of Fort Worth - continued

Chartered in 1892 (making it the oldest in Texas and one of the oldest museums in the western U.S.), this museum has evolved into a celebrated and vital showcase for works of modern and contemporary art. Great emphasis at the Modern is placed on the presentation of exceptional traveling exhibitions making a trip to this facility and others in this 'museum rich' city a rewarding experience for art lovers. **NOT TO BE MISSED:** Important collections of works by Robert Motherwell, Jackson Pollock, Anselm Kiefer, Andy Warhol and international contemporary photography.

ON EXHIBIT 1999

11/01/1998 to 01/24/1999 SELF-TAUGHT ARTISTS OF THE 20th CENTURY: AN AMERICAN ANTHOLOGY
Regarded as among the most vital and intriguing spheres of 20th century art, with an ever growing popular appeal, the work of self-taught artists continues to elude categorization. These artists work outside the mainstream art world with little or no access to galleries, museums, or other mechanisms for broad exposure. The works exhibited here span more than a century and encompass all media. Included are established artists such as Grandma Moses, Horace Pippin and Martin Ramirez as well as younger artists Purvis Young, and Ken Grimes. *Catalog Will Travel*

02/13/1999 to 04/11/1999 THE ARCHITECTURE OF REASSURANCE: DESIGNING DISNEY'S THEME PARKS
Uniquely American in its origins, the Disney theme park, whether admired or reviled, has become an international phenomenon. For the first time the intentions and methods of the Imagineers (as the design team for the parks is called) will be investigated. Approximately 300 objects, most never before available for public viewing, will be shown *Catalog Will Travel*

Modern at Sundance Square

Affiliate Institution: The Modern Art Museum
410 Houston Street, Fort Worth, TX 76102
☎: 817-335-9215　◙　www.mamfw.org
Open: 11-6 Mo-Th, 11-10 FR. SA, 1-5 Su　**Closed:** LEG/HOL
⛬　**Museum Shop**
Group Tours　Drop-In Tours　Historic Building 1929 Sanger Building, listed NRHP
Permanent Collection: AM, EU CONT ptg, sculp, works on paper, CONT photo

Opened in 1995 in the historic Sanger Building in downtown Fort Worth as an annex for both the permanent collections and temporary exhibitions of the Modern Art Museum.

Sid Richardson Collection of Western Art

309 Main Street, Fort Worth, TX 76102
☎: 817-332-6554　◙　www.txec.net/~sidr
Open: 10-5 Tu, We; 10-8 Th, Fr; 11-8 Sa, 1-5 Su　**Closed:** Mo, LEG/HOL
⛬　Ⓟ　**Museum Shop**
Group Tours　Drop-In Tours　Historic Building
Permanent Collection: AM/WEST: ptgs

Dedicated to Western Art the museum is located in historic Sundance Square in a reconstructed 1890's building. The area, in downtown Fort Worth, features restored turn-of-the-century buildings. **NOT TO BE MISSED:** 56 Remington and Russell paintings on permanent display

Contemporary Arts Museum

5216 Montrose Boulevard, Houston, TX 77006-6598

☎: 713-284-8250 ◉ www.camh.org
Open: 10-5 Tu-Sa, 10-9 Th, 12-5 Su **Closed:** Mo, 1/1, 7/4, THGV, 12/25
& ℗ **Museum Shop** ⑪: Starbucks café **Group Tours:** 713-284-8257 **Drop-In Tours Sculpture Garden**
Permanent Collection: Non-Collecting Institution

Located in a metal building in the shape of a parallelogram this museum is dedicated to presenting the art of our time to the public.

Menil Collection

1515 Sul Ross Street, Houston, TX 77006

☎: 713-525-9400 ◉ www.menil.org
Open: 11-7 We-Su **Closed:** Mo, Tu, LEG/HOL!
& ℗ **Museum Shop Group Tours Drop-In Tours Historic Building Sculpture Garden**
Permanent Collection: PTGS, DRGS, & SCULP 20; ANT; TRIBAL CULTURES; MED; BYZ

The Menil Collection was founded to house the art collection of John and Domenique de Menil. Considered one of the most important privately assembled collections of the 20th c. it spans mans' creative efforts from antiquity to the modern era. The Museum building is renowned for its innovative architecture and naturally-illuminated galleries. **NOT TO BE MISSED:** In collaboration with the Dia Center for the Arts, NY, the Cy Twombly Gallery designed by Renzo Piano is a satellite space featuring works in all media created by Cy Twombly.

ON EXHIBIT 1999

10/30/1998 to 01/17/1999 DON FLAVIN/DONALD JUDD: ASPECTS OF COLOR
In approximately 12 works by each artist their use and meaning of color will be examined .Fundamental to each artist work will be their intention to liberate color from the flat space and allow it to expand spatially.

01/29/1999 to 05/16/1999 JOSEPH CORNELL/MARCEL DUCHAMP: IN RESONANCE
An exploration of the influences and collaborations of these two artists. Cornell's "Duchamp Dossier" will be shown. This collection of 117 items ranging from Mona Lisa postcards, dry cleaning receipts, correspondence, and a study by Duchamp for his "Allegory de Genre". Included will be about 40 works by each artist examining their shared interests including film, optics, glass, games, the "portable museum" . *Catalog Will Travel*

Museum of Fine Arts, Houston

1001 Bissonnet, Houston, TX 77005

☎: 713-639-7300 ◉ www.mfah.org
Open: 10-5 Tu-Sa, 5-9pm Th, 12:15-6 Su **Closed:** Mo, THGV, 12/25
Free Day: Th **ADM: Adult:** $3.00 **Children:** F (und 5), 6-18 $1.50 **Students:** $1.50 **Seniors:** $1.50
& ℗ **Museum Shop** ⑪ **Group Tours:** 713-639-7324 **Drop-In Tours:** 12 noon and by appt **Sculpture Garden**
Permanent Collection: STRAUS COLL OF REN & 18TH C WORKS; BECK COLL: Impr; GLASSELL COLL: Af gold

Over 40,000 works are housed in the largest and most outstanding museum in the southwest. **NOT TO BE MISSED:** Bayou Bend, a 28 room former residence with 14 acres of gardens, built in 1927 and redesigned and reopened as a museum in 1966. More than 4800 works, fine and decorative arts from colonial period to the mid 19th century. Separate admission and hours. !713-639-7750 Adults,$10.00; Seniors and students,$8.50; children 10-18, $5.00. Gardens, Adults, $3.00; Children, Free

Museum of Fine Arts, Houston - continued

ON EXHIBIT 1999

ONGOING   AFRICAN GOLD: SELECTIONS FROM THE GLASSELL COLLECTION

Objects created by the Akan peoples of the Ivory Coast and Ghana as well as works from the Fulani of Mali and the Swahili of Kenya dating from the late 19th and 20th centuries are featured in this exhibition.

ONGOING   BAYOU BEND COLLECTION AND GARDENS

One of the nation's premier collections of decorative arts.

06/26/1999 to 08/15/1999   BEARING WITNESS: CONTEMPORARY WORKS BY AFRICAN AMERICAN WOMEN ARTISTS

History, ethnicity, gender, marginalization and invisibility are some of the issues addressed by these 25 prominent artists. Included are Howardina Pindell, Betye and Alison Saar, Faith Ringold, Carrie Mae Weems, and Lorna Simpson.

Rice University Art Gallery

6100 Main Street, MS-21, Houston, TX 77005

☎: 713-527-6069   ◙ www.rice.edu/ruag

Open: 11-5 Tu-Sa, 11-9 Th, 12-5 Su   **Closed:** Mo, ACAD! & SUMMER

& ℗ **Museum Shop** ⵏ: Cafeteria on campus

Group Tours   Drop-In Tours

Permanent Collection: Rotating Exhibitions, collection not on permanent display

The Gallery features changing exhibitions of contemporary art with an emphasis on site-specific installations.

KERRVILLE

Cowboy Artists of America Museum

1550 Bandera Hwy, Kerrville, TX 78028

☎: 210-896-2553   ◙ www.caamuseum.com

Open: 9-5 Mo-Sa, 1-5 Su   **Closed:** 1/1, EASTER, THGV, 12/25

ADM: Adult: $3.00   **Children:** $1.00 (6-18)   **Seniors:** $2.50

& ℗ **Museum Shop**

Group Tours   Drop-In Tours: daily !   **Historic Building   Sculpture Garden**

Permanent Collection: AM/WESTERN: ptgs, sculp

Located on a hilltop site just west of the Guadalupe River, the museum is dedicated to perpetuating America's western heritage. Exhibitions change quarterly.

LONGVIEW

Longview Museum of Fine Arts

215 E. Tyler St, Longview, TX 75601

☎: 903-753-8103

Open: 10-4 Tu-Sa   **Closed:** Mo, 12/25, 1/1

& ℗ **Museum Shop**

Group Tours   Drop-In Tours   Historic Building

Permanent Collection: CONT TEXAS ART (1958-1998)

Located in downtown Longview, this renovated building was used by many businesses in the city's history.

Longview Museum of Fine Arts - continued
ON EXHIBIT 1999
01/16/1999 to 02/28/1999   PAT MUSICK TEXAS TOUR

03/06/1999 to 04/03/1999   O. RUFUS LOVETT

04/1999 to 04/1999   STUDENT ART SHOW

05/1999 to 06/1999   39TH INVITATIONAL EXHIBIT

07/1999 to 08/1999   LONGVIEW SPOTLIGHT EXHIBIT

09/1999 to 10/1999   INVITATIONAL WINNERS EXHIBIT

11/1999 to 12/1999   ETFAA SHOW HOLIDAY MARKET & TEA ROOM

LUFKIN

Museum of East Texas
503 N. Second Street, Lufkin, TX 75901
☎: 409-639-4434
Open: 10-5 Tu-Fr, 1-5 Sa, Su   **Closed:** Mo, LEG/HOL!
  ᵺ Ⓟ **Museum Shop**
Group Tours   Drop-In Tours
Historic Building
Permanent Collection: AM, EU, & REG: ptgs; Lat/Am

The Museum is housed in St. Cyprians Church, whose original Chapel was built in 1906. An award winning wing was completed in 1990. **NOT TO BE MISSED:** Historic photographic collection covering a period of over 90 years of Lufkin's history

---

MARSHALL

Michelson Museum of Art
216 N. Bolivar, Marshall, TX 75670
☎: 903-935-9480
Open: 12-5 Tu-Fr, 1-4 Sa, Su   **Closed:** Mo, EASTER, MEM/DAY, 7/4, THGV, 12/25
Vol/Cont: Yes
  ᵺ Ⓟ **Museum Shop**
Group Tours   Drop-In Tours: 12-5 daily
Historic Building
Permanent Collection: WORKS OF RUSSIAN AMERICAN ARTIST LEO MICHELSON, 1887-1978

The historic Southwestern Bell Telephone Corporation building in downtown Marshall is home to this extensive collection.

ON EXHIBIT 1999
02/01/1999 to 03/14/1999   HELEN VAUGHN : RECENT PASTELS

09/01/1999 to 10/31/1999   BENINI AND CUNNINGHAM

TEXAS

McAllen International Museum

1900 Nolana, McAllen, TX 78504

📞: 956-682-1564   ◙ www.hiline.net/mim
Open: 9-5 Tu-Sa, 1-5 Su   **Closed:** Mo, THGV, 12/25
Free Day: 9-1 Sa   ADM: **Adult:** $2.00   **Children:** $1.00 under 13   **Students:** $1.00   **Seniors:** $1.00
 ♿ ℗ **Museum Shop** ⅋: small café
Group Tours: 956-682-1564, ext. 116   **Drop-In Tours**: 8:30-11, 12-2:30
Permanent Collection: LAT/AM: folk; AM; EU: gr 20

The museum caters to art & science on an equal level. Hands-on mobile exhibits travel to schools and community centers. **NOT TO BE MISSED:** T-Rex: King of the Dinosaurs, Jan 19 - May 16

ON EXHIBIT 1999

PERMANENT EXHIBITS   METEOROLOGY
Includes a working weather station and related exhibits

PERMANENT EXHIBITS   THE TOUCH BASE
Investigation tables and curiosity drawers all dealing with Earth Science and Ethnography.

01/19/1999 to 05/16/1999   T-REX: KING OF THE DINOSAURS

Museum of the Southwest

1705 W. Missouri Ave, Midland, TX 79701-6516

📞: 915-683-2882
Open: 10-5 Tu-Sa, 2-5 Su   **Closed:** Mo, LEG/HOL
 ♿ ℗ **Museum Shop**
Group Tours   **Drop-In Tours**: on request   **Sculpture Garden**
Permanent Collection: REG; GR; SW

The Museum of the Southwest is an educational resource in art including a Planetarium and Children's Museum. It focuses on the Southwest. Housed in a 1934 mansion and stables, the collection also features the Hogan Collection of works by founder members of the Taos Society of Artists. **NOT TO BE MISSED:** 'The Sacred Pipe', by Alan Houser, bronze

ON EXHIBIT 1999

ONGOING   THE SEARCH FOR ANCIENT PLAINSMEN: AN ARCHEOLOGICAL EXPERIENCE

ONGOING   UNDER STARRY SKIES: DEFINING THE SOUTHWEST
An interpretive installation using loan and collection works by culturally diverse artists.

09/04/1997 to 01/03/1999   AUDUBON'S TEXAS ANIMALS
13 hand colored lithographs plus one North American specimen from "The Viviparous Quadrupeds of North America"

10/18/1998 to 12/31/1998   LASTING IMPRESSIONS: THOMAS HART BENTON
Drawings and watercolors done in Benton's singular style of realism which has come to exemplify American Scene painting of the 1930s and 40s.0

Museum of the Southwest - continued

01/14/1999 to 02/28/1999   BIRDS IN ART 1998
60 selected works from the annual exhibition at the Leigh Yawkey Woodson Museum. Featured are paintings in oil, acrylic, and watercolor as well as sculpture by artists from across the globe.

01/14/1999 to 03/14/1999   OIL PATCH DREAMS: IMAGES OF THE PETROLEUM INDUSTRY
Over 50 works in a variety of media emphasizing the importance and impact of the oil industry on American life and culture. Artists include Benton, George Grosz, Rackstraw Downs, Jerry Bywaters and Andy Warhol, among others. *Will Travel*

03/05/1999 to 04/11/1999   12TH ANNUAL MIDLAND ARTS ASSOCIATION SPRING JURIED ART EXHIBITION
A showcase of works in all media from across Texas and the US.

04/08/1999 to 06/27/1999   SEEING JAZZ
A panorama of artistic response to the many rhythms and moods of jazz by renowned artists including Beardon, Basquiat, Davis, Gilliam, and Smith. The works are arranged into three sections: Rhythm, Improvisation, and Call and Response. The works are accompanied by 28 literary excerpts by Gwendolyn Brooks, Ralph Ellison, and Toni Morrison, among others. *Catalog Will Travel*

07/10/1999 to 09/19/1999   THE FRED T AND NOVADEM HOGAN COLLECTION
This collection is the core of the Museum's collection of Southwestern art. Showcased are the artist's personalized views of the Native American culture and the vast and colorful landscape of New Mexico. Featured artists include Bierstadt, Higgins, Fechin, Hurley, Moran and others.

09/01/1999 to 10/14/1999   DREAMINGS: ABORIGINAL ART OF THE WESTERN DESERT FROM THE DONALD KAHN COLLECTION
Paintings by aboriginal artists who live and work in central Australia's Western desert region. Works in this region are governed by the Aboriginal law of "Tjukurrpa", defined as the explanation of existence by two physical manifestations: the land and the people.

11/04/1999 to 01/02/2000   CURRIER AND IVES: PRINTMAKERS TO THE AMERICAN PEOPLE
The firm of Currier and Ives lasted from 1857 to 1907. During that period they produced over 7000 titles in unlimited quantities. Seventy prints from the collection of the Museum of the City of New York will be shown here.

12/02/1999 to 01/09/2000   SELECTIONS FROM THE COLLECTIONS OF THE MUSEUM

ORANGE

Stark Museum of Art
712 Green Ave, Orange, TX 77630
☎: 409-883-6661
Open: 10-5 We-Sa, 1-5 Su   **Closed:** Mo, Tu, 1/1, EASTER, 7/4, THGV, 12/25
♿ Ⓟ **Museum Shop**
Group Tours   Drop-In Tours: by appt   **Sculpture Garden**
Permanent Collection: AM: 1830-1950; STEUBEN GLASS; NAT/AM; BIRDS BY DOROTHY DOUGHTY & E.M. BOEHM

In addition to Great Plains and SW Indian crafts the Stark houses one of the finest collections of Western American art in the country. The museum also features the only complete Steuben Glass collection of 'The US in Crystal'. **NOT TO BE MISSED:** Bronze Sculptures by Frederic Remington

ON EXHIBIT 1999
06/24/1998 to 06/1999   THE INDIAN FRONTIER IN 19TH CENTURY AMERICA
More than 60 paintings, etchings and lithographs will be selected from the Museum's permanent collection by Bodmer, Catlin, Inman, Kane, King, and Lewis. These have made a significant record of the US history.

TEXAS

San Angelo Museum of Fine Arts

704 Burgess, San Angelo, TX 76903

☎: 915-658-4084   ◙ http://web2.airmail/net

Open: 10-4 Tu-Sa, 1-4 Su   **Closed:** Mo, LEG/HOL!

ADM: **Adult:** $2.00   **Children:** Free (under 6)   **Seniors:** $1.00

& ℗   **Museum Shop   Group Tours   Drop-In Tours   Historic Building   Sculpture Garden**

Permanent Collection: AM: cont cer; REG; MEX: 1945-present

The completely renovated museum building was originally the 1868 quartermaster's storehouse on the grounds of Fort Concho, a National Historic Landmark. A new museum is under construction and will open in the Fall of 1999 **NOT TO BE MISSED:** 'Figuora Accoccolata', by Emilio Greco

McNay Art Museum

6000 N. New Braunfels Ave, San Antonio, TX 78209-4618

☎: 210-805-1757   ◙ www.mcnayart.org

Open: 10-5 Tu-Sa, 12-5 Su   **Closed:** Mo, 1/1, 7/4, THGV, 12/25

& ℗   **Museum Shop   Group Tours   Drop-In Tours   Historic Building   Sculpture Garden**

Permanent Collection: FR & AM: sculp 19, 20; SW: folk ; GR & DRGS: 19, 20; THEATER ARTS

Devoted to the French Post-Impressionist and early School of Paris artists, the McNay Art Museum also has an outstanding theatre arts collection containing over 20,000 books and drawings as well as models of stage sets. It is located on beautifully landscaped grounds in a classic Mediterranean style mansion.

ON EXHIBIT 1999

01/19/1999 to 03/14/1999   THE GREAT AMERICAN POP ART STORE: MULTIPLES OF THE SIXTIES

From a ray gun and cast baked potato by Claes Oldenburg and shopping bags by Roy Lichtenstein to Robert Indiana's LOVE ring and Andy Warhol's Brillo boxes, the 100 items featured in this exhibition document the popularity of the Pop movement in the art and culture of the 1960's.

03/25/1999 to 05/31/1999   OUT OF RUSSIA

04/10/1999 to 06/06/1999   MEXICAN GRAPHICS

08/17/1999 to 10/17/1999   AFTER THE PHOTO-SECESSION: AMERICAN PICTORIAL PHOTOGRAPHY, 1910-1955

150 photographs documenting the social and artistic development of this pictorial medium between the World Wars, will be featured in the first major exhibition to focus on this subject.

San Antonio Museum of Art

200 West Jones Street, San Antonio, TX 78215

☎: 210-978-8100   ◙ www.samuseum.org

Open: 10-5 We, Fr, Sa, 10-9 Tu, 12-5 Su   **Closed:** Mo, THGV, 12/25

Free Day: Tu, 3-9   ADM: **Adult:** $4.00   **Children:** $1.75 (4-11)   **Students:** $2.00   **Seniors:** $2.00

& ℗   **Museum Shop**

Group Tours: 210-978-8138   **Drop-In Tours**: by appt   **Historic Building   Sculpture Garden**

Permanent Collection: AN/GRK; AN/R; EGT; CONT: ptgs, sculp

San Antonio Museum of Art - continued

The San Antonio Museum of Art is located in the restored turn-of-the-century former Lone Star Brewery. In addition to its other varied and rich holdings it features the most comprehensive collection of ancient art in the southwest. The new Nelson A. Rockefeller Center for Latin American Art will be the premier center in the nation devoted solely to Latin American Art. **NOT TO BE MISSED:** The spectacular Ewing Halsell Wing for Ancient Art; Kittie and Rugeley Ferguson Decorative Arts Gallery; Nelson A. Rockefeller Center for Latin American Art

ON EXHIBIT 1999

05/29/1999 to 08/08/1999   A TASTE FOR SPLENDOR: TREASURES FROM THE HILLWOOD MUSEUM
This is a rare opportunity to see the exquisite art collection of Marjorie Merriwether Post, heir to the Post cereal fortune, which never before has been seen outside her home at Hillwood. More than 160 decorative and fine arts objects created in Imperial Russia and Europe, dating from the 17th to the mid-20th c. range from 19th century French furniture to porcelains and gold boxes commissioned by Catherine The Great and treasures by Fabergé including two of the Imperial Easter Eggs.

TYLER

Tyler Museum of Art
1300 S. Mahon Ave, Tyler, TX 75701
☎: 903-595-1001
Open: 10-5 Tu-Sa, 1-5 Su   **Closed:** Mo, LEG/HOL!
🦽 Ⓟ **Museum Shop** ❗: Café open Tu-F 11-2
Group Tours   Drop-In Tours   Historic Building
Permanent Collection: PHOT; REG 20

The Museum is located in an architecturally award winning building.

WACO

Art Center of Waco
1300 College Drive, Waco, TX 76708
☎: 254-752-4371
Open: 10-5 Tu-Sa; 1-5 Su   **Closed:** Mo, LEG/HOL!
Sugg/Cont: Yes   **Adult:** $2.00   **Children:** $1.00   **Students:** $1.00   **Seniors:** $1.50
🦽 Ⓟ **Museum Shop**
Group Tours   Drop-In Tours   Historic Building   Sculpture Garden
Permanent Collection: CONT; REG

Housed in the Cameron Home, The Art Center is located on the McLennan Community College campus. It features an exhibit of sculpture on the grounds. **NOT TO BE MISSED:** 'Square in Black', by Gio Pomodoro; 'The Waco Door' 6 ½ ton steel sculpture by Robert Wilson

TEXAS

Wichita Falls Museum and Art Center

Two Eureka Circle, Wichita Falls, TX 76308

☎: 817-692-0923

Open: 9:30-4:30 Mo-Fr; 10-5 Sa   **Closed:** Su, Mo, LEG/HOL!

ADM: **Adult:** $4.00   **Children:** F (under 3) $3.00   **Students:** $3.50   **Seniors:** $3.50

♿   ℗   **Museum Shop**

Group Tours   **Drop-In Tours**: upon request

Permanent Collection: AM: gr; CONT

The art collection has the singular focus of representing the history of American art through the medium of print making. **NOT TO BE MISSED:** The 'Magic Touch Gallery' featuring hands-on science and the 'Discovery Gallery' emphasizing family programming. Also high energy, high tech laser programs and planet shows in the planetarium.

Nora Eccles Harrison Museum of Art

Affiliate Institution: Utah State University
650 N. 1100 E., Logan, UT 84322-4020
☎: 435-797-0163
Open: 10:30-4:30 Tu, Th, Fr, 10:30-8 We, 2-5 Sa, Su   **Closed:** Mo, LEG/HOL!
& ℗   **Museum Shop   Group Tours**: 435-797-0165   **Drop-In Tours   Sculpture Garden**
Permanent Collection: NAT/AM; AM: cont art, cer 20

NOT TO BE MISSED: "Moon Shot" by Arlo Acton

Salt Lake Art Center

20 S. West Temple, Salt Lake City, UT 84101
☎: 801-328-4201
Open: 10-5 Tu-Th, 10-9 F, 10-5 Sa, 1-5 Su   **Closed:** Mo, LEG/HOL!
Sugg/Cont: Yes   **Adult:** $2.00   **Children:** $1.00
& ℗   **Museum Shop** ⁐ **Group Tours   Drop-In Tours**
Permanent Collection: REG: all media

Located in downtown Salt Lake City, the Salt Lake Art Center presents changing contemporary visual art exhibitions by local, regional & national artists. Founded in 1931.

Utah Museum of Fine Arts

101 AAC, University of Utah, Salt Lake City, UT 84112
☎: 801-581-7332   ◙   www.utah.edu/umfa
Open: 10-5 Mo-Fr, 12-5 Sa, Su   **Closed:** LEG/HOL!
& ℗   **Museum Shop**
Group Tours: 801-581-3580   **Drop-In Tours   Sculpture Garden**
Permanent Collection: EU & AM: ptgs 17-19; AF; AS; EGT

With a permanent collection of over 16,000 works spanning a broad spectrum of the world's art history, this major Utah cultural institution is a virtual artistic treasure house containing the only comprehensive collection of art in the state or the surrounding region. A new Museum building is in the process of being built and is scheduled for completion in late Fall 1999.

Springville Museum of Art

126 E. 400 S., Springville, UT 84663
☎: 801-489-2727
Open: 10-5 Tu-Sa, 3-6 Su, 10-9 We   **Closed:** Mo, Major Holidays !
& ℗   **Museum Shop**
Group Tours   Drop-In Tours   Historic Building 1937 WPA Spanish-Moroccan Architecture
Permanent Collection: UTAH: ptgs, sculp; Soviet Realism; American Realism: 20

The museum, housed in a Spanish colonial revival style building, features a collection noted for the art of Utah dating from pioneer days to the present in all styles

VERMONT

BENNINGTON

Bennington Museum

W. Main Street, Bennington, VT 05201

☎: 802-447-1571
Open: 9-5 daily, Weekends 9-7, MEM/DAY-LAB/DAY   **Closed:** THGV
ADM: Y   **Adult:** $5.00, family $ **Children:** F (under 12)   **Students:** $3.50   **Seniors:** $4.50
& ℗   **Museum Shop   Group Tours   Drop-In Tours   Historic Building**
Permanent Collection: AM: dec/art; MILITARY HIST; AM: ptgs

Visitors can imagine days gone by while gazing at a favorite Grandma Moses painting at The Bennington, one of the finest regional art and history museums in New England. The original museum building is the 1855 St. Francis de Sales church.

BURLINGTON

Robert Hull Fleming Museum

Affiliate Institution: University of Vermont
61 Colchester Ave., Burlington, VT 05405

☎: 802-656-0750
Open: 9-4 Tu-Fr, 1-5 Sa, Su, call for summer hours   **Closed:** Mo, LEG/HOL!, ACAD!
ADM: Y   **Adult:** $3.00, Family #5.00   **Children:** $2.00   **Students:** $2.00   **Seniors:** $2.00
& ℗   **Museum Shop   Group Tours   Drop-In Tours   Historic Building**
Permanent Collection: AN/EGT; CONT: Eu & Am; MID/EAST; AS; AF

Vermont's primary art and anthropology museum is located in a 1931 McKim, Mead and White building.
NOT TO BE MISSED: Assyrian Relief

ON EXHIBIT 1999

01/12/1999 to 05/1999   GEORGE SMITH: RECENT SCULPTURE AND DRAWINGS

02/14/1999 to 05/16/1999   KATHLEEN SCHNEIDER: NEW WORK

09/01/1999 to 12/15/1999   STRONG HEARTS: NATIVE AMERICAN VISIONS AND VOICES
120 color and black & white photographs taken by 25 distinguished Native American photographers offer a multifaceted portrait of contemporary native Indian life.

MANCHESTER

Southern Vermont Art Center

West Road, Manchester, VT 05254

☎: 802-362-1405   ▣ www.svac.org
Open: 10-5 Tu-Sa, 12-5 Su; in winter 10-5 Mo-Sa   **Closed:** Su in winter, Mo, 1/1, COLUMBUS DAY, 12/25
Free Day: Sa, 10-1   **ADM:** Y   **Adult:** $3.00   **Children:** F (under 13)   **Students:** $0.50   **Seniors:** $3.00
& ℗   **Museum Shop**   ⊪
Group Tours   Drop-In Tours   Historic Building   Sculpture Garden
Permanent Collection: PTGS, SCULP, PHOT, GR; CONT: 20

Built in 1917, by Mr. & Mrs. W.M. Ritter of Washington D.C., the Art Center is housed in a Georgian Colonial Mansion located on 450 acres on the eastern slope of Mt. Equinox. Included in the facility is a theater with dance, music and film programs. **NOT TO BE MISSED:** Series of rotating shows as well as the permanent collection

Middlebury College Museum of Art

Middlebury College, Middlebury, VT 05753

📞: 802-443-5007

Open: 10-5 Tu-Fr, 12-5 Sa, Su **Closed:** Mo, ACAD!, 12/18-1/1

  ♿ ⓒ **Museum Shop** ❙❙ **Group Tours**: 802-443-5007   **Drop-In Tours**

Permanent Collection: CYPRIOT: pottery; EU & AM : sculp 19; CONT: GR

Designed by the New York firm of Hardy Holzman Pfeiffer Associates, the new (1992) Center for the Arts also includes a theater, concert hall, music library and dance studios. It is located midway between Rutland and Burlington. **NOT TO BE MISSED:** 'Bimbo Malado (Sick Child)', 1893 by Menardo Rosso (wax over plaster)

ON EXHIBIT 1999

ONGOING   **19TH CENTURY PAINTING FROM THE PERMANENT COLLECTION**

ONGOING   **20TH CENTURY PAINTING FROM THE PERMANENT COLLECTION**

Sheldon Art Museum, Archeological and Historical Society

1 Park Street, Middlebury, VT 05753

📞: 802-388-2117 ⓓ www.middlebury.edu/~shel-mus

Open: 10-5 Mo-Fr, 10-4 Sa June-Oct, 12-4 some Su, 10-5 Mo-Fr late Oct-late May   **Closed:** Some Su, LEG/HOL!, 1/1, MEM/DAY, 7/4, LAB/DAY, THGV

ADM: Y **Adult:** $4.00, $8.00 fam **Children:** $1.00 6-18 **Students:** $3.50 **Seniors:** $3.50

  ♿ ⓒ **Museum Shop**

Group Tours   **Drop-In Tours** **Historic Building** Y

Permanent Collection: DEC/ART; PER/RMS; ARTIFACTS

Regional Vermont's exciting and interesting history is interpreted in this century old museum located in the 1829 Judd Harris house and Fletcher History Center. **NOT TO BE MISSED:** Portraits by itinerant artist Benjamin Franklin Mason.

ON EXHIBIT 1999

Special Holiday exhibition in December each year!

T. W. Wood Gallery and Arts Center

Affiliate Institution: Vermont College

College Hall, Montpelier, VT 05602

📞: 802-828-8743

Open: 12-4 Tu-Su **Closed:** Mo, LEG/HOL!

Free Day: Su **ADM:** Y **Adult:** $2.00 **Children:** F (under 12) **Seniors:** $2.00

  ♿ ⓒ **Museum Shop**

Group Tours   **Drop-In Tours** **Historic Building** Y

Permanent Collection: THOMAS WATERMAN WOOD: ptgs; PORTRAITS; WPA WORKS

Included in the more than 200 oils and watercolors in this collection are the works of Thomas W. Wood and his American contemporaries of the 1920s and 30s including A. H. Wyant and Asher B. Durand. **NOT TO BE MISSED:** Exhibits of Vermont's artists and crafts people

VERMONT

Shelburne Museum

U.S.Route 7, Shelburne, VT 05482

☎: 802-985-3346   ◉ www.shelburne.org
Open: 10-5 daily Late-May through Late-Oct   **Closed:** 1/1,Easter THGV, 12/25
ADM: Y   **Adult:** $17.50   **Children:** $7.00 (6-14)   **Students:** $10.50
♿ ℗ **Museum Shop** ⅼⅼ
Group Tours: 802-985-3348, ext 3392   **Drop-In Tours**: 1 PM late-Oct-late May   **Historic Building**
Permanent Collection: FOLK; DEC/ART; HAVERMEYER COLL

37 historic and exhibition buildings on 45 scenic acres combine to form this nationally celebrated collection of American folk art, artifacts, and architecture. **NOT TO BE MISSED:** Steamboat Ticonderoga, "Louisine Havemeyer and her Daughter Electra" by Mary Cassatt, 1895

St. Johnsbury Athenaeum

30 Main Street, St. Johnsbury, VT 05819

☎: 802-748-8291   ◉ www.kingcon.com/athena/
Open: 10:00-8:00 Mo, We, 10:00-5:30 Tu, Fr, 9:30-4 Sa   **Closed:** Su, LEG/HOL!
Sugg/Cont: Yes   **Adult:** $2.00pp
♿ ℗ **Museum Shop**
Group Tours   **Drop-In Tours**   **Historic Building**
Permanent Collection: AM: ptgs 19; Hudson River School

The Athenaeum was built as a public library and presented to the townspeople of St. Johnsbury by Horace Fairbanks in 1871. In 1873 an art gallery, which today is an authentic Victorian period piece, was added to the main building. The collection of American landscapes and genre paintings is shown as it was in 1890 in the oldest unaltered art gallery in the US. **NOT TO BE MISSED:** 'Domes of The Yosemite', by Albert Bierstadt

CHARLOTTESVILLE

Bayly Art Museum of the University of Virginia

Rugby Road, Thomas H. Bayly Memorial Bldg, Charlottesville, VA 22903-2427

☎: 804-924-3592   ◙ www.virginia.edu/-bayly/bayly.html
Open: 1-5 Tu-Su   **Closed:** Mo, 12/24-1/2
Sugg/Cont: Yes   **Adult:** $3.00   **Students:** $3.00   **Seniors:** $3.00
🖔 Ⓟ   **Museum Shop   Group Tours:** 804-924-7458   **Drop-In Tours**
Permanent Collection: NAT/AM; MESO/AM; AF; DEC/ART 18; OM: gr; AM: ptgs, sculp, works on paper, phot 20; P/COL,

This handsome Palladian-inspired building is located on the grounds of Jefferson's University of Virginia. With its wide ranging collection it serves as a museum for all ages and interests, for art lovers and scholars alike.

ON EXHIBIT 1999

11/27/1998 to 01/17/1999   TWO VIRGINIA ARTISTS: NEW WORK BY SUSAN BACIK AND ROBERT STRINI
These two exhibitions Oct 29th-Dec. 23, 1998 and November 27-January 17, 1999 are works composed of found objects and accompanied by poems by Stephen Cushman. They explore how human beings communicate.

11/27/1998 to 01/17/1999   NIZHONI, A BEAUTIFUL RUG: THE BERTHA BROSSMAN BLAIR COLLECTION OF SOUTHWESTERN TEXTILES
Most of the 60 rugs are recent or promised gifts to the Museum. Nizhoni is Navajo for a beautiful rug.

01/09/1999 to 03/14/1999   HOT OFF THE PRESS: CONTEMPORARY PRINTS FROM THE MUSEUM COLLECTION

01/16/1999 to 03/26/1999   AFRICAN ART AND PERFORMANCE

01/29/1999 to 03/14/1999   SALLY MANN: STILL TIME
A survey of Mann's work from 1971-1991 selected by the photographer herself. *Catalog Will Travel*

03/20/1999 to 05/23/1999   DAVID BUNN: HERE THERE AND PRACTICALLY EVERYWHERE
Bunn uses rescued card catalogues from the Los Angeles Library as the basis for composing poems. These are bound together creating a circular transformation of the written word to the computerized work, to the written word.

03/26/1999 to 05/23/1999   THE PRINTED WORLD OF PIETER BREUGEL THE ELDER
Although he himself etched only one print (The Rabbit Hunt, 1566) Pieter Breugel the Elder was an artist whose work was transferred into print often in the 16th century. This exhibition presents a remarkable selection of prints that illustrate the rich and varied imagery of his world. *Catalog Will Travel*

06/05/1999 to 07/16/1999   IN HONOR OF ALAN GROH '49: A PRIVATE COLLECTION
Twentieth century art rom a private collection including works by Warhol, Indiana, Mitchell, Marca-Reli, Cornell and others.

Second Street Gallery

201 2nd Street, NW, Charlottesville, VA 22902

☎: 804-977-7284
Open: 10-5 T-Sa, 1-5 Su   **Closed:** M, LEG/HOL!
🖔 Ⓟ   **Museum Shop**
Group Tours   Drop-In Tours   Historic Building Y
Permanent Collection: Non-collecting Contemporary art space

Nationally known for its innovative programming, Second Street Gallery presents work of talented, regional, and national artists working in a variety of media from painting and photography, to sculpture and site-specific installations. The McGuffey Art Center which houses the Gallery is a historic former primary school building and is now an artist cooperative with open studios.

VIRGINIA

Second Street Gallery - continued

ON EXHIBIT 1999

01/1999   PHOTOGRAPHY TBA

02/1999   VIDEO ARTIST TBA

03/1999   SEIKO TACHIBANA, PRINTS {San Francisco, CA)

˙04/1999 to 05/1999   CRAIG PLEASANTS, MIXED MEDIA INSTALLATION (Sweet Briar, VA)

06/1999 to 07/1999   PAINTINGS, TBA

CLIFTON FORGE

Allegheny Highlands Arts and Craft Center

439 East Ridgeway Street, Clifton Forge, VA 24422

✆: 703-862-4447

Open: 10:00-4:30 Mo-Sa May-Dec, 10:00-4:30 Tu-Sa Jan-Apr   **Closed:** THGV, 12/24-01/12

 ⬄ ⓟ **Museum Shop** **Group Tours** **Drop-In Tours**

Permanent Collection: Non-collecting institution

Housed in an early 1900's building, the galleries' changing exhibits feature works produced by Highlands and other artists. **NOT TO BE MISSED:** The shop, shows, and wonderful volunteers.

ON EXHIBIT 1999

01/12/1999 to 02/20/1999   FLOWERS IN THE SNOW

02/13/1999 to 03/27/1999   ROANOKE COLLEGE FACULTY

03/30/1999 to 05/01/1999   LINSAY NOLTING

05/04/1999 to 06/12/1999   LAURA HORNER

06/15/1999 to 07/31/1999   NANCY GARRETSON

08/03/1999 to 09/04/1999   THE BEST OF SILKSCREEN

09/07/1999 to 10/09/1999   VIRGINIA 8

10/15/1999 to 11/13/1999   FALL FESTIVAL

11/16/1999 to 12/22/1999   THE SOUNDS OF CHRISTMAS

DANVILLE

Danville Museum of Fine Arts & History

975 Main Street, Danville, VA 24541

✆: 804-793-5644

Open: 10-5 Tu-F, 2-5 Sa, Su   **Closed:** Mo, LEG/HOL!

Sugg/Cont: Yes   **Adult:** $2.00   **Children:** $1.00   **Students:** $1.00   **Seniors:** $1.00

 ⬄ ⓟ **Museum Shop**

Group Tours   **Drop-In Tours:** by appt   **Historic Building** Y

Permanent Collection: REG: portraits, works on paper, dec/art, furniture, textiles

The Museum, located in Sutherlin House built about 1857, was the residence of Confederate President Jefferson Davis for one week in April 1865. **NOT TO BE MISSED:** Restored Victorian Parlor

Danville Museum of Fine Arts & History - continued

ON EXHIBIT 1999

03/20/1999 to 05/16/1999   WE SHALL OVERCOME: PHOTOGRAPHS FROM AMERICA'S CIVIL RIGHTS ERA
80 framed photographs focusing on key events and personalities of the period in American history from 1954-1968 known as the Civil Rights Era. The exhibition documents the efforts of American activists to hold this country to the promise of the Constitution.

FREDERICKSBURG

Belmont, The Gari Melchers Estate and Memorial Gallery
224 Washington St., Fredericksburg, VA 22405
☎: 540-654-1015
Open: 10-5 Mo-Sa, 1-5 Su   **Closed:** 1/1, THGV ,12/24, 12/25, 12/31
ADM: Y   **Adult:** $4.00   **Children:** F (under 6)   **Students:** $1.00   **Seniors:** $3.00
&   ℗   **Museum Shop**
Group Tours: 540-654-1841   **Drop-In Tours**: on the hour and half hour   **Historic Building** Y
Permanent Collection: EU & AM: ptgs (mostly by Gari Melchers)

This 18th century estate features many paintings by Gari Melchers (its former resident). Also on view are works by his American and European contemporaries as well as some old masters.

HAMPTON

Hampton University Museum
Hampton University, Hampton, VA 23668
☎: 757-727-5308   ▣ www.hamptonu.edu
Open: 8-5 Mo Fr, 12-4 Sa, Su   **Closed:** LEG/HOL!, ACAD!
&   ℗   **Museum Shop**
Group Tours: 757-727-5208, child 757-727-5024   **Drop-In Tours**
Permanent Collection: AF; NAT/AM: AM: ptgs 20

The Museum is housed in the spectacular, newly renovated Huntington Building, formerly the University Library. It is the oldest African American museum in the US and one of the oldest museums in Virginia. The collections include over 9000 objects including traditional African, Native American, Asian and Pacific Island art as well as a fine art collection. **NOT TO BE MISSED:** 'The Banjo Lesson', by Henry O. Tanner

ON EXHIBIT 1999

01/17/1999 to 04/18/1999   WILLIAM H. JOHNSON AND MALVIN GRAY JOHNSON

03/1999   OPENING OF NATIVE AMERICAN ART GALLERY
The Museum's collection of Native American art collected primarily between 1878 and 1923 will be permanently installed in greatly expanded space, offering access to objects never before seen.

05/02/1999 to 07/25/1999   WILLIAM E. PAJAUD

08/08/1999 to 10/10/1999   GENERATIONS: HAMPTON ARTISTS, 1950-2000

10/24/1999 to 12/12/1999   A COMMUNION OF SPIRITS: AFRICAN AMERICAN QUILTERS, PRESERVERS, AND THEIR STORIES

VIRGINIA

Maier Museum of Art

Affiliate Institution: Randolph-Macon Woman's College
2500 Rivermont Avenue, Lynchburg, VA 24503
☎: 804-947-8136 ◙ www.rmwc,edu/maier
Open: 1-5 Tu-Su Sep-May, 1-4 We-Su, June-Aug **Closed:** Mo, Acad/Hol !
⚹ ℗ **Museum Shop Group Tours Drop-In Tours:** by appt
Permanent Collection: AM: ptgs 19, 20

19th and 20th century American paintings including works by Gilbert Stuart, Winslow Homer, Thomas Eakins, Thomas Cole, George Bellows, Mary Cassatt, Georgia O'Keeffe, and Andrew Wyeth, are among the many highlights of the Maier Museum of Art. **NOT TO BE MISSED:** George Bellows' 'Men of the Docks'

ON EXHIBIT 1999
01/16/1999 to 03/17/1999 88TH ANNUAL: LOUISE BOURGEOIS PRINTS: 1989-1998

03/13/1999 to 04/25/1999 MAPPING THE WEST: NINETEENTH-CENTURY AMERICAN LANDSCAPE PHOTOGRAPHS FROM THE COLLECTION OF THE BOSTON PUBLIC LIBRARY

05/25/1999 to 08/1999 SUMMER EXHIBITION

08/1999 to 10/1999 ELENA SISTO

Peninsula Fine Arts Center

101 Museum Drive, Newport News, VA 23606
☎: 757-596-8175
Open: 10-5 Mo-Sa, 1-5 Su **Closed:** 1/1, THGV, 12/24/PM, 12/25
Vol/Cont: Yes
⚹ ℗ **Museum Shop Group Tours Drop-In Tours:** by appt **Sculpture Garden**
Permanent Collection: Non-collecting institution

Changing exhibitions of primarily contemporary art by emerging artists that often contrast with exhibitions of historical significance are featured at this fine arts center which also has a Hands On For Kids gallery. The Center is located within the Mariner's Museum Park with the Noland Trail.

ON EXHIBIT 1999
01/16/1999 to 03/21/1999 IT'S ALL RELATIVE/TWINS
An exploration of relationships and influences between family members and the art they create. How does birth order effect creativity. Inspired by Lewis Carroll's "Tweedle Dum and Tweedle Dee" these twins are mischievous, adult, perhaps dangerous, as well as childish and humorous.

04/01/1999 to 04/30/1999 THE GARDENS OF ELLEN BIDDLE SHIPMAN (1869-1950)
The life and landscape designs of one of the early twentieth century's most successful and prolific landscape architects through photographs, drawings and plans. By the time of her death she had completed over 650 projects.

05/01/1999 to 06/06/1999 MYSTERY AND ALLEGORY: 15 YEARS OF WORK: ROB EVANS
Striking in their technique, appearing smooth and polished from a distance, and textural at closer examination, Evan's work is an inventive tool for interpretation.

06/12/1999 to 08/19/1999 CONTEMPORARY CRAFTS
Craft is defined as a trade requiring manual dexterity or artistic skill. It has ceased to be mere decoration and the craftsman has become the rival of the fine artist.

08/28/1999 to 11/07/1999 JURIED EXHIBITION 1999
An annual exhibition featuring the work of local and regional artists.

NORFOLK

Chrysler Museum of Art

245 West Olney Road, Norfolk, VA 23510-1587
📞: 757-664-6200   ▣ www.chrysler.org
Open: 10-5 Tu-Sa, 1-5 Su   **Closed:** Mo, 1/1, 7/4, THGV, 12/25
Free Day: We   ADM: Y   **Adult:** $4.00   **Children:** $2.00, under 5 F   **Students:** $2.00   **Seniors:** $2.00
&   Ⓟ   **Museum Shop**   ¶: Phantoms
Group Tours: 757-664-6269 or 6283   **Drop-In Tours**   **Historic Building**
Permanent Collection: GLASS; IT/BAROQUE: ptgs; FR: 19; AN/EGT; AM: sculp, ptgs

Home to one of America's premier art collections spanning 5000 years of art history in an Italianate-Style building built on the picturesque Hague of the Elizabeth River. There are three historic houses. **NOT TO BE MISSED:** Gianlorenzo Bernini's 'Bust of the Savior'; Degas 'Dancer With Bouquet'

ON EXHIBIT 1999
07/14/1998 to 05/30/1999   THE SANDLER COLLECTION OF ITALIAN GLASS

09/22/1998 to 01/10/1999   KENNETH HARRIS WATERCOLORS

10/22/1998 to 01/10/1999   ANDY WARHOL

02/05/1999 to 05/02/1999   M. C. ESCHER: A CENTENNIAL TRIBUTE

Hermitage Foundation Museum

7637 North Shore Road, Norfolk, VA 23505
📞: 757-423-2052
Open: 10-5 Mo-Sa, 1-5 Su   **Closed:** 1/1, THGV, 12/25
ADM: Y   **Adult:** $4.00   **Children:** $1.00   **Seniors:** $4.00
&   Ⓟ   **Museum Shop**
Group Tours   **Drop-In Tours**   **Historic Building**
Permanent Collection: OR; EU; AS; 16, 17

Nestled in a lush setting along the Lafayette River is the 12 acre estate of the Hermitage Foundation Museum whose turn-of-the-century English Tudor home appears to have been frozen in time. It is, however, alive with treasures from the past. **NOT TO BE MISSED:** 1400 year old Buddha

RADFORD

Radford University Galleries

200 Powell Hall, Radford, VA 24142
📞: 540-831-5475   ▣ www.runet.edu/~rumuseum
Open: 10-4 Tu-Fr, 6-9 Th, 12-4 Su (5/1-6/15 12-6, Tu-Fr, Su)   **Closed:** Mo, Sa, LEG/HOL!, 6/15-8/15
&   Ⓟ   **Museum Shop**
Group Tours: 540-831-5754   **Drop-In Tours**: by appt   **Sculpture Garden**
Permanent Collection: Cont works in all media

Located in the New River Valley, the gallery is noted for the diversity of its special exhibitions.

VIRGINIA

Anderson Gallery, School of the Arts

Affiliate Institution: Virginia Commonwealth University
907 ½ W. Franklin Street, Richmond, VA 23284-2514
☎: 804-828-1522   ◙ www.vcu.edu/artweb/gallery/index.html
Open: 10-5 Tu-Fr, 1-5 Sa, Su   **Closed:** Mo, LEG/HOL! ACAD!
Vol/Cont: Yes   **Adult:** $3.00   **Children:** $1.00   **Students:** $1.00   **Seniors:** $1.00
 ⅃ ℗   **Museum Shop   Group Tours   Drop-In Tours**
Permanent Collection: CONT: gr, phot, ptgs, sculp

The gallery is well known in the US and Europe for exhibiting work of nationally and internationally renowned artists.

Marsh Art Gallery, University of Richmond

George M. Modlin Center for the Arts, Richmond, VA 23173
☎: 804-289-8276   ◙ www.arts.richmond.edu/~marshart
Open: 1-5 Tu-Sa   **Closed:** Su, Mo, ACAD !
 ⅃ ℗   **Museum Shop** ⫶: College Cafeteria   **Group Tours**   **Drop-In Tours**
Permanent Collection: AM: AS: EU: cer,drgs,gr,photo,ptg,sculp

The new galleries feature outstanding exhibitions of contemporary and historical art. **NOT TO BE MISSED:** The new Cram-inspired building designed by the architectural firm of Marcellus, Wright, Cox and Smith.

ON EXHIBIT 1999

01/12/1999 to 06/26/1999   JACKIE BATTENFIELD: FOUR BREATHS

01/29/1999 to 04/10/1999   THE ART OF TWENTIETH CENTURY ZEN
The first exhibition in America to present a survey of painting and calligraphy by Japan's greatest Zen masters of the 20th century.   *Catalog Will Travel*

02/18/1999 to 04/02/1999   RELIGION & POLITICS: THE RENAISSANCE PRINT IN SOCIAL CONTEXT

04/21/1999 to 06/26/1999   THE SEASONS: MONOTYPES BY JOELLYN DUESBERRY WITH POEMS BY PATTIANN ROGERS

Virginia Museum of Fine Arts

2800 Grove Ave, Richmond, VA 23221-2466
☎: 804-367-0844   ◙ www.vmfa.state.va.us
Open: 11-5 Tu, We, Fr-Su, 11-8 Th   **Closed:** Mo, 1/1, 7/4, THGV, 12/25
Sugg/Cont: Yes   **Adult:** $4.00
 ⅃ ℗   **Museum Shop** ⫶
Group Tours: 804-367-0859   **Drop-In Tours**: 2:30 Tu-Su; 6pm Th except summer   **Sculpture Garden**
Permanent Collection: AM: ptgs, sculp; LILLIAN THOMAS PRATT COLL OF JEWELS BY PETER CARL FABERGE; EU: all media (Ren to cont)

Diverse collections and outstanding special exhibits abound in the internationally prominent Virginia Museum which houses one of the largest collections in the world of Indian, Nepalese, and Tibetan art. It also holds the Mellon Collection of British sporting art and the Sydney and Francis Lewis Collection of late 19th and early 20th century decorative arts, contemporary American paintings and sculpture. **NOT TO BE MISSED:** 'Caligula', Roman, AD 38-40 marble 80 ' high. Also the largest public collection of Fabergé Imperial Easter eggs in the West. The Fabergé Gallery is closed until Spring 1999

Virginia Museum of Fine Arts - continued

ON EXHIBIT 1999

to 03/01/1999 FROM THE LOOMS OF INDIA: TEXTILES FROM THE PERMANENT COLLECTION
Many words associated with textiles come from India including calico, bandanna, dungaree, gingham etc. From the Museum's collection these are examples of textile production from the 17th to the 19th C.

10/25/1998 DISCOVER SILVER: THE JEROME AND RITA GANS COLLECTION OF ENGLISH SILVER
The remarkable gift of 18th and 19th century silver has made possible a new hands-on gallery devoted to the history and properties of silver. *Catalog*

11/13/1998 to 01/31/1999 DESIGNED FOR DELIGHT: ALTERNATIVE ASPECTS OF TWENTIETH CENTURY DECORATIVE ARTS
The international scope of the exhibition covers major stylistic developments from nouveau and art deco to pop and postmodern. Postmodern developments of the last twenty years have brought the realization that the history of modern design must take other issues into account as well. The four major themes are: The Body as Metaphor; Inversion and Transformation; Surface Enrichment; and Fantasy. Works range in media from furniture, ceramics, and glass to jewelry and metalwork. ADM: Adult $4.00; Stu $2.50 *Catalog Will Travel*

12/15/1998 to 03/14/1999 FIERY STEEDS: FRENCH ROMANTIC STUDIES BY CARLE VERNET FROM THE RITZENBERG COLLECTION
Vernet developed a realistic style of observation which bordered on satire. This gift to the Museum of 82 rapid sketches probably taken from an album, include studies of farm horses, military horses, cab horses, riderless horses and horses in every condition. Also included are 11 highly finished works from the Museum collection.

06/1999 to 11/1999 SPLENDORS OF ANCIENT EGYPT
One of the largest exhibitions of ancient Egyptian treasures to visit the US in decades, the Virginia Museum is the only East coast venue. More than 200 masterpieces will be shown ranging from 5000 years ago through the age of the pyramids to the 7th Century A.D. On view will be gilded and painted mummy cases, life-size limestone representations of pharaohs and noblemen, an 18 foot long papyrus scroll from the Egyptian Book of the Dead, gold and lapis lazuli jewelry, wall carvings and ceramics. *Catalog Admission Fee Will Travel*

ROANOKE

Art Museum of Western Virginia

One Market Square, Roanoke, VA 24011
☎: 540-342-5760 ◙ www.artmuseumroanoke.org
Open: 10-5 Tu-Sa, 1-5 Su (10-2 12/24,12/31) **Closed:** Mo, 1/1, 12/25
& ℗ **Museum Shop Group Tours Drop-In Tours Sculpture Garden**
Permanent Collection: AM & EU: ptgs 20; AM: folk, gr, phot

The Art Museum of Western Virginia is a general art museum, which presents programs and exhibitions focusing on 19th and 20th century American art by the people of Western Virginia. The Museum also houses "ArtVenture: A Children's Center," an interactive art studio offering camps, classes, and workshops to children of the area. **NOT TO BE MISSED:** Sidewalk Art Show, June 5-6, 1999

ON EXHIBIT 1999

11/06/1998 to 02/07/1999 THE ART OF THE ILLUSTRATOR: 1900-1950
American and British illustrations including works by Frank Schoonover, F. C. Yohn, and Henry Raleigh. A related exhibition will focus on illustrators from Roanoke who were active during the first half of the 20th C.

01/23/1999 to 06/27/1999 THE THEATER OF DINING: FLOYD CO. CERAMICS

02/13/1999 to 05/09/1999 GOYA: THE DISASTERS OF WAR

02/13/1999 to 05/09/1999 SPIRIT AND FLESH: PAINTINGS BY RAY ALBETYU, BILL RUTHERFORD, DOUGLAS BOURGOIS, CAROL BURCH BROWN

SWEET BRIAR

Sweet Briar College Art Gallery

Sweet Briar College, Sweet Briar, VA 24595

☎: 804-381-6248   ◉ www.artgallery.sbc.edu
Open: Pannell: 12-9:30 Mo-Th, 12-5 Fr-Su, Babcock: 9-9 daily   **Closed:** Mo, ACAD!
♿ Ⓟ **Museum Shop** ⫪: On campus
Group Tours   Drop-In Tours   Historic Building   Sculpture Garden
Permanent Collection: JAP: woodblock prints; EU: gr, drgs 19; AM: ptgs 20

The exterior design of the 1901 building is a rare collegiate example of Ralph Adams Cram Georgian Revival Style architecture. **NOT TO BE MISSED:** 'Daisies and Anemones', by William Glackens

ON EXHIBIT 1999

01/28/1999 to 03/07/1999   PAIGE CRITCHER

02/04/1999 to 03/28/1999   IT'S NOT ELEMENTARY IX

03/11/1999 to 05/02/1999   PHYLLIS MCGIBBON

04/01/1999 to 05/02/1999   JOHN MORGAN

08/20/1999 to 10/25/1999   SCOTT RIDGE

10/29/1999 to 01/31/2000   STAGE ROAD: AMHERST TO COOLWELL

VIRGINIA BEACH

Contemporary Art Center of Virginia

2200 Parks Avenue, Virginia Beach, VA 23451

☎: 757-425-0000   ◉ www.cacv.org
Open: 10-5 Tu-Fr; 10-4 Sa; 12-4 Su   **Closed:** LEG/HOL!
ADM: Y   **Adult:** $3.00   **Children:** $2.00   **Students:** $2.00   **Seniors:** $2.00
♿ Ⓟ **Museum Shop**
Group Tours   Drop-In Tours   Sculpture Garden
Permanent Collection: Non-collecting institution

The Contemporary Art Center of Virginia in a non-profit, non-collecting institution founded in 1952 to foster awareness, exploration and understanding of the significant art of our time. Regularly changing exhibitions feature painting, sculpture, photography, glass, video and other visual media from local, regional and international artists.

ON EXHIBIT 1999

11/20/1998 to 01/10/1999   JAMES CROAK: 20-YEAR SURVEY

01/23/1999 to 03/15/1999   ANDY WARHOL'S ENDANGERED SPECIES

04/17/1999 to 06/27/1999   THE ART OF GLASS 1999: CHIHULY, ANTONAKIS, STATOM AND MORRIS: 1964-1997

Abby Aldrich Rockefeller Folk Art Center

307 S. England Street, Williamsburg, VA 23185
☎: 757-220-7698   ◙ www.colonialwilliamsburg.org
Open: 11-5 daily 1/5-3/20; 10-5 3/21-12/3
ADM: Y   **Adult:** $10.00, combine
& ℗   **Museum Shop**   ¶: Café in Dewitt Wallace Gallery (separate building)
Group Tours   Drop-In Tours   Historic Building
Permanent Collection: AM: folk

Historic Williamsburg is the site of the country's premier showcase for American folk art. The museum, originally built in 1957 and reopened in its new building in 1992, demonstrates folk art's remarkable range and inventiveness in textiles, paintings, and decorative arts. The DeWitt Wallace Gallery houses the collection of English and American Decorative arts and is included in the Museums ticket cost.

ON EXHIBIT 1999

THE DEWITT WALLACE DECORATIVE ARTS GALLERY (entered through the Public Hospital Building

The gallery offers exhibitions of decorative arts, firearms, textiles and costumes.
02/1999 to 09/1999   THE KINGDOMS OF EDWARD HICKS
A major retrospective on Quaker minister and artist Hicks featuring nearly 100 of his works created between 1825 and 1840. Included is the world-renowned "Peaceable Kingdom".

Muscarelle Museum of Art

College of William and Mary, Williamsburg, VA 23185
☎: 757-221-2700   ◙ www.wm.edu/muscarelle
Open: 10-4:45 Mo-Fr, 12-4 Sa, Su   **Closed:** LEG/HOL!
& ℗   **Museum Shop**
Group Tours: 757-221-2703   **Drop-In Tours**: by appt   **Historic Building**
Permanent Collection: BRIT & AM: portraits 17-19; O/M: drgs; CONT: gr, AB, EU & AM: ptgs

The 'worlds' first solar painting' by Gene Davis, transforms the south facade of the Museum into a dramatic and innovative visual statement when monumental tubes, filled with colored water are lit from behind. **NOT TO BE MISSED:** Early Renaissance fresco fragment, St. Mary Magdalene and Donor, attributed to The Master of the Cappella di San Giorgio, Italian (Assisi), 1300-1350.

WASHINGTON

Bellevue Art Museum

301 Bellevue Square, Bellevue, WA 98004

📞: 425-454-3322   ◙ www.bellevueart.org
Open: 10-6 Mo, We-Sa, 10-8 Tu, 11-5 Su
Closed: 1/1,EASTER,7/4,MEM/DAY, LAB/DAY,THGV,12/25; THE MUSEUM IS CLOSED BETWEEN EXHIBITIONS
Free Day: Tu   ADM: Y   **Adult:** $3.00   **Children:** F, under 12   **Seniors:** $2.00
   ⅏ ℗ **Museum Shop**   **Group Tours**: 425-454-3322, ext. 100   **Drop-In Tours**: 2:00 daily
Permanent Collection: Non-collecting institution

Located across Lake Washington about 10 minutes drive from Seattle, the museum is a place to see, explore and make art.

ON EXHIBIT 1999

11/14/1998 to 01/17/1999   HANDS ON COLOR
The museum will be transformed into a giant laboratory of projected, painted, digitally generated, and natural color. Contemporary painting, sculpture and video art will help visitors understand color as an expressive element with different cultural meanings. They will also be able to experiment with the basics of color with crayons and video cameras, prisms and computer models

01/30/1999 to 04/11/1999   FRESH FLOWERS
A group exhibition surveying art in all media using flowers and floral imagery to ask questions about the relationships between nature and culture, decoration and art, decay and life.

04/24/1999 to 06/21/1999   PUBLIC/PRIVATE: A GLORIA BORNSTEIN RETROSPECTIVE
An investigation of private concerns becoming public issues. Paintings, sculpture, performances, installation and public projects revealing disturbing truths and symbolizing possible routes to reconciliation and healing. *Catalog*

07/05/1999 to 08/29/1999   1999 PACIFIC NORTHWEST ANNUAL
The 8th annual juried exhibition of work by artists from the region.

Whatcom Museum of History and Art

121 Prospect Street, Bellingham, WA 98225

📞: 360-676-6981   ◙ www.cob.org/museum.htm
Open: 12-5 Tu-Su   **Closed:** Mo, LEG/HOL!
 ⅏ **Museum Shop**   **Group Tours**   **Drop-In Tours**   **Historic Building**   **Sculpture Garden**
Permanent Collection: KINSEY: phot coll; HANSON: Naval arch drgs; NW/COAST: ethnography; VICTORIANA

An architectural and historic landmark, this museum building is situated in a 1892 former City Hall on a bluff with a commanding view of Bellingham Bay.

Valley Art Center, Inc

842-6th Street, Clarkston, WA 99403

📞: 509-758-8331
Open: 9-4 Mo-Fr, by appt other times   **Closed:** 7/4, THGV ,12/25-1/1
 ⅏ ℗ **Museum Shop**   **Group Tours**   **Drop-In Tours**   **Historic Building**
Permanent Collection: REG; NAT/AM

Valley Art Center is located in Southeast Washington at the Snake and Clearwater Rivers in the heart of the city's historic district made famous by Lewis and Clarke. **NOT TO BE MISSED:** Beadwork, Paiute Cradle Board Tatouche

GOLDENDALE

Maryhill Museum of Art
35 Maryhill Museum Drive, Goldendale, WA 98620
☎: 509-773-3733   ◙   www.maryhillmuseum.org
Open: 9-5 Daily, Mar 15-Nov 15.   **Closed:** Open HOL
ADM: Y   **Adult:** $6.00   **Children:** F (under 6)   **Students:** $1.50   **Seniors:** $5.50
&   **Museum Shop**   ⑪: café, picnic grounds
Group Tours   Drop-In Tours   Historic Building Y
Permanent Collection: AUGUST RODIN SCULP; ORTHODOX ICONS: 18; BRIT: ptgs; NAT/AM: baskets, dec/art;
FURNISHINGS OF QUEEN MARIE of ROMANIA; INTERNATIONAL CHESS SETS

Serving the Pacific Northwest, the Maryhill Museum is a major cultural resource in the Columbia River Gorge region. **NOT TO BE MISSED:** Theatre de la Mode: 1946 French Fashion collection

ON EXHIBIT 1999

02/11/1999 to 05/16/1999   FISH STORY

02/25/1999 to 06/13/1999   COMING TO LIFE: THE FIGURE IN AMERICAN ART 1955-1965

01/29/1999 to 05/30/1999   JOSIAH MCELHENY

Longview

Art Gallery, Lower Columbia College Fine Arts Gallery
1600 Maple Street, Longview, WA 98632
☎: 360-577-2300
Open: 10-4 Mo, Tu, Fr, 10-8 We, Th Sept-June   **Closed:** Sa, Su, LEG/HOL, ACAD/HOL
&   ℗   **Museum Shop**   ⑪: cafeteria in student center
Group Tours: 360-577-2314   **Drop-In Tours**
Permanent Collection: Non-collecting institution

A College Gallery that features temporary exhibitions by local, regional, and national artists.

ON EXHIBIT 1999

01/12/1999 to 02/04/1999   MASKS
An invitational show featuring masks by artists from several states.

02/12/1999 to 03/11/1999   DEBRA DAVIS/STEVE JENSEN
Paintings and Sculpture

04/02/1999 to 04/29/1999   SALLY SELLARS/HAND CRAFTED FURNITURE
Fibre art and hand crafted furniture by local furniture makers.

09/30/1999 to 10/28/1999   CONNECTING WATERS
A juried show celebrating the artists of Southwest Washington.

WASHINGTON

OLYMPIA

Washington State Capitol Museum
211 West 21st Avenue, Olympia, WA 98501
: 360-753-2580 ◉ www.wshs.org
Open: 10-4 Tu-Fr, 12-4 Sa, Su **Closed:** Mo, LEG/HOL!
ADM: Y **Adult:** $2.00, $5.00 Families **Students:** $1.00 **Seniors:** $1.75
& ℗ **Museum Shop Group Tours Drop-In Tours:** by appt **Historic Building**
Permanent Collection: REG: NAT/AM: 18,19

The Museum is housed in the Lord Mansion, a 1924 Italian Renaissance Revival Style building. It also features a permanent exhibit on the history of Washington State government and cultural history. **NOT TO BE MISSED:** Southern Puget Sound American Indian exhibit welcome healing totem pole figure.

PULLMAN

Museum of Art
Washington State University, Pullman, WA 99164
: 509-335-1910
Open: 10-4 Mo-Fr, 10-10 Tu, 1-5 Sa, Su **Closed:** ACAD!
& ℗ **Museum Shop Group Tours Drop-In Tours**
Permanent Collection: NW: art; CONT/AM & CONT/EU: gr 19

The WSU Museum of Art, in the university community of Pullman, presents a diverse program of changing exhibitions, including paintings, prints, photography, and crafts.

ON EXHIBIT 1999
01/11/1999 to 02/21/1999 COLLABORATIONS: WILLIAM ALLEN, ROBERT HUDSON, WILLIAM WILEY
Work from 1987-1997 by three significant Bay Area artists who share a 40 year friendship. Wiley's highly detailed paintings combine hand written texts and messages with energetic drawn and painted images. Hudson's sculptures juxtapose found objects with colorful, complex geometric forms. Allen produces sweeping western landscapes with surreal incidents. Over the years they have worked on highly successful collaborative projects that meld each of their artistic characters.

09/07/1999 to 10/10/1999 BEARING WITNESS: CONTEMPORARY WORKS BY AFRICAN AMERICAN WOMEN ARTISTS
History, ethnicity, gender, marginalization and invisibility are some of the issues addressed by these 25 prominent artists. Included are Howardina Pindell, Betye and Alison Saar, Faith Ringold, Carrie Mae Weems, and Lorna Simpson.

SEATTLE

Henry Art Gallery
Affiliate Institution: University of Washington
15th Ave. NE & NE 41st Street, Seattle, WA 98195-3070
: 206-543-2280 ◉ www.hentyart.org
Open: 11-5 Tu, We, Fr-Su, 11-8 Th **Closed:** Mo, 1/1, 7/4, THGV, 12/25
Free Day: Th, 5-8pm **ADM:** Y **Adult:** $5.00 **Children:** F (under 12) **Seniors:** $3.50
& ℗ **Museum Shop** ⑪
Group Tours: 206-616-8782 **Drop-In Tours:** 2nd Sa, 3rd Th each mo, 2pm **Historic Building Sculpture Garden**
Permanent Collection: PTGS: 19,20; PHOT; CER; ETH: textiles & W./Coast

Henry Art Gallery - continued

The major renovation designed by Charles Gwathmey of Carl F. Gould's 1927 building reopened in April 1997. The expansion adds 10,000 square feet of galleries and additional visitor amenities and educational facilities.

ON EXHIBIT 1999

10/08/1998 to 01/31/1999   EYE/BODY, THE FIGURE IN AMERICAN ART, 1955-1965

An exploration of the change in attitude toward figurative representation by tracing the evolution of Abstract Expressionism from the late 50s to Pop and performance art of the 60s. Included are works by de Kooning, Motherwell, Park, Arneson, Connor, Lichtenstein, Segal and Warhol as well as film and photographs by Frank, Smith, Arbus and Friedlander

11/05/1998 to 01/24/1999   DEEP STORAGE: THE ARSENAL OF MEMORY

Storage is explored as an image, a process and an enveloping issue in contemporary art and art making. Artists included art Duchamp, Beuys, Oldenburg (this work was created specifically for the American tour of the exhibition). Rauschenburg and many others. *Will Travel*

Nordic Heritage Museum

3014 N.W. 67th Street, Seattle, WA 98117

☎: 206-789-5707

Open: 10-4 Tu-Sa, 12-4 Su   **Closed:** Mo, 12/24, 12/25, 1/1

Free Day: 1st Tu each mo   ADM: Y   **Adult:** $4.00   **Children:** $2.00 (6-16)   **Students:** $3.00   **Seniors:** $3.00

  ♿ ⓒ   **Museum Shop   Group Tours:** by res   **Drop-In Tours**

Permanent Collection: SCANDINAVIAN/AM: folk; PHOT

Follow the immigrants journey across America in this museum located in Ballard north of the Ballard Locks.

ON EXHIBIT 1999

12/09/1998 to 01//1999   NORDIC FIVE

Multi media exhibition featuring California artists of Nordic descent.

02//1999 to 03/25/1999   ERIC ALLAN KARJALUOTO/ FINNISH CANADIAN

02//1999 to 04//1999   SWEDISH CRAFTS AND APPLIED ARTS: REPRESENTATIVE ARTISTS FROM ALL PROVINCES

04//1999 to 05//1999   BEV VAN BERKOM: PAINTINGS AND SERIGRAPHS BASED ON VIKING MYTHOLOGY

05//1999 to 07//1999   FINISH EXHIBIT: TIMBER CONSTRUCTION, ARCHITECTURE AND SAUNA: IN CONJUNCTION WITH FINNFEST 99

06//1999 to 07//1999   DR. DALE, NORWEGIAN AMERICAN, BRONZE SCULPTURES

08//1999 to 09//1999   FRENCH PHOTOGRAPHER IN DALAMA, SWEDEN, 1910/ AN ETHNOGRAPHIC VIEW

09/18/1999 to 11/20/1999   IB SPANG OLSEN: GRAPHICS AND BOOK PRINTING/ NULLE OIGAARD, PICTORIAL TAPESTRIES, GLASS (DANISH ARTISTS)

10//1999 to 11//1999   LYNE STEVNS JENSEN: DANISH CERAMIC AND SCRIMSHAW

12//1999 to 01//2000   JAN ROGER BRODIN: NORWEGIAN PHOTOGRAPHER

12/01/1999 to 02/28/2000   ICELANDER AMERICAN PHOTOGRAPHY: SCENES FROM THE HOMELAND AND THE LAND OF IMMIGRATION

WASHINGTON

Seattle Art Museum

100 University Street, Seattle, WA 98101-2902

📞: 206-625-8900   ▣ www.seattleartmuseum.org
Open: 10-5 Tu-Su, 10-9 Th, open Mo on Holidays   **Closed:** Mo, except Hols, THGV, 12/25, 1/1
Free Day: 1st Th, 1st Fr   ADM: Y   **Adult:** $7.00   **Children:** F (under 12)   **Students:** $5.00   **Seniors:** $5.00
  ♿ ℗ **Museum Shop**   ⫯⫯: Y
Group Tours: 206-654-3123   **Drop-In Tours:** 2 Tu-Su, 7 Th, Sp exh 1 Tu-Su, 6 Th   **Sculpture Garden**
Permanent Collection: AS; AF; NW NAT/AM; CONT; PHOT; EU: dec/art; NW/CONT

Designed by Robert Venturi, architect of the new wing of the National Gallery in London, this stunning new five story building is but one of the reasons for visiting the outstanding Seattle Art Museum. The new downtown location is conveniently located within walking distance of many of Seattle's most interesting landmarks including Pike Place Market, and Historic Pioneer Square. The Museum features 2 complete educational resource centers with interactive computer systems. **NOT TO BE MISSED:** NW Coast Native American Houseposts; 48'kenetic painted steel sculpture 'Hammering Man' by Jonathan Borofsky

ON EXHIBIT 1999

ONGOING   CONTEMPORARY NORTHWEST COAST BASKETRY
From the collection, a new case installation of masterworks by today's outstanding native weavers.

to 01/24/1999   THE PAVING OF PARADISE: A CENTURY OF PHOTOGRAPHS OF THE WESTERN LANDSCAPE
Photographs from the collection reflecting different notions of the West as a kind of paradise. Included are works by Adams, Jackson and Deal.

to 01/24/1999   GIFTS FROM THE GERBERS: MODERN PAINTINGS AND DRAWINGS
A selection of paintings and drawings including those by Kandinsky, Leger, and de Kooning.

to 03/14/1999   SILVER SERVERS
Contemporary silver servers from over 50 American and British silversmiths

08/20/1998 to 01/24/1999   DOCUMENTS NORTHWEST/THE PONCHO SERIES: WITNESS THE ART OF RQSS PALMER BEACHER AND BARBARA THOMAS
Works by two mid-career Seattle artists known for their highly imaginative, symbol laden imagery that brings personal perspectives to broad cultural issues

08/20/1998 to 01/24/1999   GEORGE TSUTAKAWA
A small memorial exhibition honoring a beloved Seattle artist who recently passed away.

08/27/1998 to 01/24/1999   ANNE GERBER EXHIBITION: CINDY SHERMAN
Works by the well known artist known for staged photographs using herself as model.

10/15/1998 to 01/10/1999   SEARCHING FOR ANCIENT EGYPT
From the display of the interior wall of a 4,300-year-old funerary chapel to an exquisite gold-covered mummy mask, this exhibition features more than 130 extraordinary objects from every major period of ancient Egypt. Many of those included have not been on public view for 30 years. *Catalog Will Travel*

02/18/1999 to 05/09/1999   CHUCK CLOSE
The full spectrum of Closes remarkable career is shown through some 80 paintings, drawings and photographs. His work has evolved over the years from harsh black and white images of uncanny scale and realism to colorful and richly patterned canvases of an almost abstract painterliness. *Catalog Will Travel*

03/04/1999 to 05/09/1999   THE VIRGINIA AND BAGLEY WRIGHT COLLECTION OF MODERN ART
Seattle residents whose collection is internationally renowned.

06/12/1999 to 08/29/1999   IMPRESSIONISM: PAINTINGS COLLECTED BY EUROPEAN MUSEUMS
An overview of the movement offering insight into acceptance by European dealers, museums and collectors. They turned it from objects of scandal to highly prized masterworks. Included are works by Gauguin, Manet, Sisley, Monet, Morisot, Pissarro, Renoir and Van Gogh. *Catalog Will Travel*

Seattle Asian Art Museum

Volunteer Park, 1400 East Prospect Street, Seattle, WA

✆: 206-625-8900   ◉ www.seattleartmuseum.org

Open: 10-5 Tu-Su, 10-9 Th   **Closed:** Mo, LEG/HOL!

Free Day: 1st Th, Sr 1st Fr, First Sa, Fr   ADM: Y   **Adult:** $3.00   **Children:** F, under 12

♿ ⓟ **Museum Shop** ⌙: Tea Garden ! for hours

Group Tours: 206-654-3123   **Drop-In Tours:** !   **Historic Building** Y

Permanent Collection: WONDERS OF CLAY AND FIRE: CHINESE CERAMICS THROUGH THE AGES (WITH PARTIAL ROTATION) A comprehensive survey of Chinese ceramic history from fifth millennium BC through 15th c AD

The historical preservation of the Carl Gould designed 1932 building (the first Art-Deco style art museum in the world) involved uniting all areas of the structure including additions of 1947, 1954, and 1955. Now a 'jewel box' with plush but tasteful interiors perfectly complementing the art of each nation. 900 0f the 7000 objects in the collection are on view.

ON EXHIBIT 1999

12/10/1998 to 04/04/1999   MASTERPIECES OF JAPANESE ART

Masterpieces of Japanese Art from the museum's collection including the 'Crow' screen, the 'Deer' scroll and the 'Hell of Shrieking Sounds' scroll.

04/29/1999 to 02/13/2000   MODERN MASTERS OF KYOTO: TRANSFORMATION OF JAPANESE PAINTING TRADITIONS 'NIHONGA' FROM THE GRIFFITH AND PATRICIA WAY COLLECTION

A third in a chronological series on Japanese painting. Featured are works from the late 19th into the 20th century. A full changeover will take place in October 1999.

SPOKANE

Cheney Cowles Museum

2316 W. First Avenue, Spokane, WA 99204

✆: 509-456-3931

Open: 10-5 Tu-Sa, 10-9 We, 1-5 Su   **Closed:** Mo, LEG/HOL!

Free Day: We, ½ price   ADM: Y   **Adult:** $4.00, Fam $10   **Children:** $2.50, 6-16   **Students:** $2.50   **Seniors:** $3.00

♿ ⓟ **Museum Shop   Group Tours   Drop-In Tours   Historic Building**

Permanent Collection: NW NAT/AM; REG; DEC/ART

The mission of the Cheney Cowles Museum is to actively engage the people of the Inland Northwest in life-long learning about regional history, visual arts, and American Indian and other cultures especially those specific to the region.

TACOMA

Tacoma Art Museum

12th & Pacific (downtown Tacoma), Tacoma, WA 98402

✆: 206-272-4258

Open: 10-5 Tu-Sa, 10-7 Th, 12-5 Su   **Closed:** Mo, 1/1, THGV, 12/25

Free Day: Tu   ADM: Y   **Adult:** $3.00   **Children:** F (under 12)   **Students:** $2.00   **Seniors:** $2.00

♿ ⓟ **Museum Shop   Group Tours   Drop-In Tours**

Permanent Collection: CONT/NW; AM: ptgs

The only comprehensive collection of the stained glass of Dale Chihuly in a public institution. **NOT TO BE MISSED:** Chihuly Retrospective Glass Collection

ON EXHIBIT 1999

through 1999   CHIHULY AT UNION STATION, 1717 Pacific Avenue, Tacoma.

WASHINGTON

Tacoma Public Library/Thomas Handforth Gallery

1102 Tacoma Avenue South, Tacoma, WA 98402

☎: 206-591-5666   ◙   www.tpl.lib.wa.us

Open: 9-9 Mo-Th, 9-6 Fr-Sa   **Closed:** Su, LEG/HOL!

♿ ℗ **Museum Shop**

Group Tours   Drop-In Tours   Historic Building Y

Permanent Collection: HISTORICAL; PHOT; ARTIFACTS

Built in 1903 as an original Andrew Carnegie Library, the Gallery has been serving the public since then with rotating exhibits by Pacific Northwest artists and touring educational exhibits **NOT TO BE MISSED:** Rare book room containing 750 prints including 'North American Indian', by Edward S. Curtice

WALLA WALLA

Donald Sheehan Art Gallery

900 Isaacs- Olin Hall, Walla Walla, WA 99362

☎: 509-527-5249

Open: 10-5 Tu-Fr, 1-4 Sa, Su   **Closed:** Mo, ACAD!

♿ ℗ **Museum Shop**

Group Tours   Drop-In Tours

Permanent Collection: SCROLLS; SCREENS; BUNRAKY PUPPETS; CER

The Sheehan Gallery administrates the Davis Collection of Oriental Art which is not on permanent display.!

CHARLESTON

Sunrise Museum

746 Myrtle Road, Charleston, WV 25314
: 304-344-8035   sunrise@citynet.net
Open: 11-5 We-Sa, 12-5 Su   **Closed:** Mo-Tu, LEG/HOL!
ADM: Y   **Adult:** $3.50   **Children:** $ **Students:** $2.50   **Seniors:** $2.50
&   P   **Museum Shop**
Group Tours   Drop-In Tours   Historic Building Y   **Sculpture Garden**
Permanent Collection: AM: ptgs, sculp, gr; SCI COLL

This multi media center occupies two historic mansions overlooking downtown Charleston. Featured are a Science Hall, Planetarium, and an art museum.

ON EXHIBIT 1999

02/06/1999 to 04/18/1999   FROM SHIP TO SHORE: MARINE PAINTING
Over 60 paintings, ranging from ship portraiture to ocean views, highlight the general fascination with marine culture since colonial times. *Will Travel*

05/01/1999 to 07/30/1999   THREE REALISTS: WORKS BY NELL BLAINE, SUSAN POFFENBARGER AND ANN SHREVE
Paintings by 3 contemporary realists will be on loan from the collection of Dr. Alfred Bader, a Milwaukee resident partial to 17th century Dutch painting.

05/01/1999 to 07/30/1999   AN INSTALLATION BY CHRIS DUTCH AND ROBIN HAMMER

HUNTINGTON

Huntington Museum of Art, Inc

2033 McCoy Road, Huntington, WV 25701-4999
: 304-529-2701   www.ianet.net/~hua
Open: 10-5 Tu-Sa, 12-5 Su   **Closed:** Mo, 1/1, 7/4, THGV, 12/25
&   P   **Museum Shop**
Group Tours   Drop-In Tours: 10:30, 11:30 Sa, 2,3 Su   **Historic Building** Y   **Sculpture Garden**
Permanent Collection: AM: ptgs, dec/art 18-20; GLASS; SILVER

The serene beauty of the museum complex on a lovely hilltop surrounded by nature trails, herb gardens, an outdoor amphitheater and a sculpture courtyard is enhanced by an extensive addition designed by the great architect Walter Gropius. The Museum is home to the state's only plant conservatory.

WISCONSIN

BELOIT

Wright Museum of Art
Affiliate Institution: Beloit College
Prospect at Bushnell, Beloit, WI 53511
☎: 608-363-2677 ◉ www.beloit.edu/~museum/index/index.html
Open: 9-5 Mo-Fr, 11-4 Sa, Su **Closed:** ACAD!
& ℗ **Museum Shop Group Tours Drop-In Tours**
Permanent Collection: AS; KOREAN: dec/art, ptgs, gr; HIST & CONT: phot

MADISON

Elvehjem Museum of Art
Affiliate Institution: University of Wisconsin-Madison
800 University Ave, Madison, WI 53706
☎: 608-263-2246
Open: 9-5 Tu-Fr, 11-5 Sa, Su **Closed:** 1/1, THGV, 12/24, 12/25
& ℗ **Museum Shop Group Tours Drop-In Tours**: !
Permanent Collection: AN/GRK: vases & coins; MIN.IND PTGS: Earnest C. & Jane Werner Watson Coll; JAP: gr (Van Vleck Coll); OR: dec/arts); RUSS & SOVIET: ptgs (Joseph E. Davies Coll)

More than 15,000 objects that date from 2300 B.C. to the present are contained in this unique university museum collection.

Madison Art Center
211 State Street, Madison, WI 53703
☎: 608-257-0158 ◉ http://users.aol.com/MadArtCtr/MadArtCt.htm
Open: 11-5 Tu-Th, 11-9 Fr, 10-9 Sa, 1-5 Su **Closed:** Mo, LEG/HOL!
& ℗ **Museum Shop Group Tours Drop-In Tours Historic Building**
Permanent Collection: AM: works on paper,ptgs,sculp; JAP; MEX; CONT

Located in the Old Capitol theatre, the Madison Art Center offers modern and contemporary art exhibitions and highlights from its permanent collections. **NOT TO BE MISSED:** 'Serenade' by Romare Bearden

ON EXHIBIT 1999

12/06/1998 to 02/07/1999 JOE WILFER: ACQUISITIONS FOR THE PERMANENT COLLECTION

03/07/1999 to 05/23/1999 TACITA DEAN

09/11/1999 to 11/14/1999 WISCONSIN TRIENNIAL

MANITOWOC

Rahr-West Art Museum
Park Street at North Eighth, Manitowoc, WI 54220
☎: 920-683-4501
Open: 10-4 Mo, Tu, Th, Fr, 10-8 We, 11-4 Sa, Su **Closed:** LEG/HOL!
Vol/Cont: & ℗
Museum Shop Group Tours Drop-In Tours Historic Building
Permanent Collection: AM: ptgs, dec/art 19; OR: ivory, glass; CONT: ptgs

Rahr-West Art Museum - continued

Built between 1891 & 1893, this Victorian mansion with its former parlors and bed chambers, carved woodwork and beamed ceiling provides an elegant setting for its fine collection. **NOT TO BE MISSED:** 'Birch and Pine Tree No 2', by Georgia O'Keeffe

ON EXHIBIT 1999

01/31/1999 to 02/14/1999	ART OF TABLESETTINGS 25TH ANNIVERSARY
04/11/1999 to 05/09/1999	PHILLIP KOCH: RECENT WORK
07/18/1999 to 08/29/1999	MIDWEST WATERCOLOR SOCIETY
09/12/1999 to 10/24/1999	FRED BERMAN
11/07/1999 to 12/05/1999	MIDWEST PHTOGRAPHY INVITATIONAL
11/21/1999 to 02/02/2000	CHRISTMAS IN THE MANSION
12/19/1999 to 01/09/2000	PERMANENT COLLECTIONS AND ACQUISITIONS

MILWAUKEE

Charles Allis Art Museum

1801 North Prospect Avenue, Milwaukee, WI 53202
☎: 414-278-8295
Open: 1-5 We Su, 7-9 We   **Closed:** LEG/HOL!
Vol/Cont: Y   ADM: Y   **Adult:** $2.00
  ♿ **Museum Shop   Group Tours   Drop-In Tours   Historic Building**
Permanent Collection: CH: porcelains; OR; AN/GRK; AN/R; FR: ptgs 19

With its diverse collection this museum is housed in a 1909 Tudor style house.

Milwaukee Art Museum

750 North Lincoln Memorial Drive, Milwaukee, WI 53202
☎: 414-224-3200   ▣ www.mam.org
Open: 10-5 Tu, We, Fr, Sa, 12-9 Th, 12-5 Su   **Closed:** Mo, 1/1, THGV, 12/25
ADM: Y   **Adult:** $5.00   **Children:** F (under 12)   **Students:** $3.00   **Seniors:** $3.00
♿ ℗ **Museum Shop**   ⑪ **Group Tours**: 414-224-3825   **Drop-In Tours   Historic Building   Sculpture Garden**
Permanent Collection: CONT: ptgs, sculp; GER; AM: folk art

The Milwaukee Museum features an exceptional collection housed in a 1957 landmark building by Eero Saarinen, which is cantilevered over the Lake Michigan shoreline. A dramatic addition designed by Santiago Calatrava is scheduled to open in 2000. **NOT TO BE MISSED:** Zurburan's 'St. Francis'

ON EXHIBIT 1999

ONGOING   THE MICHAEL AND JULIE HALL COLLECTION OF AMERICAN FOLK ART
After a cross country tour the renowned collection acquired by the Museum in 1989 will be presented in an ongoing exhibition.

11/20/1998 to 01/10/1999   HALF PAST AUTUMN: THE ART OF GORDON PARKS
All aspects of his varied career will be included in the first traveling Gorden Parks retrospective. Considered by many to be an American renaissance man, Parks, a filmmaker, novelist, poet and musician is best known as a photojournalist whose powerful images deliver messages of hope in the face of adversity. *Catalog Will Travel*

WISCONSIN

Milwaukee Art Museum - continued
01/29/1999 to 04/18/1999 SINNERS AND SAINTS, DARKNESS AND LIGHT: CARAVAGGIO AND HIS DUTCH AND FLEMISH FOLLOWERS IN AMERICA
A showcase of more than 35 paintings directly or indirectly influenced by the powerful works of Caravaggio, this exhibition will also address the history of how these paintings were acquired by museums in the US and Canada..ADM: Adults, $5.00; SR,STU, 3.00; under 12 F *Catalog Will Travel*

03/19/1999 to 05/30/1999 ESCAPE TO EDEN: THE PASTORAL VISION IN 18TH-CENTURY FRANCE

05/14/1999 to 08/08/1999 UNDER CONSTRUCTION: PHOTOGRAPHY, 1900-2000

09/10/1999 to 01/02/2000   THE LAST SHOW OF THE CENTURY: A HISTORY OF THE 20TH CENTURY THROUGH ITS ART

Patrick & Beatrice Haggerty Museum of Art
Affiliate Institution: Marquette University
13th & Clybourn, Milwaukee, WI 53233-1881
☎: 414-288-1669   ◙ www.mu.edu/haggerty
Open: 10-4:30 Mo-Sa, 12-5 Su, 10-8 Th   **Closed:** 1/1, EASTER, THGV, 12/25
Vol/Cont: Y
♿ **Museum Shop**
Group Tours: 414-288-5915   **Drop-In Tours   Sculpture Garden**
Permanent Collection: PTGS, DRWG, GR, SCULP, PHOT, DEC/ART 16-20; ASIAN, TRIBAL

Selections from the Old Master and modern collections are on exhibition continuously. The Museum also offers 10-12 temporary exhibitions per year

ON EXHIBIT 1999
PERMANENT   MODERN GALLERY:
20th century art from the collections including work by Dali, Lawrence, Man Ray and Nam June Paik.

PERMANENT   THE GREEN ROOM
Salon-style gallery hung with art from 16th-19th centuries by European Old Masters.

01/29/1998 to 03/14/1999   OSCAR WILDE

11/20/1998 to 01/31/1999   FENG MENGBO

12/03/1998 to 01/17/1999   RECENT ACQUISITIONS

02/12/1999 to 05/23/1999   CHILDREN IN ART
From Impressionism to contemporary art, a selection of drawings, paintings, and works on paper depicting children.

03/26/1999 to 05/02/1999   THE CULT OF RUINS: VISIONS OF ANTIQUITY IN THE EIGHTEENTH CENTURY
Will Travel

05/14/1999 to 07/04/1999   KENNETH KWINT

06/04/1999 to 08/08/1999   FIFTY YEARS OF CHINESE WOODBLOCK PRINTS

09/10/1999 to 10/24/1999   PROPHET WILLIAM BLACKMON

UWM Art Museum

3253 N. Downer Avenue, Milwaukee, WI 53211

☎: 414-226-6509

Open: 10-4 Tu-Fr, 12-8 We, 1-5 Sa, Su   **Closed:** Mo, LEG/HOL!

  Ⓟ   **Museum Shop   Group Tours   Drop-In Tours**

Permanent Collection: AM & EU: works on paper, gr; RUSS: icons; REG: 20

The museum works to provide its audience with an artistic cultural and historical experience unlike that offered by other art institutions in Milwaukee. It's three spaces on the campus provide the flexibility of interrelated programming.

Villa Terrace Decorative Arts Museum

2220 North Terrace Ave, Milwaukee, WI 53202

☎: 414-271-3656

Open: 12-5 We-Su   **Closed:** Mo-Tu, LEG/HOL!

ADM: Y   **Adult:** $2.00   **Children:** F (under 12)   **Students:** $2.00   **Seniors:** $2.00

  Ⓟ   **Museum Shop   Group Tours   Drop-In Tours   Historic Building**

Permanent Collection: DEC/ART; PTGS, SCULP, GR 15-20

Villa Terrace Decorative Arts Museum with its excellent and varied collections is located in a historic landmark building. **NOT TO BE MISSED:** "The Garden Renaissance Project" Help create a 16th century Italian Renaissance Garden

ON EXHIBIT 1999

01/14/1999 to 03/14/1999   THE GRAND AMERICAN AVENUE: 1850-1920

04/01/1999 to 05/16/1999   JOHN JAMES AUDUBON'S BIRDS OF AMERICA

07/18/1999 to 09/12/1999   ALLURE OF THE EAST: NEAR EASTERN DECORATIVE ARTS AND EUROPEAN ORIENTALIST PAINTINGS

The Touma Collection presents a fascinating survey of textiles, metalwork, pottery, and other decorative art forms displaying the mastery of ornament which blossomed under the influence of Islam in the Near East.   A look is offered from two perspectives: one the ideology that exists within a culture; and two, views of an alien culture by outsiders. *Will Travel*

10/10/1999 to 12/05/1999   100 YEARS OF VAN BRIGGLE POTTERY FROM THE COLORADO SPRINGS FINE ARTS CENTER *Will Travel*

OSHKOSH

Paine Art Center and Arboretum

1410 Algoma Blvd, Oshkosh, WI 54901

☎: 920-235-6903

Open: 11-4 Tu-Su, 11-7 Fr   **Closed:** Mo, LEG/HOL!

ADM: Y   **Adult:** $5.00   **Children:** F (under 12)   **Students:** $2.00   **Seniors:** $2.50

  Ⓟ   **Museum Shop**   ⑪: cafe open June-Sept

Group Tours: 920-235-6903, ext 21   **Drop-In Tours:** by appt   **Historic Building** Y   **Sculpture Garden**

Permanent Collection: FR & AM: ptgs, sculp, gr 19,20; OR: silk rugs, dec/art

Collections of paintings, sculpture and decorative objects in period room settings are featured in this historic 1920's Tudor Revival home surrounded by botanic gardens. **NOT TO BE MISSED:** 'The Bronco Buster', sculpture by Frederic Remington

Paine Art Center and Arboretum - continued

ON EXHIBIT 1999

10/18/1998 to 01/03/1999 TONES, IMPRESSIONS AND THE LANDSCAPE: AMERICAN WORKS FROM THE PAINE ART CENTER & ARBORETUM

01/15/1999 to 04/04/1999 SEND IN THE CLOWNS
The influence of the Italian "Commedia d'arte" in the design of Meissen and other European porcelain works.

04/16/1999 to 06/13/1999 MAYAN PROCESSION

06/27/1999 to 08/22/1999 UNFOLDING LIGHT: THE EVOLUTION OF TEN HOLOGRAPHERS
Holography is a process for recording images in three dimensions in which a laser is used as a light source. Invented in the 40's, it was more fully developed in the 60's. While it has many industrial and commercial applications, it also has creative properties which can be used to make works of art. Subjects explored by artists include portraits, still lifes, landscapes, etc..
Will Travel

RACINE

Charles A. Wustum Museum of Fine Arts

2519 Northwestern Ave, Racine, WI 53404

☎: 424-636-9177
Open: 11-5 Tu, We, Fr-Su, 11-9 Mo, Th, 1-5 Su   **Closed:** LEG/HOL!
Vol/Cont: Y
 ⓟ **Museum Shop**
Group Tours: Groups of six or more, 2 weeks notice   **Drop-In Tours   Historic Building   Sculpture Garden**
Permanent Collection: SCULP; WPA works on paper; Crafts

In an 1856 Italianate style building on acres of landscaped sculpture gardens you will find Racine's only fine arts museum. It primarily supports active, regional living artists.

ON EXHIBIT 1999

02/21/1999 to 04/17/1999 THE NUDE IN CLAY

02/21/1999 to 04/17/1999 EBENDORF, HANSSEN & GRANT: EPHEMERA AND RECENT WORK

05/30/1999 to 08/29/1999 MOCKING THE MASTERS: ARTISTS LOOK TO THE PAST FOR INSPIRATION

11/14/1999 to 12/30/1999 WATERCOLOR WISCONSIN '99

SHEBOYGAN

John Michael Kohler Arts Center

608 New York Avenue, PO Box 489, Sheboygan, WI 53082-0489

☎: 920-458-6144
Open: 10-5 Mo-We, Fr, 10-9 Th, 12-5 Sa, Su   **Closed:** 12/31, 1/1, EASTER, MEM/DAY, THGV, 12/24, 12/25
 ⓟ **Museum Shop   Group Tours   Drop-In Tours**: !   **Historic Building**
Permanent Collection: CONT: cer; DEC/ART

This multi-cultural center is located in the 1860's villa of John Michael Kohler, founder of the plumbing manufacturing company. Special exhibitions at the Center offer unique perspectives on art forms, artists, and various artistic concepts that have received little exposure elsewhere. The facility expansion will take place in all of 1998. The theme of all exhibitions will relate to the changes – installations that are based on process and the concepts of building, improvisation, and collaboration. Each exhibition will originate in a previous component.

WAUSAU

Leigh Yawkey Woodson Art Museum
700 North Twelfth Street, Wausau, WI 54403-5007
📞: 715-845-7010   ◉ www.lywam.com
Open: 9-4 Tu-Fr, 12-5 Sa, Su   **Closed:** Mo, LEG/HOL!
  ♿ ⓟ **Museum Shop**
Group Tours   **Drop-In Tours**: ! 9am-4pm   **Sculpture Garden**
Permanent Collection: GLASS 19,20; STUDIO GLASS; PORCELAIN; WILDLIFE; ptgs, sculp

An English style mansion surrounded by gracious lawns and sculpture gardens. A new sculpture garden features permanent installations and biennially the garden will exhibit 10-15 temporary pieces.

ON EXHIBIT 1999

01/09/1999 to 03/21/1999   CALIDO: CONTEMPORARY WARM GLASS

03/27/1999 to 06/06/1999   ART AND THE ANIMAL

06/23/2001 to 08/26/2001   THE JOHN A. AND MARGERET HILL COLLECTION OF AMERICAN WESTERN ART
The collection concentrates on works of the 20th c. with fine examples from the Taos Society of Artists, the Santa Fe School, and the American Regionalists. These included Berninghaus, Couse and Blumenschein as well as Ufer, Benton, Curry and Grant Wood.

06/12/1999 to 08/29/1999   AMERICA SEEN: PEOPLE AND PLACE
The images on view by Grant Wood, Norman Rockwell, John Stuart Curry, Thomas Hart Benton and other giants of American art working between the 1920's through the 1950's, document two world wars, the Great Depression, the New Deal, the growth of the American city and the nostalgia for simple rural life.

09/11/1999 to 11/14/1999   BIRDS IN ART
In the 24th annual presentation of "Birds in Art", artists from around the world interpret the wonder of flight and the marvel of wingtips.

11/20/1999 to 02/13/2000   DOWN UNDER/OVER HERE: ORIGINAL AMERICAN AND AUSTRALIAN CHILDREN'S BOOK ILLUSTRATION
From two continents, the 60 works on view, created by the best children's book illustrations of the 20th century, offer the visitor the opportunity to compare the ways in which artists from each culture portray the people, places and customs in books best loved by both Australians and Americans.

WEST BEND

West Bend Art Museum
300 South 6th Ave, West Bend, WI 53095
📞: 414-334-9638   ◉ www.hnet/volunteer/art.htm
Open: 10-4:30 We-Sa, 1-4:30 Su   **Closed:** Mo, Tu, LEG/HOL!
  ♿ ⓟ **Museum Shop**
Group Tours   **Drop-In Tours:** 8am-4:30pm   **Sculpture Garden**
Permanent Collection: WISCONSIN ART FROM EURO-AMERICAN SETTLEMENT TO 1950

This community art center and museum is dedicated to the work of Wisconsin's leading artists from Euro-American settlement to the present and features changing exhibitions of regional, national and international art. **NOT TO BE MISSED:** The colossal 1889 painting "The Flagellants" measuring approximately 14' x 26' first exhibited in the US at the 1893 Chicago Worlds Fair, The Columbian Exposition.

WISCONSIN

West Bend Art Museum - continued

ON EXHIBIT 1999

02/24/1999 to 04/04/1999   **WORKS FROM THE POLAROID COLLECTION**

04/07/1999 to 05/09/1999   **BEYOND THE HORIZON: SUDLOW AND JACOBSHAGEN**

05/12/1999 to 06/13/1999   **WISCONSIN WATERCOLOR SOCIETY**

06/16/1999 to 08/08/1999   **THE SCULPTOR'S LINE: HENRY MOORE PRINTS**
Prints and maquettes by Moore will be displayed with several of his full-size sculptures.

08/11/1999 to 09/19/1999   **WILLIAM WEIDNER & DENISE PRESNEL-WEIDNER**

09/22/1999 to 10/31/1999   **WISCONSIN DESIGNER CRAFTS COUNCIL**

11/03/1999 to 12/12/1999   **SHEILA HELD, FIBER**

12/15/1999 to 01/23/2000   **WASHINGTON COUNTY AND FRIENDS EXHIBITION**

01/13/1999 to 02/21/1999   **IMAGES OF A NEW ENGLAND SEACOAST**
The extraordinary light, topography, and geography of the New England Coast drew artists to the Cape Ann shore. To this day many artists teach in their studios and out of doors, for there is no "lonely garret" syndrome on the island. Together they have left a collective portrait of a New England seashore and its people.

BIG HORN

Bradford Brinton Memorial Museum

239 Brinton Road, Big Horn, WY 82833
📞: 307-672-3173
Open: 9:30-5 daily May 15-LAB/DAY, other months by appt
ADM: Y   **Adult:** $3.00   **Children:** F (under 12)   **Students:** $2.00   **Seniors:** $2.00
  ᕦ Ⓟ **Museum Shop   Group Tours   Drop-In Tours   Historic Building**
Permanent Collection: WESTERN ART; DEC/ART; NAT/AM: beadwork

Important paintings by the best known Western artists are shown in a fully furnished 20 room ranch house built in 1892 and situated at the foot of the Big Horn Mountain. **NOT TO BE MISSED:** 'Custer's Fight on the Little Big Horn', by Frederic Remington

CASPER

Nicolaysen Art Museum

400 East Collins Drive, Casper, WY 82601-2815
📞: 307-235-5247
Open: 10-5 Tu-Su, 10-8 Th   **Closed:** Mo, 1/1; THGV; 12/24; 12/25
Free Day: 4-8 1st & 3rd Th   **ADM:** Y   **Adult:** $2.00   **Children:** $1.00 under 12   **Students:** $1.00   **Seniors:** $2.00
  ᕦ Ⓟ **Museum Shop   Group Tours   Drop-In Tours:** !   **Historic Building**
Permanent Collection: REGIONAL CONTEMPORARY

The roots of this Museum reside in the commitment of Wyoming people to the importance of having art and culture as an integral part life.   **NOT TO BE MISSED:** The Discovery Center, an integral part of the museum, complements the educational potential of the exhibitions

CHEYENNE

Wyoming State Museum

Barrett Building, 2301 Central Ave., Cheyenne, WY 82002
📞: 307-777-7022 (or7024)
Open: 8:00-5 Mo-Fr   **Closed:** Su, LEG/HOL!
  ᕦ Ⓟ **Museum Shop   Group Tours   Drop-In Tours   Sculpture Garden**
Permanent Collection: PLAINS INDIAN COLLECTION; REG/W & CONT

The Wyoming State Museum is part of the Capital Complex area which includes the historic State Capitol building and the Governor's Mansion. **NOT TO BE MISSED:** Wyoming in WWII

CODY

Buffalo Bill Historical Center

720 Sheridan Ave., Cody, WY 82414
📞: 307-587-4771   ◼ www.TrueWest.com/BBHC
Open: 7am-8pm daily June-Sep; 8-5 daily Oct; 8-8 daily May; 10-2 Th-Mo Nov-Mar; 10-5 daily in April
Free Day: 1st Su in May   **ADM:** Y   **Adult:** $8.00   **Children:** 6-12 $2.00   **Students:** $4.00   **Seniors:** $6.50
  ᕦ Ⓟ **Museum Shop** 𝔦: "Great Entertainer Eatery"   **Group Tours   Drop-In Tours   Sculpture Garden**
Permanent Collection: WESTERN/ART: 19,20; AM: firearms; CULTURAL HISTORY OF THE PLAINS INDIANS; WESTERN AMERICAN HISTORY

WYOMING

Buffalo Bill Historical Center - continued
The complex includes the Buffalo Bill, Plains Indian, and Cody Firearms museums as well as the Whitney Gallery which contains outstanding paintings of the American West by such artists as George Catlin, Albert Bierstadt, Frederic Remington and contemporary artists including Harry Jackson and Fritz Scholder. **NOT TO BE MISSED:** The Whitney Gallery of Western Art

---

COLTER BAY

Grand Teton National Park, Colter Bay Indian Arts Museum
Colter Bay, WY 83012
☏: 307-739-3594
Open: 8-5 daily 5/13-6/1 & Sept, 8-8 daily 6/1-LAB/DAY, closed 10/1-5/13   **Closed:** Closed 10/1-5/13
& ℗ **Museum Shop   Group Tours   Drop-In Tours**
Permanent Collection: NAT/AM: artifacts, beadwork, basketry, pottery, musical instruments

Organized into categories and themes, the Davis I. Vernon collection of Indian art housed in this museum is a spectacular assembly of many art forms including porcupine quillwork, beadwork, basketry, pottery, masks, and musical instruments. **NOT TO BE MISSED:** Sitting Bull's beaded blanket strip,(Sioux, South Dakota, ca. 1875

JACKSON HOLE

National Museum of Wildlife Art
2820 Rungius Road, Jackson Hole, WY 83002
☏: 307-733-5771   ▣ www.infoc.wildlifeart.org
Open: 9-5 daily   **Closed:** 1/1, THGV, 12/25
ADM: Y   **Adult:** $6.00   **Children:** under 6 free   **Students:** $5.00   **Seniors:** $5.00
& ℗ **Museum Shop**   ❢❢: café   **Group Tours**   **Drop-In Tours**: daily 2pm
Permanent Collection: FINE WILDLIFE ART

One of the few museums in the country to feature wildlife, the collection is styled to sensitize visitors to wildlife and includes notable explorer, sporting and wildlife artists. PLEASE NOTE: The museum offers special admission rates for families. **NOT TO BE MISSED:** Works by Carl Rungius

---

ROCK SPRINGS

Community Fine Arts Center
Affiliate Institution: Rock Springs Library
400 "C" Street, Rock Springs, WY 82901
☏: 307-362-6212   ▣ under construction
Open: 9-12 & 1-5 Mo=-Fr; We 6-9; 10-12 & 1-5 Sa   **Closed:** Su, LEG/HOL!
& ℗ **Museum Shop   Group Tours   Drop-In Tours   Historic Building**
Permanent Collection: AM: 19, 20

The art gallery houses the nationally acclaimed Rock Springs High School Collection, and is owned by the school district. **NOT TO BE MISSED:** Loren McIver's "Fireplace", the first American women to exhibit at the Venice Biennial (1962); Norman Rockwell's "Willie Gillis: New Year's Eve" and Grandma Moses's "Staunton, Virginia"; 20th century American Art Originals.

ON EXHIBIT 1999
06/15/1999 to 07/31/1999   NATIONAL WATERCOLOR SOCIETY

Selected Listing of Traveling Exhibitions

100 MASTERPIECES FROM THE VITRA DESIGN MUSEUM
    09/18/1999 to 12/12/1999   Columbia Museum of Arts, Columbia, SC
    04/03/1999 to 06/27/1999   Phoenix Art Museum, Phoenix, AZ
    01/06/2000 to 04/16/2000   Allentown Art Museum, Allentown, PA

2000 BC: THE BRUCE CONNER STORY PART II
    10/10/1999 to 01/02/2000   Walker Art Center, Minneapolis, MN
    05/21/2000 to 07/30/2000   Fine Arts Museums of San Francisco, San Francisco, CA

A RENAISSANCE TREASURY: THE FLAGG COLLECTION OF EUROPEAN DECORATIVE ARTS AND SCULPTURE
    12/10/1998 to 03/14/1999   Smith College Museum of Art, Northampton, MA
    07/11/1999 to 09/12/1999   Memphis Brooks Museum of Art, Memphis, TN
    10/05/1999 to 12/05/1999   Iris and B. Gerald Cantor Center for the Visual Arts at Stanford University, Stanford, CA

A TALE OF TWO CITIES: EUGENE ATGET'S PARIS AND BERENICE ABBOTT'S NEW YORK
    01/28/1999 to 03/21/1999   Bowdoin College Museum of Art, Brunswick, ME
    08/1999 to 10/31/1999   University of Kentucky Art Museum, Lexington, KY

A TASTE FOR SPLENDOR: TREASURES FROM THE HILLWOOD MUSEUM
    11/21/1998 to 02/07/1999   Huntsville Museum of Art, Huntsville, AL
    02/27/1999 to 05/09/1999   Kalamazoo Institute of Arts, Kalamazoo, MI
    05/29/1999 to 08/08/1999   San Antonio Museum of Art, San Antonio, TX
    09/19/1999 to 11/28/1999   Dixon Gallery & Gardens, Memphis, TN

A WINDING RIVER: JOURNEY OF CONTEMPORARY ART IN VIETNAM
    01/1999   George E. Ohr Arts and Cultural Center, Biloxi, MS
    07/01/1999 to 09/30/1999   Bowers Museum of Cultural Art, Santa Ana, CA

AFTER THE PHOTO-SECESSION: AMERICAN PICTORIAL PHOTOGRAPHY, 1910-1955
    01/19/1999 to 03/11/1999   William Benton Museum of Art, Connecticut State Art Museum, Storrs, CT
    04/24/1999 to 07/11/1999   Laguna Art Museum, Laguna Beach, CA
    08/17/99 to 10/17/99   McNay Art Museum, San Antonio, TX

ALL THAT IS GLORIOUS AROUND US: PAINTINGS FROM THE HUDSON RIVER SCHOOL
    03/13/1999 to 06/27/1999   Worcester Art Museum, Worcester, MA
    04/14/1999 to 09/12/1999   National Academy Museum and School of Fine Arts, New York, NY

ALL THINGS BRIGHT AND BEAUTIFUL: CALIFORNIA IMPRESSIONIST PAINTINGS FROM THE IRVINE MUSEUM
    10/18/1998 to 01/24/1999   Dixon Gallery & Gardens, Memphis, TN
    03/20/1999 to 05/30/1999   Oakland Museum of California, Oakland, CA

ALLURE OF THE EAST: NEAR EASTERN DECORATIVE ARTS AND EUROPEAN ORIENTALIST PAINTINGS
    02/14/1999 to 04/11/1999   Mulvane Art Museum, Topeka, KS
    07/18/1999 to 09/12/1999   Villa Terrace Decorative Arts Museum, Milwaukee, WI
    01/09/2000 to 03/05/2000   Columbia Museum of Arts, Columbia, SC
    03/26/2000 to 05/28/2000   Arnot Art Museum, Elmira, NY

ALPHONSE MUCHA: THE FLOWERING OF ART NOUVEAU
    01/31/1999 to 03/28/1999   North Carolina Museum of Art, Raleigh, NC
    04/24/1999 to 06/20/1999   Philbrook Museum of Art Inc, Tulsa, OK
    06/09/1999 to 09/26/1999   Nevada Museum of Art/E. L. Weigand Gallery, Reno, NV

AMERICA SEEN: PEOPLE AND PLACE
    01/21/1999 to 03/14/1999   Charles H. MacNider Museum, Mason City, IA
    11/28/1999 to 01/16/2000   Scottsdale Museum of Contemporary Arts, Scottsdale, AZ
    06/12/99 to 08/29/99   Leigh Yawkey Woodson Art Museum, Wausau, WI

Selected Listing of Traveling Exhibitions

AMERICAN IMPRESSIONISM FROM THE SHELDON MEMORIAL ART GALLERY
04/18/1999 to 07/11/1999   Columbus Museum, Columbus, GA
09/13/1999 to 01/03/2000   Samuel P. Harn Museum of Art, Gainesville, FL

AMERICAN LANDSCAPES FROM THE PAINE ART CENTER & ARBORETUM
09/05/1999 to 10/24/1999   R. W. Norton Art Gallery, Shreveport, LA
04/02/2000 to 05/21/2000   Museum of the Southwest, Midland, TX

AN EXPRESSIONIST IN PARIS: THE PAINTINGS OF CHAIM SOUTINE
09/27/1998 to 01/03/1999   Los Angeles County Museum of Art, Los Angeles, CA
02/21/1999 to 05/02/1999   Cincinnati Art Museum, Cincinnati, OH

ANCIENT GOLD: THE WEALTH OF THE THRACIANS, TREASURES FROM THE REPUBLIC OF BULGARIA
10/30/1998 to 04/04/1999   New Orleans Museum of Art, New Orleans, LA
04/03/1999 to 06/06/1999   Museum of Fine Arts, Boston, Boston, MA
06/27/1999 to 08/29/1999   Detroit Institute of Arts, Detroit, MI
01/17/99 to 03/14/99   Memphis Brooks Museum of Art, Memphis, TN

ANDY WARHOL'S ENDANGERED SPECIES
01/23/1999 to 03/15/1999   Contemporary Art Center of Virginia, Virginia Beach, VA
07/02/1999 to 09/19/1999   Hudson River Museum, Yonkers, NY

ART AND NATURE: THE HUDSON RIVER SCHOOL
05/15/1999 to 07/04/1999   Museum of Art, Fort Lauderdale, Ft. Lauderdale, FL

10/15/1999 to 12/19/1999   Hudson River Museum, Yonkers, NY

ART AND THE ANIMAL
03/27/1999 to 06/06/1999   Leigh Yawkey Woodson Art Museum, Wausau, WI
11/15/2001 to 01/15/2002   Sioux City Art Center, Sioux City, IA

ART PATRONAGE IN TAOS, NEW MEXICO
05/16/1999 to 07/18/1999   Gilcrease Museum, Tulsa, OK
08/22/1999 to 11/14/1999   Snite Museum of Art, Notre Dame, IN

ARTIST/AUTHOR: THE BOOK AS ART SINCE 1980
10/10/1998 to 01/03/1999   Museum of Contemporary Art, Chicago, IL
02/18/1999 to 04/04/1999   Lowe Art Museum, Coral Gables, FL

BEARING WITNESS: CONTEMPORARY WORKS BY AFRICAN AMERICAN WOMEN ARTISTS
11/04/1998 to 01/07/1999   Gibbes Museum of Art, Charleston, SC
06/26/1999 to 08/15/1999   Museum of Fine Arts, Houston, Houston, TX
09/07/1999 to 10/10/1999   Museum of Art, Pullman, WA

BERENICE ABBOTT'S CHANGING NEW YORK 1935-1939
10/22/1998 to 01/19/1999   National Museum of Women in the Arts, Washington, DC
04/10/1999 to 05/30/1999   Frederick R. Weisman Art Museum, University of Minnesota, Minneapolis, MN

BILL VIOLA
02/14/1999 to 04/15/1999   Dallas Museum of Art, Dallas, TX
06/04/1999 to 09/07/1999   San Francisco Museum of Modern Art, San Francisco, CA
10/16/1999 to 01/16/2000   Art Institute of Chicago, Chicago, IL

BIRDS IN ART
01/14/1999 to 02/28/1999   Museum of the Southwest, Midland, TX
01/29/2000 to 03/26/2000   Saginaw Art Museum, Saginaw, MI
09/11/99 to 11/14/99   Leigh Yawkey Woodson Art Museum, Wausau, WI

400

Selected Listing of Traveling Exhibitions

BLURRING THE BOUNDARIES: INSTALLATION ART 1970-1996
01/30/1999 to 05/02/1999   John and Mable Ringling Museum of Art, Sarasota, FL
05/28/1999 to 08/29/1999   Scottsdale Museum of Contemporary Arts, Scottsdale, AZ
05/20/1999 to 08/13/2000   San Jose Museum of Art, San Jose, CA

BRASSEI: THE EYE OF PARIS
04/13/1999 to 07/04/1999   Getty Center, Los Angeles, CA
10/17/1999 to 01/16/2000   National Gallery of Art, Washington, DC

BRICE MARDEN: WORK OF THE 1990'S PAINTINGS, DRAWINGS AND PRINTS
02/14/1999 to 04/25/1999   Dallas Museum of Art, Dallas, TX
05/27/1999 to 09/06/1999   Hirshhorn Museum and Sculpture Garden, Washington, DC

CANTOS PARALELOS: VISUAL PARODY IN CONTEMPORARY ARGENTINE ART
01/16/1999 to 03/07/1999   Jack S. Blanton Museum of Art, Austin, TX
07/22/1999 to 10/03/1999   Phoenix Art Museum, Phoenix, AZ

CATHERINE MCCARTHY
01/15/1999 to 03/21/1999   Kemper Museum of Contemporary Art, Kansas City, MO
09/25/1999 to 01/10/2000   San Jose Museum of Art, San Jose, CA

CHOKWE! ART AND INITIATION OF CHOKWE AND RELATED PEOPLES
11/01/1998 to 01/03/1999   Birmingham Museum of Art, Birmingham, AL
06/13/1999 to 09/05/1999   Baltimore Museum of Art, Baltimore, MD
10/24/1999 to 01/16/2000   Minneapolis Institute of Arts, Minneapolis, MN

CHUCK CLOSE
10/15/1998 to 01/10/1999   Hirshhorn Museum and Sculpture Garden, Washington, DC
02/18/1999 to 05/09/1999   Seattle Art Museum, Seattle, WA

COLLABORATIONS: WILLIAM ALLAN, ROBERT HUDSON, WILLIAM WILEY
01/11/1999 to 02/21/1999   Museum of Art, Pullman, WA
04/03/1999 to 06/13/1999   Scottsdale Museum of Contemporary Arts, Scottsdale, AZ

COLORPRINT USA
11/04/1998 to 01/10/1999   Greenville County Museum of Art, Greenville, SC
03/07/1999 to 04/11/1999   Anchorage Museum of History and Art, Anchorage, AK

COMMON MAN, MYTHIC VISION: THE PAINTINGS OF BEN SHAHN
11/08/1998 to 03/07/1999   Jewish Museum, New York, NY
03/28/1999 to 06/27/1999   Allentown Art Museum, Allentown, PA
07/25/1999 to 10/31/1999   Detroit Institute of Arts, Detroit, MI

CONSUELO KANAGA: AN AMERICAN PHOTOGRAPHER
11/01/1998 to 01/03/1999   Samuel P. Harn Museum of Art, Gainesville, FL
01/19/1999 to 04/18/1999   Montclair Art Museum, Montclair, NJ

CROSSING BOUNDARIES: CONTEMPORARY ART QUILTS
02/28/1999 to 04/18/1999   George Walter Vincent Smith Art Museum, Springfield, MA
02/28/1999 to 04/18/1999   Museum of Fine Arts, Springfield, MA
05/09/1999 to 06/27/1999   Dane G. Hansen Memorial Museum, Logan, KS

CROSSING THE THRESHOLD
01/26/1999 to 03/07/1999   University Art Museum, Albany, NY
11/13/1999 to 02/06/2000   Mississippi Museum of Art, Jackson, MS
03/31/2001 to 05/27/2001   Sioux City Art Center, Sioux City, IA

Selected Listing of Traveling Exhibitions

DALE CHIHULY: SEAFORMS
06/22/1999 to 09/12/1999   Palmer Museum of Art, University Park, PA
10/10/1999 to 01/02/2000   Indianapolis Museum of Art - Columbus Gallery, Columbus, IN

DANCING AT THE LOUVRE: FAITH RINGOLD'S FRENCH COLLECTION AND OTHER STORY QUILTS
09/30/1998 to 12/26/1998   New Museum of Contemporary Art, New York, NY
01/27/1999 to 04/11/1999   Baltimore Museum of Art, Baltimore, MD

DIEGO RIVERA: ART AND REVOLUTION
09/12/1999 to 11/28/1999   Dallas Museum of Art, Dallas, TX
02/21/1999 to 05/02/1999   Cleveland Museum of Art, Cleveland, OH

DOWN FROM THE SHIMMERING SKY: MASKS OF THE NORTHWEST COAST
04/11/1999 to 07/11/1999   Portland Art Museum, Portland, OR
08/20/1999 to 11/07/1999   Gilcrease Museum, Tulsa, OK

EDWARD HOPPER: THE WATERCOLORS
01/30/1999 to 03/25/1999   Montgomery Museum of Fine Arts, Montgomery, AL
10/22/1999 to 01/03/2000   National Museum of American Art-Renwick Gallery -, Washington, DC

EL ALMA DEL PUEBLO: SPANISH FOLK ART AND ITS TRANSFORMATION IN THE AMERICAS
09/18/1998 to 12/31/1998   Americas Society, New York, NY
05/08/1999 to 07/25/1999   Crocker Art Museum, Sacramento, CA

ELLSWORTH KELLEY: THE EARLY DRAWINGS, 1948-1955
03/06/1999 to 05/16/1999   Arthur M. Sackler Museum, Cambridge, MA
03/06/1999 to 05/15/1999   Fogg Art Museum, Cambridge, MA
06/12/1999 to 08/15/1999   High Museum of Art, Atlanta, GA
09/11/1999 to 12/05/1999   Art Institute of Chicago, Chicago, IL

FABRIZIO PLEZZI
11/08/1998 to 01/31/1999   Museum of Contemporary Art, San Diego, La Jolla, CA
11/08/1998 to 01/31/1999   Museum of Contemporary Art, San Diego, La Jolla, CA

FOUR OBJECTS; FOUR ARTISTS; TEN YEARS
02/19/1999 to 04/09/1999   Trout Gallery, Weiss Center for the Arts, Carlisle, PA

09/05/99 to 10/31/99   Evansville Museum of Art, Evansville, IN
11/12/1999 to 01/23/2000   Philip and Muriel Berman Museum of Art at Ursinus College, Collegeville, PA

FRANCIS BACON: THE PAPAL PORTRAITS
01/17/1999 to 03/28/1999   Museum of Contemporary Art, San Diego, La Jolla, CA
01/17/1999 to 03/28/1999   Museum of Contemporary Art, San Diego, La Jolla, CA

FRENCH PHOTOGRAPHER IN DALAMA, SWEDEN, 1910/ AN ETHNOGRAPHIC VIEW
08/1999 to 09/1999   Nordic Heritage Museum, Seattle, WA
06/02/1999 to 07/28/1999   Birger Sandzen Memorial Gallery, Lindsborg, KS

FROM SHIP TO SHORE: MARINE PAINTING
07/24/1999 to 12/05/1999   Mint Museim of Art, Charlotte, NC
01/08/2000 to 03/05/2000   Montgomery Museum of Fine Arts, Montgomery, AL
02/06/99 to 04/18/99   Sunrise Museum, Charleston, WV

FULL DE DECK ART QUILTS
02/06/1999 to 03/21/1999   Indianapolis Museum of Art - Columbus Gallery, Columbus, IN
06/12/1999 to 07/25/1999   Pensacola Museum of Art, Pensacola, FL

GUSTAVE MOREAU
02/13/1999 to 04/25/1999   Art Institute of Chicago, Chicago, IL
06/07/1999 to 09/05/1999   Metropolitan Museum of Art, New York, NY

HALF PAST AUTUMN: THE ART OF GORDON PARKS
11/20/1998 to 01/10/1999   Milwaukee Art Museum, Milwaukee, WI
02/07/1999 to 04/25/1999   Detroit Institute of Arts, Detroit, MI
05/24/1999 to 08/08/1999   Edwin A. Ulrich Museum of Art, Wichita, KS
10/28/1999 to 01/09/2000   Norton Museum of Art, West Palm Beach, FL
02/05/2000 to 04/09/2000   Michael C. Carlos Museum, Atlanta, GA

HERB RITTS: WORK
02/06/1999 to 05/02/1999   Museum of Art, Fort Lauderdale, Ft. Lauderdale, FL
11/05/1999 to 01/28/2000   Kemper Museum of Contemporary Art, Kansas City, MO

HISTORY OF WOMEN IN PHILADELPHIA ART
03/01/1999 to 02/28/1999   Richmond Art Museum, Richmond, IN
09/2000 to 12/2000   Woodmere Art Museum, Philadelphia, PA

HOOSIER ARTISTS IN MUNICH: DRAWINGS AND PAINTINGS BY ADAMS, FORSYTH , RICHARDS AND STEELE
07/17/1999 to 09/26/1999   Indianapolis Museum of Art - Columbus Gallery, Columbus, IN

10/17/1999 to 09/26/1999   Indianapolis Museum of Art, Indianapolis, IN

HUNG LIU: A SURVEY 1988-1998
04/08/1999 to 06/06/1999   Bowdoin College Museum of Art, Brunswick, ME
09/19/1998 to 07/28/1999   Ackland Art Museum, Chapel Hill, NC

IKAT: SPLENDID SILKS FROM CENTRAL ASIA
02/07/1999 to 05/16/1999   Jewish Museum, New York, NY
09/30/1999 to 01/09/2000   Art Institute of Chicago, Chicago, IL

IMAGES OF THE SPIRIT: PHOTOGRAPHS BY GRACIELA ITURBIDE
02/28/1999 to 05/04/1999   San Jose Museum of Art, San Jose, CA
05/21/1999 to 08/29/1999   Mexican Fine Arts Center Museum, Chicago, IL
06/2000 to 09/2000   National Museum of Women in the Arts, Washington, DC

IMPRESSIONISM: PAINTINGS COLLECTED BY EUROPEAN MUSEUMS
02/27/1999 to 05/16/1999   High Museum of Art, Atlanta, GA
06/12/99 to 08/29/99   Seattle Art Museum, Seattle, WA

INNUENDO NON TROPPO: THE WORK OF GREGORY BARSAMIAN
01/22/1999 to 03/21/1999   Arkansas Arts Center, Little Rock, AR
04/16/1999 to 06/25/2000   San Jose Museum of Art, San Jose, CA
04/17/1999 to 06/27/1999   Polk Museum of Art, Lakeland, FL

INSIDE OUT: NEW CHINESE ART
09/15/1998 to 01/17/1999   Asia Society, New York, NY
02/26/1999 to 06/01/1999   San Francisco Museum of Modern Art, San Francisco, CA

INTERACTION OF CULTURES: INDIAN AND WESTERN PAINTING (1710-1910) FROM THE EHRENFELD COLLECTION
06/26/1999 to 08/22/1999   Fresno Art Museum, Fresno, CA
09/16/1999 to 11/07/1999   Honolulu Academy of Arts, Honolulu, HI
11/26/1999 to 01/23/2000   Cummer Museum of Art & Gardens, Jacksonville, FL

Selected Listing of Traveling Exhibitions

JOHN HENRY TWACHTMAN: AN AMERICAN IMPRESSIONIST
02/26/1999 to 05/21/1999   High Museum of Art, Atlanta, GA
06/06/1999 to 09/05/1999   Cincinnati Art Museum, Cincinnati, OH
10/09/1999 to 01/02/2000   Pennsylvania Academy of the Fine Arts, Philadelphia, PA

JOHN SINGER SARGENT
02/21/1999 to 05/31/1999   National Gallery of Art, Washington, DC
06/23/1999 to 09/26/1999   Museum of Fine Arts, Boston, Boston, MA

JOSEPH CORNELL/MARCEL DUCHAMP: IN RESONANCE
10/03/1998 to 12/06/1998   Philadelphia Museum of Art, Philadelphia, PA
01/29/1999 to 05/16/1999   Menil Collection, Houston, TX

JOSIAH MCELHENY
01/22/1999 to 04/25/1999   Isabella Stewart Gardner Museum, Boston, MA
01/29/99 to 05/30/99   Maryhill Museum of Art, Goldendale, WA

JULIA MARGARET CAMERON'S WOMEN
Fall 1999/   San Francisco Museum of Modern Art, San Francisco, CA
09/19/1998 to 01/10/1999   Art Institute of Chicago, Chicago, IL
winter 199901/27/1999 to 05/04/1999   Museum of Modern Art, New York, NY

LAND OF THE WINGED HORSEMEN: ART IN POLAND, 1571-1764
03/03/1999 to 05/09/1999   Walters Art Gallery, Baltimore, MD
06/05/1999 to 09/06/1999   Art Institute of Chicago, Chicago, IL
03/25/2000 to 06/18/2000   Philbrook Museum of Art Inc, Tulsa, OK

LARGE DRAWINGS FROM THE ARKANSAS ARTS CENTER FOUNDATION COLLECTION
01/10/1999 to 03/07/1999   Columbus Museum, Columbus, GA
04/04/1999 to 05/30/1999   Dahl Fine Arts Center, Rapid City, SD
09/11/1999 to 11/07/1999   Cedar Rapids Museum of Art, Cedar Rapids, IA
12/11/1999 to 02/06/2000   Hunter Museum of American Art, Chattanooga, TN

LESLIE LERNER:THE IMAGINED CITY
08/1999 to 09/1999   USF Contemporary Art Museum, Tampa, FL
08/1999 to 09/1999   Palo Alto Cultural Center, Palo Alto, CA

MAPPING THE WEST
01/17/1999 to 02/28/1999   Snite Museum of Art, Notre Dame, IN
03/13/1999 to 04/25/1999   Maier Museum of Art, Lynchburg, VA

MARSDEN HARTLEY: AMERICAN MODERN
01/22/1999 to 03/22/1999   Fred Jones Jr. Museum of Art, Norman, OK
04/11/1999 to 06/20/1999   Parrish Art Museum, Southampton, NY
08/15/1999 to 11/21/1999   Memphis Brooks Museum of Art, Memphis, TN
01/2000 to 03/2000   Norton Museum of Art, West Palm Beach, FL
04/11/2000 to 06/18/2000   McNay Art Museum, San Antonio, TX

MARY CASSATT: MODERN WOMAN
10/13/1998 to 01/10/1999   Art Institute of Chicago, Chicago, IL
06/06/1999 to 09/06/1999   National Gallery of Art, Washington, DC

MASAMI TERAOKA: FROM TRADITION TO TECHNOLOGY, THE FLOATING WORLD COMES OF AGE
01/23/1999 to 03/07/1999   David Winton Bell Gallery, Providence, RI
04/09/1999 to 06/06/1999   Allen Memorial Art Museum, Oberlin, OH
03/26/1999 to 05/02/1999   University of Oregon Museum of Art, Eugene, OR

MASTER DRAWINGS FROM THE WORCESTER ART MUSEUM
11/07/1998 to 01/17/1999	University of Michigan Museum of Art, Ann Arbor, MI
01/16/1999 to 04/11/1999	Colorado Springs Fine Arts Center, Colorado Springs, CO
02/07/1999 to 04/11/1999	Davenport Museum of Art, Davenport, IA
05/08/1999 to 07/11/1999	Michael C. Carlos Museum, Atlanta, GA

MAXFIELD PARRISH, 1870-1966
06/19/1999 to 09/26/1999	Pennsylvania Academy of the Fine Arts, Philadelphia, PA
11/26/1999 to 01/23/2000	Currier Gallery of Art, Manchester, NH
05/26/2000 to 08/06/2000	Brooklyn Museum of Art, Brooklyn, NY

MEXICAN MASKS OF THE 20TH CENTURY: A LIVING TRADITION
11/29/1998 to 01/17/1999	Arts & Science Center for Southeast Arkansas, Pine Bluff, AR
09/05/1999 to 10/24/1999	Mesa Southwest Museum, Mesa, AZ

MIRIAM SCHAPIRO WORKS ON PAPER
01/16/1999 to 03/07/1999	Tucson Museum of Art, Tucson, AZ
09/01/1999 to 11/15/1999	Art Museum of Missoula, Missoula, MT

MODERN AMERICAN REALISM: THE SARA ROBY FOUNDATION COLLECTION FROM THE NATIONAL MUSEUM OF AMERICAN ART
11/21/1998 to 01/31/1999	Heckscher Museum of Art, Huntington, NY
03/05/1999 to 05/23/1999	Everson Museum of Art, Syracuse, NY

MODOTTI AND WESTON: MEXICANIDAD
05/01/1999 to 06/27/1999	Joslyn Art Museum, Omaha, NE
08/07/1999 to 10/03/1999	Dayton Art Institute, Dayton, OH

MONET AT GIVERNY: MASTERPIECES FROM THE MUSÉE MARMOTTAN
09/18/1998 to 01/03/1999	Portland Art Museum, Portland, OR
05/23/1999 to 08/29/1999	Albright Knox Art Gallery, Buffalo, NY
09/18/1999 to 01/02/2000	Phoenix Art Museum, Phoenix, AZ

NEW WORLDS FROM OLD: AUSTRALIAN AND AMERICAN LANDSCAPE PAINTING OF THE NINETEENTH CENTURY
09/11/1998 to 01/03/1999	Wadsworth Atheneum, Hartford, CT
01/27/1999 to 04/20/1999	Corcoran Gallery of Art, Washington, DC

ON THE ROAD WITH THOMAS HART BENTON: IMAGES OF A CHANGING AMERICA
08/22/1999 to 10/17/1999	Lauren Rogers Museum of Art, Laurel, MS
11/14/1999 to 01/09/2000	George Walter Vincent Smith Art Museum, Springfield, MA
11/14/1999 to 01/09/2000	Museum of Fine Arts, Springfield, MA
07/23/2000 to 09/24/2000	Knoxville Museum of Art, Knoxville, TN
01/21/2001 to 03/18/2001	Fort Wayne Museum of Art, Fort Wayne, IN

PARIS 1900: THE "AMERICAN SCHOOL" AT THE UNIVERSAL EXPOSITION
09/28/1999 to 01/19/2000	Montclair Art Museum, Montclair, NJ
02/12/2000 to 04/16/2000	Pennsylvania Academy of the Fine Arts, Philadelphia, PA

PHILIPPE HALSMAN: A RETROSPECTIVE
11/06/1998 to 02/07/1999	National Portrait Gallery, Washington, DC
03/27/1999 to 05/23/1999	Center for Creative Photography, Tucson, AZ
11/1999 to 01/2000	Toledo Museum of Art, Toledo, OH

PICASSO: GRAPHIC MAGICIAN--PRINTS FROM THE NORTON SIMON MUSEUM
11/07/1999 to 01/16/2000	Toledo Museum of Art, Toledo, OH
winter 99/	Iris and B. Gerald Cantor Center for the Visual Arts at Stanford University, Stanford, CA

Selected Listing of Traveling Exhibitions

POSTERS: AMERICAN STYLE
01/23/1999 to 03/21/1999   Santa Barbara Museum of Art, Santa Barbara, CA
06/01/1999 to 08/15/1999   Oakland Museum of California, Oakland, CA

POWERFUL IMAGES: PORTRAYALS OF NATIVE AMERICA
09/26/1998 to 01/03/1999   Eiteljorg Museum of American Indians and Western Art, Indianapolis, IN
02/20/1999 to 05/16/1999   Autry Museum of Western Heritage, Los Angeles, CA
11/13/1999 to 03/19/2000   Heard Museum, Phoenix, AZ

PURE VISION: AMERICAN BEAD ARTISTS
01/31/1999 to 03/14/1999   Philbrook Museum of Art Inc, Tulsa, OK
06/10/1999 to 07/31/1999   Lowe Art Museum, Coral Gables, FL

RAOUL DUFY: LAST OF THE FAUVES
03/27/1999 to 06/06/1999   Norton Museum of Art, West Palm Beach, FL
06/27/1999 to 09/05/1999   Dixon Gallery & Gardens, Memphis, TN
10/02/1999 to 11/28/1999   New Orleans Museum of Art, New Orleans, LA

REFLECTIONS OF A JOURNEY: ENGRAVINGS AFTER KARL BODMER
11/07/1998 to 01/03/1999   Mitchell Museum, Mount Vernon, IL
03/28/1999 to 05/09/1999   Mesa Southwest Museum, Mesa, AZ
01/18/2000 to 03/26/2000   Museum of the Southwest, Midland, TX

REFUGE: THE NEWEST NEW YORKERS
Mid September 1999   Roberson Museum Science Center, Binghamton, NY
02/03/1999 to 05/30/1999   New-York Historical Society, New York, NY

REVEALING THE HOLY LAND: THE PHOTOGRAPHIC EXPLORATION OF PALESTINE
02/23/1999 to 05/23/1999   Saint Louis Art Museum, St. Louis, MO
06/08/1999 to 08/28/1999   Dahesh Museum, New York, NY

ROBERT COLESCOTT: RECENT PAINTINGS
01/15/1999 to 03/21/1999   Portland Art Museum, Portland, OR
09/24/1999 to 01/02/2000   Sheldon Memorial Art Gallery and Sculpture Garden, Lincoln, NE

ROBERT GWATHMEY
02/18/1999 to 05/09/1999   Morris Museum of Art, Augusta, GA
09/15/1999 to 10/17/1999   Dahl Fine Arts Center, Rapid City, SD
06/2000 to 09/2000   Pennsylvania Academy of the Fine Arts, Philadelphia, PA

RODIN: SCULPTURE FROM THE IRIS AND B. GERALD CANTOR COLLECTION
12/08/1998 to 01/31/1999   J. B Speed Art Museum, Louisville, KY
02/17/1999 to 05/16/1999   Palm Springs Desert Museum, Inc., Palm Springs, CA

ROY DE CARAVA: A RETROSPECTIVE
10/17/1998 to 01/04/1999   Corcoran Gallery of Art, Washington, DC
02/13/1999 to 04/25/1999   Minneapolis Institute of Arts, Minneapolis, MN

SALLY MANN: STILL TIME
01/29/1999 to 03/14/1999   Bayly Art Museum of the University of Virginia, Charlottesville, VA
04/06/1999 to 05/30/1999   Mount Holyoke College Art Museum, South Hadley, MA

SANDY SKOGLUND: REALITY UNDER SEIGE
02/12/1999 to 05/16/1999   Toledo Museum of Art, Toledo, OH
06/04/1999 to 08/01/1999   Delaware Art Museum, Wilmington, DE

SARAH CHARLESWORTH: A RETROSPECTIVE
    03/22/1998 to 06/14/1998   Museum of Contemporary Art, San Diego, La Jolla, CA
    03/25/1999 to 05/30/1999   Rose Art Museum, Waltham, MA

SEA CHANGE: THE SEASCAPE IN CONTEMPORARY PHOTOGRAPHY
    02/11/1999 to 04/25/1999   Museum of Photographic Arts, San Diego, CA
    06/12/1999 to 09/16/1999   International Center of Photography, New York, NY

SEARCHING FOR ANCIENT EGYPT
    10/15/1998 to 01/10/1999   Seattle Art Museum, Seattle, WA

    03/27/1999 to 05/25/1999   Joslyn Art Museum, Omaha, NE
    10/03/1999 to 01/16/2000   Birmingham Museum of Art, Birmingham, AL
    03/15/2000 to 07/23/2000   Honolulu Academy of Arts, Honolulu, HI

SELF-TAUGHT ARTISTS OF THE 20th CENTURY: AN AMERICAN ANTHOLOGY
    10/31/1998 to 01/24/1999   Amon Carter Museum, Fort Worth, TX
    11/01/1998 to 01/24/1999   Modern Art Museum of Fort Worth, Fort Worth, TX
    05/15/1999 to 08/15/1999   Wexner Center for the Arts, Columbus, OH

SHAMANS, GODS AND MYTHIC BEASTS: COLUMBIAN GOLD AND CERAMICS IN ANTIQUITY
    10/31/1998 to 01/10/1999   Michael C. Carlos Museum, Atlanta, GA
    01/29/1999 to 04/11/1999   Mingei International Museum of Folk Art, San Diego, CA
    04/20/1999 to 07/11/1999   Orlando Museum of Art, Orlando, FL
    10/29/1999 to 01/09/2000   Bowers Museum of Cultural Art, Santa Ana, CA

SILVER AND GOLD: CASED IMAGES OF THE CALIFORNIA GOLD RUSH
    10/30/1998 to 03/07/1999   National Museum of American Art-Renwick Gallery -, Washington, DC
    08/13/1999 to 10/10/1999   Crocker Art Museum, Sacramento, CA

SINNERS AND SAINTS, DARKNESS AND LIGHT: CARAVAGGIO AND HIS DUTCH AND FLEMISH
FOLLOWERS IN AMERICA
    01/29/1999 to 04/18/1999   Milwaukee Art Museum, Milwaukee, WI
    05/08/1999 to 07/18/1999   Dayton Art Institute, Dayton, OH

SPLENDORS OF ANCIENT EGYPT
    10/04/1998 to 03/27/1999   Phoenix Art Museum, Phoenix, AZ
    06/1999 to 11/1999   Virginia Museum of Fine Arts, Richmond, VA

STRONG HEARTS: NATIVE AMERICAN PHOTOGRAPHY
    03/27/1999 to 06/13/1999   Herbert F. Johnson Museum of Art, Ithaca, NY
    09/01/99 to 12/15/99   Robert Hull Fleming Museum, Burlington, VT

SUNLIGHT AND SHADOW: AMERICAN IMPRESSIONISM, 1885-1945
    03/09/1999 to 04/23/1999   Elizabeth Myers Mitchell Art Gallery, Annapolis, MD
    02/19/2000 to 04/12/2000   Tucson Museum of Art, Tucson, AZ

TACITA DEAN
    11/14/1998 to 01/03/1999   Institute of Contemporary Art, Philadelphia, PA
    03/07/1999 to 05/23/1999   Madison Art Center, Madison, WI

THE ARCHITECTURE OF REASSURANCE: DESIGNING DISNEY'S THEME PARKS
    02/13/1999 to 04/11/1999   Modern Art Museum of Fort Worth, Fort Worth, TX
    10/06/1998 to 01/10/1999   Cooper-Hewitt, National Design,Museum, Smithsonian Institution, New York, NY

THE ART OF TWENTIETH CENTURY ZEN
    01/19/1998 to 01/10/1999   Japan Society Gallery, New York, NY
    01/29/1999 to 04/10/1999   Marsh Art Gallery, University of Richmond, Richmond, VA

Selected Listing of Traveling Exhibitions

THE BUFFALO SOLDIER: THE AFRICAN-AMERICAN SOLDIER IN THE US ARMY, 1866-1912 FROM THE COLLECTION OF ANTHONY L. POWELL
04/16/2000 to 06/04/2000	Mesa Southwest Museum, Mesa, AZ
12/10/2000 to 01/28/2001	Afro-American Historical and Cultural Museum, Philadelphia, PA

THE CECIL FAMILY COLLECTS: FOUR CENTURIES OF DECORATIVE ARTS FROM BURGHLEY HOUSE
02/13/1999 to 04/07/1999	Society of the Four Arts, Palm Beach, FL
05/08/1999 to 07/03/1999	New Orleans Museum of Art, New Orleans, LA
07/31/1999 to 10/10/1999	Santa Barbara Museum of Art, Santa Barbara, CA
01/22/2000 to 03/19/2000	Columbia Museum of Arts, Columbia, SC

THE CHARLESTON RENAISSANCE
12/02/1998 to 03/07/1999	Greenville County Museum of Art, Greenville, SC
04/03/1999 to 06/06/1999	Columbia Museum of Arts, Columbia, SC
09/09/1999 to 11/07/1999	Morris Museum of Art, Augusta, GA
09/12/1998 to 09/06/1999	Gibbes Museum of Art, Charleston, SC

THE FRAME IN AMERICA
01/21/1999 to 03/16/1999	Texas A&M University/J. Wayne Stark University Center Galleries, College Station, TX
08/28/1999 to 04/14/1999	Memorial Art Gallery, Rochester, NY

THE GREAT AMERICAN POP ART STORE
08/01/1999 to 09/12/1999	Muskegon Museum of Art, Muskegon, MI
01/19/99 to 03/14/99	McNay Art Museum, San Antonio, TX

THE GREAT EXPERIMENT: GEORGE WASHINGTON AND THE AMERICAN REPUBLIC
10/06/1998 to 05/30/1999	Huntington Library, Art Collections and Botanical Gardens, San Marino, CA
09/16/1999 to 01/02/2000	Morgan Library, New York, NY

THE HASKELL COLLECTION OF CONTEMPORARY ART
03/21/199 to 06/27/1999	North Carolina Museum of Art, Raleigh, NC
07/01/1999 to 09/26/1999	Cummer Museum of Art & Gardens, Jacksonville, FL

THE INTIMATE COLLABORATION: PRINTS FROM THE TEABERRY PRESS
03/14/1999 to 05/02/1999	Museums of Abilene, Inc., Abilene, TX
12/17/2000 to 02/04/2001	Kennedy Museum of Art, Athens, OH
07/15/2001 to 09/02/2001	Blanden Memorial Art Museum, Fort Dodge, IA

THE INVISIBLE MADE VISIBLE: ANGELS FROM THE VATICAN
11/08/1998 to 01/03/1999	Walters Art Gallery, Baltimore, MD
01/23/1999 to 04/04/1999	Norton Museum of Art, West Palm Beach, FL

THE JOHN A. AND MARGERET HILL COLLECTION OF AMERICAN WESTERN ART
01/24/1999 to 04/04/1999	Owensboro Museum of Fine Art, Owensboro, KY
07/04/1999 to 08/22/1999	Amarillo Museum of Art, Amarillo, TX
09/12/1999 to 10/31/1999	Art Museum of South Texas, Corpus Christi, TX
11/21/1999 to 01/09/2000	Louisiana Arts and Science Center, Baton Rouge, LA
04/04/2000 to 05/28/2000	Sunrise Museum, Charleston, WV
06/18/2000 to 08/16/2000	Frederic Remington Art Museum, Ogdensburg, NY
11/05/2000 to 12/21/2000	Sioux City Art Center, Sioux City, IA
06/23/2001 to 08/26/2001	Leigh Yawkey Woodson Art Museum, Wausau, WI

THE JUDY CHICAGO RETROSPECTIVE: WORKS ON PAPER
02/12/1999 to 04/04/1999	Florida State University Museum of Fine Arts, Tallahassee, FL
09/01/1999 to 10/31/1999	Indiana University Art Museum, Bloomington, IN

THE KINGDOMS OF EDWARD HICKS
Fall 99/	Philadelphia Museum of Art, Philadelphia, PA
02/1999 to 09/1999	Abby Aldrich Rockefeller Folk Art Center, Williamsburg, VA

THE PHILADELPHIA TEN: A WOMEN ARTIST GROUP 1917-1945
01/23/1999 to 03/20/1999	Old Jail Art Center, Albany, TX
04/16/1999 to 06/11/1999	Concord Art Association, Concord, MA
07/17/1999 to 10/03/1999	James A. Michener Art Museum, Doylestown, PA

THE PRINTED WORLD OF PIETER BREUGEL THE ELDER
03/26/1999 to 05/23/1999	Bayly Art Museum of the University of Virginia, Charlottesville, VA
12/12/1999 to 02/13/2000	Memphis Brooks Museum of Art, Memphis, TN

THE SCULPTOR'S LINE: HENRY MOORE PRINTS
11/06/1998 to 01/03/1999	George D. and Harriet W. Cornell Fine Arts Museum, Winter Park, FL
06/16/1999 to 08/08/1999	West Bend Art Museum, West Bend, WI

THE STONEWARES OF CHARLES FERGUS BINNS: FATHER OF AMERICAN STUDIO CERAMICS
01/24/1999 to 03/14/1999	Museum of Arts and Sciences, Daytona Beach, FL
04/11/1999 to 06/27/1999	Muscatine Art Center, Muscatine, IA
09/12/1999 to 11/02/1999	Butler Institute of American Art, Youngstown, OH
09/12/1999 to 11/02/1999	Dahl Fine Arts Center, Rapid City, SD
04/30/2000 to 06/18/2000	Memorial Art Gallery, Rochester, NY

TO CONSERVE A LEGACY AMERICAN ART FROM HISTORICALLY BLACK COLLEGES AND UNIVERSITIES
03/10/1999 to 06/27/1999	Studio Museum in Harlem, New York, NY
07/1999 to 10/1999	Addison Gallery of American Art, Andover, MA

TRANSIENCE: CHINESE ART AT THE END OF THE 20TH CENTURY
02/18/1999 to 04/18/1999	David and Alfred Smart Museum of Art, Chicago, IL
07/1999 to 09/1999	University of Oregon Museum of Art, Eugene, OR

TRASHFORMATIONS: RECYCLED MATERIALS IN CONTEMPORARY AMERICAN ART AND DESIGN
02/13/1999 to 04/25/1999	Boise Art Museum, Boise, ID
11/07/1999 to 01/02/2000	Anchorage Museum of History and Art, Anchorage, AK
04/29/2000 to 07/25/2000	Yellowstone Art Museum, Billings, MT

TREASURES FROM THE ROYAL TOMBS OF UR
10/04/1998 to 01/03/1999	Bowers Museum of Cultural Art, Santa Ana, CA
05/30/1999 to 09/05/1999	Dallas Museum of Art, Dallas, TX
10/17/1999 to 01/17/2000	Arthur M. Sackler Gallery, Washington, DC

TREASURES OF CHINESE GLASS WORKSHOPS: PEKING GLASS FROM THE GADIENT COLLECTION
01/24/1999 to 05/30/1999	Museum of Fine Arts-St. Petersburg Florida, St. Petersburg, FL
11/02/1999 to 01/30/2000	Lowe Art Museum, Coral Gables, FL

TREASURES OF DECEIT: ARCHAEOLOGY AND THE FORGER'S CRAFT
02/18/1999 to 04/04/1999	Lowe Art Museum, Coral Gables, FL
04/25/1999 to 06/13/1999	Lyman Allyn Art Museum, New London, CT
07/07/1999 to 08/22/1999	George Walter Vincent Smith Art Museum, Springfield, MA
07/07/1999 to 08/22/1999	Museum of Fine Arts, Springfield, MA
11/26/98 to 01/17/99	Memphis Brooks Museum of Art, Memphis, TN

Selected Listing of Traveling Exhibitions

TWENTIETH CENTURY AMERICAN DRAWINGS FROM THE ARKANSAS CENTER FOUNDATION
COLLECTION
12/11/1998 to 01/30/1999	Philharmonic Center for the Arts, Naples, FL
02/20/1999 to 04/18/1999	Fort Wayne Museum of Art, Fort Wayne, IN
11/07/1999 to 01/09/2000	Mobile Museum of Art, Mobile, AL
01/30/2000 to 03/26/2000	Art Museum of Southeast Texas, Beaumont, TX

UNFOLDING LIGHT: THE EVOLUTION OF TEN HOLOGRAPHERS
01/31/1999 to 03/28/1999	Hofstra Museum, Hempstead, NY
06/27/1999 to 08/22/1999	Paine Art Center and Arboretum, Oshkosh, WI
09/12/1999 to 11/07/1999	Tweed Museum of Art, Duluth, MN
11/27/1999 to 01/23/2000	Canton Museum of Art, Canton, OH

URSULA VON RYDINGSVARD: SCULPTURE AND DRAWINGS
05/09/1998 to 03/28/1999	Nelson-Atkins Museum of Art, Kansas City, MO
12/05/1998 to 01/31/1999	Chicago Cultural Center, Chicago, IL
05/1999 to 04/2000	Indianapolis Museum of Art, Indianapolis, IN

WALKER EVANS SIMPLE SECRETS: PHOTOGRAPHS FROM THE COLLECTION OF MARIAN AND
BENJAMIN A. HILL
12/11/1998 to 02/24/1999	Whitney Museum of American Art at Champion, Stamford, CT
04/14/1999 to 06/27/1999	Detroit Institute of Arts, Detroit, MI

WALTER O. EVANS COLLECTION OF AFRICAN AMERICAN ART
12/17/1998 to 02/07/1999	Lowe Art Museum, Coral Gables, FL
02/21/1999 to 05/28/1999	Meadows Museum of Art of Centenary College, Shreveport, LA

WHEN TIME BEGAN TO RANT AND RAGE: TWENTIETH CENTURY FIGURATIVE PAINTING FROM
IRELAND
10/29/1998 to 12/19/1998	Drawing Center, New York, NY
02/10/1999 to 05/01/1999	University of California Berkeley Art Museum & Pacific Film Archive, Berkeley, CA
06/25/1999 to 07/31/1999	Grey Art Gallery and Study Center, New York, NY

WILLIAM SIDNEY MOUNT: PAINTER OF AMERICAN LIFE
08/1998	Museums at Stony Brook, Stony Brook, NY
11/13/1998 to 01/10/1999	Frick Art Museum, Pittsburgh, PA
02/05/1999 to 04/04/1999	Amon Carter Museum, Fort Worth, TX

WITNESS AND LEGACY: CONTEMPORARY ART ABOUT THE HOLOCAUST
03/25/1999 to 05/23/1999	Oklahoma City Art Museum, Oklahoma City, OK
09/2000 to 10/2000	Tucson Museum of Art, Tucson, AZ

WORLDWIDE

Discount Coupon

Present this coupon at the Acoustiguide Counter
and receive $1.00 off on an Acoustiguide Tour

Discount Coupon

Selected Listing of Exhibitions
with Acoustiguide Tours Available

As of the closing date of this publication, these are the temporary exhibitions for which Accoustiguide tours are currently planned. This list is subject to change. Additional exhibitions are frequently added throughout the year. For an up-to-date listing, or an inquiry on a specific exhibition, please call 212-974-6600

ANCIENT GOLD: THE WEALTH OF THE THRACIANS, TREASURE FROM THE REPUBLIC OF BULGARIA
10/31/98-1/3/99   New Orleans Museum of Art Louisiana

ANCIENT GOLD, THE WEALTH OF THE THRACIANS, TREASURES FROM THE REPUBLIC OF BULGARIA
01/17/99-03/14/99 Memphis , TENNESSEE

ANCIENT ART: THE WEALTH OF THE THRACIANS, TREASURES FROM THE REPUBLIC OF BULGARIA
06/20/99-08/29/99 Detroit Institute of Arts, Michigan

THE CECIL FAMILY COLLECTS: FOUR CENTURIES OF ART FROM BURGHLEY HOUSE
11/18/99-1/4/99 Cincinnati Ohio

DELACROIX: THE LATE WORKS
09/20/98-01/03/99 Philadelphia Museum of Art, Philadelphia, PA

HALF PAST AUTUMN: THE ART OF GORDON PARKS
02/07/99-04/25/99 Detroit Institute of Arts, Detroit, MI

THE INVISIBLE MADE VISIBLE: ANGELS OF THE VATICAN
11/8/98-01/03/99 Walters Art Gallery, Baltimore, MD

JACKSON POLLOCK
11/01/98-02/05/99 Museum of Modern Art, New York, NY

MARY CASSAT: MODERN WOMAN
6/6/99-9/6/99 National Gallery of Art, Wash, D.C.

PICASSO AND THE WAR
10/10/98-1/3/99 Fine Arts Museum of San Francisco, CA

JOHN SINGER SARGENT
2/28/99-5/31/99 National Gallery of Art, Wash, D.C.

A TASTE FOR SPLENDOR: TREASURES FROM THE HILLWOOD MUSEUM
11/21/98-02/0799 Huntsville Museum of Art, Huntsville, AL

VAN GOGH'S VAN GOGHS From the National Museum in Amsterdam.
10/4/98-1/10/99 National Gallery of Art, Washington, DC

Accoustiguide Audio Tours
of Permanent Collections in 1999

Graceland, Memphis TN
Museum of Modern Art, New York City, New York
Allentown Art Museum, Allentown, PA
Antietam, Sharpsburg, MD
Ellis Island, New York City, New York
Chrysler Museum, Norfolk, VA
Frick Collection, New York City, New York
Hermitage, Hermitage, TN
Historic Annapolis, Annapolis, MD
Houston Decorative Center, Houston, TX
Isabella Stewart Gardner Museum, Boston, MA
Mashantucket Pequot Tribal Nation, Mashantucket, CT
San Diego Museum of Contemporary Arts, La Jolla, CA
Mercer Museum, Doylestown, PA
Monterey Bay Aquarium, Monterey Bay, CA
Montpelier, Montpelier Station, VA
Museum of Contemporary Art, Chicago, IL
New England Aquarium, Boston, MA
National Cryptologic Foundation, Ft. George Meade, MD
New York Botanical Garden, Bronx, New York
National Gallery of Art, Washington, D.C.
Oregon Coastal Aquarium, Newport, OR
California Palace, Legion of Honor, San Francisco, CA
Pennsylvania Academy of the Fine Arts, Philadelphia, PA
San Diego Zoo, San Diego, CA
Scriptorium, Grand Haven, MI
John G. Shedd Aquarium, Chicago, IL
Monticello, Home of Thomas Jefferson, Charlottesville, VA
Toledo Museum, Toledo, OH
Tulsa Zoo and Living Museum, Tulsa, OK
Virginia Historical Society, Richmond, VA
Walker Art Center, Minneapolis, MN
Whitney Art Museum, New York City, NY
World Golf Village, Hall of Fame, St. Augustine, FL

Alphabetical Listing of Museums

Alphabetical Listing of Museums

Alphabetical Listing of Museums

Alphabetical Listing of Museums

Alphabetical Listing of Museums

Alphabetical Listing of Museums

Alphabetical Listing of Museums

Alphabetical Listing of Museums

Alphabetical Listing of Museums

ABOUT THE AUTHOR

Judith Swirsky has been associated with the arts in Brooklyn as both staff and volunteer for more than forty years. The recipient of many awards, she has held both curatorial and volunteer administration positions at The Brooklyn Museum. While Executive Director of the Grand Central Art Galleries Educational Association she coordinated the 1989 Moscow Conference. She is now an independent curator and artists' representative. She is listed in *Who's Who of American Women.*